BROTHERS AT WAR

Also by Sheila Miyoshi Jager

Ruptured Histories: War, Memory, and the Post-Cold War in Asia
(with Rana Mitter, eds.)

Narratives of Nation-Building in Korea: A Genealogy of Patriotism

BROTHERS AT WAR

The Unending Conflict in Korea

SHEILA MIYOSHI JAGER

PROFILE BOOKS

First published in Great Britain in 2013 by
PROFILE BOOKS LTD
3A Exmouth House
Pine Street
London ECIR OJH
www.profilebooks.com

First published in the United States of America in 2013 by
W. W. Norton & Company, Inc.

10 9 8 7 6 5 4 3 1

Book design by Kristen Bearse
Printed and bound in Great Britain by
Clays, Bungay, Suffolk

A CIP catalogue record for this book is available from the British Library.

ISBN 978 1 84668 067 0
eISBN 978 1 84765 202 7

The paper this book is printed on is certified by the © 1996 Forest Stewardship
Council A.C. (FSC). It is ancient-forest friendly. The printer holds FSC chain
of custody SGS-COC-2061

FSC
www.fsc.org
MIX
Paper from
responsible sources
FSC® C018072

FOR JIYUL

CONTENTS

Abbreviations Used in Text

AEC: Atomic Energy Commission

ASPAC: Asia-Pacific Council

CCP: Chinese Communist Party

CPKI: Committee for the Preparation of Korean Independence

CPV: Chinese People's Volunteer

DMZ: demilitarized zone

DPRK: Democratic People's Republic of Korea

IAEA: International Atomic Energy Agency

ICRC: International Committee for the Red Cross

JCS: Joint Chiefs of Staff

KATUSA: Korean Augmentation to the United States Army

KCIA: Korean Central Intelligence Agency

KCP: Korean Communist Party

KDP: Korean Democratic Party

KMAG: Korean Military Advisory Group

KPG: Korean Provisional Government

KPR: Korean People's Republic

KSC: Korean Service Corps

LST: landing ship tank

LWR: light-water reactor

MACV: Military Assistance Command Vietnam

NAM: Nonaligned Movement

NKPA: North Korean People's Army

NKWP: North Korean Workers' Party

NPT: Nuclear Nonproliferation Treaty

NVA: North Vietnamese Army

PDS: Public Distribution System

PLA: People's Liberation Army

POW: prisoner of war

PRC: People's Republic of China

ROK: Republic of Korea

SACEUR: Supreme Allied Commander Europe

SCA: Soviet Civil Administration

SCAP: Supreme Commander for the Allied Powers

SKWP: South Korean Workers Party

SOFA: Status of Forces Agreement

TF: Task Force

UNC: United Nations Command

UNRC: United Nations Reception Center

UNCURK: United Nations Commission for the Unification and Rehabilitation of Korea

USAFIK: United States Army Forces in Korea

USAMGIK: United States Military Government in Korea

VPA: Vietnam People's Army

WFP: World Food Program

ACKNOWLEDGMENTS

My first opportunity to study the Korean War in depth came in 2006 when I was offered a two-year research fellowship at the U.S. Army War College in Carlisle, Pennsylvania. Affiliated with the War College is the U.S. Army Military History Institute, which houses the largest collection in the United States of oral history archives on the Korean War. One of the major benefits I saw of working with oral histories at the onset of this project was the visceral connection I was able to make with the subjects of my research. Although oral histories are not always reliable and must be handled with care, they are invaluable for re-creating the mood and emotions of the battlefield that underlay the actions and attitudes of the soldiers who fought there.

I was also fortunate during my research at the Institute to run into a group of South Korean researchers from South Korea's Truth and Reconciliation Commission (TRC). The South Korean government had established the Commission in 2005 to investigate various incidents in Korean history, and in particular numerous atrocities committed by various government agencies during Japan's occupation of Korea, the Korean War, and the successive authoritarian governments. The Commission was disbanded in 2010. As I sat down with the TRC researchers one evening over coffee, I discussed my project, and they offered their help. As the primary researcher on the Commission at that time, Suh Hee-gyŏng not only shared with me thousands of pages of unpublished and published reports and photos of the Commission's findings, but also helped me navigate the daunting Korean bureaucracy in securing permission to use them. She also provided invaluable assistance in assembling materials pertaining to the mass killings that occurred early on during the Korean War. Kim Dong-ch'un, former standing commissioner of the Commission, also provided important materials; it was he who showed me what I regard as one of the most haunting photos of the war, the remains of 114 bodies discovered at Buntegol, Chŏngwŏn, Ch'ungbuk province, in 2007, which appears in this book.

I am also indebted to Balázs Szalontai for sharing some of his unpublished work with me. The book is much richer because of it. Katalin Jalsovszky, the archivist at the Hungarian National Museum, quickly and efficiently helped me to secure some rare North Korean photos of the war. I am thankful to Balázs and Chris Springer, who brought these amazing photos to my attention. John Moffett, librarian at the Needham Institute in the United Kingdom, was helpful in taking the time to locate, scan, and send dozens of photos of Joseph Needham's trip to China in 1952. Mitchell Lerner steered me to some of his and other recent work on the USS *Pueblo* incident from which the book has greatly benefited. Choe Yong-ho of the Korea Institute of Military History, Ministry of National Defense, Republic of Korea, helped me to track down books, articles, and data on Korea's involvement in the Vietnam War. Raymond Lech generously provided me with copies of transcripts of pretrial interviews, appellate reviews, memos, and letters concerning U.S. Korean War POWs. Ray allowed me to borrow this extraordinary collection—filling more than fifteen boxes—to use at my leisure before he deposited them at the U.S. Army Military History Institute, where the collection now resides. New materials about the war from the Soviet, Chinese, East German, Hungarian, and Romanian archives, all available online at the web site for the Cold War International History Project at the Woodrow Wilson International Center for Scholars, have enabled scholars to adopt a truly multinational approach in their study of the cold war. We now know more about the views of "other" major players in the cold war than ever before. This book is a direct beneficiary of the tremendous contributions the Wilson Center has made to advancing cold war scholarship. Finally, I would like to acknowledge Oberlin College for granting me a two-year leave during which time the bulk of the research for this book was done. I also benefited greatly from three summer research grants awarded by Oberlin for travel to Korea and other research libraries in the United States. I consider myself lucky to be teaching in such a supportive academic environment. My colleagues Ann Sherif, Pauline Chen, and Qiusha Ma have been not only wonderful mentors but also supportive friends.

During the writing phase of the project, Daniel Crewe, my editor at Profile Books in the United Kingdom, read so many drafts of this book that I have lost count. Several of the major sections of the present text were completely revised and rewritten in response to his suggestions and questions. Allan R. Millett, who read an early draft of the book, was pointed in his critical comments but made it all that much better. Retired U.S. Army Colonel Don Boose also read through an earlier draft of the manuscript and provided excellent feedback, especially on the later chapters. For her enthusiastic and unfailing support of this project, I am grateful to my editor at W. W. Norton, Maria Guarnaschelli, and her assistant, Melanie Tortoroli: Maria, for having such faith and insight into the book even as the manuscript grew longer, and Melanie, for helping me at critical points in the rewriting and for keeping everything else on track. I would also like to acknowledge my copy editor, Mary Babcock, whose meticulous attention to every detail of the book helped to improve it tremendously. Kim Preston and Bonnie Gordon have seen me through some of the more grueling stages of the book's evolution, and I also wish to thank them here for their warm friendship and support.

My older kids, Isaac and Hannah, also contributed to this project early on: Isaac, now a cadet at West Point, for spending an entire summer with me at the Military History Institute pouring over after-action reports and writing them up, and Hannah, for her computer wizardry in organizing all my books, papers, computer files, and photos. In addition, both helped care for their younger siblings, Emma and Aaron, when mom was at work in the attic, good deeds for which I am thankful. All four kids grew up with this book, patiently tolerating my own "unending" obsession with the war without too much complaint while also providing the necessary perspective as only one's children can do.

My greatest debt is owed to my husband, Jiyul, without whose contribution this book might never have been written. We covered a great deal of ground together; his help in surveying a broad range of materials, reading and rereading through numerous drafts of the manuscript, and above all, his enthusiasm for debating—and often correcting—the finer points of Korean War history, made the final product a much better book. These conversations became part of our daily routine and contributed to the overall richness of our daily lives. For that, I will always be grateful.

———

A note on source, transliteration, and naming convention. Considerations of space have precluded the inclusion of a separate bibliography. The notes include the full citation of each source when it appears for the first time in a particular chapter. Throughout the text, I have employed the McCune-Reischauer system of romanization for all Korean words and names, with the exception of well-known nonstandard romanized names, such as Syngman Rhee, Park Chung Hee, Kim Il Sung, and Kim Jong Il. As a rule, Chinese names are romanized according to the pinyin system. Korean, Chinese, and Japanese personal names are, with the exception of Syngman Rhee, written with family name first and given name last.

Sheila Miyoshi Jager
Oberlin, Ohio
December 2012

BROTHERS AT WAR

Introduction

The War Memorial, Seoul. (PHOTO BY AUTHOR)

MY INTEREST IN THE KOREAN WAR began with a visit to a memorial. In the summer of 1996 my family relocated to South Korea when my husband, a U.S. Army officer, was assigned to work at the U.S. embassy in Seoul. Just a few minutes away from the main gate of the Yongsan U.S. Army base, where we lived, is the War Memorial, and over the next four years I made frequent trips to visit it. Ostensibly, it commemorates South Korea's military war dead, but other wartime events, including Korea's thirteenth-century struggles with the Mongols and sixteenth-century defense against the Japanese, are also represented in the exhibitions. Inclusion of these earlier conflicts appears to reinforce the idea that the Korean War was part of the nation's long history of righteous struggle against adversity—in this case, South Korea's struggle against

North Korean communists. Situated on five acres along a wide boulevard that bisects the army base, the War Memorial encompasses a rare, large open space in crowded Seoul. Originally conceived and planned under the No T'ae-u (Roh Tae-Woo) administration (1988–93), the complex opened its doors in 1994. It includes a museum as well as an outdoor exhibition area featuring tanks, airplanes, statues, and a small amusement area for children. It has become a popular destination for school field trips.

What struck me most about the memorial was the paradox of what it represented. How does one commemorate a war that technically is not over? While the Korean War, at least for Americans, "ended" in 1953, the meaning and memories of the war have not been brought to closure in Korean society because of the permanent division of the peninsula. How does one bring closure to a war for which the central narrative is one of division and dissent, a war whose history is still in the process of being made?

In South Korea, the official view of the Korean War has always had, unsurprisingly, an anti–North Korean character. One striking feature of the memorial, however, is the relative absence of depictions of the brutal struggle between the North and the South. Although its purported task is to memorialize the war, the main purpose of the memorial appears to be to promote reconciliation and peace. There are few exhibits of bloody battle scenes, but most conspicuously is the lack of any reference to known North Korean atrocities committed during the war. The successive purges of South Korean sympathizers after the North Korean People's Army occupied Seoul in June 1950 and the execution of prisoners of war are represented nowhere. Evidence of the widely publicized executions of an estimated five thousand South Korean civilians during the last days of the North Korean army's occupation of Taejŏn in September 1950—an event highlighted in the history books from previous South Korean military regimes—is also missing. For a war that was particularly remembered for its viciousness, the memorial seems to be promoting a tacit kind of forgetfulness. This is in sharp contrast to earlier representations of the conflict that proliferated during the cold war, when North Korean brutality played a central role in the story of the war.

It was not difficult to understand why this sudden shift in memory had occurred. By the time the memorial had opened its doors, the cold war had ended and South Korea had come out on top. Following its global coming-out party during the 1988 Seoul Olympics, South Korea had clearly "won" the war against the North, but it could not afford to bask in its glory if it wanted to foster North-South rapprochement and the reunification of the peninsula. The memorial's designers were thus faced with the dilemma of how to memorialize a brutal war while at the same time leaving open the possibility for peninsular peace.

When I returned to the Memorial a decade later, the pendulum of politics in South Korea had swung sharply to the Right. The conservatives had gained power and opposed improving relations with the P'yŏngyang regime. I was in Seoul in 2006 when North Korea test-fired missiles, including a long-range Taep'odong-2 with the theoretical capacity to reach the continental United States. These acts of defiance were followed by the testing of North Korea's first nuclear device on October 9, 2006, and then again on May 25, 2009. South Koreans were furious. When the conservative presidential candidate Yi Myŏng-bak (Lee Myung-bak) assumed office in 2008, he abruptly renounced the policy of engagement with the North that previous administrations had pursued. The North responded with vitriolic attacks against the new South Korean government. Relations between the two Koreas spiraled downward from there. By then, it had become quite apparent that the Korean War would not end as optimistically as the War Memorial planners had hoped. Rather, the memorial itself had become part of the history of the war, one "phase" of its never-ending story.

That initial visit to the War Memorial in 1996 spurred me to think more closely about the war. Eventually, I made the memorial the subject of several essays and book chapters and then finally undertook a major research project on the Korean War itself. This entailed exploring the policies and actions of all the major players of the war, including the sixteen UN countries that sent troops to aid South Korea, the military history, and a wide variety of popular and academic writings about the conflict. But I never lost sight of my original fascination with the war and its continuing and evolving impact on the two Koreas and on the rest of the world.

Since the late nineteenth century, the Korean peninsula has been a focal point for confrontation and competition among the Great Powers. First China, then Japan, Russia, and the United States in succession, exerted some form of control over the peninsula. No other place in the world has assumed such symbolic importance to these four countries. The Second World War, however, left only two Great Powers vying for influence over Korea: the United States and the Soviet Union (formerly Russia).

But by then the Koreans had already divided themselves into partisan camps under the tutelage, and with the support, of these two patrons. Two antagonistic regimes were born: communists in the North and conservatives in the South, each with dreams of reunifying the Korean peninsula under their rule, but without any means of achieving this ambition on their own. Their diverging visions of what kind of modern nation Korea was to become made the possibility of conciliation and unity increasingly remote and exploded into war in 1950.

The main issues over which the war was fought had their origins immediately after Korea's liberation from Japan in 1945. The division of the peninsula at the 38th parallel by the United States and the Soviet Union gave rise to a fractured polity whose political fault lines were exacerbated further by regional, religious (Christians versus communists), and class divisions. Open fighting among these groups eventually claimed more than one hundred thousand lives, all before the ostensible Korean War began. Prior to the founding of the Republic of Korea in August 1948, the Americans organized a constabulary force in their zone to augment the national police, primarily to conduct counterinsurgency operations against leftist guerillas. While the record of their operations remains controversial, the security forces successfully suppressed the insurgency by the spring of 1950. The decision by North Korea's leader, Kim Il Sung, with the backing of Joseph Stalin, to launch a conventional attack across the 38th parallel on June 25, 1950, thus resumed the fighting by other means.

The Korean War, in the midst of the rapidly developing cold war, reestablished China, now Communist China, as a Great Power, setting up a triangular struggle over the peninsula between the United States, the Soviet Union, and Communist China. The irresolution of the Korean War, owing to the lack of a peace treaty, with only a military armistice signed in 1953, stoked the fire of simmering confrontation and tension between North and South Korea as well as their Great Power overseers. But the most important fuel that kept the flame of confrontation alive was the implacable nature of the two Korean regimes. This is all the more remarkable as Korea had been unified since the seventh century.

Today, the essentially continuous war between the Koreas threatens to reach beyond their borders, as North Korea continues to develop nuclear weapons and long-range missiles. How did we get to this point? This book is the story of Korean competition and conflict—and Great Power competition and conflict—over the peninsula: an unending war between two "brothers" with ramifications for the rest of the world. If a resolution to the conflict is ever to be found, this history must be understood and taken into account.

I develop two major but overlapping themes in this book. The first one emphasizes the evolution of the war through time. Because the Korean War technically ended in an armistice and not a peace treaty, it continued to influence regional events even though the significance of the war dramatically changed. Hence, the conflict evolved from a civil war in 1948–49 to an international war from June 1950 to 1953, to a global cold war after 1953, only to undergo yet another transformation in the late 1960s, when the focus of the conflict was no longer on containing communism per se, but ensuring the region's stability. By the mid-1970s, the stalemated Korean War kept American forces in South Korea because the conflict had ironically become a source of regional stability during a period of significant changes in Asia: Sino-American rapprochement, the Sino-Soviet split, and increasing Sino-Vietnamese tensions. Although the Korean War continued to be waged as a series of "local wars" along the demilitarized zone (DMZ) dividing the North from the South, the nature of the conflict had fundamentally changed since the armistice. In the post–cold war period, the Korean War was defined by a series of crises over the North Korean nuclear weapons program and the potential collapse of the North. Should fighting ever resume on the Korean peninsula, it will not resemble the first phase of the war. No one will mistake another North Korean attack on the South as a communist challenge or a war by proxy.

As much as the war has transformed over the years, it has also stayed very much the same. By titling this book *Brothers at War*, I highlight the second major theme: the continuous struggle between North and South Korea for the mantle of Korean legitimacy. It was this competition, after all, that had given rise to Kim Il Sung's ambition to reunify the peninsula by force in June 1950. Although Kim did not succeed in this endeavor, he never gave up on his dream of "liberating" the South. By the late 1960s, when it appeared that South Korea was winning the legitimacy war against the North, owing to the South's rapid economic growth and greater international stature, Kim embarked on a series of provocative actions in the hope of toppling the South Korean regime. These events were remarkable for the brazenness in which Kim tried to co-opt his allies, the Soviet Union and China, to back him in starting a second Korean War. While these efforts ultimately failed, they reveal Kim's increasing desperation to undermine the South's growing global stature and influence. By the 1990s, few people could deny that North Korea had lost its legitimacy war with the South. The contrast between the two "brothers" could not have been more stark. Today, North Korea is an aid-dependent nation, wracked by hunger, repression, and a looming legitimacy crisis. This book puts this legitimacy struggle in a longer historical perspective to consider how the fraternal conflict has influenced, and continues to influence, East Asia and the world.

This book is also a military history of the war. The critical importance I give to military campaigns and operations arises from my conviction that it was during the life-and-death struggles in Korea that cold war antagonisms were hardened and perceptions of the enemy were formed. I argue that these perceptions were just as important in understanding American and Chinese behavior after the armistice, for they continued to influence America's view of China and China's view of America. Certainly, the two "lost" decades in Sino-American relations between the outbreak of the war in 1950 and Nixon's opening to China in 1972 came about because of attitudes forged by both parties during the war.

At the same time that the Korean War influenced the cultural perceptions of the enemy, it transformed society at home. When the armistice was signed in 1953, the United States, for the first time in its history, emerged staunchly anticommunist, with a large permanent standing army, a huge defense budget, and military bases around the world. The war did much to forge a new China too. China had lost nearly half a million men, but Mao Zedong emerged with his reputation intact and his power greatly enhanced. Emboldened by his success, Mao applied what he learned during the war to building his communist utopia at home, stoking the flames of Sino-Soviet competition in the process. The war significantly transformed the two Koreas as well. The military on both sides of the DMZ became the strongest, most cohesive, best-organized institutions in Korean life. For the first time since the twelfth century, a military regime took power in South Korea in 1961, marking the beginning of its extraordinary path toward economic development and the source of its eventual "triumph" in its legitimacy struggle with the North.

Something about North Korea invites people to view it hermetically, not unlike the way Westerners wrote about the "Hermit Kingdom" after their travels to Korea in the nineteenth century. "It can hardly be a cause of surprise," observed the German businessman and traveler Ernst Oppert in 1879, "that a system so strictly and severely carried out, combined with a reputation for inhospitality not altogether undeserved, would have been thought sufficient to deter others from any attempt to form a closer acquaintance with this country. It naturally follows that foreigners have found it next to impossible to collect any reliable information on the subject there, and Corea has remained to us like a sealed book, the contents of which we have yet to study."[1] Similar observations could be made about North Korea today. The place is uniformly characterized in the West as "bizarre," "erratic," or simply "baffling." North Korean experts also tend to isolate and insulate North Korean uniqueness, focusing on Kim Il Sung's cult of personality and the regime's Stalinist-Confucian system. For many, the regime's behavior is explained either as a ruthless ploy to maintain its hold on power and privilege or as a "rational" response to the legitimate threats posed by hostile foreign powers, namely, the United States.[2] Both interpretations have focused on the actions of the regime in which North Korea's ongoing legitimacy war with the South plays little or no role.

North Korea's main security threat, however, is not the United States. It is the prosperity, wealth, and prestige of South Korea. The greatest challenge of the North Korean regime is not how it will feed its own people; it is how it will come to terms with its own humiliating defeat. South Korea's miraculous story of economic growth and democratic progress threatens the regime's hold on power precisely because the more North Koreans know about the South, the less likely they are to put up with the conditions of poverty and repression at home. It is the regime's pending legitimacy crisis that drives it to act in "irrational" ways. This is why it explodes nuclear devices, launches missiles, fires on South Korean naval vessels, and shells remote islands. A North Korean poster sums up these anxieties: "We will reckon decisively with anyone, anywhere who meddles with our self-respect."[3] Any reforms that would make North Korea look more like the South cannot be accepted, for they would undermine the entire legitimacy of the regime and spell the end of the Kim dynasty.

More than sixty years after North Korea invaded South Korea, the first major hot war of the cold war has yet to end. The fighting resolved nothing of the internal Korean issues that had caused the war in the first place, and the status quo ante was restored. Today, the Korean peninsula remains roughly divided where the conflict began, and the DMZ that separates North and South Korea is the most heavily fortified border in the world. Two million soldiers face each other along a two-and-a-half-mile-wide strip of land straddling the 155-mile-long Military Demarcation Line. President Bill Clinton once called the DMZ "the scariest place on earth." This is hardly an exaggeration. Should fighting break out again on the Korean peninsula, the ramifications on the region and the world would be catastrophic. There is also reason to hope, however, that given the regional powers' experience in dealing with this sixty-year-old conflict, they will eventually come up with a solution to finally end it. China is the key and has the best potential to bring this about.

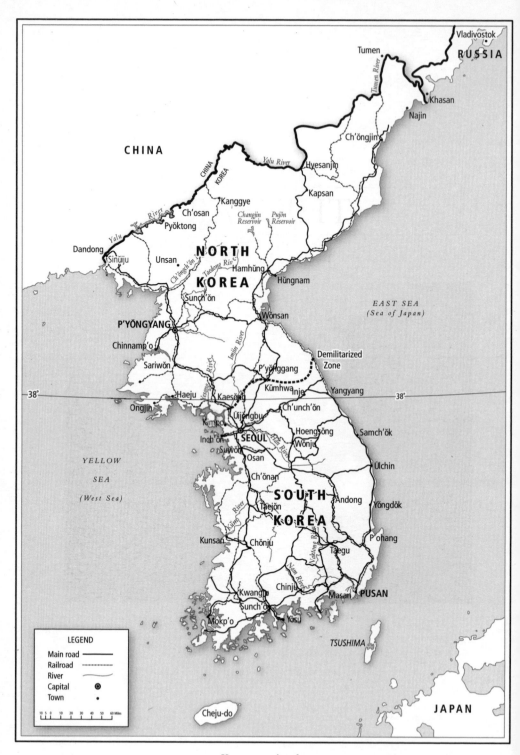

Korean peninsula

PART I

THE WAR

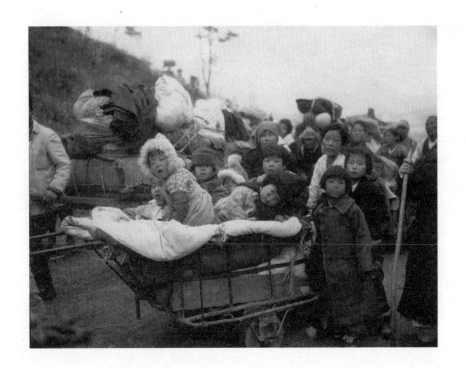

In 1943, in the middle of World War II, President Franklin D. Roosevelt, Premier Joseph Stalin, and Prime Minister Winston Churchill discussed the fate of Korea at the Cairo Conference, in anticipation of Korea's liberation from Japanese rule. Roosevelt hoped to grant Korea independence "in due course" after a period of trusteeship under the Allied Powers. This did not sit well with the Korean people. The Korean nation had been in existence far longer than any of the Allied Powers. By the seventh century, Korea was a unified nation with its own language, culture, monarchy, state bureaucracy, and centuries of high civilization comparable to that in neighboring China and Japan. Korea had been an independent nation for over a thousand years when Japan annexed it in 1910.

Korea's fate after World War II was not decided by a trusteeship, but by military conditions on the ground. Roosevelt anticipated there would be heavy losses in defeating the Japanese forces in China and Korea. Hoping to leave those operations to Soviet forces, he agreed at the Yalta Conference in February 1945 that for entry into the war against Japan, Stalin would get the southern Sakhalin and the Kurile Islands, the lease of ports at Dairen [Dalian] and Port Arthur [Lüshun], and control of key railroads in northeast China, formerly Manchuria. At the Potsdam Conference in July 1945, news of the successful testing of the atomic bomb significantly dampened President Harry Truman's enthusiasm for a quick Soviet entry into the war. Japan surrendered virtually overnight in August soon after the atomic bombings of Hiroshima and Nagasaki, coupled with rapid Soviet advances in Manchuria. Truman, who had become president after Roosevelt's death in April, proposed that the occupation of Korea be shared, divided along the 38th parallel. To his surprise, Stalin agreed. Although the entire peninsula had been his for the taking, Stalin was focused more on consolidating control over Eastern Europe. Control over the northern half of Korea was enough to secure Soviet interests without unduly antagonizing Washington. Eventually, the two zones were to be united under a trusteeship, but as the cold war heated up in Europe, it soon became clear that no reconciliation between the superpowers, and their respective zones, would be possible.

Violent upheavals by communists and leftists plagued the American zone. In the face of Soviet opposition, a UN-sponsored election for a national assembly was conducted but only in the South in May 1948. The new national assembly chose an aging and fiery nationalist, Syngman Rhee, to be the first president of the

Republic of Korea. Four months later, in September 1948, the Democratic People's Republic of Korea was established in the north, headed by a young former Soviet Army captain and anti-Japanese guerilla fighter, Kim Il Sung. By the end of 1948, two antithetical and antagonistic regimes were formed, each with its own vision of Korea's future.

Stalin gave Kim Il Sung the green light to launch the invasion of South Korea, which took place at dawn on June 25, 1950. Within a week, American forces, under the UN flag, were committed in the fighting. Kim Il Sung's war of liberation had turned global, and China's entry in October 1950 risked expansion into World War III. The unfinished war, the first hot war of the cold war, intensified global confrontation and competition between the United States and the Soviet Union. Paradoxically, the new international order that resulted from the fighting signifi- cantly reduced the possibility of a world war by establishing a stable balance of power that neither side was willing to upset.

CHAPTER ONE

Liberation and Division

S hortly before noon on August 15, 1945, Kim Eun-kook turned on the radio. His grandfather told the young boy that an important announcement was to be broadcast at noon and that they would listen to it together. The day before, the police had come through his neighborhood in Hamhŭng city to remind everyone to listen to the radio because the emperor would be speaking. "The emperor was going to say something about a 'fantastic weapon' invented by Japan," the old man told the boy. The weapon was supposed to "wipe out the Americans in no time" and win the war for Japan.

Eun-kook and his grandfather sat together on the veranda while they listened to the crackling notes of the Japanese national anthem. Although they had been reminded by the police to face the radio and touch the floor with their foreheads when the emperor spoke, they did no such thing. Both remained sitting upright and cross-legged. Then the emperor spoke. Eun-kook translated the speech for his grandfather because the old man could not understand Japanese. At first the young boy had a hard time making sense of the emperor's words. Neither he nor his grandfather, or any of the emperor's subjects for that matter, had ever heard the voice of the emperor before.

"Well, what is he saying?" asked the old man. "Has he said anything important yet?" The boy shook his head. The emperor spoke in a complex form of Japanese that few people could understand. Eun-kook turned up the volume. Suddenly, he straightened up, jolted by what he had just heard. He told his grandfather that the emperor had just announced that Japan had lost the war and would surrender unconditionally to the Allied Powers. The old man grasped the boy and began sobbing. Hearing the cries, the boy's grandmother ran out to the veranda. She too began weeping openly when she learned the news. Before the emperor had finished speaking, Eun-kook abruptly turned off the radio. He ran outside and took down the Japanese flag that hung by the door. Showing it to his grandmother, he asked what he should do with it. "Burn it," she said.[1]

End of Empire

For tens of millions of Koreans who listened to the Japanese emperor's announcement that afternoon, August 15 was a day of joyous celebration, marking freedom from thirty-five years of colonial servitude. Despite the fervor of the moment, however, liberation carried a heavy price. Korea was not liberated by Koreans, and so Korea was subjugated to the will and wishes of its liberators. While thousands of Japanese flooded the trains and ferries to go back to Japan, the Americans and Soviets took control. American planners had only a vague notion of what would happen to Korea after Japan's collapse. Korea had never been important to the United States. Forty years earlier, President Theodore Roosevelt had taken a cold-eyed, realistic view of the situation in northeast Asia. He had accepted Japan as the regional hegemon and praised Japan's success and progress from a feudal state to world power in less than four decades. Roosevelt's recognition of Japan's "special interest" in Korea after it defeated Russia in the Russo-Japanese War (1904–5), a war he helped end by negotiating a peace treaty, for which he received the Nobel Peace Prize, had facilitated Korea's colonization. For this Japan had agreed to recognize America's special interest in the Philippines.

Theodore Roosevelt's complicity in Korea's colonization would be rectified in 1945 by his cousin's vision of a free and independent Korea. After World War II, Franklin Delano Roosevelt (FDR) embraced a new world order that would fundamentally transform the status of Japanese and European colonies. He advocated the virtues of representative democracy, aid to the oppressed, free trade, and open markets. But before full independence could be granted to Korea and other former colonies, FDR envisioned a period of trusteeship by the Allied Powers to oversee internal affairs and prepare them for independence and self-rule. He was also careful to ensure that postcolonial nations would not orient themselves against American interests. Although at first opposed, Churchill agreed, because the Cairo Declaration did not specifically infringe on

Britain's own colonial holdings and named only Korea for trusteeship. The Declaration, published on December 1, 1943, contained the first Great Power pledge by the United States, Great Britain, and China to support Korean independence "in due course." Stalin responded positively about the trusteeship idea when FDR told him about it at their meeting in Tehran shortly after the Cairo Conference, but Stalin thought the period of trusteeship should be as short as possible.[2]

The proposal, however, was ill defined and lacked specifics on how a joint trusteeship in Korea was supposed to work. In the end, it was not resolved through an agreement, but by military events on the ground. More than FDR's grand design for a new world order, it was the sudden collapse of Japan that would determine Korea's future, as well as the post–World War II order in Asia. At Yalta in February 1945, as the end of World War II approached, FDR and Stalin agreed that Soviet forces would liberate Korea while the Americans would invade the Japanese mainland.[3] Stalin expected much in return for liberating Manchuria and Korea. American General Douglas MacArthur, the Supreme Commander for the Allied Powers (SCAP) for the Japanese occupation, warned, "They would want all of Manchuria, Korea, and possibly parts of North China. The seizure of territory was inevitable, but the United States must insist that Russia pay her way by invading Manchuria at the earliest possible date after the defeat of Germany."[4] Roosevelt tacitly agreed. Without consulting Churchill or the Chinese leader Chiang Kaishek (Jiang Jieshi), FDR made a secret deal with Stalin conceding the Kurile Islands, the southern half of Sakhalin, and special privileges in Manchuria for Soviet entry into the war against Japan.[5]

By the time the Potsdam Conference was held in July following Germany's surrender, the situation had changed dramatically, owing to the death of FDR in April and the success of the atomic bomb program. The main goal of the Potsdam Conference was to establish a vision for the postwar world order, but the bomb's existence had complicated matters between the United States and the Soviet Union. American Secretary of War Henry Stimson told President Harry Truman at the conference that the atomic bomb would be ready in a matter of days for use against Japan. Truman then approached Churchill to discuss what they should tell Stalin. If they told him about the bomb, he might try to enter the war against Japan as soon as possible. The bomb provided the possibility of circumventing a costly invasion of Japan, and the need for Soviet help became far less pressing. Truman decided to tell Stalin as late as possible and to describe it in the vaguest terms, not as an atomic bomb but as "an entirely novel form of bomb."[6]

Stalin, however, had already known of the bomb's existence for some time.[7] Andrei Gromyko, the Soviet ambassador to the United States at the time, recalled that Stalin was angry at the Americans' apparent lack of trust. "Roosevelt clearly felt no need to put us in the picture," Stalin later told Gromyko. "He could have done it at Yalta. He could simply have told me the atom bomb was going through its experimental stages. We were supposed to be allies."[8] Stalin told Truman that his forces would be ready for action by mid-August. With the atomic bomb on the table, however, Stalin secretly decided to advance the date of the attack by ten days, as Truman and Churchill had feared. He would outmaneuver the Americans, who had hoped to force Japan's surrender without the Soviet Union's entry into the war. At 11 p.m. on August 8, two days after "Little Boy" was dropped on Hiroshima, the Soviet Union declared war on Japan. Soviet forces began crossing into Manchuria an hour later on August 9. For just a week's worth of fighting, the Soviet Union reclaimed the territory lost in the Russo-Japanese War. Truman had lost the race to induce Japan's surrender before Soviet tanks rolled into Manchuria.[9]

Japan's sudden collapse caught everyone by surprise. The fate of the Korean peninsula suddenly became of interest to the Americans. The Soviet advance through Manchuria was so rapid that it would be able to occupy all of the Korean peninsula before the Americans could get there. It was one thing to give up Korea to save American lives and quite another to simply hand it over to the Soviets. The United States realized that talks of joint trusteeship would be moot if the Soviets occupied all of Korea. The Americans decided to approach the Soviets with a proposal to divide the peninsula into American and Soviet zones of occupation, with the ultimate goal of creating a unified Korea under joint American and Soviet tutelage. But before such a request could be offered, a decision on where to divide the peninsula had to be made. This task fell on two U.S. Army colonels from the War Department staff, Charles Bonesteel, future commander of U.S. and UN forces in Korea in the late 1960s, and Dean Rusk, future secretary of state under Presidents John F. Kennedy and Lyndon B. Johnson. Using a *National Geographic* map and working late into the night under great pressure, they chose the 38th parallel. Rusk later recalled that "we recommended the 38th Parallel even though it was further north than could realistically be reached . . . in the event of Soviet disagreement," but to the surprise and relief of everyone, Stalin agreed.[10]

Why did he agree when Soviet forces could have easily occupied the entire peninsula? Rather than territorial gain, Stalin's main concern was to eliminate Japanese political and economic influence in the region. "Japan must forever be excluded from Korea," stated a June 1945 Soviet report on Korea, "since a Korea under Japanese rule would be a constant threat to the Far East of the USSR."[11] Stalin accepted a divided occupation in Korea because the Americans could help in neutralizing Japan. Japanese victory in the Russo-Japanese War had forced Russia to forfeit its interests in Korea and Manchuria for nearly half a century and to give up Russian territory in southern Sakhalin. Japan's demise gave Stalin the chance to regain Russia's pre-1905 position in the Far East. As Stalin triumphantly noted in a radio speech on September 2, the date of Japan's formal surrender, "The defeat of the Russian troops in the period of the Russo-Japanese War left grave memories in the minds of our people. It fell as a dark stain on our country. Our people trusted and awaited the day when Japan would be routed and the stain wiped out. For forty years we, the men of the older generation, have waited for this day. And now this day has come."[12]

Red Army in Korea

The first weeks of Soviet occupation did not bode well for the Koreans. The soldiers were not the Red Army's finest and lacked discipline. The initial wave of Russian troops behaved with widespread and indiscriminate violence toward the local population. Within days of their arrival, disturbing reports of rape and pillage filtered into the American zone from beleaguered Japanese and Korean refugees.[13] Harold Isaacs of *Newsweek* described a harrowing visit to Sŏngdo city, about fifty miles north of Seoul and now known as Kaesŏng, which the Russians had mistakenly occupied and then retreated from as it lies south of the 38th parallel. During their ten-day stay, the Russians had thoroughly ransacked the city's shops, wineries, and warehouses.[14] Moscow claimed northern Korea's economic resources as compensation for its week-long war against Japan. Industrial complexes in North and South Hamgyŏng provinces were particularly hard hit as Russian forces dismantled steel plants, textile mills, and dock facilities and shipped the parts back to the Soviet Union.[15]

Reports of the Soviet pillaging led many Americans to believe that support for the Russians in northern Korea would be short-lived. Remarkably, however, Korean resistance to Soviet occupation did not last long. Stalin ordered the commander of the Soviet occupation force to take control of the situation and "to explain to the local population ... that the private and public property of the citizens of North Korea are under the protection of Soviet military power ... [and] to give instruction to the troops in North Korea to strictly observe discipline, not offend the population, and conduct themselves properly."[16] By late September 1945, discipline markedly improved, and the harassment of the local population ended as the Soviet occupiers quickly began to establish control over their zone.[17] Ethnic Koreans already in service with the Soviet government and others were mobilized to help with the administration of the Soviet zone. While the occupation of northern Korea found the Soviets almost as unprepared and untrained for the task as the Americans were in the south, the available pool of these Soviet Korean citizens who were committed communists, spoke both Korean and Russian, and understood the political and cultural nuances of Korean society made the transition to Soviet-occupied northern Korea a fairly easy one.

The history of the Soviet Korean community is intimately intertwined with the turbulent history of Russo-Japanese relations. Although Korean emigration to the Russian Far East goes back to the mid-nineteenth century, the flow increased significantly after the Russo-Japanese War and Japanese colonization of the peninsula. Tens of thousands of Koreans during this period fled the Japanese colony and sought refuge in Russia. Following the Russian Revolution of 1917, many Korean communists joined the Bolsheviks in Russia's civil war. Japan's invasion of Manchuria in September 1931 and Stalin's pledge to aid Chiang Kai-shek's Nationalist forces against the Japanese further consolidated Soviet Koreans behind the Soviet regime in their fight against Japan. In 1932, all Soviet Koreans were granted Soviet citizen-

Ethnic Korean families living in the Soviet Far East, like Hum Bung-do and his wife (above), were the first among many ethnic minorities to be subjected to the hardships of deportation by the Soviet leadership in 1937. Their resettlement in Kazakhstan and Central Asia also offered a partial solution to depopulation in these areas. Forced collectivization, famine (1931–33), epidemics, and other hardships had killed some 1.7 million people in Kazakhstan alone. These losses created severe labor shortages, which were partly filled by the new Korean settlers. (COPYRIGHT KORYO SARAM: *THE UNRELIABLE PEOPLE*)

ship, but it did not spare them from Stalin's Great Purge of the late 1930s. Japan's invasion of China in 1937 was used as a pretext to forcibly relocate, at great human cost, the entire Korean community away from the Soviet Far East on the suspicion that they were instruments of the Japanese.[18] Between September and November 1937, some 180,000 Koreans were involuntarily resettled in the Soviet interior in Kazakhstan and Uzbekistan.[19] It was from these same communities that Stalin later recruited ethnic Koreans to help administer the Soviet zone.

The first cohort of Soviet Koreans arrived in P'yŏngyang in September 1945 to help set up the Soviet Civil Administration (SCA), the Soviet military government for the northern zone. "We call this period the 'Age of the Translators,'" wrote Lim Ŭn, a former North Korean official who defected to the Soviet Union in the 1960s. "The interpreters were powerful ambassadors of the Soviet Army Headquarters."[20] By quickly replacing top colonial Japanese and Korean officials and civil servants, the Soviets righteously claimed a sharp break from the colonial past. Marshal Aleksandr M. Vasilevsky, the commander in chief of the Soviet forces in the Far East, put Korean anti-Japanese sentiments to work on behalf of his troops. On August 9, the same day the Soviets invaded Manchuria, Vasilevsky issued an "Appeal by the Commander-in-Chief of the Soviet troops in the Far East to the People of Korea" that linked Korea's anti-Japanese colonial struggle to Russia's struggle against Japan:

> The dark night of slavery over the land of Korea lasted for long decades, and at last, THE HOUR OF LIBERATION HAS COME! The Red Army has, together with the troops of the allied armies, utterly destroyed the armies of Hitler's Germany, the permanent ally of Japan ... Now the turn of Japan has come. Koreans! Rise for a holy war against your oppressors ... Remember, Koreans, that we have a common enemy, the Japanese! Know that we will help you as a friend in the struggle for your liberation from Japanese oppression![21]

While the occupation was overseen by Soviet officers, law and order was maintained by a Soviet Korean bureaucracy that worked directly with the Korean population. Soon after liberation, several hundred self-governing People's Committees sprang up throughout the country, in both the north and the south, to help secure law and order in the immediate aftermath of liberation, but they quickly evolved into local governing groups with their own peacekeeping duties. Rather than banning them as the Americans had done in their zone, the Soviets used them by turning them "into core institutions of the pro-Soviet regime."[22]

Senior Soviet officers in Korea were not specialists in foreign affairs, let alone experts on Korea, but many of the key officers were, interestingly, veterans of the Russo-Finnish War of 1939–40, a fact that would later have consequences when the operational plan for the invasion of South Korea was formulated. Marshal Kirill Meretskov, who commanded the

Soviet forces attacking Manchuria and Korea and then became chief of the SCA, was a senior commander in the Finnish War and was personally chosen by Stalin for his proven ability in that conflict. "The wily man of Iaroslavl [Meretskov's headquarters in the Finnish War] would find a way of smashing the Japanese," Stalin said.[23] Another veteran of the Finnish War who played a key role in the occupation was Maj. Gen. Nikolai Lebedev. A political officer with limited military training, Lebedev participated in the liberation of Manchuria and northern Korea and became the head of the SCA in 1947. The most important personage was another Finnish War veteran, Col. Gen. Terentii Fomich Shtykov, head of the Soviet delegation to the United States–Union of Soviet Socialist Republics Joint Commission on Korea, the brainchild behind the creation of the SCA, and the first Soviet ambassador to North Korea. Khrushchev, future leader of the Soviet Union, described him as "brilliant."[24] Shtykov was known as Moscow's "Mr. Korea." He was, according to the historian Charles Armstrong, "instrumental in formulating Soviet policy toward Korea, had direct access to Stalin, and exercised close supervision of the political events in northern Korea."[25] Lebedev later said that "there was not an event in which Shtykov was not involved."[26]

With the Soviet Koreans working directly with the populace, Soviet authorities were able to control their zone unobtrusively while promoting Soviet policies. Yet, despite their central role in running the Soviet zone, the Soviet Koreans' influence over the Korean people was limited. Most of them had been born and raised in the Soviet Union and therefore had few if any close personal ties to the land or the people. Thus, there was an early recognition of the need for an indigenous Korean leader who had legitimacy in the Korean community while still being receptive to Soviet influence. The Soviets' first choice was Cho Man-sik. A devout Christian and nationalist who commanded great respect for his refusal to adopt a Japanese name in the 1940s, Cho was perhaps the most admired political figure in all of Korea and thus could have been an effective Soviet proxy.[27] Since the communist movement in northern Korea was virtually nonexistent, its main strength being in the south, there was no pool of Korean communists for the Soviets to choose from. The Soviets hoped to leverage Cho's popularity and prestige to put together a broad coalition of leftists and nationalists as a base of support for their policies and plans to create a pro-Soviet regime.

It was soon apparent, however, that Cho was not amenable to such an arrangement. Yu Sŏng-ch'ŏl, a Soviet Korean who later became chief of the North Korean army's Operations Bureau, recalled that Cho opposed Soviet policies and "refused to cooperate with the Soviet Occupation Forces." Even after Cho's refusal, "the Soviet Occupation Forces tried to recruit Cho through many different people. However, they were never successful in their attempts, and [because of] this the Soviets lost interest."[28]

The other logical choice was Pak Hŏn-yŏng, one of the key leaders of the Korean Communist Party (KCP). But Pak was from Seoul and was neither well known nor completely trusted in the north. "The decisive cause of Pak's failure," wrote Lim Ŭn, "was that he was unable to get 'a sign of wings' [a check mark next to his name] from Stalin." The Soviets also discounted Korean communists who had fought with the Chinese communists in the Chinese civil war, because they could not be trusted. Kim Mu-chŏng, more commonly known simply as Mu Chŏng, was perhaps the most prominent member of this faction. He participated in and survived the Long March with Mao Zedong in 1934–35 and was considered by his contemporaries as a "matchless star." "He won popularity as he was an eloquent speaker of great resources," observed Lim Ŭn. But it was precisely because of his strong ties to the Chinese communists "that the Soviets felt that they could not trust him."[29] This left one final group of Korean communists who might be tapped, the small band of former anti-Japanese guerillas in Manchuria who had found refuge in the Soviet Far East. Among them was a boyish thirty-three-year-old captain in the Soviet Army named Kim Il Sung. Yu Sŏng-ch'ŏl recalled that Kim had "considerable authority among the . . . partisans who, along with Kim, had risked their lives conducting anti-Japanese resistance operations . . . in Manchuria."[30]

Compared to Cho Man-sik, Pak Hŏn-yŏng, and Mu Chŏng, Kim Il Sung had far less experience as either a political leader or a military commander. The 88th Brigade at Khabarovsk, to which Kim Il Sung had been assigned as a young Soviet captain, was a reconnaissance unit that infiltrated into Japanese areas to gather information.[31] Yu, who met Kim in the 88th Brigade, recalled only one instance when Kim directly commanded a reconnaissance mission: "On June 4, 1937, Kim Il Sung led a group of some 200 partisans . . . across the border in an assault on the border village of Poch'ŏnbo killing several Japanese police and retreating after obtaining rations and funds from landlords there." A month after the Japanese surrender, Kim Il Sung and Yu Sŏng-ch'ŏl arrived in Wŏnsan. "At the time," recalled Yu, "I was not quite sure how the Soviets intended to use us in North Korea, but I believe there was no definite plan. Even at this time, none of us was thinking that Kim Il Sung would become the new leader of North Korea."[32] Still, visible interest in Kim Il Sung was shown when Col. Gen. Ivan Chistiakov, commander of the Soviet occupation army, personally greeted him. The first sign of Kim's rising star came at a mass rally in mid-October to honor the Soviet Army. It was there that Kim was introduced to the citizens of P'yŏngyang. Cho Man-sik was also asked by the Russians to give his blessing to the event by appearing alongside Kim.

By all accounts the event was a flop. When Lebedev, chief of the SCA, opened the rally and presented Kim as a national hero and an "outstanding guerilla leader," many were astonished and even angry. O Yŏng-jin, Cho Man-sik's personal secretary, recalled the public's reaction:

> [The people had anticipated a gray-haired veteran patriot] but they saw a young man of about 30 with a manuscript approaching the microphone ... His complexion was slightly dark and he had a haircut like a Chinese waiter ... "He is a fake!" All of the people gathered upon the athletic field felt an electrifying sense of distrust, disappointment, discontent, and anger ... There was the problem of age, but there was also the content of the speech, which was so much like that of the other communists whose monotonous repetitions had worn the people out.[33]

The Soviet authorities were alarmed and bewildered by the negative reaction, but they stuck with their choice and thereafter "placed enormous emphasis on improving Kim Il Sung's image through propaganda activities."[34]

In late 1945, Chistiakov announced that the People's Committees would be allowed to participate in political affairs if they interacted with proper Russian authorities.[35] This was followed by a requirement for all "anti-Japanese parties and democratic organizations" to register with the SCA and provide a roster of its members. The SCA was thus able to identify "activists" and control organizations that were deemed potentially subversive. Parties identified as anticommunist or sympathetic to the United States were banned.[36] Many Koreans reacted with outrage. In addition, contrary to the hope that the People's Committees would abolish the state purchase of grains, a policy the Japanese had forced on Korean farmers, no such reforms occurred. Instead, on August 20, the People's Committees officially announced plans for the state to purchase grain. For the average North Korean farmer, very little had changed before and after liberation.[37]

On November 23, riots broke out in Sinŭiju, a northwestern city on the Yalu River. Secondary-school students demonstrated against "the provincial police headquarters, People's Committee, and the provincial [communist] party headquarters calling for the removal of Communist and Soviet military rule." One account stated that "the police and Soviet troops opened fire killing 23 students and wounding some 700."[38] Soon after the uprising, a stream of people began to flow to the south. From early December 1945, six thousand refugees a day poured into the American zone, straining the U.S. military command's ability to handle them.[39] Student riots in the port city of Hamhŭng on the east coast in March 1946 exacerbated the situation.[40] By July 1947, the *New York Times* reported, nearly two million refugees had moved south from the Soviet zone.[41]

The Soviets welcomed this exodus, for it removed much of the anti-Soviet and anticommunist factions in their zone. Still, the uprisings in Sinŭiju and elsewhere were warnings to Kim Il Sung and his Soviet backers of the potential hazards from social unrest. Lebedev was particularly alarmed by reports of scattered violence. Political opponents shot and killed the chairman of a township People's Committee in the county of Haeju, and an ex-landlord attempted to murder a peasant committee member in the same province. There were reports of water tanks being poisoned and a food depot set on fire.[42] The Soviet response was to tighten control over political groups and activities. Kim Il Sung declared that social and political unrest had occurred because the Korean Communist Party (KCP) had weak ties to the masses. He called for the merging of "democratic forces" in northern Korea to create a united front. New members needed to be properly screened and trained, and old members vetted to purge reactionary elements. Local cells were brought under centralized party control. By December 1945, the contours of the future North Korean regime had already begun to take shape.[43]

General Hodge Goes to Korea

The Americans faced greater difficulties in governing their zone despite the initial goodwill of the Koreans. Many Koreans were familiar with the American missionaries who had been in Korea since the mid-nineteenth century. Moreover, a large number of prominent Korean leaders in the south, as in the north, were devout Christians. Few believed that American soldiers would act like the Russians and expected, with tremendous excitement, the prospect of independence and freedom.

The goodwill quickly evaporated soon after Lt. Gen. John R. Hodge and his XXIV Corps arrived in September 1945. A capable and blunt-speaking field commander, Hodge went to Korea with the simple goal of disarming the Japanese and sending them back to Japan. With the trusteeship plan still not fully settled, American policy in East Asia was focused not on the occupation of Korea, but on the occupation of Japan. The focus on Japan would have lasting implications for Korea. General MacArthur adopted an "enlightened" policy, treating the Japanese not as America's conquered foe, but as a new and liberated friend. Arriving

Parade welcoming the Americans on September 16, 1945. Many of the welcoming parades also featured Soviet flags as the Korean people were not sure whom their liberators would be. (U.S. NATIONAL ARCHIVES AND RECORDS ADMINISTRATION)

in Tokyo at the end of August, MacArthur believed that the occupation should make maximum use of existing institutions to govern "from above" while seeking to induce radical changes "from below." America, he said, would lead the Japanese by example. Setting out to reform the Japanese of their "backward" and "feudalistic" culture, MacArthur sought to reweave Japan's political, social, cultural, and economic fabric and revise the very way the Japanese thought of themselves. It was a role he relished.[44] But America's occupation policy for Japan had confusing implications for Korea. If the Japanese were to be reformed and treated as friends, where did that leave the Koreans, victims of Japan's brutal colonial regime?

Hodge did not give much thought to the question since his primary concern was to disarm and repatriate the Japanese. He was also unsure of the reception he and his troops would receive when they arrived in Korea. Colonel Kenneth Strother of the XXIV Corps staff recalled Hodge's uneasy reaction: "At the time and in the atmosphere which had been generated by four years of combat with the Japanese, the thought of trusting the lives of a small group of American soldiers to the Japanese Army [in Korea] was startling." Moreover, there had also been some doubt as to whether the Japanese were in full control of the situation in Korea. "The Japanese government was having plenty of trouble between their surrender and the arrival of the American occupation forces," observed Strother. "As we later learned, a conspiracy against the government to prevent national surrender developed on August 16 into an open revolt by the garrison troops of Tokyo. This was put down with bloodshed, leaving serious question as to the attitude we might expect in the Japanese troops stationed in Korea."[45] The precarious state of affairs in liberated Korea and the potential for violence led Hodge to decide that he would have to rely on incumbent Japanese officials to carry out the essential functions of governance. To his relief, Hodge and his men were received peacefully and courteously, dispelling fears that they might face a hostile or unstable situation in Korea. However, the Koreans reacted with outrage when Hodge announced that Japanese officials, including the hated Governor General Abe Nobuyuki, would continue to administer the American zone. Hoping to placate their anger, Hodge announced that "Abe's position would be analogous to that of the Emperor of Japan," meaning that he would "merely be a figurehead." For a people who had been oppressed by this "figurehead" for the last thirty-five years, these were hardly reassuring words.[46]

On September 9, Hodge and Abe signed the formal surrender document. As Abe reached over to sign with the pen, he began to tremble. "His complexion suddenly took on an alarming green cast," recalled Strother. Turning his head away, Abe "vomited quietly in his handkerchief before affixing his own signature." Hodge was deeply affected. As a professional military man, Hodge respected the Japanese as loyal soldiers and empathized with the pain of their defeat. Earlier, Abe had requested that he and his family remain in the official residence for a few extra days because his wife was ill with pneumonia. Strother recalled that "Hodge, a stern-looking, tough talking man, replied with obvious compassion that the Abes could stay in residence as long as they wanted."[47] Such acts of compassion toward the Japanese, mostly because Japanese cooperation was essential, enraged the Koreans. They deeply resented the Americans treating the Koreans as a conquered people while conferring with the Japanese on the future of their country. They also questioned American motives. Just what kind of liberators would allow a defeated nation to remain in power? What kind of deal was being struck? The situation smacked of the Great Power jostling over Korea that had occurred at the end of the nineteenth century and had led to subjugation under Japan.

The Americans soon realized that retaining Japanese officials was harming their ability to govern. MacArthur wrote to Hodge, "For political reasons it is advisable that you should remove from office immediately: Governor-General Abe, Chiefs of all bureaus of the Government-General, provincial governors and provincial police chiefs." He concluded, "You should furthermore proceed as rapidly as possible with the removal of other Japanese and collaborationist Korean administrators." This was easier said than done. Could the Americans govern without the Japanese? H. Merrell Benninghoff, the State Department political advisor to Hodge, thought that the "removal of Japanese officials is desirable from the public opinion standpoint," but they must be relieved "only in name [because] there are no qualified Koreans for other than the low-ranking positions, either in government or in public utilities and communications." The question was how long Hodge and his staff would have to rely on the Japanese. Benninghoff pointed out a possible way out: "Seoul, and perhaps southern Korea as a whole, is at present politically

divided into two distinct political groups. On the one hand there is the
so-called democratic or conservative group, which numbers among its
members many of the professional and educational leaders who were
educated in the United States or in American missionary institutions in
Korea. In their aims and policies they demonstrate a desire to follow the
western democracies." On the other hand, "there is the radical or communist group. This apparently is composed of several smaller groups
ranging in thought from left of center to radical. The avowed communist group is the most vocal and seems to be supplying the leadership."
Benninghoff believed that the U.S. Army Military Government in Korea
(USAMGIK) would be able to work with the so-called conservative
group. He also optimistically concluded, "Although many of them have
served with the Japanese, that stigma ought eventually to disappear."[48]

Early in the occupation, USAMGIK had attempted to be neutral in
its treatment of the various and often hastily organized Korean political
groups. But this policy proved to be increasingly difficult. For practical
purposes, the Americans needed Koreans who spoke English, but "it so
happened that these persons and their friends came largely from the mon-
eyed classes because English had been a luxury among Koreans." They
were therefore part of the privileged conservatives far removed from the
masses.[49] The Americans also needed Koreans who supported the occupation's aims, which meant that these Koreans required American support
to remain in power. The "radical" group identified by Benninghoff did not
fit either of these categories.

Ironically, it was the Japanese who were largely responsible for the
viability of the so-called "radical" group. On August 14, Abe met with
Yŏ Un-hyŏng, a moderate leftist who was rumored to be a member of a
Korean communist group in Shanghai. Abe said that the Japanese were
planning to surrender the following day, and asked Yŏ to organize a
group to help maintain order. Yŏ agreed. Within a few weeks, the organization that was meant to keep the Koreans in line during the transition period until the arrival of the Americans had transformed into
a self-declared and de facto Korean government. Two days before the
Americans' arrival, Yŏ declared that his newly established organization
was not only a political party but also the government of the Korean
People's Republic (KPR). The KPR group attracted many populist and
left-leaning nationalists whose paramount concern was not ideology, but
the establishment of an independent Korean state.[50]

On the morning of September 8, three leading members of the KPR group, including Yŏ, went to meet Hodge. Yŏ viewed the American occupation command as a transitional authority between the Japanese colonial government and the newly established KPR. The members had come to offer their services as a liaison between the American military command and the Korean people. They were also emphatic about removing the Japanese from Korea as quickly as possible. Hodge, ironically, refused to meet them because the KPR group was formed with Japanese support. He considered it "unwise to give even the slightest possible appearance of favoring any political group."[51] In a double irony, it also became apparent that the allegedly "pro-Japanese" KPR was not supported by the Japanese, who considered Yŏ to be a "political opportunist with communist leanings." The Americans were warned that the KPR was "better organized and more vocal" than any other political group in Korea, and that "the nature and the extent of actual communist (Soviet Russia) infiltration cannot be stated with certainty, but may be considerable."[52]

More alarming was the KPR's unwillingness to cooperate with USAMGIK. By mid-September, the KPR began organizing numerous subsidiary groups throughout the country. The group released political prisoners, assumed responsibility for public safety, and organized food distributions. In addition, the KPR called for a national election as early as March 1946. Realizing that the authority of the occupation was being undermined by the KPR, Maj. Gen. Archibald Arnold, the military governor of Seoul, issued a strongly worded statement against the organization for "confusing and misleading" the Korean people. He declared that "there is only one Government in Korea south of the 38 degrees north latitude"; it is the government "created in accordance with the proclamations of General MacArthur, the General Orders of Lieutenant General Hodge and the Civil Administration order of the Military Governor." Arnold also mocked the KPR's "self-appointed 'officials,' 'police,' groups, big (or little) conferences," which he said were "entirely without any authority, power or reality," and warned the KPR leaders that the "puppet show" must end. "Let us have no more of this," he declared. "For any man or group to call an election as proposed is the most serious interference with the Military Government, an act of open opposition to the Military Government and the lawful authority of the Government of Korea under the Military Government."[53]

Arnold's proclamation appalled the KPR leaders. While his statement was meant to show who was in charge, its demeaning tone and condescending language resulted in further alienating the KPR and ordinary Koreans from the Americans. In response, the KPR published *The Traitors and the Patriots*. The pamphlet began with an exposure of allegedly pro-Japanese officials who were advising USAMGIK. It attacked the notion that USAMGIK was the only legitimate government south of the 38th parallel. The KPR, the pamphlet asserted, "was the duly constituted organ of the people," and Arnold's statement was condemned as an "insult to the Korean people."[54]

By mid-October 1945, Hodge understood that the KPR could have no future role under the American occupation. USAMGIK gave its support to the Korean Democratic Party (KDP), the group of conservatives first identified by Benninghoff. What the Americans needed most at this time was bilingual, educated, and above all, cooperative allies to deal with rising discontent and revolutionary sentiments. Hodge was less worried about the KPR's leftist ideology than its deliberate attempts to subvert his authority. A crackdown on the KPR soon ensued. His willingness to accept leftist organizations as long as they did not challenge USAMGIK's authority also reflected MacArthur's tolerance of leftists and communists in Japan at the time.

Hodge miscalculated in thinking that disbanding the KPR would end the challenges to USAMGIK's authority. Many Koreans were by now deeply disillusioned by the failed expectations of liberation. Especially critical was land reform and rice supply. USAMGIK seized Japanese-owned land but did not turn it over to Korean farmers. Theoretically, former Japanese land was to be held in escrow for redistribution as part of a land reform plan, but lack of planning led to rumors that the land would be given to wealthy landlords, those who had collaborated with the Japanese, and supporters of the American occupation. Many Koreans believed that the Americans were reestablishing the same system of land ownership and political dictatorship that had prevailed under the Japanese. Furthermore, in the fall of 1945, USAMGIK abolished the price controls on rice. The bumper crop in 1945 led many to expect that for the first time in decades, Koreans would have an ample supply of rice since no rice would be sent to Japan, as had been the practice during the colonial period. But just the opposite result occurred. With price

General Hodge broadcasting to the United States about the conditions of American troops in Korea, April 18, 1948. (U.S. NATIONAL ARCHIVES AND RECORDS ADMINISTRATION)

controls gone, speculators bought up the rice they could find, driving up the price. Greedy farmers withheld rice in anticipation of greater profits. USAMGIK did little to stop the hoarding, while hungry Koreans demanded that price ceilings be reinstituted. In March 1946, the Americans were forced to issue directives for rationing, but these controls only reminded Korean farmers of the former Japanese system. To make matters worse, the average Korean received only half the amount of rice he or she had received under the Japanese.[55] "As a result of its handling of the rice problem, the Koreans arrived at a complete loss of faith in the Military Government," lamented an attorney who served in Korea during this period.[56]

The Americans also had a problem the Soviets did not: the repatriation of several hundred thousand Japanese soldiers and civilians.[57] In October alone, more than eighty-eight thousand were evacuated, creating enormous administrative and logistical pressures on the relatively small American force. Meanwhile, hundreds of thousands of Korean refugees from the Soviet zone and Manchuria added to the south's economic plight. "The refugee crisis," stated an embassy report, "is making living conditions increasingly hard. Three-quarters of the population of Korea is now in our hands and the Koreans are looking to us for a solution to their problem."[58] Inflation, black markets, scarcity of consumer

The rice shortage in Pusan came to a head on the evening of July 6, 1946, when a mob of hungry people attempted to break into a rice distribution center. (U.S. NATIONAL ARCHIVES AND RECORDS ADMINISTRATION)

goods, and an unbalanced wage scale added to the economic and political confusion in the American zone.

The morale of the Americans was a problem as well. Charles Donnelly, an economic advisor to the U.S. Army Forces in Korea (USAFIK was the overall military command in Korea and oversaw USAMGIK), noted that "the shortage of typewriters, stencils, and chairs is scandalous."[59] Empty shelves in the post exchange glumly revealed the reality of being at the end of a long supply line from the United States. One reporter counted the following items for sale in early December: "ten cartons of cigarette, five bars of candy, six toothbrushes, several packages of razor blades, and a few pads of writing paper, all for 500 soldiers." Americans, who "just a few weeks ago were selling cigarettes to the Koreans, are now buying them back at a high cost . . . grumbling soldiers and officers are complaining that folks at home don't seem to care, now that the war is over, whether we are getting supplies or not."[60] Another chronic problem was theft. "Thievery here is rampant," Donnelly complained. "My felt hat was stolen from my office. Miss Carol's handbag with sixty dollars in it was taken from her desk while she was in the restroom. Simon lost his hat and top coat. A resident in the Bizenya [a hotel] awoke to find that his room was literally stripped of everything except the bed in which he was sleeping." Relations between the Americans and the Koreans were increasingly strained. The Koreans resented the occupation while the Americans increasingly disliked the Koreans because they acted "like difficult spoiled children." "The Koreans are unwilling to take the time to develop political and economic know-how," wrote Donnelly. "All they want is for Americans to get out of their country so that they can run it by themselves."[61] By the end of 1945, the Americans were struggling to gain control over an increasingly chaotic and demoralizing situation. Something had to be done.

Two Koreas

Prior to 1945, Stalin had been vague in committing to a joint trust-eeship for Korea, and now that the Soviets had successfully set up a relatively stable, friendly, and well-functioning government in their zone, he became less enthusiastic. The Soviets were barely responsive to American initiatives to unify the economy or to relax travel restrictions between the two zones. Hoping to exchange a trainload of supplies for coal, Hodge was shocked to learn that the Soviets not only refused to send the coal, but also kept the train.[1] The Americans faced far greater economic and political turmoil than the Soviets. Hodge and his staff identified the uncertainty of Korea's future as the greatest source of political discontent. Establishing an independent, united, and democratic Korea was clearly a priority. The turmoil provided an ideal condition for leftist and communist groups to flourish. Edwin Pauley, an advisor to President Truman who visited Korea in early 1946, warned Truman that "communism in Korea could get off to a better start than practically anywhere else in the world. The Japanese [had] owned the railroads, all the public utilities including power and light as well as all of the major industries and natural resources." Now the communists could "acquire them without any struggle of any kind." For this reason "the United States should not waive its title or claim to Japanese external assets located in Korea until a democratic (capitalist) form of government is assured."[2] But how was such a government to be established? Joint trusteeship leading to independence seemed to be the only viable option to avoid a divided Korea. Until an agreement was concluded with the Soviets, however, USAMGIK would be forced to tighten control, build closer relationships with more conciliatory groups like the KDP and prevent a takeover by the leftists. While Washington was considering trusteeship with the Soviets, Americans on the ground were strengthening their control over their zone and hence deepening the division between the two zones.

The contradiction frustrated the Americans in Korea. They were critical of the trusteeship idea. William Langdon, Hodge's political advisor, pointed out the obvious: that Koreans of all political persuasions would protest fervently against it. "After one month's service in liberated Korea and with background of earlier service in Korea," Langdon wrote to the secretary of state in Washington, "I am unable to fit trusteeship to the actual conditions here or to be persuaded of its sustainability from moral and practical standpoints and, therefore, believe we should drop it." As an alternative, Langdon proposed a trusteeship plan to begin in the American zone. He noted that during the transition period between USAMGIK and the formation of an independent Korean government, the Soviets should be invited to participate in the process. But if the Soviets were not forthcoming, the United States should carry out the plan in the southern zone. The deteriorating political situation in the south required immediate action for transition to independence with or without the Soviets. "It is imperative that the U.S. act," warned Langdon, as "[only such actions] will convince the Korean leaders that our intentions of their independence are genuine and in this way we can win their support in fighting communism, unrest, and the hostility of the masses toward us."[3]

Hodge and his staff, as well as MacArthur and his staff, agreed with Langdon. The issue boiled down to promising Koreans their independence by backing political leaders and groups conciliatory to American interests. But whom? The KDP's leaders had always had the ears of the Americans, but the group's political power base was weak due to its lack of contact with the masses and past associations with the Japanese. Someone without links to the colonial regime, but with nationalist standing among the Koreans, was needed. KDP leaders suggested Syngman Rhee (Yi Sŭng-man). In many ways, Rhee was the perfect candidate. He had spent much of his life overseas, mostly in the United States, where he earned a PhD from Princeton in 1910. After a two-year stint in Seoul as a Christian educator and missionary, he returned to the States in 1912. In 1919 he was elected the first president of the Korean Provisional Government (KPG), a government in exile in Shanghai. He went back to the United States in 1925 after being expelled by the KPG and remained there until the end of World War II. While in the States, he was politically active in the Korean independence movement. He was fluent in English as well as untainted by association with the colonial regime. Rhee was seventy years old in 1945, but vigorous. He was also difficult, stubborn, and fiercely patriotic. Francesca Rhee, his Austrian wife whom he met in Geneva in 1933, wistfully wrote in a letter to a friend, "When I married Dr. Rhee, I married Korea."[4]

Rhee's stint as president of the KPG was marked by strife. He tried hard to get American recognition of the KPG as the legitimate government of Korea during the colonial period. Some in the State Department found him and other KPG leaders "personally ambitious and somewhat irresponsible" and downplayed the clout of the KPG "even among exiles."[5] Nevertheless, Hodge and his advisors were eager to embrace him, believing that the legitimacy Rhee could bring to the KDP and the promise of Korean independence might be enough to stem the tide of political chaos in their zone. The State Department, however, still intent on pursuing trusteeship, dragged its feet. With backing from the War Department and MacArthur, however, Hodge prepared to create a governing body in the American zone. In any case, Hodge knew that the Soviets had already created a de facto government in the north, whether the State Department wanted to admit this or not. In the end, Washington settled on a two-track policy, building up "a reasonable and respected government" in the south that would deepen the division between the two zones, while pursuing trusteeship in the hope that the two could eventually be reunited.

After much pressure, the Soviets agreed to discuss trusteeship. In mid-December 1945, the U.S. secretary of state and foreign ministers from Great Britain and the Soviet Union met in Moscow to discuss a variety of post–World War II issues. Korea was high on the agenda. The Moscow Decision that came out of the conference included provisions for establishing a unified Korean government through Soviet-American cooperation to end zonal occupations. A joint commission formed from the Soviet and American occupation authorities was to formulate recommendations for establishing a single government. However, in preparing its recommendations, the agreement stated, "the Commission shall consult with the Korean democratic parties and social organizations." Once a provisional government was established, the Soviet Union,

Members of the U.S.-U.S.S.R. Joint Commission. From left to right: Brig. Gen. John
Weckerling; Col. Koruklenko; Mr. Tunkiv, Dr. Arthur Bunce; Lt. Gen. John Hodge,
Col. Gen. Terentii Fomich Shtykov; Maj. Gen. Albert E. Brown; Maj. Gen. Nikolai
Lebedev; Calvin M. Joyner; B. M. Balasonov; William R. Langdon; and Col. Lawrence
L. Lincoln, June 1, 1947. (U.S. NATIONAL ARCHIVES AND RECORDS ADMINISTRATION)

China, Britain, and the United States would oversee it in a trusteeship
for a period of up to five years.

Not surprisingly, the plan was greeted by wild protests in the south.
Schools were closed down, as were factories, stores, and public transportation, while people demonstrated in the streets. Hodge, who had
predicted the violent reaction, called on Song Chin-u, a leading member
of the KDP, and asked him to endorse the trusteeship plan. A haggard
Song tentatively agreed. The next morning, Hodge awoke to the dread-
ful news that Song was dead. He had been shot in the head in front of
his house.[6]

Other southern Korean leaders protested and claimed independence
from the Americans. Rhee, publicly distancing himself from Hodge,
spoke out against the Moscow Decision. He declared that the "self
respect of his nation would not permit the acceptance of this decision
or of anything short of full independence."[7] Kim Ku, a staunch rightist
and the last president of the KPG in Shanghai, called for a general strike
and insisted on immediate recognition of the KPG. Left-wing groups
were similarly outraged. The KCP denounced trusteeship. Opposition

by the Right and the Left opened the possibility for a powerful coalition
to challenge the trusteeship plan. On New Year's Day 1946, southern
communist party leader Pak Hŏn-yŏng signed a public anti-trusteeship
statement with members of the Kim Ku group. That same day, Pak met
with Hodge to tell him directly his opposition to trusteeship. A huge
"Citizens Rally against Trusteeship and for the Acceleration of National
Unification" was planned for January 3. For the first time since liberation,
the Right and the Left joined in a common cause to oppose the American and Soviet plan.[8]

But the cooperation did not last. Pak was summoned to P'yŏngyang
on January 2. He returned a changed man. He told party members that
the North Korean leadership had decided to support the Moscow Decision and trusteeship. Although many members balked, Pak made support
of trusteeship an issue of party loyalty. In an extraordinary about-face,
the January 3 rally, planned as an anti-trusteeship demonstration by Pak
and other Korean communists, became a rally in support of the Moscow
Decision. Moderate leftists were stunned and appalled. It was evident
that Soviet authority wielded far greater control over the northern zone
and the Korean communist movement than had been previously thought.
Compared to the Americans' unsuccessful efforts to get the KDP and
other conservative groups to support trusteeship, the Soviets were able,
within a matter of a few days, to quickly put their house in order. This
was the turning point the Americans needed to stabilize their zone.

Fierce opposition to trusteeship in the south temporarily united the
moderate Left and the Right. A full-blown anticommunist/anti-Soviet
movement enabled the Right to mobilize popular support for its policies for the first time. The communists were now painted as servants
of a foreign, anti-Korean, anti-independence pro-Soviet regime. While
the trusteeship controversy temporarily bolstered the American zone
by fracturing the Left, and provided greater legitimacy to the KDP and
other right-wing groups, the controversy had even greater consequences
in the Soviet zone, where it created a political crisis and the end of challenges to the regime.[9]

On January 1, 1946, the chief of the SCA, Maj. Gen. Andrei Romanenko,
asked Cho Man-sik to publicly endorse trusteeship and promised that
he would be made the first president of Korea if he did so. Cho refused
and was arrested, never to be heard from again. It was rumored that he

was executed in October 1950 along with other political prisoners soon after the Inch'ŏn landing.[10] Cho's arrest was followed by a roundup of other Korean nationalist leaders as the Soviets made an all-out effort to create a pro-Soviet proto-government in the north. In early February, the Soviets oversaw the creation of the Central People's Committee as a provisional government. Kim Il Sung became its chairman, making him, in effect, the interim premier. "Parting with Cho Man-sik without regret, Shtykov made up his mind to support Kim Il Sung as the head leader of democratic Korea and suggested this to Stalin," Lim Ŭn recalled.[11] With Cho Man-sik out of the way and the arrest of other "reactionaries," there was no longer a viable opposition leader or party in northern Korea.

The opening weeks of 1946 also saw dramatic changes to the situation in the American zone. Hodge realized the benefit of the KDP and other right-wing groups using the Moscow Decision as a catalyst for political unity. He allowed the belief to circulate in the south that it was the Soviets, not the Americans, who advocated trusteeship. Never in favor

The first formal meeting of the American-Soviet commission in Seoul. General Hodge is seated on the left, with General Shtykov in the middle and a female interpreter on the right, January 16, 1946. (U.S. NATIONAL ARCHIVES AND RECORDS ADMINISTRATION)

of the trusteeship idea, Hodge stepped out of bounds of his authority by openly siding with the Right in its opposition to the Moscow Decision. Shtykov was angry that Hodge had allowed newspapers in the American zone to falsely report that it had been the Soviets who forced trusteeship down Washington's throat. On January 22, the Soviet newspaper *Izvestia* published a strongly worded article accusing the southern rightists of "fermenting enmity against the Soviet Union."[12] Four days later at a press conference, Shtykov provided a detailed history of the trusteeship idea, declaring that it was "the Americans who had called for 'guardianship' for Korea for at least five years and possibly ten years, but that the Soviets opposed this and succeeded in obtaining adoption of the Russian plan."[13] Embarrassed over the flap, the State Department asked Hodge to clear up the "misunderstanding" and announce that Shtykov's account was essentially correct. Hodge sent back a blistering response: "It [the State Department request] is in itself complete evidence that the Department has paid little attention either to the information painstakingly sent in from those actually on the ground [in Korea] as to the psychology of the Korean people or to the repeated urgent recommendations of the commander and State Department political advisors . . . Just after the quelling of the revolt and riots brought about by the announcement of the trusteeship, our position here was the strongest since our arrival."[14]

Hodge was right. It was his opposition to the Moscow Decision that had temporarily elevated USAMGIK's status among Koreans in the south. Going against the will of the people by endorsing trusteeship would have destroyed American credibility and led to further chaos. He saw no hope in any future cooperation with the Soviets through a joint trusteeship plan or on any other basis. Hodge's remedy for Korea was to create a separate government in the south that would give the Koreans the independence they craved while shielding it from the "ruthless political machinery" in the north. Contrary to State Department officials, Hodge understood that the Moscow Decision was unworkable.

Hodge did not have to wait long for his view on the trusteeship to be vindicated. In the weeks leading up to the first meeting of the U.S.-U.S.S.R. Joint Commission tasked to establish an interim government, set for March 20, tensions had been building. On March 5, Winston Churchill delivered his fiery speech in Fulton, Missouri, in which he warned that "an iron curtain has descended across the [European] Continent." An angry Stalin fired back in an interview with *Pravda* that Churchill was nothing more than "a second Hitler." He defended his actions in Eastern Europe, stating that "it was only natural that the Soviet Union would welcome friendly nations on its borders." Picking up on Stalin's words about "friendly" nations, Hodge warned the Soviets before the first meeting that "the purpose of the American delegation is to see that a government [in Korea] corresponds to the views of the majority, not the minorities, no matter how vocal and well organized they are, or how energetic they may be in their political activities."[15] Clearly, Hodge was worried that the Soviets would favor "friendly" groups amicable to Soviet interests and exclude right-wing organizations from participating in the interim government.

Shtykov's opening speech proved Hodge correct. The Soviet officer attacked what he called "reactionary and anti-democratic groups" in the south that were offering "furious resistance" to the creation of "a democratic system in Korea." He called for a "decisive battle" against them. The criterion to determine whether a group was reactionary or anti-democratic was to be based on its support for the Moscow agreement. In other words, groups that opposed the Moscow Decision, which meant all right-wing and moderates in the south, were to be excluded from participating in the provisional government.[16] The Americans were stunned. After six weeks of fruitless discussion, the Joint Commission adjourned. Trusteeship seemed dead, and the path to permanent division appeared more certain than ever. Chistiakov later defended the Soviet position by stating that the reestablishment of Korea as an independent state required "the liquidation of the ruinous after-effects of long Japanese domination in Korea." Since the Soviet delegation was "guided by the aims and spirit of the Moscow Decision," whose purpose was to oversee the liquidation of Japanese influences, "it would therefore not be right to consult on the question of methods of fulfilling the Moscow Decision with those parties which had voiced opposition to this plan for Korea."[17] By insisting that all "pro-Japanese/anti-democratic" forces be *excluded* from the political process, the Soviets would be assured that Korea would rest in "friendly" hands. "If they [pro-Japanese forces] seize power in the [Korean] government," Shtykov told Hodge, "the government would not be loyal to Russia, and its officials would be instrumental in organizing hostile actions on the part of the Korean people against the Soviet Union."[18] These concerns underscored the extent to which the Russians feared the resurrection of Japanese power.

Failed Revolution

Suspension of the Joint Commission ushered in a period of armed struggle in the American zone. Pak Hŏn-yŏng returned to Seoul in July 1946 with instructions from Shtykov to merge the main leftist parties in the south to form the South Korean Workers Party (SKWP). In late September, a rail strike in Pusan spread throughout the American zone. More strikes followed, by postal employees, electrical workers, printers, and laborers in other industries. Students joined in, and USAMGIK faced its first real major crisis. By the end of September, the strikes became violent. On the evening of October 1, the Autumn Rebellion (also known as the Taegu Uprising) began. The police fired on striking workers at the Taegu railway station, killing one. An angry crowd assembled in front of the city police headquarters. Major John Plezia, an American advisor who was inside the headquarters, called for help from nearby American units. By the time American troops arrived, mob attacks had spread to other police stations. The next day, violence continued with vehemence. "It was open season on the police and all other natives who held jobs with the U.S. Military Government," stated one eyewitness account. "Mobs killed them on the streets, stormed police boxes and public offices and rooted them out of their homes and hiding places for slaughter." Rioters ransacked the homes of Korean officials, looting and killing. Hodge declared martial law and a crackdown. Thousands of alleged leftists were arrested. As order was restored over the following weeks, policemen and their rightist allies exacted revenge.[19]

The Americans believed that the communists and, in particular, Pak Hŏn-yŏng had instigated the strikes. Shtykov's diary clarified the Soviet involvement. The Soviets did not instigate the strikes, but their occurrence "provoked the intervention of Soviet leaders in the north." Shtykov provided advice and funneled large sums of money to support the general strike and the Autumn Rebellion. As unsettling as the uprising was for the Americans, it proved to be counterproductive for the communists. The riots resulted in loss of popular support for the Left and the emergence and rise of more extreme and less accommodating organizations from the Right. "There are no moderate groups in Korea anymore," Francesca Rhee lamented to a friend. "There are only Rightists and communists."[20] The forced merger of the Left into the SKWP had also alienated many moderate leftists, and the base of communist support shrunk to extremist groups. The successful repression of the uprising also revealed that the communists did not have the organizational strength necessary to bring about a revolution in the south. This, in turn, consolidated the forces of the Right, which became more powerful than ever before.

The most significant development was that the extreme violence perpetrated by both sides laid bare the pretense that reconciliation between the northern and southern zones was even possible. Although the United States and the Soviet Union were still officially bound to follow the Moscow Decision and the trusteeship plan, Syngman Rhee and other right-wing politicians began to actively petition to form a separate government in Seoul. "If anyone says Dr. Rhee should unite with the Reds or anyone else," wrote Rhee in a letter to his friend and advisor Robert Oliver, "tell him that Dr. Rhee will never cooperate with smallpox."[21] In January 1947, Rhee publicly repudiated the Moscow Decision. In a long and bitter diatribe against the Joint Commission, Rhee warned the Americans, "We will not accept the plan for a four power trusteeship for our country . . . It is ridiculous to believe that a nation with a 4,000 year old history of independence needs to be shepherded through a period of 'political tutelage.'"[22]

Hodge was in a difficult position. The political complications were accompanied by deteriorating living conditions in the American zone. Meanwhile, the Russians were simply biding their time. "They [the Russians] are playing now a game of waiting, a game of out-waiting us with the idea that we will tire and get out," Hodge told the U.S. House Appropriations Committee in May.[23] The Russian position had produced a deadlock. Southern rightist groups would never allow themselves to be excluded from the Joint Commission process, yet the Soviet position on excluding them was immutable. General Chistiakov expected his intransigence to pay off in terms of growing instability in the American zone. The longer the Joint Commission dragged on, the stronger the rightists' pressure in the south. The stalemate was bound to result in the splintering of the moderate center and confrontation between the Americans and the extreme Right. "If this trend continues," stated a 1947 interagency report, "it is apparent that our position in Korea will soon weaken to a point where it may become untenable. The Korean people are daily growing more antagonistic in their attitude toward the Military Government, toward U.S. objectives in Korea, and even toward the U.S. itself." The only alternative to continuing beyond the impasse was to form a separate government in the south, in effect creating an independent South Korea, but such a course was fraught with difficulties. Recognizing Korean independence in the southern zone would not solve its basic economic problems. "Only unification and a program of outside aid in rehabilitation can do that," wrote one political advisor, and the United States was "the only reliable source for such aid." In addition, the United States would have to establish safeguards to ensure that an independent southern Korea would not fall under Soviet domination, which meant a continued presence of American troops.[24] Two years after the liberation of Korea, the Americans still lacked a clear policy on their interest there. Unanswered was a basic question: Was the survival of a noncommunist Korea of sufficient importance to U.S. interests to undertake the risks, economic burden, and responsibility of supporting a separate South Korean regime? The unspoken consensus seemed to be "no," but many thought abandoning Korea would hurt American credibility and prestige in the emerging cold war environment.

In late September 1947, at the final Joint Commission meeting, Shtykov made a surprising proposal. He said the Koreans should be given the opportunity and responsibility for forming their own government. The Soviets were prepared to withdraw their troops from the northern zone if the Americans agreed to withdraw all their troops from the south.[25] The joint withdrawal could take place as early as 1948. The proposal seemed to provide a way for the Americans to extricate themselves from the Korean quagmire. A mutual withdrawal of troops would still preserve American prestige since it could be explained that the Koreans were getting what they had always wanted: independence. But it would also mean abandoning Korea to a likely bloody civil war and the all-but-certain takeover of the peninsula by the communists.

The Soviet proposal was studied in Washington for nearly three weeks. The Pentagon, tired of footing the bill for the occupation, had long called for a graceful exit. Korea was of little strategic value, defined as defending Japan, and the occupation was costly.[26] The State Department, however, believed that the loss of Korea would undermine America's prestige and threaten Japanese and Pacific security. It had been a year since Churchill's "Iron Curtain" speech at Fulton and George Kennan's "Long Telegram" warning of the Soviet aim to dominate the world. Communist parties were growing in France and Italy. In a weak and divided China, the Soviet Union was in position to exert greater influence than any other country. The Truman Doctrine, established in March 1947, committed U.S. support for democracies and fighting communism worldwide. How, then, could the Americans abandon Korea to the communists? On October 17, the Russians received their answer:

> In view of the continued inability of the Soviet and the United States Delegations in the Joint Commission to agree on how to proceed with their work and the refusal of the Soviet Government to participate in discussion on this problem with the other Governments adhering to the Moscow Agreement on Korea, the United States Government considers it obligated to seek the assistance of the United Nations in order that, as the Secretary of State said on September 17, "the inability of two powers to reach an agreement" should not further delay the early establishment of an independent, united Korea.[27]

The Americans thus passed the issue to the United Nations. Under UN auspices, elections for a national assembly were scheduled for May 1948, and the assembly would in turn select the president. The Soviets were invited to participate in the northern zone, but they refused, claiming that the UN could not guarantee fair elections. The specter of a permanently divided Korea was becoming a reality.

Yŏsu, Sunch'ŏn, and Cheju-do

In April 1948, Kim Il Sung hosted a conference in P'yŏngyang with southern political leaders to discuss Korea's future. It was his response to the UN's approval of separate elections in the South. He declared that Koreans must not allow other Great Powers to decide their fate. Sensing a ruse to postpone the elections, Rhee refused to attend. His rivals, the right-wing Kim Ku and moderate Kim Kyu-sik, however, agreed to go. Rhee was proved correct; the conference was a Soviet ploy. The conference "agreement" was announced with great fanfare, but it offered nothing that the Soviets had not put forth before, reiterating the same proposals laid out to the Americans in September 1947. The agreement did add one major new item that was bound to raise the ire of southern leaders: "separate elections in South Korea, if held, cannot express in any way the will of our nation, and will be regarded as a fraud."[28] Kim Ku, the staunch anticommunist and nationalist, had risked his political career by going to P'yŏngyang. He returned to Seoul disgusted. Charges of being soft on communism dogged him. A year later, a South Korean military officer, Lt. An Tu-hŭi, assassinated him.[29]

By the fall of 1946, after the Autumn Rebellion, the need for a larger indigenous security force in the American zone was apparent. Hodge envisioned an upgraded and larger security force consisting of an army of forty-five thousand, a navy and coast guard of five thousand, and a national police of twenty-five thousand.[30] While the War Department and the State Department generally backed the idea, Secretary of State George Marshall was concerned about the Soviet reaction. In 1946, the Americans were still committed to negotiating some kind of modus vivendi with the Russians, and he thought the establishment of a separate army would be interpreted as an attempt to create a separate regime. Hence, instead of "army," the ground force would be called the Korean Constabulary.

One of the men chosen to work in organizing the Constabulary was Capt. James H. Hausman, an infantry officer who had become battle-hardened in Europe during World War II. He was thirty-two years old and, at over six feet tall, an imposing figure. He was not a career officer, but a prewar sergeant. Trying to find a place for himself in the post–World War II army, Hausman had volunteered for occupation duty in Japan. He went instead to Korea as an advisor in the Military Advisory Group (commonly known in 1949 as KMAG, for Korean Military Advisory Group) that assumed responsibility for helping to organize the newly created Korean Constabulary. As an alternative force with no direct links to the hated Japanese colonial regime—a lasting legacy that the Korean police were hard-pressed to deal with—the Constabulary would help bring order to the American occupied zone without having all the obvious residual colonial associations attached to it. Volunteers accepted into the Constabulary would be chosen based on ability and merit. However, under pressure to recruit rapidly, background checks were often perfunctory. This situation would later have serious repercussions for the Constabulary and the nation. As Hausman later admitted, "We actually created a safe haven for many communists [and] we suffered the ill-effects of this many times in the months and years ahead."[31]

The Constabulary's first test came in early April 1948. While Kim Ku and Kim Kyu-sik were fuming in P'yŏngyang, a storm had gathered in the southern island of Cheju-do. On April 3, 1948, communists and leftists attacked the local government, police, and rightist youth organizations. The SKWP had ordered them to take actions to disrupt the planned general elections on May 10. Pak Hŏn-yŏng, the head of the SKWP, emphasized that actions be limited to disruptive activities to avoid bloodshed. Despite this, the rebellion became violent and spread throughout the island. It also received substantial outside help. Colonel Rothwell Brown, an American advisor, reported that the SKWP had infiltrated "over six thousand agitators and organizers" from the mainland and, with the islanders, established cells in most towns and villages. In addition, he estimated that "sixty to seventy thousand islanders had joined the party," and they were, for the most part, "ignorant, uneducated farmers and fishermen whose livelihood had been profoundly disturbed by the post-war difficulties."[32]

Thousands of police and Constabulary troops were sent to the island under orders from USAMGIK, but they could not end the unrest by election day. By May 10, the violence had become so rampant that few people dared to go to the polls. "During election week," wrote one Korean observer, "there were fifty assorted demonstrations, disorders, arson cases, and attacks, in addition to attacks on three government buildings."[33] The voting on Cheju-do was declared invalid, as the voting rate was only 20 percent, compared to the nearly 90 percent turnout on the mainland.

The end of the voting did not stop the mayhem. Instead, it became more vicious and widespread, eventually developing into a full-blown insurgency. Reports of atrocities began to surface with increasing frequency. "Stories were told of raided villages where there were found the bodies of hanged women or women and children run through with spears.

Korean students in Seoul pass out election handbills to passersby on May 4 in preparations for the elections on May 10, 1948. (U.S. NATIONAL ARCHIVES AND RECORDS ADMINISTRATION)

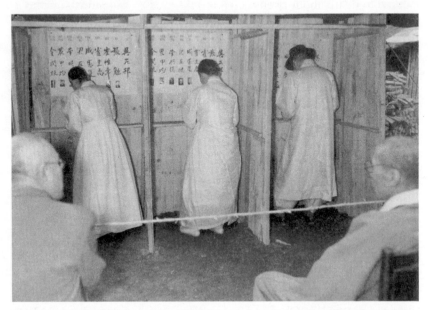

Voters marking their ballots during the UN-supervised elections on May 10, 1948. (U.S. NATIONAL ARCHIVES AND RECORDS ADMINISTRATION)

Tales of villages utterly wiped out kept coming in," wrote an American observer. "A number of rightist and police were also kidnapped, then hanged or beheaded."[34] A violent pacification campaign ensued. Government forces established fortified strategic hamlets manned by local militia, and conducted sweeps to locate the insurgents. Innocent civilians were invariably caught up in the sweeps.

The establishment of the Republic of Korea (ROK) on August 15, 1948, did little to curb the violence on Cheju-do. At the founding ceremony, President Rhee, selected by the newly elected National Assembly, urged the audience not to forget the division of the nation and that it would be his mission to reunify the peninsula. Meanwhile, vigilance against the forces of "alien philosophies of disruption" must be forcibly put down.[35] By August 15, the operation to put down the insurgents had reached a feverish pitch. In the hunt for the agitators, whole villages became targets, innocent suspects were beaten and hanged, and women and children massacred. A reign of terror largely perpetuated by government forces, the police, and the Republic of Korea Army (ROKA, as the Constabulary was renamed after the founding of the republic) gripped the island. "There was the occasion when ROKA personnel on Cheju-do speared to death about twenty civilians (allegedly communists) without benefit of a trial," remembered Hausman.

> Unfortunately, a picture was taken later and was given to Ambassador Muccio [first U.S. ambassador to the ROK]. I might add, a Korean Military Advisor Group sergeant had witnessed this act and he was plainly recognizable in that picture. I was ordered to report to the Ambassador. When confronted with the facts of the picture, I told the Ambassador that this was a good sign because in the past, similar groups of two hundred or more had been summarily executed and now the number was down to twenty. This was progress! I won't repeat the Ambassador's reply to me. I wouldn't want to give you the impression that he was short-tempered and uncouth.[36]

Meanwhile, in the Soviet zone, the DPRK was founded on September 9, 1948, an uneventful affair that provided a study in contrasts: a cohesive, peaceful, and highly disciplined North against the increasingly chaotic, violent, and unstable South.

As the turmoil on Cheju-do grew worse, a battalion in the 14th Regiment of the ROK Army stationed at the southern port city of Yŏsu received orders in mid-October to deploy to the island. For some time Hausman had been wary of the 14th Regiment because of doubts about its political reliability. There were a number of red flags that should have made him even more cautious. Rumors of leftists and SKWP members infiltrating its ranks abounded. The regimental commander, Maj. O Tong-gi, a fervent anticommunist, had also just been sacked, providing an opportunity for leftists and communists to organize a mutiny. On October 19, on receipt of the deployment order, the regiment mutinied. By the following morning, mutinous soldiers had murdered their officers, gathered thousands of supporters, seized control of Yŏsu, and then occupied the nearby city of Sunch'ŏn. "People's Courts" meted out summary justice. The Cheju-do Rebellion had now spread to the mainland, presenting the first major challenge to the newly established ROK. Brigadier General William Roberts, chief of KMAG, having great confidence in Hausman, selected him over more senior officers to go to Kwangju city, in the southwest, to take operational control of the suppression campaign. At Kwangju, Hausman was told that the 4th Regiment had also apparently mutinied. The 4th Regiment had been ordered to help suppress the rebellion in Sunch'ŏn, but it had disappeared en route. Meanwhile, underground members of the SKWP and local People's Committees began taking over parts of Kwangju. "In essence," wrote Hausman, "all hell had broken loose and we had nothing to stop the onslaught."[37]

On October 21, Hausman received the first good news: the "lost" 4th Regiment had not mutinied after all and was "found" in the hills west of Sunch'ŏn. Hausman organized a patchwork of ROK Army units to reclaim the city and put down the rebellion. Sunch'ŏn was retaken on October 23. ROK soldiers discovered that the mutineers had massacred as many as five hundred police and civilians, including women and children. Elmer Boyer, an American missionary living in Sunch'ŏn at the time, recalled what happened before the ROK Army units arrived:

> Most of the police were killed and hundreds of civilians. In one pile of bodies, where they had been shot, bound and tied in bunches of about ten, I counted ninety-eight persons . . . In the police yard, there were about eighty bodies . . . Just below our house, twenty-four were shot. I buried these and another Christian young man together in a long grave near here.[38]

By October 28, most of the towns and villages held by the rebels were recaptured. The Korean police exacted revenge. Keyes Beech, reporting for the *Chicago Daily News*, was in Sunch'ŏn days after the city fell and recalled the scene: "Before each square stood police, some attired in old Japanese uniforms and wearing swords. One by one, the citizens were called forward, to kneel before the police. Every question was punctuated by a blow to the head or back, sometimes with a rifle butt, sometimes from the edge of a sword. There was no outcry, no sound at all except for the barked questions and the thud of blows. That was what made the scene so terrifying, the utter, unprotesting quietness."[39] Many identified as rebels were summarily executed.[40]

By the spring of 1949, the last of the original leaders of the Cheju-do Rebellion were eliminated. The police killed Yi Tŏk-ku in early June and hung his mutilated body on a cross. Later that month, Kim Chi-hoe, "the greatest guerilla leader" and a native of Cheju-do, was killed. "When his capture appeared imminent," remembered Hausman, "we issued strict instructions to bring his body to Seoul (It was customary to mutilate bodies and display them for people to see) . . . One morning, I found a square five-gallon gas tank in my office. On inspection, I found it contained one highly bloated head, Kim Chi-hoe's." By the end in June 1949, an estimated thirty thousand had been killed in Cheju-do, many of them innocent civilians massacred by government forces.[41] The last of the American troops, except for KMAG, left South Korea in July 1949. It was nearly a year since the ROK had been established. KMAG, authorized with five hundred officers and soldiers as advisors and trainers, including Hausman, continued the task of building, organizing, and training the young ROK security and military forces. But the Soviets had been ahead of the Americans, by withdrawing from North Korea the previous fall and leaving behind a Soviet military advisory group to help build the North Korean armed forces.

Not surprisingly, Rhee was anxious about the departure of the Americans and especially how the United States would regard an invasion by the North. "In case of an attack by outside powers," he asked, "would the Republic of South Korea be able to count upon all-out military aid?"[42] President Truman made no promises, but he tried to calm the old man's fears by requesting from Congress a $150 million aid package. The suppression of the uprisings, especially Yŏsu-Sunch'ŏn, was seen as a success

ROK Army Chief of Staff Maj. Gen. Ch'ae Pyŏng-dŏk ("Fat Chae") addresses officers of the newly created ROK Army. Captain James Hausman is in the dark uniform, on the right, September 26, 1949. (U.S. NATIONAL ARCHIVES AND RECORDS ADMINISTRATION)

for the fledgling nation, although low-level guerilla war continued until early 1950. More importantly, the uprising had revealed and allowed the purging of leftists and communists in the ROK Army who could have caused far greater difficulties in the future. In Cheju-do, the SKWP had been prematurely forced into an armed struggle that it was unable to win.

Kim Il Sung's dream of reuniting the peninsula under his rule by provoking a general uprising in the South had been thwarted. Having twice failed to foment an internal revolution in the South, with the Autumn Rebellion in 1946 and the Cheju-do Rebellion in 1948–49, Kim now considered another way to communize the South. In March 1949, Kim Il Sung went to see Stalin.

CHAPTER THREE

Momentous Decisions

K im's trip was his first official visit to Moscow after the establishment of the DPRK. His main goal was to obtain Stalin's approval and support to use force for reunification. "Now is the best opportunity for us to take the initiative into our own hands," he told Stalin. "Our armed forces are stronger, and in addition, we have the support of a powerful guerilla movement in the South. The population of the South, which despises the pro-American regime, will certainly help us as well." Although Stalin did not oppose the idea on principle, he remained unconvinced that the conditions were right. American forces were still in the South, and North Korean forces were not yet strong enough. Moreover, Stalin believed that the Americans would intervene, setting the stage for a direct U.S.-Soviet confrontation that he wanted to avoid at all costs. "You should not advance south," he told Kim. Instead, he advised patience, to wait for the South to attack first. "If the adversary has aggressive intentions, then sooner or later it will start the aggression. In response to the attack you will have a good opportunity to launch a counterattack. Then your move will be understood and supported by everyone."[1] Kim returned to P'yŏngyang disappointed but not despairing. Stalin had not categorically rejected Kim's plan, but had merely qualified his support based on the right conditions. Kim would simply have to be patient and wait for the right opportunity.

While Kim was brooding about the future, the Chinese civil war, which had raged for almost two decades, was finally coming to an end. The war had reached a turning point by December 1947 after Nationalist forces suffered a series of disastrous defeats. "[A year earlier] our enemies were jubilant," wrote Mao, "and the U.S. imperialists, too, danced with joy . . . Now [they] are gripped by pessimism."[2] Stalin began to have doubts about how he approached the Chinese situation. Writing to Yugoslav leader Milovan Djilas in early 1948, he admitted that he had erred in supporting the Nationalists and demanding Mao's cooperation with Chiang Kai-shek. Mao, he told Djilas, had been right all along.[3] A year later, as the People's Liberation Army (PLA) routed the Nationalists, Stalin made what amounted to a public apology. He told Liu Shaoqi, Mao's second in command, that "all victors are always right . . . you Chinese comrades are too polite to express your complaints. We know that we have made a hindrance to you, and that you did have some complaints . . . We may have given you erroneous advice as the result of lacking understanding of the true situation in your country."[4]

The speed of the Nationalist collapse astonished everyone. By May 1949, Chiang abandoned the mainland for the island of Formosa (Taiwan). On October 1, Mao proclaimed the birth of the People's Republic of China (PRC) from the Gate of Heavenly Peace (Tiananmen), the entrance to the Imperial Palace, and the beginning of a new era in China's history. "The Chinese people, comprising one quarter of humanity, have now stood up," he triumphantly declared. "[Today] we have closed our ranks and defeated both domestic and foreign oppressors through the People's War of Liberation and the great people's revolution, and now we are proclaiming the founding of the People's Republic of China. Ours will no longer be a nation subject to insult and humiliation."[5] The next day the Soviet Union became the first country to establish diplomatic relations with Beijing, severing its ties with the Nationalists. Not long thereafter, Mao began to prepare for his first visit abroad, to Moscow.

Mao urgently needed economic and technical assistance from the Soviet Union to rebuild a nation ruined by decades of war. He also needed Moscow's military umbrella while the People's Liberation Army (PLA) concentrated on suppressing the last pockets of internal resistance and liberating Taiwan. Stalin's ill-treatment of the Chinese Communist Party (CCP) had not been forgotten, however, and Mao knew that Stalin was not likely to meet his needs without some kind of quid pro quo. Months earlier Mao had explained to Anastas Mikoyan, a senior member of the Soviet Politburo sent by Stalin on a fact-finding mission, that the policy of "leaning to one side" would involve a degree of diplomatic isolation and dependence on Russia. Yet, Mao had been careful not to cast Stalin's "help" as Chinese dependence, but in the spirit of friendship

North Korean leader Kim Il Sung (hatless, looking to the left) and Pak Hŏn-yŏng (second from the right, with glasses) are greeted by Soviet officials in Moscow, March 1949. (LIBRARY OF CONGRESS)

and allegiance to a common cause. "You must lean to one side," Mao had said. "To sit on the fence is impossible. In the world, without exception, one either leans to the side of imperialism or to the side of socialism."[6] Mao was acutely aware that he had to make good on his promise to the Chinese people to establish a new, proud, and independent China, a China that had finally "stood up." Mao was trying to maintain a delicate balance. Although he needed Soviet help, he would not allow his country to be subservient to Soviet interests and policies. The new China had to expunge the last remnants of its "century of national humiliation."

The first test of Mao's balancing act came in late 1949 when he met Stalin for the first time since the founding of the PRC. Arriving in Moscow on a bitterly cold afternoon in mid-December, his welcoming ceremony had been curtailed due to the weather, and Mao was asked to provide the Soviets with a copy of his arrival speech instead of delivering it in person at the station. The speech outlined Mao's main objective: Soviet economic, technical, and military assistance. Mao also expected the Soviets to abrogate the Sino-Soviet Treaty of Friendship signed with Chiang Kai-shek in August 1945 as an appendix to the Yalta accords, which most

Chinese saw as a national disgrace for it gave Moscow extraterritorial rights in China.[7]

Mao and Stalin met on the evening of December 16. According to the Soviet version, Mao began by stating his goal of replacing the 1945 treaty with a new one. Stalin pointedly refused: "As you know, this treaty was concluded between the USSR and China as a result of the Yalta Agreement," and therefore the terms of the treaty involved other parties (the United States and the United Kingdom) and could not be changed or abrogated without their consent. Mao and Stalin did not meet again for five days. Meanwhile, Mao waited in Stalin's dacha a few miles outside of Moscow. He had been left alone to brood in isolation. "Since Stalin neither saw Mao nor ordered anyone else to entertain him," Nikita Khrushchev later recalled, "no one dared to see him."[8] On December 21, Mao was invited to attend ceremonies marking Stalin's seventieth birthday. Stalin then subsequently canceled talks that had been scheduled for two days later. Mao was furious. "I have only three tasks here," he shouted to his bodyguard. "The first is to eat, the second is to sleep and the third is to shit!"[9] Mao cabled home on January 2, 1950, that "up to now, I have had no chance to go out to speak face to face with any [of the Soviet leaders] alone."[10]

This clash of wills might have gone on longer had it not been for Western press reports that the Soviets were mistreating Mao. Some even speculated that Mao was under house arrest. This prompted Stalin to send a Soviet correspondent to interview Mao. Mao indicated that he would stay in Moscow as long as it would take to get a new treaty. "The length of my sojourn in the USSR," Mao said, "partly depends on the period in which it will be possible to settle questions of interest to the People's Republic of China. These questions are, first and foremost, the existing Treaty of Friendship and Alliance between China and the USSR."[11] Stalin at last decided to meet Mao and to negotiate a new Sino-Soviet treaty. When Mao saw Stalin on January 22 and asked about Yalta, Stalin responded, "To hell with it. Once we have taken up the position that the treaties must be changed, we must go all the way. It is true that for us this entails certain inconveniences and we will have to struggle against the Americans. But we are already reconciled to that."[12]

Several explanations have been proposed for why Stalin changed his mind. Britain's recognition of the PRC in early January had given

Stalin pause. Others—Sweden, Denmark, Switzerland, and Finland—followed, fueling Stalin's paranoia that China might tilt toward the West. While congressional conservatives in the United States denounced London's decision, many in the State Department, including Secretary of State Dean Acheson and George Kennan, who was in charge of planning, thought the United States should follow suit. Nonrecognition would simply drive the Chinese communists closer to the Soviets.

Stalin also saw that the Truman administration was backing away from Chiang Kai-shek, which signaled the possibility of U.S.-PRC relations. Acheson, Kennan, and others in the State Department thought the United States should sever ties with the corrupt Chiang regime, but Truman took an ambiguous position. Truman reaffirmed both the Cairo Declaration of December 1943 and the Potsdam Declaration of July 1945, which promised the restoration of Taiwan, formerly a Japanese colony, to "China," but he would not formally end Washington's commitment to Chiang. The United States, he declared, "had no desire to obtain special rights or privileges or to establish military bases on Formosa or to detach Formosa from China." Washington would send no military aid to Chiang or continue any involvement "in the civil conflict in China."[13] Acheson's presentation at the National Press Club on January 12, 1950, further clarified the extent and limit of U.S. interest and policy in East Asia. Acheson accused the Soviet Union of acting to annex parts of China, a "process that is complete in Outer Mongolia ... and nearly complete in Manchuria." He reconfirmed America's hands-off policy regarding the future of Taiwan, while excluding, fatefully as it turned out, South Korea from America's defensive perimeter in the western Pacific. Britain's recognition of the PRC, Truman's assurances of neutrality in China's civil war, and Acheson's affirmation of Washington's hands-off policy vis-à-vis Taiwan gave Stalin the impression of an emerging relationship between China and the West and the United States in particular.[14] Stalin thus had to reconsider his relationship with Mao. If the United States was willing to allow China to "liberate" Taiwan without interference, it could eventually lead to the normalization of Sino-American relations and a wedge in Sino-Soviet relations. And that was unacceptable to Stalin.[15]

A final consideration for Stalin was Japan. By late 1949, as the cold war intensified, the Americans had adopted a "reverse course" policy in

Japan that, through economic revitalization and remilitarization, aimed to turn Japan into an anticommunist bulwark in northeast Asia. Stalin was fearful of a remilitarized Japan. "Japan still has cadres remaining," Stalin told Mao, "and it will certainly lift itself up again, especially if Americans continue their current policy." Mao seized on Stalin's thoughts: "Everything that guarantees the future prosperity of our countries must be stated in the treaty of alliance and friendship, including the necessity of avoiding a repetition of Japanese aggression."[16] Both Mao and Stalin saw Japan as a serious potential threat, perhaps even greater than a threat from the United States. Russian enmity with Japan went back to the nineteenth century, and China had suffered two ruinous wars in 1894–95 and 1931–45 that were then, and remain today, fresh in the memory of the Chinese people.

On February 14, 1950, Foreign Ministers Zhou Enlai and Andrei Vyshinsky signed the "Treaty of Friendship, Alliance and Mutual Assistance" as Stalin and Mao looked on.[17] The negotiations had been difficult. Stalin had balked at Mao's request for a Soviet commitment to aid China in the event of an American attack; Stalin would agree only on the condition that a war was formally declared. Mao had also been irritated by Stalin's demands for special privileges in Xinjiang in western China and Manchuria in the northeast. Despite these and other compromises, Mao basically obtained what he had wanted and was satisfied that he had the basis to establish a new place for China in the world, one that would instill pride in all Chinese.[18] Soon after Mao's departure, Stalin invited Kim Il Sung to Moscow.

War Drums

Kim was supremely confident in the spring of 1950. North Korea was politically and economically stable, and his regime was firmly in control. He was also sure that with Soviet support he could successfully use force to reunite the peninsula. There was little doubt that the NKPA was better trained and equipped than its southern counterpart. Although Stalin had not given approval for an invasion of the South during Kim's March-April 1949 visit, he promised to significantly increase military assistance to create a modern military force. Over four hundred Soviet advisors were authorized by January 1950. All were officers, with the majority (72 percent) being lieutenant colonels.[19] The NKPA, as well as the small navy and air force, was organized, trained, and prepared for war by a far more professional and experienced cadre of advisors than the ROK armed forces, for the vast majority of the Soviet advisors were veterans of the epic battles of the eastern front in World War II.[20] The NKPA's professional capacity and battle readiness increased further in the late spring of 1950, when Mao allowed the transfer of tens of thousands of ethnic Korean veterans who had fought for him in the Chinese civil war.

Eager to start a war that was certain of a quick victory, Kim Il Sung approached Shtykov in mid-January 1950 and told him that the time had come "to take up the matter of the liberation of Korea." He was becoming restless. "Thinking about reunification makes it impossible for me to sleep at night," Kim confided. Shtykov noted that Kim "insists on reporting to Stalin personally to gain permission for North Korea to attack the South."[21] Stalin's response was brief and to the point: "An operation on such a large scale demands preparation. It is necessary to organize the operation in such a way as to minimize risk. I am ready to see the man."[22] An excited Kim, along with Pak Hŏn-yŏng, who had moved to North Korea to join forces with Kim around August–September 1948, when the two separate Korean states were established, departed for Moscow on March 30. At their meeting, Stalin told them that the international environment had "sufficiently changed to permit a more active stance on the unification of Korea." He was optimistic that the communist victory in China was an important psychological blow to the West, proving "the strength of Asian revolutionaries and shown the weakness of Asian reactionaries and their mentors in the West." He also believed that China would help in the quest for unification. In apparent reference to the Koreans in the PLA, he told Kim, "China has at its disposal troops which can be utilized in Korea without any harm to the other needs of China." Furthermore, the Soviet Union's possession of the atomic bomb, successfully tested in August 1949, and its treaty alliance with China would make "the Americans even more hesitant to challenge the Communists in Asia." Nevertheless, Stalin was still worried about the possibility of an American intervention. Kim reassured Stalin on this point. Since the "USSR and China are behind Korea and are able to help," Kim reasoned, "the Americans will not risk a big war." Moreover, "the attack will be swift and the war will be won in three days," and the Americans will not have enough time to even deliberate about intervention. As for China, Kim did not want Mao's help. "We want to rely on our own force to unify Korea," Kim said emphatically.[23]

Stalin asked if there would be support in the South for such an invasion. Kim assured him that the "guerilla movement in the South has grown stronger and a major uprising can be expected." Pak added that "200,000 party members will participate as leaders of the mass uprising." Stalin remarked that they "should not count on direct Soviet participation in the war because the USSR had serious challenges elsewhere to cope with, especially the West." He told Kim to secure Mao's commitment to help as a condition for his assent to an attack. Stalin warned them, "If you should get kicked in the teeth, I shall not lift a finger. You have to ask Mao for all the help."[24] Stalin had transferred the burden of decision to Mao. He thought that regardless of the outcome, the Soviet Union would benefit. Success meant a communist Korea that expanded Russia's "friendly" borders. A failure, conceivable only if the United States intervened, would result in Chinese assistance to North Korea and a Sino-American confrontation that would end all possibilities of a Sino-American rapprochement. This is what Stalin had feared most, and Kim's invasion could help prevent it. Stalin had everything to gain by supporting the invasion plan and appeared to have little to lose. Still, Stalin premised his support of Kim's war on his calculations that the United States would not intervene.

Kim went to see Mao in mid-May 1950. Rather than try to persuade him to commit to supporting the plan, Kim matter-of-factly "informed Mao of his determination to reunify his country by military means." The war would be won quickly, Kim assured Mao, and Chinese help would not be needed. Peng Dehuai, later the commander of Chinese forces in Korea, recalled that Mao disagreed with Kim's proposal because he thought that the Americans might intervene, but Mao could not reject it since Kim had presented it as a fait accompli approved by Stalin.[25] Having just concluded the Sino-Soviet treaty, which was seen as essential for the PRC's future, Mao felt he could not refuse. Mao also needed Stalin's help to "liberate" Taiwan, and he could not use the argument about possible American intervention in Korea to oppose Kim's plan since a similar argument could be used to deny Soviet support for the invasion of Taiwan. Mao, reluctantly, gave his support.[26]

Endgame

While Kim and Stalin were meeting in April, Paul Nitze was finishing an explosive secret report on the future of America's military and national security posture. Nitze had recently replaced George Kennan as the director of policy planning at the State Department, and over the course of the winter of 1949–50 he had produced National Security Council Paper 68 (NSC 68), which eventually became, through its proposal for military buildup and containment of communism, the American master plan for the cold war. In the document delivered to President Truman in April, Nitze and his staff introduced an ominous theme from the very beginning: "The assault on free institutions is world-wide now, and in the context of the present polarization of power, a defeat of free institutions anywhere is a defeat everywhere ... Thus unwilling our free society finds itself mortally challenged by the Soviet system." Nuclear weapons were insufficient to thwart this ominous threat, as the Soviets were expected to achieve nuclear parity by 1954. Dramatic measures, a massive military buildup, would be required to counter the Soviet challenge. The cost would be $40 to $50 billion a year, three times the annual defense budget that Truman and the War Department had estimated for the early 1950s.[27]

Truman was not persuaded. NSC 68 might dramatically point out the perilous state of American security against a theoretical Soviet threat, but with midterm elections coming up in the fall of 1950, he was resistant to expanding defense expenditures when Americans still expected continuation of the peace dividend from the victory in World War II. Truman set off in May to Washington state, where he was scheduled to speak at the ceremony dedicating the Grand Coulee Dam. He did not mention during the two-week trip the possibility of a major Soviet threat or that it may require a national call to arms. On the contrary, he projected confidence and hopefulness about the global situation and America's security. At his weekly press conference on June 1, Truman assured the American people that the world was "closer to peace than at any time in the last five years."[28] NSC 68 was politely ignored.

Stalin was encouraged by Truman's talk about peace and prosperity. The Americans, he surmised, were simply tired of war and had also withdrawn their forces from Korea the year before. Nevertheless, with planning for the invasion rapidly moving forward, Stalin remained cautious about American intentions. Stalin rejected Kim's request for Soviet advisors to operate ships for an amphibious assault, a request that Shtykov advised should be granted. When Shtykov conveyed another request from Kim on June 20, the eve of the attack, for Soviet advisors to be assigned to frontline combat units, Stalin admonished the ambassador. "It is necessary to remind you that you are a representative of the USSR and *not* of Korea," he wrote. "Send necessary numbers of our advisors to headquarters and to army groups dressed in civilian uniforms posing as *Pravda* correspondents. You will be held personally responsible if any of these men were taken prisoner."[29] Stalin wanted to minimize the risk of Soviet casualties or prisoners lest it lead to a direct U.S.-Soviet confrontation in Korea.

On June 15, Shtykov informed Stalin that the operational plan, written by the Soviet advisory group, was ready. The attack would start in the early morning on Sunday, June 25 (the evening of June 24, Washington time). "At the first stage, formations and units of the NKPA will begin action on the Ongjin peninsula [on the far western end of the 38th parallel] like a local operation and then deliver the main strike along the western coast of Korea to the South," he related.[30] Key to the plan was to disguise the attack as a counteroffensive reacting to a South Korean provocation. The offensive would then spread eastward along the 38th parallel over the following days. In its overall conception, the plan was similar to Russia's attack on Finland in 1939, which was not surprising since most senior Soviet officers in North Korea were veterans of the Finnish War. As in Korea, the Finnish plan had contained a ruse, the shelling of a Russian village near the Finnish border, Mainila, before the start of the Soviet invasion. A Soviet mobile artillery unit had been secretly deployed deep into the woods near the Soviet-Finnish border and had shelled Mainila. Soviet troops, located near Mainila, had then reported receiving Finnish artillery fire. This had become a pretext, albeit fabricated, for a general attack against Finland. General Vladimir Razhubayev, chief of the Soviet Advisory Group from early 1951 to 1953, stated that in North Korea "the People's Central Committee was full of experts who were working on a way to pull a similar pretext off." Shtykov himself had led a major part of the invasion force against Finland.[31]

As June 25 approached, Stalin received alarming news from Shtykov, who relayed an urgent message from Kim that "the Southerners have learned the details of the forthcoming advance of the NKPA." Kim urged modification of the plan. "Instead of a local operation at the Ongjin peninsula as a prelude to the general offensive," relayed Shtykov to Stalin, "Kim Il Sung suggests an overall attack on 25 June along the whole front line." Stalin approved "an immediate advance along the whole front line," but he stipulated that it still must be made to look like a counterattack.[32] The stage was set for the invasion, but Stalin and Kim failed to foresee how the United States and the rest of the world would view it. The two leaders also completely failed to consider the possibility that they would be testing the effectiveness of the collective security mechanism of the newly established United Nations.

CHAPTER FOUR

War for the South

The opening shots of the attack in the predawn hours of Sunday, June 25, 1950, surprised few, and yet all were caught unprepared. Localized skirmishes and even major actions along the parallel had occurred with regularity over the previous year, and nothing in the way the North Korean attack began gave any indication that it was different this time. Almost nightly, the North Koreans infiltrated patrols to probe, ambush, or take prisoners. The South Koreans retaliated with their own patrols. These actions sometimes involved hundreds of men. Not infrequently, artillery duels were waged. A year earlier, North Korean shelling near Kaesŏng, located just south of the parallel, was of such ferocity that the American Methodist Mission there was forced to stay in a shelter for three days.[1] Border skirmishes had continued unabated since January, but in May, border incidents suddenly dropped off sharply, making Capt. Joseph Darrigo of KMAG suspect that something was afoot. North Korean farmers were evacuated from the border zone. Captain Darrigo reported his concerns to his superior, Lt. Col. Lloyd H. Rockwell, but it was lost in the cacophony of similar warnings that had become almost routine in Seoul and Washington.[2]

The five hundred U.S. military advisors of KMAG were under the leadership of Brig. Gen. William Roberts, who was nearing his mandatory retirement in July. KMAG's mission was to train and build functioning ROK security forces, especially the army. It was a daunting challenge requiring patience and skill. But Roberts was an optimist. The ROK Army had, after all, been battle-tested in the Yŏsu-Such'ŏn uprisings and in the numerous clashes along the border. It had proved its loyalty and its mettle. Roberts reported to Washington that the ROK Army could meet any test the North Korean army might impose on it.[3] The optimistic assessments were also voiced by the ambassador to South

Korea, John Muccio, who confirmed that progress in military training had been "heartening," and the ROK Army "had kept pace" with the North Koreans.[4] The official view from Washington was summed up by Republican Senator H. Alexander Smith (New Jersey), a recent guest of Ambassador Muccio, who reported that the ROK forces were "thoroughly capable of taking care of South Korea in any possible conflict with the North."[5]

President Syngman Rhee disagreed. He interpreted the stream of positive assessments of the fledgling army, which had no tanks, no heavy artillery, and no fighter aircraft, as a deceptive ploy to deny him military aid and equipment. He complained to Muccio and Roberts that the ROK Army was woefully underequipped to repel a North Korean attack. In Washington, however, denial of Rhee's repeated requests for more arms was thought to be prudent and justified. There was legitimate concern that the difficult and fiercely patriotic Rhee might start a war of reuni-

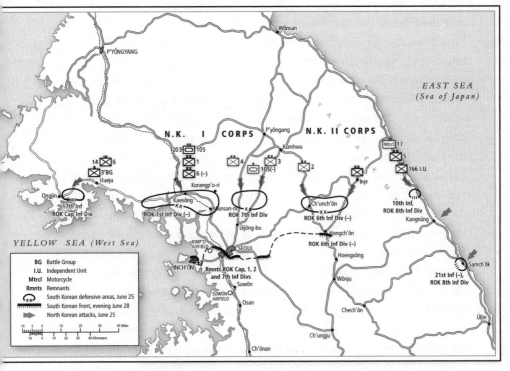

North Korean Invasion, June 25–28, 1950. (MAP ADAPTED FROM ROY B. APPLEMAN, *SOUTH TO THE NAKTONG, NORTH TO THE YALU* [U.S. GOVERNMENT PRINTING OFFICE, 1960])

fication on his own if he were given the tanks, artillery, and aircraft he demanded. A week before the outbreak of war, Muccio wrote to Acheson, "The Korean Army has made enormous progress during the past year. The systems and institutions set up through the instrumentality of KMAG are now such that reductions in advisory personnel can well be made," and he recommended a 50 percent reduction by the end of 1950.[6] More important was a definitive shift in reducing South Korea's strategic value to the United States. Democratic Senator Tom Connally (Texas), chairman of the Senate Committee on Foreign Relations, told a reporter that "I am afraid it [the United States abandoning South Korea] is going to be seriously considered because I'm afraid it is going to happen, whether we want it to or not."[7] The praises heaped on the ROK military provided political cover for drawing down American commitments. Rhee had reasons to be concerned.

Captain Darrigo was the only American officer at the 38th parallel on the morning of June 25. He was the KMAG advisor to a regiment of the ROK First Division, and he lived in Kaesŏng. Darrigo jumped out of bed when he heard artillery shells land nearby, ran to his jeep, and sped away, reaching the division's headquarters in Munsan, about twenty miles to the south, to sound the alarm. Unfortunately, the very capable division commander, Col. Paek Sŏn-yŏp, perhaps the best officer in the ROK Army who later became its first four-star general, was absent. Lieutenant Colonel Rockwell, chief KMAG advisor to the ROK First Division, was also absent. He had gone to Seoul for the weekend to visit family and friends. By the time they were notified later that morning and hurriedly made their way back, Kaesŏng had fallen and NKPA tanks were rolling toward Seoul.

The NKPA conducted six sequenced thrusts across the 38th parallel, beginning in the Ongjin Peninsula on the west and then rolling eastward. KMAG advisors with the ROK 17th Regiment on Ongjin had also been jolted from their beds by artillery. Without heavy weapons, the regiment had little chance. At first, many ROK soldiers fought bravely. "Acting without orders from their officers," recalled Paek, "a number of them broke into suicide teams and charged the T-34s clutching explosives and grenades. They clambered up onto the monsters before touching off the charges."[8] But the futility of the "human bomb" attacks soon led to "T-34 fear," and the troops began to run away. "The symptoms of the disease were straightforward," Paek later wrote. "As soon as the men even heard the word 'tank' they fell into a state of terror."[9]

When news of the North Korean invasion reached Washington in the early evening of Saturday, June 24, many officials, including Truman and Acheson, were away for the weekend. Truman was at his home in Independence, Missouri. Acheson called from his country house in Maryland to inform the president of the news. He also told Truman that he had requested an emergency session of the UN Security Council.[10] While Truman returned to Washington, the UN Security Council met and unanimously adopted an American resolution calling for the immediate cessation of hostilities and the withdrawal of North Korean troops. There was no Soviet vote, and hence no veto, because the Soviet representative had walked out earlier that year to protest the UN's refusal to seat the PRC in the council instead of Taiwan. Truman gathered his principal advisors for a crisis meeting. All agreed that the Soviet Union was involved. Acheson recommended that MacArthur be instructed to airdrop supplies, food, ammunition, and weapons to strengthen the South Korean forces. No direct U.S. military involvement was discussed, as it was still widely believed that the ROK Army was capable of handling the NKPA. This belief was reinforced by the first of many cables from Ambassador Muccio: "The Korean defense forces are taking up prepared positions to resist northern aggression. There is no reason for alarm."[11]

Muccio's reports became more ominous the following day: "I earnestly appeal to Department to back up to such extent as may be necessary KMAG's appeal for additional ammunition. Without early receipt of such ammunition and assuming hostilities continue at present level, is feared most stocks in Korean hands will be exhausted within ten days time."[12] Faced with bleaker reports about the situation on the front, and with rumors running wild that the NKPA was about to take Seoul, Muccio ordered the evacuation of American civilians. On the morning of Tuesday, June 27, nearly seven hundred American women and children boarded a Norwegian ship at Inch'ŏn and sailed for Japan. More Americans were evacuated the following day, and Muccio went to Suwŏn, twenty-five miles south of Seoul. Rhee and the ROK government had departed earlier that morning and were on their way farther south to the city of Taegu. Ordinary Koreans were on their own. Some stayed, but many left, becoming faceless actors in innumerable tragedies on the refugee trail. In just two days, Seoul was in chaos and its residents in full flight.

Not everyone was eager to leave the city, however. Four American journalists, Keyes Beech of the *Chicago Daily News*, Frank Gibney of *Time*, Marguerite Higgins of the *New York Herald Tribune*, and Burton Crane of the *New York Times,* arrived on one of the last evacuation planes from Tokyo on June 27 to cover the fall of Seoul.[13] They were greeted at ROK Army headquarters by Col. W. H. Sterling Wright, KMAG's acting chief, and a skeleton crew of KMAG officers. KMAG's chief Brig. Gen. Roberts had departed just days before to retire and his replacement had not yet arrived. Despite the bleak situation, Wright was hopeful. He and others had been bolstered by MacArthur's message earlier that day that "momentous events are in the making."[14] It was after midnight when the group finally decided to turn in. Colonel Wright suggested that Marguerite Higgins, together with a group of other KMAG officers, accompany him to his quarters in the KMAG housing area. Meanwhile, Beech, Gibney, and Crane went with Maj. Walter Greenwood, who offered the men a place on the sofa and floor to sleep. But no sooner had they closed their eyes when they were awakened by the phone. Beech heard Green shout, "They are in the city! Head for Suwŏn!" It was raining hard that night as Gibney, Beech, and Crane jumped into their jeep. "The whole city was on the move," recalled Beech. "It was toward the Han River Bridge."

The pitiful human mass, wet and trudging through the dark, created an eery scene. Caught in the streaming mobs of people, oxcarts, trucks, and bicycles, the three reporters saw Capt. James H. Hausman ahead of them as they approached the bridge. Suddenly everything came to a halt. "We sat in the jeep waiting," Beech recalled. "Then it seemed that the whole world exploded in front of us. I remember a burst of orange flame; silhouetted against the flame was a truckload of Korean soldiers. The truck lifted into the air. I felt our own jeep in motion, backwards."[15] Crane and Gibney were wounded by flying glass and bled from their heads, but they were conscious and able to walk. Beech noticed the truckload of soldiers whose vehicle had shielded them from the blast. All of the soldiers were dead, their bodies strewn haphazardly in heaps on the ground. And so were hundreds of other innocent people who had died in the explosion or who had simply drowned in the dark river waters below. Someone had blown up the Han River Bridge with people still on it.

Hausman's group had been luckier. They were safely across the river when the bridge blew. "It was a tremendous explosion," he recalled, "Our jeep actually left the road, vertically."[16] Meanwhile, Wright and Higgins, who had not yet crossed the bridge, were unharmed although they now found themselves, like Gibney, Crane, and Beech, trapped on the wrong side of the Han River. Fortunately they were able to make it safely across on makeshift rafts. The KMAG party, including the four American journalists, had come through the ordeal miraculously, without loss of life.

The premature destruction of the bridge was not only a humanitarian disaster but a military one as well. Seoul was still in ROK hands at the time, and trapped on the northern side of the Han River were over thirty thousand ROK soldiers. Colonel Paek, whose men had fought heroically to hold back the attack, was devastated: "I cried tears of blood on that day. I saw no way to rescue the men of the proud ROK 1st Division, scattered as they were over miles of threatening terrain."[17] Brigadier General Yu Chae-hŭng, commander of the ROK Seventh Division, led just over one thousand men to safety. The other two ROK divisions that were still relatively intact, the ROK Sixth Division in Ch'unch'ŏn to the east and the Eighth at Samch'ŏk on the East Sea, were now isolated and utterly helpless.

On June 28, three days after the attack, the ROK Army could account for only twenty-two thousand men of the nearly hundred thousand that had made up its rolls on the twenty-fifth. Most of its heavy weapons, transport, and supplies were lost. General Roberts's "best doggone shooting army outside of the United States" was not just defeated, it was destroyed.[18]

MacArthur's survey team, sent to assess the situation and led by Brig. Gen. John Church, landed in Suwŏn on June 27, just hours before the fall of Seoul. Church was shocked by the utter chaos. Hausman, who had just arrived in Suwŏn, related the horrific story of the Han River bridge explosion and the ROK Army's dire predicament. Church notified Tokyo that "it will be necessary to employ American ground forces" to reestablish ROK positions at the 38th parallel and to recapture Seoul.[19] That evening, MacArthur radioed Church that a senior officer would be arriving the next morning. That senior officer turned out to be MacArthur himself. A distraught Rhee greeted MacArthur. Church and

Wright briefed them on the deteriorating situation. Returning to Tokyo that evening, MacArthur cabled Washington: "The only assurance for holding the present line and the ability to regain later the lost ground is through the introduction of United States ground combat forces into the Korean battle area. Unless provision is made for the full utilization of the Army-Navy air team in this shattered area, our mission will at best be needlessly costly in life, money and prestige. At worst, it might even be doomed."[20] But Truman had already decided to intervene. Later, he said that committing American troops to combat in Korea was the most difficult decision of his presidency, more so than the decision to use the atomic bomb against Japan in 1945. He did not want to get into a war, but he thought that failure to act in Korea could lead to another world war, this time with the Soviet Union.

On June 27, congressional leaders, the secretary of state, the secretary of defense, and the Joint Chiefs of Staff (JCS) joined Truman for a meeting. He informed them that that morning he had authorized the use of air and sea forces. The congressional leaders approved that the crisis be managed on the basis of presidential authority alone, without calling on Congress for a declaration of war. That evening, the UN Security Council passed Resolution 83 authorizing the use of force to halt North Korean aggression, testing for the first time the UN principle of collective security. In the days leading to the UN resolution, the American people's anxiety and doubt over what to do about Russia's "testing" of America's resolve in Korea had suddenly given way to a new clarity and sense of purpose. Three days later, on June 30, Truman authorized the deployment of American ground forces.

The response of the American people, the media, and Congress was overwhelmingly positive. The press unanimously praised Truman for his "decisiveness" and his "bold and courageous decision." The *Christian Science Monitor*'s Washington Bureau chief, Joseph Harsh, gushed, "Never before have I felt such a sense of relief and unity pass through the city."[21] Truman had drawn the line, and the American public firmly backed him. Yet, there was still confusion concerning exactly what the crisis was all about. At a June 29 press conference, Truman was asked whether the United States was at war. "We are not at war," Truman replied. A reporter asked, "Would it be correct . . . to call this a police action under the United Nations?" "Yes," replied Truman, "that is exactly what it amounts to."[22] Calling Korea a "police action" would later haunt Truman when the bloody and brutal reality of a full-blown war became apparent. Throughout the hot months of July and August 1950, American soldiers were stunned and humiliated as they were repeatedly thrown back by the North Korean "bandits." For the time being, however, Truman's euphemism served to downplay the seriousness of the crisis and provided the illusion that the "police action" would be a relatively quick and simple affair.[23]

Less than six days after the North Korean attack, American soldiers were committed to the fighting. The former Japanese colony that few had ever heard of and had been on the periphery of America's postwar interests suddenly became the epicenter of America's first armed confrontation against communism. Truman had drawn the line in Korea between freedom and slavery. Haphazardly and fatefully, Korea's localized civil war morphed into a war between the centers of power in the post–World War II order.

Desperate Days

The first American troops arrived in Korea confident that the North Koreans could be stopped quickly. Virtually nothing was known about the enemy, but everyone thought that once the North Koreans saw that they were fighting Americans, they would retreat in panic. Overconfidence and arrogance ruled the day. "We thought they'd back off as soon as they saw American uniforms," Lieutenant Philip Day recalled. Lieutenant John Doody echoed the sentiment: "I regarded the episode as an adventure that would probably last only a few days."[24] Their first encounter with the NKPA abruptly exploded their illusions. More important, the confrontation between the world's most powerful nation and a nation of "bandits" was a brutal wake-up call to Washington, for it showed just how much American military readiness had deteriorated. America's precipitous demobilization and slashed defense budgets after World War II, the peace dividend, and the "soft" occupation in Japan exacted an unforgiving outcome in the violence of combat. It was glaringly apparent that despite its vaunted nuclear supremacy, America was unprepared to fight a conventional war.

MacArthur selected the Twenty-Fourth Infantry Division as the first unit to deploy. The division and its commanding general, Maj. Gen. William Dean, seemed well suited for the job. Dean was the only one of the four division commanders in the Eighth U.S. Army, the American occupation force in Japan, to have commanded troops in combat. He had also served as commanding general of the Seventh Infantry Division and as military governor of South Korea under Lt. Gen. John R. Hodge from 1947 to 1948. Dean took command of the Twenty-Fourth Division after the dissolution of USAMGIK following the elections in May 1948. MacArthur instructed Dean to send a battalion task force, as quickly as possible, to be followed by the remainder of the division. Dean chose the 1st Battalion of the 21st Infantry Regiment commanded by Lt. Col. Charles Smith as the core of the task force. Smith had fought in the Pacific in World War II and was considered the most experienced and competent of the battalion commanders in the division. But the unit was only at two-thirds strength and most of the soldiers had no combat experience, having joined after World War II. The unit also lacked training, owing to the "soft" occupation duty in Japan. The equipment was in poor shape, and antitank weapons were inadequate against the tanks of the NKPA. Task Force (TF) Smith was the best that MacArthur could send, a unit of ill-trained, undermanned, underequipped, and underexperienced men.[25] Dean's instructions to Smith were simple: "Contact Brig. Gen. John Church and if you can't locate him, go to Taejŏn and beyond if you can . . . Good luck to you and God bless you and your men."[26]

Brigadier General Church greeted TF Smith at Taejŏn on the morning of July 2. Brimming with confidence, Church assured Lieutenant Colonel Smith that all that was required to stop the NKPA was a few Americans who would not run from tanks. Smith was ordered to block the enemy north of the village of Osan. The NKPA's primary avenue of attack was along the main road from Seoul, which ran through Osan and farther south through Taejŏn and Taegu to Pusan. It was the only avenue of attack from the Chinese border to the southern coast that was free from the mountains dominating most of the peninsula. To this day, this corridor is the key line of communication and transportation and therefore the backbone of South Korea's bustling economy. It was also the traditional invasion path through the peninsula whether coming from the north or from the south. The Mongols in the thirteenth century and the Manchus in the seventeenth century followed it going south; the Japanese followed it north during their invasion in the sixteenth century. The NKPA, in other words, was using a well-worn path. As TF Smith deployed north of Osan, the Twenty-Fourth Infantry Division's 34th Infantry Regiment, led by Col. Jay Lovless, arrived in P'yŏngtaek south of Osan. Dean deployed the regiment around P'yŏngtaek to block any enemy that got through TF Smith.

Smith and his men caught sight of the North Korean soldiers on the morning of July 5. Over thirty tanks rolled toward their positions. The Americans fired recoilless rifles and bazookas at point-blank range, but to their surprise, even direct hits had no effect. The artillery battery attached to TF Smith destroyed four of the tanks, but still nearly thirty had gotten through and headed south toward the 34th Infantry Regiment digging in at P'yŏngtaek. By early afternoon, Smith ordered a withdrawal. Soon thereafter, "things slowly began to go to pieces," Lt. Philip Day recalled. "All crew served weapons were abandoned, as well as all the dead and some 30 wounded. Confusion rapidly became rampant."[27] A quarter of the unit, 150 men, was lost at Osan.[28]

Reports that TF Smith was overrun reached Lovless the next morning. Fearful that the understrength battalion at P'yŏngtaek might not be able to hold, Lovless ordered it to fall back to Ch'ŏnan, about eight miles farther south. Meanwhile, a battalion at Ansŏng to the east fell apart. Dean was furious that P'yŏngtaek was abandoned without a fight, and he ordered Lovless to go back, but it was too late because P'yŏngtaek had already been taken by the NKPA. By this time, Ch'ŏnan's defenses rapidly fell apart, and the hasty withdrawal from P'yŏngtaek and Ansŏng now turned into a frantic flight. The men abandoned equipment, weapons, and comrades who had been killed or wounded. "I was thoroughly disgusted with this exhibition," recalled John Dunn. "It was more than a lack of aggressiveness and initiative, it bordered on cowardice."[29] Dunn, who was taken prisoner at Ch'ŏnan, spent the rest of the war in a POW camp. It took just a few days for the cocky and confident American soldiers to become a disoriented mob of terrified men.

As bewildered American and ROK troops were flung back, MacArthur decided to commit the whole of the Eighth U.S. Army. Lieutenant General Walton "Johnnie" Walker, its commander, was known as a "GI's

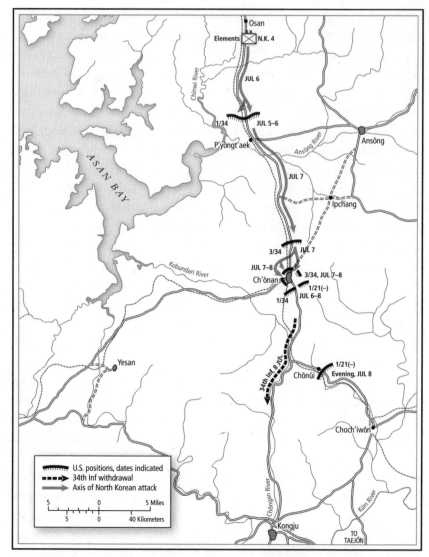

Delaying actions, 34th Infantry Regiment, July 5–8, 1950. (MAP ADAPTED FROM ROY B. APPLE-
MAN, *SOUTH TO THE NAKTONG, NORTH TO THE YALU* [U.S. GOVERNMENT PRINTING OFFICE, 1961])

general." A modest and unpretentious man who "smiled infrequently
and rarely voiced a remark worthy of being remembered," Walker made
a personal assessment of the situation by visiting Dean at Taejŏn in early
July.[30] His assessment was crucial in MacArthur's decision to use all of
the Eighth Army. Walker's operational control included the remnants of

the ROK Army, conceded by President Rhee on July 14.[31] The unified U.S.-ROK forces gave hope of establishing a coherent defense.

Much has been made of the ROK Army's poor performance, but this ignores the heroic efforts made to successfully rebuild the ROK Army on the run.[32] The South Koreans were able, against great odds, to piece their shattered forces back together while fighting a delaying action without collapsing, despite their inferiority in men, arms, equipment, and training. "We started greatly under-strength and bereft of heavy weapons and equipment and were obliged to reorganize, replenish and even re-arm while keeping ahead of a pursuing enemy," recalled Paek Sŏn-yŏp. "In what I regard as one of the minor miracles of the war, some four or five thousand of the men we lost crossing the Han rejoined the division during our withdrawal to the Naktong [River]."[33] ROK forces reached their prewar strength by the end of August.[34] Kim Il Sung later acknowledged that "our greatest mistake was failing to encircle and completely annihilate the enemy, and giving them enough time to reorganize and reinforce their units while withdrawing."[35]

Walker's immediate task was to delay the enemy advance. In the west, location of the NKPA's main effort, Walker established a defensive line along the south bank of the Kŭm River. In the east, Walker used the mountains and the narrow coastal corridor to delay the North Korean advance. The purpose of the delay was to buy time for reinforcements, not only from the United States, but also from over a dozen other UN nations, to arrive and set the conditions for a counteroffensive. The Kŭm River was the first defensible river line south of the Han along the path of North Korea's advance. Less than fifteen miles beyond it was Taejŏn, the first major city after Seoul along the invasion route. Walker wanted Dean's Twenty-Fourth Division to hold the Kŭm River line to protect Taejŏn, a key nexus of road and rail networks. But Dean's forces could not hold, and the North Koreans easily penetrated the Kŭm River line and then began assaulting Taejŏn on July 20. Whereas Dean's tactical sense called for withdrawing from Taejŏn as it was being surrounded, he was ordered to hold on to gain time for reinforcements to arrive from Pusan. It was a fateful delay. Dean became trapped as NKPA forces closed in from all sides. Escaping the city on foot, he survived in the mountains for thirty-six days before being captured, and spent the rest of the war as a POW. Dean was the highest-ranking POW, and in January 1951, Truman, not knowing whether he was alive, awarded him the Medal of Honor.

By the end of July, the Twenty-Fourth Division was in very bad shape. It had lost more than half of its men.[36] It had been a desperate, agonizing, and bitter month. Many soldiers felt that their leaders, from Truman on down, had failed them. They had been told that their sojourn in Korea would be an easy affair, a mere "break" from the boredom of the occupation in Japan. Moreover, the difficulty of identifying friend from foe, because some NKPA troops infiltrated UN lines by disguising themselves in the same white-cotton clothes that refugees wore, led American troops to commit appalling deeds, including shooting at women and children, because they did not know what else to do.

Near the village of Nogŭn-ri, about a hundred miles southeast of Seoul, several hundred refugees were killed in late July by soldiers of the 7th Cavalry Regiment from the First Cavalry Division and by American aircraft. The American soldiers, who believed North Korean soldiers were hiding among the villagers, had told the villagers to gather by the railroad tracks. There are contradictory accounts of what happened next. One Korean witness recalled spotting an American plane that suddenly swooped down and strafed the area. An American soldier recalled receiving fire from the refugee group.[37] Whatever triggered the mayhem, the terrified villagers ended up in a nearby tunnel, where they sought cover and ended up trapped.[38] Yang Hae-chan, nine at the time, recalled that they were "fired upon by American soldiers, bullets rained down on the crowd."[39] Another eyewitness said they were "packed tightly inside with little or no room to move," and recalled having to "drink bloody water from the stream that flowed through one of the tunnels." The killing lasted several days, and "dead bodies were piled up on the tunnel entrance" to protect those inside from the oncoming fire. Two hundred and forty-eight people, including many women and children, are alleged to have been killed in the incident.[40]

Early August brought more despair but also new hope. American and ROK forces set up a defense line behind the Naktong River. It was a thinly held front and the last line of defense. On the map, the Pusan perimeter looked like a tiny toehold at the southeastern corner of the peninsula. Walker dramatically declared, "There will be no Dunkirk, there will be no Bataan . . . We must fight until the end . . . I want everybody to understand that we are going to hold this line. We are going to win."[41] The soldiers were exhausted, bitter, and dispirited. The monsoon season had just ended, but it was abnormally hot and dry. Lack of water forced the soldiers to drink from paddies and ditches, causing severe cases of dysentery. Yet, despite the exhaustion, the heat, and the sickness, Walker's line held.

One key to this success was the delaying action of the ROK Sixth Division, which had put up a tenacious fight in Ch'unch'ŏn thirty miles east of Seoul against overwhelming odds.[42] A KMAG advisor recollected that the Sixth Division was driven from the city but "counterattacked and recaptured Ch'unch'ŏn and then held it for five days until ordered to withdraw because of failure along the rest of the front."[43] Shtykov reported on June 26 to Gen. Matveyev Zakharov, head of a special mission from the Soviet General Staff to oversee the operations, that "the invasion ran into trouble from the beginning especially because the Soviet plan did not take into account the severe terrain that slowed down mechanized units and especially the unexpectedly courageous defense of the ROK 6th Division at Ch'unch'ŏn."[44] The ROK Sixth Division's delaying actions threw off the NKPA's timeline and probably bought time for the establishment of the Pusan perimeter and the arrival of UN reinforcements.[45]

Shtykov was worried. He wrote to General Zakharov that NKPA units were operating on an ad hoc basis without direction from senior staff. The quality of staff work was poor, "[the command staff] does not have battle experience," he complained, and "after the withdrawal of Soviet military advisers they organized the battle command poorly, they use artillery and tanks in battle badly and lose communications."[46] On June 28, Shtykov reported to Stalin that without more Soviet advisors on the ground, "it would be difficult for the NKPA to conduct smooth operations."[47] On July 8, Shtykov cabled Stalin to convey Kim Il Sung's personal appeal for more Soviet advisors for frontline units: "Being confident of your desire to help the Korean people rid themselves of the American imperialists," Kim pleaded, "I am obliged to appeal to you with a request to allow the use of 25–35 Soviet military advisers in the staff of the Front of the Korean Army and the staffs of the 2nd Army Group, since the national military cadres have not yet sufficiently mastered the art of commanding modern troops."[48] Kim confided to Shtykov that without the advisors, "the invasion would fail." Shtykov wrote to Stalin "that he had never seen Kim Il Sung so dejected and hopeless."[49] Stalin acquiesced. That Stalin would have allowed Soviet advisors to serve in the front lines and risk a direct confrontation with Americans revealed how critical the situation had become.[50] By mid-July, the NKPA had largely lost its momentum.

The next Eighth Army unit to arrive was the Twenty-Fifth Infantry Division, which included the all-black 24th Infantry Regiment. Following the Twenty-Fifth was the First Cavalry Division in mid-July and the 5th Regimental Combat Team from Hawaii, which arrived on July 25. The Second Infantry Division followed in early August and then a provisional U.S. Marine brigade. With these reinforcements, a defensive line was established along the Naktong River in southeastern Korea. The Eighth Army was responsible for the seventy-mile western flank of the Pusan perimeter, while the ROK Army was responsible for the fifty-five miles of the front on the northern boundary. With overextended supply lines and increasing UN strength, North Korea estimated that it had about a month at most to break the Pusan line and bring the war to a conclusion in its favor. Throughout August and early September, the NKPA maintained unrelenting pressure, but the perimeter held.

War for the North

As the situation in Korea stabilized, Truman sent W. Averell Harriman, a senior White House advisor, to Japan. Truman had been disturbed by MacArthur's highly publicized trip at the end of July to Taiwan, where he had met Chiang Kai-shek and publicly praised the generalissimo's "indomitable determination to resist communist domination."[51] Secretary of State Acheson was upset, but he put MacArthur's trip down to politics. "Before 1950 General MacArthur had neither shown nor expressed any interest in Formosa," wrote Acheson. "But the General was not deaf to political reports coming to him from the United States, particularly those emanating from the Republican right wing, which found our Far Eastern policy repulsive and occasionally mentioned the General as the charismatic leader who might occasionally end the obnoxious Democratic hold on the White House."[52] It was well known

that MacArthur had looked favorably on Chiang's offer of Nationalist troops for Korea, but Truman rejected the offer for fear of drawing
China into the war. Truman told Harriman to tell MacArthur to stay
clear of Chiang Kai-shek and to find out MacArthur's future plans for
Korea.[53] Harriman returned with an encouraging report. Concerning
Chiang Kai-shek, MacArthur would do as the president ordered. For
the war, Harriman reported on MacArthur's plan for victory with a bold
amphibious landing at Inch'ŏn, behind enemy lines, to surround and
destroy the North Korean forces.

MacArthur's audacious plan carried great risks. The greatest were
Inch'ŏn's tremendous tides of thirty feet or more and the lack of suitable landing beaches. The landing could take place only at high tide,
which lasted just two hours. General Omar Bradley, chairman of the
JCS, thought it was the riskiest plan he had ever seen. General Joseph
"Lightning Joe" Lawton Collins, army chief of staff, thought the plan
should be modified by making the landing site at Kŭnsan instead of at
Inch'ŏn. Kŭnsan was located 130 miles south of Inch'ŏn. Geographically,
it was more hospitable and accommodated more easily the amphibious
landing MacArthur proposed. But it was precisely the "impracticalities" of the operation that could ensure Inch'ŏn's success, MacArthur
argued, "for the enemy commander will reason that no one would be
so brash as to make such an attempt."[54] The Joint Chiefs were not convinced. Secretary of the Army Frank Pace Jr. noted that "the almost
universal feeling of the Joint Chiefs was that General MacArthur's
move was very risky and had very little chance of success."[55] Whether
MacArthur was angered by the reluctance of the Joint Chiefs or simply frustrated by the events in Korea, he almost lost all support for
the Inch'ŏn plan when he challenged Truman's Far East policy in late
August. In response to an invitation by the Veterans of Foreign Wars to
send a message to its annual convention, MacArthur chose to address
the thorny issue of Taiwan. As he did during his trip to the island a
few weeks earlier, MacArthur argued for Taiwan's strategic value and
attacked those who opposed supporting Chiang Kai-shek. "Nothing
could be more fallacious than the threadbare argument by those who
advocate appeasement and defeatism in the Pacific that if we defend
Formosa, we alienate continental Asia," he declared. Drawing on his
claim of intimate knowledge of the "Oriental mind," he concluded,

"Those who speak thus do not understand the Orient. They do not grant that it is in the pattern of Oriental psychology to respect and follow aggressive, resolute and dynamic leadership, to quickly turn on a leadership characterized by timidity or vacillation."[56] Widely covered by the media, MacArthur's message represented exactly the kind of dabbling in politics that Truman had warned MacArthur against. Truman, however, appeared swayed in favor of the Inch'ŏn plan by a strong memorandum of support from Lt. Gen. Matthew B. Ridgway, the U.S. Army's deputy chief of staff for operations and administration and a World War II hero, who had gone to Japan with Harriman.[57]

MacArthur chose his chief of staff, Maj. Gen. Edward Almond, to command the landing force, X Corps, for Inch'ŏn. Almond had a relatively undistinguished record as a division commander in World War II, and the appointment surprised many, including Almond himself. Almond was concerned about his ability to execute two jobs, as MacArthur's chief of staff and as commander of X Corps. "Well, we'll all be home by Christmas," MacArthur reassured him. "It is only a short operation. You'll continue as my Chief of Staff and you can get any assistance you like."[58] Almond was a fiercely driven and competitive man with an all "consuming impatience with incompetence,"[59] but he inspired little affection from his peers or subordinates. The mutual dislike between Almond and Maj. Gen. O. P. Smith, the commanding general of the First Marine Division assigned to X Corps, was well known. Smith, a cautious commander who believed that "you do it slow, but you should do it right," was deeply suspicious of Almond. He later told the commandant of the Marine Corps, Gen. Clifton Cates, that he had "little confidence in the tactical judgment of [Almond's] X Corps or in the realism of their planning."[60] Their poor relations would have tragic consequences later in the war.

Despite the doubts and worries, the landing was a great success. At high tide early on September 15, the marines easily seized the small island of Wŏlmi-do, which controlled access to Inch'ŏn. The main force from the First Marine Division landed that afternoon in the next high-tide cycle. The landing caught the North Koreans by surprise; only a token force of two thousand North Korean soldiers defended the Inch'ŏn area. Within three days nearly seventy thousand men were put ashore.[61]

The Joint Chiefs and General Walker assumed that X Corps would be placed under the Eighth U.S. Army, but MacArthur kept it directly under his own control. MacArthur's decision to divide the command surprised many. "When MacArthur insisted on keeping the X Corps under his own control, the feeling was that the Eighth Army was being slighted in favor of MacArthur's 'pets,'" recalled Ridgway. "While there was never any open expression of jealousy or unwillingness to cooperate, there was no mistaking the fact that the atmosphere of mutual trust so necessary to smooth cooperation was lacking."[62] The arrangement had lasting consequences. "The relationship between Almond and Walker was horrible," recalled Col. John Michaelis. "I used to be in Walker's office, briefing him or something, and the phone would ring. 'Walker this is Almond.' This is a two-star general talking to a three-star general. 'I want you to do so and so.' And Walker would ask, 'Is this Almond speaking or Almond speaking for MacArthur?' They just couldn't get along."[63] Walker resented Almond's special access to MacArthur. "Walker was very suspicious of Almond," remembered Maj. Gen. John Chiles, Almond's operations officer. "He thought Almond was putting words in MacArthur's mouth because he was close to MacArthur and Walker wasn't."[64] Almond's position was an unenviable one. William McCaffrey, a regimental commander in X Corps, recalled that "Almond's complete mystical faith in General MacArthur and his duties to his troops placed him in an extraordinary position of inner conflict."[65] This inner conflict became notably manifest in Almond's relationship with his subordinate commanders, who felt that he was unresponsive to their needs and fighting conditions, because his greater goal was always to please the "big man" in Tokyo.

By September 25, the marines had entered Seoul. MacArthur declared it retaken even though less than half of the city was in UN hands. MacArthur's gamble had paid off. The North Korean army, faced with encirclement and annihilation, rapidly retreated and disappeared "like wraiths into the hills."[66] For MacArthur, success of the Inch'ŏn plan and the liberation of Seoul were both a vindication and a professional triumph. Doubts expressed by General Omar Bradley, Collins, and other members of the JCS had fed into MacArthur's paranoia that Washington was conspiring against him. But everything had gone just as MacArthur said it would. His honor and reputation had been strengthened to epic proportions. He saved South Korea. It was *his* brilliant plan that

General MacArthur addresses guests at a ceremony held at the Capitol Building in Seoul to restore the capital of the Republic of Korea to its president, Syngman Rhee (in the background with glasses). (U.S. NATIONAL ARCHIVES AND RECORDS ADMINISTRATION)

would bring victory. MacArthur was indignant when the Joint Chiefs questioned his authority to restore Syngman Rhee's government, which, they said, "must have the approval of a higher authority." "Your message is not understood," replied MacArthur. "The existing government of the Republic has never ceased to function."[67] The Joint Chiefs simply allowed the matter to rest. It was the first of a series of MacArthur's actions in Korea that the JCS failed to directly challenge. Ridgway later remarked, "A more subtle result of the Inch'ŏn triumph was the development of an almost superstitious regard for General MacArthur's infallibility. Even his superiors, it seemed, began to doubt if they should question *any* of MacArthur's decisions."[68] The more troubling result of Inch'ŏn, however, was that MacArthur ceased to have any doubts about himself.

South Korean prisoners shot by retreating North Korean troops, October 6, 1950. (U.S. NATIONAL ARCHIVES AND RECORDS ADMINISTRATION)

Savage War

Soon after Seoul's liberation, disturbing reports of North Korean atrocities began to surface. "Everywhere the advancing columns found evidence of atrocities as the North Koreans hurried to liquidate political and military prisoners held in jails before they themselves retreated in the face of the U.N. advance," stated the official U.S. Army history.[69] The Associated Press reported that "mass graves, large and small, are being found daily in South Korean communities."[70] The *Washington Post* called a massacre site at Yangyŏng, thirty-five miles south of Seoul, "Red Buchenwald," reporting that "in this Korean Red murder camp, 700 Korean civilians including children were executed."[71] The *New York Times* conveyed that at "Chunghǔng, near Kunsan, Communist soldiers armed with bamboo spears last Monday impaled eighty-two men, women and children after they took the village food supply."[72]

The *Jefferson City Post* reported that "seeing the massacre stung the imagination." It was a "coldly calculated massacre. Each man had been shot individually. Many apparently were clubbed to make sure they were

Captured North Korean soldiers guarded by ROK Military Police remove the bodies of sixty-five political prisoners of the North Korean army that had been dumped into wells in the city of Hamhŭng, North Korea, October 19, 1950. (U.S. NATIONAL ARCHIVES AND RECORDS ADMINISTRATION)

UN forces make another grim discovery of a North Korean massacre near Hamhŭng, where roughly three hundred bodies were taken out of a tunnel, October 1950. (U.S. NATIONAL ARCHIVES AND RECORDS ADMINISTRATION)

In the courtyard of the Taejŏn central police station, a film crew records the oral testimony of a survivor of the Taejŏn massacre, October 31, 1950. These on-site recordings by survivors played an important role in creating the Taejŏn massacre as an iconic symbol of Red terror in both American and South Korean memories of the war. (U.S. NATIONAL ARCHIVES AND RECORDS ADMINISTRATION)

dead. One man had a hatchet sticking to his head."[73] An American survivor of a massacre in Chinju related how the North Koreans had first made them dig their own graves before mowing them down with machine guns. "They tied us all together and shot us," said Pvt. Carey Weinald. "I played dead."[74] North Korean soldiers and local leftists wantonly killed thousands. Women, the elderly, and children were not spared. In one especially brutal incident at Muan county on October 3, families selected for execution were bound and taken to the shore, where the adults were killed with knives, clubs, bamboo spears, and farm implements and then thrown into the sea. Children under ten were thrown into a deep well. The majority of those killed were women and children.[75]

The North Korean massacres at Taejŏn prison became endowed with particularly powerful symbolic significance. The official U.S. history of the war described what had happened in Taejŏn as "one of the greatest mass killings of the entire Korean War," estimating that five to seven thousand civilians and soldiers had been slaughtered.[76] Private Herman

Nelson described the horror of what he saw when he entered the prison: "After a GI thought he saw a body in an open well in the prison camp, an American officer ordered the well searched. A total of twenty-nine dead American soldiers were fished out of the well." Over the next few days, more gruesome discoveries were made: "We discovered a church basement full of women slaughtered by the North Koreans. It was the same sickening sight we had witnessed a few days earlier."[77] Yi Chun-yŏng, who had been a South Korean prison guard at Taejŏn prison before the North Koreans came, vividly recalled the scene when he returned to the prison in early October:

> I entered the prison and walked around and discovered the corpses. They were black and covered with flies. I was speechless. I couldn't believe how cruelly these civilians were killed . . . Some had been shot and others seemed to have been killed by a blunt force that had cracked open their skull. I went to wells and found them full of bodies. We considered what to do . . . We obtained seven suspected communist prisoners and told them to line up the bodies. But the bodies were so decomposed that when we tried to pick them up, the flesh just slipped off. If they were clothed we could have picked them up by their clothing, but most were naked. The communist prisoners asked to be killed rather than handle these bodies, so we returned them to jail. I went to the Taejŏn City Hall to ask for help . . . By the next day, they had mobilized 300–400 people to clear up the bodies. I had them dig holes in the hill behind the prison to bury them . . . It took 2–3 days to do it. At first I thought of burying them individually, but there were just too many bodies, so we buried them in groups in larger holes. I don't have an exact count, but it was between 400–500 people.[78]

The discovery of mass murder solidified in the minds of Americans and others that they were dealing with an "unnatural" enemy, one who had "no regard for human life" or who observed "no rules of war or humanity." Like the "Mongolian hordes" of Asia's past, this enemy "fights with a blend of Asiatic fatalism and Communist fanaticism." "We are facing an army of barbarians in Korea," wrote Hanson Baldwin of the *New York Times*, "but they are barbarians as trained, as relentless, as reckless of life, and as skilled in the tactics of the kind of war they fight as the hordes of Genghis Khan." The North Korean "hordes," like their Russian masters, inherited the particular "Mongolian penchant for cruelty" and used "weapons of fear and terror."[79]

If the horrors of Taejŏn were a glimpse of an enemy not bound by laws of warfare, it was also apparent that the South Koreans were just as brutal. "[The South Korean security forces] murder to save themselves the trouble of escorting prisoners to the rear," wrote an appalled John Osborne of *Time* and *Life*. "They murder civilians simply to get them out of the way or to avoid the trouble of searching and cross examining them. And they extort information . . . by means so brutal that they cannot be described."[80] The *New York Times* reported on July 13 that twelve hundred suspected communists had been executed by the South Korean police since the outbreak of hostilities, an estimate that was woefully inadequate. In the early days of the war, little effort was made by North or South Koreans to hide their atrocities. Telford Taylor, the former chief counsel for prosecution at Nuremberg, incensed by what he was reading in the newspapers, wrote to the *New York Times* that "it seems apparent, if we may take the press accounts at face value, that the atrocities have not all been the work of the North Koreans. The laws of war and war crimes trials are not weapons like bazookas and hand grenades to be used only against the enemy. The laws of war can be 'law' in the true sense only if they are of general application and applied to all sides." He concluded, "We will make ourselves appear ridiculous and hypocritical if we condemn the conduct of the enemy when at the same time troops allied with us are with impunity executing prisoners by means of rifle butts applied to backbones."[81]

The commission of atrocities by South Koreans was not the only issue that would make the Americans appear "ridiculous and hypocritical" to the world. From the beginning, the Americans faced a moral dilemma over what to do with the thousands of Korean refugees. It was a different kind of war from World War II, where the enemy was clearly identifiable on the battlefield. North Korean soldiers easily mixed with the refugees by disguising themselves in the ubiquitous white-cotton peasant clothing. "Time after time an American soldier would pass an innocent-looking bearded Korean farmer hoeing a rice paddy only to be confronted with the same figure throwing grenades at him in a dawn attack," wrote Marguerite Higgins.[82] In late July, the Associated Press reported an announcement by the South Korean government that civilians found making "enemy-like actions" would be executed.[83] "The enemy has used the refugees to his advantage in many ways," reported Ambassador Muccio on July 26, "by forcing [the refugees] south and so clogging the roads as to interfere with military movements, by using them as a channel for infiltration of agents, and most dangerous of all, by disguising their own troops as refugees, who after passing through our lines proceed, after dark, to produce hidden weapons, and then attack our units from the rear. Too often such attacks have been devastatingly successful." Muccio also described a meeting at the South Korean Home Ministry on July 26 between American and South Korean officials where they concluded that leaflets warning people not to proceed south, and that if they did, they risked being fired upon, would be dropped north of the U.S. lines. "If refugees do appear from north of US lines they will receive warning shots, and if they then persist in advancing they will be shot."[84] These instructions were consistent with eyewitness accounts. No one willingly wanted to shoot innocent civilians, particularly women and children, but the nature of the war often forced American soldiers to do so. Colonel Paul Freeman, a regimental commander, admitted in an interview twenty years later, "This was the first time we had really encountered Communist cruelty ... When we first met some of these North Korean attacks, they were driving civilians, elderly people, in front of them as shields. We had a very difficult time making our men fire into them. But if we didn't fire into them, we were dead. I mean our people were dead. This was a very hard thing to do."[85]

Another measure involved air strikes. "We heard numerous stories about American planes strafing civilians," recalled H. K. Shin, who was just sixteen when he joined the ROK Military Police.[86] One observer recalled that the First Cavalry Division's commanding general, Maj. Gen. Hobart Gay, ordered a "scorched earth" policy: "In any withdrawal, all rural structures would be leveled, burned to the ground. No cover would be left for the enemy. Further, after a posted period, any Koreans found in the area between UN lines and the enemy would be considered hostile and shot on sight."[87] Distinctions between civilians and soldiers were blurred, and the brutality of the violence disturbed even the most seasoned soldier. "Much of this war is alien to the American tradition and shocking to the American mind," observed John Osborne. "The attempt to win it is to force our men in the field to commit acts and attitudes of the utmost savagery." This was not, he thought, "the inevitable savagery of combat in the field, but savagery in detail, the blotting out of villages where the enemy *may* be hiding, the shooting and shelling of refugees who *may* include North Koreans . . . or who *may* be screening an enemy march upon our positions."[88]

Some of the worst atrocities were committed by South Koreans against South Koreans. In July 1950, the South Korean military and police conducted mass executions of suspected leftists before the arrival of the North Korean army.[89] At Chŏngwŏn in central South Korea, the police killed hundreds of suspected communists. Pak Chŏng-gil, a young boy at the time, remembered the "perfidious" activities of the fleeing South Korean police: "I think they killed several thousand people there. Every day for seven straight days I saw four trucks in the morning and three trucks in the afternoon loaded with people." The trucks, he said, all came back empty at night. At Nanju, in the southwest, police officers disguised as North Koreans stormed the village. When the people welcomed them, they were rounded up, taken to a field, and summarily executed.[90] These and other massacres throughout South Korea in 1949 and 1950 demonstrated that the end of the Cheju and Yŏsu-Sunch'ŏn Rebellions had not stopped the fratricidal bloodshed. South Korean

Remains of 114 Bodo League victims executed in July 1950 at Chŏngwŏn, Ch'ungbuk province, excavated by the Truth and Reconciliation Commission in 2007. Remains of the victims reveal that they had been shot to death. (ROK TRUTH AND RECONCILIATION COMMISSION)

security forces purged the army of leftists and communists and did their ruthless best to rid the countryside of communist guerilla groups formed by the remnants of the Yŏsu-Sunch'ŏn rebels who had escaped into the mountains. Caught in the roundup of suspected leftists and communists were innocent civilians, including women and children who were summarily executed in the thousands in the name of fighting the communists. It is estimated that at least a hundred thousand South Koreans were killed in the summer of 1950. Most were members of the Bodo League (*kungmin podo yŏnmaeng*, National Guidance League), ostensibly created by the Rhee government in the summer of 1949 to rehabilitate leftists, but in reality it was a form of totalitarian state control of the people. Its logic required hapless and often illiterate farmers and fishermen to be enticed to join the league with promises of jobs, food, and other benefits to meet the quota imposed from Seoul. When North Korea invaded, the South Korean regime hastily took measures to eliminate those who might help the communists, and Bodo League members, mostly innocent of leftist leanings, were arbitrarily and summarily executed all over the country. Indeed, the hundred thousand estimate might be on the conservative side, as there were three hundred thousand members on the rolls of the league on the eve of the North Korean invasion.[91]

In an interview in November 2007, Chŏng Kwang-im recounted how her young farmer husband, who had joined the Bodo League in 1949, was summarily arrested and executed at Taejŏn:

> One day the police came and asked where my husband, Pak Man-ho, was and I told them that he went away to make some money. They then arrested me. I spent the night in the jail. The next morning my husband came to the police station with our two children who had been crying for me all night. After he arrived they called for me. They gave me the children and took my husband without any chance for us to talk. At the urging of other people I awaited outside the prison. Around five in the morning a siren rang and trucks came. They loaded the trucks with prisoners, one at a time. We didn't know where they were being taken to. I heard later they were taken to Sannae village.

Pak was executed in a remote valley near Sannae village. Chŏng later went to recover his remains, but she could not find him because the bodies had rapidly decomposed in the July heat. She never remarried and

The remains of twenty-nine bodies were unearthed at the third site of the Kolryŏnggol, Sannae, Taejŏn in 2007. They were found face down with their knees bent, which suggests that the victims were killed execution-style. (ROK TRUTH AND RECONCILIATION COMMISSION)

lived a life of suffering with her two sons, ostracized by her husband's past as an alleged communist sympathizer.[92]

Many American advisors, concerned and revolted by what they saw, filed reports with photographs. But the senior-level American response was decidedly ambivalent. Lieutenant Colonel Rollins Emmerich reported on the situation in Pusan, which had never fallen into enemy hands. He discovered that the local ROK Army commander, Col. Kim Chŏng-wŏn, planned "to execute some 3,500 suspected Communists." He told Colonel Kim that the enemy would not reach Pusan soon and that "atrocities could not be condoned." But "Colonel Kim was told that if the enemy did arrive to the outskirts of Pusan he would be permitted to open the gates of the prison and shoot the prisoners with machine guns." Emmerich faced a similar situation in Taegu, where he managed to persuade South Korean authorities not to execute forty-five hundred prisoners. Taegu soon was threatened by the presence of North Koreans on its outskirts, and hundreds of the prisoners were executed. Donald Nichols, an air force intelligence officer, witnessed, photographed, and reported on the execution of eighteen hundred prisoners in Suwŏn,

just south of Seoul. A North Korean press report that a thousand prisoners were executed in Inch'ŏn in late June 1950 was corroborated by
an Eighth Army report on the execution of "400 Communists" there.
Attempts were made to restrain the South Koreans, but the authorities receiving these reports, including MacArthur, were ambivalent. He
had received numerous reports of the killings and atrocities committed by South Korean forces under his command, but he deferred to
Ambassador Muccio, who merely asked the South Korean government
to execute humanely and only after due process. MacArthur considered
the situation a Korean "internal matter" and took no action.[93]

Ironically, one of the most egregious massacres by the South Koreans
took place in the very vicinity where the North Koreans were accused
of committing their most heinous war crimes. In early July, three weeks
before Taejŏn fell to the NKPA, South Korean security forces executed
thousands of suspected communists and leftists. Details of this incident have only recently been reported in South Korea. "After receiving news of the North Korean attack on Taejŏn," reported the *Wŏlgan
chosŏn*, a prominent South Korean monthly, in June 2000, "high ranking
government and prisoner officials were too busy retreating to worry
about the prisoners at Taejŏn prison." As a result, "the responsibility ultimately fell on lower-ranking prison officials who did not want
their men butchered alone by the revolting prisoners."[94] Yi Chun-yŏng,
the Taejŏn prison guard who saw victims of North Korean killings in
October, recalled the chaotic events in the days before the city fell. "We
received a phone call from the Chief Prosecutor of the Justice Ministry
and were ordered to execute all the leaders and officials of the Communist Party." Seeking confirmation, Yi found the justice minister at
the train station getting ready to evacuate south. The minister coolly
told Yi "to tell the Commandant in charge to take action based on his
own judgment." Yi was furious. "If there hadn't been others around, I
would have shot him then and there," Yi recalled indignantly. "The
nation was in peril because people like him didn't take any responsibility for any decision."[95] Minutes later, the minister was gone, taking one
of the last trains out of Taejŏn.

There were only twenty-two men to guard and control the thousands
of prisoners. Most were political prisoners charged with communist and
leftist leanings. The local military police unit, led by Lt. Sim Yŏng-hyŏn,
had arrived. Sim directed the prison guards to identify for execution

any prisoners who had violated the Special Security Law, who had been involved in the 1948 Yŏsu-Sunch'ŏn Uprising or the 1948–49 Cheju-do Rebellion, or who had been indicted for spying, and anyone else who had received a sentence of ten years or more. But time was short and they could not complete the sorting. In the end, all prisoners were executed. "The Commandant said that [executing all the prisoners] may become a political problem in the future, but there was nothing that could be done about the situation as there was no time to sort through all their backgrounds."[96] The prisoners, men and women, with their hands tied behind their backs, were loaded onto trucks. "Men from nearby villages were mobilized to dig trenches." The prisoners were driven to various sites in the outskirts of the city and "taken to the trenches in groups of about ten. They were forced to kneel at the trench and bow their heads. The firing team was composed of military and civilian policemen. They put the barrel against the back of the head and fired."[97] "Even at point blank range, some were not killed outright," Yi recalled. "Lt. Sim ordered me to confirm the executions and finish off those who were not dead. I was carrying a 45 caliber pistol unlike other guards who had smaller caliber pistols. I shot those who were still alive and squirming as I walked by them. I did as I was ordered." There was one moment, however, that Yi will never forget:

> As I walked by I heard behind me, "Sir, sir, I am not dead yet, please, sir, shoot me." I turned around and saw a man who had worked in the mess hall. He had been imprisoned for theft and had one year left to serve out his ten year term . . . Why didn't he say, "Hey you bastard, I am not dead. Shoot me, you bastard." Why did he call me "sir" instead? He had no hostility towards me, and I suddenly felt a rush of anguish and respect for this man. He asked me to shoot him because he was suffering and I did.[98]

Yi later blamed higher authorities for what happened: "I don't regret the death of communists who were convicted and sentenced to death, but the others . . . I wonder what kind of people led our nation who allowed them to be executed as well."[99] Although scattered reports about the mass executions managed to find their way into the foreign media, few stories ever reached the mainstream press because they were dismissed as communist propaganda. Alan Winnington, a British journalist for the communist *Daily Worker*, wrote what he had witnessed in Taejŏn when he arrived there with the NKPA:

Civilians about to be executed by South Korean security forces, Taejŏn, July 1950. (U.S. NATIONAL ARCHIVES AND RECORDS ADMINISTRATION)

Try to imagine Rangwul Valley, about five miles south-east of Taejon on the Yongdong road. Hills rise sharply from a level floor of 100 yards across and a quarter of a mile long. In the middle you can walk safely, though your shoes may roll on American cartridge cases, but at the sides you must be careful for the rest of the valley is thin crust of earth covering corpses of more than 7,000 men and women. One of the party with me stepped through nearly to his hip in rotting human tissue. Every few feet there is a fissure in the topsoil through which you can see into a gradually sinking mass of flesh and bone. The smell is something tangible and seeps into your throat. For days after I could taste the smell. All along the great death pits, waxy dead hands and feet, knees, elbows, twisted faces and heads burst open by bullets, stick through the soil . . . All six of the death pits are six feet deep and from six to twelve feet wide. The biggest is 200 yards long. Local peasants were forced at the rifle point to dig them, and it was from these that I got the facts. On July 4, 5 and 6, all prisoners from the jails and concentration camps around Taejon were taken in trucks to the valley, after first being bound with wire, knocked unconscious and packed like sardines on top of each other. So truckloads were driven to the valley and flung into pits. Peasants were made to cover the filled sections of the pits with soil.[100]

Few believed him at the time. When the city was retaken, victims of the earlier massacre perpetrated by the ROK forces were conflated with victims of the North Korean killings. Buried beneath the story of the

North Korean slaughter, literally, was the forgotten story of the South Korean carnage. The raw brutality of a civil war wracked by deep and polarized ideological divide and decades of pent-up personal animosities exploded in the first few months of the war, causing a wound in Korean society, North and South, that remains raw to this day. The tides of cruelty continued with the tides of war as North and South Koreans tried to outdo each other in eliminating suspected collaborators and sympathizers of the other side as the front line moved north and south. In the context of the cold war, where clear lines between the "free world" and the "slave world," and "civilization" and "barbarism," needed to be starkly drawn, the messy civil war in Korea, with its moral ambiguities and vengeful deeds, had to be simplified. Historical forgetting, selective reporting, propagandistic self-deception, and a truly savage war and war crimes played major roles in the demonization of the other side. While the Western press continued to report on North Korean atrocities, particularly the merciless treatment of American POWs, critical coverage of South Korean brutality and U.S. operational excesses largely disappeared. Already, in the opening weeks of the war, a subtle yet distinct process of "forgetting" was beginning to take place.

CHAPTER FIVE

Uncommon Coalition

At the end of August 1950, UN ground forces began to arrive in Korea, starting with the first contingent of British troops. The passage of UN Security Council Resolution 83 on June 27, 1950, obligated UN member states to consider sending assistance "to the Republic of Korea as may be necessary to repel the armed attack and to restore international peace and security in the area." Fifty-one member states were part of the United Nations upon its founding in 1945, and by the time of the Korean War, only eight more had joined. Out of these fifty-nine nations, forty-eight offered or sent forces or aid to South Korea. Seven non–UN member states also sent aid, bringing the total to fifty-five nations. Japan was under Allied occupation when the war started, but it was a critical support base for the war and was thus a member of the coalition. Germany was also under occupation but provided nonmilitary aid. Adding South Korea brought the final count of the coalition to fifty-eight. Of these, twenty-two nations, including one non–UN member, with "boots on the ground" in Korea formed the core of the coalition. Never before in modern history had so many nations committed themselves to a common political and military endeavor as they did during the Korean War (see appendix).[1]

There was a fundamental difference in the way the coalition in Korea was organized and operated compared to coalitions in other wars, such as the two world wars and the more recent conflicts in Iraq and Afghanistan. Coalitions formed in wars before and after the Korean War normally consisted of discrete national units under national command, with coalitional integration or command and control achieved only at the highest level of command. For example, in World War II, the major Allied forces in the European theater of operations did not mix different nationalities below the corps level, except for very minor exceptions for specialized operations. In Korea, necessity, expedience, improvisation, and politics demanded a wholly different kind of coalition.

The unique character of the Korean coalition arose from a number of factors. First, the South Korean military was placed under UN/U.S. control because of its severely depleted and disorganized state after the first two weeks of fighting.[2] Second, as an extension of the first, two pools of manpower were provided to UN/U.S. forces. One comprised the tens of thousands of Korean men known as KATUSA (Korean Augmentation to the United States Army) soldiers assigned to U.S. units, an arrangement that was later expanded to include British, Australian, Canadian, French, Dutch, and Belgian units. Most of the KATUSA soldiers were integrated down to the lowest level, the squad of some dozen men. The other pool of manpower was the Korean Service Corps (KSC), civilian laborers who were organized and led by ROK Army leaders to provide dedicated support to all UN/U.S. units. The ratio of laborers to soldiers was roughly one to two. Finally, non-U.S./Korean UN ground forces were sent not as large units or with a complete support structure and thus could not operate independently. Britain, Turkey, and Canada sent brigades (3,000–5,000 men), but most non-U.S./Korean UN ground forces were battalion size (about 1,000 men). All units were integrated into American divisions and corps. By 1952, every American division and corps had KATUSA soldiers and at least one UN battalion or brigade. The British Commonwealth ground forces (United Kingdom, Australia, Canada, New Zealand, and India) did combine into a single division in the summer of 1951, an arrangement unprecedented for the Commonwealth, but it was subordinated to a U.S. corps and relied on American logistical support. The flow of campaigns and battles from late 1950 to mid-1951, under constant reorganization and re-subordination, led to complex mixes of nationalities.[3]

By the end of 1950, ten nations (in the order of arrival: the United Kingdom, the Philippines, Australia, Turkey, Thailand, the Netherlands, France, Greece, Canada, and New Zealand) had sent ground combat forces to join the Koreans and the Americans. Four more nations (Belgium, Luxembourg, Ethiopia, and Colombia) sent combat forces by the middle of 1951. Medical units from five other nations (Sweden, India, Denmark, Italy, and Norway) arrived by the end of 1951, while the United Kingdom, Canada, Australia, and New Zealand significantly increased their contingents. By the end of 1951, the total strength of the non-U.S./ ROK force was 35,000. This would grow to nearly 40,000 by July 1953.[4]

The British Commonwealth forces formed the majority of the coalition forces, about 60 percent (21,000–24,000). These forces went through several stages of reorganization, from the Commonwealth Brigade of British, Australian, Canadian, and Indian units in 1950 to, with reinforcements in 1951, the unique First Commonwealth Division formed in the summer of 1951. The unprecedented formation of the Commonwealth Brigade and the Commonwealth Division created political and high-level military difficulties, but at the lower level it was a relatively smooth process done efficiently and effectively, owing to a shared military heritage and culture and the use of English as a common language. The assignment of the Norwegian mobile army surgical hospital (NORMASH) also was done without significant problems. The Commonwealth units were the only forces besides the U.S. military that established a separate logistical system, easing the burden of support from the Eighth U.S. Army, which still had to provide fuel and fresh food.

Integrating an Army

The arrival of the 5,000 men of the Turkish Brigade in October 1950, however, posed far greater challenges. As soon as the situation stabilized after the victory at Inch'ŏn, a centralized transition and training center, the United Nations Reception Center (UNRC), was established near Taegu to help "clothe, equip, and provide familiarization training with US Army weapons and equipment to UN troops." As the first UN troops to be processed, the Turks, during their three-week stay, provided the UNRC a much clearer picture of the kinds of problems the American commanders would be facing in commanding an international coalition. For example, bathing proved to be an unexpected challenge. "When showers were set up, it was found out that only one Turkish soldier at a time would bathe, until the problem of their unexpected modesty was solved by the soldiers themselves. Each man formed an individual cubicle by wrapping shelter halves around himself."[5]

Language differences also posed a formidable barrier. Greek, Turkish, Thai, French, Flemish, Spanish, and Dutch as well as a number of other

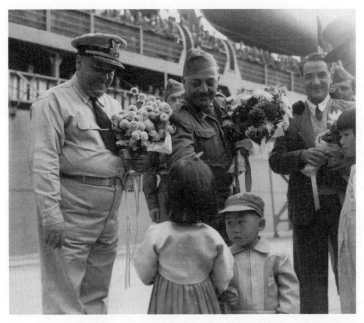

South Korean children present flowers to a Turkish officer (center) in
charge of the first contingent of Turkish troops on their arrival in Pusan,
October 18, 1950. (U.S. NATIONAL ARCHIVES AND RECORDS ADMINISTRATION)

dialects "were among the tongues used in the UN ground [combat]
units." Added to these difficulties were the "Swedish, Norwegian, Italian, and several regional languages used by medical units supporting the
combat forces." Although the language barriers were never completely
overcome, English was the lingua franca, and the burden of translation
was left to UN units that "provided English-speaking personnel to translate training materials, operational orders and supply instructions into
their own languages."[6]

Feeding the Turks was a special challenge, for most of them were
Muslims and forbidden to eat pork. The Eighth Army devised a porkless
diet manufactured by a Japanese fish cannery. The Turks also procured
their "own stronger brand of coffee." Since the staple of the Turkish diet
was bread, they were given "three times the amount of bread issued to a
US regiment as well as greater quantities of vegetable oil, olives, vinegar,
dehydrated onions, and salt."[7]

As with the Turks, culinary differences with the units from other
countries initially posed great problems and stressed the U.S. ration

Troops in the Greek army prepare for a pork barbecue behind UN lines in Korea. Like other nationalities, the Greeks had their own unique dietary requirements, such as olive oil, raisins, and special flour, which were provided in sufficient quantities through their own channels. (U.S. NATIONAL ARCHIVES AND RECORDS ADMINISTRATION)

Indian cooks prepare traditional "chapati" flat bread. Unlike troops from Asian and European nations, which required large quantities of rice and potatoes, respectively, Indian troops required large quantities of wheat. (U.S. NATIONAL ARCHIVES AND RECORDS ADMINISTRATION)

system. It was difficult, for example, to get the Thai to eat "any sort of food except rice and pots of boiled vegetables, thick with peppers and hot sauces." The Greeks did not eat corn, carrots, and asparagus and required olive oil for cooking. The Indians were mostly vegetarians. The Filipinos required additional rice, while the Belgians, French, and Dutch consumed greater quantities of bread and potatoes than the Americans did. The Greeks required special meals for religious days: "On Good Friday, they desired no meat in their rations, whereas for Greek Orthodox Easter, they required fifteen live lambs for their traditional feasts."[8]

Clothing also produced its share of difficulties. The Thai, Filipino, and Greek soldiers required smaller clothing. A major challenge was combat boots. "It must be remembered that some of these troops were accustomed to wearing sandals, and therefore their feet were wide at the ball and narrow at the heel," noted an American officer. Ethiopians were generally taller than Americans and their feet longer and narrower.[9]

The most critical area, weapons and ammunition, was not a major issue. Most UN troops, except for the Commonwealth units, were given American arms. Some contingents arrived already familiar with the U.S. Army, its procedures, and weapons. The Philippine army had been trained by the United States for many years, while the Greek army had recently undergone intense American training and equipping under Lt. Gen. James Van Fleet, to fight its communist insurgency. Van Fleet's assumption of command of the Eighth Army a few months after the Greek battalion's arrival no doubt provided an additional level of comfort to the Greeks.

The greatest challenge of the coalition, however, was integrating the ROK Army with the Eighth U.S. Army. Until the breakout from the Pusan perimeter in September 1950, ROK Army units were kept together at their own part of the front and controlled through the ROK Army headquarters. When the Eighth Army was reorganized for the breakout, the ROK First Division was assigned to an American corps, thus beginning the process of integrating ROK units with American forces.[10]

The need for men was so great in the summer of 1950 that the KATUSA program expanded rapidly, and by September over 19,000 KATUSA soldiers were assigned to the Eighth Army and X Corps.[11] Integration of these Korean soldiers presented major difficulties at all

American and KATUSA soldiers of the 27th Infantry Regiment advance toward Chinese forces at Kyŏngan-ri February 17, 1951. (U.S. NATIONAL ARCHIVES AND RECORDS ADMINISTRATION)

levels of command. The success of the Inch'ŏn landing demonstrated the surprising efficiency of UN operations even at this early phase in the war. While most accounts of the operation have focused on the epic battles of the U.S. X Corps and its two American divisions, the First Marine Division and the U.S. Army Seventh Infantry Division, what is rarely noted is the role that the Korean soldiers and marines in the two divisions played in the events. The simpler arrangement was the attachment of the ROK Marine Corps Regiment to the U.S. First Marine Division.[12] Such an attachment was routine and natural, and the regiment fought as a unit. However, the situation in the Seventh Division was quite different, because fully one-third of the division was composed of KATUSA soldiers.

The Seventh Division had been on occupation duty in Japan at reduced strength. It became further depleted when men were transferred to the Twenty-Fourth and Twenty-Fifth Infantry Divisions as they deployed to Korea in July 1950, thereby reducing the Seventh to less than half strength by late July. Essentially the division was not combat ready.[13] Two measures were taken to bring it up to strength after it was selected for the Inch'ŏn operation. First, a large portion of the replacement flow from the United States was sent to the division. Second, MacArthur requested that the South Korean government provide Korean recruits to make up for the remaining shortfall. In mid-August nearly 9,000 Koreans arrived at Yokohama, Japan, "stunned, confused, and exhausted."[14] General "Johnnie" Walker reported to MacArthur, "They are right out of the rice paddies, and have nothing but shorts and straw hats."[15] Many had literally been dragged off the streets and arrived in Japan "in their native civilian clothes, white baggy cotton pants, small white jackets, [and] rubber shoes," according to Maj. Spencer Edwards, the Seventh Division's replacement officer.[16] They had less than a month to become soldiers and get ready for an amphibious landing, one of the most complex and riskiest of military operations. In three weeks, 8,600 Koreans were clothed, equipped, and trained, however minimally, to join the 16,000 Americans of the Seventh Division embarking for Inch'ŏn.[17] The challenges and obstacles were huge. Few, if any, spoke English. They had no military background or experience. Stocks of small-size uniform items were quickly exhausted. For many, the standard American rifle (the M1) was too long. Instead of forming all-Korean units, they were apportioned throughout the division at the rate of a hundred men per company or battery and integrated to the lowest echelon. Given that a standard company or battery may have about two hundred men, this was an enormous challenge. A buddy system of pairing individual Koreans with an American was used for assimilation, training, and control.[18] The operational risks of the Inch'ŏn plan were magnified by the huge tactical risk of employing a division composed of the greenest troops, American and Korean, in which a third of the fighting force did not understand English.[19]

Fortunately, the First Marine Division, which landed first, was able to quickly secure a beachhead, allowing the Seventh Division to land without fighting for one. The Seventh Division soon entered combat to cut off the North Korean army's retreat and to liberate Seoul. Their actions on the battlefield were predictably mixed. Major Edwards recalled that "some of the ROKs participated heroically and some of them disappeared at the first sign of danger. The great majority behaved just as any other troops with less than three weeks' training would have—they just didn't know what was going on." Korean civilians watched in amaze-

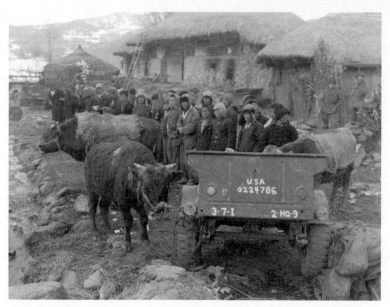

Korean Service Corps (KSC) laborers, near Suwŏn, February 5, 1951. In addition to the KATUSAs serving in U.S. units, the other pool of manpower was the KSC. Affectionately referred to as the "A-Frame Army" by American soldiers because of their wooden backpacks, at its peak the KSC had over 130,000 Koreans who were organized to provide direct support to non-Korean soldiers. The unarmed members of the KSC moved ammunition, supplies, and food to the front lines, traversing steep and rugged terrain that was otherwise inaccessible by vehicles. They also helped in the evacuation of wounded and deceased soldiers and the construction of defensive positions. (U.S. NATIONAL ARCHIVES AND RECORDS ADMINISTRATION)

KSC laborer, near Suwŏn, February 5, 1951. (U.S. NATIONAL ARCHIVES AND RECORDS ADMINISTRATION)

ment as thousands of Koreans marched through the streets wearing the patch of an American unit that had been part of the occupation force in South Korea between 1945 and 1949. By the end of the Inch'ŏn-Seoul operations on October 3, the Seventh Division had suffered 572 casualties, of which 166 were KATUSA soldiers. By this time, thousands of other KATUSA soldiers had been assigned to and were fighting in all U.S. Army divisions.[20]

Japanese nationals also played an important role in these operations. The majority of the landing ship tanks (LSTs) that the First Marine Division used at Inch'ŏn, thirty-seven of forty-seven, were, in fact, manned by Japanese crews.[21] Furthermore, twenty Japanese minesweepers were contracted to help clear mines along the coastal areas. One was sunk during mine-clearing operations in Wŏnsan Harbor.[22] Japanese nationals thus participated directly in combat operations. One Japanese national was even listed as an exchanged POW after the armistice.[23] In addition to providing LST crews and minesweepers, Japan was literally the unsinkable base of support for the fighting. Nearly all military forces and supplies to Korea came from or transited through Japan. It also provided bases for air and naval operations.[24] Troops were trained there before deployment, were treated there after being wounded, and played there during R&R leave. Japanese firms provisioned the UN forces and repaired their equipment.

Calling the Eighth Army a "U.S. Army" was thus a significant misnomer by the summer of 1951. More appropriate would have been the "UN Army in Korea" since less than half of its half-million men were Americans. Indeed, more than 50 percent of the fighting force were Koreans, of whom 20,000 were integrated into U.S., French, Dutch, and Belgian units. Some 28,000 soldiers from nineteen other nations joined them. The Eighth Army's strength increased to nearly one million men by the time of the armistice, with 300,000 Americans, 590,000 Koreans, and 39,000 soldiers from other nations.[25] No U.S. division since August 1950 was purely American, as KATUSA soldiers filled the ranks through all echelons.[26] The U.S. divisions also had at least one UN battalion or brigade attached. Every U.S. corps had at least one ROK division. I Corps was probably the most diverse, composed of U.S. Army, ROK, and British Commonwealth divisions, which also included Turkish, Greek, and Norwegian contingents. Furthermore, since the summer of 1950 all non-

Korean UN ground units were supported by the ROK Army's KSC. At its height the Eighth Army's KSC had 130,000 men to support 300,000 non-Korean soldiers.[27]

Common Cause

So why had all these nations come together under the UN flag to fight in Korea? Although each nation had its own reason to participate in the war, there was a broad commonality of factors, especially for the nations that sent combat forces. First and foremost, the war was seen as a test for the young United Nations and the concept of collective security it was supposed to uphold. Invoking the UN also invoked its most important member, the United States, and support to the UN also implied support for the Americans. Demonstrating this support became critical in the aftermath of World War II, for the United States emerged from the war as the most powerful and prosperous nation in the world, a world devastated by the destruction of that war and the ensuing strife and unrest of postcolonial struggles for independence, many involving indigenous communist movements. Communist insurgencies in Malaya for the United Kingdom and Indochina for France were particularly troubling. The United States had also been helping the Philippines battle its growing communist threat. In 1949, the Dutch pulled out of Indonesia, conceding defeat in the Indonesian War of Independence. Its new president, Sukarno, was sympathetic to communism. Most noncommunist member states of the United Nations thus felt an obligation to uphold the UN Charter and its principle of collective security. No member state felt this obligation more keenly than the three Western permanent members of the Security Council: the United States, the United Kingdom, and France. Anticommunism and collective security were major shared ideologies of the nations that sent aid to Korea, especially those that deployed combat forces. The line was to be drawn against communism in general and against the Soviet Union in particular.

But idealistic ideology alone could not produce the kind of assistance the war called for, as most nations lacked the resources to provide it. Furthermore, many nations either were dependent on or wanted American assistance or commitment for economic development and security.

Soldiers of the Argyll and Sutherland Highlanders arrive in Pusan. Originally, the British government had decided to mobilize and deploy the Twenty-Ninth Infantry Brigade, a unit in the British strategic reserve force, but the brigade would not be ready on time. As a result, the Twenty-Seventh Brigade from Hong Kong was sent to Pusan as a quick stop measure until the Twenty-Ninth Brigade could be deployed. Only two of the brigade's three battalions, the Argyll and Sutherland Highlanders and the Middlesex battalions, were sent, however. In order not to deplete the Hong Kong garrison completely, the Leicesters were left behind. Arriving on August 29 to bolster the Pusan perimeter, the Twenty-Seventh Brigade was the first non-U.S. UN ground force to enter the war. (U.S. NATIONAL ARCHIVES AND RECORDS ADMINISTRATION)

Britain was particularly keen to maintain a "special relationship" with the United States and to secure an American commitment for Western European security. France, already deeply embroiled in a protracted war with Ho Chi Minh's forces in Indochina, was eager to obtain American assistance for its own "cold war struggle" in Asia. France had convinced the Americans that, far from fighting a selfish colonial war, it was in fact defending the principles of freedom against communist world dictatorship. For its efforts in Korea and in Indochina, President Truman believed that France was entitled to a generous measure of American military and financial assistance since "these were two fronts in the same struggle."[28] Many nations reasoned that providing a contribution, especially combat forces, would serve not only their idealism but also, by getting in America's good graces, their national interests. Largely

On November 20, 1950, the 60th Indian (Parachute) Field Ambulance, a mobile army surgical hospital, arrived and became part of the Twenty-Seventh Brigade. Britain pressured India for a large combat force, but Prime Minister Jawaharlal Nehru wanted to position India, which had only recently won its independence in 1947, as a leader of the underdeveloped countries in the UN and nonaligned with any major power. Nehru decided to contribute a medical unit as a commitment to the UN rather than to the Commonwealth, a symbol of its noncombatant status. The 60th Field Ambulance was an elite regular unit with personnel who were veterans of the Burma campaign during World War II serving in the British army. (U.S. NATIONAL ARCHIVES AND RECORDS ADMINISTRATION)

because of their participation in the Korean War, Greece and Turkey, for example, were admitted to NATO in 1952. This was a triumph especially for Turkey, which had struggled to be accepted as part of Europe. Its large contribution in Korea, the legendary Turkish brigade, served to prove Turkey's commitment to the West and its willingness to make sacrifices to uphold it.[29]

For Thailand, participation in the war helped to solve the special problem it had faced following the Second World War. Thailand had been a member of the Axis after signing an armistice with Japan in December 1941. Fighting in Korea largely "rehabilitated" the Thai in the eyes of the

A group of smiling Turkish officers pose with Korean Boy Scouts who welcomed their arrival at Pusan, October 19, 1950. (U.S. NATIONAL ARCHIVES AND RECORDS ADMINISTRATION)

free world. Japan's role in the Korean War was not so much as a willing participant, since it was still under American occupation in 1950, as it was of an unsuspecting bystander of a conflict from which it reaped tremendous benefit. The war was, as Prime Minister Yoshida Shigeru once famously proclaimed, "a gift from the gods." A war boom, stimulated by U.S. procurements for the war, put Japan's economy back on track. Japanese industrial production during the conflict also laid the technological foundation for the subsequent development of the country's industry.[30] Japan's central role in enabling the support of the UN forces created a paradox regarding the ending of the Allied occupation and the restoration of sovereignty. At first, military necessity made it preferable to delay any plans for Japanese independence until the Korean War was over. The Americans needed Japan's full compliance for their war efforts in Korea. However, as the level of occupation forces dwindled and Japanese civil society became crucial in maintaining military support for the Korean War, the logic of denying the Japanese their independence was turned on its head as the Americans began to realize the necessity for placating, and even appeasing, the Japanese people as a prolonged occupation could degrade their cooperation and support. Nothing could have done this more powerfully than the end of the occupation, which occurred in April 1952. At the same time, even though the Japanese postwar constitution, drafted by the Americans, specifically forbade the maintenance of a military, the Korean War convinced both the Americans and the Japanese that Japan needed to be rearmed to defend itself against the communist and Soviet threat. Japan regained not only sovereignty, but a military as well. [31]

India, too, provided an interesting case. Although it sent a military medical unit that served with the Commonwealth forces, its motive was not to strengthen ties with Britain or the United States. Rather, India wanted to demonstrate its nonaligned and nonbelligerent policy. In line with this position, India agreed to chair the Neutral Nations Repatriation Commission, which later oversaw the repatriation of POWs from both sides and provided a brigade-size custodial force to supervise the POW exchange after the armistice was signed. It also accepted a significant number of POWs from both sides who did not want to be repatriated to their countries. India's record in Korea helped to validate its nonalignment policy and its position as a leader of the Nonaligned Movement (NAM) during the height of the cold war. [32]

Ultimately, the most important outcome of the Korean War for all these nations was the legitimization of the United Nations. The failure of the League of Nations to confront Japan after it invaded Manchuria in 1931 had loomed large for many UN members. The successful coalition that fought in Korea erased doubts that the UN might be an equally empty promise; it had become a credible and effective international organization for peace and cooperation. For most countries that sent military forces to Korea, it was the first time in their history to participate in a war in a foreign land not for conquest, occupation, or defense of colonial territory. MacArthur's spectacular victory at Inch'ŏn, however, would test the promise of that noble endeavor when UN forces were ordered to cross the 38th parallel into North Korea.

CHAPTER SIX

Crossing the 38th Parallel

By the end of September 1950 the mandate of the original UN Security Council resolution had been fulfilled: the aggressors had been repelled and the original boundary restored. However, unfulfilled was the second and more ambiguous mandate of the June 27 resolution, which called for restoration of "international peace and security in the area." Many assumed that this required establishing conditions ensuring that another attack could not be mounted after UN forces withdrew—in other words, for the UN to eliminate North Korea and reunify Korea. Yakov Malik, the Soviet permanent representative to the UN, challenged this interpretation and the meaning of restoring "international peace and security in the area." Malik argued that peace and security could be restored only if Korea was reunified, and this required the withdrawal of all foreign troops to allow the Koreans to work out their own reunification. To avoid a Soviet veto in the Security Council, the United States turned to the General Assembly to introduce a resolution providing political guidance for military operations in Korea. The resolution called for the establishment of "conditions of stability" throughout Korea with a unified government followed by "a prompt withdrawal of troops." The Soviets opposed the resolution, and so did India and Yugoslavia, who argued that it exceeded the original limited objective of repelling the invasion. The resolution passed on October 7.[1]

The resolution stipulated that UN forces "should not remain in any part of Korea longer than necessary once the goal of achieving stability and a unified democratic Korea had been attained." It did not explicitly call for UN forces to cross the 38th parallel, and this ambiguity reflected the delicate nature of the political situation surrounding the "artificial dividing line." Most members of the UN, including the United States, sought to evade the issue by playing down the significance of the 38th parallel, "to allow the UN commander to be guided by tactical considerations when he reached the parallel."[2] In any case, General MacArthur had already received authority to conduct military operations north of the 38th parallel even before the UN resolution was passed.

On September 27, MacArthur received the crucial directive from the Joint Chiefs of Staff authorizing his advance into North Korea. It stated, "Your military objective is the destruction of the North Korean Armed Forces. In attaining this objective you are authorized to conduct military operations . . . north of the 38th Parallel in Korea, provided that at the time of such operation there has been no entry into North Korea by major Soviet or Chinese Communist Forces, no announcement of intended entry, nor a threat to counter our operations militarily in North Korea." The directive explicitly stated that "under no circumstances, however, will your forces cross the Manchurian or USSR borders of Korea," and included a prohibition: "As a matter of policy, no non-Korean ground forces will be used in the northeast provinces bordering the Soviet Union or in the area along the Manchurian border."[3] But the directive was complicated by the new secretary of defense, George Marshall. Marshall wrote to MacArthur, "We want you to feel unhampered tactically and strategically to proceed north of the parallel. [However] announcement [of this] . . . may precipitate embarrassment in the U.N. where evident desire is not to be confronted with necessity of a vote on passage of 38th Parallel, rather to find you have found it militarily necessary to do so." Marshall wanted MacArthur to recognize the political sensitivity of crossing the "artificial line" and to cross the line only under absolute military necessity while keeping it low key. MacArthur's reply, however, gave cause for concern. "Parallel 38 is not a factor in the military employment of our forces . . . in exploiting the defeat of the enemy forces, our own troops may cross the parallel at any time," he wrote back. "Unless and until the enemy capitulated, I regard all of Korea open for our military operations."[4]

While the UN and the Truman administration were deliberating over the issue of the 38th parallel, the ROK Third Division simply crossed it on the clear autumn day of October 1, a week before the UN resolution was passed. Colonel Kim Chŏng-sun, the commander of the lead regiment, later recalled, "It was overwhelming. I thought that that damned

American soldiers gaze at portraits of Stalin and Kim Il Sung. Such portraits were commonly found in villages and towns liberated by UN forces, November 7, 1950. (U.S. NATIONAL ARCHIVES AND RECORDS ADMINISTRATION)

line, which had separated our people and the country for so long, was about to crumble, and we would be reunified. We were all so excited that we practically ran across the 38th Parallel."[5] There had been strong indications that ROK troops would cross the line regardless of UN authorization, as President Syngman Rhee had repeatedly stated that he had no intention of halting his forces at "the artificial border" and they would stop only at the Yalu River on the Chinese line. "We have to advance as far as the Manchurian border until not a single enemy soldier is left in our country," announced Rhee at a mass rally on September 19.[6]

This climactic moment was followed by a remarkable phase of pursuit. By October 10, ROK forces had captured Wŏnsan, the major port city on the east coast. On October 17, they occupied the northern cities of Hamhŭng and Hŭngnam and thereby secured North Korea's main industrial hub on the east coast. Meanwhile, in the west, UN forces advanced rapidly against little opposition, and ROK units entered the city of Ch'osan on the Yalu River on October 26. In a little over a month since the Inch'ŏn landing, the tide of war had completely turned.

Lessons of History

In 1592, the Japanese military ruler Toyotomi Hideyoshi launched an invasion of the Korean peninsula. Intent on building a great East Asian empire, Hideyoshi set his sights on Ming China. Control of the Korean peninsula was necessary to secure the invasion route into China. The Japanese invasion force landed just off Pusan and then advanced up the Pusan-Taegu-Seoul corridor. After taking Seoul, the soldiers marched to Kaesŏng, meeting little opposition.[7] Once in Kaesŏng, however, the Japanese did not advance farther north as a unified force. Instead, Hideyoshi divided his army. Konishi Yukinaga commanded the western force, which continued northward through flat open terrain to P'yŏngyang and beyond to the Yalu River. Katō Kiyomasa led the eastern force, which advanced to the northeast through a mountainous and wild region toward the Tumen River on the Manchurian border. Petty rivalries put the two commanders at odds, and the result was that the two armies operated without coordination. Hideyoshi's decision to divide his army was a fatal one. With Katō side-tracked in the wilderness of northeastern Korea, the strength of Konishi's thrust toward P'yŏngyang and beyond, strategically the more important axis, was effectively cut in half. Eventually, the Japanese faced a dilemma. They needed more men to secure the peninsula, but the Korean navy's successful interdiction of shipping prevented reinforcements. Faced with the approaching winter, Konishi hunkered down in P'yŏngyang while his army was whittled away by hunger, disease, and the cold. Katō's army, meanwhile, was scattered across northeastern Korea. It was at this moment, when the Japanese forces were at their weakest, that Ming China attacked, turning the tide of the war.[8]

Substitute the UN for Japan, MacArthur for Hideyoshi, Walker for Konishi, and Almond for Katō, and you have exactly what happened in Korea in late 1950. MacArthur divided his command like Hideyoshi, sending the Eighth Army up the western half of North Korea, while the weaker ROK forces advanced along the eastern coast, and the X

Corps embarked to conduct an amphibious landing at Wŏnsan on the east coast. The forces would link up at the "waist" of the Korean peninsula, a line stretching from P'yŏngyang to Wŏnsan, and then advance north, still under separate commands.[9] General Omar Bradley, chairman of the JCS, later wrote, "Too many North Koreans had slipped through the trap [of the encirclement between the X Corps forces advancing east and south after the Inch'ŏn landing and the Eighth Army advancing northward], perhaps a third of the 90,000 North Korean troops in South Korea . . . The military textbook solution to the existing problem was 'hot pursuit.' That is, to drive forward at utmost speed with all the UN forces at hand before the North Koreans could dig in defensively."[10] Instead, MacArthur stopped the pursuit, pulled the X Corps from the lines, loaded it aboard ships, and sent it on a long voyage to the other side of the peninsula to conduct a landing of dubious value. Walker's Eighth Army, tired from months of fighting and strung out from attacking and moving from Pusan, was left to continue the pursuit. As it turned out, ROK forces occupied Wŏnsan a week before the X Corps's amphibious "assault." Another week of delay was caused by mines in the harbor. When the X Corps finally landed, on October 25, they discovered to their dismay that even Bob Hope's USO show had beaten them to Wŏnsan, much to MacArthur's embarrassment and chagrin.

Pilgrimage to Wake

At this moment Truman decided to meet MacArthur, for the first time. MacArthur was upset by the president's "summoning." Ambassador John Muccio later recalled, "The general appeared irked, disgusted, and at the same time somewhat uneasy" during the plane ride there. "In the course of his exposition, he used such terms as 'summoned for political reasons' and 'not aware that I am still fighting a war.'"[11] The two met on October 15 at Wake Island in the middle of the Pacific, the site of a heroic American stand against the Japanese in the opening days of World War II. Truman's main concern was the possibility that China would enter the war. MacArthur assured Truman that Chinese intervention was unlikely, and even if they did decide to fight, UN forces would be able to handle it and "the victory was won in Korea."[12] During the meeting, neither Truman nor his advisors questioned MacArthur's declarations. At one point, Assistant Secretary of State Dean Rusk, alarmed by the superficiality of the questions posed by the president and the speed in which he was firing them off, passed a note to him suggesting he slow down. Truman scribbled a reply back, "Hell no! I want to get out of here before we get into trouble!"[13] MacArthur's answer to the most important issue facing Truman, and indeed the future postwar world order, was not challenged.

So why did Truman travel so far to meet MacArthur? Truman's own explanation was that he had sought a better rapport with MacArthur and wanted a chance to explain to him in person the goals of U.S. foreign policy. "Events since June had shown me that MacArthur had lost some of his contacts with the country and its people in the many years he had been abroad," Truman later wrote. "I had made efforts through Harriman and others to let him see the world-wide picture as we saw it in Washington, but I felt that we had little success. I thought he might adjust more easily if he heard it from me directly."[14] If this had been Truman's intention, it had clearly failed. The meeting had created more friction than friendship. MacArthur turned Truman down for lunch, saying that he needed to get back to Tokyo as quickly as possible. "Whether intended or not," Bradley later wrote, "it was insulting to decline lunch with the President, and I think Truman was miffed, although he gave no sign."[15] Truman and MacArthur said good-bye before lunchtime that same morning. The president had been on Wake Island for just five hours. They never saw each other again.[16]

After returning from the meeting, MacArthur removed all restraints on the advance of UN forces. It was a violation in spirit of the September 27 directive from the Joint Chiefs. In response, the JCS meekly queried MacArthur, who replied that "the instructions contained in [my message to my subordinate commanders to advance north] were a matter of military necessity." As for the provision to use only ROK forces, "not only are the ROK forces not of sufficient strength to initially accomplish the security of North Korea, but the reactions of their commanders are at times so emotional that it was deemed essential that initial use be made of more seasoned and stabilized commanders." MacArthur saw "no conflict with the directive . . . dated 27 September, which merely enunciated the provision as a matter of policy." He continued that "the necessary latitude for modification was contained also in [the message] dated 29

September from the Secretary of Defense [Marshall] that he should 'feel unhampered . . . to proceed north of the 38th Parallel.'" He concluded haughtily that "this entire subject was covered in my conference at Wake Island."[17]

The die was cast. "As in the case of the Inch'ŏn plan, it was really too late for the JCS to do anything about the order," Bradley recalled.[18] While all seemed aware that something was terribly amiss, there was no consensus over what should be done about it. "We were all deeply apprehensive," recalled Dean Acheson. "We were frank with one another, but not quite frank enough." Had Marshall and the JCS proposed a halt at the P'yŏngyang-Wŏnsan line, the "waist" of the peninsula, Acheson continued, "disaster would probably have been averted."[19] But such a stance would have meant a fight with MacArthur, and everyone, it seemed, was more afraid of MacArthur than they were of a potential conflict with the Chinese. As UN forces advanced deeper into North Korea, Chinese troops were massing along the Manchurian border, just as they had done nearly 360 years earlier when the Ming army had lain in wait for the approaching Japanese.

"If War Is Inevitable, Let It Be Waged Now"

Ten days after the Inch'ŏn landing, Gen. Nie Rongzhen, the acting chief of staff of the PLA General Staff and military governor of Beijing, dined with K. M. Panikkar, India's ambassador to China. The conversation quickly turned to Korea. "General Nie told me in a quiet and unexcited manner that the Chinese did not intend to sit back with folded hands and let the Americans come to the border," recollected Panikkar. "This was the first indication that I had that the Chinese proposed to intervene in the war." Panikkar impressed on Nie, "a pleasant-spoken man, friendly and ready to discuss matters with an air of frankness," how destructive a war with the United States would be, how "the Americans would be able to destroy systematically all the industries of Manchuria and put China back by half a century." But Nie "only laughed." "We have calculated all that," he told the ambassador. "They may even drop atom bombs on us. What then?" Not long after this conversation, Premier Zhou Enlai spoke on the first anniversary of the founding of the PRC, on October

1, and warned that the Chinese people "will not tolerate foreign aggression and will not stand aside should the imperialists wantonly invade the territory of their neighbor." Just after midnight on October 3, Panikkar was abruptly awakened. Zhou had sent a message for him to come to his residence at once. Zhou explained that China had reached a decision regarding Korea. "If the Americans cross the 38th Parallel," Panikkar recalled, "China would be forced to intervene in Korea. Otherwise, he was most anxious for a peaceful settlement."[20]

Panikkar's cable to New Delhi was passed through London to Washington, where it was retransmitted to MacArthur. MacArthur considered the warning a bluff: the Chinese had not intervened when the tide of war was in their favor, so why would they enter when the tide was against them? Truman was skeptical, but his skepticism was less an issue of strategy than of credibility. The problem with the Indian ambassador's warning, according to Truman, was that "Mr. Panikkar had in the past played the game of the Chinese Communists fairly regularly, so that his statement could not be taken as that of an impartial observer. It might very well be no more than a replay of Communist propaganda." Furthermore, a key vote on the UN resolution was due the following day, and "it appeared quite likely that Zhou En-lai's 'message' was a bald attempt to blackmail the United Nations by threats of intervention in Korea."[21]

As Panikkar's message was being considered in Washington, Kim Il Sung, facing imminent defeat, was close to panic. He and Pak Hŏn-yŏng had been completely wrong about the South Korean people's reaction. A senior North Korean communist cadre, Lim Ŭn, remarked, "We all steadfastly believed the boasting of Pak Hŏn-yŏng that once we first occupied Seoul, the 200,000 South Korean Worker's Party (SKWP) members, who were in hiding throughout South Korea, would rise up and revolt, toppling the South Korean regime." Kim had no contingency plan for failure. When the anticipated revolt did not happen, Kim threw all his troops into the attack to try to end the war as quickly as possible. "He was engrossed only in marching forward," according to Lim.[22]

Kim faced total defeat since his forces were cut off by the landing at Inch'ŏn. He begged Stalin for help, pleading to him on October 1, "We are determined to overcome all the difficulties facing us so that Korea will not be a colony of the U.S. imperialists . . . This notwithstanding, if the enemy does not give us time to implement the measures which we plan, and, making use of our extremely grave situation, steps up its offensive operations into North Korea, then we will not be able to stop the enemy troops solely with our own forces. Therefore, dear Iosif Vissarionovich, we cannot help asking you to provide us with special assistance."[23] Stalin wrote to Mao and Zhou that he had warned the North Koreans to expect an amphibious landing at Inch'ŏn and "had admonished the North Koreans to withdraw at least four divisions from the South immediately." But the North Koreans had failed to heed his warning and now "our Korean friends have no troops capable of resistance in the vicinity of Seoul." Stalin concluded, "I think that if in the current situation you consider it possible to send troops to assist the Koreans, then you should move at least five-six divisions toward the 38th Parallel at once," adding that "the Chinese Divisions could be considered as volunteers, with Chinese in command at the head, of course."[24]

Mao's reply was unexpected.[25] Going back on his initial promise to aid the North Koreans, Mao wrote that his forces were not strong enough to take on the Americans: "We originally planned to move several volunteer divisions to North Korea to render assistance to the Korean comrades when the enemy advanced north of the 38th Parallel. However, having thought this over thoroughly, we now consider that such actions may entail extremely serious consequences." Mao explained that a clash with the United States would ruin his plans for peaceful reconstruction. He believed it would be better "to show patience . . . and actively prepare our forces" for a moment when the situation was more advantageous. Mao added, "Of course, not to send out troops to render assistance is very bad for the Korean comrades," but while the Koreans will "temporarily suffer defeat, [this] will change the form of the struggle to partisan war."[26]

Stalin asked Mao to reconsider. He thought the Americans would not start a major war and would agree on a settlement that favored the communists. Under such a scenario, China might also resolve the Taiwan issue. A passive "wait and see policy" as Mao suggested would be counterproductive: "China would fail to get back even Taiwan, which at present the United States clings to as its springboard, not for Jiang Jieshi [Chiang Kai-shek] who has no chance to succeed, but for themselves or for a militaristic Japan." Stalin then made his most compelling argument for Chinese intervention: "If a war is inevitable, then let it be waged now, and not in a few years when Japanese militarism will be restored as an ally of the USA and when the USA and Japan will have a ready-made bridgehead on the continent in a form of the entire Korea run by Syng-man Rhee."[27]

Mao spent many sleepless nights that early October trying to decide. He convened an urgent meeting of the Politburo Standing Commit-tee to tell its members he had decided in favor of intervention, but he met strong opposition. Lin Biao, Mao's old comrade in arms during the civil war, was firmly against it. China, he said, was not ready for such a monumental undertaking. What the country needed was to recuper-ate after decades of warfare. Nor had the Chinese revolution been fully completed, as there were still more than a million "bandits" roaming the countryside and party control was not completely secure. And, he argued, the PLA's outdated arsenal was no match against the Ameri-cans and would lead to a great slaughter. For Lin Biao, the wiser and safer decision was to accelerate the buildup of the Chinese air, naval, and artillery forces and to assist North Korea in fighting a guerilla war without direct intervention.[28] Mao's response echoed Stalin's, that if the Chinese did not fight the Americans now, they might be forced to do so at a later date. Since America's plan to occupy North Korea was part of a grand strategy to dominate the whole of East Asia, the task of defending China would be that much harder if the Americans gained a foothold on the Korean peninsula. Given the deployment of the U.S. Seventh Fleet to the Taiwan Straits and MacArthur's belligerence toward China, Mao was convinced that such a confrontation was only a matter of time.

He also appealed on moral grounds: "It would be shameful for us to stand by seeing our neighbors in perilous danger without offering any help."[29] China would lose face before its North Korean comrades, many of whom had fought in the PLA. Moreover, if China did not help North Korea, the Soviet Union might do nothing if China were in peril, and "internationalism would be empty talk."[30] General Peng Dehuai, a bril-liant military leader and another of Mao's close civil-war comrades, summed up the main thrust of Mao's argument: "The tiger wanted to eat human beings; when it would do so would depend on its appetite."[31] Mao prevailed. Stalin wrote, "Mao expressed solidarity with the main ideas of my letter and stated that he would send nine, not six, divisions to Korea."[32] Mao had also based his decision to enter the war on the under-standing that China would receive air support from the Soviet Union.

On October 8, the day after the UN passed the resolution empowering UN forces to unify Korea, Mao cabled Kim Il Sung: "In view of the current situation, we have decided to send volunteers to Korea to help you fight against the aggressors."[33] China, it was decided, would enter the Korean War on October 19.

Just as the Korea question seemed to be finally settled, it took another startling turn. While Mao was deciding about China's intervention in Korea, Stalin was considering what, if any, involvement there should be for the Soviet Union. The Politburo agreed with him that a direct confrontation with the United States must be avoided, even if it meant abandoning North Korea.[34] The best option was a proxy in the form of China. When Zhou went to Moscow to finalize the details of Sino-Soviet military cooperation in Korea, he was shocked to learn from Stalin that the Soviet Union would seek to avoid all direct involvement in the conflict. It would not provide Soviet air forces to protect Chinese troops in Korea as promised earlier.[35] Zhou told Stalin that the decision would put the Chinese in a quandary as to whether to proceed without the promised air cover. He cabled Mao and the CCP leadership and asked them to reconsider the decision to intervene in light of the Soviet "betrayal."[36]

Mao suspended his intervention order, and the Politburo convened to deliberate. As before, two main points were raised: China was unprepared for a conflict with the Americans, and the intervention could not be done without Soviet help.[37] "Comrade Mao Zedong remained undecided even when our forces reached the Yalu River," recalled Nie Rongzhen. "He racked his brain and indeed thought about this many times before he made up his mind."[38] An exhausted Mao, who had not slept for days, finally decided to proceed with the intervention. His reasoning had not changed: the UN forces would not stop at the Yalu and war with the United States was inevitable. The others conceded, and Mao informed Zhou in Moscow that "the consensus is that it is still advantageous to send our troops to Korea."[39]

Chinese troops began crossing the Yalu on October 19, embarking on a risky venture that would determine the fate of China and its revolution. Stalin's "betrayal" clarified for Mao the limits of the Sino-Soviet alliance and reinforced the slide toward an eventual Sino-Soviet split. The betrayal also strengthened Mao's determination to be self-reliant in national security.[40] Domestically, Mao's "far-sighted" and "brilliant" decision to confront the American "imperialists" in Korea would lead to his complete monopoly on power and the radicalization of China's political and social affairs. Once China's external enemies were defeated abroad, Mao would turn to China's "internal" enemies at home. Less than two weeks after crossing the Yalu, the Chinese People's Volunteer (CPV) army launched an attack that would determine the course of China's future for decades to come.

First Strike

In less than two weeks, 200,000 Chinese soldiers crossed the Yalu River into North Korea undetected by the United Nations Command (UNC).[41] On October 25, the Chinese initiated their first major attack. The main effort, in what Peng Dehuai called "First Phase Offensive," was against the Eighth Army. Peng targeted the ROK Army sectors for they were weaker and more vulnerable. ROK II Corps, part of the Eighth Army that occupied the eastern half of the army's area of operations, received the first blow. Within a few days, II Corps was largely destroyed, and all of the Eighth Army was put in peril. By early November, however, General Walker was able to rally his troops and establish a defense line along the Ch'ŏngch'ŏn River north of P'yŏngyang. The Chinese also engaged the X Corps on Korea's east coast, but only on a limited scale. General Almond ordered the X Corps, scattered widely in the rugged mountains of the northeast region, to mop up remnants of the NKPA and reach the Yalu as quickly as possible. A short but bloody engagement with the Chinese took place in early November near Changjin (Japanese: Chosin) Reservoir, but the Chinese forces mysteriously disappeared as quickly as they had appeared, instilling a false sense of security.[42]

Despite the scale of the Chinese actions and their consequences in the Eighth Army sector, MacArthur's chief of intelligence, Maj. Gen. Charles A. Willoughby, refused to believe it was a major intervention. He estimated that about 16,500, but no more than 34,000, Chinese were in Korea.[43] Willoughby's lack of alarm was not only supported by MacArthur, but also shared by Walker and Almond. According to Walker, the "Chinese" presence had merely indicated the introduction of North Korean reinforcements taken from China.[44] This assessment

First group of captured Chinese held near Hamhŭng, October 30, 1950. (U.S. NATIONAL ARCHIVES AND RECORDS ADMINISTRATION)

was repeated in MacArthur's report to the UN, which concluded that "there is no such evidence that Chinese Communist units, as such, have entered Korea."[45] Considering the damage inflicted on the Eighth Army, these assessments were excessively optimistic, if not delusional. MacArthur provided the JCS with his personal "appreciation" of the situation and presented four possible scenarios to explain the sudden appearance of the Chinese: first, a full-scale invasion; second, covert military assistance; third, permitting volunteers to help North Korea; or fourth, provisional intervention predicated on encountering only ROK units in the border provinces. He thought "the last three contingencies, or a combination thereof, seem to be the most likely condition at the present moment." MacArthur "warned against hasty action and specifically discounted the possibility that the intervention of the Chinese Communists was a 'new war' "[46]

Privately, however, MacArthur seemed to have had some doubts. On November 6, he told his air commander, Lt. Gen. George Stratemeyer, to plan for a bombing campaign of North Korea. "General MacArthur wanted an all-out air effort against communications and facilities with every weapon to stop and destroy the enemy in North Korea," wrote Stratemeyer in his wartime diary.[47] A key target was the bridge over the Yalu River at Sinŭiju, to stop or delay the flow of Chinese troops. Recognizing the political sensitivity of the mission, Stratemeyer contacted Air Force Chief of Staff Gen. Hoyt S. Vandenberg, who in turn got in touch with Deputy Secretary of Defense Robert A. Lovett and Secretary of State Acheson. They agreed that such a mission was unwise due to the risk of accidentally bombing Chinese territory, which could provide a casus belli for China and perhaps even the Soviet Union. Moreover, such action violated the U.S. commitment not to take any action that would affect Manchuria without prior consultation with the British. Truman, who was in Independence to cast his vote on Election Day, November 7, received an urgent call from Acheson. He told Acheson that he would "approve this bombing mission only if there was an immediate and serious threat to the security of our troops." Truman also asked Acheson to find out "why MacArthur suddenly found this action necessary" since his earlier cable had given no hint that such drastic actions were being contemplated. The JCS canceled the mission less than two hours before the bombers were scheduled to take off. MacArthur was requested to "forward his estimate of the situation and his reasons for ordering the bombing of the Yalu River bridges."[48] It was the first time the JCS had countermanded an order from MacArthur.

MacArthur's reply was unexpected. In a sudden and inexplicable change from his report just a few days earlier, MacArthur wrote that "men and material in large force are pouring across all bridges over the Yalu from Manchuria. This movement not only jeopardizes but threatens the ultimate destruction of the forces under my command." "The only way to stop this reinforcement of the enemy is the destruction of these bridges and the subjection of all installations in the north area supporting the enemy advance to the maximum of our air destruction," he declared. "I cannot overemphasize the disastrous effect, both physical and psychological, that will result from the restrictions which you are imposing. I trust that the matter [will] be immediately brought to the attention of the President as I believe your instructions may well result in a calamity of major proportion for which I cannot accept the responsibility without his personal and direct understanding of the situation."

The JCS was jolted by the cable's accusatory and hysterical tone. Bradley recollected that "we had little choice but to authorize the mission." Truman agreed.[49]

Two days later, MacArthur again changed his tune. "The introduction of Chinese Communist forces in strength into the Korean campaign had completely changed the overall situation," he wrote on November 9, but he had every confidence that with his superior airpower he could interdict Chinese reinforcements from Manchuria and destroy those already in Korea. MacArthur was now so confident that he planned to resume the offensive on November 15 to occupy all of North Korea.[50] On November 7, the JCS had received the startling report that Chinese and North Korean troops had completely broken contact with UN forces and "disappeared." These developments appeared to support MacArthur's initial assessment that the Chinese had intervened only in moderate numbers and, having been successfully "rebuffed," lost their nerve for further fighting.[51] The JCS decided that MacArthur would "continue military operations in accordance with current directive," but the directive should be "kept under review." "We read, we sat, we deliberated," recalled Bradley, "and, unfortunately, we reached drastically wrong conclusions and decisions."[52] The JCS was lulled by MacArthur's optimistic predictions of a quick victory, the sudden disappearance of the Chinese, and "wildly erroneous" estimates of the scale and intent of the Chinese intervention.

If the Americans appeared blissfully ignorant of China's real intentions, the North Koreans were downright unhappy. China's entrance had significantly marginalized Kim Il Sung and North Korea, which now played only a supporting role. Keenly aware of his diminishing influence, Kim had hoped to reorganize his forces with the help of the Soviet Union even as China was preparing to launch its second offensive at the end of November. Ambassador Shtykov wrote to Stalin with a plea from Kim Il Sung: "Our North Korean friends will withdraw to Manchuria with the personnel for organizing nine divisions . . . Once again, our comrades in North Korea are requesting that ninety Soviet advisors and education and training specialists remain with them to help them organize the nine divisions and establish education and training institutions. The North Koreans state that if they do not have this help, it will take them a year before they can prepare for combat on their own."[53] Kim believed that with Soviet help he could reconstitute his tattered NKPA in time to make a difference in the outcome of the war. His fear of Chinese domination of the Korean peninsula was understandable. Given the long history of Chinese interventions in Korea, Kim was loath to give China control over military operations.

Disgusted by the turn of events, Stalin refused to help, deciding instead to distance himself from Korean military matters all together. When Shtykov told Kim that his request had been denied, "he was silent for a moment," then turned to Pak Hŏn-yŏng and said, "How can matters have come to this?"[54] To add to Kim's misery, Stalin replaced his team in North Korea. First to go was Gen. Nicolai Vasiliev, chief of the Soviet Military Advisory Group, who was replaced by Gen. V. N. Razuvaev. Ambassador Shtykov was recalled at the end of December, demoted to lieutenant general in early 1951, and then forced to retire, a precipitous fall reflecting Stalin's displeasure at his performance. Shtykov's departure had far-reaching consequences for future North Korean–Soviet relations. He had been Stalin's personal envoy to North Korea since 1945 and had enjoyed direct access to the Soviet dictator. Razuvaev, who also replaced Shtykov as ambassador while remaining chief of the Soviet Military Advisory Group, did not enjoy the same close relationship with Stalin. With Shtykov gone, Kim Il Sung no longer had a valuable ally with a direct line to Stalin. To Kim's dismay, Mao became the new conduit to the Soviet leader. North Korea had been treated as an independent agent by Stalin since 1945, but with the Chinese entering the war, North Korea became relegated to a satellite of China. A perceptible split between Kim and Stalin was beginning to emerge, sowing the seeds for future conflict and driving Kim to seek a more independent path from the Soviet Union.

CHAPTER SEVEN

An Entirely New War

The war in Korea was on everyone's mind as Americans sat down to enjoy their Thanksgiving feast. Truman reminded the American people "in church, chapel and synagogue, in their homes and in the busy walks of life, every day and everywhere, to pray for peace."[1] Cardinal Francis Spellman of New York made a plea "for clothing, blankets and money for the destitute in Korea."[2] Americans, Commonwealth soldiers, and other UN allies in Korea, some of whom had never eaten turkey, were treated to a lavish Thanksgiving dinner. The logistics of transporting tens of thousands of frozen turkeys, then thawing, cooking, and serving them on the front lines was an immense undertaking. And just so the American people would know what would be served, newspapers published the menu. Many soldiers later said it was the best meal they had ever eaten.

ARMY'S HOLIDAY MENU[3]

Roast turkey
Cranberry sauce
Sage dressing and giblet gravy
Snowflake potatoes and candied sweet potatoes
Fresh green peas and whole kernel corn

Waldorf salad
Lettuce, Thousand Island dressing
Ice cream and pumpkin pie
Mincemeat pie. Fruitcake.

Parker house rolls
Bread
Butter

Mixed shelled nuts
Fresh fruit

Coffee
Fruit punch

   The lavishness of the meal enhanced the optimism of the moment. Everyone thought the war was just about over and the "boys" would be home for Christmas. MacArthur stated that "regardless of Chinese intervention, the war will be finished by the end of the year."[4] The meal was as much a victory feast as it was a tribute to the sacrifices of the UN forces. Few knew that for many of these soldiers it would be their last good meal for months and for some, their last Thanksgiving meal.

   The Eighth Army and X Corps resumed their advance the next morning. With MacArthur's reassurance that the war would be over by the end of the year, there was little else on anyone's mind but the upcoming Christmas holidays that promised a trip home. Everything had been

Inspecting Thanksgiving dinner preparations at a mess hall, November 23, 1950. (U.S. NATIONAL ARCHIVES AND RECORDS ADMINISTRATION)

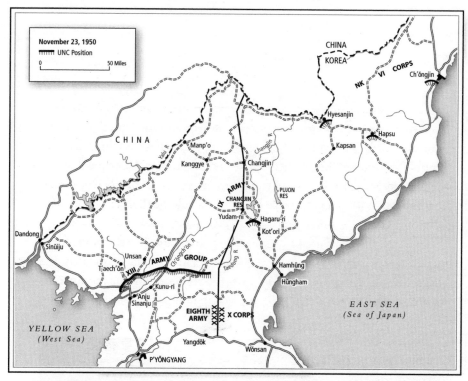

The battlefront, November 23, 1950. (MAP ADAPTED FROM BILLY C. MOSSMAN, *EBB AND FLOW*, U.S. GOVERNMENT PRINTING OFFICE, 1990)

going remarkably well. MacArthur was certain that Stratemeyer's bombing campaign had destroyed all significant targets between the UN front lines and the Yalu River. Stratemeyer recalled MacArthur's visit to Korea on November 24: "[He] was thrilled with the entire operation as was everyone in his party."[5] When IX Corps commander Maj. Gen. John Coulter told him that his troops were eager to reach the Yalu, Earnest Hoberecht of the United Press overheard MacArthur's reply: "You can tell them when they get up to the Yalu, Jack, they can all come home. I want to make good my statement that they will get a Christmas dinner at home."[6] No one suspected, least of all MacArthur, that at that very moment almost 400,000 Chinese troops were about to strike.

The CPV attacked ROK II Corps, again, on the evening of November 25. The gravity of the situation was not immediately apparent to General Walker. By nightfall, he received disquieting news from ROK II Corps that its divisions had encountered strong CPV "resistance." Walker made

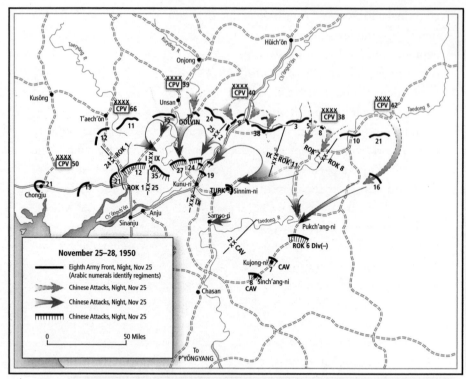

Battle of the Ch'ŏngch'ŏn, second Chinese offensive against the Eighth Army in North Korea, November 25–28, 1950. (MAP ADAPTED FROM MOSSMAN, *EBB AND FLOW*)

no effort to reinforce the South Koreans.[7] He soon realized that ROK II Corps was under a strong CPV attack that threatened to expose the army's eastern flank. As ROK forces collapsed, the CPV began encircling the Eighth Army. In the face of the irresistible Chinese onslaught, Walker ordered the Eighth Army to break contact and retreat to more defensible terrains north of Seoul. Within ten days the Eighth Army had retreated 120 miles.

In the eastern sector, a large CPV force was planning to launch an attack against the X Corps, whose units were widely dispersed over hundreds of square miles of freezing barren mountains. The core of X Corps, the First Marine Division with elements of the Seventh Infantry Division, was scattered around the Changjin Reservoir. On November 27, the X Corps resumed its advance northward, unaware of the disaster that was unfolding against the Eighth Army. The winter of 1950–51 turned out to be one of the harshest on record. Temperatures were so cold that soldiers were routinely afflicted with frostbite, weapons did not function, vehicles and generators did not start, artillery shells failed to explode, and food always arrived frozen. Treating the wounded was particularly challenging. "Everything we had was frozen," recalled Chester Lessenden, a medic. "Plasma froze and the bottles broke. We couldn't use the plasma because it wouldn't go into the solution and the tubes would clog up with particles. We couldn't change dressings because we had to work with our gloves on to keep our hands from freezing." The journalist Keyes Beech wrote that "it was so cold that men's feet froze to the bottom of their socks and the skin peeled off when the socks were removed."[8] Two weeks earlier, Maj. Gen. O. P. Smith, the First Marine Division commander, had confided his deep concerns about the precariously exposed deployment of X Corps to the commandant of the Marine Corps. General Almond, he angrily vented, was pushing Smith to advance too fast and without taking the necessary precautions. This resulted in the division being strung out along a sixty-mile dirt road dominated by high grounds on both sides under harsh winter conditions, a situation Smith thought resulted from an unsound operational plan. "Time and again I have tried to tell the Corps Commander [Almond] that in a Marine division, he has a powerful instrument, but that it cannot help but lose its full effectiveness when dispersed," Smith fumed.[9]

Disaster struck on the night of November 27, and thus began one of the greatest epic tales of tragedy and triumph in the annals of American military history.[10] The CPV hit the widely dispersed X Corps everywhere simultaneously. Piecemeal destruction of the First Marine Division was prevented by Smith's decision to concentrate the bulk of his division at three key villages around and near the Changjin Reservoir: Yudam-ni, on the northern side; Hagaru-ri, on the southern side about ten miles from Yudam-ni; and Kot'o-ri, a farther ten miles south of Hagaru-ri. It was another fifty miles from Hagaru-ri to Hŭngnam port, which was the X Corps's main port for supply and evacuation, should it be necessary. Smith ordered the marines on the western side of the reservoir to fall in on Yudam-ni, and the task force from the Seventh Infantry Division, commanded by Col. Allan MacLean, on the eastern side to fall back to Hagaru-ri. On the morning of November 28, Almond made an impromptu visit to Hagaru-ri to confer with Smith and then visited the Seventh Division task force. Almond told MacLean to take the offen-

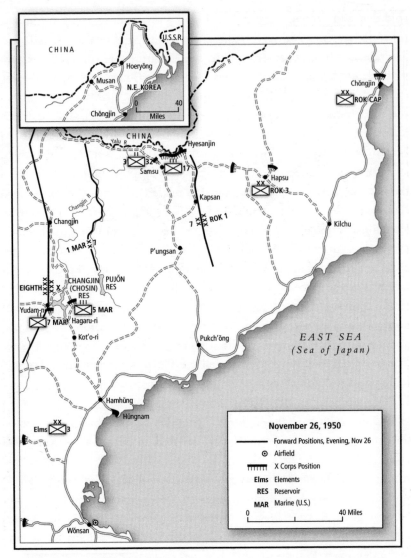

The X Corps zone, North Korea. (MAP ADAPTED FROM MOSSMAN, *EBB AND FLOW*)

sive. "The enemy who is delaying you for the moment is nothing more than remnants of Chinese divisions fleeing north," Almond assured him. "We're still attacking and we're going all the way to the Yalu. Don't let a bunch of Chinese laundrymen stop you."[11] However, with dire reports from the Eighth Army, MacArthur knew something was wrong and sent an alarmist cable to the JCS proclaiming that America now faced an

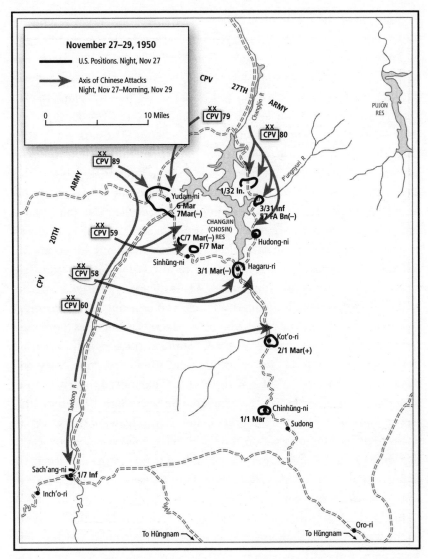

November 27–29, 1950

━━━━ U.S. Positions. Night, Nov 27

━━▶ Axis of Chinese Attacks
Night, Nov 27–Morning, Nov 29

0 ────────────── 10 Miles

Battle of the Changjin Reservoir, North Korea, November 27–29, 1950. (MAP ADAPTED FROM MOSSMAN, *EBB AND FLOW*)

"entirely new war." It had finally dawned on him that the Chinese had come in with both feet. He ordered an immediate withdrawal.

It was almost too late. During the night of November 28–29, the CPV besieged MacLean's strung-out force. He ordered withdrawal at 2:00 a.m. "The snow was coming down in earnest," recalled Maj. Hugh

Robbins, "and the footing had become extremely slippery. Columns of foot soldiers had formed on the road on each side of the vehicles and had moved out in front . . . Many vehicles, which simply could not start because of the cold, had to be left behind, but none of the wounded was without transportation." As the task force made its way south toward Hagaru-ri, MacLean was killed. Lieutenant Colonel Don Faith, a battalion commander under MacLean, took charge. The task force continued its treacherous march toward Hagaru-ri. Faith called for close air support to hold off the Chinese, and marine aircraft responded with napalm. But tragedy struck as some of the napalm hit the task force. "It hit and exploded in the middle of my squad," recalled Pvt. James Ransone. "I don't know how in the world the flames missed me . . . Men all around me burned." Soon thereafter, Faith was killed and his command fell apart. "It was everyone for himself," recalled Staff Sgt. Chester Bair. "The chain of command disappeared." Over the next few days, survivors of the task force came limping, stumbling, and crawling across the great sweep of ice covering the reservoir to Hagaru-ri. The marines there used sleds to help them. A marine recalled, "Some of these men from Faith's outfit were dragging themselves on the ice, others had gone crazy and were walking in circles." "I was disoriented, exhausted, nearly frozen, hungry, and vomiting blood," remembered Sergeant Bair. "The temperature at night was 20 or more degrees below zero. The wind was so strong it was hard to stand or walk on the ice."[12] The marines rescued about a thousand of the original twenty-five hundred troops of the task force. Of these, only four hundred were fit enough to continue to serve. The rest were evacuated to Japan.

As the disastrous drama unfolded on the eastern side of the reservoir, on the western side the marines successfully fell back to Yudam-ni. They were then ordered to withdraw farther south and join the marines at Hagaru-ri. Afterward, the whole force was to withdraw still farther south to Kot'o-ri to rejoin the rest of the First Marine Division and then move to Hŭngnam for evacuation. The marines from Yudam-ni broke through the Chinese forces and arrived at Hagaru-ri on December 4–5, creating a surge of confidence that they were going to survive the ordeal after all. Smith made headlines around the world when he refused to call the withdrawal a retreat. "Retreat hell!" he said. "We are not retreating. We're just advancing in a different direction."[13] The truth of the matter was that there was no front or rear, and therefore nowhere to retreat to. What the marines were doing *was* attacking in another direction.[14] The epic withdrawal of the marines at Changjin Reservoir became a cause for celebration. Headlines announced that calamity had been miraculously averted. "Marines Return Full of Fight after a Nightmare of Death," announced the *New York Times*.[15] "Marine Guts Turn Disaster into Day of Moral Triumph," blazed the *Washington Post*. Jack Beth reported for the paper that "American Marines walked out of 12 days of freezing hell. These thousands of Leathernecks did it on guts. They turned their encirclement into one of the fightingest [*sic*] retreats in military history."[16] *Time* magazine wrote admiringly, "The running fight of the Marines and two battalions of the Army's 7th Infantry Division from Hagaru . . . was a battle unparalleled in U.S. military history . . . It was an epic of great suffering and great valor."[17]

The "triumph" might have been as much due to Chinese miscalculations as the bravery of the Americans. Had the Chinese hit Hagaru-ri on the night of November 27, they could have isolated the marines and soldiers to the north and thus destroyed in piecemeal most of the First Marine Division and the Seventh Division task force. Smith later told the *New York Times*, "They knew all about us all right, where we were and what we had, but I can't understand their tactics. Instead of hitting us with everything at one place, they kept hitting us at different places. Had the Chinese decided to knock out the small Marine garrison at Hagaru-ri, the task of regrouping the forces into a full division would have been made immeasurably more difficult."[18] What Smith did not know is that the CPV had also taken a terrible beating from the cold, had suffered from lack of food, and had been tremendously hampered by UN air attacks. Tens of thousands of soldiers of the CPV Ninth Army Group died from freezing. The Chinese soldiers were supposed to have been issued winter uniforms, but many did not get them. They wrapped themselves in cotton scarves or covered themselves with "carpets."[19] Moreover, incessant UN air attacks limited movement to the nights. "We have no freedom of activities during the daytime," General Peng complained to Mao. "Even though we have several times of the armed strength to surround them on four sides, fighting cannot end in a night."[20]

Two weeks into the Chinese offensive, Mao worried about the adequacy of the CPV logistical network. "Are you entirely sure about supplying our army's food and fodder by drawing on local resources?" an anxious Mao wrote to Peng. "Have the railroad lines from Sinŭiju and from Manp'o to P'yŏngyang been under rush construction? When will the construction be completed? Is it really possible for both railroads to transport all military supplies to the P'yŏngyang area?"[21] The answers were apparent by the end of December, when the offensive began to run out of steam. Marshal Nie Rongzhen, who oversaw CPV logistics, described in his memoirs how he had stockpiled supplies, but that the "preparations had not been sufficient."

> During the Second Campaign, we had originally planned that two armies plus two divisions could handle campaign responsibilities in the western sector of the advance. But because we couldn't transport the required amounts of rations up to the front, we were forced to cancel the two extra divisions ... In the eastern sector, the troops which entered Korea had not made sufficient preparations and faced even greater difficulties. Not only did these troops not have enough to eat, their winter uniforms were too thin and could not protect their bodies from the cold. As a result, there occurred a large number of non-combat casualties. If we hadn't had these logistical problems as well as certain other problems, the soldiers would have wiped out the U.S. First Marine Division at Changjin Reservoir.[22]

By late December, over a hundred thousand men in the X Corps, Americans and South Koreans, and, in a humanitarian triumph of the Changjin epic, more than ninety-eight thousand refugees were evacuated.[23] After great pressure, Almond approved the evacuation of refugees despite concerns over the presence of communist infiltrators. One of the approximately two hundred ships assembled for the evacuation at Hŭngnam was the SS *Meredith Victory*, a merchant ship built during World War II. Commanded by Capt. Leonard LaRue, the vessel was later credited with "the greatest rescue operation by a single ship in the history of mankind." As a cargo ship, the *Meredith Victory* was designed to accommodate fewer than sixty people, but Captain LaRue and his crew somehow managed to load fourteen thousand refugees on board. After a harsh three-day journey, the refugees, who had suffered cold, hunger, and lack of facilities, and grown by five newborns, were landed at Kŏje island on Christmas Day. There was not a single casualty, and the *Meredith Victory* became known as the "Ship of Miracles."[24]

North Korean refugees attempting to board U.S. Navy ships at Hŭngnam, December 1950. (U.S. NATIONAL ARCHIVES AND RECORDS ADMINISTRATION)

"Defeat with Dignity and Good Grace"

China's intervention shocked the American public. "The nation received the fearful news from Korea with a strange-seeming calmness," *Time* wrote. "It was the kind of fearful, half-disbelieving matter-of-factness with which many a man has reacted on learning that he has cancer or tuberculosis." Unlike Pearl Harbor, which had "pealed out like a ball of fire," the numbing facts of the defeat in Korea "seeped into the American consciousness slowly." Days passed before it became apparent that UN forces had met a "crushing defeat." The disaster and its implications became the subject of endless shocked conversations. "Some of them were almost monosyllabic, men meeting on the street sometimes simply stared at each other and then voiced the week's oft-repeated phase, 'It looks bad. Very bad.' "[25]

It did not take long for recriminations to follow. There were "peeved cracks" about MacArthur's "home by Christmas" remarks, as well as criticism of the Truman administration. While most Americans accepted that war with China, perhaps even World War III, was now inevitable, it was MacArthur who had the greatest difficulty coming to terms with the disaster. Almost immediately, he launched a public attack on the administration. In late November he "cast discretion to the wind" and publicly expressed his frustration and resentment. He began with a written statement in the *New York Times* justifying his march north. "Every strategic and tactical movement made by the United Nations Command has been in complete accordance with United Nations resolutions and in compliance with the directives under which I operate," MacArthur insisted. "It is historically inaccurate to attribute any degree of responsibility for the onslaught of the Chinese Communist armies to the strategic course of the campaign itself." The next day, in an interview with *U.S. News & World Report*, MacArthur criticized the limitations the Truman administration had placed on "hot pursuit" and the bombing of Manchurian bases as "an enormous handicap, without precedent in history." MacArthur also wrote to Hugh Baillie, president of United Press International, and came close to questioning the motives of allies, particularly the British, by suggesting that their "selfish" and "short-sighted" vision had been responsible for withholding support for his forces.[26]

Truman was predictably angry. Of this latest incident of MacArthur "shooting off his mouth," Truman later wrote in his memoir that "he should have relieved General MacArthur then and there." The reason he did not "was that I did not wish to have it appear as if he were being relieved because the offensive failed. I have never believed in going back on people when luck is against them and I did not intend to do it now." Nevertheless, MacArthur "had to be told that the kinds of public statements he had been making were out of order."[27] On December 5, the president issued two directives that, though generally applicable to all "officials of the departments and agencies of the executive branch," were really meant for MacArthur. The first required that "all public statements by U.S. government personnel, civilian and military, had to be cleared in advance by the State and Defense Departments." The second ordered all officials and commanders to "exercise extreme caution in public statements . . . and to refrain from direct communication on military or foreign policy with newspapers, magazines, or other publicity media in the United States."[28] While Truman never directly blamed MacArthur for the failure of the UN forces, he did blame the general "for the *manner* in which he tried to excuse his failure."[29] Everyone in his administration had a share in the blame for the disaster, but MacArthur alone was unable to deal with the defeat with "dignity and good grace." He had panicked, lashed out at the administration, and then lapsed into a profound depression.

The JCS met on December 3 to discuss the situation in Korea. MacArthur had written to the JCS that unless ground reinforcements "of the greatest magnitude" were promptly sent, hope for success "cannot be justified and steady attrition leading to final destruction can reasonably be contemplated." For Bradley and the rest of the JCS, "this message and all it conveyed was profoundly dismaying. It seemed to be saying that MacArthur was throwing in the towel without the slightest effort to put up a fight."[30] The JCS seemed paralyzed about what to do and unable to leap beyond MacArthur's doom and gloom.

In the end, it was the State Department that took control of the situation. It was thought that perhaps the United States should try to negotiate a cease-fire with the Russians. George Kennan, who was recalled from leave at the Institute for Advanced Study in Princeton to be an advisor to Secretary of State Acheson, counseled that engaging in negotiations with the Russians at such a time of weakness would do more harm than good, since "they would see no reason to spare us any of the humiliation of military disaster." "The prerequisite to any satisfactory negotiation . . . is the demonstration that we have the capability to stabilize the front somewhere in the peninsula and to engage a large number of Communist forces for a long time."[31] UN forces had to stand firm to exert pressure on the enemy to force a cease-fire. Kennan, aware that Acheson was surrounded by "people who seemingly had no idea how to take defeat with dignity and good grace," composed a note to raise the secretary's spirits and strength to face what would no doubt be a trying period:

> Dear Mr. Secretary:
>   There is one thing I would like to say in continuation of our discussion yesterday evening. In international, as in private, life what counts most is not really what happens to someone, but how he bears what happens to

him. For this reason almost everything depends from here on out on the manner in which we Americans bear what is unquestionably a major failure and disaster to our national fortunes. If we accept it with candor, with dignity, with a resolve to absorb its lessons and to make it good by redoubled and determined effort—starting all over again, if necessary along the pattern of Pearl Harbor—we need lose neither our self-confidence nor our allies nor our power for bargaining, eventually, with the Russians. But if we try to conceal from our own people or from our allies the full measure of our misfortune, or permit ourselves to seek relief in any reactions of bluster or petulance or hysteria, we can easily find this crisis resolving itself into an irreparable deterioration of our world position—and of our confidence in ourselves.[32]

Acheson, moved, read the note to his staff. "We were being infected by a spirit of defeatism emanating from headquarters in Tokyo," Acheson declared. The essential problem facing Washington's political leaders was how to begin "to inspire a spirit of candor and redouble and determine our effort." Acheson thought that the main issue was that "the Korea campaign had been cursed . . . by violent swings of exuberant optimism and the deepest depression and despair . . . what was needed was dogged determination to find a place to hold and fight the Chinese to a standstill." This would be better than to consider withdrawal from Korea.[33] Secretary of Defense George Marshall agreed. Acheson met with Truman and the matter was settled. Kennan recalled, "We lunched with Secretary Acheson. He had just been talking with the President. The President's decision was, as always in great crises, clear, firm and unhesitating. He had no patience, Mr. Acheson told us, with the suggestion that we abandon Korea. We would stay and fight as long as possible."[34]

Truman asked Army Chief of Staff J. Lawton Collins to go to Tokyo and Korea to assess the situation. Collins reported that although the military situation "remained serious, it was no longer critical." The Eighth Army and X Corps were "calm and confident," Collins recalled. "Throughout my visit, [Walker] seemed undismayed. While the situation was tight, I saw no signs of panic and left the next morning for the X Corps reassured that the Eighth Army could take care of itself." Further, he anticipated "no serious trouble" in evacuating the X Corps from Hŭngnam. Collins concluded that the best solution was to evacuate the X Corps to Pusan, and the Eighth Army "should be gradually withdrawn toward Pusan," where the united force could hold a defensive line "indefinitely." Collins's assessment was greeted "like a ray of sunshine."[35]

While the crisis was unfolding, British Prime Minister Clement Attlee arrived in Washington on the afternoon of December 4 for urgent talks with Truman. The British were alarmed by Truman's mention of the possible use of atomic weapons in Korea. If the prospect of a third world war in Korea was not enough to deal with, now came the unwelcome visit from "a Job's comforter" in the form of Attlee. Acheson found Attlee "persistently depressing," whose thoughts resembled "a long withdrawing, melancholy sigh." As soon as Attlee was reassured by Truman "that alarm over the safety of our troops would not drive us to some ill-considered use of atomic weapons," the real purpose of his trip emerged. What Attlee wanted was to end the war in Korea so that the United States could "resume active participation in security for Europe." He also wished that Britain be allowed "some participation . . . in any future decision to use nuclear weapons." To end the fighting in Korea, Attlee urged Truman and Acheson to consider giving China UN membership and cutting Taiwan loose. Attlee argued that the UN position in Korea was so precarious that a price must be paid to extricate UN forces out of that conflict. Giving China a seat at the UN and withdrawing from both Korea and Taiwan would not be too high a price to pay, Attlee argued, for "there was nothing more important than retaining the good opinion of Asia." Moreover, China was not a Soviet satellite, and if handled properly, "it might become an important counterpoise to Russia in Asia and the Far East."[36]

Acheson vehemently disagreed. "To cut, run and abandon the whole enterprise was not acceptable conduct. There was a great difference between being forced out and getting out," he responded.[37] Furthermore, the security of the United States was more important than anyone's "good opinion," and the preservation of America's defenses in the western Pacific and the Asian people's confidence in America also provided "a path to securing their good opinion." The only way to fight communism, he said, "was to eliminate it." In the end, the British agreed to stay the course in Korea and accepted the United States' refusal to rush to negotiations with China. In return, Truman implicitly agreed to keep the fighting limited and to abandon any plans for Korean unification. Truman also privately assured Attlee that he was not considering

Alarmed by rumors that the United States might use atomic weapons in Korea, British Prime Minister Clement Attlee (center) makes an urgent visit to Washington for talks with President Truman, December 4, 1950. (TRUMAN LIBRARY)

use of the atomic bomb and agreed to a broad pledge of close U.S-UK consultations on all global crises.[38] Truman had, in effect, promised not to risk World War III without consulting the British. Talks with Attlee ended with a clear consensus, but they stirred up consternation in other circles. Republican Senator William Knowland from California, a severe critic of Truman and a strong supporter of Chiang Kai-shek who was known as the "Senator from Formosa," said he saw "the making of a Far Eastern Munich."[39] Korean President Rhee stated he was "tremendously disappointed" that the Truman-Attlee conference ended "without a call for complete mobilization of the democratic world to fight against communism," and thought that "it would have been better if the United Nations had not helped us at all if we are to be abandoned now."[40] But the furor eventually died down. UN forces would stay in Korea until a truce was negotiated. Once the front stabilized, a political basis for negotiations to end the conflict could begin. What no one could have guessed was just how long the negotiations would take.

Meanwhile, as the X Corps was evacuating, the Eighth Army continued to fall back. General Walker ordered the evacuation of P'yŏngyang on December 3 and a "scorched earth policy" to destroy everything that might be of use to the enemy. Corporal Leonard Korgie, one of the last Americans to abandon the city, recalled the scene:

> We went through P'yŏngyang at night and the whole city looked like it was burning. In one place, the engineers burned a rations dump about the size of a football field. God, it was a shame to see it in a land of hunger all the food going up in smoke. There was U.S. military equipment everywhere. I don't know how much was destroyed . . . I believe we set on fire most of the villages we passed through. We weren't going to give the Chinese too many places to shelter in during the rest of the winter.[41]

While the measure was to deny the enemy shelter and supply, the more immediate impact of the wholesale destruction of towns and villages was on the civilian population. North Korea was already a barren land with few resources, and the measure created an enormous refugee crisis in the middle of a harsh winter. When word spread that UN forces would not defend P'yŏngyang, three hundred thousand people living there fled. Barges and small boats ferried people across the Taedong River, but the UN forces destroyed many of these to prevent the refugees from crossing and clogging the roads the military needed for its own withdrawal. The civilians were also barred from crossing over bridges, so they sought alternative crossing routes. Some made their way over the ruins of the great steel bridge destroyed by American bombers earlier that summer. Others tried to wade across through freezing water. It was clear that nothing but inhumane suppression by force could deter the refugees.[42] Captain Norman Allen recalled his torment about the refugees' plight:

> The refugees, awful moments there, deep memories. So pitiful, so desperate; they also hampered our movement by day and threatened our positions at night. Oh my God, what to do about them? The problem drove me wild. Once there were hundreds of them in one valley, maybe four hundred yards wide. We were tied in on the road with a company of another battalion. They came right up to our lines and we had to fire tracers over their heads to stop them from overrunning us . . . Shortly thereafter, both companies began receiving incoming mortar fire. The

other company reported one of its platoons was overrun by the enemy
who had mixed with refugees . . . When our road block reported that the
refugees were pressing in on them and the pressure was growing, the men
requested permission to fire. I asked who the refugees were, men, women,
what? They replied: "Mostly women and children, but there are men
dressed in white right behind them, men who look to us to be of military
age." I paused. The pause went on. The roadblock came on again, urgent,

Fearing communist reprisals, refugees crawl perilously over the shattered girders
of a bridge across the Taedong River in their desperate attempt to flee P'yŏngyang
once it became clear that UN troops would not defend the city, December 4, 1950. (U.S.
NATIONAL ARCHIVES AND RECORDS ADMINISTRATION)

desperate, requesting permission to fire . . . I instructed the roadblock to fire full tracer along the final protective line, then to fall back to the high ground . . . I could not order firing on those thousands upon thousands of pitiful refugees.[43]

Some soldiers did open fire, and aircraft sometimes strafed the refugees. Hong Kyŏng-sŏn and his grandmother were among the refugees. Hong, a nineteen-year-old student and a Christian, had been part of the crowd that welcomed the UN liberation of the city in October. The news that the Americans had decided to abandon the city just three months later was an unbelievable shock. An even greater shock occurred when they were strafed by an aircraft with South Korean markings.[44] At Chinnamp'o, a port thirty miles southwest of P'yŏngyang, UN forces were trying to evacuate the thousands of refugees who had streamed in. But of the fifty thousand refugees, only twenty thousand could be evacuated. On December 3, U.S. Navy Transport Squadron 1, which was en route to Japan from Inch'ŏn, was ordered to divert to Chinnamp'o to aid in the evacuation. The following morning, five ships reached the port and began loading the refugees. Lt. Jim Lampe, an officer in the squadron, had been born in Korea in a missionary family and had gone to school in P'yŏngyang as a child. His return to North Korea was a homecoming. Lampe was ordered to help evacuate those who had worked for the UN forces, as they would be the most likely targets for retribution. But, as Lampe wrote to his wife, this proved to be exceedingly difficult:

I had the police form a line of all those who worked for us, who hadn't gotten out on the junks, to form a line, four abreast, with their families, along the pier area, to be taken to an LST by our small boats. It was morning now and that line was the most pathetic thing I had ever seen. We got into trouble when a group of several thousand who hadn't worked for us, but wanted to get out, crashed through the guards and into the line . . . Each of these people had a pitiable small bundle with them [and] each thought that their life depended on their getting on one of those boats. Noon passed . . . all but twelve of our guards were pulled out and we backed down to the loading ramp. The crowd had absolutely no semblance of order now; it was just a solid mass of people, several thousand, all pushing . . . Women, the old ones, young girls and half naked babies in the cold, all crying, pleading . . . The last boat out. I felt like a monstrous murderer. A devil with a gun and pistol condemning these people to death . . . I was ashamed and embarrassed to be leaving and these helpless ones had to stay. I had to actually kick my foot free from a woman's hand as I stepped in the boat. I felt like killing these people for making me feel like a murderer, and I wanted to blow my brains out for being the murderer. Big, warm, well-armed American! . . . I vowed never to go near Chinnamp'o again. How could I look at these people in the eyes![45]

The refugees themselves also had to leave the more unfortunate behind. H. K. Shin remembered one tragic scene in which a small child, perhaps a year or two old, was crying at the side of the road next to her dead mother while a stream of refugees passed by. He recalled, "People passed by the child and dead mother shaking their heads as a desperate gesture of hopelessness and pity, but no one stopped to help the crying child. War had forced them to close their hearts and care for their own burdens."[46]

December Massacres

The reaction in Seoul to the fall of P'yŏngyang was deadly. In the seemingly endless cycle of violence and retribution that characterized the war since it began, the South Korean government rounded up suspected "enemies" for summary execution. By the second week of December, mass executions of alleged communists by South Korean security forces took place on a large scale. An earlier period of retributive atrocities had taken place after the success of Inch'ŏn. The *London Times* on October 25, in a story titled "Seoul after Victory," reported that "290 men and women and seven babies were detained . . . They squatted on the floors, unable to move or to lie down . . . (and) were beaten to insensibility" with rifle butts and bamboo sticks, and tortured "with the insertion of splinters under the finger nails." The story concluded that while "the scene described has been, as is still being, repeated throughout Korea," UN forces "feel either too helpless to intervene or believe attention drawn to the reprisals would be excellent material for Communist propaganda."[47] The daily executions after the fall of P'yŏngyang became too egregious to ignore. According to Western news sources, eight hundred persons described as convicted communists, collaborators, saboteurs, and murderers were executed during the second week of December alone. "A wave of disgust and anger erupted through American and British troops who either have witnessed or heard the firing squads in action in the Seoul area," reported the *Washington Post*.[48] A worried Muccio reported to Acheson that "17 persons had been killed, according to a British report, in a 'brutal,' and 'criminal fashion' raising concerns about the international backlash against the Rhee regime."[49]

The British were also alarmed. A December 19 cable from the Foreign Office reported that "a massacre of 34 prisoners including women and children by South Korean police was witnessed by men of the Northumberland Fusiliers," causing deep consternation among the British troops.[50] Private Duncan, one of the witnesses, wrote to his member of Parliament.

> Sir:
> I wish to report an incident that occurred at a place three miles north of Seoul in Korea on December 12, 1950. Approximately forty emaciated and very subdued Koreans were taken about a mile from where I was stationed and shot while their hands were tied and also beaten by rifles . . . I myself saw the graves and also one of the bodies as they were very cruelly buried. The executioners were South Korean military police and the whole incident has caused a great stir and ill-feeling among the men of my unit . . . I write to tell you this as we are led to believe that we are fighting against such actions and I sincerely believe that our troops are wondering which side in Korea is right or wrong. Also my own feelings are so strong that I felt I must make known to someone of power this cruel incident.[51]

Other eyewitness accounts, like those of Fusilier William Hilder, were widely quoted by news organizations: "A truckload of prisoners was shot less than 150 feet from the camp where the British were eating their breakfast. The guards led them in groups of 10 into the trenches and then shot them in the back of the head. The women were screaming and the men wailing . . . Some of the guards went around with a machine gun firing bursts into those who didn't die immediately. I walked away when the kiddies were shot. I didn't like to see it."[52]

President Rhee and other South Korean officials denied the killing of children, calling the reports "irresponsible and vicious slander," but the on-site response was immediate and intense.[53] Brigadier Tom Brodie, commander of the British Twenty-Ninth Infantry Brigade, was so incensed that he ordered his men to shoot any South Korean policemen attempting to carry out executions on the so-called Execution Hill, which was near his troops' encampment. Brodie vehemently said that "he would not have people executed on my doorstep. My officers will stop executions in my area or within view of my troops."[54] Father Patrick O'Connor of the *Catholic News Agency* of Washington, D.C., and Father George Carroll, two priests in Seoul, sought to stop the executions by appealing directly to Rhee. Constantine Stavropoulos, principle secretary of the United Nations Commission for the Unification and Rehabilitation of Korea (UNCURK), demanded that Cho Pyŏng-ok, South Korea's Home Minister, conduct an immediate investigation. UNCURK was created in October 1950 in anticipation of a reunified Korea as a result of UN operations. It was charged with overseeing the unification, reconstruction, and security of Korea as directed by the UN General Assembly. It arrived in Korea only days before the massive Chinese intervention at the end of November.[55] The American mission requested that UNCURK itself conduct an investigation, which it did. The investigation largely confirmed the reports.[56] Eventually, Rhee, who had initially ordered the executions speeded up, backed down and, conceding to international pressure, suspended the mass executions.[57] Muccio reported, "Owing to public furor caused by second day's executions and foreign correspondents cabling stories of mass executions without trial ... government has suspended executions for time being."[58]

Nevertheless, the credibility and legitimacy of the South Korean government, and by extension, the UN intervention, had already been badly damaged. Journalist René Cutforth reported on an Australian officer's reaction to the inhumane and dire conditions of the Sŏdaemun (West Gate) Prison, which summed up the general mood: "This, my God, is a bloody fine set-up to waste good Australian lives over. I'm going to raise hell!"[59] It was a sentiment shared by many who seriously questioned their country's involvement in what was obviously a vicious civil war. The American public was angered and disgusted. Allen Neave of Highsville, Maryland, wrote to the *Washington Post* reflecting the prevalent feeling:

> It has been said that the United Nations Troops are now fighting in Korea to preserve, among other things, decency. Are South Korean massacres more decent than others? Those same South Koreans are imploring the

United Nations to hold off the bloody hordes from the North. Why? So that they can match, drop for drop, the quantity of mother's and children's blood spilled? Surely some of my buddies are not fighting for this!![60]

International outrage forced Rhee to order an "inquiry into the conduct of the executions." He also gave assurances to the British that "no further executions in the British area" would be carried out and that "the lieutenant in charge of the firing party is being held for court martial proceedings." Rhee announced that he had accepted UNCURK's recommendation for the mitigation of death sentences. He also announced amnesty for political prisoners.[61] Finally, he assured the UN that "in the future, all executions will be carried out individually and not in groups of persons."[62]

James Plimsoll, the Australian representative to UNCURK, was pleased by "the very satisfactory response" regarding the amnesty and future ROK policy on prisoners. Nevertheless, he could not help but wonder "to what extent this policy was actually being carried out." In a February 1951 report to Canberra, Plimsoll admitted that "the Commission has no way of being sure that mass executions are not occurring; and the United States Embassy is equally in the dark." Being in the dark, however, was exactly where the UN wanted to be. There were, after all, practical matters to consider in the conduct of the war. Although everyone deplored the mistreatment of prisoners, the UN was limited in what it could do to prevent it in the future because UN forces had come to depend on South Korean security forces to "check the infiltration of North Korean spies and agents, and in fighting guerillas in some regions." Undermining their morale at such a critical time would make an already precarious situation worse. Internal reform of the security forces was needed, Plimsoll believed, not international censure. Plimsoll explained, "Some members of the Commission wanted a scathing report on the executions to be submitted to the General Assembly of the United Nations, but the majority opposed this." He concluded, "No advantage can be gained by an act which might weaken the international support now being accorded the United Nations' effort in Korea." Plimsoll's assessment was largely shared by MacArthur's staff. Public condemnation of the executions could undermine the UN war effort and threaten the safety of UN troops. Humanitarian concerns had to give

Thousands of terror-stricken Koreans pack all the roads leading southward, fleeing the advance of the communists. In this picture, two families combine their efforts in a cart pulled by the fathers and pushed by the mothers and older children, January 5, 1951. (U.S. NATIONAL ARCHIVES AND RECORDS ADMINISTRATION)

way to the military realities on the ground, which required cooperation with the South Koreans, who were responsible for the major share of the fighting. After the initial public outcry died down, MacArthur imposed censorship on all media dispatches of UN operations.[63]

"Revolt of the Primitives"

Confusion over the morality of the war, uncertainty over the reasons why American soldiers were fighting and dying, and fear of World War III with China's intervention led to increasing alarm and skepticism in the American public that translated into an angry backlash against the Truman administration and against Acheson in particular. Truman's approval rating plummeted to an all-time low, and his critics attacked him with increasing ferocity. In mid-December congressional Republicans overwhelmingly voted for the removal of Acheson from his office. Republican Senator Joseph McCarthy of Wisconsin asserted that "the Korea deathtrap" could be laid squarely at "the doors of the Kremlin and those who sabotaged rearming, including Acheson and the President."[64] Even those who were disgusted by McCarthy's anticommunist scare tactics questioned Acheson's continued effectiveness. Walter Lippmann, whose liberal "Today and Tomorrow" column in the *New York Herald Tribune* was enormously influential, called on Acheson to resign, charging that the administration's actions had led to "disaster abroad and disunity at home."[65] Nor did the revered George Marshall escape the barrage of attacks. Senator William Jenner, Republican from Indiana, accused him of playing the "role of a front man for traitors." As a result, he said, the government had been turned into a "military dictatorship, run by communist-appeasing, communist-protecting, betrayer

Harry Truman (center) with Dean Acheson (left) and George Marshall, in good spirits despite an extremely difficult December. In one of his press conferences at the height of the attacks, Acheson was asked how the attacks were affecting him. He replied with a story of a poor fellow who had been wounded during the Indian wars in the West. "He was in bad shape," said Acheson, "scalped, wounded with an arrow sticking into his back, and left for dead. As the surgeon prepared to extract the arrow, he asked the man, 'Does it hurt very much?' to which the wounded man replied, 'Only when I laugh.'"[66] (TRUMAN LIBRARY)

of America, Secretary of State Dean Acheson."[67] Acheson weathered the "shameful and nihilistic orgy" of abuse with humor. "Humor and contempt for the contemptible," wrote Acheson, "proved as always, a shield and buckler against the 'fiery darts of the wicked.'"[68]

While humor enabled Acheson to endure what John Miller of the *London Times* had called "a revolt of the primitives against intelligence," his only real protection against the vicious attacks was the complete confidence of Truman.[69] On December 20, four days after he declared a state of emergency because the United States was in "great danger created by the Soviet Union," Truman delivered an impassioned defense of his secretary of state. "How our position in the world would be improved by the retirement of Dean Acheson from public life is beyond me," Truman declared. "If communism were to prevail in the world, as it shall not prevail, Dean Acheson would be one of the first, if not the first, to be shot by the enemies of liberty and Christianity."[70] Truman knew that Acheson's departure would not be the end of "the revolt of the primitives," but would merely become an invitation for further attacks against his administration, because the source of the anger was not Acheson or even the administration's foreign policy, but the hysterical fear of communist subversion heightened by China's unexpected entrance into an unpopular war.

The campaign against Acheson and Truman exacted a heavy toll. It tore at the fabric of American democracy and threatened to widen the war to mainland China. "[The McCarthyites] were operating on the principle that there can be no such thing as an honest difference of opinion, that whoever disagreed with them must be a traitor," wrote Elmer Davis of *Harper's Magazine*.[71] Thus, while fighting a war against communism abroad, Americans were engaged in a "cold civil war" at home. The result, according to Acheson, was that "the government's foreign and civil services, universities, and China-studies programs took a decade to recover from this sadistic pogrom."[72] The situation could have been far worse, however, had it not been for the new commander of the Eighth Army, Lt. Gen. Matthew B. Ridgway, who was able to quickly reverse the situation in Korea. Ridgway's leadership prevented a defeat in Korea that would surely have allowed anticommunist forces to paralyze America's democratic institutions and give credence to MacArthur's belligerent calls to expand the war to China and hence World War III. Ridgway could offer only the possibility of a limited victory, but the stabilization of the battlefield eventually led to the demise of the "revolt of the primitives."

Wrong Way Ridgway

Ridgway's appearance in Korea was the result of a traffic accident in which General Walker was killed on his way to Ŭijong-bu north of Seoul.[73] Before his death, serious questions had been raised about Walker's leadership. His decision to abandon P'yŏngyang without a fight was seen as "one of the most important tactical mistakes of the war."[74] With uncontested airpower and strong armor forces, the Eighth Army had a good chance of turning back the Chinese. Some correspondents thought the withdrawal was an "uncontrolled bug-out," nothing like the measured, successful retreat and evacuation of the X Corps. Walker became despondent; his professional reputation was now stained by the disastrous retreat while his leadership during the desperate days of the Pusan perimeter seemed all but forgotten.[75]

Walker's apprehension about his future was warranted. Only a few weeks earlier General Collins had had a discussion with MacArthur about replacing Walker with Ridgway. When news of the tragic traffic accident reached MacArthur and the Joint Chiefs, Collins was able to obtain almost immediate clearance for Ridgway's assignment. Three days after Walker's death, Ridgway was on his way to Tokyo. MacArthur and Ridgway had been acquaintances for years, but they were never particularly close. Ridgway had served under MacArthur at West Point in 1919 when the latter was the superintendent of the academy. Unlike his flamboyant boss, Ridgway was known for his no-nonsense, hands-on approach. His trademark habit of strapping a hand grenade to the webbing harness on his chest was interpreted as showmanship, but Ridgway explained that "[The grenades] were purely utilitarian ... Many a time in Europe and Korea, men in tight spots blasted their way out with hand grenades."[76] If anything, the grenades symbolized his view of himself as both a leader and a common soldier.

MacArthur greeted Ridgway warmly at their first meeting, in Tokyo on the day after Christmas 1950. Ridgway asked whether he might go on the offensive should an opportunity present itself. MacArthur simply replied, "The Eighth Army is yours, Matt. Do what you like with it."[77] MacArthur's latitude for Ridgway, something that he had not extended to either Walker or Almond, was not so much a reflection of special confidence as it was an indication of his troubled state of mind. MacArthur had become deeply despondent over the consequences of China's intervention. He had staked his reputation on the Chinese not entering, or if they did, that he could easily deal with them. "The Red Chinese had made a fool of the infallible 'military genius'," Bradley later observed.[78] Now the situation appeared close to hopeless. What else could MacArthur do but give Ridgway his full support? MacArthur was unsure that UN forces could hold the Chinese back, and he continued to urge expanding the war to mainland China. The Joint Chiefs, however, strongly disagreed. Their directive of December 29 stated that "Korea is not the place to fight a major war" and that MacArthur must continue to defend while "inflicting such damage to hostile forces in Korea as is possible." Instead of following the directive, MacArthur challenged the Joint Chiefs, arguing that the Chinese war-making capacity should be crippled by air and by a naval blockade. He also urged acceptance of Chiang Kai-shek's offer of Nationalist troops. MacArthur presented the JCS with two alternatives: expand the war to China or withdraw to Japan. In arguing for the former, he risked World War III, a risk the Truman administration was not willing to take.

While the JCS and MacArthur sparred, Ridgway was planning to go on the offensive. He thought the notion of withdrawing to Japan absurd. UN forces had complete control of the skies and the seas and had vastly superior weapons and logistical support at its disposal. There was no reason why the Eighth Army could not get back on its feet. "My morale was at the highest of all times," he later confided. "I didn't have the slightest doubt that we would take the offensive. It was just a question of giving us a little time."[79] Upon his arrival in Korea on December 27, Ridgway called on Ambassador Muccio and President Rhee. Muccio was deeply worried about the rumors that UN forces were preparing to evacuate to Japan. Ridgway reassured both men that he and the UN were staying. He told them that "he planned to go on the offensive again as soon as we could marshal our forces."[80] Ridgway then toured the front, in an open jeep in freezing weather, and within forty-eight hours had met every corps commander and all but one division commander. He did not like what he saw, later writing, "Every command post I visited gave me the same sense of lost confidence and lack of spirit. The leaders, from sergeants on up, seemed unresponsive, reluctant to answer my questions."[81] The challenge was infusing this demoralized force with renewed spirit. His first step was to take formal control of the X Corps and unify the UNC under him. As William McCaffrey, Almond's deputy chief of staff, recalled, "Ridgway told him [Almond] how things were going to go in Eighth Army from now on. Almond got the point, and that's how it went. There wasn't any question as to who was the army commander. Ridgway straightened out that ridiculous situation the first day."[82]

Ridgway made other major changes as well. Major General Coulter of the IX Corps, who had performed badly when the Chinese attacked, was promoted out of his position. Ridgway retained his friend Maj. Gen. Frank Milburn, commander of I Corps, who also did not do well, but kept him under close rein. Officers who did not perform up to standard or who were deemed wanting were sent packing. Once, Ridgway attended a briefing given by Colonel Jeter, the I Corps operations officer, who was briefing his plans for "defending in successive positions." Ridgway interrupted him and asked what his attack plans were. Puzzled, Jeter said there were no attack plans since the Eighth Army was in retreat. Ridgway relieved him on the spot.[83] News of Jeter's fate spread quickly among the ranks. While some within I Corps staff resented Ridgway's treatment of Jeter, it did have the kind of shock effect that the new commander had hoped for. Ridgway made it clear that he intended to move the Eighth Army forward, not backward. Thus was born a grudging nickname that, while originally intended as an insult, soon became a badge of honor: "Wrong Way Ridgway."

While dramatic changes were made at the top, Ridgway also sought to inspire transformation from the bottom. He visited the troops, listened to their complaints, and shared in their hardships. "It is the little things that count," he recalled of his efforts to uplift his soldiers. One soldier had complained to him that there was never enough stationery to write letters home, so the general "had somebody send up a supply of stationery." Ridgway became known for passing out extra gloves. "Any soldier up there, you know, the temperature is down below or around zero and his hands are cold and raw, and sure would like to have a pair of gloves;

a thousand and one little things like that." Ridgway was strict about officers setting good examples. "I never would permit a senior officer to ride
about in an automobile, I mean of any kind. He had to be in an open jeep
with the top down for safety. That does the GI good too, to see his commander up there, as cold as hell."[84] Blessed with a phenomenal memory,
Ridgway astonished his soldiers by remembering their names. According to one account, Ridgway could recall "without hesitation four or five
thousand names, half of whom were enlisted men."[85] It was his acute
attention to detail, and to the names and needs of his men, that made
Ridgway's leadership so effective, especially with soldiers who believed
that they had been ill treated, betrayed, and forgotten. His aide-de-camp,
Walter F. Winton Jr., recalled,

> If you had been a betting man, you would not have bet an awful lot on the
> United Nations Forces at this juncture in history. A short summation of
> the situation: weather terrible, Chinese ferocious, and morale stinko. The
> Eighth Army Commander, General Ridgway, took hold of that thing like
> a magician taking hold of a bunch of handkerchiefs out of a hat, like so
> ... He didn't turn the Army around by being mean to people, by shooting
> people, by relieving people, by chopping people's heads off, or by strik-
> ing fear; quite the opposite. He breathed humanity into that operation
> ... He effected gradual and orderly relief. He kept alive the old spirit of
> the offensive, the spirit of the bayonet; call it what you will. Talk about
> practicing what he preaches. During the time he was in command of the
> Eighth Army, in Korea, I can hardly think of half a dozen days when he
> was not under hostile fire. This impressed me. The troops knew it and
> once they got the idea that somebody was looking out for them, and not
> for himself, the miracle happened.[86]

As Ridgway was breathing new life into his army, the Chinese continued their long trek south. Rest halts were few. It was deathly cold. Almost
everything had to be carried on men's backs or by pack animals since
they had little motorized transport. Each man carried rations for about
a week consisting of soya flour, tea, rice, some sugar, and perhaps a small
can of meat.[87] The lengthening supply line meant that replenishing even
these meager supplies became more difficult. Hunger became endemic.
UN air raids disrupted the CPV's march and supply lines, and the bombing of villages left few places for the soldiers to seek shelter. One Chinese soldier recalled, "One night it was reported to me that an entire
squad's post collapsed in the snowstorm. When I rushed to the squad's

Generals Matthew B. Ridgway (left) and Edward Almond, February 15, 1951. (U.S. NATIONAL ARCHIVES AND RECORDS ADMINISTRATION)

post in the trench, I was dumbfounded by the scene, all nine unconscious and covered by layers of snow. As those bodies under the thin uniforms began to turn cold, I also realized that their food bags were empty. None of them survived to participate in the offensive attack."[88]

By January 1951, the Chinese army was badly in need of a rest. General Peng, cautious by nature, understood the limitations of his army and what he could achieve against a technologically superior force with near-total command of the skies. He was wary of underestimating the enemy. After the CPV's victorious second campaign in late November, Peng requested permission to regroup his forces and rest over the winter. Logistical problems, hunger, cold, and exhaustion had made it almost impossible to continue. "Let [the troops] stop in areas dozens of *li*s north of the parallel, allowing the enemy to control the parallel, so that we will be able to destroy the enemy's main force the next year," Peng wrote to Mao. But Mao was impatient and wanted the third offensive to begin as soon as possible, by no later than early January, much earlier than what Peng thought wise or feasible. "Our army must cross the 38th parallel," Mao wrote back to Peng in mid-December. "It will be

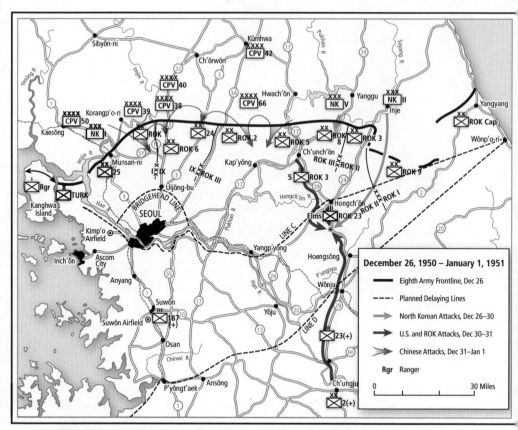

Chinese third offensive, December 1950–January 1951. (MAP ADAPTED FROM MOSSMAN, *EBB AND FLOW*)

most unfavorable in political terms if [our forces] don't reach the 38th parallel and stop north of it." Peng warned Mao of "a rise of unrealistic optimism for a quicker victory from various parts" and suggested a more prudent advance.[89] Peng continued to press his case to Mao, laying bare the full horror of what his army was facing in Korea: "Most of the overcoats for the various corps have not yet arrived, nor have the cotton-padded shoes for the 42nd Army." By this time, the shoes had been mostly worn out, and some of the soldiers had been forced to go barefoot. "Cooking oil, grain, and vegetables are either unavailable or late in arrival, and the physical strength of our army unit has weakened, with increasing numbers of sick soldiers." The situation was going from bad to worse, Peng warned Mao. "If there is no remedy for quick relief, the war will be protracted."[90] But Mao could not be persuaded to postpone the offensive. Peng arrived at a compromise solution: he would scale down the size of the military operation and stop whenever it became necessary.[91] The CPV would adopt a "gradual plan of advancement."[92] He knew that UN morale was low, but there were still a quarter of a million UN forces, and Peng worried that as they began to dig in, it would become increasingly costly to assault them and their wall of firepower. Mao finally agreed.

The CPV attack pushed UN forces across the Han River.[93] Seoul fell on January 4, the third time the city had changed hands since the war began. While the withdrawal was not without some disorder, Ridgway had by this time, less than ten days after his arrival, revived the Eighth Army's spirits. Ridgway established a strong defensive line about sixty miles south of Seoul. After Seoul's fall, Peng pushed south for a few more days and then ordered a general halt. His exhausted soldiers were simply in no condition to continue, and he feared that UN forces were trying

Refugees again flee from Seoul, January 5, 1951. (U.S. NATIONAL ARCHIVES AND RECORDS ADMINISTRATION)

to lure his army into vainly assaulting fortified positions. Peng's forces, including the NKPA, withdrew several miles to rest and regroup. When the third offensive ended, China had "only 280,000 poorly supplied and very exhausted troops facing 230,000 well-equipped UN and ROK forces."[94] Peng's forces had been reduced in half, and the winter months were making it difficult to get supplies through to those who remained.[95] Zhang Da, who was only seventeen years old when he enlisted to fight in Korea, remembered that many soldiers continued to "suffer severe frost-bite to their hands and their feet." The food was also very poor, with the main staple being "baked dry flour with rice, sorghum or ship biscuits."[96] A captured diary written by a Chinese officer vividly recounted what Peng and his army were up against during that harsh winter:

> Difficulties: 1) We have been troubled on the march due to icy roads. 2) we are exhausted from incessant night marches. To make matters worse, when we should be resting during the day, we cannot take a nap due to enemy air activity. 3) Due to a shortage of shoes, almost all the soldiers are suffering from frostbite. 4) We have had to cross rivers with our uniforms on during combat, which has resulted in severe frostbite. 5) The fighting is becoming critical due to lack of ammo and food. 6) Lack of lubrication causes untimely rifle jams when firing. 7) We have had to carry heavy equipment on our backs, we are always heavily burdened when marching. 8) The physical condition of the soldiers has been getting worse as they have to hide in shelters all day long, and fight only at night or during enemy air assaults. 9) When reconnoitering at night disguised in civilian clothing, it is very difficult to carry out the mission because of language difficulties.
>   Morale of the soldiers of our unit: Enemy air strikes frighten the soldiers most of all. The most unbearable labor they have to endure is to carry heavy equipment on their backs when climbing mountain ridges. Their conviction that they will win the war is wavering.[97]

On January 11, Mao instructed Peng to reorganize the CPV and defend Seoul, Inch'ŏn, and the areas north of the 38th parallel, while the NKPA was to be resupplied and continue their attack south. Kim Il Sung was delighted. Kim, Pak Hŏn-yŏng, and Peng met to discuss the new plan. Peng was wary. He thought Kim's focus on expanding territory without destroying the enemy was pointless. Furthermore, sending the North Koreans ahead alone assumed that the communists held the advantage and that UN troops would eventually retreat from the peninsula, something Peng did not believe was likely to happen. He knew that the NKPA was not strong enough to destroy the UN forces on its own, and with the latter's well-defended positions and superior firepower, the NKPA would surely fail. But Pak countered that the UN forces need not be annihilated, only *pursued*. Recent reports from Moscow indicated that the UN forces would soon withdraw from the peninsula. All they needed was a little prodding. Peng retorted that a few more American divisions would have to be destroyed before the UN forces withdrew. Kim responded by suggesting again his idea of sending NKPA forces south now and CPV forces to follow after resting for a month. Peng impatiently "raised his voice" and emphatically declared that "they [Kim and Pak] were wrong and that they were dreaming." "In the past, you said that the US would never send troops," he fumed. "You never thought about what you would do if they *did* send troops. Now you say that the American army will definitely withdraw from Korea, but you are not considering what to do if the American army doesn't withdraw." He scolded the Koreans for "hoping for a quick victory," which was "only going to prolong the war" and "lead . . . to disaster." Peng concluded that "to reorganize and re-supply, the Volunteer Army needs two months, not one day less, maybe even three [months]. Without considerable preparation, not one division can advance south. I resolutely oppose this mistake you are making in misunderstanding the enemy. If you think I am not doing my job well, you can fire me, court martial me, or even kill me." When Stalin was informed of the heated exchange, he sensed a crack in the alliance and sided with Peng. "The leadership of the CVA [Chinese Volunteer Army] is correct. Undoubtedly the truth lies with commander Peng Dehuai."[98]

While the Chinese halted, MacArthur continued his calls to widen the war with China. What disturbed the JCS most, however, was MacArthur's "negative and defeatist tone about the Eighth Army," painting the bleakest possible picture of the situation in Korea. This was all the more puzzling since it was in sharp contrast to the optimistic reports from Ridgway. "It indicated," wrote Bradley, "that MacArthur might well be completely out of touch with the battlefield." MacArthur reported that the UNC was not strong enough to hold Korea and protect Japan. He reported gloomily that his troops were "embittered" and tired and that "their morale will become a serious threat to their battlefield efficiency unless the political basis upon which they are asked to trade life for time is clearly delineated, fully understood, and so impelling that the hazards of battle are cheerfully accepted."[99]

MacArthur's message of potential doom was received grimly in Washington. Truman was deeply disturbed.[100] Rusk later remarked that "when a general complains of the morale of his troops, the time has come to look at his own." Acheson, unconvinced by the general's ominous predictions, was also suspicious and privately concluded that MacArthur was "incurably recalcitrant and basically disloyal to the purposes of the Commander-in-Chief."[101] The JCS told MacArthur to hold out as long as possible and to withdraw to Japan if no other recourse was available, while the administration considers contingency military and nonmilitary courses of action against China. Generals Collins and Vandenberg then flew to Japan and Korea on a fact-finding mission. What they found surprised and heartened them. Ridgway was optimistic and confident. Both men were impressed with how Ridgway had revived the Eighth Army. There was no doubt in their minds that the UN forces could and would stay and fight in Korea. "Morale very satisfactory considering condition," reported Collins to Washington. "On the whole, Eighth Army now in position and prepared to punish severely the enemy."[102] It was their opinion that, short of Soviet intervention, the Eighth Army could continue operations in Korea without endangering the security of either itself or Japan. From then on, there was no further discussion about blockading or bombing China. Ridgway had made that option moot.

But Ridgway's success was also MacArthur's failure, for it undercut his power to direct and influence events in Korea. The JCS distrusted MacArthur and sought information on Korea directly from Ridgway, as MacArthur was seen as untrustworthy. "There was a feeling," wrote Bradley, "that MacArthur had been 'kicked upstairs' to chairman of the board and was, insofar as military operations were concerned, mainly a prima donna figurehead who had to be tolerated."[103] MacArthur had become what he feared most: ignored and irrelevant. He was stung by public criticisms characterizing his actions in Korea as "a momentous blunder," a "gross miscalculation," and a "great tragedy."[104] As the war in Korea stabilized in January 1951, MacArthur had probably already decided that he would challenge the president in order to regain the influence and power he had lost after the Inch'ŏn landing. He would gamble his career and reputation in a public spat with the increasingly unpopular Truman administration to redeem his honor and kick-start a new career in politics. It was a calculated risk and one that only MacArthur, courageous, flamboyant, brilliant, but supremely egotistical, could have taken.

Lost Chances

On January 14, Mao cabled Peng his estimate on the future intentions of the UN forces: they could, under pressure from the CPV and NKPA, retreat from the peninsula after "symbolic" resistance; or they could retreat to Taegu and Pusan, wage a stubborn defense as in 1950, and then retreat. Either way, Mao thought, "they will finally retreat from Korea after we have exhausted their potential."[105] It was now Mao's turn to underestimate the enemy. His drastic miscalculation about American tenacity and its ability to spring back from defeat cost the Chinese the opportunity to gain a greater victory at far less cost than what they would get later, after another two and a half years of war. The success of the third offensive, and especially the recapture of Seoul, had convinced Mao that China now held the upper hand. China's victories, just like MacArthur's success at Inch'ŏn, had made Mao hungry for total victory in Korea. This overconfidence led him to reject the UN Cease-Fire Commission's peace plan, which included many of Beijing's earlier demands. Presented to the UN on January 11, the plan proposed a five-step program: (1) cease-fire; (2) a political meeting for restoring peace; (3) a withdrawal by stages of all foreign forces; (4) arrangement for an immediate administration of all Korea; and (5) an establishment of an "appropriate body" composed of the United States, the United Kingdom, the Soviet Union, and China to settle Far East problems, including the status of Taiwan and China's representation in the UN.

This was a poor deal for Washington, for the "appropriate body" charged with settling affairs in Korea was clearly stacked against the United States. The United Kingdom was likely to support a motion to seat the PRC instead of Taiwan in China's seat at the UN, as it had promoted such a shift since the founding of the PRC. China's admission to the UN would lead to a complete loss of UN support for Taiwan. This would not play well domestically, since the Truman administration was already under fire for having "lost" China, and the "primitives" were getting louder in their calls for Acheson's head. The cease-fire, proposed to take place at the 37th parallel, therefore farther south than the 38th, would also yield considerable new territory to North Korea, including Seoul. South Koreans would undoubtedly oppose it bitterly. Acheson recalled, "The choice whether to support or oppose this plan was a murderous one threatening, on the one side, the loss of the Koreans and the fury of Congress and press and, on the other, the loss of our majority and support in the United Nations." Nevertheless, Acheson decided to gamble by recommending support, calculating that the Chinese would reject it. After painful deliberations, Truman supported the recommendation. Acheson later wrote, "The President—bless him—supported me even this anguishing decision."[106] As Acheson and Truman "held their breath," the Chinese unequivocally rejected the UN cease-fire plan. Acheson's gamble, which he admitted had almost brought the administration to "the verge of destruction domestically," had paid off.[107]

With China's rejection of the cease-fire, Washington could claim the moral high ground, for it was China's decision to continue the war. On January 20, a resolution condemning China as an aggressor was introduced in the UN. Britain and other allies thought the condemnation of China was gratuitous, but Acheson, with an eye toward American public opinion, lobbied unapologetically for the resolution.[108] It was a triumph of poker-player diplomacy and Acheson had played his cards beautifully. China was now thrust into a pariah status as an aggressor, while the Truman administration suffered little domestic political consequences. Getting the British to support the resolution had been a particularly hard sell, but with Acheson's private assurances that the administration would not use the resolution as an excuse to widen the war, the British finally agreed. The UN General Assembly resolution condemning China passed on February 1.

Meanwhile in Korea, Ridgway was taking his own great gamble. He launched a probe in mid-January to find the CPV, which seemed to have disappeared. He was wary of a possible trap and repeating the mistake of November, when MacArthur recklessly urged an advance to the Yalu. There were other concerns as well. The Russians had greatly built up the Chinese air force in recent weeks. By January 1951, some estimates gave the Chinese as many as 650 combat aircraft.[109] The question on every-one's mind was whether this new airpower would be used against UN forces. Ridgway considered two options: dig in and wait for the Chinese to make their next move, or take the initiative and go on the offensive. Unsurprisingly, Ridgway chose to go on the offensive, even though the Eighth Army was not completely recovered. Run right, his plan would have an incalculable psychological benefit. He needed to show his sol-diers, and the badly mauled ROK forces, that the Eighth Army was no longer in retreat. He also desperately needed to know about the enemy: "There were supposed to be 174,000 Chinese in front of us at that time but where they were placed, in what state of mind, and even that they were there at all was something we could not determine. All our vigor-ous patrolling, all our constant air reconnaissance had failed to locate any trace of this enormous force."[110]

Ridgway's probe discovered the Chinese withdrawing. Furthermore, the feared Soviet-backed Chinese air force had failed to materialize. Ridgway's actions made clear to Mao and Kim that Peng's calculation had been correct: the UN forces were not defeated nor would they with-draw from the peninsula without a fight. Thus, by the end of January 1951, the communists' euphoria about the war began to decline sharply. While tensions between America and its allies, and especially with Brit-ain, had eased significantly by early 1951, relations between Stalin and Mao were strained. Mao realized that Stalin was doing his utmost to keep the Soviet Union out of direct participation in the war.[111]

On January 25, Ridgway launched a general offensive that caught Peng by surprise. Peng reported on February 4, "We are obliged to begin the 4th phase of operations. The battle begins under unfavorable conditions. Our period of rest is interrupted and now, when we are not yet ready to fight."[112] The fourth phase of the Chinese offensive might have been forced to be launched prematurely, but at least the UN forces did not know where the attack would come.

By early February, the Eighth Army had reestablished full contact with the CPV, but it did not know if the Chinese were establishing a defensive line or preparing a counteroffensive, and if so, where. Intel-ligence indicated that Chinese forces had shifted from the west to the mountainous central region. Ridgway could not be sure where the Chi-nese might strike along this central region, but the most likely path of

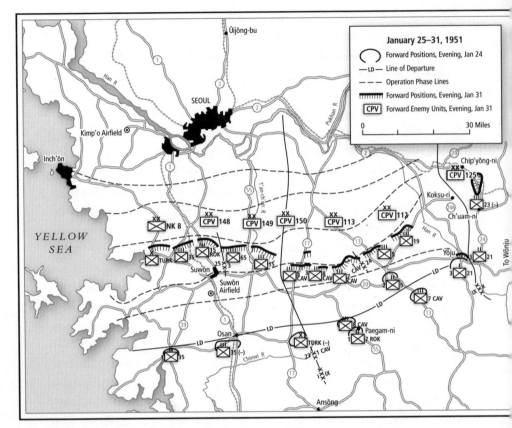

First phase of the UN counteroffensive, January 25–February 11, 1951. (MAP ADAPTED FROM MOSSMAN, *EBB AND FLOW*)

enemy advance would be down the Han River valley toward Wŏnju. Chinese control of Wŏnju would allow them to be within striking distance of Taegu. And once Taegu was taken, the Chinese would be poised to take Pusan. Major action was anticipated for the X Corps, which was deployed in the central region.[113] Ridgway was thus prepared to go to the defensive, taking advantage of the rugged terrain in the central region. His objective was "to advance and then hold along the general line Yangp'yŏng-Hoengsŏng-Kangŭng" from west to east. Ridgway intended to dig in behind this defensive line and slaughter Chinese forces during their attempt to cross it.[114]

On February 5, the X Corps launched its offensive. The attack plan was to move about thirteen miles north of Hoengsŏng to Hongch'ŏn to disrupt North Korean forces that could threaten the X Corps. Almond's plan of advance placed the lightly armed and weaker ROK divisions of his command in the lead, followed by the heavier American units. The result of this disposition proved to be disastrous. On February 11, three CPV divisions hit the ROK Eighth Division in a frontal assault in broad daylight and destroyed it within hours. Its collapse imperiled the U.S. Second Infantry Division at Hoengsŏng. "Our people fought desperately to extricate themselves from certain destruction," recalled one veteran. "On the afternoon of February 13, I received an order to proceed [south] to Wŏnju immediately. Upon my arrival late in the day, I was informed of the catastrophe suffered by our people and the expectation that the Chinese would resume their attack the next morning."[115] A tally of casualties a few days later revealed a disastrous outcome: over 1,500 Americans and Dutch (the Netherlands Battalion was attached to the Second Division) killed, wounded, and missing and nearly 8,000 casualties for the ROK Eighth Division.[116] UN losses at Hoengsŏng were so appalling that MacArthur's headquarters (Far East Command) tried to suppress the story. When the Seventh Marines passed through the same area later in March, they were shocked to discover corpses still littering the battlefield. It was, recalled Bill Merrick, "like an enormous graveyard."[117] More than 250 bodies of American and Dutch soldiers, including the Dutch battalion commander, Marinus den Ouden, were recovered. Many of the bodies had been looted of shoes and clothes, and several had been bound and shot in the back. Sickened by the sight, the marines erected this sign:

MASSACRE VALLEY.
SCENE OF HARRY TRUMAN'S POLICE ACTION.
NICE GOING, HARRY.

Meanwhile, another drama was unfolding at the little town of Chipyŏng-ni, fifteen miles northwest of Wŏnju. Colonel Paul Freeman, commander of the Second Division's 23rd Infantry Regiment, received the news of X Corps's withdrawal to Wŏnju with a sense of foreboding. The disaster at Hoengsŏng opened Freeman's right flank, exposing his forces to encirclement. Freeman's request for permission to withdraw was denied by Ridgway, an unusual skip-echelon command since Ridgway went over the heads of the corps and division commanders. He

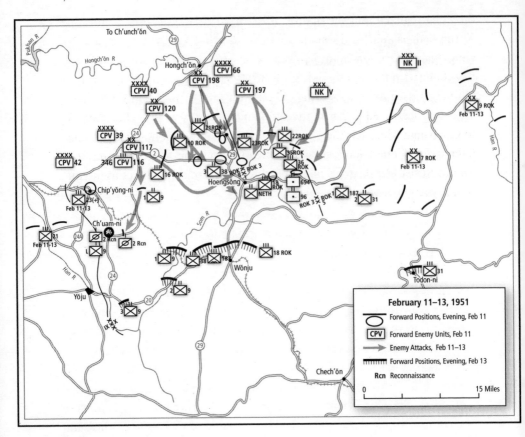

Battle of Hoengsŏng, February 11–18, 1951. (MAP ADAPTED FROM MOSSMAN, *EBB AND FLOW*)

ordered Freeman to stay and hold Chipyŏng-ni, which was now the vital "left shoulder" holding back the CPV penetration. As important rail and road hubs, both Wŏnju and Chipyŏng-ni had to remain in the hands of the Eighth Army.

The crucial battles for Wŏnju and Chipyŏng-ni demonstrated the UN force's enormous advantages, which proved decisive in defeating the CPV. Control of roads and railways with abundant motor transport meant that troops could be rapidly repositioned and supplies could flow unimpeded. Extensive communications provided the capacity to respond quickly to developing situations and close air-ground coordination. The battle of Wŏnju in mid-February in particular, which was known as the "Wŏnju shoot" for the prodigious use of artillery by UN forces, was a devastating blow for the communists and a major turning point of the war. From then on, Peng realized that the opportunity for quick and decisive victory in Korea had passed. The fourth offensive that had begun with a bloody bang against UN forces on February 11 at Hoengsŏng ended just fifteen days later with the bloody defeat of the CPV at Wŏnju and Chipyŏng-ni. Chinese losses were staggering. The better part of fourteen CPV divisions was destroyed.[118] An anguished Peng went to see Mao. "I explained to Chairman Mao that the Korean War could not be won quickly," Peng later wrote. "The Chairman gave a clear instruction for conducting the War to Resist U.S. Aggression and Aid Korea, 'Win a quick victory if you can; if you can't, win a slow one.'"[119]

CHAPTER EIGHT

Quest for Victory

By the end of February 1951, the Eighth Army was again on the offensive and advancing steadily. On March 15, Seoul, now a devastated city, was abandoned by the enemy without a fight, and changed hands for the fourth time in less than nine months. Unlike the festive mood that had surrounded the recapture of the city in September, there were no ceremonies and no grand speeches to mark the occasion. The ROK troops who first entered the city simply took down the North Korean flag and raised their own at the Capitol Building. The war-beaten residents appeared almost too weary to notice. Soon, the issue of whether to cross the 38th parallel once again became a matter of discussion. The political and military situation was entirely different from what it was in September 1950. The kind of sustained drive into North Korean territory after Inch'ŏn appeared unlikely against the still-formidable Chinese force. Nevertheless, MacArthur pressed for unifying the peninsula and taking the war to China. On February 15, he asked for the removal of military restrictions, to permit bombings to disrupt the supply line from the Soviet Union into North Korea. The JCS denied the request. On February 26, MacArthur asked for authorization to bomb the hydroelectrical power facilities along the Yalu. The JCS did not give it to him, for "political reasons." A frustrated MacArthur issued a public statement on March 7, in direct violation of Truman's gag order on public discussion of policy matters, predicting that the "savage slaughter" would continue and the war would evolve into one of attrition and indecisiveness unless Washington's policies changed.

The first opportunity to bring an end to the war came in March when the exhausted Chinese forces abandoned Seoul and retreated north, allowing the UN forces back to the 38th parallel. With status quo ante bellum essentially restored, the UNC, as George Kennan had predicted, was finally in a position to negotiate a settlement from "something approaching an equality of strength." On March 20, the Joint Chiefs informed MacArthur that the president was about to implement a peace initiative: "Strong UN feeling persists that further diplomatic efforts towards settlement should be made before any advance with major forces north of 38th parallel," they wrote. "Time will be required to determine diplomatic reactions and permit new negotiations that may develop." Rather than responding directly to the initiative, MacArthur simply reiterated his earlier position: "I recommend that no further military restrictions be imposed upon the United Nations Command in Korea ... The military disadvantages arising from restrictions ... coupled with the disparity between the size of our command and the enemy ground potential render it completely impracticable to attempt to clear North Korea or to make any appreciable effort to that end." The JCS was puzzled by the cable. His "brilliant but brittle mind" seemed to have snapped, recalled Bradley, but no one in Washington was prepared for what MacArthur did next.[1]

The General and the Statesman

On March 24, MacArthur issued a public statement that challenged the pride of China and the authority of his Washington superiors, sabotaging any chance for a peace settlement. MacArthur's "communiqué" began by taunting China for its lack of industrial power and poor military showing against UN forces. More seriously, he raised the possibility of a widened war: "The enemy, therefore, must by now be painfully aware that a decision of the United Nations to depart from its tolerant effort to contain the war to the area of Korea, through an expansion of our military operations to his coastal areas and interior bases, would doom Red China to the risk of imminent military collapse."[2] He concluded with words that seemed calculated to upstage the president: he, MacArthur, personally "stood ready at any time" to meet with the Chinese commander for a settlement. The White House and the State Department were bombarded with queries by allied leaders and the press demanding to know whether there was now a new direction in U.S. policy in Korea. The French newspaper Le Figaro mocked MacArthur's negotiation offer as "an olive branch with a bayonet hidden amongst the leaves." London's *Daily Telegraph* observed that "the U.N. General Assembly becomes embarrassed, resentful or merely incredulous when General MacArthur . . . speaks again of carrying the war to the Chinese mainland." Soviet Foreign Minister Andrei Vyshinsky probably best summed up the general reaction of the foreign press when he announced that MacArthur was "a maniac, the principal culprit, the evil genius" of the war.[3]

That evening, Deputy Secretary of State Robert A. Lovett, Dean Rusk, and others gathered at Acheson's home to discuss the uproar that MacArthur had created. Lovett, Acheson recalled, "was angrier than I had ever seen him." The general, he said, "must be removed at once." Acheson shared Lovett's anger: "[MacArthur's statement] can be described only as defiance of the JCS, sabotage of an operation of which he had been informed, and insubordination of the grossest sort to his Commander-in-Chief." The following day, Lovett, Acheson, and Rusk met with Truman. "The President," recalled Acheson, "although perfectly calm, appeared to be in a state of mind that combined disbelief with controlled fury."[4] In his memoirs, Truman confided that he decided that day to relieve MacArthur, although it was not yet clear to him when and how he would do it. "[MacArthur's statement] was an act totally disregarding all directives to abstain from any declarations on foreign policy . . . By this act MacArthur left me no choice. I could no longer tolerate his insubordination." Yet, despite the seething anger in the room, the president coolly asked the group to check his directive prohibiting comments on policy to see if there was any ambiguity. They told him it was crystal clear. Truman then instructed Lovett to send a priority message to MacArthur "that would remind him of his duty under the order."[5] Given the circumstances, Truman's mild reprimand appeared to be yet another instance of Washington's leaders caving in to MacArthur. The general had, after all, violated the December order repeatedly, including his statement earlier in March predicting a "savage slaughter" in Korea, and nothing much was said then. Despite his "controlled fury," Truman appeared to be wavering again.

However, it was different this time. Truman's outward restraint was due to not only his sense of caution, but also what others called "political guile." As during other crises, Truman refused "to act impulsively or irresponsibly, whatever his own feelings."[6] His ability to remain cool, calm, and collected under fire was a trait that his staff had come to admire.[7] On this occasion, there was an additional motive. For all his anger, Truman understood that MacArthur remained an enormously popular figure. The mood of the country favored the general, not the president. A mid-March Gallup poll showed the president's public approval rating at an all-time low of just 26 percent. War casualty figures were appalling and further soured the national mood (the Defense Department reported that the United States had suffered a total of 57,120 casualties since June 1950).[8] People were becoming fed up with the war, and MacArthur at least spoke of a way to victory and end. Patience was required to bring down MacArthur. Premature or rash action would hurt only Truman and his administration. Thus, far from being timid, Truman's calm rebuke was actually a calculated response aimed, in Acheson's words, at "laying the foundation for a court-martial."[9]

Truman did not have to wait long. In early April, House Minority Leader Joe Martin took the floor with an explosive revelation. A long-time MacArthur admirer, Martin told the House that he had sent the general a copy of a speech he had made in February. Martin called for the use of Nationalist Chinese forces in Korea and accused the administration of a defeatist policy. He asked for MacArthur's views "to make sure my views were not in conflict with what was best for America."[10] MacArthur's response carried no stipulation of confidentiality, and Martin announced it dramatically in Congress: "It seems strangely difficult for some to realize that here in Asia is where the Communist conspirators have elected to make their play for global conquest, and that we have joined the issue thus raised on the battlefield . . . if we lose the war to communism in Asia the fall of Europe is inevitable, win it and Europe most probably would avoid war and yet preserve freedom."[11]

The Martin letter and renewed doubts about MacArthur's loyalty could not have come at a more inopportune time. The Joint Chiefs had just received alarming intelligence that the Soviet Union was preparing for a major military move. "One suggestion," recalled Bradley, "taken with utmost seriousness, was that they would intervene in Korea. Another was that they might attempt to overrun Western Europe."[12] It appeared that the situation in Korea had reached a new crisis point. In conveying these reports to Truman, Bradley also provided the JCS's recommendation that MacArthur be authorized to retaliate against air bases and aircraft in China in the event of a "major attack."[13] He convinced Truman that the Chinese and the Russians might be preparing to push the United States out of Korea and that the air force needed to be prepared to respond quickly. Deeply shaken, Truman called for the chairman of the Atomic Energy Commission (AEC), Gordon Dean, who controlled all nuclear warheads, and told him that he had decided to deploy bombers and atomic warheads to the Pacific because of the serious situation in Korea.[14] Dean recalled, "He [Truman] said that if I saw no objection, he would sign the order directing me to release to the custody of General Vandenberg, Chief of Staff, USAF, nine nuclear ****[*sic*]."[15] Truman said that he was not giving the air force a green light to drop the nuclear bombs; he still hoped the need to use them would never arise. He was sending them as a contingency, and no decision would be made without consulting the National Security Council's special committee on atomic energy. The next day, the 99th Medium Bomb Wing was ordered to pick up atomic bombs for trans-shipment to Guam. By this time, Truman and Acheson had approved a draft order to MacArthur authorizing him, in the event of a "major" air attack on UN forces originating outside of Korea, to retaliate against air bases in China, but not with nuclear weapons without Truman's release.

MacArthur never received the order. Bradley later explained, "I was now so wary of MacArthur that I deliberately withheld the message and all knowledge of its existence from him, fearing that he might, as I wrote at the time, 'make a premature decision in carrying it out.'"[16] MacArthur had lost Bradley's trust. By sending nuclear bombs and approving a directive that conditionally authorized their use, Truman strengthened the argument for MacArthur's relief: if nuclear weapons were to be used in Korea, it was absolutely essential to have a trustworthy commander in the field. Furthermore, Truman had shown that although he disapproved of MacArthur's public statements, he was willing to consider the strategic concepts underlying them.[17] While Truman and the JCS were in agreement with MacArthur on what had to be done in case of an attack, they were also in agreement that MacArthur was the wrong person to be entrusted with such a difficult mission.[18] It was this confluence of events—MacArthur's letter to Martin, the crisis in Korea, and the decision to deploy nuclear weapons—that led to the conclusion to dismiss MacArthur. Acheson, Bradley, George Marshall, and Averell Harriman (the "Big Four") unanimously agreed that MacArthur should be relieved of duty.[19]

Truman insisted that MacArthur be notified with courtesy and dignity. Secretary of the Army Frank Pace Jr. was en route to Japan and Korea, and Marshall decided to have him deliver the order of relief personally to MacArthur on the morning of April 12 (evening of April 11, Washington time) before it was publicly announced. But a chain of actions made the notification neither courteous nor dignified. On the evening of April 10, the information had leaked, and the *Chicago Tribune*, a staunch critic of the Truman administration, queried for confirmation and details. An emergency White House meeting considered whether to stick to the original plan or to make an immediate announcement. The fear was that the *Tribune* would notify MacArthur, and he might try to trump the president by dramatically resigning before the public announcement. The risk could not be taken. A special press conference was called at 1:00 am on April 11, Washington time, to tell the reporters, bleary-eyed and bewildered, of the extraordinary news. Although an attempt was made to inform MacArthur shortly before the press conference, radio broadcast of the order reached Tokyo first.[20] MacArthur learned of his dismissal from his wife, Jean, after she was notified by a member of the personal staff who had heard the news on the radio. MacArthur was seventy-one years old and had been in Asia for fourteen years. Ridgway was chosen to replace him.

Ridgway did not know of his promotion until a reporter congratulated him. Flustered, the general shrugged it off. Not long thereafter, he received official word from Secretary Pace and the next day flew to Japan for his last meeting with MacArthur. Ridgway recollected, "He was entirely himself, composed, quiet, temperate, friendly, and helpful to the man who was to succeed him."[21] Nevertheless, MacArthur's rancor against Truman was palpable. He told Ridgway that an "eminent medical man" had confided to him that "the President was suffering from malignant hypertension" and that "this affliction was characterized by bewilderment and confusion of thought." Truman, MacArthur declared, "would be dead in six months."[22]

MacArthur left Tokyo amid much emotional fanfare. The Japanese Diet passed a resolution praising him. Prime Minister Yoshida and other top officials publicly expressed their gratitude for his "outstanding" service to Japan. Throngs of Japanese densely lined the route from the embassy to the airport to offer their farewells. A nineteen-gun salute was rendered and a large formation of jet fighters flew in formation over the airport in his honor.[23] "The farewells were an ordeal," commented William Sebald, the American ambassador to Japan. "Many of the women were sobbing openly, and a number of the battle-hardened men had difficulty suppressing their tears."[24] MacArthur turned and waved to the crowd one last time before boarding his famed *Bataan*. "You'd think he was a conquering hero," said one observer, "not at all a demeanor of a man who'd just been fired."[25]

MacArthur received a tumultuous reception on his return to the United States. It was his first visit to the continental United States in fourteen years. He was greeted with one of the biggest ticker-tape parades ever staged in New York, and he delivered a stirring farewell speech to a joint session of Congress that Congressman Dewy Short of

Japanese crowds line the road to the airport to say good-bye to General MacArthur, April 16, 1951. (U.S. ARMY MILITARY HISTORY INSTITUTE)

"Bon Voyage" and "God Be with You" from Japanese well-wishers, April 16, 1951. (U.S. ARMY MILITARY HISTORY INSTITUTE)

Missouri characterized as "the voice of God."[26] The reaction to MacArthur's firing was stupendous. In San Gabriel, California, students hanged an effigy of Truman. In Ponca City, Oklahoma, a dummy representing Acheson was soaked in oil and then burned. At MacArthur's birthplace in Little Rock, Arkansas, citizens lowered the flags to half mast. In Lafayette, Indiana, workers carrying signs "Impeach Truman" paraded in the rain. Senator Richard Nixon from California reported that he had received more than six hundred telegrams on the first day of the news of MacArthur's recall, and most were in favor of impeachment of Truman. "It is the largest spontaneous reaction I've ever seen," said Nixon, who demanded MacArthur's immediate reinstatement. Before the day was over, the White House had received seventeen hundred telegrams about MacArthur, three to one against his removal.[27] Republicans spoke threateningly of "impeaching" the president. Pro-administration voices, however, were heard in the two houses of Congress, both controlled by the Democrats, Truman's party. House Speaker Sam Rayburn spoke for many of the president's supporters when he declared, "We must never give up [the principle] that the military is subject to and under the control of the civilian administration."[28]

Throughout Europe, MacArthur's dismissal was greeted as welcome news, as the Europeans had long feared his mercurial ambition and desire to widen the war. "The removal of MacArthur will be received with dry eyes; yes with extraordinary relief," reported the Danish newspaper *Afterbladet*, which described Truman's decision as "the most daring during his career." The French, reported Janet Flanner in *The New Yorker*, were "solidly with Truman." Britain's Conservative leader Winston Churchill expressed his approval, stating that "constitutional authority should control the action of military commanders." Ironically, the Russians and the Chinese also approved. But the most impressive support for Truman's decision was the weight of editorial opinion at home. The *New York Times*, *New York Herald Tribune*, *Washington Post*, *Boston Globe*, *Atlanta Journal*, *Minneapolis Tribune*, and *Christian Science Monitor* all endorsed his decision. Truman remained calm throughout the political storm because, as he later confided, "I knew that once all the hullabaloo died down, people would see what he was." As he anticipated, the "hullabaloo" did subside. After Senate hearings investigating MacArthur's dismissal had shown that Truman's decision to relieve the general had been unanimously backed by Secretary of Defense Marshall and the JCS, public opinion turned in favor of the president. In mid-May, Democratic National Committee Chairman William Boyle pronounced that "the public 'furor' over MacArthur's dismissal appeared to be subsiding," and that the Senate hearings had "helped to blow away much of the fog and bring out the facts."[29]

Spring Offensive

While the Truman administration settled on limiting the war, the Chinese decided to make one last effort to drive UN forces out of the peninsula. Although the defeats at Wŏnju and Chipyŏng-ni had demonstrated that a quick victory would be elusive, Mao believed that success was possible with sufficient forces. He thought a million men could do it. This was nearly three times the number of soldiers who had pushed back the UN forces the previous fall and winter.[30] The spring offensive from mid-April to mid-May 1951 would be the last effort for a communist victory and the largest campaign of the Korean War. Peng had reservations about the logistical capacity to support such a massive offensive, but he agreed with the plan, believing that it was more favorable for the CPV to fight now than later, because "the enemy is tired, its troops have not been replenished, its reinforcements have yet to gather, and its military strength is relatively weak."[31] By launching the spring offensive, the CPV could "regain the initiative."[32]

Lieutenant General James Van Fleet replaced Ridgway as the commander of the Eighth Army just before the spring offensive was launched. Only days after taking over, he would be in charge of defending against the massive communist assault. Van Fleet was coming off a highly successful assignment in Greece. In the post–World War II period, Greece had become fertile ground for communism. With Moscow's support, Greek communists initiated an insurgency. At first, Britain provided military and economic assistance, but by early 1947 the British had run out of resources, bankrupted by World War II, the loss of colonies, and the crisis it supported in Europe. Britain asked the United States to accept responsibility for continuing the aid, and it did, thus establishing the Truman Doctrine in March 1947 that committed the United States to help fight communism around the globe. Van Fleet arrived in Greece in late February 1948 to revamp the Greek army, which, among other things, "lacked an offensive spirit" and was shot through with "incompetent older officers."[33] He did such a remarkable job that by August 1949 the Greek army was able to put the communist insurgents on the run. It was a great victory for the Truman Doctrine and a personal triumph for Van Fleet.

Truman and others saw the situations in Korea and Greece as similar, and so it was thought that Van Fleet's success in Greece might be replicated in Korea. Both countries were poor, peninsular with mountainous terrain, and wracked by a brutal civil war with communists who were supported by border states (Soviet support for the Greek communists had been channeled through Yugoslavia, although Tito's split from Stalin closed this route and was a major factor in the defeat of the insurgency). The long-term solution for Korea, like Greece, was thought to be the creation of reliable and effective indigenous security forces that could stand up to the communist threat. Bittman Barth, who served under Van

Fleet in France in 1944, recalled that Van Fleet inspired his men with "quiet self-assurance" that transmitted "a feeling of confidence." The Greeks "admired him tremendously," as would the South Koreans, who later honored him with the epitaph "Father of the ROK Army."[34]

Ridgway told Van Fleet, when he arrived on April 14, that although he would give Van Fleet "the latitude and high respect his ability merited," he would keep a tight rein on operations in Korea: "I undertook to place reasonable restrictions on the advances of the Eighth and ROK Armies. Specifically, I charged Van Fleet to conduct no operations in force beyond the Wyoming Line [the farthest line of advance of UN forces, located slightly north of the 38th parallel] without prior approval of GHQ. I made my wishes unmistakably clear to General Van Fleet with respect to the tactical latitude within which he was to operate."[35] Ridgway's decision to closely oversee Eighth Army operations was warranted because he was concerned that Van Fleet might share MacArthur's view on the war and might, perhaps inadvertently, initiate actions that could widen it. One of Ridgway's first official acts as the new head of Far East Command was to issue a "directive" to his senior commanders that succinctly laid out the basic principles on which the war was to be waged to support the UN and U.S. policy for limiting the war:

> The grave and ever present danger that the conduct of our current operations may result in the extension of hostilities, and so lead to a worldwide conflagration, places a heavy responsibility upon all elements of this Command, but particularly upon those capable of offensive action. In accomplishing our assigned missions, this responsibility is ever present. It is a responsibility not only to superior authority in the direct command chain, but inescapably to the American people. It can be discharged ONLY if every Commander is fully alive to the possible consequences of his acts; if every Commander has imbued his Command with a like sense of responsibility for its acts; has set up, and by frequent tests, has satisfied himself of the effectiveness of his machinery for insuring his control of the offensive actions of his command and of its reactions to enemy action; and, in final analysis, is himself determined that no act of his Command shall bring about an extension of the present conflict . . . International tensions within and bearing upon this Theater have created acute danger of World War III. Instructions from higher authority reflect the intense determination of our people, and of all the free peoples of the world, to prevent this catastrophe, if that can be done without appeasement, or sacrifice of principle.[36]

Ridgway also issued a more specific "Letter of Instructions" to Van Fleet designed "to prevent expansion of the Korean conflict." He instructed Van Fleet that "your mission is to repel aggression against so much of the territory (and the people therein) of the Republic of Korea, as you now occupy and, in collaboration with the Government of the Republic of Korea, to establish and maintain order in said territory . . . Acquisition of terrain in itself is of little or no value."[37] Bradley later wrote, "It was a great relief to finally have a man in Tokyo who was in agreement with the administration's views on containing the war."[38]

The spring offensive was launched on April 22, just eight days after Van Fleet's arrival. The communist forces struck in two tremendous and simultaneous blows: a main effort in the west by Chinese troops and a supporting attack in the east, through rugged mountains, by the North Koreans. In the west, 250,000 Chinese attacked the I and IX Corps with the aim of capturing Seoul by May 1. Most of the units of the two corps were American, but I Corps also included the Twenty-Ninth British Brigade, and each corps had an ROK division, which, given its weaker strength, proved to be an Achilles' heel. The ROK Sixth Division in the IX Corps was overwhelmed and collapsed, threatening the U.S. Twenty-Fourth Division to its west and the First Marine Division to its east with envelopment. The collapse of the ROK Sixth Division symbolized for many, then and since, the weakness of the ROK Army. Some blamed the inadequacy of the unit's weaponry and training against overwhelming Chinese force, but many others blamed poor leadership and cowardice. It was an ignoble fate for a division whom some credited for having saved the nation by mounting an effective and stubborn defense in the Ch'unch'ŏn area in the opening days of the war, an action that threw off the North Korean schedule and bought time for UN forces to arrive.

The First Marine Division, with an exposed flank, was forced to fall back. The U.S. Twenty-Fourth Division's exposed eastern flank posed an even more serious challenge. It appeared that the Chinese plan was a wide envelopment of Seoul from the east in concert with the main thrust from the north. Fortunately, the Twenty-Seventh Commonwealth Infantry Brigade, consisting of British, Canadian, Australian, New Zealand, and Indian units, made a heroic stand at Kapyŏng and checked the eastern arm of the offensive. In the west, the Chinese attack concentrated on the weakest part of the front line, the sector held by the ROK First

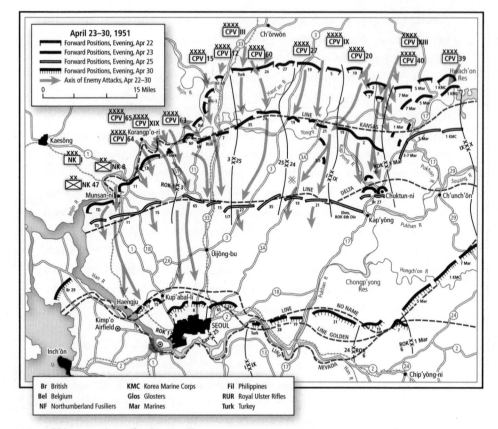

Chinese spring offensive, April 22–30, 1951. (MAP ADAPTED FROM MOSSMAN, *EBB AND FLOW*)

Division occupying the westernmost end. To its eastern flank was the British 29th Infantry Brigade. These forces held the gates to Seoul, and if they collapsed, not only Seoul but the entire front would be in danger of being rolled up.

The capture of Seoul seemed to be the communists' main objective. Though Ridgway had not changed his view about not holding real estate just for its own sake, he believed that for psychological and symbolic reasons, Seoul had become an overwhelming stake for Mao, especially after the defeats at Wŏnju and Chipyŏng-ni. Ridgway instructed Van Fleet to make a strong stand for Seoul: "I attach considerable importance to the retention of Seoul. Now that we have it, it is of considerable more value, psychologically, than its acquisition was when we were south of the Han."[39] Van Fleet agreed and thought that losing the capital would also have a deleterious effect on ROK forces. "Seoul had been given up twice before," Van Fleet later recalled. "I felt that to give it up a third time would take the spirit out of a [Korean] nation. It would destroy morale completely to lose their capital."[40] The war devolved to a battle for Seoul. Given the CPV's logistical shortcomings, Van Fleet estimated that holding them up for several days north of Seoul with delaying or blocking actions would be sufficient to exhaust their supplies and give the UN force enough time to establish a strong defensive line. This critical mission largely fell on the British 29th Brigade with its attached Belgian battalion. It was deployed widely along the Imjin River at the most traditional crossing point, where armies had swept north and south through the peninsula over the past centuries. It was no different this time, as the main thrust of the Chinese pointed at the heart of the brigade. Due to the wide front that the British and Belgians had to hold, the line was not continuous, islands of companies being separated by wide-open stretches. Holding back the Chinese main assault would be a difficult if not an impossible task.

Magnificent Glosters

The British 29th Brigade had arrived in Korea in early November 1950, just in time to be initiated into the war with the Chinese intervention and the UN retreat. As with all British formations, its units possessed long and proud martial histories, going back as far as the seventeenth century, and had served in some of the most storied and exotic corners of the British Empire. Many of the soldiers were reservists who had been in World War II, and at an average age of thirty, many were married with children when they were called back to duty. The Belgian battalion with its Luxembourg platoon was attached to the brigade on the eve of the battle at Imjin River.

The Chinese struck on the night of April 22. In the initial assault, the Belgian battalion was surrounded and cut off. For twenty-four hours the Belgians' situation was precarious, but they held off the Chinese until they could be rescued and fall back. The next day, two British battalions, the Glosters (1st Battalion of the Gloucestershire Regiment) and the Royal Ulster Fusiliers, were besieged by Chinese forces. The incredible mobility of the Chinese on foot over the rough terrain enabled them to surround these units by infiltrating through the open stretches in the line. By mid-morning the battalions were forced to contract to hilltop perimeters. The Chinese also put terrific pressure on the ROK First Division, which was covering the British brigade's western flank. While it did not collapse like the ROK Sixth Division, it was nevertheless driven back several miles, exposing the Glosters' flank. The Glosters, anchoring the brigade's western end, found themselves in considerable difficulty as the Chinese completed their encirclement. The battalion, having suffered many casualties, was tightly ensconced atop a single hill, Hill 235. Its commanding officer, Lt. Col. James Carne, inquired about a possible withdrawal before the noose became too tight. Brigadier Tom Brodie, the brigade commanding officer, told Carne to stay put and hold out for just a few more hours. "I understand the position quite clearly," Carne replied. "What I must make clear to you is the fact that my command is no longer an effective fighting force. If it is required that we shall stay here, in spite of this, we shall continue to hold."[41]

Brodie assured Carne that a rescue mission was on its way. By this time, however, the Chinese had penetrated so far behind the lines that a rescue mission was increasingly becoming unfeasible. Ammunition, food, water, and medical supplies were running dangerously short. The men were more thirsty than hungry. "The heat of the day and the loss of sweat in the march up to the night position made them thirsty, and there was no water," recalled Capt. Anthony Farrar-Hockley, the battalion's adjutant. Aerial resupply was attempted, but the perimeter was small and located atop a steep hill surrounded by the Chinese, making accurate air drops nearly impossible. One pilot asked if "there (was) any means of marking a dropping zone." Farrar-Hockley said he felt like shouting over the radio, "Tell them to aim for a high rock with a lot of Chinese around it!" Many of the bundles rolled down the hillsides to the Chinese. Substantial air support was also committed, but it did not relieve the situation.[42]

Early on the morning of April 25, after nearly three days of intense fighting, the 29th Brigade received orders to withdraw. Carne explained the situation to his men and told them that the battalion could not carry on as a unit. He gave them the option of surrendering or fighting their way out as separate groups. All opted to make their way out. Three of

Top of Gloster Hill (Hill 235) shortly after the battle. (SOLDIERS OF GLOUCESTERSHIRE MUSEUM)

the four companies along with the staff at battalion headquarters headed south directly toward the UN line. Very few made it through, and most of them were captured, including Carne. The fourth company's commander, Capt. Mike Harvey, decided on a counterintuitive route and proceeded north. This took his men straight into the Chinese rear, where they were able to swing around to the west and then south toward the UN line. For the next few miles Harvey and his group did not encounter any Chinese. Adding to their good fortune, they were spotted by a UN aircraft, which began guiding them homeward through the hills. Suddenly, they came under heavy fire from the Chinese, but then they saw American tanks just ahead of them down the valley. As they raced toward the tanks, however, the Americans mistook them for Chinese and opened fire, killing six. Horrified, the aircraft pilot flew frantically over the tanks and dropped a note from the sky. Realizing their mistake, the Americans ceased their fire, and the Glosters rushed forward for cover behind the tanks. The Americans were heartsick over their mistake. The lieutenant in charge asked how many were killed. Captain Harvey did not want to make the Americans feel any worse than he had to, so he did not answer.[43]

Of the original 699 men, only 77 made it out.[44] A large number were captured and spent over two years in POW camps. Van Fleet described the Glosters' action as "the most outstanding example of unit bravery in modern warfare." Although there was much recrimination about who was responsible for the debacle—some blamed Brodie for not giving the withdrawal order earlier, while others blamed Carne for not communicating more clearly the dire situation—Van Fleet concluded that the loss of the Glosters had not been in vain: "This is one of those great occasions in combat which called for a determined stand," he later wrote. "The loss of 622 officers and men saved many times that number."[45] The British 29th Brigade had held for sixty crucial hours, which had not only severely gutted the Chinese force but also seriously disrupted their schedule and momentum. It had also bought enough time to establish a firm defense line to protect Seoul. On the night of April 27–28, the Chinese made one final effort, but they were unable to overcome the defense

Glosters taken prisoner are on a break while on their way to a POW camp on the Yalu River. (SOLDIERS OF GLOUCESTERSHIRE MUSEUM)

Brigadier Tom Brodie, commander of the British 29th Brigade, unveiling a memorial to the men who lost their lives during the battle at Imjin River, July 5, 1951. (U.S. NATIONAL ARCHIVES AND RECORDS ADMINISTRATION)

line or sustain their attack. By April 29, there was a palpable diminution of the offensive. "After we had turned back the enemy's first greatest onslaught by April 28," recalled Van Fleet, "we dug in and waited for him to come. We waited and waited and he did not come."[46] Despite the huge losses, the Chinese had not yet given up hope. Turning their sights eastward, they planned a "second phase" of the spring offensive.

Victory Denied?

Detecting the CPV's shift eastward, Van Fleet thought the Chinese were planning to attack down the Pukhan River valley to envelope Seoul from the southeast.[47] Unexpectedly, the offensive was launched on May 16 much farther to the east than Van Fleet had estimated. Massive CPV and North Korean forces struck UN forces situated from the central region to the east coast. Van Fleet had placed his units mainly to defend Seoul and now faced an all-out attack on his weaker eastern sector. The main

CPV effort was against X Corps and ROK III Corps, with a supporting attack against ROK I Corps deployed by the east coast. The four ROK divisions in X Corps and ROK III Corps rapidly collapsed. This exposed the U.S. Second Division's right flank in a replay of the events of November 1950, when the collapse of the ROK Sixth Division placed the entire Second Division in a similar predicament that had led to its virtual destruction. The objective of the attack in the east was uncertain, but one possibility was to advance to Pusan. "This was a startling development," recalled General Almond.[48]

The communist offensive met initial success, especially in the exploitation of the gap opened by the collapse of the ROK units. U.S. units to the west of the gap and ROK units from I Corps to the east were forced to fall back, creating a large bulge in the UN lines. But the shoulders held with rapid reinforcements and a shifting of forces from the western sector. Punishing artillery and air attacks exacted an enormous toll on the Chinese troops. By the third day, the offensive began to wane. Sensing the enemy's exhaustion and with Ridgway's urging, Van Fleet and Almond formed a counteroffensive plan that would, if successful, turn the game around and surround the bulk of the communist forces. IX Corps supported by I Corps would attack from the west and cut off lines of communication, supply, and, most importantly, reinforcement or withdrawal routes in the western half. X Corps, supported by ROK I Corps, would attack in the east to cut off similar lines in the eastern half. It was a bold plan nearly worthy of the Inch'ŏn operation in its ambition and objective. If successful, the entire eastern half of the front would be torn wide open, and a majority of the communist forces neutralized.

On May 20, merely four days after the communist offensive started, the western attack was initiated, joined by the eastern attack on May 23. Peng decided on May 21 to cut his horrendous losses and not only halt the offensive, but rapidly pull his forces back to a line about ten miles north of where they had started, because it was more defensible. The UN attacks were overly cautious and slow and allowed the bulk of the enemy to escape. By July 1, UN forces had pushed the communists back twenty-five to fifty miles north all across the front, establishing a line that more or less remained static for the next two years, until the armistice.

Despite the failure to completely destroy the attacking communist forces, the outcome was a triumph for the UN forces in general and the

U.S. Army, and especially X Corps, in particular. During the opening days of the counteroffensive, wrote Van Fleet, UN forces "offered no resistance at all in the east or along the coast." He concluded, "The Red soldier in that advance must have thought it was a very easy war." However, on the third day, "we launched a counterattack in the main area of battle and instead of being outflanked by the Reds who had poured down the mountains and roads east for as much as 50 miles, we pinched them off and disposed of them at leisure."[49] Van Fleet had beaten the Chinese at their own game.

The success of the counteroffensive presented an opportunity to destroy the Chinese army and, by extension, a chance to win the war. Years later, Van Fleet would bitterly recall that the chance to end the war in May–June 1951 was squandered. This was not November 1950,

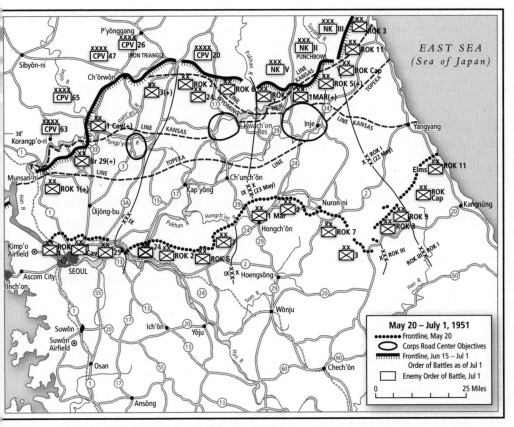

Eighth Army advance, May 20–July 1, 1951. (MAP ADAPTED FROM MOSSMAN, *EBB AND FLOW*)

when MacArthur had made his foolhardy plunge to the Yalu to face a fresh, strong, and eager Chinese army. After the huge casualties and deprivations suffered by the Chinese forces since the winter, Van Fleet believed they were tired, weak, and perhaps morally defeated. "The mission to which we had been assigned, to establish a defensive line across the peninsula, was accomplished," recalled Van Fleet, "though we could have readily followed up our successes and defeated the enemy, but that was not the intention of Washington."[50] Sensing Van Fleet's frustration, Ridgway wrote to him, "Because of this particularly sensitive period politically, I would like you and your most senior officers . . . meticulously to avoid all public statements about the Korean situation which pass beyond the purely military field."[51] Ridgway did not want another MacArthur-esque fiasco. Had the political will existed, a military victory might have been possible since the communist front lay wide open. "We met the attack and routed the enemy," Van Fleet later wrote. "We had him beaten and could have destroyed his armies. Those days are the ones most vivid in my memory, great days when all of the Eighth Army, and we thought America too, were inspired to win."[52]

But Washington and its allies wanted only to bring the fighting to an end. No one could determine for sure what Mao would do if UN forces once again advanced to the Yalu. Surely, the Chinese forces would regroup and continue the fight. Then there was the issue of what Stalin might do if the war was extended to China. There was also little likelihood that North Korean communists would have simply accepted their defeat. Given the nature of the vicious civil war that preceded June 1950, disaffected Korean communists, northern and southern, would undoubtedly have taken up arms and continued the fight in an insurgency. With objectives to bring about "an end to the fighting, and a return to the status quo" achieved, Acheson told the Senate on June 7 that UN forces would accept an armistice. It was time to end the Korean War.

CHAPTER NINE

The Stalemate

S ecretary of State Dean Acheson was cautious but receptive to the overture for a cease-fire and an armistice from the Soviet ambassador to the UN, Yakov Malik, on June 23, 1951. There were doubts about the Soviets' sincerity, but Acheson nonetheless responded quickly to seize an opportunity to end the fighting.[1] General Ridgway was more skeptical. Although he found the prospect of a cease-fire "not unwelcomed," he deeply distrusted the communists. He sent a message to "all commanders" in the field lest they began to let down their guards. "Two things should be recalled" about the Soviets, he warned: "One is the well-earned reputation for duplicity and dishonesty," and "the other is the slowness with which deliberative bodies such as the [UN] Security Council produce positive action." He cautioned General Van Fleet to "personally assure yourself that all elements of your command are made aware of the danger of such a relaxation of effort and that you insist on an intensification rather than a diminution of the United Nations' action in this theater."[2]

Ridgway was right to be cautious. In light of recent evidence, the Soviet proposal appears to have been disingenuous. In a cable to Mao in early June, Stalin stated that the best strategy to pursue was "a long and drawn out war in Korea." By then, the Eighth Army's successful counteroffensive had seriously disrupted the communist forces. A cease-fire would have been advantageous to the communists, as it would have allowed the Chinese and the North Koreans to rest and regroup. "The war in Korea should not be speeded up," Stalin advised Mao, "a drawn out war, in the first place, gives the possibility to Chinese troops to study contemporary warfare on the field of battle and in the second place, shakes up the Truman regime in America and harms the military prestige of the Anglo-American troops."[3] Given the fighting and casualties suffered since October, the Chinese leadership probably thought they had learned enough. But Mao's exchanges with Stalin indicate that he was willing to continue the war. His reaction to a potential end of hostilities appeared ambivalent.[4] Although Mao responded favorably to an offer made by Ridgway, as the UNC commander, on June 29 to discuss an armistice, Mao's message to Stalin two weeks earlier gave no indication that Mao was thinking about an armistice at all. "The position at the front in June will be such that our forces will be comparatively weaker than those of the enemy," he wrote. "In July we will be stronger than in June, and in August we will be even stronger. We will be ready in August to make a stronger blow to the enemy."[5]

In June, Mao's intention was to use the operational pause during armistice negotiations to rebuild his forces and eventually resume the offensive, but his communications in July and August indicated that he was willing to conclude an armistice if it was accomplished in a manner that would not undermine China's prestige.[6] Mao was anxious to avoid unfavorable armistice terms that would threaten not only his leadership position, but the revolution itself. The Chinese regime was careful in how it presented the new strategy of ending the war to the Chinese people. On July 3, the Central Committee issued "Instructions on the Propaganda Affairs Concerning the Peace Negotiations in Korea," which began with the point that "peace has been the very purpose of the CPV's participation in the anti-aggression war in Korea."[7] The United States was to be portrayed as the weaker party, "that it was the American leadership who had solicited negotiations and an armistice" and not China.[8] Mao already viewed the war as a victory for China: it had fought the world's greatest superpower to a standstill, and he was not about to sabotage this perception. The British reporter and communist sympathizer Alan Winnington noted, "This is the first time Oriental Communists have ever sat down at a conference table on terms of equality with Americans, and they intend to make the most of it."[9]

Ridgway had no interest in enhancing China's or Mao's prestige. He identified several points that he did not like in Beijing's response accepting his June 29 proposal for a meeting to discuss an armistice. The most important clause was: "We agree to suspend military activities and to hold peace negotiations," meaning, first stop fighting and then talk.[10] In passing Beijing's message to the JCS, Ridgway wrote that a suspension of military activities would "gravely prejudice the safety and security of UN forces" and would be "wholly unacceptable." For their part, Chinese leaders believed that the fighting thus far had taught the Americans that neither side could achieve military victory, and therefore assumed that suspension of fighting and restoration of the 38th parallel as the border would be acceptable.[11]

Both sides had valid concerns. But whereas Mao was seeking ways to preserve and enhance China's and his prestige, using the armistice negotiations with the world's most powerful nation for domestic propaganda purposes, Ridgway had no intention of compromising on anything. Why should he yield anything to the Chinese when the UN forces were strong and had the advantage? When armistice negotiations started in July, Ridgway told the UN team's chief delegate, Vice Adm. C. Turner Joy, that the basic UN position was an "implacable opposition to communism." In his "Guidance Memo," Ridgway instructed the delegates that they were "to lead from strength not weakness." Ridgway concluded that if UN negotiators could "cap the military defeat of the Communists in Korea" with skillful handling of the armistice talks, "history may record that communist military aggression reached its high water mark in Korea, and that thereafter, communism itself began its recession in Asia."[12]

Truce Talks

Each side's negotiating team consisted of five principal military delegates. Admiral Joy, commander of U.S. Naval Forces Far East, led the UN team, which included Maj. Gen. Paek Sŏn-yŏp, the commanding general of the ROK I Corps, who represented the ROK but only as an observer. On the communist side, the senior delegate was Lt. Gen. Nam Il, the NKPA's chief of staff and a veteran of the Soviet Army in World War II, where he participated in some of the greatest battles including Stalingrad. The Chinese, however, took control of all major policy decisions at the talks, but only after coordination with Moscow. The initial meeting was held on July 10 at Kaesŏng. The UN team soon realized that it had been a mistake to agree to meet in this ancient capital city. The supposed "neutral zone" was a facade as it was full of Chinese and North Korean

The UN delegation arrives at the negotiation site in Kaesŏng, July 10, 1951. (U.S. ARMY
MILITARY HISTORY INSTITUTE)

soldiers. The situation was particularly galling for Ridgway, because UN
forces had held Kaesŏng before the talks and withdrew to make it "neutral." He also appeared to be unaware of Kaesŏng's symbolic importance
to the North Koreans until after the talks began. Over a thousand years
earlier, Kaesŏng had been the capital of the ancient kingdom of Koguryŏ,
whose territory encompassed all of North Korea as well as a large part
of Northeast China. Koguryŏ was conquered by a southern kingdom,
Silla, in the unification wars of the seventh century. Silla's ancient territory was now part of South Korea. For North Korea, seeing itself as
part reincarnation of Koguryŏ and engaged in another war of unification,
Kaesŏng symbolized, if not the possibility of a reversal of that ancient
defeat, at least the continued preservation of the northern "kingdom."

It was soon apparent that the Kaesŏng arrangement was a propaganda stage rather than a sincere venue for talks. The UN delegation
was required to arrive bearing a white flag as if in surrender and to be
escorted by communist troops, journalists, and photographers. The UN
press corps, much less soldiers, were prevented from entering the area.
The UN, or more specifically, the Americans, were portrayed as coming

to Kaesŏng to plead for peace. The talks got off to a predictably rocky start. "At the first meeting of the delegates," recalled Admiral Joy, "I seated myself at the conference table and almost sank out of sight. The communists had provided a chair for me which was considerably shorter than a standard chair." Meanwhile, "across the table, the senior Communist delegate, General Nam Il, protruded a good foot above my cagily diminished stature. This had been accomplished by providing stumpy Nam Il with a chair about four inches higher than usual." Other indignities followed. During a recess, Joy was threatened by a communist guard "who pointed a burp gun at me and growled menacingly." Joy's courier, who had been instructed to carry an interim report to Ridgway, was halted and forcibly turned back. A guard posted "conspicuously besides the access doorway wore a gaudy medal which he proudly related to Col. Andrew J. Kinney was for 'killing forty Americans.'" Joy had had enough. On July 12, the UN delegation walked out. The talks resumed three days later after the armed communist personnel were withdrawn.[13]

After much haggling over the physical arrangement of the negotiation room, the discussion finally turned to the agenda. The UN delegation presented three main items: establishment of a truce line, exchange of POWs, and an enforcement mechanism for the armistice. The communists agreed to these but added one more: the withdrawal of all foreign armed forces from Korea. Joy rejected this item as a political matter, which it was, and not appropriate to the armistice talks, which were limited to military matters. A few days later the communist side agreed to drop the withdrawal issue after the UN team stood uncompromisingly firm against its inclusion. The communists then raised the stakes by proposing that the 38th parallel be the line of truce and that a cease-fire be declared during the negotiations. When the talks started, UN forces were in possession of a significant amount of territory in good defensible terrain north of the 38th, especially in the eastern and the central regions. Using the 38th as the truce line would be highly disadvantageous to the UN. Mao confided to Stalin that "it is possible there will be some divergence," but "our proposal is extremely just and it will be difficult for the enemy to refute."[14] Since the 38th had been recognized as the boundary before the war, the communists advocated that it be simply restored. The UNC rejected the proposal outright, stating that the 38th parallel "has no significance to the existing military situation."[15] A proposed cease-fire was also rejected as it was seen as a ruse to build up and strengthen the communist forces.

The communists were angered by the UN response. General Nam described the UN position as "incredible," "naïve and illogical," and "absurd and arrogant." Nam then proposed the 38th parallel as the truce line with a twelve-mile-wide demilitarized zone, in contrast to the UN's proposal for a twenty-mile-wide zone. The talks deadlocked. A perturbed Mao wrote to Stalin for advice. A month had passed, and no progress had been made. The truce line was, thus far, the only issue discussed. Mao had come to believe that "from the entire course of the conference and the general situation outside the conference, it is apparent that it is not possible to force the enemy to accept the proposal about the 38th parallel." He concluded, "We think that it is better to think over the question of cessation of military operations at the present front line than to carry on the struggle for the 38th Parallel and bring the conference to a breakdown."[16] Under pressure from Washington, the UN team made a concession: to accept the communist proposal for a twelve-mile-wide demilitarized zone. The communists stated that they were considering the line of military contact, as proposed by the UN, for the truce line.[17]

The communists abruptly broke off the talks on August 23, alleging that an American aircraft had bombed a neutral area near Kaesŏng. They also alleged that a few days earlier "enemy troops, dressed in civilian clothes, made a raid on our security forces in the neutral zone in Kaesŏng," killing a Chinese soldier and wounding another.[18] The UN delegation refuted the allegations after its own investigations.[19] Yet, given Mao's earlier message to Stalin that he wanted to avoid a breakdown in the negotiations "at all costs," it is difficult to understand why such incidents would have been staged. It is likely that the ground raid was the work of South Korean partisans conducted without coordination or permission from the UNC. The ROK Army and partisan operations had been responsible for a number of previous violations in the area, and it is possible that President Rhee, who vociferously opposed the talks, ordered them to disrupt the negotiations. Mao wrote to Stalin in late August that "the enemy, in justifying himself, stated that this was [committed by] partisans from the South Korean partisan detachment active in our region, and therefore he does not take any responsibility

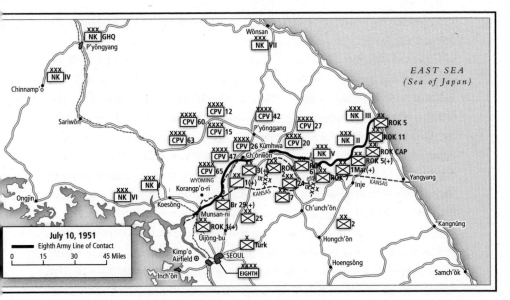

The front line in early July 1951. (ADAPTED FROM WALTER G. HERMES, *TRUCE TENT AND FIGHT-ING FRONT*, U.S. GOVERNMENT PRINTING OFFICE, 1996)

for it ... The negotiations will not be resumed until we receive a satis-factory answer."[20]

The talks remained suspended for the next two months, during which time the UNC conducted a series of limited-objective attacks that pushed the front line north an average of fifteen miles. In the mean-time, Ridgway had been fighting a less visible, but no less hotly contested battle with Rhee. The old patriot was adamantly opposed to a truce of any kind. In mid-July, Rhee pressed Ridgway to continue the war to vic-tory. Van Fleet alerted Ridgway to "rumors to the effect that the ROK Army was prepared in the event of any settlement along the 38th parallel, to continue the fighting regardless of the consequences." Ridgway then reminded Rhee that "if the UN troops were withdrawn from Korea, the country would be united in slavery."[21] Truman warned Rhee that "it is of the utmost importance that your Government takes no unilateral action which would jeopardize the armistice discussions."[22] Truman implied that should Rhee continue to oppose the talks or threaten unilateral action, the U.S. and other UN forces were prepared to withdraw from Korea. Temporarily chastised, Rhee nevertheless continued to disrupt the armistice talks in other ways, hoping that the UN team's mounting frustration with the communists would eventually lead to the end of the negotiations and a resumption of an all-out effort to "win" the war.

Meanwhile, other nations, especially the British, were pulling Washington in the opposite direction, urging a more flexible stance to get the talks moving and an armistice signed.[23] India proposed that the foreign ministers of the major powers meet to get the talks back on track.[24] While the Truman administration had no intention of broadening the number of participants in the negotiations, Washington was also aware that the longer the talks dragged on, the greater the pressure of "world opinion" to resolve matters quickly. To make matters even more complicated, Ridgway insisted that the site of negotiations be moved from Kaesŏng to a neutral zone. The communists refused, accusing the Americans of "creating a pretext for breaking off negotiations." The impasse finally ended in early October when the Chinese agreed to move the venue to P'anmunjŏm, south of Kaesŏng, in no-man's land between the two sides. The talks resumed later in October, with the truce-line issue at the top of the agenda. Despite pressure from the allies, Ridgway showed no flexibility in terms that now included the return of Kaesŏng to UN control in exchange for territory on the east coast.[25]

Facing another deadlock, the communists made a surprising offer. In what many rightly viewed as a breakthrough and a major concession, they offered to accept the battle line, instead of the 38th parallel, as the truce line, provided the UN agreed to its implementation immediately. In effect, they proposed that the fighting stop before other issues are resolved and an armistice is put into effect. The UN team rejected the offer. Suspending all military operations would mean a de facto ceasefire, which would end any leverage the UN might have to influence the communists' behavior. "The agreement to this proposal," argued Ridgway, "would provide an insurance policy under which the communists would be insured against the effects of the UNC military operation during the discussions of other items on the agenda."[26] If the proposal was accepted, the communists could indefinitely drag on negotiations on the remaining agenda items without fear of UN military reprisal.

Washington was upset at Ridgway's rejection. The UN team's rigid position threatened to drag the war on unnecessarily and was affecting public support for it. An opinion poll in October 1951 revealed that 67 percent agreed with the proposition that the war in Korea was "utterly useless." Senator Robert Taft (Ohio), a Republican presidential candidate for 1952, attacked the administration: "Stalemated peace is better than a stalemated war . . . we had better curtail our losses of 2,000 casualties a week in a war that can't accomplish anything."[27] The British, America's most important ally, in particular, were concerned by what they perceived as "American intransigence."

With public and official opinion in the United States and abroad swinging in support of the communist proposal, the State–Defense committee that oversaw the negotiations in Washington informed Ridgway, through the JCS, of the following: "Throughout we have taken as basic principle that the demarcation line should be generally along the battle line. Communists now appear to have accepted this principle. We feel that in general this adequately meets our minimum position re DMZ [demilitarized zone]." Regarding Ridgway's concern that the communists would drag on the negotiations indefinitely while a de facto cease-fire was in effect, the message proposed provisional acceptance "qualified by a time limitation for completion of all agenda items."[28] This meant that the truce line would become void if an armistice was not completed within the deadline.

But Ridgway was still not amenable. He was convinced that without the leverage of constant UN military pressure, the communists would lose a sense of urgency and incentive to make progress in the talks and would continue to strengthen their forces during the respite. The service chiefs disagreed. They felt that the provisional truce was not a de facto cease-fire and certainly did not affect air and naval actions. The truce-line agreement was finalized on November 27 over Ridgway's strong objections. It would expire if other issues were not finalized by December 27. After nearly six months of frustrating negotiations, the first significant agreement had finally been reached. The talks now turned to the remaining agenda items: an armistice enforcement mechanism and the exchange of POWs.

Voluntary Repatriation

Admiral Joy requested an exchange of POW rosters and immediate admission of representatives from the International Committee of the

Red Cross (ICRC) to the communist POW camps. Neither side knew the names or precise number of prisoners held by the other side. Ridgway was initially instructed to seek a POW exchange on a one-for-one basis until all UN prisoners had been returned, and then repatriate the remaining communist prisoners. But there were problems with this scheme. Dean Rusk pointed out that the UNC held about 150,000 prisoners, mostly North Koreans, compared to "less than 10,000 United Nations personnel in enemy hands," and thus the repatriation of all communist POWs "would virtually restore intact to North Korean forces equivalent to the number it possessed at the time of the aggression."[29] This was a moot point under the Geneva Convention, which required repatriation of all POWs by the detaining powers. Although the United States had yet to ratify the 1949 convention, it felt bound to abide by its provisions. However, there was undoubtedly a desire to find a way to limit or delay the reconstitution of the NKPA. Ambassador Muccio raised a related point to Acheson: the long-standing ROK claim that forty thousand of the POWs were South Koreans who had been forced to serve in the NKPA.[30] But how could one distinguish between a genuine and committed North Korean soldier, an anticommunist North Korean conscript, an impressed South Korean civilian, a North Korean who may pretend to be an impressed South Korean, and a pro-North South Korean who had willingly joined the NKPA but claimed otherwise? The situation was further complicated, because at least half of the Chinese prisoners appeared to have been former Nationalist soldiers who were impressed into the CPV.

Brigadier General Robert McClure, the U.S. Army chief of psychological warfare, suggested that prisoners be repatriated voluntarily. Citing moral and humanitarian considerations, McClure was concerned that Koreans and Chinese who had been impressed into the NKPA and the CPV would be "sentenced to slave labor, or executed" upon their return. He pointed out the propaganda value of allowing prisoners to choose where they wanted to be repatriated. A significant number of Chinese prisoners seeking repatriation to Taiwan instead of China "would be a formidable boon to Washington's Asian policies."[31] Furthermore, "if word of it got around, it might encourage other disaffected Chinese soldiers to surrender."[32]

The plan was forwarded to the National Security Council. Acheson vigorously objected to it. While he recognized "the possible psychological warfare advantages of the proposed policy," it was "difficult to see how such a policy could be carried out without conflict with the provisions of the 1949 Geneva Convention which the United States and the Unified Command has expressed its intention of observing in the Korean conflict."[33] The Geneva article pertaining to the treatment of POWs required that all "prisoners of war shall be released and repatriated without delay after the cessation of hostilities."[34] There the matter would probably have died had it not been for Truman's strong interest in the issue. Truman opposed an all-for-all exchange since it was "not on an equitable basis." Nor did he want to send back prisoners who had surrendered or cooperated with the United Nations, "because he believed they [would] be immediately done away with." Truman's position was strongly supported by a State Department counselor, Charles Bohlen, who "personally witnessed the anguish of Russian prisoners forcibly returned home from German prison camps at the end of World War II, many of whom committed suicide rather than reencounter Stalinism."[35] Truman's position, tinged with emotionalism and humanitarianism as well as cold war ideology, violated the Geneva Convention, which had no provisions for either the need for equity in the number of POWs exchanged or exceptions to the all-for-all arrangement. In retrospect, the Geneva code was too black and white, a reaction to the huge numbers of unrepatriated and abused German and Japanese POWs held by the Soviet Union after the end of World War II and the forcible repatriation of Soviet prisoners who did not want to go back and wound up executed. It did not consider the possibility that some POWs did not want or could not be repatriated for legitimate reasons.[36]

But many had reservations about voluntary repatriation. The JCS pointed out that the enemy POWs had been captured while they fought against UN forces, and thus "we had no obligation to let them express their wishes, much less give the other side any pretext for retaining UN troops."[37] General Bradley favored returning all prisoners, "including, even if necessary, the 44,000 ROK personnel [forcibly impressed into the NKPA]."[38] Ridgway was also against voluntary repatriation: "We [the UN team] believe that if we insist on the principle of voluntary repatriation, we may establish a dangerous precedent that may be to our disadvantage in later wars with communist powers," he argued. "Should they ever hold a preponderance of POWs, and then adhere to their adamant stand against any form of neutral visit to their POW camps, we would have no recourse if they said none of our POWs wanted to be repatriated."[39] In early December it was agreed that, at least initially, the UN maintain its position on one-for-one exchange, which would allow the UNC to retain certain classes of prisoners who did not wish repatriation.

The POW rosters were exchanged in mid-December, and each side had cause to complain. North Korea had boasted of capturing over 65,000 ROK prisoners in the early months of the war, and by the end of 1951 the ROK Army identified over 88,000 missing, and yet the North Korean roster contained the names of a little over 7,000 ROK POWs. Part of the discrepancy could be accounted for by the thousands of former ROK Army soldiers who were classified as North Koreans and were therefore among the NKPA POWs. Still, there were tens of thousands who remained unaccounted for. Furthermore, the 4,400 UN POWs listed by the Communists contrasted sharply with the nearly 12,000 Americans and several thousand other UN soldiers identified as missing.[40] Likewise, the communists protested that over 40,000 of their soldiers were missing from the UN list. They claimed 188,000 missing while the UN roster listed only 132,000 (95,000 North Koreans, 21,000 Chinese, and 16,000 South Koreans who joined the NKPA). The UNC claimed that 37,000 were determined to be South Korean civilians impressed into the NKPA and were reclassified as civilian internees and thus not included on the roster. The communists protested "that it was not the place of residence but the army in which a man served that determined whether he should be repatriated or not."[41] While both sides cried foul, the striking disparity in the number of POWs made one thing clear: the communists were unlikely to accept the proposal for an initial one-for-one exchange, followed by repatriation of the remaining prisoners. A decision was therefore made to put the voluntary repatriation principle on the table.

The proposal was introduced in early January 1952, with a predictably explosive reaction from the other side. Maj. Gen. Yi Sang-ch'o, a member of the communist delegation, branded the proposal as "a barbarous formula and a shameful design," which they "absolutely cannot accept."[42] The communists accused the UNC of forcibly holding prisoners and "bluntly violat[ing] the regulations of the Geneva Joint Pledge on POWs' Rights."[43] After weeks of acrimonious exchange, Joy gloomily concluded that "the commies will never give up in their determination to bring about the unconditional release and repatriation of all of their POWs."[44] The thirty-day time limit on the truce line expired on December 27. As Ridgway had feared, the communists had rested and strengthened their forces during the month-long respite. It appeared that the continuation of a stalemated war was inevitable.

With another deadlock, voluntary repatriation faced, according to U. Alexis Johnson, a "serious rearguard defection in the Pentagon."[45] Robert Lovett, who had become secretary of defense in September 1951 after Marshall retired, searched for another solution. Admiral William Fechteler, chief of Naval Operations, and General Hoyt Vandenberg, air force chief of staff, were now firmly opposed to voluntary repatriation. Joy also expressed doubts, believing that the communists would never concede on the issue. He raised the ethical issue of a policy that would prolong the suffering of American POWs instead of seeking their immediate release: "Voluntary repatriation placed the welfare of ex-communist soldiers above that of our own United Nations Command personnel in communist prison camps"[46] However, with Truman still adamantly in favor with the support of the State Department, Lovett agreed not to oppose the idea when discussing it with the president.[47] Prime Minister Churchill, who replaced Attlee in October, also agreed with voluntary repatriation for the same reasons Truman wanted it, and played a key role in building a consensus for the policy in the international community. Other European leaders were concerned about the legality and practical implementation of voluntary repatriation, but key allies from the British Commonwealth, Canada and Australia in particular, were assuaged in their doubts by Churchill's strong support. Doubters also included British Foreign Secretary Anthony Eden, who reminded Churchill that humanitarianism worked both ways and that British prisoners should not be forgotten. How could the British government back a policy that would seek to put the welfare of communist prisoners before that of their own citizens languishing in enemy camps? Churchill, however, was undeterred. In time, Eden came around. "I did not know that our legal grounds were so poor," he wrote at the time, "but this doesn't make me like the idea of sending these poor devils back to death any worse."[48]

The crucial challenge was selling it to the communists. The first task

North Korean prisoners who wanted to remain in the South, June 25, 1952.
(U.S. NATIONAL ARCHIVES AND RECORDS ADMINISTRATION)

was to find out how many communist POWs would opt for repatriation. U. Alexis Johnson, who was visiting Ridgway in early February, wrote, "Hints dropped by communist correspondents at Panmunjom, and other data led us to believe that, as Ridgway put it, numbers and nationalities of the POWs returned, rather than the principles involved, appears to be the controlling issue."[49] If the number of those wanting repatriation was high enough, the communists might be amenable. Ridgway's staff estimated that about 16,000 would choose not to be repatriated, leaving about 116,000 who would.[50] When the communists were given these figures in early April, they did not balk and instead proposed that the issue be deferred until both sides determined the exact number of prisoners to be exchanged. The UNC had reached a point of no return. By agreeing to carry out the screening process, the UNC was now fully committed to the principle of voluntary repatriation and would henceforth be honor-bound not to return those who had identified themselves as anticommunists.

The results of the UN screening were as unexpected as they were astonishing. "Our procedures," recalled Johnson, "were actually designed to favor repatriation. Within the camps, we publicized a command offer of amnesty to all POWs who chose repatriation, stressing that refusing to go home might open their relatives to reprisals, made clear that those refusing repatriation might have to stay on Kŏje Island [UNC POW camp] long after others had gone home, and promised nothing about what eventually would become of them." The screening revealed that only 70,000, a little over half, wanted to return home, rather than the estimated 116,000. The communists angrily denounced the result when informed of it in late April. With the number of non-repatriates so large, even Johnson admitted, "The possibility of their ever accepting voluntary repatriation seemed remote."[51] Eager to keep the talks going, the UN team responded that they were prepared to return all 70,000 immediately in exchange for the 12,000 UN POWs in an all-for-all arrangement. As for those who did not want repatriation, it was proposed that they be screened again by a neutral international organization.

The communists refused, recessing the talks indefinitely. "We believed that world opinion needed to follow closely what was going on at the negotiations," wrote Chai Chengwen, a staff member of the communist delegation. "The people who wanted an early end to the war should know where the obstacles really lay." On May 9, 1952, the *People's Daily* published a prominent editorial where "voluntary repatriation" was interpreted as "forced repatriation" *against* the communist side. "They said that releasing all the prisoners would mean enhancement of our military manpower," observed Chai. "Our answer was that the Americans' argument showed that what they really were concerned with was not prisoners' rights and happiness, but competition in combat forces and military power."[52] The situation seemed insoluble. Sending back those who did not want to be repatriated would mean certain death or imprisonment. The impasse meant either an indefinite prolongation of the existing stalemate or renewed attempts to end the war quickly through drastic action. "So there we sit," wrote a sullen Walter Lippmann, "or rather, there sit the unhappy prisoners of war, waiting."[53]

CHAPTER TEN

"Let Them March Till They Die"

The first large group of Western prisoners was captured in early July 1950. Among them were fifty-eight Western missionaries, including Rev. Larry Zellers, a Methodist missionary from Texas who had come to Korea fresh out of college to teach English at the Methodist Mission in Kaesŏng, and Bishop Patrick Byrne, an American who along with his secretary, Father William Booth, had willingly stayed in Korea when the war started. "Byrne's only concern was with the question of where he could serve the Church best," recalled Father Philip Crosbie, an Australian who was captured at Ch'unch'ŏn. "Since a Church overrun by communists would have more need of such aid as he could offer, he decided to remain in his headquarters in Seoul."[1] Father Byrne had a remarkable record of missionary work in Japan and Korea. He was the director of the Maryknoll Mission in Kyoto when World War II started in the Pacific, but he was not detained by the Japanese. When the war ended he was transferred to Korea to become the bishop.[2]

Commissioner Herbert Arthur Lord, a fluent Korean speaker, had come to Korea in 1909 at the age of twenty-one, on the eve of Japan's annexation of Korea. In 1935, he was sent to British Malaya and then to Singapore, where he was taken prisoner by the Japanese in 1942 and interned until the end of the war. He returned to Korea in 1949, nearly sixty years old, to run the Salvation Army branch there. At the outbreak of the war, he remained in Seoul to continue his work. He, along with the French missionaries Father Paul Villemot, Mother Beatrix Edouard, and Mother Eugenie Demeusy, was taken into custody by the North Koreans in early July. Father Villemot was eighty-two years old and in poor health. Mother Beatrix was a frail woman of seventy-six who had spent most of her life in Korea looking after Korean orphans. Within days of the invasion, these Western missionaries found themselves in a school located on the outskirts of P'yŏngyang that had been transformed into a concentration camp for prisoners.

They were soon joined by over seven hundred American soldiers. Among them was Maj. John Dunn, who had been captured at Ch'ŏnan. At the camp, Dunn met Capt. Ambrose Nugent, who had been taken prisoner near Osan. Nugent had been beaten, starved, threatened, and marched on foot from Seoul. He was forced to take part in the first of many propaganda broadcasts that would later haunt him after the war. In early October, the prisoners were moved north to the city of Manp'o. They were aware that something dramatic had happened. News filtered in that UN forces had landed at Inch'ŏn and were moving north. Elated, they thought they would be freed any day, and excitedly prepared for liberation. "We took it for granted that our captors would keep us in Manp'o until the United Nations Forces could reach us," recalled Father Crosbie. "It seemed that the only other way they could prevent our early liberation would be to take us across the Yalu to Chinese territory, and we reasoned that the Chinese would not want us on their hands."[3] Much to their surprise and disappointment, however, they were told that they would be going north with the retreating NKPA. The North Koreans, it seems, had use for them.

Death March

After P'yŏngyang was captured by UN forces in mid-October, the prisoners were marched to the Yalu River to go by boat to a village more than a hundred miles away. But the boats never arrived. "The organizing abilities of our captors were the subject of much bitter criticism as we plodded back with our loads to our old home," recalled Father Crosbie.[4] In Manp'o they met their new commandant, known simply as "The Tiger." For the next nine days, the prisoners would endure a bitter ordeal that left few survivors. The Death March, as it later became known, began with a warning from the Tiger. On the evening of October 31, he told the prisoners that they had a long walk ahead of them and that they must proceed in military formation. Commissioner Lord voiced concerns for the entire group. "He pointed out that many of the party would find it impossible to march like soldiers, and at a

military pace; that for some the attempt would surely be fatal." The
Tiger roared, "Then let them march till they die! That is a military
order."[5] And so, at dusk, the prisoners—diplomats, soldiers, elderly
missionaries, women, and seven children, all captured at the start of the
war—set out on a march toward Chung'an-ni. No one was prepared or
equipped to handle a long march or deal with the approaching winter.
Nearly everyone was still wearing the same summer clothes they had
worn when captured in July. Major Green, who had been captured with
Nugent and Dunn near Osan, recalled that "a lot of the guys didn't
have clothing and a lot of them were barefooted, and a lot of people
had dysentery." "We began in the evening," recalled Father Booth. "We
camped in a cornfield not far outside of Manp'o. It was bitterly cold
at the time and we slept, or tried to sleep, on the ground." The next
morning it began to snow. Chilled to the bone, the first of many prisoners began to fall out. Nugent recalled that "the merciless pressure
was especially weakening for the many who were suffering from severe
dysentery, which seemed to be rife among the GIs." When the marching
finally stopped for the day, the prisoners had to spend another night in
the open, huddling against each other for warmth.[6]

Over the next few days, more prisoners, too weak to go on, were left
by the side of the road. When the Tiger saw what was happening, he
halted the march. The prisoners had been organized into five groups,
with an American officer responsible for each. The Tiger ordered the
group leaders to step forward and told the five men they would be executed for disobeying orders. Lord pleaded for their lives, explaining that
the guards had given permission to leave behind those who could not
keep up and that they would be picked up later by oxcarts. The Tiger
scoffed and decided to execute one of the officers and singled out Lt.
Cordus Thornton of Longview, Texas. As he stepped forward, Thornton whispered to Lord, "Save me if you can, sir." In a scene burned into
the memory of everyone on the Death March, the Tiger convened an
impromptu court-martial, found him guilty, and pronounced death. One
witness vividly recalled what happened:

> "There, you have your trial," The Tiger announced. "In Texas, sir, we
> would call that a lynching," Lieutenant Thornton responded . . . The
> Tiger asked Thornton if he wished to be blindfolded. Hearing an affirma-
> tive answer, The Tiger handed a small towel to a guard. Another towel

was used to tie the victim's hands . . . The Tiger moved smartly to face the victim and ordered him to turn around. Pausing for a moment, The Tiger pushed up the back of Thornton's fur hat. But like Father Crosbie, I had seen too much already; my eyes snapped shut just before The Tiger fired his pistol into the back of Thornton's head. When I opened my eyes, I saw that the brave young man lay still without even a tremor. The Tiger knew his business well. Quickly putting away his pistol, The Tiger called for Commissioner Lord to come to his side and translate. "You have just witnessed the execution of a bad man. This move will help us work together better in peace and harmony." In that brief speech, The Tiger managed to outrage both the living and the dead.[7]

Thornton's death had a salutary effect on the prisoners. Perhaps it was the sheer bravery and dignity with which Thornton had faced his death that inspired them. During the long march many showed great acts of kindness. Monsignor Thomas Quinlan and someone else assisted Father Charles Hunt, a large Anglican priest with a foot problem who found it difficult to keep up with the march. "Monsignor and his partner were supporting Father Hunt's upper body, while the lower lagged behind about three feet"[8] Natalya Funderat, "a stout Polish woman who was having great difficulty keeping up, was helped for a time by Commissioner Lord, who tied a rope around her waist and pulled her along like a farmer with an ox."[9] Sagid, a seventeen-year-old Turkish boy, was lugging a large suitcase full of clothes for his youngest brother, Hamid. He was the oldest of six children of the Salahudtin family, who had come to Korea as traders. All of them walked except Hamid, who was just one year old. Father Byrne had come down with a serious cold. At night, the others tried their best to warm him with their bodies and protect him from the winter air. The French consul and his staff carried Mother Beatrix for a time. By the fourth day the old woman simply could not go on. When the Korean guards pushed the old woman to get up, Mother Eugenie pleaded with them. She told them the woman they were beating "was seventy-six years old and had spent nearly fifty of those years in caring for the sick and the poor orphans of their country." Her appeals were in vain. She was executed for exhaustion.[10]

After nine days the group arrived at Chung'an-ni, later known as Camp 7, where they were quartered in an old school. By then, winter had arrived and temperatures dropped to below freezing. Surveying the sick and dying prisoners, the Tiger believed that exercise would cure their health problems, and ordered everyone outside the next morning. Lord and Quinlan vainly tried to reason with the Tiger that exercise under such conditions was madness. The Tiger responded by placing his pistol to Lord's head. Father Villemot was carried out into the freezing cold even though he could barely stand. He weakly went through the motions but died three days later. The Combert brothers, both French priests, who had arrived in Korea at the turn of the century, died two days later. More deaths followed. Father Byrne died on November 25. Father Canavan told the others, "I'll have my Christmas dinner in heaven" and passed away on December 6. Almost everyone was suffering from dysentery. The room that Major Green occupied was so crowded that when the guards wouldn't let people out, they ended up defecating on themselves and on the people around them. Beatings were also a regular occurrence. Green recalled that "one of their favorite methods was to have a man kneel and kick him in his chin, and they took some of the guys that they got it in for and would make them kneel down against the building and butt their heads against the building till they gave out, fell over."[11] But more than the starvation diet, the illness, the continual beatings, and the deplorable sanitary conditions, it was the "merciless grinding down of men, the dehumanizing process that went on, the attempt to turn human beings into sheep" that Father Crosbie recalled most vividly.[12] Many of the prisoners began to lose the will to live. Camp 7 was the first of many POW camps that sprang up along the Manchurian border during the winter of 1950–51. But unlike other camps, which would be administered by the Chinese or jointly by the North Koreans and the Chinese, Camp 7 was run solely by the North Koreans at least until October 1951. The death rate was appalling. Approximately two-thirds of the 750 men, women, and children who marched in October were dead by the following spring.[13] At this rate, no prisoners would soon be left alive at Camp 7.

Valley Camp to Camp 5

While Major Dunn, Captain Nugent, Father Booth, and other prisoners were out in the cold cornfields near Manp'o at the end of October, Maj. Harry Fleming, an American regimental advisor in the ROK Sixth

Division, reached the Yalu. He was the only American during the war to look across the Yalu into China. Farther south, another advisor was fighting for his life. Major Paul Liles had only recently arrived in Korea and was assigned to advise a sister regiment to Fleming's in the ROK Sixth Division. Liles reached his regiment while the unit was heavily engaged with the Chinese. "The first battle with the Chinese was already going on when I arrived," he later recalled. "The battle went on all night … and the next morning it became obvious that we were cut off by a road block in the rear." The ROK soldiers panicked at being surrounded, and the regiment soon fell apart. Liles was able to evade the Chinese for three days, but then was captured.[14]

Meanwhile, Fleming was contemplating victory as he stood on the banks of the Yalu. He firmly believed that the war was over. "I listened to the radio from Seoul," he recalled later. "I heard speeches that were being made as to the tremendous victory by the United Nations in Korea, and our morale was pretty good." That afternoon, however, Fleming received the disturbing message that "[someone] told me that the Second Regiment [Liles's], which was my support regiment, had been completely decimated in battle, with great loss, and that my regiment was to return to a place called Unsan which was about 75 miles to our rear, and there, rejoin the Division." As news of the disaster began to hit him, he realized how vulnerable he and the regiment really were: "We had extended our supplies and communications to the point where we just had no contact with the rear whatsoever except through radio." For the next four days, the regiment fought their way south. Surrounded and out of supplies, Fleming and his party were overtaken by a Chinese patrol. "My interpreter, a Korean by the name of Quan, hit the ground with me," Fleming recalled. Fleming had fainted temporarily but had come round just in time to see his assistant, Captain Roesch, struggling with a Chinese soldier. "He [the Chinese soldier] stood over Captain Roesch with this burp gun and opened it up into him, killed him." Shortly thereafter, Fleming was captured.[15]

Fleming was taken to a collection point called Valley Camp. Located ten miles south of the Manchurian border, the compound, like so many other camps, was originally constructed by the Japanese as living quarters for Korean miners during the colonial period. Each of the mud-walled houses, with three small rooms and a kitchen, housed roughly sixty prisoners. "This meant that the width that each individual had on the floor was so narrow that everyone on one side of the room had to lie on the same side at the same time. You could not lie on your back and when you moved everyone had to move in unison." There were about 750 men at Valley Camp. "At this time," recalled Fleming, "I had marched quite a ways, and I hadn't much to eat, and what I had had, I couldn't eat, except on very rare occasions. Water was practically non-existent." Food consisted of cracked corn twice a day and a few frozen turnips. The weather was bitterly cold. Fleming found Liles in the camp, but he was desperately ill. "At the time," recalled Fleming, "Major Liles was more dead than alive from ulcers on his legs, and a general debilitated condition." Both men agreed that while Liles was the senior officer, Fleming was physically better able to take command and organize the prisoners.[16]

The camp was jointly administered by the Chinese and the North Koreans, and the first thing Fleming did was to meet with them to seek permission to visit the entire camp. He did not get far with the North Korean commander, Maj. Kim Dong-suk. Kim insisted that the UN soldiers were not POWs, but war criminals, and should be treated as such. But the Chinese camp commander, Yuen, who was apparently the senior or at least had greater authority than his North Korean counterpart, was more pliable and agreed that Fleming could visit the various compounds within the camp to determine what was needed to improve living conditions. Fleming was shocked by his tour: "Actually the men were suffering from hunger such as we were at the time, [*sic*] were having hallucinations about food, and I actually got many requests, believe it or not, for things such as chocolate bars, or candy and other things."[17] Everything was filthy, and the men were covered in lice. All suffered from dysentery and many had pneumonia. There was also a serious discipline problem. The Chinese promoted this by causing dissent between the officers and the enlisted men. "The first statement the Chinese made to us," recalled Liles, "was that 'you are no longer members of your armed forces' and to the enlisted men they told them that they wouldn't have to follow the order of their officers."[18] In their desperate situation, however, the prisoners welcomed the strong leadership that Fleming provided.

One of the first things that Fleming did was to enforce sanitation.

The soldiers were told to relieve themselves in a make-shift latrine instead of anywhere, as they had been doing. Water had to be boiled before drinking it. This was a difficult rule to enforce since boiling water was time-consuming and took more energy than most could muster on their starvation diet. A lice-picking routine was also enforced. Fleming's measures soon began paying off. Of the approximately 750 prisoners at Valley Camp, only 22, or just 3 percent, died.[19] Captain Sidney Esensten testified after the war that "the morale of this camp was pretty good and I think that is why our death rate was so low."[20] But there was a price to be paid. Liles recalled, "Major Kim offered to improve rations only if the officers would sign surrender leaflets. We refused."[21] They did, however, sign a leaflet announcing the entry of the Chinese into the war. Soon there were more demands to endorse a pro-communist propaganda. "Kim repeated his warning that all who refused to cooperate would perish," Fleming later testified. "The younger, stronger officers believed that U.S. forces would arrive to rescue us in a few weeks, and we should tell Kim to go to hell." But Liles was not so sure: "I had seen on the roads, on the mountainous terrain, the complete absence of U.S. aircraft after 1 December 1950. I predicted a long hard struggle for UN forces before they could again reach the Yalu. My fellow officers called me a traitor, saying I had lost my faith in my own troops. I was more concerned with keeping myself and my men alive, however, than in preserving my own honor and reputation, priceless though it had been, because I was the senior officer."[22] The price for better treatment was the acceptance of some sort of "accommodation" with the communist authorities.

After a two-month stay at Valley Camp, the prisoners marched six miles to Camp 5 at Pyŏkdong in mid-January 1951. It was much larger than Valley Camp, accommodating approximately three thousand men. In the following months, POWs from other temporary camps were transferred to Camp 5. The majority of them came from a temporary collection site called "Death Valley," so named because of its high mortality rate. Many of the prisoners there had been captured at Kunu-ri at the end of November, where the Second U.S. Infantry Division was nearly destroyed. "The men were more or less down to an animal stage," recalled Lieutenant Erwin. "They would sit and watch with a wolfish look and if a man was unable to eat, or anything like that, they would always grab it away from him."[23] Men died rapidly at Camp 5. "The camp held about 3,200 by the end of January 1951," Liles later said. "At this time, the death rate at Pyŏkdong (Camp 5) was 7 per day average, and the corpses were collected by a Korean bullock cart, reminding me of stories of the Great Plague in London."[24]

Unlike Valley Camp, Camp 5 was administered only by the Chinese. The conditions, however, were far worse, and once again Fleming began the task of organizing the men to care for themselves. Many compounds did not establish a common latrine. Starvation was making men unruly, hostile, and then passive. Captain Charles Howard, a survivor of Camp 5, recalled, "You don't think as clearly as you would under normal conditions. A man's instinct goes back to self-preservation and I know my own personal thoughts were devoted mostly to food. I didn't think too much about home or my wife, family, because I was primarily interested in food."[25] Some men eventually had no desire for food or life and simply laid down and died. Despite the dire conditions, Fleming attempted to bring order and discipline to alleviate the situation. He organized details to make clean water available, sleeping arrangements so the men would have equitable sleeping space, and a kitchen to control rations so all would have their fair share.[26]

In late January, Major Kim, the former commandant of Valley Camp, made an unexpected visit. He told the Chinese commandant that he needed twenty prisoners to take with him to P'yŏngyang for ten days to make radio broadcasts. Although the prisoners had already guessed at Kim's sinister motivations, he assured them that those selected for the trip would be able to broadcast letters to their families. He also promised that they could broadcast the names of the POWs in Camp 5. This was especially enticing to the prisoners, since the North Koreans had not yet released such a list to the ICRC. Ten officers and ten enlisted men, including Liles and Fleming, were selected. Among the other officers were Lieutenant Erwin and Captain Galing, both of whom had come to Camp 5 from Death Valley, and Capt. Clifford Allen, a black officer who had recently arrived at Camp 5 from Bean Camp, another notorious collection center where an estimated 280 of 900 prisoners had died. As dawn broke on the cold winter day of January 30, 1951, the twenty prisoners from Camp 5 set off by truck for the 110-mile ride to P'yŏngyang. They would not return to Pyŏkdong until nearly a year later.

Camp 10

While prisoners at Camp 5 and Camp 7 were slowly starving to death, another group of captured soldiers were in a comparatively better situation. In December 1950 about 250 prisoners captured at the Changjin Reservoir were brought to Kanggye, where they were housed in what once was a large village. There were no barbed wires or any enclosures around Camp 10, only a Chinese soldier who stood guard at each house. Camp 10 was administered solely by the Chinese. The prisoners were provided sufficient food, clothing, and medical attention to sustain a reasonably comfortable life. Only twelve prisoners at Kanggye died, most from battle wounds, between December 1950 and March 1951, a remarkable figure considering that nearly twice that many prisoners died every day at Death Valley and seven daily at Camp 5 during the same period. The reason for the high survival rate at Camp 10, however, had less to do with Chinese benevolence than with experimentation of new methods of thought and behavior modification. The Chinese wanted to know whether they could turn loyal UN soldiers into loyal communists. These experiments, later popularized in the Western press as "brainwashing," attempted to control the prisoners' minds through psychological pressure, social conditioning, and reward. The articles published in the camp newsletter, *New Life*, starting in January 1951, contained pro-communist and anti-American themes. The experiment seemed to be working. The newsletter featured articles like "Truman a Swindler," "Truth about the Marshall Plan," "We Were Paid Killers," and "Capitalism and Its Aims," and appeared to have been written by the prisoners voluntarily. With "proper" guidance and training, it seemed that UN soldiers could be transformed into pliant communists. At least, this is what the Chinese believed, and they diligently set about working with the prisoners at Camp 10 to accomplish this task.

Prisoners at Camp 10 were told that they were not prisoners but "students," that "they were fools for being in Korea, for being duped into it, and had no business there." The Chinese dangled the idea of early release, "the quicker you learn what we have to teach you, the sooner you will be released and sent back to your lines."[27] The men were organized into ten-man squads, each with a leader who was responsible for overseeing the group's "education." Private Theodore Hilburn of the First Marine Division later testified, "[The squad leaders] would give us these papers and books and they would mark off a column for us to read and study and he [Camp Commandant Pan] would have the squad leader read to us and then would have us discuss it. They called it going to school."[28] The prisoners were also required to attend larger meetings run by the Chinese. The first such meeting occurred on December 22 with a Christmas party for the prisoners. They were given hot white rice and pork, an expensive treat given that the Chinese soldiers on the front had far worse rations. "The party was held in a large warehouse," recalled Marine Sgt. Leonard Maffioli. "They had a banner tacked up on all four walls with 'Fight For Peace' and such slogans as that. They had two Christmas trees with little candles burning on them."[29]

The Chinese also distributed presents, a few pieces of candy, a handful of peanuts, and a pack of cigarettes. Music was played. Some of the prisoners even danced. After the festivities, the Chinese asked for volunteers to give a speech. Master Sergeant William Olson, a veteran of Omaha Beach in Normandy in 1944 who had served in the army for seventeen years, was the first to stand up. Olson told the assembled POWs that they were lucky to have been captured by the Chinese, who had given them food, warm clothing, and tobacco. Conditions at the camp were far better than what Allied POWs had experienced under the Nazis. He praised China's lenient policy and thanked his captors. The speech was short, but it elicited considerable reactions among those who heard it. "I was shocked to tell the truth," recalled Master Sgt. Chester Mathis, "that he would get up and talk like that in that short a period because we hadn't received any indoctrinations or lectures to speak of, and I was really amazed."[30] Lieutenant Charles Harrison recounted, "There seemed to be a general feeling of anger, confusion and distrust amongst everybody."[31] The following week, parts of Olson's speech, entitled "If the Millionaires Want War, Let Them Take up the Guns and Do the Fighting Themselves," was published in *New Life*:

> The Germans were Christians. But they did not allow us to spend our Christmas happily. The Chinese do not observe Christmas, but they have arranged this fine party for us. The Nazis beat their prisoners. They spat on us and forced us to stand for intolerably long hours at a time. Some of us who could not stand this torture would urinate in their trousers. BUT

THE CHINESE HAVE GIVEN US WARM CLOTHES, BED-
DING AND EVEN HAND TOWELS. THEY HAVE SHARED
THEIR FOOD WITH US AND GIVEN US THE BEST THEY
HAD. This has taught me a lot of things, I can tell you. When I get home
this time, they would not get me in the army again. If the millionaires want
war, let them take up guns and do the fighting themselves.[32]

Many prisoners wrote articles for *New Life*. The general approach to
the indoctrination program was to do just enough to survive. "I think I
could best explain this passive attitude in the little bits of advice that
we were able to get from Major McLaughlin," recalled Harrison. "He
told us that to save lives he saw nothing wrong with going along with
the program to a certain extent."[33] To McLaughlin, the senior officer
at Camp 10, the articles appearing in *New Life* were merely a "parody
of Communist ideology." None of the prisoners were physically threat-

American POWs at an unidentified camp, undated. (U.S. ARMY MILITARY HISTORY INSTITUTE)

ened. "There were no threats of violence," recalled Joseph Hammond, "just subtle hints that if we learned and studied their so-called truth, we would be released to go home."[34] On March 1, after four months, Camp 10 was closed, and the remaining prisoners were transferred to other POW camps. The experiment appeared to be a success. Prisoners would cooperate with the right amount of pressure and incentives applied incrementally and persistently. Plans were made to expand the "reeducation" program to other camps.

Camp 12

Fleming, Liles, Allen, and the other seventeen prisoners from Camp 5 arrived in P'yŏngyang on February 1. Over the next several months, they were interned in various locations in and around the capital city and then settled at Camp 12. They had to attend "indoctrination" classes for three weeks and, as at Camp 10, conduct daily readings and discussions. But conditions were much worse than those at Camp 10. Fleming recalled, "It was through these conditions of life, these predatory conditions of life I should say, that the communists reduced us to a very, very servile state; where they almost got us to the point that we would do anything they wanted us to do, because we had nothing to fall back on, no strength left, and no source of strength. When a man is sick and starving and freezing, he loses his ability to rationalize."[35]

After the indoctrination period the prisoners were asked to make propaganda radio broadcasts. Fleming stated that they were told "that anyone who refused would be marched back to Pyŏkdong [Camp 5], which was a distance of 160 miles. In our weakened condition, it was tantamount to death." Everyone agreed to make the broadcasts, although only five, including Fleming, were selected to participate. The main theme was that "the United States foreign policy should return to that of the Roosevelt era of 'good-will all over the world'." Liles later testified that "the broadcast was cleverly written by Major Fleming and was purposely very vague and nebulous."[36] To the prisoners' great disappointment, they were unable either to broadcast the names of POWs at Camp 5 as had been promised or to read letters to their families.

The prisoners at Camp 12 were the victims of the most intense indoctrination pressure endured by any POW in North Korea. Between February and December 1951, POWs at Camp 12 made over two hundred propaganda radio broadcasts. Some contained outright lies, such as Fleming's statement that all POWs had received treatment that "[was] in strict accordance with the principles of humanity and democracy." Other broadcasts were critical of the United States, accusing it of a "grave error in interfering in Korean internal affairs" and demanding that UN forces "should leave at once." An appeal "inviting UN troops to surrender and promising kind treatment by the communists" was broadcast in late spring during the Chinese offensive. A broadcast in mid-December addressed an Eighth Army report (Hanley Report) that accused the Chinese of killing 2,513 American POWs and 250 other UN prisoners since November 1950 and the North Koreans of killing at least 25,000 South Korean POWs and 10,000 North Korean "reactionaries." Outraged by the report, which later proved accurate, the Chinese forced the prisoners at Camp 12 to denounce it. Most, if not all, of the POWs later profoundly regretted what they had done. Major Clifford testified after the war, "I was ashamed of the whole recording. I was very pointedly, very, very pointedly, ashamed of any portion of the recording that referred to the Korean War. So far as my name and identity was concerned, I shouldn't have even done that."[37]

There was a constant fear of being purged. Nothing frightened the men at Camp 12 more than the threat of being sent to a camp known as "The Caves."[38] Lieutenant Bonnie Bowling described the Caves as a place of horror where prisoners were sent to die. "The conditions were such that I don't know anyone who stayed there more than six months and survived," recalled Capt. Lawrence Miller.[39] Lieutenant Chester Van Orman remembered passing the camp on his way to get rations: "There were many Korean, South Korean, bodies that were frozen and laid up on the ground over the entrance of the caves."[40] Captain Allen remembered the Caves as nothing more than "holes in the ground with mounds of dirt piled on top." The prisoners there "were skeletons, living skeletons or walking corpses . . . The Caves was a place where life absolutely could not be maintained."[41] Captain Anthony Farrar-Hockley of the Glosters was one of a handful who survived the Caves. After his capture during the battle at Imjin River, and several failed escape attempts that led to a stay at the notorious interrogation and torture center called Pak's Palace, where two of his ribs were cracked under torture, the British officer was brought to the Caves. "Except when their two daily meals of boiled maize were handed through the opening," wrote Farrar-Hockley later, "they [the prisoners] sat in almost total darkness. A subterranean stream ran through the cave to add to their discomfort, and, in these conditions, it was often difficult to distinguish the dead from the dying."[42] The exact number of men who died will never be known.

The beginning of the armistice talks in July 1951 brought significant changes in the treatment of the POWs. There was now concern over the number of POW deaths. The communists realized that if conditions were not changed, few, if any, prisoners would be alive by the time the armistice was signed. "The only time we started getting food," recalled Lt. Col. John Dunn from Camp 7, "was after we were turned over to the Chinese, and that was after the peace talks had started. Up to that time, we were practically living on nothing." He added, "When they were winning the war, they were a pack of raving animals. They had no respect for anything and would not hesitate a moment about killing a man . . . The period up until the time these negotiations started was characterized by mass starvation . . . After that period, they just started feeding people."[43] By the end of 1951, when POW rosters were exchanged, deaths at the camps had all but ceased. "Life at Camp 5 seemed pretty good," according to Liles, who had returned after Camp 12 was disbanded in December. "Food was excellent (compared to what we had been eating). POWs got rice, steamed bread, pork and potato soup . . . POWs had blankets, warm winter clothes, were fat and healthy."[44] Beginning in 1952, the Chinese permitted the prisoners to write two censored letters home every month, their first communication with their families since their capture. Together with the better food, clothing, and medical care, the prisoners entered a new period of relative "normalcy" in which daily existence in the POW camps became tolerable.

As their physical conditions improved, the POWs faced a new challenge: the increasing attempt to attack their minds. The Chinese began to systematically apply lessons from Camp 10 at all camps. They pitted prisoners against each other, creating an insidious division between the so-called progressives (collaborators) and the reactionaries (recalcitrants). These divide-and-conquer tactics worked wonders for the communists, as they preyed on weaker prisoners to perform their propaganda work, which in turn exacerbated the social isolation they felt among their

This photo was taken by Wang Nai-qing, a former Chinese POW guard at Pyŏkdong (Camp 5). Although the picture is undated, it is clear that it was taken in late 1951 or sometime in 1952 when conditions in the camp had markedly improved. The prisoners are well dressed and look generally well fed and healthy. (COURTESY OF WANG NAI-QING)

peers. But the most insidious aspect of the divide-and-conquer tactics was that whoever had collaborated with the enemy in the past now found themselves stuck in the role of the so-called progressives. This included the prisoners from Camp 12, all of whom had been captured during the fall and winter of 1950–51 and therefore had experienced firsthand the horrors of the POW camps before the conditions changed for the better. For prisoners captured later on, and especially those captured after the truce talks started, it was easy to overlook the intense physical and mental deprivations of the POWs captured earlier. Moreover, almost every POW had collaborated to some degree to survive, whether it was participating in study group sessions or signing unknown documents, but censoring others as "progressives" helped many of them cleanse their own sense of guilt. Some even found a new status. Major Harold Kaschko later recollected, "In late 1952 the food and camp conditions improved sufficiently that a number of prisoners became self-proclaimed heroes, brightening their own reputation by spattering on others."[45]

Soon after Camp 12 prisoners were moved to Camp 5, Fleming, Allen, and other officers were transferred to an officer's compound, Camp 2, located about ten miles northeast of Pyŏkdong at the village of Pingchŏng-ni. Camp 2 was the only POW camp for officers. The 350 officers there were quartered in a large school that also included a spacious yard. The compound was enclosed by barbed wire and guarded by two hundred Chinese soldiers. After arriving at Camp 2, the officers from Camp 12 immediately sensed that something was wrong. They were greeted by their fellow officers with hostile, stony stares. When one of the newcomers, Maj. David McGhee, went up to a group of Americans, he was asked, sarcastically, "So how's everything in Traitors' Row?" It was an indication that the prisoners from Camp 12 would be "treated as pariahs."[46] In the case of McGhee, the question seemed particularly unfair. McGhee was a survivor of both Pak's Palace and the Caves. He had been sent to the Caves because he had refused to make broadcasts. Yet now he was labeled a collaborator and traitor simply because he had been at Camp 12. "The thing that the men held most against us," McGhee later testified, "was that we had gone to that group voluntarily, or you might say, with our eyes open. Its announced purpose was propaganda, we had volunteered to go, and it was resented specifically, or most intensely, by the company grade officers [lieutenants and captains]."[47]

Also taken by Wang Nai-qing, this photo shows UN POWs attending a typical study lecture session at Pyŏkdong (Camp 5). (COURTESY OF WANG NAI-QING)

Major Nugent, whom Liles later described as a "physical and mental wreck" at the time, was similarly disdained. Captain Waldron Berry later testified about Nugent: "I do not recall ever having spoken to him," he said contemptuously. "His reputation as a collaborator effectively precluded any conversation with him so far as I was concerned."[48] Captain John Bryant recollected that "collectively, [we] had a very low opinion of Nugent and perceived him with the same lack of trust and confidence as was reserved for other members of Traitors' Row," adding, "My personal opinion was that Nugent, or other officers who were members of Traitors' Row . . . were unfit to be officers of the United States Armed Forces."[49] The prisoners from Traitors' Row did their best to cope with the ostracization. Liles became withdrawn and depressed. Fleming also withdrew and spent most of his time in the camp "library," rarely speaking to other prisoners. Captain Allen reacted with anger: "Camp 5 and Camp 2 were living much better than Camp 12 . . . We [at Camp 12] were the worst off bunch, and still, we were the ones who were called traitors, which is a nasty name. There were a lot of loud mouths there, a lot of self-professed patriots, waving the Flag and calling other people nasty names."[50]

By early 1952, deep factional divisions within the camps had emerged. The result was a mini-war of suspicion among the prisoners that played havoc on their morale. "Throughout the thirty-two months that I was prisoner the things that we discussed or things we would plan would invariably get out to our captors," recalled Lieutenant Chester Van Orman. "It resulted in people getting mighty suspicious of one another."[51] Many thought the Chinese planted rumors or provided special treatment to a particular prisoner to arouse suspicion, to keep the prisoners divided. Only the British officers appeared to be immune from the communists' tactics. Lieutenant Sheldon Foss thought their "discipline was better than ours and they were, for the most part, a unit. I know some British officers who are still alive and to my knowledge never went along with them [the Chinese]. These included Colonel Carne, commanding officer of the Gloucestershire Regiment; Major Joseph Ryan who was with the Royal Ulster Rifles; and Major Sam Weller of the Gloucestershire Regiment."[52]

Fleming, Nugent, and many other POWs emerged from their captivity emotionally shattered and with intense resentment against communism. Commander R. M. Bagwell later noted that "on many occasions in private conversation with Fleming, we discussed the communist menace,

Major Ambrose Nugent, Fort Sill, Oklahoma, January 1955.
Nugent was court-martialed in 1955 on charges that he collaborated with the enemy by making propaganda broadcasts and
signing leaflets urging American soldiers to surrender. After the
six-week trial ended, he was cleared of all charges and promoted
to lieutenant colonel. Nugent retired from the Army in 1960 and
died in 1988 at the age of seventy-eight. (U.S. NATIONAL ARCHIVES AND
RECORDS ADMINISTRATION)

and he shared my feelings, he had an extreme dislike bordering on hatred
for any part of that system."[53] Similarly, Nugent "was outspoken in his
hatred [of the communists]," Maj. Filmore Wilson McAbee later testified.
"He appeared to have an intense, almost pathological hatred for them."[54]
Despite daily exposure to communist doctrine, very few UN prisoners
emerged from their prison camp experience transformed into communists.

Return of the Defeated

Return of the Defeated (*Toraon p'aeja*), a unique and incisive personal
account of a South Korean POW's experience, was published in 2001. Its

author, Pak Chin-hŭng, had been a soldier in the ROK Sixth Division in the very same regiment where Maj. Harry Fleming had served as its chief American advisor. It was the only UN unit to reach the Yalu River. Pak was nineteen years old when he voluntarily enlisted in the army. At the time of his enlistment he had been a first-year medical student at the Taegu medical school. Fifty years later, at the age of seventy, Pak published his memoir. It was one of a small handful of memoirs written by former South Korean POWs that began to be published in the wake of democratization in the 1990s.[55] That Pak had waited so long to write had been as much due to political necessity as personal choice. South Korea until the early 1990s was authoritarian, virulently anticommunist, and inhospitable to former South Korean soldiers who had ended up as POWs in communist prison camps. They were suspected of being sympathetic to communism or worse: being closet communist spies. South Korea's democratization allowed Pak to freely revisit his past, but he did not take much satisfaction from it. He is a man consumed by bitterness and regret at having been long rejected by the country he so loyally served.

Pak's regiment was under a Chinese onslaught in late November 1950. After two days of grueling fighting, he faced the unpleasant realization that the officers in his unit had deserted. Pak was captured by the Chinese at Tŏkch'ŏn. After being interrogated, he was marched north to a former Japanese coal mine in Hwap'ung that was used by the NKPA as a temporary holding camp for prisoners. The Chinese forced Pak to carry wounded Chinese soldiers through the arduous mountain paths, but he did not mind. He was impressed by their commitment not to leave their wounded behind. Certainly, this contrasted sharply with his own experience when his officers simply got up and abandoned him and the hundreds of wounded at Tŏkch'ŏn.

At Hwap'ung, the Chinese handed the South Korean prisoners over to the North Koreans. Living conditions were deplorable, but the North Korean guards were hardly better off. Prisoners were given just 150 poorly cooked kernels of corn per day. They were bitterly cold, sick, and starving. Nevertheless, Pak was able to take comfort in the warm camaraderie among the prisoners. "There was no discrimination based on rank, age or authority or wealth," he wrote. "We all shared equally." One day, Pak unexpectedly found a pot of salt hidden in the ceiling. This was liter-

ally manna from heaven. All the prisoners had been suffering from salt
and vitamin deficiency. He informed the others in his room and carefully
divided the salt equally among them. "I could not believe how delicious
the salt tasted," Pak later recalled. "It was unbelievably delicious. Sweet,
salty, just beyond words. I put a kernel of corn in my mouth, licked the
tip of my finger and carefully picked up one grain of salt and put it in my
mouth. We could hardly describe how delicious the corn tasted!"[56]

In January 1951, life at Hwap'ung came to an abrupt end and the prisoners made an arduous winter march north to Camp 5 in Pyŏkdong, the
same camp to which the Americans from Camp 12 would be transferred.
Pak recalled "the death march to Pyŏkdong as the most difficult time
of my life. None of us had an overcoat and the cold wind swept down
from the mountains and up the valley. We constantly fell. We had to
shorten our stride to prevent from falling, but that meant jogging rather
than walking." When they arrived, the camp was already full of prisoners.
South Korean prisoners were separated from other UN soldiers, but they
all lived under the same deplorable conditions. They were given a starvation diet of two meals a day consisting of roughly seventy corn kernels.
The death toll of South Korean prisoners was horrendous, twenty to
fifty per day according to Pak. But their deaths were not wasted. "When
someone died, all his clothes would be taken off and divided among the
living. The dead were disposed completely naked," Pak wrote. Even the
lice-infested clothing from typhoid victims was prized among the prisoners. Since typhoid is transmitted by lice, wearing these clothes was a
dangerous undertaking. Pak came up with a simple solution. Every night
he would take off one pair of clothes to hang outside, and by the morning
the lice were frozen to death. "They don't fall off easily, so I have to beat
the clothes with a stick. This is how I killed them. On very cold nights,
even the eggs died. It was much more efficient and effective than catching them by hand."[57]

In the midst of the misery, the North Korean guards still insisted on
calling the prisoners "Liberated Soldiers," liberated from American
imperialism. Like other UN prisoners, South Korean prisoners were
forced to undergo "ideological educational studies," but they were meant
to appeal more to the stomach than to the mind. "During these study
sessions we expected propagandistic lectures with extravagant claims.
But they weren't . . . the gist of the sessions was: don't stay here starv-

ing, volunteer for the People's Army. Fight for the fatherland and eat rice and meat. They didn't try to agitate or incite us. It wasn't coercive like asking those to volunteer to step forward. They used persuasion." In other words, the prisoners could risk dying of disease and starvation in the camps, or they could join the NKPA and risk dying on the battlefield for their nation and their people with glory and honor. In the meantime, they would also be better fed and clothed. Pak was conflicted about what to do. If he stayed in the camp, he thought he would certainly die if conditions did not improve. On the other hand, he thought about the future. If he joined up with the NKPA, he would never be able to see his family again. Moreover, what kind of life could he expect in North Korea? There was certainly no chance of him ever becoming an officer. How would he, a former South Korean soldier, expect to be treated in North Korea? Still, the offer was tempting as he was consumed by thoughts of food. "The only thing I wished for was to eat. I only thought about food. I could not stop thinking about rice no matter how hard I tried. I was unable to feel sadness or any other emotion. I was becoming an animal but so was everyone else."[58]

Not surprisingly, many prisoners signed up. "Most argued that it would be better to volunteer and live rather than stay in the prison camps and die of starvation or typhoid," Pak lamented. Pak did not volunteer. The painful choice was made all the more poignant when Pak learned that an old classmate from medical school in the same camp decided to join. Pak was shocked by the news. His classmate told him, "How can we survive here. Every day 20 to 50 of us die. How can I survive until the end? We don't know when the war will end, and if we stay we will surely die. I want to join so I can live."[59] Pak tried to persuade his friend that the war would soon be over and reminded him about his family back home. What about his future in North Korea? But his friend's mind was made up. As a last favor, he asked Pak to visit his family if Pak survived the war. He wanted his mother and father to know what had happened to him. Pak memorized his address.

> After I was repatriated and returned home, the very first place I went to was his house. He hadn't told us, but he was married and had a daughter. When I conveyed the news everyone broke down in tears. I left his house in a hurry . . . I felt horrible, as if I had committed a sin by surviving and returning home.[60]

Pak remembered a similarly tragic encounter just before he was repatriated. His train stopped at Sariwŏn on the way to P'anmunjŏm in August 1953. A North Korean private approached him and said, "I can't return home even though I used to be a prisoner of the People's Army like you, because I volunteered. Please tell my family that I am alive."[61] Pak couldn't forget his tear-streaked face.

In the summer of 1951, South Korean prisoners were moved to another camp located near the town of Anbyŏn in the northern part of Kangwŏn province. The camp was an abandoned school, and unlike Camp 5 the floors were covered with wood. "It seemed like paradise compared to the hell of Pyŏkdong camp," recalled Pak.[62] The prisoners were issued unmarked North Korean uniforms and were fed boiled corn instead of the rock-hard uncooked kernels they had eaten before. They were put to work. Owing to the threat of UN air attacks during the day, they worked only at night. They loaded sacks of rice and corn on a rail car, which they then pushed across a wooden bridge. On the other side, other prisoners transferred the cargo onto freight cars. These were then pushed into a tunnel to avoid detection from the air. Before dawn the rails were disassembled for the same reason. At dusk, the rails were reassembled and the cycle was repeated. Through these laborious measures, supplies continued to get through to the front lines.

Given the stable situation and relatively good living conditions, Pak and a group of prisoners, calling themselves the "Resurrection Band" to signal their "rebirth" as free men, began planning an escape. They would live off the land. They had stolen bayonets and grenades and hid them under the roof tiles. A few days before the plan was to be executed, however, "lightning struck" when one of the men betrayed the group.[63] The group was apprehended and interrogated, and Pak, as the alleged leader of the plot, was sent off to P'yŏngyang to be questioned further. In retrospect, it may have been a blessing for Pak that the plan had failed. Unlike American, British, and other non-ROK UN POWs whose chances of a successful escape were limited by their conspicuous appearance, Pak probably could have made it to UN lines. He spoke the language, blended into the surroundings, and otherwise could roam the countryside relatively anonymously. Yet, it was precisely this advantage that became a huge liability for South Korean POWs. Once captured, or recaptured, there was nothing he could do to actually prove his national loyalty. Tragically, many ROK POWs who had successfully made their escape to the South were again incarcerated, this time in UN POW camps, as suspected North Korean spies and infiltrators.

Pak told of one such story involving a Mr. Cho. Like Pak, Cho joined the ROK Army at Taegu and fought with the ROK Sixth Division. He was captured by the Chinese and then sent to a North Korean prison camp. To his surprise, the commandant of the camp turned out to be a close high school classmate. This classmate had fled to the North in 1948 following the suppression of the Yŏsu-Sunch'ŏn Rebellion. He recognized Cho immediately. Deeply moved to see an old friend, the North Korean officer helped Cho escape. After an arduous trek south, Cho reached UN lines held by Americans. "But the Americans treated him as a North Korean soldier and took him prisoner," wrote Pak. "He ultimately ended up classified as a North Korean and was sent to Kŏje Island!"[64] Cho's family tried everything they could to get him released, writing petitions to various agencies and producing his South Korean army serial number as evidence of his service in the ROK Army, but to no avail. Cho was identified as a North Korean POW. He was finally able to return home through the anticommunist prisoner release in July 1953 that had been secretly engineered by President Rhee to sabotage the armistice.

And then there were those who were forced to remain in North Korea as virtual slaves. Many of the ROK prisoners were unaware that an armistice had even been signed. "One day I found it rather strange that I could not hear the sound of airplanes overhead," recalled Cho Ch'ang-ho, who was able to escape and return to South Korea in 1994 after nearly fifty years of detainment in a political camp in Manp'o and forced labor in various mines in North Korea. "Later, I found out the reason the skies had fallen silent: the war was over."[65] In his memoir, *Return of a Dead Man* (*Toraon saja*), published in 1995, Cho claimed that thousands of South Korean POWs were as oblivious to the war's end as he was.[66] Kim Kyu-hwan, a POW who escaped to the South in 2003, testified that he had been forced to work in a mine for thirty-five years and had no idea when the war ended. "Six hundred and seventy South Korean POWs were confined to hard labor at the Aogi coal mine in 1953," he wrote. "There are no more than 20 left now. Over the past five decades, many have died in working accidents, and others have died of old age."[67] According to former POWs who escaped, most South Korean prisoners were sent to work in mines in the hinterlands of the northeast along the Chinese border, the most remote part of North Korea. Since 1994, sixty-five former South Korean POWs have escaped to South Korea through China.[68]

At the end of the war, 11,559 UN POWs were repatriated, including 3,198 Americans and 7,142 ROK soldiers. According to official figures from the South Korean Ministry of National Defense, however, 41,971 South Korean soldiers remained unaccounted for.[69] Assuming that the 41,971 had not been killed in action, what had happened to the missing soldiers? An intriguing Soviet embassy report dated December 3, 1953, was recently discovered in the Soviet archives by a Chinese scholar.[70] The report stated that 42,262 ROK soldiers "voluntarily" joined the NKPA, while 13,940 were forced to stay in North Korea after the war as laborers, coal miners, and railway workers. According to a former South Korean POW who escaped to the South in 1994, 30,000 to 50,000 ROK POWs were forcibly held by North Korea and unrepatriated. Another source puts that number at 60,000.[71] Thus the number of South Korean POWs who were forcibly held back and unrepatriated ranged from 13,940 to 60,000, depending on the source. These figures do not include the South Koreans who "voluntarily" joined the NKPA, which, as the Soviet report pointed out, were in the tens of thousands, even though one can hardly describe the choice made by starved and abused prisoners to survive by joining the NKPA as "voluntary." Thus, the Soviet figure of 42,262 "voluntary" nonrepatriates seems rather meaningless. Nevertheless, if the figures are correct, the document does provide insight into the enormous number of South Koreans who were not repatriated after the war. If the December 1953 Soviet report is taken at face value, then a minimum of 56,202 South Korean POWS (42,262 + 13,940) were not repatriated, voluntarily or forcibly, and this is a far higher number of unaccounted South Koreans than the official Ministry of National Defense figure of 41,971. The individual and familial tragedies that lie behind these enormous numbers are staggering.

Considering the fate of many thousands of South Korean POWs, Pak was one of the lucky ones. He had survived and was repatriated in August 1953. At the time, however, he did not feel so lucky. He was elated to hear that he was going to Inch'ŏn when he boarded a bus at P'anmunjŏm. But when he was told that he and his fellow prisoners would continue their journey by ship, his joy suddenly turned to fear. The ship took him and others to Yongch'o Island off South Korea's southern coast. Yongch'o had been a POW camp for North Korean prisoners. Pak's fear turned into rage: "We couldn't believe it!! How could we be placed in a camp for North Korean POWs!"[72] Yongch'o served as a holding camp for the South Korean authorities to screen repatriated prisoners for their political "purity." Over the next few months the "released" prisoners found themselves prisoners once again, this time by their own government. They felt lonely, anxious, and betrayed, having been given no information when they might return home. For all Pak knew, he would be waiting out the rest of his life on this small, rocky, isolated island. But the worst was his deep sense of betrayal. He had done nothing wrong. He had served his country loyally. What did all his suffering mean if his country did not even recognize his sacrifice?

Adding insult to injury and fueling the sense of betrayal was Pak's back pay for the three years he was a prisoner. The amount came to a little more than a few dollars. Furious, Pak "wanted to throw on the ground the pittance I received as compensation for the thirty-three months of suffering." Not wanting to handle the money himself, he asked a fellow prisoner to buy something with it. "I thought the money was unlucky and didn't want to put it in my pocket, but when I saw what he came back with from the camp store, I could only sigh. He held one bottle of cheap liquor and a few cans of meat."[73] This was what three years in a North Korean prison camp was worth to his country, he thought. He and his friends drank the cheap wine "made with potato liquor and food coloring" and fell into a deep, troubled sleep. He had blown his three years of back pay in one night of drunken slumber.

Not long thereafter, prisoners began committing suicide. Rather than fling themselves off the cliffs of the island where their bodies would be swept away by the ocean, they chose the most gruesome method possible, hanging themselves in the latrine. "I saw an unbelievably shocking sight. How could this happen, I thought! I reopened my closed eyes and saw my fellow prison-mates hanging on ropes. Not just one or two, but 10 of them! I couldn't tell who they were. Nobody moved but simply stared at the hanging figures. Another 7–8 prisoners hung themselves the next day and another 4–5 the following day." The camp commandant prevented the suicides by increasing security and surveillance, but this only heightened the stress on the prisoners as they now had less freedom to move about: "All we did was eat and let time flow by."[74]

Confined to barracks on this isolated island in the middle of nowhere, Pak slumped into a deep depression. One day he was informed of the screening process that the detainees would have to go through. The screening would determine whether they were ideologically "fit" to reenter South Korean society. "In the 1950s, everyone thought that if you had been exposed to communism, even for a few days, you could be turned into a communist," complained Pak. "This is something we all had to go through."[75] The prisoners were uneasy. If the screening process determined that a prisoner was a communist, they would have no future in South Korea. Their fate hinged on the decision of the screener. To his relief, Pak passed the screening. He was determined to be "ideologically sound" and could leave Yongch'o Island and his life as a POW. He was given a two-week leave to visit his family in Taegu, and was to report to the recruiting office at Tongnae, near Pusan, where he would be given his new assignment. Despite his three-year service in the war, he would not be discharged from the army.

At home in Taegu, Pak realized the great gulf that now existed between himself and his former life. Some childhood friends invited him to a coffee shop to talk about old times. When he arrived, he felt out of place. His classmates were dressed in stylish clothes and wore their hair long. They laughed easily and freely. When Pak asked them how they had passed the war years, they told him that they had avoided military service so that they could continue their studies. How was it possible that he was the only one of the group who had volunteered? "I was the only fool here," he thought to himself. To make matters worse, a policeman approached them and singled Pak out. Someone had reported him as a suspicious character, and the policeman wanted to see his identification papers. He said that he had left them at home. A commotion ensued. Pak was humiliated and indignant: "How dare they who didn't serve in the army much less seen a battlefield, living safely in the rear, ask me, who had not only fought in the war but had suffered as a POW, for identification papers!" The next evening, still boiling with anger, he thought of his classmates. "I thought of their easy-going laughing faces. Some welcomed me while others secretly jeered. I also thought about the contemptuous looks of the young women at the coffee shop. I thought about the disabled veteran in shabby clothes with a crutch who came into the coffee shop. He didn't even have a prosthetic leg so one of his pants legs flopped around. He had given one of his legs for his country but became a beggar. Compared to those who avoided military service, he was condemned to live in the shadows of society for the rest of his life. I could only pity him."[76]

After his two-week leave, Pak reported for duty to his new unit and was sent to the DMZ. The cold and deprivation reminded him of his days in the prison camps. "I could barely contain my hunger," he remembered. "I could barely put up with my misery and self-pity. How did I wind up like this, suffering like this in this mountain valley while others were studying."[77] He had given so much for his country, and yet others who had shirked their duty were living comfortably at home. How could this be? Pak was at last discharged from the army in March 1954. He decided that he would try to forget the past. He would resume his medical studies and become a doctor. He would not let the trauma of war and his bitterness ruin his life.

Then, one day in 1995, Pak read about a POW who had escaped from North Korea. After the fall of the Soviet Union in 1991 and the death of Kim Il Sung in 1994, it appeared that North Korea was on the verge of collapse. Escapees and defectors trickling out of the country began to tell stories of famine and extreme hardship. South Korea, too, was undergoing a period of unprecedented transition. Kim Dae-jung was elected president in 1997, the first opposition leader to be elected in South Korean history. Kim initiated a new policy to engage North Korea (Sunshine Policy), ushering in a period of unprecedented cooperation between the two Koreas. Pak no longer had to suffer the stigma of silence that he felt imposed on him by South Korea's former military dictatorships. Ironically, though, in the new age of North-South rapprochement, the South Korean government did not want to publicize any harsh criticisms of North Korea for fear that it might wreck the delicate negotiations between the two countries. And so Pak's story remained "undesirable."

Pak began writing about his experiences as a South Korean POW for an obscure daily, *Yŏngnam Today*, in 1999. He felt as if he and other POWs had been doubly forgotten, first by the anticommunist military regimes and then by a democratic South Korean government that was focused on establishing a close relationship with P'yŏngyang. The South Korean government was not interested in pursuing old wounds from the past. Pak's anger was suddenly rekindled. Why wasn't the government doing more to locate former South Korean POWs and demand their release from the North Korean regime? Why wasn't more being done to obtain from the North Korean regime an accurate accounting of the tens of thousands of South Koreans who had disappeared after the war? Why were the South Korean people forgetting the war crimes committed by the North against their own citizens?

Pak read about a former POW, Yang Sun-yŏng, who had escaped to South Korea from the North in 1997. He was owed back pay for the time he was a POW, and the government offered him 2,200,000 won, or about $1,600, for the forty-four years and six months of imprisonment. "I could not suppress my anguish when I heard about this," wrote Pak. "It amounted to 45,393 won [$33] per year or just 3,782 won [$2.78] per month. That was the pay for an enlisted soldier back then." Couldn't the government have found another way to compensate him adequately? "How was it," he asked, "that the government could give hundreds of millions of won to prevent a bank from going under, but give Yang a mere pittance for his 44 years of hardship as a POW?"[78] Pak could not understand. Did his and other former South Korean POWs' service and suffering for their country mean so little?

Yang was furious too. He refused to accept the compensation money.

CHAPTER ELEVEN

Propaganda Wars

When the armistice talks stalled over the POW issue in the fall of 1951, incendiary raids reminiscent of those during World War II were carried out against the North with such effectiveness that Air Force Chief of Staff General Hoyt Vandenberg complained, "We have reached the point where there are not enough targets left in North Korea to keep the air force busy."[1] Charles Joy, chief of the Korean mission of CARE (Cooperative for Assistance and Relief Everywhere) and witness to World Wars I and II, wrote, "In twelve successive years of relief work in different parts of the world, I have never seen such destitution and such widespread misery as I have seen here."[2] Similar observations were made by the Hungarian chargé d'affaires, Mária Balog, who reported in February 1951,

> Korea has become a pile of ruins. There are no houses or buildings left [presumably in P'yŏngyang]. Cities and villages have been blown up, or destroyed by bombings, or burned down. The population lives in dugouts in the ground. The people are literally without clothes or shoes. They cannot even be sent to work, at least until the weather starts warming up. There is no food. Cholera, which the Soviet physicians managed to eradicate in the last five years, may emerge, since it occurred in a district of P'yŏngyang as late as last summer . . . They are not prepared against these epidemics; there is no medicine and there are not enough medical personnel. There is no soap.[3]

The rapid descent into the hell of an all-out war left many Americans stunned. Freda Kirchwey, senior editor of *The Nation*, angrily observed, "Someday soon the American mind, mercurial and impulsive, tough and tender, is going to react against the horrors of mechanized warfare in Korea . . . liberation through total destruction cannot be the answer to the world's dilemma."[4] An appalled Harold Ickes of the *New Republic* wrote,

"They [Koreans] had welcomed us to South Korea with shouts of joy. We were deliverers, bringing aid and comfort and unity. Apparently we were bringing other things, wounds and dismemberment and death. Bombs falling from the air or bullets from machine guns being fired into a hurrying or huddled mass, cannot distinguish between the sexes, or between the ages and infants."[5] Upton Sinclair, the Pulitzer Prize–winning author and social activist, worried that devastation by bombing was counterproductive because it fomented a "hatred of Americans in Asia."[6] In Britain, prominent clergymen protested the use of napalm. Emrys Hughes, a renowned Welsh Labour politician, requested permission to exhibit photographs of the P'yŏngyang bombings in the House of Commons, where a similar exhibition of the "Mau Mau atrocities" in Kenya had been allowed in the past, but the request was denied.[7]

In the end, what determined the debate on the bombing was not the moral argument, but the acceptance by both American and European leaders that the destruction of North Korea was necessary to prevent a greater evil, the possibility of another world war. "Korea is merely one engagement in the global contest," ran an editorial in the *Washington Post*. "If we can punish the Chinese severely enough in Korea, a settlement

Napalm victims, February 4, 1951. (U.S. NATIONAL ARCHIVES AND RECORDS ADMINISTRATION)

P'yŏngyang, 1953. By the end of the war, only three major buildings remained standing. "The gleaming-white building of the bank stands out grotesquely in the center
of the city, one of the few buildings that can still be restored. It was used as a hospital
by the [UN] interventionists who had evacuated in too great a hurry to blow it up.
But beyond it, all the way to the railway station, there is nothing but ruins, a forest of semi-demolished walls and blackened chimneys."[8] (COURTESY OF THE HUNGARIAN
NATIONAL MUSEUM).

can be achieved . . . This sober analysis carries little of the glitter or glib
promises of the MacArthur formula. But it shows a lot more regard for
military risks and realities."[9] With the war at a stalemate by the fall of
1951, Western leaders were of the opinion that bombing campaigns were
necessary to punish the communists and force them to the negotiating
table. Despite the destruction of North Korean cities, towns, and villages, the success of the bombing was measured by its utility in forcing a
settlement and thus preventing a larger war.[10]

Tunnel War

To a certain extent, the air campaigns were effective in achieving that
goal. UN strategic bombing had added to the communist difficulty in
sustaining the war. Coping with relentless attacks from the air, Chinese

logistical problems multiplied as battle lines moved southward. The UN air interdiction campaign against North Korean rail and road networks was particularly devastating to the Chinese forces.[11] General Hong Xuezhi, deputy commander of the CPV force in Korea and also its chief of logistics, recalled that "on 8 April 1951, American napalm bombing runs set 84 rail cars afire, destroying 1,500 tons of grain, 408,000 uniforms, and 190,000 pairs of boots." As much as 40 percent of all supplies had been destroyed in the bombing raids, and CPV troops were going hungry.[12] During the fifth campaign (April 22–June 10), Marshal Nie Rongzhen, who oversaw CPV logistics at the Central Military Commission headquarters in Beijing, described the Chinese troops as "unable to break through enemy lines in the Xianli Sector because they didn't have food or bullets and they stopped the attack for three days and lost the initiative."[13] With all railways virtually gone, the CPV was forced to resort to trucks, donkeys, and corvée labor to transport supplies from the Yalu to the front, facing great hazards. The countryside had become a moonscape of huge craters filled with water. Trucks operating at night without lights for fear of detection or being attacked by night bombers often drove into the craters, wrecking the vehicle and sometimes killing the driver. General Hong complained, "Even with a hundred men it took forever to fill in a crater."[14]

With the front virtually static and under constant air attack, the Chinese were forced to go underground. Tunnels, bunkers, and trenches became the backbone of China's defensive strategy. Each soldier "had a rifle in one hand and a shovel in the other," wrote General Hong. The tunnels were constantly expanded under arduous conditions. "The big 'orchestra' composed of our soldiers and commanders played a new 'movement' in constructing tunnel fortifications," recalled Yang Dezhi, an army group commander. "This approach meant operating inside the mountains, dealing with rocks, sandy grit, and cave-ins. Lacking technology or advanced tools, we were depending largely on our hands. Pickaxes were worn down so that they ended up looking like rounded iron blocks about the size of a hammer . . . broken glass and metal plaques were also used at tunnel entrances to reflect sunshine inside during the daytime . . . They worked so hard that their palms blistered, then became thick and badly calloused." By August 1952 the Chinese had dug 125 miles of tunnels and 400 miles of trenches. By the end of the war the Chinese had built an astonishing 780 miles of tunnels that formed underground cities. On August 4, 1952, almost two years after China entered the war, Mao optimistically reported, "The problem of food, that is, how to guarantee the provision lines, had been for a long time a real question. We did not know, until last year, that digging up grottos for storing food was the solution. Now we are aware of it. Each of our divisions has enough food for three months. All have their storage and ceremonial halls. They are well off."[15]

Despite satisfaction with the underground facilities ("one could find all kinds of facilities, such as dorms, canteens, and latrines . . . There was also what our soldiers called the underground mansion 'our club hall'"), life was difficult and stressful.[16] Under constant air attack, soldiers spent weeks underground. Coping with the darkness was a challenge. Meager light was provided by oil lamps made from tin cans and shell casings, and keeping the lamps lit used up precious cooking oil. Smoke from the lamps caused headaches and dizziness in the congested and poorly ventilated space. Moreover, the lack of sunlight and poor diet led to nutrient deficiencies with serious effects such as night blindness and diarrhea. Urgent calls were made for shipments of proper food, but "because the shipments were small in quantity, the troops vast in numbers, these shipments were a drop in the bucket and the problem was not solved." A solution was found through a local Korean folk remedy. Korean peasants showed that night blindness could be cured by drinking bitter "pine needle tea." The already denuded Korean landscape became ravaged even more by marauding Chinese soldiers searching for the proper nourishment. Tadpoles became a favorite dietary supplement as they were a rich source of vitamins and also helped cure night blindness. General Hong recalled "taking a handful of the little tadpoles from a crater, pop them into a tea pot with some water, best with some sugar but okay without, and gulp them down alive three times a day, and in two days you begin to see results. We got every unit mobilized to play with this clever beverage . . . once again, the night returned to us."[17]

Although the constant bombardment from the air had slowed the communist advance, and thus stalemated the war, it did little to force the communist leadership to a settlement. Despite the destruction, there was little evidence of a collapse of will. As in World War II, intensive strategic bombing could inflict catastrophic damage on a society without defeating it.[18] The Chinese and the North Koreans had simply adapted. It soon became clear that the stalemate war could not be won on the battlefield. Rather, it would have to be waged in the court of world opinion. For the communists, this would entail an all-out effort to win condemnation of the United States by discrediting the integrity of the UN war effort in Korea as well as undermining the legitimacy of the principle of nonforcible repatriation.

American Bugs

In early 1951, intelligence reports describing a devastating epidemic sweeping across North Korea reached General MacArthur's desk. The reports recounted many cases of communist soldiers and civilians dying from a mysterious disease whose symptoms appeared to resemble the bubonic plague. As the Eighth Army advanced northward to recapture Seoul, verification of these reports became a priority. The bubonic plague can sweep though a population like wildfire, blazing a path of death that is difficult to extinguish. A bubonic plague north of Seoul would obviously impact on potential future UNC operations. MacArthur directed Brig. Gen. Crawford Sams, his chief of public health and welfare, to find the truth. It would be a difficult and hazardous task since the allegedly infected area was in enemy territory. Moreover, no one, including Sams, had firsthand experience with the plague. "Not too many of our doctors in America have seen the bubonic plague, and so far as I knew there were none in the Far East at the time," Sams later wrote. Several reports stated that hospitals in the Wŏnsan area were filled with plague patients. Sams "felt that he should go to Wŏnsan in an attempt to investigate these cases for himself." Thus began one of the most astonishing episodes of the war.[19]

The journey posed seemingly insurmountable challenges. Sams decided to enter behind enemy lines by sea. He would travel to near Wŏnsan by ship at night and then get ashore on a row boat. Once he was on land, the journey to find a patient would become more perilous, since he was "an Occidental among Orientals in the dead of winter" and thus without vegetation for cover. He would have to kidnap the patient, take him to the coast, put him on a rubber raft, and then transport him to a waiting ship. "We could then . . . make our laboratory determination."[20] The operation had to be done quickly and surreptitiously. It seemed like an impossible task, but given the importance of the mission, Sams decided that he had to take the risk. For twelve days in March, Sams tried various ways of getting ashore. Ten teams of Korean agents had been sent in advance to support the operation from ashore, but nothing had been heard from them for several days, and apparently all of them had been captured or killed and the mission compromised. Sams recollected, "Unfortunately, in the torturing which preceded death or execution of these agents, apparently some yielded to such fantastic pressure as the oriental mind can devise in torture, and the communists were aware of the fact that I was trying to get into Korea from that location." The odds of success appeared nil, and any sane mind would have canceled the operation. But providence struck as the last team of agents, apparently safe, made contact, and Sams decided to proceed.

Sams and Yun, a Korean commando, approached the shore south of Wŏnsan by a little village called Chilso-ni. Yun made contact with the advance team. Over the next few days, Sams hid in a cave while Yun and the other agents scouted nearby villages for victims of the plague. Although unable to capture a patient, Sams was nevertheless able to determine, through the agents who had actually seen many sick people, that there was indeed an epidemic, but it was not the plague. Rather, it appeared to be "a particularly virulent form of smallpox, known as hemorrhagic smallpox." The "Black Death," as the epidemic was called, "was as fatal as the bubonic plague except that it was a different disease" and could be more easily controlled through immunization inoculations and medical treatment.[21]

Sams returned safely with the good news. The communists were furious that Sams had avoided capture. "They executed some twenty-five people in the little village of Chil-So-Ri whom they suspected of having collaborated with us and our agents," Sams later wrote. But more significantly for the course of the war, Sams's mission incited a new but still largely uncoordinated charge by the communists that would later erupt into one of the most explosive issues of the Korean War: the accusation that UN forces were engaged in biological warfare. On May 4, 1951, the *People's Daily* reported that Sams's mission was "to spread the plague" and that the ship that had taken him to Wŏnsan was a biological warfare vessel designed to "carry out inhuman bacteriological experiments on Chinese People's Volunteers."[22]

Biological or germ warfare was not a new issue in China. During the Second Sino-Japanese War (1937–45) the Japanese established a number of units in occupied China where they worked on developing biological weapons using Chinese prisoners and internees as subjects for gruesome experiments. The most important activity took place at Unit 731 in Harbin commanded by Lt. Gen. Ishii Shirō. The Americans granted Ishii, his subordinates, and members of other Japanese biological warfare units immunity from prosecution for war crimes in exchange for the technical information they had gathered. In the emerging cold war environment, a calculated determination was made that rebuilding Japan, rather than punishing Japanese war criminals, would better serve the long-term security interests of the United States and the free world. In one of the most blatant cases of injustice, Ishii's men, their past hidden, became ostensibly respectable members of Japanese society as deans of medical schools, senior science professors, university presidents, and key technicians in industries.[23] The Soviets put to trial in Khabarovsk the few members of Unit 731 they had captured. The biological warfare methods that the Chinese alleged that the Americans used were *precisely* the same as those described in evidence and testimonies that came out at the trials.[24]

After raising the issue of bacteriological warfare in early 1951 following General Sams's extraordinary mission to North Korea, the communists backpedaled. By mid-May 1951, charges of bacteriological warfare almost disappeared from the communist press. With the prospect of a truce, continuing the accusations seemed unwise. By July 1951, when the armistice talks began, they were dropped completely. It was not until early 1952, after truce talks became deadlocked, that the communists once again raised the charges of bacteriological warfare. In February 1952, North Korean Foreign Minister Pak Hŏn-yŏng accused the United States of repeatedly dropping large numbers of insects carrying cholera and other diseases. The Chinese followed up with charges of their own. In a front-page editorial, the *People's Daily* condemned "the appalling crimes of the American aggressors in Korea in using bacteriological warfare." The accusations gained worldwide publicity with Premier Zhou's statement on February 24 that called on all nations to condemn the "U.S. Imperialists War Crimes of germ warfare."[25] The communists claimed that one thousand biological warfare sorties were flown by UN aircraft between January and March 1952 in northeast China.

In early April the *People's Daily* began publishing eyewitness accounts of germ warfare attacks. An account by a Chinese journalist described how a twin-engine plane had sprayed germ-carrying "poisonous insects" near Xipuli, China, on March 23. Another report relayed how a British reporter witnessed insects being released from an American plane on April 2 in the same area.[26] Between mid-March and mid-April, germ warfare allegations with descriptions of strange insects and mysterious airborne voles filled China's media as the country went on a nationwide insect and rat extermination campaign. The communists also imple-

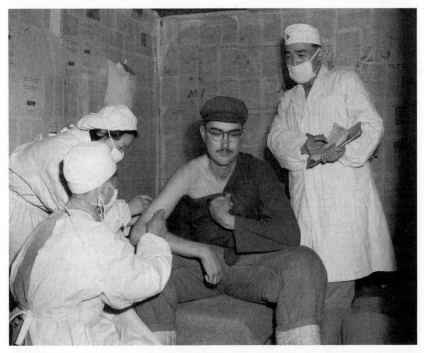

Lieutenant Ralph R. Dixon, prisoner of war, gets inoculated at a POW camp, April 3, 1952. Facing a long and protracted war, Mao inaugurated the Patriotic Hygienic Campaign in 1952 to mobilize thousands of students, housewives, and workers to reduce the incidence of disease and to "crush the enemy's germ warfare." In addition, hundreds of thousands of Chinese citizens, including UN POWs, were inoculated against the dreaded disease. Mao also instigated a widespread purge of counterrevolutionaries during this same period. Those who were not immediately executed were systematically "cleansed" of their bourgeois ideology and their "disease-laden" Western inclinations in reeducation camps that began to spring up throughout the country. (U.S. NATIONAL ARCHIVES AND RECORDS ADMINISTRATION)

mented a national inoculation campaign. By October, 420 million people had been inoculated against smallpox. "In our large towns and seaports," wrote Fan Shih-shan, general secretary of the Chinese Medical Association, "small pox has been completely wiped out . . . Constant measures taken to destroy rodents and fleas, mass vaccination of local populations, early diagnosis, efficient isolation and energetic treatment have succeeded in controlling the disease."[27]

During his captivity in North Korea, Gen. William Dean experienced firsthand the effects of this national campaign when he too was vaccinated. "Everybody, soldiers, civilians, adults and children, received four separate inoculations and revaccination," recalled Dean. "They were monster shots and all of North Korea had fever and sore arms."[28] American POWs languishing in prison camps along the Yalu were also informed of the germ warfare. William Banghart at Camp 5 recalled that "the bacteriological warfare orientation given to us by the Chinese" consisted of "an elaborate display of pictures, photostatic copies of confessions or statements made by [air force pilots] Lieutenants Quinn and Enoch, and a great quantity of printed matter . . . One thing I remember clearly is the report I read on the pictorials supplied to the company libraries by the Chinese concerning a Japanese war criminal called Shirō Ishii, who had been released from military prison in Japan and flown to the U.S. where he was supposed to have conferred with President Truman and MacArthur. Every man in the company was given a written test on his feelings on Bacteriological Warfare."[29] One popular slogan was, "One fly, one American soldier; the enemy drops them, we will eliminate them!"[30] Political cartoons depicting U.S. imperialism as the Grim Reaper riding the back of a housefly reinforced the notion that the American enemy, and anyone associated with him, was an enemy of China.[31] Slogans such as "Resist Germ Warfare and American Imperialism" were calculated to stir hatred for the Americans as disease-laden pests.

The innumerable eyewitness accounts of germ attacks, the lure of war memory, the power of rumor, the fear of epidemic diseases, and the reality of a frustrating war transformed charges of germ warfare into a belief that gripped the Chinese public in terror. Whipped into frenzy, Chinese farmers, housewives, students, and factory workers became citizen-soldiers ready to battle against the unseen and disease-bearing American enemy. This enemy came in many forms. As early as 1949 the

CCP leadership had begun launching a campaign to rid the new nation of its counterrevolutionary forces in the guise of the "Suppress Counter-revolutionary Campaign." The CCP arrested thousands of religious sect leaders, alleged Nationalist spies, and gang leaders, and executed many hundreds. A wide-scale program was launched to crack down on beggars, prostitutes, and criminals. The war in Korea ("Resist America, Aid Korea") merely intensified the CCP dread of these "internal" enemies. The germ warfare charges arose simultaneously with several new campaigns launched in 1952 that were aimed at the professional classes. The "Three-Anti campaign" and "Five-Anti campaign," which began at the end of 1951 and in January 1952, respectively, were designed to undermine the authority of China's capitalists and business managers as well as the rural landlords.[32] In February 1952, the CCP also inaugurated the "Patriotic Hygiene Campaign," which mobilized housewives, students, and workers, equipped with gauze masks, cotton sacks, and gloves, to fight against the American-delivered germs. "Let us get mobilized," Mao wrote in a memorial to the National Heath Conference in Beijing. "Let us attend to hygiene, reduce the incidence of disease, raise the standards of health, and crush the enemy's germ warfare."[33]

At the same time, the "Thought Reform Campaign" began penetrating institutions of higher learning and professional services. Intellectuals, who had previously thought of themselves as benignly apolitical, or even progressive, were now forced to publicly announce their allegiance. Thought reform classes included not only instructions in proper work ethic, but also the abandonment of "Western influenced elitism."[34] Between February and July 1952, germ warfare was transformed from a regional military-related issue in northeast China into a national mobilization campaign aimed to rid China of all "foreign" influences. Foreign jazz was banned in early 1952. The teaching of English ceased.[35] In the hunt for American germs, anyone remotely associated with America—the Nationalists, capitalists, religious leaders, Western-trained intellectuals, businessmen, or managers—was considered a menace to the national body-politic and caught in the same net as insects and rats. In radio broadcasts, mass meetings, and daily newspapers, the Chinese state called on its citizens to expose evildoers, confess crimes, and eliminate poisonous germs from their homes and workplaces.[36]

The publication of confessions by captured American pilots intensified the popular hysteria. Some wondered why the POWs were even kept alive. In a widely distributed brochure prepared by the China Medical General Association entitled "General Knowledge for Defense against Bacteriological Warfare," the linkage between the war against germs at home and the war against enemies abroad was made explicit. In both cases, the best defense was vigilance and the eradication of "impure" elements within Chinese society in order to maintain the nation's health. "It is possible to defend against bacteriological warfare," the brochure stated. "Under the leadership of Chairman Mao and the Communist Party, we can overcome any kind of weapon, because it is the men holding the weapons, and not the weapons [themselves], that can decide the victory and defeat of the war."[37] By linking American germ attacks with a disease prevention movement aimed to rid China of both its biological and its political impurities, the CCP leadership was able to transform popular dread of American germs into fear of China's internal enemies that would eventually lead to the persecution of hundreds of thousands of Chinese businessmen, intellectuals, and landowners.[38]

The hallmark of Mao's design to purge counterrevolutionaries was his decree on February 21, 1951, which extended the death penalty or life imprisonment to virtually any kind of antigovernment activity. What exactly constituted that activity, however, was never clearly defined. Arrests and purges soon became routine occurrences. The Hong Kong newspaper *Wah Kiu Yat Po* reported that more than "20,000 persons had been killed in the southeastern districts of Kwangsi [Guangxi], a troublesome southern province," in March 1951 alone.[39] The same newspaper reported the arrests of thousands of people in northeast China. "Mao said that in the struggle against counterrevolution 650,000 persons were executed in the country," recounted V. V. Kuznetsov, Soviet ambassador to the DPRK, noting as an aside that "some number of innocent people apparently suffered."[40] The goal of the "purification" campaigns was to eliminate entire groups of people from the fabric of Chinese society, and the fear of American bugs provided the perfect pretext to do it.

While Chinese and North Korean officials had little trouble persuading their people that biological warfare was real, persuading the international community was a far more difficult task. The Soviet Union leveled charges of biological warfare through the UN and took the lead in this task. The first official U.S. denial came on March 4, 1952. Secretary of

State Dean Acheson angrily stated, "We have heard this nonsense about germ warfare in Korea before [in 1951]," and denied the charges "categorically and unequivocally." He said he welcomed "an impartial investigation by an international agency such as the Red Cross."[41] General Matthew Ridgway told Congress on May 22 that the allegations "should stand as a monumental warning to the American people and the Free World about the extent to which the communist leaders will go in fabricating, disseminating and persistently pursuing these false charges."[42] A week after calling for an investigation, Acheson sent a request to the ICRC requesting an on-site investigation, under the auspices of the UN, of the allegedly affected areas as soon as possible. Neither China nor North Korea responded to the ICRC's request for such an inspection. Three additional requests were made, and when they were all ignored, the ICRC considered their request rejected. The only acknowledgment made of the requests was at the UN, where Soviet delegate Yakov Malik formally rejected them on behalf of China and North Korea. Malik charged that a UN-sponsored ICRC investigation would be biased in favor of the United States and the West, and therefore an impartial investigation could not be guaranteed. The UN Political Committee, however, approved the ICRC investigation in early April. It was only on the verge of this expected approval that the Soviet Union offered to withdraw the charge of biological warfare "as proof of its sincere striving for peace."[43]

Although the Soviets dropped the charges, the drama was not over. The allegations by the communists had stirred anger among many of America's leading scientists. Unable to conduct on-site investigations, they examined whatever evidence was available, in this case nine photographs published by the *People's Daily* of the alleged insects and voles dropped by the Americans as disease vectors. Scientific experts discredited the photographs as fakes.[44] Under pressure of widespread skepticism in the noncommunist press, CCP leaders were unable to let the allegations simply drop because they had staked their regime's reputation and the basis for national "purification" campaigns on the charges. The ICRC and the UN's World Health Organization were deemed untrustworthy, but an investigation by neutral outsiders with Chinese oversight would be acceptable. For such an investigation to be legitimate, however, the Chinese government needed a credible group of Western scientists to verify its claims.

To lead the international group, the Chinese invited Joseph Needham, a Cambridge University don from the United Kingdom. Needham was a polymath, one of those exceptionally rare individuals who could rightly be called a Renaissance man. Needham's scientific credentials were impeccable. He was at the time one of the world's leading scientists, a pioneering biochemist who had written leading works on biochemistry and embryology. But he also possessed special qualifications in dealing with Chinese matters and especially Mao's Communist China. He was an avowed leftist and rejoiced in Mao's victory and the establishment of the PRC, believing that a communist utopia would follow. This view would be tempered later, especially after the Cultural Revolution of the late 1960s to early 1970s, but in 1952 no such suspicion entered Needham's mind. In 1942, the British government posted Needham to wartime China to head a new office in Chongqing, the Sino-British Science Co-operation Office, as a sort of cultural attaché to help spread British goodwill and material assistance among the Chinese academic community. He had never been to China, but had developed a lifelong passion for the country in the late 1930s, even learning the language fluently enough to read classical texts. He stayed for four years and during that time traveled the country widely, amassing a huge amount of material on the history of science and technology in China and establishing a wide network of contacts in the Chinese scientific community. The material he collected formed the basis for a monumental project on the study of scientific and technological developments in China that would prove not only the vastness of China's achievements but also the indebtedness of the world to China's genius. It would put to rest the prevailing view that China was backward and had contributed little to the development of mankind. The first volume of his work, *Science and Civilization in China*, was published in 1954. It is arguably the most important study of China's scientific history ever undertaken and from a man who was trained neither as a historian nor as a Sinologist.

When Mao invited Needham to investigate the biological warfare allegations, he was in the midst of writing the first volume of his work, and he enthusiastically accepted the chance to return to China and to meet his old acquaintances, including Zhou Enlai.[45] Needham was intrigued about the allegations since he had been convinced earlier that the Japanese had used fleas to spread plague in China. He also had to

Joseph Needham (seated) and N. N. Zhukov-Verezhnikov examining specimens, 1952.
(NEEDHAM RESEARCH INSTITUTE)

wonder about the connection between the alleged outbreak of "inexplicable" illness in 1951 and the American decision to grant amnesty to Japanese scientists involved in biological warfare in exchange for their experimental data. Needham looked forward to employing his scientific and language skills in the service of the struggling new regime.

Another key expert invited by the Chinese was N. N. Zhukov-Verezhnikov, a bacteriologist and vice president of the Soviet Academy of Medicine who was also intimately familiar with Ishii's Unit 731 program. Zhukov-Verezhnikov had served as a medical expert in the Khabarovsk trials of members of Unit 731. Needham and Zhukov-Verezhnikov, along with four other left-leaning Western scientists from Italy, France, Brazil, and Sweden, constituted the International Scientific Commission, formed by the Soviet-bloc World Peace Organization in the spring of 1952, to investigate allegations of germ warfare. The team arrived in June and worked tirelessly over the summer. Their report presenting the findings of Chinese scientists, with commentaries and final conclusions by the commission, was issued on September 15, 1952.

It confirmed everything China had claimed: "These [biological weap-

Members of the International Scientific Commission (left to right): Olivo Oliviero (Italy),
Jean Malterre (France), N. N. Zhukov-Verezhnikov (USSR), Andrea Andreen (Sweden),
Samuel Pessoa (Brazil), and Joseph Needham (UK). (NEEDHAM RESEARCH INSTITUTE)

ons] have been employed by units of the U.S.A. Armed Forces, using a
great variety of different methods for the purpose, some of which seem
to be developments of those applied by the Japanese army during the
Second World War."[46] Curiously, although commission members had
significant scientific credentials and were responsible for writing, organizing, translating, and editing the final report, they themselves conducted no direct scientific investigations. Instead they heard testimonies
and viewed a vast array of evidence presented to them by Chinese scientists, including an amazing variety of supposed vectors—voles, spiders,
nonbiting flies, and other insects.[47]

Needham appeared to put particular stake in the reputation of the
dozens of Chinese scientists who had participated in the investigations
and submitted the evidence, writing later that "they were first rate bacteriologists . . . and of whom I know well personally and can vouch for."[48]
At the same time, he appeared blissfully unaware that the germ warfare
investigations were taking place in the midst of a tense climate of political repression, "Thought Reform," reeducation, and the execution of

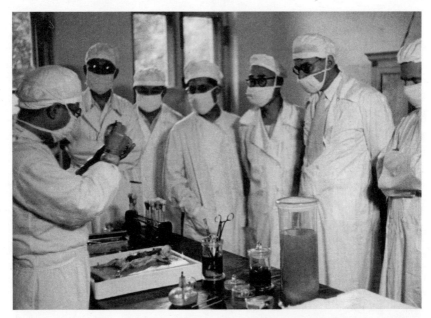

Plague lab, 1952. After spending the summer of 1952 investigating claims of bacteriological warfare presented by Chinese scientists, the International Scientific Commission published a 665-page report on September 15. Archibald Vivian Hill, the 1922 Nobel laureate in physiology and medicine, summed up the Western reaction to the report by proclaiming it to be "a prostitution of science for the purposes of propaganda." As for Needham, he was proclaimed a persona non grata by the British academic establishment. Needham was also blacklisted by the U.S. State Department and banned from travel to the U.S. until the mid-1970s. (NEEDHAM RESEARCH INSTITUTE)

hundreds of thousands of counterrevolutionaries.[49] Neither Needham nor the other Western scientists considered how politics might have compromised scientific truth. Nor did they seem aware that Chinese bacteriologists and entomologists were under intense pressure to cook the evidence and back the government's claims of American germ warfare. Needham simply could not believe that profound political changes might have influenced the conclusions of the scientists with whom he had become and remained close. He told Dr. Alfred Fisk, an American scientist and colleague, "If anyone insists on maintaining that a large number of scientists or scholars who were excellent men before automatically becoming scoundrels on the same day that a government such as that of Mr. Mao Tse-tung [Mao Zedong] comes into power (a government which, by the way, I am convinced has the support of the overwhelming majority of the people), I do not argue with him."[50]

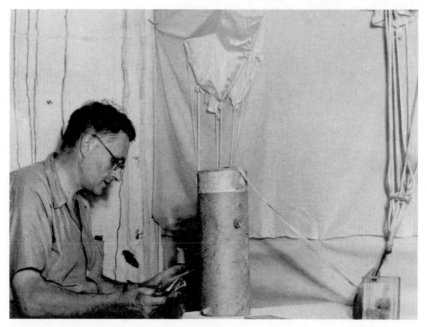

Joseph Needham examining an alleged biological warfare canister dropped from American bombers. (NEEDHAM RESEARCH INSTITUTE)

In his field notes, however, Needham hinted that many of these exhibitions might have been staged for his benefit. He was uncertain of what he might find when he visited Gannan county, the site of the first reports of purported droppings of germs. After he was invited to observe a technician in full protective gear examining microscopic slides that had been set up in a mobile bacteriological laboratory, he later wrote to his wife, "I have the feeling that this may have been a mise-en-scene for one person."[51] Nevertheless, he gave the Chinese the benefit of the doubt.[52] At a press conference following his return home, Needham was asked "what proof he had that samples of plague bacillus actually came from an unusual swarm of voles as the Chinese had claimed." "None," he answered. "We accepted the word of the Chinese scientists. It is possible to maintain that the whole thing was a kind of patriotic conspiracy. I prefer to believe the Chinese were not acting parts."[53]

Curiously, there were no epidemics in China or North Korea in 1952. The head of the UN World Health Organization, Dr. Brock Chisholm, noted that "North Korean and Chinese reports of epidemics in enemy territory . . . did not indicate the use of germ warfare because bacteriological weapons would bring far heavier casualties than indicated by the accounts of epidemics." He concluded that if germ warfare had been waged, "millions of people would die suddenly" and there would be "no mystery as to whether bacteriological weapons had been used."[54] Alternatively, one could also conclude that the hygienic measures put in place were done quickly and widely enough to have prevented epidemics from biological weapons. However, the Western public dismissed the whole episode as a hoax, yet another example of the dangers of communism and how a communist regime promoted lies over truths by subordinating science to politics. It was not simply the cynicism of the untruths that was unsettling, but the darker power of what those untruths revealed about the enemy. "The alarming thing," the *New York Times* wrote, "is the demonstration that the power we are fighting is not simply a great, militant and aggressive empire on the make, it is the power of *evil*. It could be said of the ruling mind in Russia that it has lost

Members of the International Scientific Commission with Korean and Chinese officials. Needham, with glasses, is seventh from the left. Kim Il Sung is seventh from the right, summer 1952. (NEEDHAM RESEARCH INSTITUTE)

the sense of truth. To this mind anything it desires is good, and any lie is truth that serves its end."[55]

In January 1998 the Japanese newspaper *Sankei shinbun* uncovered twelve Soviet-era documents. They provided the first evidence that the biological warfare allegations had been fabricated. The documents describe how the North Koreans and the Chinese, with Soviet help, created false evidence.[56] One document described how the hoax was carried out. General Razuvaev, the Soviet ambassador to the DPRK, reported, "With the cooperation of Soviet advisers a plan was worked out for action by the Ministry of Health . . . False plague regions were created, burials of bodies of those who died and their disclosure were organized, measures were taken to receive the plague and cholera bacillus. The adviser of MVD [Ministry of Internal Affairs] DPRK proposed to infect with the cholera and plague bacilli persons sentenced to execution, in order to prepare the corresponding [pharmaceutical] preparations after their death."[57]

What was the reason for the elaborate hoax? Chinese commanders in the field made the initial charges. Mao ordered scientific investigations to confirm the reports before making them public, but the North Koreans prematurely made their charges before the tests were completed. Mao realized that the charges were false, but he decided to take advantage of the opportunity to discredit and embarrass the United States, to maintain China's revolutionary momentum while purging its internal enemies.[58] This happened while the armistice talks were deadlocked over the issue of voluntary repatriation of POWs, and thus allegations of germ warfare could also be exploited for their propaganda value to gain an edge at the talks. Domestically, it came at an opportune moment for Mao. Fear of political impurity and invisible enemies could help mobilize the nation under Mao's leadership to be prepared for a protracted war. Mao exhorted the people to report pro-American attitudes in the intellectual and business communities. The germ warfare campaign would make the link between American biological warfare and spiritual contamination of the Chinese body-politic direct and tangible. Internationally, the charges would expose the hypocrisy of the UN policy of voluntary repatriation. While such heinous war crimes are being committed, the insistence that POWs freely choose where they wanted to be repatriated after the war would appear calculated and shallow.

The Soviet Union went along with the hoax until the spring of 1953, when the Soviet delegation at the UN was ordered to "no longer show interest in discussing this question." Even more strikingly, Moscow told Beijing and P'yŏngyang that the Soviet government was now aware that the allegations claiming that the United Sates had used biological weapons were false. A May 1953 resolution of the presidium of the USSR Council of Ministers (which ran the Soviet Communist Party immediately after Stalin's death in March 1953) noted that "the Soviet Government and the Central Committee of the CPSU [Communist Party of the Soviet Union] were misled" and concluded that "the accusations against the Americans were fictitious." In order to remedy the situation, the resolution recommended that "publication in the press of materials accusing the Americans of using bacteriological weapons in Korea and China" cease and that "the question of bacteriological warfare in China (Korea) be removed from discussion in international organizations and organs of the UN."[59] Apparently, the Soviets had resolved to distance themselves from the hoax because it "damaged Soviet prestige."[60]

Regardless of the decisions made by the Soviet Union's new leadership to abruptly end the propaganda campaign, the allegations had already begun to die down by the summer of 1952. This is because another scandal, tragically of Washington's own making, did far more damage to America's image abroad and UN credibility on the POW repatriation issue than communist allegations of bacteriological weapons ever did.

Kŏje-do

On May 7, 1952, the new UN commander in chief, Gen. Mark Clark, landed at Haneda Airport in Tokyo. General Ridgway was glad to see him. After a year as commander of both the UNC and the Far East Command, Ridgway was relieved to be leaving. "The negotiations with the communists were my major concern throughout most of my remaining tenure in the Far East Command," Ridgway later wrote. "They were tedious, exasperating, dreary, repetitious and frustrating."[61] Ridgway was going to Paris to be the Supreme Allied Commander Europe (SACEUR), replacing General Dwight Eisenhower, who had decided to try for the Republican nomination in the 1952 presidential election.

Clark had become well known as commander of the Fifth Army in the Italian Campaign during World War II. He had also gained a reputation for being vainglorious. A former superior, Gen. Jacob Devers, described Clark as a "cold, distinguished, conceited, selfish, clever, intellectual, resourceful officer."[62] Clark would have to rely on all of those traits in dealing with the communists at P'anmunjŏm. He had no illusions about the difficulty he faced: "I had been in on much of the Korean planning in Washington and knew that this would be the toughest job of my career."[63] What Clark did not know was that on the very day of his arrival, he would be confronted with one of the biggest crises of the Korean War. On Kŏje Island (Kŏje-do), some thirty miles off the southeast coast of Korea and the site of the main UNC POW camp, Brig. Gen. Francis Dodd, the camp commandant, was taken hostage by North Korean prisoners. They threatened to kill him if their demands were not met.

By December 1951, there had been indications of serious problems in the camp. The first problem was overcrowding. Between September and November, over 130,000 prisoners had been taken, owing to the success of the Inch'ŏn operation. The UNC had not anticipated nor was it prepared to hold such a large number of prisoners. In January 1951, with the number of POWs reaching 140,000, the prisoners were consolidated into one complex of compounds on Kŏje-do to ease the task of holding them and to reduce the number of guards needed. The camp was originally designed to hold 5,000.[64] The prisoners were literally packed in with minimal fencing, which permitted them to communicate freely among themselves as well as with local villagers. Through sympathetic villagers and refugees, the Chinese and North Korean authorities were able to pass messages back and forth to the POWs. As a result, the communist prisoners received instructions from and coordinated with P'yŏngyang and Beijing to instigate mass demonstrations, riots, and other disturbances. The inadequate guard force was another major problem. There were simply not enough guards nor were they of a quality "to insure the alertness needed to detect prisoners' plots or to identify and isolate the ringleaders."[65] As a virtual civil war raged between the prisoners, with former Chinese Nationalist and anticommunist Koreans (many of whom had been forcibly enlisted in the NKPA) clashing with their pro-communist opponents, beatings, mock trials, and murders became a daily occurrence. The UN guards, especially the Americans charged

Pro–North Korean compound, May 31, 1952. The banner says, "Long live General Kim Il Sung, the acclaimed leader of our people and the supreme commander of the Korean People's Army." (U.S. NATIONAL ARCHIVES AND RECORDS ADMINISTRATION)

with administering the camp, were intimidated or indifferent and did not take actions to prevent the incidents.

In mid-February, a large riot broke out when thousands of staunch North Korean communists refused to allow UN personnel to enter their compound to conduct preliminary prisoner screening. "There were approximately 3,000 civilian Korean internees in Compound no. 62," wrote Sir Esler Dening, the first British ambassador to Japan after World War II, who was then serving as political advisor to the UNC. "Amongst them were a fairly high proportion of fanatical communists, and the Americans had reasons to believe that these latter were using strong arm tactics to coerce 'deviationists' (e.g. anti-communists) amongst the internees into line." The result was a clash between UN guards and the prisoners that resulted in the death of dozens of prisoners. The incident was the first real indication that something was terribly wrong at Kŏje-do. "Unfortunately, the episode is a very disagreeable one and I fear, brings the United Nations Command nothing but discredit," concluded Dening.[66] R. J. Stratton, chief of the China and Korea Department in the British Foreign Office, was sufficiently alarmed to ask Sir Oliver Franks, the British ambassador to the United States, to raise the issue with the U.S. secretary of state: "If you see no objection, it might be well to draw Mr. Acheson's attention informally to the possibility of repercussions in the House of Commons, which, as he knows, has a long tradition of humanitarian interest in cases of alleged brutality."[67] The implied "repercussion" pertained to continued British participation in the war.

Camp conditions deteriorated rapidly. P. W. Manhard from the American embassy reported that leaders in the pro-Nationalist Chinese compounds "exercise[d] discriminatory control over food, clothing, fuel, and access to medical treatment," and pro-Nationalist prisoners controlled former CPV soldiers by means of "beatings, torture, and threats of punishment." He feared that "mounting resentment among the Chinese POWs [against the pro-Nationalist leaders] constituted an increased threat to the security within the UN POW camp."[68] A detailed public report by UNCURK after the commission's visit in mid-March described a situation that was clearly out of control. G. E. Van Ittersum, the Dutch representative, wrote that "no American ever enters the compounds . . . In many compounds there is no sewage. Dead and seriously wounded people are hardly ever extricated."[69] Pro-communist compounds were strewn "with banners and placards with such slogans as 'Down with American Imperialism.'" General Dodd told the commission that "he did not have enough guards to have these signs removed." In another pro-communist compound the commission "found about 5,000 communist prisoners formed round a square beating drums and shouting communist songs." Dodd, "fearing a hostile incident," requested that commission members quickly withdraw. The commission was barred from entering a third pro-communist compound. The prisoners, he said, "had not allowed any American to enter the camp on the two previous days." Moreover, during the commission's visit, "this compound was being bombarded with stones thrown across the road from a non-communist compound." Unmistakenly shocked, UNCURK concluded, "The visit to Koje-do made clear to the commission members the possibility of further political disturbances." As for Dodd, "he is living on the edge of a volcano and on any day there might be fresh outbreaks of violence and more deaths."[70]

On the evening of May 6, members of Compound 76 asked for a meeting with Dodd to discuss their complaint over beatings by Korean guards and poor living conditions. Compound 76 contained some 6,400 North Korean prisoners who were categorized as "zealous communists" and had violently refused to be screened by UN personnel in April. In exchange for a meeting they agreed to be rostered and fingerprinted. UN personnel had not been able to enter the camp for many weeks, and Dodd was directed to complete a roster of the remaining POWs. Dodd agreed and arrived on the afternoon of May 7 with five guards. He spoke to the prisoners through the fence. Shortly after the meeting began, a work detail of forty prisoners was permitted to pass through the gate under the supervision of two guards. The gate was opened, allowing some of the prisoners talking with Dodd from the inside to step outside. The last few men of the detail suddenly rushed Dodd as they were about to pass the gate and dragged him inside. Bewildered, some of the American guards swung their weapons to their shoulders, but Dodd shouted, "I'll court-martial the first man who shoots." The prisoners closed the gates and then raised a sign painted on ponchos, about twenty-five feet in length, which read, in stilted English:

WE CAPTURE DODD AS LONG AS OUR DEMAND WILL BE SOLVED, HIS SAFETY IS SECURED. IF THERE HAPPEN BRUTAL ACT SUCH AS SHOOTING, HIS LIFE IS DANGER[71]

News of Dodd's kidnapping quickly reached Ridgway. Ridgway informed the Joint Chiefs that the prisoners were capable of a mass breakout, which might result in the capture of the island itself. An American infantry battalion and a company of tanks were immediately dispatched to the island. General Van Fleet appointed Brig. Gen. Charles Colson to take charge of the camp and to negotiate Dodd's release.

Soon after his capture, Dodd sent a message that he was unharmed but that he would be killed if force was used to try to rescue him. He passed on the prisoners' demand that two delegates from each of the other compounds be brought to Compound 76, "where a conference would be held to discuss grievances and settle the terms on which he would be released."

The next morning, May 8, Dodd was confronted by representatives from all compounds, Chinese and North Koreans. One by one they spoke, "each having prepared a good deal of evidence" for their accusations of violence and abuse allegedly suffered. It was an extraordinary account of "concentrated and unvarnished tale of murder, torture, and thuggery, rape (for there were delegates from the women's compound) and of the unrelieved brutality of the men under his [Dodd's] command."[72] One described how some prisoners had been beaten by other prisoners because they wanted to return to North Korea. Others displayed evidence of torture, claiming that the scars on their bodies had been inflicted by the South Korean guards. "The warehouse bookkeepers explained how the camp supplies were sold by ROK soldiers to the black market. Two female prisoners told their stories about frequent rapes and gang rapes by both guards and prisoners." The prisoners drew up a list of nineteen counts of death and injury caused by the South Korean guards. One Chinese prisoner recalled that "[Dodd] became nervous and sometimes seemed touched by the stories. He just said: 'I can't believe it. I can't believe it.'"[73] On May 10, three days after Dodd's capture, Colson received a statement written in Korean, with a poor but comprehensible English translation, that the prisoners said he must sign to secure Dodd's release.

> 1. Immediate ceasing the barbarous behavior, insults, torture, forcible protest with blood writing, threatening, confinement, mass murdering, gun and machine gun shooting, using poison gas, germ weapons, experiment object of A-bomb, by your command. You should guarantee PW's human rights and individual life with the base on the International Law.
> 2. Immediate stopping the so-called illegal and unreasonable volunteer repatriation of NKPA and CPVA [Chinese People's Volunteer Army] PW's.
> 3. Immediate ceasing the forcible investigation (Screening) which thousands of PW's of NKPA and CPVA be rearmed and falled in slavery, permanently and illegally.
> 4. Immediate recognition of the PW Representative Group (Commission) consisted of NKPA and CPVA PW's and close cooperation to it by your command. This Representative Group will turn in Brig. Gen Dodd, USA, on your hand after we receive the satisfactory declaration to resolve the above items by your command. We will wait for your warm and sincere answer.[74]

Colson was appalled. He could not sign such a document. He responded with a revised version. Dodd offered to modify Colson's draft so that it was acceptable to both sides. Over the next few hours, Dodd, Colson, and Senior Col. Lee Hak-ku, the POW spokesman, engaged in furious back-and-forth exchanges until a final statement was agreed upon.[75] That evening, Colson signed the document and Dodd was released.

It was now up to General Clark to clean up the Kŏje-do mess and make sure that it never happened again. "As Ridgway waved good-bye," remembered Clark, "I visualized him throwing me a blazing forward pass." Clark was unsure whether he was ready to catch the ball. Earlier that morning, Clark had written a public statement denouncing the text of the POW demands and of Colson's agreement. Clark was upset not only that Dodd and Colson had accommodated the prisoners' demands but also that Colson signed a letter containing incriminating language that could be used against the UN negotiators in P'anmunjŏm:

> I do admit that there have been instances of bloodshed where many PW have been killed and wounded by UN Forces. I can assure that in the future that PW can expect humane treatment in this camp according to the principles of International Law. I will do all within my power to eliminate further violence and bloodshed. If such incidents happen in the future, I will be responsible.[76]

Clark stated that "the allegations set forth in the first paragraph are wholly without foundation," and that "any violence that has occurred at Kŏje-do has been the result of the deliberate machinations of unprincipled communist leaders whose avowed intent has been to disrupt the orderly operation of the camp and to embarrass the UNC in every way possible."[77] Dodd also released a statement including an account of his capture. He ended it with a justification of sorts: "The demands made by the PWs are inconsequential and the concessions granted by the camp authorities were of minor importance."[78] Clark could not have disagreed more. Colson's statement and the entire Dodd affair had greatly damaged the UN position. Ridgway agreed: "The United Nations Command was asked to plead guilty to every wild and utterly baseless charge the Red radio had ever laid against us."[79] By admitting that there had been "instances of bloodshed" and that "prisoners of war had been killed or wounded by UN Forces," Colson had undermined the moral foundation of the UN, and in particular, the principle of voluntary repatriation, which was based on the assumption of fair and equal treatment. Dodd and Colson were punished by being demoted to colonel.[80]

Clearly changes had to be made at Kŏje-do. Clark sent Brig. Gen. Hayden Boatner, the "tough, stocky and cocky" assistant commander of the Second Infantry Division, to replace Colson. The compounds were broken up, and some prisoners and all civilian internees were moved to other camps. Routine inspections were enforced, and anti-UN or pro-communist banners and signs were forbidden. But the UNC had suffered a severe blow to its credibility. "At the time of the Secretary of State's statement in the House on the repatriation question on May 7, we had no reason to doubt the validity of the screening process," wrote Charles Johnston from the China and Korea Department of the British Foreign Office. "The revelations which we now have of the conditions in the camps must give us serious misgivings on the fairness and accuracy of the census." He concluded, "We still stand firmly on the principle of voluntary repatriation; but we must be sure that the factual foundation on which that principle rests is sound."[81]

Acheson told Foreign Secretary Anthony Eden in late May that "the incident on Kŏje Island had greatly weakened the moral position of the United Nations Command," and that it was "urgently necessary to restore this."[82] Johnston lamented that Britain's image had been tarnished by the whole affair. He was angry that the British had been kept out of the loop on the Kŏje-do incident. The Foreign Office, however, had been well aware of the troubling conditions on Kŏje-do for quite some time. In December 1951 it had raised concerns about the camp but had been rebuffed. "Is U.S. State Department now in a position to supply the authoritative statement on recent events on Kŏje requested in our telegram No. 2039 of 16 May?" Johnston demanded. "It would be regrettable and embarrassing if the results of the United Nations Command's enquiry into these recent disturbances on Kŏje were withheld from us, as were those on the 18 February and the 13 March riots."[83] From then on the Foreign Office insisted on being kept directly informed about the POW situation. Some members of the British House of Commons even began whispering that "the troubles of Kŏje-do would probably never have happened if the prison camps had been under British control." Many British officials were privately "scathing on the subject," although they did their best to hide their disdain publicly.[84]

It was only months later that Clark realized the full extent of the "civil war" and general lawless conditions that had existed at Kŏje-do. There were whisperings that Dodd and Colson had been unfairly scapegoated and that Ridgway and Van Fleet deserved much of the blame. But the anticipation of an imminent truce meant that the POW problem was largely soft-pedaled in the hope that a quick armistice would resolve all the problems. Any public revelation of the conditions at Kŏje-do, it was thought, would give the communists another excuse to delay the talks. The irony is that the armistice did not resolve the problems at Kŏje-do. Rather, the situation at Kŏje-do complicated the problem of reaching an armistice. The Dodd affair and everything that it revealed about the conditions of the camp had seriously compromised the principle of non-forcible repatriation. It gave the communists fodder for refusal based on claims that the screening process had been unfair. By May 1952, the war seemed to have reached a moral and physical stalemate. It would take a new American president to move the struggle forward, even at the risk of a nuclear war.

CHAPTER TWELVE

Armistice, at Last

President Truman's approval rating sank to 22 percent by February 1952. The war remained an unresolved nightmare, mired in petty haggling at P'anmunjŏm and punctuated by fierce battles over a landscape that resembled the horrors of World War I trench warfare. Many thought Korea was a conflict that was neither noble nor necessary. Edith Rosengrant of Springfield, Colorado, a widowed mother of six children, wrote a stinging letter to Truman, enclosing her son's posthumously awarded Purple Heart: "Soldiers need help when they are fighting ... Dick's life was thrown away by his own country's cowardly leaders."[1] Halsey McGovern of Washington, D.C., lost two sons in Korea, Lt. Robert McGovern, who won the Medal of Honor, and Lt. Jerome McGovern, who won the Silver Star. They died within eleven days of each other in early 1951. Mr. McGovern took an even more dramatic and unprecedented action than Mrs. Rosengrant to express his bitterness. He notified the Pentagon that he would not accept the Medal of Honor, the nation's highest award for valor, or the Silver Star on behalf of his sons because the president was "unworthy" to "confer them on my boys or any other boys."[2]

Donna Cooper of Memphis, Tennessee, also returned the Purple Heart awarded to her fallen son, Pvt. Paul Cooper, who was killed in October 1951. She wrote:

> Dear Mr. President:
>
> Today I buried my first-born son. Having known the depth of his soul, I can find no place among his memories for the Purple Heart or the scroll. I am returning it to you with this thought: To me, he is a symbol of the 109,000 men who have been sacrificed in this needless slaughter, a so-called police action that has not and could never have been satisfactorily explained to patriotic Americans who love their country and the ideals it stands for. None of us appreciate the degradation and ridicule we have to suffer because of a pseudo war. If there had been a need for armed con-

Robert McGovern and Francis McGovern as students at St. Johns College High School in Washington, D.C. Robert McGovern was a member of Company A, 5th Cavalry Regiment, First Cavalry Division. He was awarded the Medal of Honor for his actions near Kamyangjan-ni on January 30, 1951. Eleven days later, his brother, Francis McGovern, posthumously earned the Silver Star for his actions near Kŭmwang-ni while serving with Company I, 9th Infantry Regiment, Second Infantry Division. (COURTESY OF CHARLES MCGOVERN)

flict to preserve the American way of life, I could have given him proudly and would have treasured the medal. However, since there was nothing superficial in his whole life, I cannot mar his memory by keeping a medal and stereotyped words that hold no meaning and fail to promise a better tomorrow for the ones he died for.[3]

Recrimination and disillusionment over Korea, rabid McCarthyism, and personal attacks against Truman and Acheson brought with them a thirst for profound political change. Eisenhower's declaration of his candidacy for president in 1952 led many to express optimism that his experience in foreign policy and moderate position on domestic issues made him just the right person to replace Truman.

"I Shall Go to Korea"

Polls showed that the war was the foremost issue on the American people's minds, and the election would largely become a referendum on Korea. Eisenhower addressed the issue directly on October 24, when, in a blistering speech, he promised to forgo "the diversions of politics" and concentrate on the task of closing the war that "has been the burial ground for 20,000 American dead." Korea, he said, "has been a sign, a warning sign, of the way the Administration has conducted our world affairs" and "a measure, a damning measure, of the quality of leadership we have been given." If elected, Eisenhower declared dramatically, "I shall go to Korea." The speech drew high praise and rave reviews from the press. The *New York Times* hailed the speech and endorsed Eisenhower. For Emmet Hughes, Eisenhower's speech writer, "psychologically, this declaration ("I will go to Korea") probably marked the end of the campaign. Politically, it was later credited . . . with sealing the election itself."[4] Truman, however, thought using the tragic Korean situation for political gains was contemptible. "Ike was well informed on all aspects of the Korean War and the delicacy of the armistice negotiations," recalled the chairman of the JCS, General Omar Bradley. "He knew very well that he could achieve nothing by going to Korea."[5] Still, the speech was a masterful political stroke, for it put the Democrats on the defensive, and Eisenhower's promise to go to Korea, while not offering a specific policy proposal to end the war, nevertheless offered a chance at something new.

Eisenhower won in a landslide against Adlai Stevenson. Keeping his campaign promise, the president-elect announced that he would go to Korea on November 29. He was not yet sure how he would end the war, but he did possess one significant advantage. Republican critics such as Senators Robert Taft and William Knowland would be silent, at least for the time being, and this gave the incoming administration much greater freedom to maneuver.

As soon as news of Eisenhower's planned trip reached Seoul, President Syngman Rhee announced that he would be given a rousing reception, including a mass rally, parades, and dinners. Rhee saw the visit as an opportunity to convince the new president to resume the offensive to achieve Korean unification. Rhee thought Eisenhower would be sympathetic to the cause of "total victory" both as a military man and as a Republican. "I expect General Eisenhower to bring peace and unity to Korea," the South Korean president told the *New York Times*. "We are depending on him."[6] The JCS instructed General Clark to tell Rhee that there would be no public receptions or appearances for Eisenhower

Korean civilians during a rally held in anticipation of President-elect Eisenhower's forthcoming visit to Seoul, November 25, 1952. (U.S. NATIONAL ARCHIVES AND RECORDS ADMINISTRATION)

because it was too dangerous. The visit would be brief, and Eisenhower's advisors cautioned him to avoid Rhee. "President Syngman Rhee is old and feeble," warned John Foster Dulles, Eisenhower's choice for secretary of state, before his trip. "His will is still powerful and he has three obsessions: (1) To continue power; (2) to unite all of Korea under his leadership; (3) to give vent to his life-long hatred of the Japanese." Dulles recommended "that political matters be discussed as little as possible with Rhee."[7]

Eisenhower's time in Korea consisted almost entirely of touring the front and visiting units. He saw his son John, who was serving in the Third Infantry Division. When Eisenhower declined to attend a welcoming ceremony in Seoul, Rhee refused to take no for an answer. On December 4, Rhee went to downtown Seoul where a large "U.S. President-Elect Eisenhower Welcome Rally" at the Capitol Building had been organized. A huge crowd bearing American flags and "Welcome Ike" banners had gathered to see and greet Eisenhower that afternoon. General Paek Sŏn-yŏp recalled the disappointment: "Rhee sat on the stand and waited for the Americans to change their minds and for Eisenhower to show up. I accompanied President Rhee and shook from the cold, as some one hundred thousand Seoul residents waited in bitter weather, sitting on the plaza in front of the Capitol. We waited for Eisenhower, but he never came."[8] Realizing that Eisenhower would not show up, Rhee went to the presidential residence to wait for the president-elect's courtesy call. Paek was furious. "Whatever the Americans' real reasons [for not meeting Rhee]," Paek later reflected, "this communication dealt a severe blow to the prestige of a sovereign head of state." Paek immediately got in touch with General Clark, telling him that in no uncertain terms he could not imagine a "greater affront" to South Korea. "If the president-elect does not visit President Rhee," Paek threatened, "you will insult President Rhee, of course, but you will also offend the Korean people. If a meeting between the two men does not materialize, any and all future cooperation between the ROK Army and the United States will be jeopardized." Taken back by the vehemence of Paek's response, Clark immediately got on the phone with his staff. A meeting was arranged.[9]

On December 5, the day the president-elect was due to depart, Eisenhower finally met with the South Korean president and his cabinet. The meeting lasted just forty minutes, and nothing substantive was discussed. Rhee nevertheless made sure that the meeting was recorded for posterity. General Clark recalled that the "newspaper people were there, including still and movie photographers. Rhee was certain he was going to have a fine record of the Eisenhower visit."[10] The old patriot needed to save face, but he was angry and confused. He had thought Eisenhower had a grand strategy to drive the communists out of Korea. Eisenhower made it clear, however, that he would not seek unification but rather a truce in Korea, and pursued an alternative strategy to end the war: "My conclusion, as I left Korea, was that we could not stand forever on a static front and continue to accept casualties without any visible result. Small attacks on small hills would not end the war."[11]

On December 5, as Eisenhower was flying from Seoul to Guam, MacArthur delivered a speech to the National Association of Manufacturers at the Waldolf Astoria Hotel in New York City, where he announced that he had come up with a solution on how to end the war in

Korea. Eisenhower was informed of MacArthur's proposal, and a meeting between the two men was quickly arranged. Despite mutual antipathy (MacArthur once dismissed Eisenhower as a "mere clerk, nothing more"), Eisenhower was curious to know what the old general had to say. They met in New York City on December 17. MacArthur handed him a copy of his "Memorandum for Ending the Korean War." The plan called for a two-party conference between the president and Stalin to "explore the world situation as a corollary to ending the Korean War" and to agree that "Germany and Korea be permitted to reunite under forms of government to be popularly determined upon." If Stalin refused such a meeting, the president should inform him that it was the intention of the United States "to clear North Korea of enemy forces . . . through the atomic bombing of enemy military concentrations in North Korea and sowing the fields with suitable radioactive materials . . . to close major lines of enemy supply and communication leading south from the Yalu." The president should also threaten to "neutralize Red China's capability to wage modern war." The memo, MacArthur explained, presented "in the broadest terms a general concept and outline." He would also "be glad to elaborate as minutely as desired."[12]

Eisenhower listened patiently and said, "General, this is something new. I'll have to look at the understanding between ourselves and our Allies in the prosecution of this war." Privately, Eisenhower was appalled. "He didn't have any formal peace program at all," Eisenhower later confided. "What he was talking about was the tactical methods by which the war could be ended."[13] But the nuclear question remained a central question when Eisenhower deliberated on how best to end the war. Sharp disagreements over how atomic weapons might be used became the focus of intense debate. The air force and the navy believed that atomic bombs might constitute sufficient pressure to force China to accept reasonable armistice terms. The army strongly disagreed. Army Chief of Staff Joe Collins noted that the Chinese and North Koreans were dug in underground across the front and provided poor targets for atomic weapons. Bradley was concerned that casualties in a new offensive would be so great that "we may find that we will be forced to use every type of weapon that we have."[14]

There was also concern about the impact of the use of nuclear weapons on the UN coalition in Korea. Between February and May 1953, the

National Security Council conducted a series of meetings that were far more "discursive than decisive" in an effort to find a way to end the war.[15] Notwithstanding interservice differences, the threat of Soviet retaliation, and the "disinclination" of allies to go along with a military proposal that included nuclear weapons, Eisenhower wanted to take a more "positive action against the enemy" and concluded that "the plan selected by the Joint Chiefs of Staff was most likely to achieve the objective we sought." The JCS plan included the option of employing atomic weapons "on a sufficiently large scale to insure success." Secretary of State Dulles, then on a trip to India, told Prime Minister Nehru that "if the armistice nego- tiations collapsed, the United States would probably make a stronger rather than a lesser military exertion, and that this might well extend the area of conflict." He also told Nehru that "only crazy people could think that the United States wanted to prolong the struggle, which had already cost us about 150,000 casualties."[16] Dulles's intent was for Nehru to pass the message to the Chinese that the United States was prepared to use nuclear weapons if an armistice agreement was not soon forthcoming. But Nehru apparently passed no such message to the Chinese and later denied having any role in conveying Washington's atomic warning.[17]

Whether Nehru's denial is to be believed or not, the Chinese were aware that Eisenhower was considering the nuclear option. The new American ambassador to the Soviet Union, Charles Bohlen, was instructed to "emphasize" to the Soviet foreign minister the "extreme importance and seriousness of the latest UNC proposals" by pointing out "the lengths to which the UNC has gone to bridge [the] existing gap" and "making it clear these represent the limit to which we can go." Furthermore, Bohlen was to point out that "rejection [of] these propos- als and consequent failure [to] reach agreement in the armistice" would create a situation that Washington is "seeking earnestly to avoid."[18]

Most Americans and others around the world at the time believed that the threat of nuclear war coerced the communists to reach an armi- stice agreement. "We told them we could not hold it to a limited war any longer if the communists welched on a treaty of truce," Eisenhower told his assistant, Sherman Adams. "They didn't want a full scale war or an atomic attack. That kept them under some control."[19] But had nuclear coercion really worked in Korea? Was the threat of nuclear warfare the most important factor in forcing the communists to reach an armistice agreement?[20] The answer is, probably not. First, Chinese leaders were well aware of the potential of an American nuclear attack. Indian Ambassador K. M. Panikkar recalled that when Truman raised the possibility that atomic weapons might be used in Korea in late November 1950, "the Chinese seemed totally unmoved by this threat." General Nie Rongzhen told Panikkar early in the war that "the Americans can bomb us, they can destroy our industries, but they cannot defeat us on land. We have calculated all that. They may even drop atom bombs on us. What then? After all, China lived on farms."[21] The Eisenhower administration's alleged threat of nuclear war was also issued nearly two months *after* the communists had already made a significant compromise at P'anmunjŏm. An unexpected breakthrough occurred in March 1953 when the communists suddenly became conciliatory. On March 30, Zhou Enlai declared that the communists would agree to voluntary repatriation.[22] Whatever happened to change the communists' minds between October 1952, when the armistice talks were suspended, and March 1953, it could not have been the nuclear threats made in May. The forces of peace were already in motion in Korea *before* any alleged threat of nuclear war was made.[23]

What, then, had happened to change the communists' mind? Why had they finally come around on the POW voluntary repatriation issue after two years of fruitless talks? If not "atomic brinkmanship," what suddenly pushed them to the path toward peace?

Death of a Dictator

On March 4, 1953, the Soviet people awoke to the radio bulletin that Stalin was gravely ill. He had suffered from a "sudden brain hemorrhage" with loss of consciousness and speech.[24] The world soon learned that Stalin was dead. Power was assumed by a coalition of four men: Georgi Malenkov was appointed premier. Lavrenti Beria retained his position as minister of the interior, while V. M. Molotov, who had known Stalin longer than anyone else, became foreign minister. Nikita S. Khrushchev became Central Committee secretary. There was other startling news. Sweeping changes in the government and party hierarchies were announced.

In the months before his death, Stalin appeared intent on keeping the flames of the war burning bright. In August and September 1952, Stalin and Zhou met to discuss the war's course. Zhou wanted a settlement in Korea, but he approached the matter with Stalin cautiously, seemingly to agree with Stalin's hard-line stance while attempting to explore the possibility of a negotiated settlement. Zhou noted that "the [North] Koreans were suffering greatly" and were anxious to bring the war to a close. Stalin responded caustically that "the [North] Koreans have lost nothing except for casualties." The Americans, he said, "will understand this war is not advantageous and they will have to end it." He claimed that the "Americans are not capable of waging a large-scale war at all," because "all of their strength lies in air power and the atomic bomb." Stalin advised that "one must be firm when dealing with America"; patience was required to beat them. "The Americans cannot defeat little Korea," Stalin mockingly declared. "The Germans conquered France in 20 days. It's already been two years and the USA has still not subdued little Korea. What kind of strength is that?" Belittling America's alleged weakness was probably galling to Zhou since it was the Chinese, not the Russians, who were fighting and dying in Korea. Zhou stated that if the United States "makes some sort of compromises, even if they are small, then they should accept" them, but only "under the condition that the question of the remaining POWs will be resolved under mediation by some neutral country, like India, or the remaining POWs transferred to this neutral country, until the question is resolved."[25] Zhou was trying to find a way to end the impasse over the POW issue. But Stalin continued to discourage the Chinese premier's desire for flexibility. He reiterated his hard-line stance to Mao in late December.[26]

General Clark anticipated communist rejection of the proposal made on February 22, 1953, for the exchange of sick and wounded POWs: "There was dead silence for over a month," he recalled.[27] Three weeks after Stalin's death, the silence was broken. The communists not only agreed to exchange the sick and wounded but also proposed a resumption of the talks, which had been suspended for nearly six months. The communists had abruptly changed their tune and became conciliatory. Stalin's death was a turning point in the war, although few had been prepared for it.

Many had believed that post-Stalinist Russia would experience a great upheaval. "Some in the West predicted that the Soviet Union would surely undergo a bloodbath," recalled Ambassador Bohlen. But the predictions proved wrong. Within days of Stalin's death, it appeared that the so-called guardians of unity—Malenkov, Beria, Molotov, and Khrushchev—were firmly in charge.[28] They ushered in a striking shift in foreign policy. Malenkov announced a "peace initiative" in mid-March, stating that "there is no litigious or unresolved question which could not be settled by peaceful means on the basis of the mutual agreement of the countries concerned ... including the United States of America."[29] A few days later, Radio Moscow admitted, for the first time since the end of World War II, that the United States and Great Britain had played a role in the defeat of the Axis Powers. Stalin's "Hate America Campaign" of 1952 was abruptly suspended.[30] During Stalin's final days, Moscow had been festooned with anti-American propaganda: "Placards portraying spiderlike characters in America military uniform ... stared down at us from every fence throughout the city," George Kennan observed.[31] These disappeared. The Russians also agreed "to intervene to obtain the release of nine British diplomats and missionaries held captive in Korea since the outbreak of the Korean War." The changes were not confined to Korea. The Soviet government withdrew Stalin's 1945 claim to the Turkish provinces of Kan and Ardahan and control of the Dardanelles. After weeks of refusal, Moscow agreed to the appointment of Dag Hammarskjöld as the new secretary general of the United Nations. Moscow also proposed the possibility of a meeting between Malenkov and Eisenhower to discuss "disarmament and atomic energy control." On June 8, Molotov told the Yugoslav chargé d'affaires that Moscow wanted to send an ambassador to Belgrade, "the first move toward repairing the rupture with Tito."[32]

It was all breathtaking, but the biggest change was Moscow's desire to end the Korean War. On March 19, the Soviet Council of Ministers adopted a resolution that was a complete review of Soviet policy in Korea. In "tortuously convoluted language" that reflected the Kremlin's unease at fundamentally altering Stalin's Korea policy, the resolution declared,

> The Soviet Government has thoroughly reviewed the question of the war
> in Korea under present conditions and with regard to the entire course of
> events of the preceding period. As a result of this, the Soviet Government
> has reached the conclusion that it would be incorrect to continue the line

on this question which has been followed until now, without making those alterations in that line which correspond to the present political situation and which ensue from the deepest interests of our peoples, the peoples of the USSR, China, and Korea who are interested in a firm peace throughout the world and have always sought an acceptable path toward the soonest possible conclusion of the war in Korea.[33]

The resolution outlined "statements that should be made by Kim Il Sung, Peng Dehuai, the government of the PRC, and the Soviet delegation at the UN" to quickly achieve an armistice.[34] Two weeks later, the communists responded positively to Clark's proposal for exchanging sick and wounded prisoners while also announcing their intention to obtain a "smooth settlement of the entire question of prisoners of war."[35]

Despite the breakthrough, Clark was suspicious: "I could not help but think, as I read the proposal to resume armistice talks, that perhaps it was the anesthetic before the operation."[36] The feeling was widely shared in Washington and London. Dulles, in particular, was highly suspicious of the new Soviet leadership and their "peace offensive." British Foreign Secretary Eden also shared the skepticism, arguing that what changes there seemed to be in Russian policy might be "tactical" moves to dupe the West. Eden, like Dulles, believed that the Soviet Union merely wanted to be more accommodating to gain time to consolidate the new leadership. The Kremlin, according to Dulles, was trying to "buy off a powerful enemy and gain a respite." Moreover, he argued, it would be an "illusion of peace" if there was "a settlement [in Korea] based on the status quo." The United States needed to make "clear to the captive people that we do not accept their captivity as a permanent fact of history."[37]

Despite Dulles's reservations, Eisenhower wanted to take advantage of the moment and responded with his own peace offensive in a speech on April 16. He called it "The Chance for Peace." Eisenhower said he welcomed the recent Soviet statement, but he could accept them as sincere only if the words were backed by concrete deeds. He called for a Soviet signature on the Austrian treaty, an agreement for a free and united Germany, and the full independence of the Eastern European nations. He also called for the conclusion of an "honorable armistice" in Korea. "This means the immediate cessation of hostilities and the prompt initiation of political discussions leading to the holding of free elections in Korea." In exchange, Eisenhower said, he was prepared to conclude an arms-limitations agreement and to accept international control of atomic energy to "insure the prohibition of atomic weapons."[38] There was no reference to Taiwan or China. It was an expression of the American vision of the conditions of peace in Europe and Asia. The persuasive power of the speech was essentially reactive, not proactive. For critics of the Eisenhower administration, the speech was more political posturing than an actual compromise effort to achieve détente with the Soviet Union.[39]

Still, the speech was well received. Sherman Adams called it "the most effective of Eisenhower's public career and certainly one of the highlights of his presidency."[40] Walter Lippmann commended the president for "seizing the initiative" and for beginning discussion and negotiations of the greatest complexity and consequence."[41] But nothing significant was achieved because of it. Moreover, incredibly, it was during this time that the Eisenhower administration began contemplating the use of nuclear weapons to achieve a quick end to the Korean War. Ambassador Bohlen in Moscow believed the United States had missed an important opportunity to fundamentally change its relationship with the Soviet Union after Stalin's death: "I wrote Dulles that the events could not be dismissed as simply another peace campaign designed solely or even primarily to bemuse and divide the West."[42] Three years of fighting an angry and frustrating war in Korea had embittered Americans against the Soviet Union, and thus it was probably no surprise that Bohlen's observations fell on deaf ears in Washington. The temporary thaw between the Americans and the Soviets after Stalin's death did not bring about measurable changes in their relationship, but it did make possible the exchange of sick and wounded prisoners in Korea. In mid-April an agreement was reached at P'anmunjŏm, and Operation Little Switch repatriated seven hundred UNC POWs and seven thousand communist POWs between April 20 and May 3. Only one item remained for resolution for an armistice: the selection of neutral nations to serve as custodians of the prisoners refusing repatriation. But this issue was relatively minor compared to previous hurdles. "Despite these annoyances," recalled General Clark, "progress toward an armistice appeared to be rapid. None of the disagreements that still existed appeared to be too difficult to overcome."[43]

Divided Nation

The talks at last reached the point of settlement in early June. The final issue of selecting neutral nations to supervise voluntary non-repatriates was settled when the communist side agreed to establish a Neutral Nations Repatriations Commission with five members—Poland, Czechoslovakia, Switzerland, Sweden, and India. These countries would share in the task of maintaining custody of the non-repatriates in their original places of detention. India would be in physical custody of the non-repatriates. Communist and UN authorities would question the non-repatriates for final verification that their decision was made voluntarily and free of coercion.[44] As the negotiators began working out the last details, Clark reported that "the resolution of the POW issue will now make the signing of the armistice agreement possible in the near future and possibly as early as June 18."[45]

After nearly two years of negotiations, peace was finally in sight. But one final obstacle remained: Rhee refused to get on board. "An armistice without national unification was a death sentence without protest," he declared.[46] After meeting Rhee just before the POW terms were agreed on, Clark reported that "he had never seen him [Rhee] more distracted, wrought up and emotional." Rhee had always held out hope that the armistice negotiations would fail. Clark later wrote, "My relations with South Korea's venerable, patriotic and wily chief of state had been excellent right up to the moment the United States indicated clearly it intended to go through with an armistice that might leave his country divided. Then I became a whipping boy for his bitterness and frustration."[47] Proclaiming the right of self-determination, Rhee insisted that peace must be restored by the Koreans themselves: "We reassert our determination to risk our lives to fight on to a decisive end in case the United Nations accepts a truce and stops fighting. This is imperative because the presence of Chinese Communist troops in Korea is tantamount to denying us our free existence."[48]

Washington had assumed that Rhee's threat to continue fighting alone was a bluff and that he would sign the armistice, and so the administration was caught off-guard by the emotional intensity of his opposition and the scale of popular support from the South Korean people.

Clark suggested a mutual security treaty to placate Rhee and the South Koreans. Eisenhower agreed and wrote to Rhee that while he empathized with the South Korean leader's "struggle for unification," the time had nevertheless come "to pursue this goal by political and other methods." The enemy "proposed an armistice which involves a clear abandonment of the fruits of aggression," and since the cease-fire line would follow the front lines, "the armistice would leave the Republic of Korea in undisputed possession of substantially the territory which the Republic administered prior to the aggression, indeed, this territory will be somewhat enlarged." He also agreed to negotiate "a security pact . . . which would cover the territory now or hereafter brought peacefully under the administration of the ROK" in addition to providing "substantial reconstruction aid to South Korea." He concluded, "Even the thought of a separation [between the United States and the ROK] at this critical hour would be a tragedy. We must remain united."[49] On June 18, Eisenhower received Rhee's reply. Rhee surreptitiously ordered the ROK Army to release twenty-seven thousand anticommunist North Korean prisoners held in its custody. Clark remembered that "all hell broke loose, at Rhee's order."[50]

The release of the prisoners had been carefully planned. The idea had originated with Rhee himself. Former prime minister Chŏng Il-kwŏn, a senior army commander at the time, recalled that the "release was planned in top secret between retired Maj. Gen. Wŏn Yŏng-dŏk [as provost marshal general in charge of the Korean guard force] and Rhee," and that he himself had been kept in the dark.[51] Only at the last minute was the plan disseminated to key subordinates. At 2:30 a.m. on June 18, Wŏn's men abetted the prisoners' escape by "cutting the barbed wire and killing the camp lights." Meanwhile, the Americans, under orders to fire only in self-defense, tried to turn back the mass of prisoners with tear gas, "but the gas proved useless."[52] When news of the escape was made public, Rhee immediately acknowledged his role in the plan.[53]

Eisenhower was aghast at Rhee's perfidy: "What Syngman Rhee had done was to sabotage the very basis of the arguments that we had been presenting to the Chinese and North Koreans for all these many months. In agreeing that prisoners should not be repatriated against their will, the communists had made a major concession. The processing of the prisoners was observed by representatives of both sides. This condition

was negated in a single stroke by Rhee's release of the North Koreans."
Eisenhower immediately sent a warning to Rhee: "Persistence in your
present course of action will make impractical for the UN Command to
continue to operate jointly with you under the condition which would
result there from. Unless you are prepared immediately and unequivocally to accept the authority of the UN Command to conduct present hostilities and to bring them to a close, it will be necessary to effect
another arrangement."[54] But what other arrangements could there be?
The South Koreans could not possibly win the war against China by
themselves and yet they constituted the bulk of the UN fighting force.
Rhee could order ROK forces to withdraw from the UNC. This possibility deeply worried the Americans and other UN participants. Rhee
could sabotage not only the armistice but also the fate of the UNC,
the credibility of the UN itself, and the idea of international collective
security. Prime Minster Nehru laid out these concerns in a memo to
the president of the UN General Assembly: "In view of [Rhee's] action,

Anti-armistice demonstrations, April 1953. (AP PHOTOS)

armistice terms become unrealistic and the United Nations has been put in a most embarrassing position which will undoubtedly affect their credit and capacity for future action." Furthermore, "Chinese and North Koreans can, with reason, object to signing any armistice terms which have not been and are not likely to be carried out." As a result, "the position of United Nations Command in Korea becomes completely anomalous and the question arises whether United Nations Policy must be subordinated to President Rhee's policy." Nehru suggested that the matter be taken up at once by the UN General Assembly since "the whole future of the United Nations is jeopardized."[55]

The South Korean people overwhelmingly supported Rhee's actions. On June 25, the third anniversary of the start of the war, Rhee appeared before a cheering crowd and vowed to unify the nation and "fight communism to the death." With "tears in his eyes," his voice "broken as the loudspeaker carried his words to the crowds and all over the nation through Seoul radio," he declared, "What we want, because we know we will die if we follow our Allies, is to be given the opportunity to fight by ourselves. We simply ask to be allowed to decide our fate by ourselves." The crowd roared and hysterically waved banners that said, "Don't sell out Korea" and "Down with the Armistice."[56] Daily anti-armistice demonstrations in Seoul and other cities and increasing bitterness threatened to sever U.S.-ROK relations. An alarmed Dulles wrote to Rhee,

Dear Mr. President:

I speak to you as a friend of your nation. As you know I have long worked for a free and united Korea. In 1947 and again in 1948 in the United Nations, I initiated for the United States steps which led to the establishment of your government and international acceptance of the proposition that Korea ought to be free and united . . . I pledged our nation's continuing support of that goal. Also, because aggression was an ever-present threat and because your people felt alone, I asserted that free world unity was a reality, and I concluded: "you are not alone." You will never be alone so long as you continue to play worthily your part in the great design of human freedom.

That pledge of unity was hailed throughout South Korea. It was quickly put to the test, for within six days, the aggressor struck, within a few hours, the brave army of the Republic of Korea was overwhelmed by superior forces and the territory of the Republic of Korea was overrun. Then you pleaded for the help of the Free World. It came. The United Nations acted and the United States responded quickly and largely to its appeal on your behalf. We responded because we believed in the principle of free world unity.

The principle of unity cannot work without sacrifice. No one can do precisely what he wants. The youth of America did not do what they wanted. Over one million American boys have left their homes and families and their peaceful pursuits, to go far away to Korea. They went because, at a dark hour, you invoked the sacred principle of free world unity to save your country from overwhelming disaster ...

Your nation lives today, not only because of the great valor and sacrifices of your own armies, but because others have come to your side and died besides you. Do you now have the moral right to destroy the national life which we have helped save at a great price? Can *you* be deaf when *we* now invoke the plea of unity?[57]

The call for unity and the moral outrage against Rhee's actions were echoed around the world. London's *Daily Mail* condemned Rhee for his "treacherous" and "insolent" act, which brought up "a simple, but all-important question: Who is to be in charge in South Korea, the United Nations or Syngman Rhee?" If an armistice failed to materialize, "such is the enormity of Rhee's offense," it declared. "He has demonstrated he is not to be trusted. He should be replaced by someone with a sense of responsibility. If necessary, his whole Government should be bundled out." London's *Daily Herald* was similarly outraged: "The present position is utterly intolerable and the disaster for the world would be incalculable." India's *Delhi Express* stated that "Rhee should be removed at once to a place far from the scene of mischief." The *Times of India* responded that "the situation calls for an all-out action to save peace," while Tokyo's *Jiji shimpō* suggested that the United States depose of "the unscrupulous dictator."[58]

Only the communists reacted coolly. They wanted to end the fighting. Their letter to Clark in early July included the usual vitriol against the Syngman Rhee "clique" for "unscrupulously violating the prisoner of war agreement," but the letter, signed by both Kim Il Sung and Peng Dehuai, nevertheless ended on an upbeat note: "To sum up, although our side is not entirely satisfied with the reply of your side, yet in view of the indication of the desire of your side to strive for an early armistice and in view of the assurances given by your side, our side agrees that the delegations of both sides meet at an appointed time to discuss the question

of implementation of the armistice agreement and the various preparations prior to the signing of the armistice agreement."[59] An uncharacter-
istically generous response, it indicated the communists' determination
to conclude an armistice. The communists also saw Rhee's provocative
actions as an opportunity to splinter the U.S.-ROK alliance. In their
assessment and response to the current state of armistice negotiations,
the Soviet leadership suggested that the Chinese "achieve a common
point of view with the U.S. on the issue of an armistice in order to isolate
Rhee . . . and deepen the domestic and foreign differences of the American side." It was a policy that Kim Il Sung would continue to exploit
in his future dealings with the United States. As the Chinese Deputy
Minister of Foreign Affairs Wu Xiuquan later quipped, "In this case, a
paradoxical situation will be created inasmuch as we and the U.S. are
sort of acting together against Syngman Rhee."[60]

A grim Eisenhower opened an emergency National Security Council
meeting on June 18 lamenting "the terrible situation" for UN forces. How
could UN forces "conduct the defense of South Korea while ignorant
of what ROK forces in their rear would do next?" he asked. If the UNC
was unable to trust Rhee, "how can we continue to provide ammunition
for the ROK forces when we have no idea what their next move would
be?"[61] Removing Rhee, an option considered, no longer seemed possible.
He had gained enormous domestic prestige for his bold defiance. Getting rid of him could create a politically explosive situation that could
lead to mass defections within the ROK Army. The only viable option
was negotiation to get South Korea to agree to the armistice. Walter Robertson, the assistant secretary of state for East Asian and Pacific affairs,
would lead the American team. U. Alexis Johnson, the deputy assistant
secretary of state overseeing Japan and Korea policy, later said, "In Robertson, Rhee had met his match. Garrulous, earthy, charming as it was
possible to be, Robertson could out-talk even Rhee; and his voice had
the kind of soothing richness that could tame even this crotchety mono-
maniac."[62]

Robertson was optimistic. Rhee told him that his arrival in Korea
was "like a hand to a drowning man." Robertson reported to Dulles
that Rhee was "a shrewd and resourceful trader" who was also "highly
emotional, irrational, illogical, fanatic, and fully capable of attempting to lead his country into national suicide." Still, Robertson believed

there was room for compromise. If the Americans could not persuade Rhee to accept an armistice, they would scare him into compliance. Eisenhower told the National Security Council on July 2 that "we can do all sorts of things to suggest to Rhee that we might well be prepared to leave Korea, but the truth of the matter is, of course, that we could not actually leave . . . We must only take actions which imply the possibility of our leaving."[63] The new Eighth Army commander, Lt. Gen. Maxwell Taylor, who replaced General Van Fleet in January 1953, announced on July 6 plans "for the withdrawal of American and British divisions from the battle line with or without the cooperation of the South Korean Army in the event of a truce being signed with the communists."[64] The story was picked up by newspapers around the world, including *The Times of London*, which reported, "An inspired dispatch from Washington even speaks of a possible withdrawal of American and allied forces; and the expectation in the United Nations is that, unless Mr. Rhee is brought to terms, the United Command will proceed to the signature of an armistice without him."[65] Patience and politicking paid off. On July 9, Rhee indicated that he was prepared to cooperate with the United States and not disrupt the armistice talks. In exchange, Rhee received "informal assurances" that the U.S. Senate would ratify the mutual security treaty and provide additional economic and military support. Rhee's bold move had paid off handsomely. Dulles later confided that "we had accepted it [mutual security treaty and aid] as one of the prices that we thought we were justified in paying in order to get the armistice."[66]

With the prospect for peace just around the corner, the communists decided to give Rhee a "bloody nose" just to make sure he would not try another ploy to disrupt the armistice agreement. On July 13 they launched their final offensive. ROK II Corps was driven back six miles and suffered more than ten thousand casualties. The communists had made their point. General Paek Sŏn-yŏp later noted, "The outcome of the Kŭmsŏng battle had dealt a serious blow to the President's prestige."[67] The attack undermined Rhee's credibility that ROK forces could face the Chinese alone. The Chinese had called Rhee's bluff, and thereafter there was no more talk of South Koreans going north.

There was one final obstacle to the signing of the armistice: inside the wooden building in P'anmunjŏm where the armistice was to be signed hung a copy of Picasso's *The Dove*, a painting that had been adopted by the communists as their symbol of peace. Clark ordered this "Red Symbol" removed. After a heated exchange, Picasso's *Dove* painting was finally covered up.

At 10:00 a.m. on July 27, 1953, Lt. Gen. William Harrison, the Eighth Army deputy commander who had replaced Admiral Joy as chief UN delegate in May 1952, and Lt. Gen. Nam Il signed the eighteen-page armistice agreement. They did so in twelve minutes and in complete silence. When finished, they simply got up and left without saying a word. "That's the way it had been throughout the negotiations," said Clark later. "Never during the talks did the delegates of either side nod or speak a greeting or farewell during the daily meetings."[68]

Immediately afterward, the document was taken to Clark at his forward headquarters in Munsan. Three hours after the signing in P'anmunjŏm, Clark sat down at a long table in front of newsreels and TV cameras to sign the document again. He then addressed the audience:

> I cannot find it in me to exult in this hour. Rather, it is time for prayer, that we may succeed in our difficult endeavor to turn this armistice to the advantage of mankind. If we extract hope from this occasion, it must be diluted with the recognition that our salvation requires unrelaxing vigilance and effort.[69]

Many in Korea shared Clark's ambivalence. "The cease-fire caused a measure of anguish in the officers and men of the South Korean army because it perpetuated the division of our nation," wrote Paek. "The lengthy armistice negotiations had given us enough time, however, to accept the reality that we could do nothing about it."[70] There were no victory celebrations in the United States, no cheering crowds in Times Square, no sense of triumph. "The mood," wrote one observer, "appeared to be one of apathy."[71] Yet Eisenhower considered the armistice to be one of his greatest achievements. He had promised to go to Korea and end the killing and this he did. Although Stalin's death and other events played a greater role in ending the war than either Eisenhower or Dulles ever cared to admit, the president had nevertheless put his prestige behind the settlement. He also knew that only a Republican president could have done it. The same settlement coming from a Democratic administration, especially one that had been blamed for "losing" China, would have had a far more divisive effect on the country.[72] Still, the armistice did not resolve the fundamental problem that had precipitated Kim Il Sung's invasion of South Korea. The nation remained divided.

Although the killing had stopped, the war continued, solidifying cold war arrangements for the next fifty years. The Korean War has officially outlasted the cold war, since no formal peace treaty between the belligerents has been signed, and it has persisted in influencing global events, giving birth to a new world order that would directly impact not only the politics and societies in America and China, but also those in the East Asian region and beyond.

PART II
COLD WAR

What impact did the Korean War have on the cold war? Since no peace treaty was signed to formally end the conflict, the Americans and the Chinese continued to view each other warily, setting the stage for another potential superpower confrontation in Asia. What lessons did the United States and China take away from the Korean War that helped them shape their respective responses to the growing conflict in Indochina? How did their experiences in Korea influence their domestic and foreign policies, especially with regard to the Soviet Union? Finally, how did South Korea become the unexpected beneficiary of this continuing cold war struggle, with lasting implications for its own ongoing legitimacy war with North Korea?

Although the fighting in Korea ceased in 1953, the war continued to shape events. The United States emerged staunchly anticommunist with, for the first time in its history, a large permanent standing army, an enlarged defense budget, and military bases around the world. The Korean War also did much to forge Chinese self-perceptions. The Chinese had lost nearly half a million men in Korea, but they had fought the world's greatest superpower to a standstill and emerged with their reputation and self-esteem greatly enhanced. The Korean War led to mass mobilization campaigns that aimed to eradicate the "impure" and "foreign" elements of Chinese society and inspire a politically motivated popular nationalism that Mao used to consolidate his power.

After a brief repose (1954–57) during which China cultivated a new international image to correspond with its claims of peaceful coexistence, as reflected in its role in ending the First Indochina War in Geneva in 1954, China once again reverted to themes of war, revolution, and mass mobilization in the wake of Khrushchev's denunciation of Stalin in 1956. In 1958, Mao started the Great Leap Forward movement for economic development, which led to widespread famine and the deaths of millions. He also initiated military actions against Taiwan in 1958 and India in 1959, partly to divert domestic attention away from the failure of the Great Leap.

China's new radicalism caused strains in the relationship between Mao and Khrushchev. China accused the Soviet Union of abandoning the true principles of Marxism-Leninism by seeking accommodation with the West. It was during this period that China provided substantial military aid to the Vietnamese communists in their struggle to "liberate" South Vietnam. The CCP's claim of leadership of the world revolutionary movement directly challenged the Soviet Union. To China's leaders, the Vietnam War essentially served a similar purpose in radicalizing the Chinese masses as the Korean War had done a decade earlier. In each case, "resisting America" became a rallying cry to mobilize the Chinese population along Mao's revolutionary lines.

Meanwhile, the responses by Presidents John F. Kennedy and Lyndon B. Johnson to the growing awareness of Chinese radicalism and the Sino-Soviet split informed Washington's view of the war in Vietnam and their retrospective view of the war in Korea. Both presidents believed Vietnam to be a test of whether Moscow's seemingly more benign form of communism or Beijing's radical Bolshevism would triumph in the international communist movement. Vietnamese communist success, it was believed, would dramatically encourage the radical national liberation doctrine espoused by China. The dominant assumption was that the Chinese communists were the vanguard of the most aggressive wing of world communism and had to be stopped. The crucial moment that led America down the path to tragedy in Vietnam took place in July 1965, when Johnson committed American power to seek a military solution.

The "lessons" of the Korean War played a significant role in Johnson's decision. Although Eisenhower had opposed American intervention in the First Indochina War on the grounds that he did not want a repeat of Korea, Johnson saw the lessons of that war quite differently. The frustrations of an indecisive victory in Korea had been tempered in time by the domino theory and the notion that the communist threat in Asia had, at least, been contained. The Korean War was now seen as an extension of the cold war and the global struggle against communism. Korea was held up as a model of how the battle line for freedom had been successfully drawn.

Along with the decision to deepen American commitment in Vietnam, Johnson sought to internationalize the war by seeking combat forces from other countries. South Korea's President Park Chung Hee responded positively. Major General Park had come to power in 1961 after a decade of economic stagnation. South Korea during the 1950s appeared to be losing its legitimacy war with the North. Mired in hopeless poverty and plagued by corruption, the gap in economic performance between the South and the North was increasing. In April 1960, a popular uprising, led by labor and student groups, overthrew the Rhee regime. The post-Rhee government floundered. In May 1961, Park Chung Hee and some thirty-six hundred troops staged a coup, steering the country into a new direction.

Park portrayed involvement in Vietnam to his own people as repayment to the free world for saving South Korea during the Korean War, but he also saw an opportunity to strengthen South Korea's security and economy. Washington provided an extensive list of economic and military incentives. Vietnam also furnished a compelling replay of the Korean situation that Park used to rally support for national construction and anticommunism. "Re-fighting" the communists in Vietnam provided South Korea the foundation for the nation's spectacular growth in the coming decades. South Korea's involvement in America's second major cold war struggle in Asia thus brought about enormous advantages for the Park regime, largely because the first struggle in Korea between the United States and China had remained unresolved.

In addition, Park abandoned Rhee's anti-Japanese attitude and normalized relations with Japan. In June 1965 the two countries signed the Treaty of Basic Relations, and South Korea obtained Japanese grants and loans for Park's modernization program. This step had troubling implications for Kim Il Sung, since Japan had recognized the ROK as the only lawful government in Korea. Moreover, the economic benefits accrued to South Korea for help in Vietnam led Kim to believe that South Korea would soon catch up to the North. Time was quickly running out if he was to achieve the "liberation" of South Korea.

Under these conditions and fearful that the South would soon surpass the North in economic and military power, Kim Il Sung began to embark upon a series of provocative actions against the South, setting the stage for a new "phase" of the Korean War.

CHAPTER THIRTEEN

Lessons of Korea

On August 5, 1953, Maj. Ambrose Nugent, former POW from Camp 12, arrived at Freedom Village in Munsan and began weeping uncontrollably. Released as part of Operation Big Switch (the final exchange of prisoners that took place between August 5 and December 23, 1953), Nugent felt elated and relieved, but also confused. "Having been a prisoner of war in the hands of the Asiatic Communists," he later recalled, "and having gone through these periods that we did over there—the death, the starvation, the deprivation, the threat of never being able to return home—reaching Freedom Village was like coming out of a black night. Over the course of the next month, I felt like I was dreaming."[1]

Awakening from that dream turned out to be far ruder than he, or any other prisoner of war, might have expected. Almost immediately after repatriation, the prisoners realized that they would not be going home as heroes, but as suspected collaborators. Even before their homecoming, journalists and military officers began painting a disturbing picture of undisciplined soldiers in Korea who were lacking in camaraderie and patriotism. As many as one-third of the prisoners were suspected of having collaborated in one form or another. Twenty-three American airmen, including a senior marine pilot, Col. Frank H. Schwable, had publicly confessed to germ warfare and other war crimes. Twenty-one American POWs had decided to remain with the enemy. Many prisoners had made public statements against the UN effort in Korea, with particular criticisms of America's conduct in the war. Fourteen former POWs, including Major Nugent, Lt. Col. Harry Fleming, and Lt. Jeff Erwin, all survivors of the 1950 winter death march, were court-martialed for their alleged collaboration with the enemy. Major William Mayer, an army psychiatrist and outspoken critic of the POW behavior, summed up what many Americans thought about the prisoners' "misconduct": "Too many of our soldiers in prison fell far short of the historical American standings of honor, character, loyalty, courage, and personal integrity." He concluded, "The fact that so many yielded to the degree that they did presents a problem of fantastic proportions and should cause searching self-examination by all Americans, both in and out of uniform."[2]

The lack of a clear victory in Korea made questions about the character flaws of the American soldier all the more urgent. What could explain the nation's less-than-total victory in its first confrontation with communism? Some devious force had to be at work, whether this was "Red" infiltration at home or a deep spiritual flaw within American society itself. Whatever the cause, Korean War POWs became associated with all that was wrong with American society: materialistic, pampered, and overindulgent ways had produced men wholly unprepared to face America's ideologically dedicated adversaries. By the end of 1953, Americans were inundated with daily anecdotal evidence of treason. Headlines like "The GIs Who Fell for the Reds," "The Colonel's Korean Turncoats," "Why Did the Captives Cave In?" or simply "The Rats" fed a growing sense of crisis that American society was somehow failing.[3]

Feminized Nation

These concerns were also taken seriously by the Department of Defense and the armed forces. In the aftermath of the POW "debacle," the secretary of defense's Advisory Committee on Prisoners of War was established in June 1955 to provide "recommendations on various aspects of the POW problem, which entailed provisions for a new Code of Conduct" as well as a "program of training and education to make the Code effective."[4] "We must view the communist treatment of prisoners of war as only another weapon in the world-wide war for the minds of men," declared Gen. John E. Hull, the new commander of the Far East Command, to the committee. The foundation of a soldier's strength, he announced, "lies not in armament and training alone" but is "derived in large part from his early environment which shapes his beliefs, builds his loyalty and molds his stature."[5] As symbols of an effete and indulgent society,

Korean War POWs became linked to deep anxieties about the American character. New measures to strengthen American society were therefore deemed necessary.[6] The Korean War experience sharpened Americans' anxieties about their nation's "apathy" in the face of the communist threat by painting the American struggle against these alien forces as a contest between two ways of life: freedom and individualism versus slavery and conformity.

Popular concerns over the apparent loss of manly vigor in the wake of the Korean War also found expression in popular cold war cinema. American films made during this period repeatedly returned to fear of an overwhelming "feminine" force that threatens American manhood/ nationhood. *My Son John* (1952), for example, explores the unhealthy relationship between mother and son that eventually turned John into a communist.[7] Popular science fiction films of the 1950s reinforced these anxieties. As the film scholar Michael Rogin observed, "Biology is out of control in these films ... and reproduction dispenses with the father."[8] In *The Thing from Another World* (1951) the aliens are able to quickly multiply, through detachable body parts. Likewise, in *Invasion of the Body Snatchers* (1956) the ovarian pods take over the body of their victims as they sleep. *Them!* (1954) literally makes the connection between communists and the matrilineal society of giant ants whose multiplying colonies threaten to overrun the free world.

Behind these anxieties lay the emergence of a strong and hostile China. Like the giant insects/aliens that made their appearance onto the Hollywood screen, the Chinese also became associated with these ant- like creatures in the popular mind, made all the more striking by their nocturnal fighting habits and their propensity to dig underground pas- sages and build "nests." "They [the communists] continue unceasingly to burrow and tunnel to advance their positions against the citadels of free- dom," Dulles once famously declared.[9] Moreover, because the end of the fighting in Korea had not settled the contest between freedom and slav- ery, it was feared that the Chinese would take the struggle to other parts of Asia.[10] It was this fear of the Chinese communist threat that had led the Truman administration to support the French in their effort to reestablish their former colonial power in Indochina after World War II. "The loss of Vietnam," Eisenhower was convinced, "would have meant the surren- der to Communist enslavement of millions."[11] Secretary of State Dulles advocated a harsh approach to China, "a policy of containment through isolation" because it held out the promise of ultimately dividing Moscow from Beijing.[12] Chinese forced dependence on the Soviet Union, he believed, would inevitably lead to conflict between them. The Chinese would realize the drawbacks of their dependence, while the Soviets in turn would tire of supporting the Chinese. "My own feeling," explained Dulles, "is that the best way to get a separation between the Soviet Union and Communist China is to keep pressure on Communist China and make its way difficult so long as it is in partnership with Soviet Russia." Yugoslavia's Tito did not break with Stalin because the West was nice to him. "On the contrary, we were very rough on Tito."[13]

The policy also had the concomitant benefit of soothing the domestic forces of the right wing in Congress, which blamed the Truman administration for China's "fall" in 1949. The Eisenhower administration was very aware of the power of the Taiwan-China lobby and the need to cultivate a fervently anticommunist Chinese image to defend itself against potential attacks.[14] Such a policy also allowed the administration to pursue a partial improvement in Washington's relationship with Moscow.

Isolating China would also help to limit the status it gained from holding back the world's greatest superpower in Korea. In his speech before the Oversea Press Club on March 29, 1954, Dulles outlined the administration's position toward Communist China as well as the threat it posed to Indochina. The United States was opposed to recognizing China, he declared, and the reasons were simple: "Will it help our country," Dulles asked, "if by recognition we give increased prestige and influence to a regime that actively attacks our vital interests? Will it serve the interests of world order to bring into the United Nations a regime which is a convicted aggressor, which has not purged itself from that aggression, and which continues to promote the use of force in violation of the principles of the United Nations?"[15] Dulles also believed that by holding back on recognition with Beijing, the United States would enhance the prestige of the anticommunist leaders in Asia. For those "defenders of freedom" it was necessary to show a positive spirit that America and her anticommunist allies would stand strong against the forces of defeatism and tyranny. The new importance of Indochina after Korea thus became part of a developing concern about anti-Western and communist activity in the Third World.

As the architect of Eisenhower's foreign policy, Dulles was also aware that many of the "new nations" that had emerged since World War II "harbored mistrust and fear of the West."[16] Touting American values of freedom while supporting old colonial powers, like the French in Indochina, clearly presented a problem for the Eisenhower administration. And this is exactly what made the Chinese communists so dangerous. They were seen to be taking advantage of the fervor of anticolonialism and independence movements in Asia to enslave them under communism. Any accommodation with China, Dulles believed, would certainly "sow discouragement" among the anticommunist leaders in Asia, since communism would be seen as "the wave of the future"[17] The United States needed to confront the Chinese communists head-on in their battle for the Third World by showing that the "boundless power of human freedom" was stronger than the enslaving myths of communism.[18] "We should be dynamic, we should use ideas as weapons, and these ideas should conform to moral principles," Dulles declared. "That we do this is right, for it is the inevitable expression of a faith ... But it is also expedient in defending ourselves against an aggressive, imperialistic despotism."[19] Smaller countries in Asia needed to be encouraged to take sides. They also had to be presented with a stark moral choice that any accommodation with the Chinese communists would mean turning their back on the self-evident truths of freedom and goodness. This is why the United States would remain implacably opposed to Communist China. "It ... is one thing to recognize evil as a fact," Dulles announced on March 29, 1954. "It is another thing to take evil to one's breast and call it good. That we shall not do."[20]

Dulles's fear of the dynamism of the Chinese communists as the potential "wave of the future" was also a reflection of his anxieties about America's moral decline in the wake of the Korean War. The Chinese represented an "acute and imminent threat" precisely because they were "dizzy with success" and "have an exaggerated sense of their own power."[21] American reaction to this threat had been lukewarm, and he criticized the Truman administration for its "passive" policies. Although he was quick to commend Truman for his forthright decision to respond to the North Korean attack, he believed that the administration's response had merely been reactive. To counter this passive response, a new "policy of boldness" was required. "It is ironic and wrong that we who believe in the boundless power of human freedom should so long have accepted a static political role," he observed. "It is also ironic and wrong that we who so proudly profess regard for the spiritual should rely so utterly on material defenses while the avowed materialists have been waging and winning a war with social ideas, stirring humanity everywhere."[22]

The attempt to rally the nation by invoking themes of boldness and strength also deeply resonated with the American national character. The historian Rupert Wilkinson identified the national preoccupation with national vigor with what he called "the fear of winding down," which "rests on the traditional belief that Americans are people of energy and reach who nevertheless fear the loss of their vigor and competence."[23] Dulles claimed that to defend freedom in Asia, Americans needed to act boldly and thereby "seize the initiative."[24] "We were from the beginning a vigorous, confident people, born with a sense of destiny and of mission," he reminded the nation. "That is why we have grown from a small and feeble nation to our present stature in the world."[25] The anxiety that China might provide an alternative model emulated by other Asian nations thus propelled both Eisenhower and Dulles to proclaim that the United States must act boldly and repulse the Chinese hordes from sweeping over Vietnam and the rest of Southeast Asia. "The violent battles now being waged in Viet-Nam and the aggressions against Laos and Cambodia are not creating any spirit of defeatism," Dulles told the nation on April 19, 1954. "On the contrary, they are rousing the free nations to measures which we hope will be sufficiently timely and vigorous to preserve these vital areas from Communist domination."[26]

The call to action was also in response to a vulnerable Japan. Dulles was concerned over what a communist victory in Vietnam might mean for Japan's future growth. The "workshop of Asia" would be deprived of access to the vital raw materials—tin, tungsten, and rubber—from Southeast Asia that it needed. A communist victory could also undermine Japan's confidence in America's protection. "The situation of the Japanese is hard enough with China being a commie," Dulles declared. If Indochina fell, "the Japs would be thinking how to get on the other side." As he reassessed the repercussions of a communist victory, Dulles concluded that "the Indochina situation" was even "more important than Korea, because the consequences of loss there could not be localized, but would spread throughout Asia and Europe."[27] China's success in Korea had created a new "breeding ground" for communists. Although that "plague on freedom" had been temporarily stopped at the 38th parallel, this did not mean that the communists would not try and find other outlets to reproduce themselves. Admiral Arthur Radford, chairman of the JCS, spoke of Korea simply being "one tentacle" of Chinese communism "that has been denied the prize for which it was reaching." Indochina and then the rest of Southeast Asia were seen as the most viable other prizes. This region "was a very real part of the over-all conflict between the free world and Communism."[28]

Beyond the familiar imagery of communism as a "plague" on human freedom, the fear of a French loss in Indochina had awakened in the Eisenhower administration old fears associated with Japanese conquest, the Greater East Asia Co-Prosperity Sphere and the Yellow Peril. Vietnam was one of the launching pads for the Japanese conquest of Southeast Asia in World War II, and a communist victory in Vietnam could also provide a similar launching pad for other communist conquests. "Communist conquests, if Indochina falls," wrote the *U.S. News & World Report*, "may well follow the pattern set by the Japanese, as officials here see it. In 1940, Japanese 'protective forces' took over Indo-China after the fall of France. That gave Japan a base from which to seize other countries of Southeast Asia."[29]

Linked to concerns regarding American vigor, or lack thereof, was the administration's "New Look" policy, which focused on, among a variety of issues, the role of nuclear weapons both to deter and to defeat communist aggression. Dulles laid out the details of the New Look policy in the April 1954 issue of *Foreign Affairs*, where he explained that the capacity for instant retaliation was the most effective deterrent against a surprise attack. Asserting that the Chinese and the Soviets would always resort to battle conditions involving manpower, which favored them, Dulles observed that "the free world must devise a better strategy for its defense based on its own special assets." These assets included "air and naval power and atomic weapons which are now available in a wide range, suitable not only for strategic bombing but also extensive tactical use."[30] This did not mean, Dulles emphasized, turning every local war into a world war. It did mean, however, "that the free world must maintain the collective means and be willing to use them the way which most effectively makes aggression too risky and expensive to be tempting." In this way, "the prospective attacker is not likely to invade if he believes the probable hurt will outbalance the probable gain." Korea had been the first test of the policy of massive retaliation since, according to Dulles and Eisenhower, it was the threat of massive nuclear retaliation that had finally pushed the communists to settle the conflict. "The essential thing is that a potential aggressor should know in advance that he can and will be made to suffer for his aggression more than he can possibly gain."

Yet, for all his rhetorical power, which the journalist Richard Rovere once characterized as "one of the boldest campaigns of political persuasion ever undertaken by an American statesman," Dulles's repeated calls to "preserve" Indochina from the communists were ambivalently received by the American people.[31] To the administration, attempting to determine the best response to what looked to be, in mid-1954, the inevitable defeat of France in Indochina, a central question was whether Americans would support another war in Asia.

The "Never Again Club"

On March 13, 1954, the Vietnam People's Army (VPA) besieged and assaulted Dien Bien Phu, a major French strongpoint located in northern Vietnam and manned by ten thousand men. As the siege developed, it became clear that the French had underestimated the Communist Vietnamese strength. The possibility of a French defeat loomed, and such an outcome would be a decisive military and psychological victory for the communists. In late March, General Paul Ely, the French Armed Forces chief of staff, arrived in Washington. His mission was to secure American military aid in the form of bombers and a commitment of American air support in the event of a Chinese air attack.[32] Dulles and Admiral Radford were noncommittal about Ely's query regarding Chinese intervention, although the request for bombers was approved. According to Ely, however, he received a promise from Radford that he would push for an approval of airstrikes to relieve the siege. The plan, code-named VULTURE, called for massive strikes against the Communist Vietnamese positions from bombers based on U.S. carriers and in the Philippines.

Radford's plan generated little support among the Joint Chiefs. General Matthew B. Ridgway, then the army chief of staff, was the most vocal in his opposition. Ridgway thought that Radford saw Indochina as a place to "test the New Look" strategy of placing primary reliance on airpower and the threat of massive retaliation to deter communist aggression. To Ridgway, the war in Indochina was an uncomfortable reminder of Korea. He later recalled, "In Korea, we had learned that air and naval power alone cannot win a war and that inadequate ground forces cannot win one either. It was incredible to me that we had forgotten that bitter lesson so soon that we were on the verge of making the same tragic error."[33] Ridgway felt sure that "if we committed air and naval power . . . we would have to follow . . . immediately with ground forces in support." He responded with an "emphatic and immediate 'No'" when asked for his view on the desirability of U.S. military intervention.[34] There was also the question of possible Chinese intervention in Indochina and the widening of the war, which might lead to World War III. UN forces had narrowly escaped this fate in Korea, and Ridgway saw no reason to test that possibility again in Indochina. For him, "no more Koreas" also meant "no more unilateral intervention close to the Chinese border."[35]

To Ridgway and other members of what later became known as the "Never Again Club," the lessons of Korea proved to be a strong incentive against involvement in Vietnam. Vice Admiral A. C. Davis in the office of secretary of defense, for example, warned that "involvement of US forces in the Indochina War should be avoided at all practical costs," because, as he warned, "one cannot go over the Niagara Falls in a barrel only slightly."[36] It was a sentiment echoed throughout the country. One reader wrote to the editor of the *New York Times*,

> We, the American people, have only recently finished (I hope) with the Korean War. This so-called police action cost us over 100,000 casualties and an increased cost of living with higher prices, that we can ill-afford. After reading Secretary Dulles' March 29 statement on Indochina, I wonder if we are going to be again dragged into another "Korea" in Indochina, with more casualties and sacrifices.[37]

Similar concerns were expressed by members of Congress. Many of them opposed the limited air and naval intervention proposed by Dulles and Radford on the ground that such a venture would be a repeat of Korea. Senate Majority Leader William Knowland expressed the unanimous concerns of his fellow congressmen when he said that there should be no congressional action until the administration has secured the commitment of political and material support from America's allies. "We want no more Koreas with the United States furnishing 90% of the manpower," he stated. However, if "satisfactory commitments" could be obtained, "the consensus was that a Congressional resolution could be passed, giving the president power to commit armed forces to Indochina."[38] In effect, Congress insisted that the United States could intervene only as part of a coalition. Dulles later dubbed this plan "United Action." The idea was to create a coalition composed of the United States, the United Kingdom, France, Australia, New Zealand, Thailand, and the Philippines for the joint defense of Indochina and the rest of Southeast Asia against the communist threat. This would also allow the United States to take control of the Indochina situation from the French while at the same time "remove the taint of waging the war for French colonialism."[39] Cooperation from the British and French was vital to the plan's success.

Dulles flew to Europe in April in a frantic round of "shuttle diplomacy" before the Geneva Conference, set up to resolve the Indochina crisis, opened on the twenty-sixth. He had hoped to persuade the British to answer his call for "United Action" to save Indochina, while holding out the prospect of U.S. intervention to France if it remained committed to the fight in Indochina and resisted a negotiated settlement in Geneva. French Foreign Minister Georges Bidault refused, saying that such a commitment would jeopardize the success of the Geneva negotiations. British Foreign Secretary Anthony Eden also made it clear that no decision regarding Dulles's proposal of "United Action" would be made before the Geneva meeting. The looming memory of Korea informed his view: "I did not believe that anything less than intervention on a Korean scale, if that, would have any effect in Indo-China," he later wrote. "If there were such intervention, I could not tell where its consequences would stop." Echoing Omar Bradley's famous dictum made at the MacArthur hearings in 1951, Eden concluded, "We might well find ourselves involved in the wrong war against the wrong man in the wrong place." Eden was also wary of the administration's motives: "Once President Eisenhower had been assured that the United Kingdom would participate in this declaration, he would be prepared to seek Congressional approval for intervention." Prime Minister Churchill shared Eden's concerns. He later confided to Eden, "What we were being asked to do was to assist [Dulles] in *misleading* Congress into approving a military operation." If the United Kingdom acceded to this latest American proposal, "we should be supporting direct United States intervention in the Indo-China war, and, probably, later American action against the Chinese mainland." The best Eden could do was to promise Dulles to revisit the issue in the event that the talks at the upcoming conference failed. More cautious than either Dulles or Radford, Eisenhower was forced to concur: "Without allies . . . the leader is just an adventurer like Genghis Khan."[40]

The Geneva Conference

The prospect of sitting down with the Chinese in an international forum meant to confer both legitimacy and prestige on the PRC was extremely distasteful to the Eisenhower administration. Earlier in 1954 in Berlin, when Soviet Foreign Minister V. M. Molotov proposed a conference in Geneva with representatives from the United States, France, Britain, the Soviet Union, and China to both conclude the Korean War with a peace treaty and end the Indochina War, the Americans at first refused.[41] Dulles, in particular, wanted nothing to do with a conference that provided China equal status. But the deteriorating events in Indochina had forced his hand. Dulles had to go to Geneva if he hoped for cooperation from the French and the British, but not without taking some heat from the Republican right wing and the China lobby, which characterized the conference as nothing more than a "second Yalta" and an "appeasement to communism."

In the weeks leading up to the Geneva Conference, Dulles had thus been forced to walk a fine line between not doing anything that might enhance China's prestige and building an international consensus about Indochina and Korea. By the time the conference began on April 26, it was also clear that the United States, France, and Britain were on the defensive. "One only has to look across the room to poor Bidault, pale, apprehensive, doomed, to see how far we have fallen back since last year," observed Evelyn Shuckburgh, Eden's private secretary. "The serried ranks of yellow faces and blue suits, the confident hand-shakes between Molotov and Premier Zhou Enlai after the latter's speech, the

ashen anger of Dulles" demonstrated that it was the Chinese who were
now on top. Dulles's proposal "to reactivate the UN Neutral Nations
Commission for Korea and try to unite the country, by the withdrawal of
Chinese troops from North Korea," was met with predictable resistance
from the communists. Even the British were perturbed by Dulles's "mor-
alistic denunciations" of the Chinese, which failed to further the discussions. According to Shuckburgh, Eden was "concerned" by the fact that
"with regard to the Korea issue, no reasonable proposition has yet been
put forward from the Western side—nor can be, because the Americans
felt obliged to give further run to the ridiculous South Korean proposal
of elections in North Korea only." Very quickly, it had become apparent
that no solution to Korean unification would be forthcoming.[42]

Nevertheless, the Korean War overshadowed the events. As during
the armistice negotiations at P'anmunjŏm, symbolism became extremely
important. U. Alexis Johnson, who served as the coordinator of the U.S.
delegation, recalled that he was under considerable pressure "to satisfy
Dulles' stringent and convoluted seating requirements" aimed to deny
China its due status as an equal participant of the conference. "This was
China's first major international conference, but we did not want to give
its government any added status." Dulles refused, for example, "to sit
at a table with Zhou Enlai, thus requiring an auditorium-type seating
arrangement"[43] The secretary of state also purportedly refused to shake
hands with Zhou. Zhou never forgot the rebuke, and the incident was
often recounted to visitors with "an air of injured innocence."[44] Despite
American attempts to marginalize the Chinese, however, the Communist
Vietnamese victory at Dien Bien Phu on May 7 significantly enhanced
China's hand. The French defeat and the rising crisis in Algeria made the
French even more desperate to extract themselves from Indochina. The
victory also made the British more skeptical of military intervention.[45]
Eden stalwartly refused to answer Dulles's call for United Action. Chinese Vice Foreign Minister Wang Bingnan recalled that "when the news
of Dienbienphu [sic] came we spread it to each other. We were very much
encouraged and felt more confident in solving the Indo-China issue."[46]
With the aim of breaking the American policy of isolation toward China
by adopting a moderate line, Chinese leaders hoped to win over British
and French support on Indochina by driving a wedge between them and
the United States.[47]

To a large extent, the Chinese were successful. Nevertheless, Zhou and other Chinese leaders were still concerned that the Americans might intervene unilaterally. According to Khrushchev, who had by then become the de facto leader of the Soviet Union, "Zhou Enlai told him before the Geneva Conference that 'China could not meet Ho Chi Minh's demands to send Chinese troops to Vietnam.'" Zhou had also told Ho that "we've already lost too many men in Korea—that war cost us dearly. We're in no condition to get involved in another war at this time."[48] After fighting in Korea, the Chinese wanted to focus on domestic affairs and rehabilitate their economy. Although the French defeat had raised the possibility that the Communist Vietnamese might be able to end the war more or less on their own terms, the Chinese nevertheless pressed their Vietnamese allies into accepting a divided Vietnam to settle the conflict. The Vietnamese were also pressured into agreeing to proposed elections that would eventually unify all of Vietnam. Rather than driving for maximum advantage for their Vietnamese comrades, the Chinese pushed them hard for a compromise solution. Eventually, and not without some resentment, Ho accepted the 17th parallel as a temporary dividing line. Nationwide elections were scheduled to follow in 1956.

The Geneva Conference had thus ended the First Indochina War, although the Korean War remained without resolution. And it was the Korean War experience that had played a decisive role in President Eisenhower's decision *not* to intervene in Indochina in 1954. That decision also began to raise doubts about his New Look strategy and its reliance on "massive retaliation." It had become clear to Dulles and Eisenhower that the threat of massive retaliation would not have saved the situation in Indochina. America and her allies would not risk nuclear war over interests that were, despite all the heated rhetoric, still considered peripheral. Thus, Eisenhower's reaction to the Indochina situation was actually very much in line with Truman's reaction to Korea. Richard Rovere wrote in 1956, "About all that seems to be left of the New Look now is a budget that strengthens the Air Force at the expense of ground forces. But if the worst happens in Indochina, where atomic bombs would be useless as crossbows, the ground forces will have to be restored to their former strength—and then some."[49] Rovere would be proved right.

Eisenhower's Warning

"How can a liberal society provide for its military security when this requires the maintenance of professional military forces and institutions fundamentally at odds with liberalism?"[50] This paradox, first posed by Samuel Huntington in his classic work *The Soldier and the State*, became particularly acute after the Korean War when U.S. foreign policy shifted its emphasis from political and economic "containment" of communism to military security from it.[51] For Huntington, there were three possible answers to this dilemma: The first was to return to the pre-1940 pattern of civil-military relations, that is, "cutting military forces to the bone, isolating military institutions from society, and reducing military influence to negligible proportions." In this way, American society would remain true to its liberal tradition based on the idea that military and democratic values were antithetical and that a large standing army posed a threat to liberty. However, the pursuit of liberty would be realized at the expense of the nation's military security.

The second solution was "to accept increased military authority and influence but to insist that military leaders abandon their professional outlook and that military institutions be reformed along liberal lines." The drawback of this solution was that while it would provide for the continuation of liberalism in American society, it might have to accomplish these goals at the expense of military effectiveness. Finally, the third solution was for society to adopt "a more sympathetic understanding and appreciation of the military viewpoint and military needs." This would require, however, "a drastic change in the basic American liberal ethic."[52] Although none of these solutions was followed exclusively, it was the third solution—the militarization of American society—that was ultimately adopted in the aftermath of the Korean War. Why?

At first, Eisenhower had tried to adhere to the traditional American stance that military and democratic values were antithetical. He recognized early on in his presidency the threat that a large standing army and huge defense expenditures posed to American society. As a staunch Republican, he accepted his party's time-honored view that balanced budgets and low taxes were essential factors in maintaining a healthy economy. Vowing to put the nation on the course to achieve both security and solvency, Eisenhower aimed to eliminate the national deficit, racked up during the Truman administration, by targeting defense for major cuts. For him, "the foundation of military strength, was economic strength."[53] Eisenhower's New Look policy would thus rely almost exclusively on nuclear weapons at the expense of a large permanent standing army. The principle of "massive retaliation" would make war obsolete since, as the American military strategist Bernard Brodie put it, "war and obliteration are now completely synonymous."[54]

But beyond the concern for balanced budgets, Eisenhower was also fearful that huge defense expenditures would lead to America's slide toward becoming a "garrison state." Would America have to become a garrison state in order to fight one? The New Look was Eisenhower's answer to this paradox and to the heightened tensions between the military imperatives of security and the maintenance of a liberal society.

Yet Korea had shown that atomic weapons did not make war obsolete. As Ridgway, Taylor, and other military leaders would later argue, a "properly balanced" force was necessary to prepare for a wide range of contingencies, and only such a force could claim real credibility as a deterrent.[55] Moreover, committing the nation to a strategy that reduced war to the threat of annihilating entire civilian populations also meant that force was no longer an instrument of policy, since such a strategy undercut the very purpose of war itself. Such sentiments, widespread among army leaders during the mid-1950s who deplored the way that nuclear weapons had "corrupted American thinking about war," had given rise to a fierce backlash against the New Look among army leaders. As a result of the New Look, wrote one Army officer,

> we have accepted civil destruction as an object of war and a means of war where formerly it was an incident of war. The question raised is not of humanity but of reality—whether we have forgotten that war is still a political instrument which must have political objectives and methods . . . This error leads to the brutalization of war without purpose, to a preoccupation with mass destruction, to the neglect of political realities.[56]

Ultimately, Eisenhower's New Look failed. By relying on nuclear weapons, Eisenhower had attempted to balance military imperatives and democratic values, but the solution proved unworkable. His strategy of massive retaliation had offered only two choices: the initiation of general nuclear war—Armageddon—or compromise and retreat.[57]

Thus when John F. Kennedy came into office in 1961, the stage was set for a new defense policy. Although Kennedy was not adverse to the use of nuclear weapons, the main tenet of his defense strategy, Flexible Response, was the resurgent role that the army would play "to put out a brushfire war before it becomes a conflagration." Kennedy believed that the security of the free world required that the United States "have military units capable of checking Soviet aggression at any scale of violence."[58]

Flexible Response also aimed to reinvigorate U.S. global power through the expansion of the range of options available to policy makers, by demonstrating a U.S. willingness to fight non-nuclear wars. During President Kennedy's first year in office, military outlays rose 15 percent. Between 1961 and 1962, the army's budget increased, and 207,000 soldiers were added to its rolls. The number of active-duty divisions increased from eleven to sixteen. Kennedy also dispatched additional ground troops to West Germany "to bolster U.S. commitment to NATO." In 1961, he dispatched four hundred American Green Berets to South Vietnam; by 1963, there were sixteen thousand American military personnel in that country, a huge increase from Eisenhower's nine hundred advisors.[59] Whereas Eisenhower had tried, and failed, to resolve the fundamental tensions in civil-military relations through reliance on nuclear weapons, Kennedy had opted to resolve these same tensions by adopting Huntington's third solution: making American society more militarized.

Military influence during this period had indeed extended throughout the government, and from there to virtually every area of American life. Few developments more dramatically symbolized the new status of the military than the links forged between the business community and the armed forces. While military spending helped to revive the flagging aviation industry in New England, it also contributed enormously to the economic boom of the American West. Civic and local leaders in places like California, Colorado, New Mexico, and Utah organized sustained efforts to capture a large share of the defense budget, which in turn shaped, often dramatically, the growth patterns in those regions. The *Denver Outpost*, for example, began tracking the economic benefits of government procurements, which included more than $1.5 billion for metal mining in western states.[60] Utah's defense industry complex, in particular, grew very rapidly. By 1963, the state was receiving $408 million in defense contracts, an absolute gain of 1700 percent since the outbreak of the Korean War, and the largest gain recorded by any state for the same period.[61] These expenditures helped to reopen hundreds of mines, add new jobs, and increase the state's income, all of which in turn laid the foundation for new industries.[62] A similar dynamic affected California, which dominated the fast-growing military aviation, missile, and electronics industries that accounted for the bulk of military procurements. Nearly 25 percent of all persons employed in manufacturing, equivalent to one out of every fifteen of those employed in the state, worked in the defense industry.[63]

Although traditional isolationists like Republican Senators Robert Taft and William Jenner would continue to hammer away on the point that the national purpose was "to maintain the liberty of our people" rather than "reform the entire world or spread sweetness and light and economic prosperity to peoples who have lived and worked out their own salvation for centuries," the Korean War had made these isolationist views largely irrelevant.[64] The Great Debate of 1951, between the Old Right "isolationists" like Senator Taft and the cold war liberal interventionists like Dean Acheson, had by 1961 been firmly settled in favor of the new ideology of national security, which had made it impossible for the United States to retreat from globalism or to reduce its defense spending to the comparatively modest levels of the pre–Korean War period.[65] The influential columnist James Reston of the *New York Times*, in describing the Korean War as a major turning point in American history, wrote that the United States was going to have to live with permanently higher defense budgets, less spending on nondefense programs, and a large peacetime army." "Whether we like it or not," observed Reston of America's new global identity, "we have inherited the role played by the British" of maintaining world peace, and "this role must be organized, not on a temporary, but on a permanent basis."[66]

Eisenhower was keenly aware of the problems that Korea raised. He had won the 1952 presidential election by promising to end the fighting there, but he knew the conflict was not over. The unfinished war would continue to shape events, channeling American policy and state-making into a direction that he feared was wrong for the country. In his farewell address to the nation on January 17, 1961, one of the most important presidential speeches ever given in American history, Eisenhower conceived his good-bye to America as a warning. "A vital element in keeping the peace is our military establishment," he told the nation. "Our arms must be mighty, ready for instant action, so that no potential aggressor may be tempted to risk his own destruction." But the new role of the military in American society raised troubling questions. One was the rising defense budget. "We annually spend on military security more than the net income of all United States corporations," he noted, and the conjunction of "an immense military establishment and a large arms industry is new in the American experience." Eisenhower continued, "We recognize the imperative need for this development. Yet we must not fail to comprehend its grave implications." Then he warned,

> In the councils of government, we must guard against the acquisition of unwarranted influence, whether sought or unsought, by the military industrial complex. The potential for the disastrous rise of misplaced power exists and will persist. We must never let the weight of this combination endanger our liberties or democratic processes. We should take nothing for granted. Only an alert and knowledgeable citizenry can compel the proper meshing of the huge industrial and military machinery of defense without peaceful methods and goals, so that security and liberty may prosper together.[67]

Eisenhower's warning went largely unheeded. The militarization of American society and the ever-growing military-industrial complex had become the Korean War's enduring legacy.

CHAPTER FOURTEEN

Deepening the Revolution

T he Chinese people emerged from the ashes of the Korean War supremely confident. The war had imbued them with a sense of national pride for having fought the greatest superpower to a standstill and affirmed Mao's promise that China would indeed overcome its "century of national humiliation." Mao declared "a great victory in the war to resist U.S. aggression and aid Korea"[1] Recognizing China's new status, Khrushchev assumed a solicitous stance toward Mao and China by ending all unequal agreements between the two nations and by providing Beijing with the necessary economic and military assistance to help China get back on its feet. Khrushchev welcomed the emergence of a strong communist neighbor. The historian William Taubman noted that between 1953 and 1956, "the Soviets agreed to build, or aid, in the construction of 205 factories and plants valued at about $2 billion, with $727 million financed with Soviet credits, all at a time when the Russians themselves suffered shortages."[2] The scale of Soviet largesse was impressive: technological support to initiate or upgrade 156 industrial projects for the First Five-Year Plan; giving up the Soviet share in four Soviet-Sino joint ventures; a corps of experts to tutor the Chinese in everything from road construction to factory management; and blue prints of entire factories.[3] In 1955, Moscow provided nuclear technology, purportedly for peaceful purposes.[4] Moscow even offered to give Beijing a sample nuclear bomb in 1957.[5] "We gave everything to China," recalled Khrushchev. "We kept no secrets from the Chinese."[6]

Besides helping China economically, Soviet leaders were also generous in offering diplomatic and military support. The Soviets insisted on Beijing's participation in the 1954 Geneva Conference on Indochina and Korea. When Mao began shelling the offshore islands of Jinmen (Quemoy) and Mazu (Matsu) in late 1954, during the First Taiwan Strait

Crisis, Khrushchev backed him, even though he was trying to improve relations with the West. The Chinese were also invited to attend the founding meeting of the Warsaw Pact in 1955.[7] Khrushchev later wrote, "We considered the people of the Soviet Union and China to be brothers, and we felt this world was useful not only for us but also for the international communist movement."[8]

But Khrushchev was disappointed with the outcome of Soviet generosity. Even when the Sino-Soviet relationship was at its most harmonious during the mid-1950s, growing tensions were becoming apparent. This happened because Mao was no longer willing to play second fiddle to Khrushchev as he had done with Stalin. He had never forgotten that Stalin had reneged on his promise to provide crucial air support at the start of China's entry into the Korean War, leaving Mao's forces to face the Americans alone. In Mao's view, China had earned its newfound respect and international prestige from the Chinese blood spilled on the battlefields of Korea, and he sought to uphold the memory of these enormous sacrifices by asserting China's equality, and indeed, superiority, with the Soviet Union. No amount of aid or solicitous treatment from Khrushchev would diminish Mao's desire to show just who ruled the roost.[9]

Khrushchev's memories of his first visit to Beijing in 1954 are replete with resentments. For example, when he offered to withdraw Soviet troops from Port Arthur and Dairen and restore the two ports to China, Mao insisted that the Soviets leave their heavy artillery behind. Surprised, Khrushchev refused to do so without payment.[10] Khrushchev had also raised the question of Chinese guest workers coming to Siberia, to help with the cutting of timber. "We thought it was of mutual interest and to some degree would be of assistance to China," wrote Khrushchev, but Mao's reply angered him. "Everyone looks at China as a kind of reserve source of labor," Mao said. "In China this attitude toward the Chinese people is considered insulting." The matter was quickly dropped, though Khrushchev resented Mao's haughtiness. "It seemed to me that Mao could not reconcile himself to the circumstances necessary for healthy relations among socialist countries, circumstances in which each country and each ruling party hold a position of equality with all the others," Khrushchev later declared. "He was aspiring to hegemony of the world Communist movement!"[11]

It was the Polish and Hungarian crisis of 1956 that had brought these private tensions into public awareness. Khrushchev had not consulted the Chinese in advance about his secret speech at the Twentieth Congress in 1956 that denounced Stalin. While Mao had his own grievances against Stalin, he believed it was unwise to undermine the cult of personality. "Mao had an almost mythical faith in the role of the leader," observed Mao's personal physician, Li Zhisui. "He was China's Stalin, and everyone knew it. He shared the popular perception that he was the country's messiah." Khrushchev's attack against Stalin raised uncomfortable questions about Mao's own leadership style and "cult of personality," which was by then well orchestrated throughout the country. Li observed, "For Mao to agree to the attack against Stalin was to admit that attacks against himself were permissible as well." Just as important, Mao saw foreign manipulation in the denunciation. "Mao saw Khrushchev's attack as playing into the hands of the Americans, the imperialist camp," Li later wrote. He also quoted Mao as saying that "[Khrushchev] is just handing the sword to others, helping the tigers harm us."[12]

Khrushchev's handling of the Polish and Hungarian crises of 1956 merely reconfirmed Mao's view of the Soviet leader's deficiencies. His vacillation in the face of the crises, and his apparent reliance on Chinese advice to use force to crush the Hungarian rebellion made it seem, at least to the Chinese, as if they were coaching the Soviets, in a stark reversal of roles.[13] By the end of 1956, Mao began to harbor serious doubts about Khrushchev's competence to lead the communist movement, as Mao had come to believe that the Polish and Hungarian crises had been the direct outcome of Khrushchev's "foolish" denunciation of Stalin. "The sword of Stalin has now been discarded by the Russians," he proclaimed in November 1956, "and some people in Hungary have picked it up to stab at the Soviet Union and to oppose so-called Stalinism." Mao added that "we Chinese have not thrown it away." Mao was becoming increasingly critical of Khrushchev's principle of "peaceful coexistence" between the socialist and nonsocialist worlds. He accused Khrushchev of abandoning the class struggle. Mao asserted that "the Western world had simply used the Hungarian incident to mount an anti-Soviet, anti-communist tide," and he, not Khrushchev, was the more qualified to lead the communist revolution and to dictate the principles underlying the relations between and among socialist countries since he was the true Marxist-Leninist.[14] "Mao thought he was God," Khrushchev complained. "Karl Marx and Lenin were both in their graves and Mao thought he had no equal on earth."[15]

Mao could hardly hide his disdain for his Soviet hosts during his trip to Moscow in November 1957, the first since 1949–50. "The arrangements for Mao and his entourage had been made with the greatest care," reported Li Zhisui. Yet Mao received the Russian hospitality with contempt. "Look how differently they're treating us now," he snapped. "Even in this communist land, they know who is powerful and who is weak. What snobs!" Although two Russian chefs were assigned to him, Mao refused to eat the food they prepared, preferring instead "the Hunanese fare concocted by his favorite chef." Taken to see a performance of *Swan Lake* at the Bolshoi, Mao was immediately bored and announced at the end of the second act that he was leaving. He seemed, in the words of his physician, to be "deliberately refusing to appreciate Russian culture."[16] Khrushchev noticed Mao's "aloof manner." "You could already sense that he placed himself above the rest," Khrushchev angrily recalled. "Sometimes he allowed himself to do things that in general were impermissible, and he did it all without paying the slightest attention to others." The Soviet leader also complained that Mao flirted with his wife during the meetings, saying "indecent things to her laughing." Khrushchev was appalled.[17]

Relations between the two leaders worsened in 1958. Following the harsh crackdown of the failed Hundred Flowers campaign, which had been introduced in 1956 to encourage open criticism of the government and its policies, Mao launched the Great Leap Forward campaign, a new mass mobilization movement to consolidate his power and maintain China's revolutionary momentum.[18] Sino-Soviet tensions escalated during this period as Mao sought to both radicalize China's domestic policies and distance himself from Soviet economic practices. His realization of China's economic backwardness coupled with a new confidence to claim authority in the world communist hierarchy led him to launch the movement, which was intended to turn China into an industrialized power in just a few years. Mao wanted to prove that he was the true successor of Marx and Lenin.

It was at this moment, when Mao decided to assert China's independence from Moscow, that Khrushchev proposed a joint venture: establishment of a communication station on China's coast to serve not only

Soviet submarines in the Pacific but also a joint Soviet-Chinese sub-marine fleet. The Soviets would build the radio station themselves, but the technology would be "in the common interest of the entire socialist camp" since, as Khrushchev put it, "all military resources of the socialist countries were all serving one common cause, to be prepared to repel the imperialists if they unleashed a war against us."[19] Mao's reaction was unexpected. He accused the Soviet Union of "big power chauvinism" and charged them with "looking down on the Chinese people." Further-more, "if the Soviets wanted joint ownership and operation of a subma-rine fleet," Mao sarcastically told Soviet Ambassador Pavel Yudin, "then let us turn into joint ownership and operation of our army, navy, air force, industry, agriculture, culture, education." Or better still, "[you] may have all of China's more than ten thousand kilometers of coastline and let us only maintain a guerilla force." Mao told Ambassador Yudin, "Please report all my comments to Comrade Khrushchev . . . You must tell him exactly what I have said without any polishing so as to make him uneasy. He has criticized Stalin's [policy] lines but now adopts the same policies as Stalin did."[20]

Alarmed by Yudin's report, Khrushchev rushed to Beijing. Between July 31 and August 3, 1958, the two leaders met four times. Khrushchev was mistaken in thinking a personal visit would smooth Mao's ruffled feath-ers, for Mao treated him shabbily if not with contempt. "Mao returned the extravagant hospitality given him in the Soviet Union [in 1957] with a slap in Khrushchev's face," observed Li Zhisui.[21] After four days of inten-sive meetings, an agreement on the construction of the long-wave radio station was eventually signed, but it had been hard fought and revealed the growing discord between the two leaders. Mao would later recall that "the overturning [of our relations with] the Soviet Union occurred in 1958, and that was because they wanted to control China militarily."[22]

Even more alarming than Mao's boorish behavior during the 1958 meetings from Khrushchev's point of view was his view of nuclear war. "Mao regarded as the top priority not the question of peaceful coex-istence, but the question of preparing for war with the aim of crush-ing our enemies in a war, no matter how great the losses such a war might bring to the socialist countries." Mao was not afraid of nuclear war: "The size of the population is decisive, as in the past, in deciding the balance of forces. We have plenty of people . . . There is no country that can succeed in defeating us." Khrushchev was stunned by Mao's bravado. Mao advised that if there was an attack on the Soviet Union, the Russians should offer no resistance. Instead, "you should withdraw gradually," Mao told Khrushchev. "Retreat for a year or two or three. You would force the enemy to extend his lines of communication and thereby weaken him. Then, with our combined forces, we would attack him and crush him." "But where would Soviet forces retreat to?" asked an astonished Khrushchev. "Didn't you retreat as far as Stalingrad? For two whole years you retreated, so why can't you retreat for three years to the Urals or Siberia?" Was Mao playing the fool simply to annoy the Soviet leader? Khrushchev couldn't be sure. Mao's wild rants about preparing for nuclear war worried Khrushchev: "If he [Mao] actually believed that his arguments made sense in terms of military strategy, it's hard to believe that an intelligent person would be capable of thinking that way. To this day, it remains a total mystery to me. I still don't know whether he was being provocative or was simply incapable of thinking clearly."[23]

The talks ended abruptly. Khrushchev had originally planned to stay a week but left after only three days. Mao's churlish behavior and his talk of Soviet forces retreating to the Urals in the event of a nuclear attack had angered and confused him. According to Li Zhisui, however, this had been Mao's intention all along: "The chairman was deliberately playing the role of emperor, treating Khrushchev like the barbarian come to pay tribute. It was a way, Mao told me on the way back to Beidaihe, of 'sticking a needle up his ass.'"[24]

If Khrushchev returned to Moscow believing that the worst of his troubles with Mao were over, he had been sorely mistaken. On August 23, 1958, the Chinese began bombarding the offshore Taiwanese islands of Jinmen and Mazu, initiating the Second Taiwan Strait Crisis without any advanced warning to Moscow. In response, the Americans mounted a massive show of force in the Taiwan Strait. Dulles announced Washington's intention to defend the offshore islands. A Sino-American war would very likely draw in the Soviet Union. Khrushchev secretly sent Foreign Minister Andrei Gromyko to Beijing to find out what Mao was up to. He was relieved by Gromyko's report. Mao's intention was not to provoke a war with the United States, but rather to draw the world's attention to the Taiwan question and to divert American strength from the rest of the world. With these assurances, Khrushchev sent a letter to Eisenhower declaring his country's solidarity with Beijing. The Soviet Union would abide by the Sino-Soviet Treaty of 1950 and would regard an attack on China as an attack on itself.[25] Khrushchev thought as well that the show of solidarity would reduce the threat of war since he believed that Washington would not risk conflict, one that could go nuclear, over Taiwan. Still, Khrushchev was infuriated by Mao's actions. It appeared that Mao's intent was to derail Khrushchev's pursuit of détente with the United States and to undermine his quest for "peaceful coexistence." The shelling may have been Mao's way of declaring war on Khrushchev's "revisionism" and announcing his independence from the Soviet regime. These assumptions proved correct. Mao later confided to Li Zhisui: "The islands are two batons that keep Khrushchev and Eisenhower dancing, scurrying this way and that." For Mao, "the shelling of Quemoy and Matsu was pure show, a game to demonstrate to both Khrushchev and Eisenhower that he could not be controlled, and to undermine Khrushchev in his new quest for peace."[26]

More important than international considerations, however, was Mao's main concern in the summer of 1958 on how to propel the Great Leap Forward movement into its most radical phase, the communization and militarization of the entire Chinese population.[27] On August 17, at a meeting of the Politburo of the CCP, Mao discussed the idea of shelling Jinmen and Mazu. The crisis would help in the mobilization effort of the Great Leap Forward, Mao reasoned, for "tension can help increase steel as well as grain [production] . . . To have an enemy in front of us, to have tension, is to our advantage."[28] Wu Lengxi, the director of Xinhua (New China News Agency) and editor of *People's Daily*, the two main propaganda organs, recalled, "Chairman Mao said that the bombardment of Jinmen, frankly speaking, was our turn to create international tension for a purpose." That purpose was to mobilize the people and to re-create the revolutionary fervor of the civil war and Korean War days. "The shelling of Jinmen-Mazu was a continuation of the Chinese civil war," Mao explained. "No foreign country or international organization should be allowed to interfere in China's affairs."[29] By linking the 1958 Taiwan Strait crisis and the Great Leap Forward, Mao wanted to galvanize the people by evoking their nationalist pride and profound victim mentality. Jinmen and Mazu were part of China's territory that had been "lost" as a result of imperialist aggression (by

Japan and later by the United States), Mao explained. They therefore needed to be recovered. "Taiwan keeps the pressure up," Mao told Li Zhisui. "It helps maintain our internal unity. Once the pressure is off, internal disputes might break out."[30] In the meantime, significant fissures had opened between Beijing and Moscow. Khrushchev departed Beijing after his visit in the summer of 1958, having grave doubts about Mao's "methods for building socialism" and his capacity to deal with the capitalist world in "a rational, cooperative way."[31]

The Tragic Demise of Peng Dehuai

The man who had led Chinese forces in Korea had never been shy about bringing bad news to Mao. Peng Dehuai had always been honest with Mao. When Mao pushed Peng to pursue and drive UN forces from the Korean peninsula during the winter of 1950–51, Peng protested, stating that doing so was foolhardy and would lead to certain defeat. He halted his army near the 38th parallel instead, insisting that his men needed to regroup and rest. Nine years later, Peng warned Mao that he was pushing his people too hard and too fast: grain targets were unrealistic; there was excessive reliance on production of steel of dubious quality from backyard furnaces; the people were exhausted. Peng's conclusion that disaster was looming came from firsthand observations. In October 1958, Peng traveled to the northwestern province of Gansu, which he had liberated from Nationalist forces almost a decade earlier. What he saw shocked him. At an infantry school, classes and training had been canceled because all instructors and students were laboring at backyard furnaces, with "their clothes black as soot." The school staff told him that houses and fruit trees were used for fuel. He saw fields with ripe crops ready for harvest and inquired why they were being left to rot. The reply he received was that there were not enough people to harvest because they had to work at the furnaces. At an iron and steel works, Peng saw "smashed cooking vessels being used as raw materials simply to produce more iron. Useless lumps of it were lying resting on the ground." The whole operation was "futile," Peng told the local cadre and "compared it to beating a gong with a cucumber."[32] Although they agreed, they told him their quota had to be filled.

Peng visited his home province, Hunan, where he met with old friends in his home village, Wushi, not far from Mao's birthplace in the same county, Xiangtan. It was the first time he had visited since the 1920s. The mood of the people was somber. He met aged peasants who were angry, even mutinous. "The youth can tighten their belts; the old can grit their teeth," said one farmer, "but babies? They can only cry." They hated the daily militarized routine, the forced communal living, and the destruction of family life that had been the center of Chinese society for millennia. There was not enough food. He was shown a "dish of vegetables with a few grains of rice" as a typical meal. Peng could see from their physical condition that they were not deceiving him. The cadres, they explained, were under constant pressure to outdo rival communes, which led to chronic exaggeration of crop yields. A set percentage of the yield was taken for provisioning the cities, and when this was applied to the exaggerated yields, there was virtually nothing left for the farmers. The Great Leap was a huge lie. "The old folk indicated to Peng that they could cope with natural disasters, but man-made ones were another matter."[33]

Assessing the success or failure of the Great Leap was not in Peng's portfolio as defense minister, but so great was his distress, especially what he witnessed in his own home town, that Peng decided to write a private letter to Mao on his observations. "By the evening of July 12, I had formed the opinion that serious disproportions had now emerged in China," he later wrote. "This became the burden of my letter dated July 14, 1959. In that letter, I merely set out in general terms several relatively important issues, but made no comment on the causes that had given rise to these problems, indeed, at that time I could not explain the causes." The letter was hand-delivered to Mao at Lüshan, where the Central Committee, the highest authority of the party, was meeting to discuss the Great Leap.

Peng was not prepared for the fury of Mao's response. Instead of handling the letter as a private communication from a trusted colleague, Mao copied and circulated it to the 150 senior cadres attending the meeting. Mao attacked Peng, "declaring that the letter constituted an 'anti-Party program of right-wing opportunism'."[34] He presented a stark choice to the Central Committee: side with Peng and he, Mao, would "go away to the countryside, to lead the peasants and overthrow the government," or side with Mao. He added a direct challenge to the leaders of the PLA. If they did not want to follow him, he would raise another army, a truly Red one this time, and continue the revolution.[35] They sided with Mao, and Peng was censured. Virtually overnight, Peng had become persona non grata. He was forced to move out of his large home to a half-ruined house. For the next six years he lived under virtual house arrest cleaning sewers and collecting refuse.

On December 28, 1966, at the start of the Cultural Revolution, Peng was arrested. His niece said he was continuously beaten and tortured. "During the decade of trouble, uncle was subjected to harsh persecution," she wrote. "After the CPC [Communist Party of China] Central Committee had reviewed uncle's case, I came across one document ... prepared for the group for the Cultural Revolution." The document described Peng's tragic demise:

> Yesterday, at the Peking Aviation Institute, there was a meeting of struggle with Peng Dehuai attended by 30–40 people. Peng Dehuai was at the meeting and was beaten several times. He was wounded in the forehead, and there were internal injuries in the regions of the lungs: tomorrow there will be a new round ... After the meeting of struggle on July 19, 1967, Peng lay on the bed to rest, he had chest pains and difficulty in breathing, groaned constantly and in the evening could not even spit. When he was ordered to write down material, he said: "I cannot write now." On the 22nd—today—the pain in his chest expanded in every direction and became even more serious. He had difficulty getting up off the bed ... and could not speak. The doctor diagnosed two broken ribs, a rapid pulse and high blood pressure, and there were internal injuries.[36]

By the time of his death on November 29, 1974, Peng was unable to speak and had to be fed intravenously.[37] The old revolutionary and hero of the Korean War died of untreated pneumonia in an empty, unheated building at the Municipal Party Committee headquarters in Beijing.[38]

Meanwhile, Peng's predictions about the Great Leap had come true. The Soviets had warned Mao of the coming disaster, but Mao did not want to listen. "They wanted to show us how to build communism," Khrushchev later quipped. "Well, all they got was a stink, nothing else."[39] In 1957, the average annual amount of grain per person in the countryside was 450 pounds. The following year, it dropped to 443 pounds and then to 403 pounds in 1959, and in 1960, it was 348 pounds, a drop of 112 pounds per person in just three years.[40] The result was famine on a grand scale. An estimated 45 million Chinese people starved to death between 1959 and 1962.[41] In the wake of the crisis, the distrust between Moscow and Beijing deepened while the specter of a radical and hostile China increased the fear and loathing of Mao's regime in Washington. From Mao's perspective, however, his management of the crisis had been masterful. He had successfully promoted domestic mobilization by provoking international tensions. Mao's handling of China's domestic and external policies in the late 1950s was a foretaste of what was to come.[42] That is, in the same way Mao used the Korean War to consolidate his power and spur on the revolution, he used succeeding international crises to further that revolution. The next "opportunity" came in Vietnam.

Khrushchev, Korea, and Vietnam

Khrushchev visited Mao in September 1959 immediately following his twelve-day visit to the United States. He and Eisenhower had agreed, in their meeting at Camp David, that "the question of general disarmament is the most important one facing the world today."[43] The visit had made a positive impression on Khrushchev, who later insisted to his skeptical colleagues that Eisenhower was a reasonable "good hearted" man who could be dealt with through personal diplomacy.[44] Mao had not been consulted about the U.S. trip, and he wondered whether "peaceful co-existence" and talks about general disarmament concealed a secret agreement at China's expense. In China, Khrushchev spoke of the "Camp David spirit" of cooperation between East and West, which Mao perceived as an insult since Khrushchev was visiting to celebrate the tenth anniversary of the founding of the PRC and to give homage to the Chinese Revolution and China's victory over foreign imperialism.[45] At Eisenhower's request, Khrushchev asked Mao to release five U.S. citizens held on espionage charges. His awkward mediation further antagonized Mao. As the historian Sergey Radchenko noted, "The Soviet leader lacked the tact to understand that Mao needed no one, least of all Khrushchev, to deal with the West."[46]

Khrushchev and other Soviet leaders became increasingly alarmed by what they considered Mao's "Stalinist tendencies." Mikhail Suslov, a powerful and influential member of the Soviet Politburo, reported on the 1959 meeting, with stinging criticism of Mao's leadership style:

> One should not omit the fact that . . . mistakes and shortcomings in the field of domestic and foreign policy of the Communist Party of China are largely explained by the atmosphere of the cult of personality of com. [comrade] Mao Zedong. Formally, the CC [Central Committee] of the Communist Party of China observes the norms of collective leadership, but in effect the most important decisions are made single-handedly, and thus are often touched by subjectivism, and in some instances are simply not well thought through. Glorification of com. Mao Zedong is visibly and unrestrainedly on the rise in China. In the party press one can increasingly find such statements as "we, the Chinese, live in the great epoch of Mao Zedong," comrade Mao Zedong is portrayed as a great genius. They call him the beacon illuminating the path to communism, the embodiment of communist ideas. The name of com. Mao Zedong is equated with the party, etc. One presents the works of com. Mao Zedong in China as the last word of creative Marxism, of the same rank as the works of the classics of Marxism-Leninism. In effect, the works of com. Mao Zedong are at the foundation of all educational work in the party and in the last two–three years has been reduced to the study of Mao's works. All this, unfortunately, pleases com. Mao Zedong, who, by all accounts, himself has come to believe in his own infallibility. This is reminiscent of the atmosphere that existed in our country during the last years of I.V. Stalin.[47]

Tensions in Sino-Indian relations complicated the situation between Mao and Khrushchev. Prime Minister Nehru's accommodation of the Dalai Lama in the spring of 1959 after a failed Tibetan uprising against Chinese rule had led to a Sino-Indian clash along the Indo-Tibetan border. Khrushchev's decision to maintain a neutral position in the dispute further infuriated Mao, for whom the neutrality indicated that Moscow "had virtually adopted a policy to support India's position."[48] In February 1960, both sides publicly aired their differences at a Warsaw Pact meeting in Moscow. The purpose of the meeting had been to endorse Khrushchev's policy of peaceful coexistence and disarmament proposals in advance of the Soviet leader's big-four summit meeting with Eisenhower scheduled for that spring. Chinese delegates opposed peaceful coexistence, condemning it as being merely a "bourgeois pacifist notion."[49]

The two sides were now on record with "diametrically opposed analysis of world affairs and prescriptions for bloc policies."[50] Two months later, on April 22, 1960, Mao publicly attacked the Soviet Union's foreign policy, using the occasion of the ninetieth anniversary of Lenin's birth to extrapolate on his themes of war and revolution. Citing Lenin, Mao declared that war was the "inevitable outcome of systems of exploitation and the source of modern wars is the imperialist system." As long as imperialism existed, "wars of one kind or another will always occur." Furthermore, "in the light of bloody facts both of the historical past and of the modern capitalist world," peaceful coexistence between capitalist and socialist worlds was a chimera, a myth created by communist revisionists like Khrushchev.[51] Lashing out against Soviet "revisionism," he accused Khrushchev of pursuing policies that were ideologically incompatible with the teachings of Marx and Lenin. Moreover, unlike the Soviet Union, which was unwilling to support national liberation struggles in the Third World, China was the natural ally of the oppressed peoples.

An open clash followed as both sides began canvassing support among other communist parties. For the first time, Khrushchev publicly denounced Mao by name at the Romanian Party Congress in June 1960, calling him an "ultra-Leftist, ultra dogmatist and left wing revisionist who, like Stalin, had become oblivious to any interests but his own."[52] The next month, Khrushchev notified Mao that he would be withdrawing all Soviet advisors and experts from China. Ratified agreements on economic and technological aid were suspended, and hundreds of cooperative scientific and technological projects came to an abrupt halt mid-completion. Khrushchev also reneged on his promise to provide a sample atomic bomb. Mao was shocked and furious.[53] Several weeks after the Soviets withdrew, the CCP leadership left Beijing to escape the summer heat at a seaside resort. Mao vented his anger to the Vietnamese leader Ho Chi Minh, who joined him there:

> Khrushchev can cooperate with America, England and France. He can cooperate with India and Indonesia . . . He can even cooperate with Yugoslavia, but only with China is it impossible on the grounds that we have divergent opinions. Does that mean that his views are identical with America, England, France and India to allow whole-hearted cooperation? [He] withdraws the experts from China and doesn't transfer technology, while sending experts to India and giving technology. So what if China doesn't have experts? Will people die, I don't believe it.[54]

Nikita Khrushchev, Mao Zedong, and Ho Chi Minh at a banquet in Beijing celebrating the tenth anniversary of communist rule in China, October 1, 1959. China's support of Vietnam's struggle began to take a radical turn in 1962 and early 1963 that further strained relations with the Soviet Union. Competition with Moscow for influence in Vietnam drove the two nations further apart but also made the situation difficult for Hanoi, which was now forced to navigate between two contending powers. Moreover, after the catastrophe of the Great Leap Forward, Mao saw an opportunity afforded by the crisis in Vietnam to strengthen his hold on power. In the same way that Mao used the crisis in Korea to instigate the Thought Reform Campaign and the Patriotic Hygiene Campaign to mobilize the masses and consolidate his hold on power, the Chinese leader used the tensions caused by the war in Vietnam to attack Soviet "revisionists" and launch the Cultural Revolution. (AP PHOTOS)

Ho had come to China hoping for assistance for the armed struggle in South Vietnam. Throughout the late 1950s, Mao had counseled Ho on the wisdom of adopting the Bandung line of peaceful coexistence, a policy first advocated by Zhou Enlai in Bandung, Indonesia, when Zhou and Ho met in April 1955. When in 1958 an increasingly frustrated Vietnamese Politburo formally requested China's help in reviving a revolutionary war to bring about a communist victory in the South, Chinese leaders advised caution: "The realization of revolutionary transformation in the South was impossible at the current stage."[55] By the fall of 1959, however, Mao had softened his position because of increasing tensions with the Soviet Union, and agreed to provide the military aid Ho requested. Nevertheless, Chinese leaders were uneasy that Ho might prematurely escalate the conflict from guerilla war to conventional war. It would be better to wage a protracted guerilla war "for three to five years, even eight or ten years."[56] Chinese leaders were wary of provoking a wider war with the Americans in Vietnam. China's policy toward

Vietnam underwent a major shift in late 1962 and early 1963, owing to increased military support to Saigon from the Kennedy administration. The North Vietnamese feared that American forces would attack the North. Alarmed, Mao substantially increased military aid.[57]

In addition, China's economy had begun to recover by the end of 1961, and Mao felt personally vulnerable. The myth of his "eternal correctness" had been called into question for the first time by the disaster of the Great Leap Forward. His colleagues favored more moderate policies by allowing family households to grow produce in their own private plots, offering more freedoms and status to intellectuals, and moderating China's foreign policy toward its principle antagonists, namely, the Soviet Union, the United States, and India.[58] Mao feared the influence of Soviet-style "revisionists" within his own ranks. Moreover, the abrupt withdrawal of Soviet aid in July 1960 had cast China into deep isolation from the rest of the world. Mao believed that his apocalyptic vision of the inevitable struggle between the forces of revolution and reaction was in the process of being fulfilled. He was not about to be marginalized on the eve of this fateful struggle.

Finally, the lessons of the Korean War had instructed Mao on the profound linkage between war and revolution. Renewed militancy abroad would serve his purpose by creating militancy at home. Throughout 1962–64, Mao repeatedly emphasized that the Chinese people were facing reactionary forces both from within and from outside their country. They needed to be prepared for the inevitable war. "In our country, we must . . . admit the possibility of the restoration of reactionary class," Mao declared at the Central Committee's Tenth Plenum in September 1962. "We must raise our vigilance and properly educate our youth . . . Otherwise, a country like ours may yet move toward its opposite. Therefore, from now on, we must talk about this every year, every month, every day . . . so that we have a more enlightened Marxist-Leninist line on the problem."[59]

Although Mao's emphasis on war and revolution played an important role in plotting his comeback, it was the debate over Vietnam policy where Mao attempted to gain an advantage in any challenge to his authority. Vietnam crystallized the essential tenets of Mao's revolutionary ideology: his rejection of the possibility of peaceful coexistence and his view of China's new and central role as supporter of Third World liberation movements. The contest between Mao's revolutionary goals and the more moderate policies favored by so-called revisionists was brought to a head during the spring and summer of 1962, when Wang Jiaxiang, head of the CCP's International Liaison Department, openly challenged Mao. Wang had been deeply affected by the failures of the Great Leap. While he was convalescing from an illness in Canton, he received a report about the mass starvation in Hunan Province and "became emotional and wept." Believing that the CCP needed to concentrate on China's domestic problems and adopt a more moderate line to reduce international tensions, Wang warned the party's leadership against becoming involved in another war with the United States, this time in Vietnam. He criticized the tendency to overrate the dangers of world war and underestimate the benefits of peaceful coexistence. As for supporting revolutionary movements in Asia, Africa, and Latin America, Wang advocated reducing the costs of foreign entanglements. "At times like the present economic crisis, China had to consider very carefully what it spent overseas and not go overboard."[60]

Wang Jiaxiang's ideas came under heavy attack by Mao during a conference of party members held in Beidaihe in August 1962. The Chinese leader condemned Wang for promoting the policy of "three reconciliations and one reduction" as appeasement to imperialism, revisionism, and international reactionism, and reduction of assistance to support anti-imperialist forces in other countries.[61] He rejected the idea that the "Soviet Union of today" would be "China's tomorrow," saying that he sought a different future for China.[62] By the end of 1962, Mao was able to reassert his control over China's foreign and domestic policies. His decision to censure Wang and other revisionists, including future leader Deng Xiaoping, came hand in hand with the adoption of a more radical policy toward Vietnam.[63]

However, when the United States launched its first air strike against North Vietnam in August 1964, Mao wanted to avoid the apparent mistake he had made in Korea by selecting the wrong channel to convey China's warning. Mao did not want a direct Sino-American clash. The Chinese believed that one of the reasons why the Americans had ignored the warning in October 1950 against crossing the 38th parallel in Korea was because the Truman administration did not trust the messenger, Indian Ambassador Pannikar, who was thought to be anti-American and thus unreliable.[64] This time Mao chose an American ally, Pakistan, through its president, Ayub Khan, who was scheduled to visit Washington the following spring, to deliver a warning. Zhou Enlai asked Khan to convey to President Lyndon Johnson that "if the United States expands the war, the war will gradually be expanded to China. We are prepared both materially and spiritually."[65] The Americans would not dismiss a message coming from their Pakistani ally so quickly.

But the visit was unexpectedly canceled. The Chinese attempted other channels. They sent the warning for Washington to Burmese leader Ne Win and Cambodia's Prince Norodom Sihanouk. On April 20, Zhou himself delivered the message in a speech to leaders of the NAM in Bogor, Indonesia, at a gathering to mark the tenth anniversary of the Bandung Conference. He stated that "if the United States bombs China, that means bringing the war to China. The war has no boundary. This has two meanings. First, you cannot say that only an air war on your part is allowed, and the land war on my part is not allowed. Second, not only may you invade our territory, we may also fight a war abroad." In order to emphasize the seriousness with which the Americans should take China's warning, Zhou declared that "the Korean War can be taken as evidence." On May 16, Zhou reassured a visiting Vietnamese National Liberation Front (Vietcong) delegation of China's solidarity with their cause, telling them that "we will go to Vietnam if Vietnam is in need, as we did in Korea." Finally, the British senior diplomat in China, chargé d'affaires Donald Hopson, was summoned to a rare meeting on May 31 with Foreign Minister Chen Yi. Chen told Hopson that he would be "grateful" if Hopson could pass on the warning to the Americans.[66]

The Korean analogy thus set the stage for escalating the war in Vietnam for the purpose of radicalizing the Chinese masses and leading them toward the Cultural Revolution. At the same time, warnings to the Americans *not* to expand the war to China were based on the lessons of Korea and were clear indications that Mao wanted to avoid another Korean-style confrontation.[67] What Mao did not anticipate was how his Vietnam policy would lead to the complete breakdown of Sino-Soviet relations. Ironically, their joint support of North Vietnam contributed to the growing acrimony between them. As China plunged into the chaos of the Cultural Revolution, Mao faced the possibility of a war with the Soviet Union.

CHAPTER FIFTEEN

Korea and Vietnam

I would suggest to you that if we had not gone into Korea, I think it would have been very unlikely that we would have gotten into Vietnam.

—GEORGE BALL, July 1986[1]

We are duty-bound and obliged to defend a friendly ally from Communist aggression, just as the 16 allies of the free world, led by the United States, saved us in the Korean War of 1950.

—PARK CHUNG HEE, February 1965[2]

By 1965 the Sino-Soviet split had become obvious. But these new developments did not mean that the communist threat to the free world had diminished in any way. Both the Kennedy and Johnson administrations saw the split and Sino-Soviet competition in the communist world as actually leading to greater efforts on the part of Moscow, and Beijing, to exert communist control over the Third World. "We see stepped up attempts to subvert, to undermine, and to spread Communist revolution," the elder statesman W. Averell Harriman observed.[3] Staunch anticommunists like W. W. Rostow echoed the same theme: "The impulse in Moscow to seek the expansion of Communist power is so deeply rooted and institutionalized that Soviet leaders will feel an almost historic duty to exploit gaps in the capacity, unity and will of the West."[4]

It is not surprising that the Kennedy administration saw the fate of Vietnam tied to new concerns about communist activities in the Third World. These concerns were carried over into the Johnson administration after Kennedy's death in November 1963. In a key speech on April 7, 1965, Johnson explained why America had to be involved in Vietnam. Directly, America had a moral duty to honor the pledge made at the Geneva Conference in 1954 to protect Vietnamese independence. More broadly, Vietnam was part of the American commitment to protect the free world order, and stopping the communist threat in Vietnam was especially vital to halting the Chinese threat to that order. "The central lesson of our time is that the appetite of aggression is never satisfied. To withdraw from one battlefield means only to prepare for the next," Johnson passionately stated.[5] William Bundy, assistant secretary for Far Eastern affairs, echoed the charge:

> We recognize the profound implications of the Sino-Soviet split and the possibility that it may lead to greater tensions between the U.S.S.R. and Communist China in the northern regions. But we doubt that the U.S.S.R. has yet abandoned her Communist expansionist aims, and certainly not to the point where in the foreseeable future she could be relied upon to play a constructive role in assisting other nations to defend themselves against Communist China . . . And let us recognize too that, to the extent that Soviet policy has changed, or may change in the future, this will be in large part due to the fact that we, in partnership with other free-world nations, have maintained a military posture adequate to deter and to defeat any aggressive action. We do not aim at overthrowing the Communist regime of North Vietnam but rather at inducing it to call off the war it directs and supports in South Vietnam . . . If Hanoi and Peiping prevail in Vietnam in this key test of the new communist tactics of "wars of national liberation," then Communists will use this technique with growing frequency elsewhere in Asia, Africa and Latin America.[6]

America's challenge in Vietnam was to prevent these "wars of national liberation" from spreading. When asked in April 1965 how Americans could hope to compete with China in influencing Southeast Asia, "which is virtually a Chinese backyard," Secretary of State Dean Rusk replied, "Why not? These countries in Southeast Asia have a right to live out their own lives without being overrun by the outside . . . their national existence depends upon it. If we were to abandon that idea then the great powers would—what? Revert to the jungle?"[7] For Rusk the problem of South Vietnam essentially boiled down to a replay of the war in Korea: North Vietnam, with the backing of China and the Soviet Union, was waging a war of aggression against a sovereign state.

In 1954, as senator, Johnson, along with Senator Richard Russell Jr., the chairman of the Senate Armed Services Committee, had been the loudest and strongest opponent of American military intervention in Indochina. And yet, as president, Johnson embarked on a series of intervention actions in Vietnam, the sort he had advised Eisenhower against a decade earlier. Why? Why had the "lessons" of Korea, which had provoked such a strong reaction by members of the "Never Again Club" and Congress *against* American involvement in Indochina in 1954, now emerged as a preeminent consideration *for* intervention in 1965?

Part of the answer had to do with the fact that perceptions of the Korean War had changed. The frustrations over the inconclusive and protracted nature of the war in Korea had, by the mid-1960s, been tempered by time, while the communist threat in Asia had at least been contained. The Korean intervention was viewed through the prism of the wider global cold war struggle and was eventually cast as an American victory.[8] Korea had become an example where the battle line for freedom had been successfully drawn and had stood firm.

Lyndon B. Johnson: Refighting the Korean War

By the time of President Kennedy's death, in November 1963, there were sixteen thousand American advisors and support troops in Vietnam. Three weeks earlier, the president of South Vietnam, Ngo Dinh Diem, was killed in a military coup that had been quietly sanctioned by Washington. Johnson had inherited a chaotic and unstable situation in Vietnam made all the more difficult because his interests and strengths were not in foreign affairs but domestic policy. According to McGeorge Bundy, who served as the national security advisor to Kennedy and Johnson, Johnson's main concern during the first months of his presidency was the upcoming 1964 presidential elections, which "served as powerful deterrent for Johnson to take any definitive action regarding American commitment to Vietnam." For a year Johnson was tremendously constrained, as he could ill afford a major escalation of the Vietnam conflict during an election year, but neither could he afford to lose South Vietnam and be blamed for a communist victory on his watch. "My own impression, then and through the early summer, was that he [Johnson] wanted firmness and steadiness in Vietnamese policy, but no large new decisions," Bundy recalled.[9]

The opportunity to show his serious commitment to Vietnam came on August 2, 1964, when the North Vietnamese attacked an American destroyer in the Gulf of Tonkin. Two days later, new gunboat attacks were reported. Although doubts were later raised about whether a second attack had actually occurred, Johnson responded by ordering retaliatory raids against North Vietnam. The incident provided Johnson with enough leverage to extract from Congress almost unlimited authority to escalate American involvement in Vietnam. The Gulf of Tonkin Resolution that Congress passed gave the president the authority to respond to any armed attack against the United States without congressional approval. Johnson attempted to quell concerns over this unprecedented presidential power by reassuring the American public that "we still seek no wider war." In a speech on August 5, he declared, "To any who may be tempted to support or to widen the present aggression, I say this: there is no threat to any peaceful power from the United States of America. But there can be no peace by aggression and no immunity from reply."[10] The resolution provided the president with just enough political cover to convince the American people that he was tough on communism without appearing overly belligerent.

Johnson won a landslide victory that November. Domestic political considerations continued to shape his decisions on Vietnam. On the one hand, he feared that Vietnam would drag down his domestic agenda. He was keenly aware that the stalemated war in Korea had prevented Truman from seeking a second term. At the same time, he thought that "losing" South Vietnam to the communists would damage his power and America's credibility and standing in the free world. The Vietcong had stepped up their military pressure, and by the spring of 1965 it appeared that all of South Vietnam was on the verge of being overrun by the communists. The choice was remarkably stark: withdraw or escalate. The Korean analogy largely informed how Johnson thought about the two issues.[11]

Advocates of a negotiated neutralization of South Vietnam and eventual American withdrawal included two influential Democratic senators, Richard Russell of Georgia and Wayne Morse of Oregon. Russell was convinced that the U.S. mission in Vietnam was doomed and that negotiations and withdrawal were the only viable options. He warned the president that Vietnam "would be a Korea on a much bigger scale and worse." He also heeded the historical lessons of the French colonial wars. "The French reported that they lost 250,000 men and spent a couple of billions of our dollars down there and just got the hell whipped out of them." When Johnson brought up the subject of bombing North Vietnam, Russell retorted, "Bomb the North and kill old men, women and children? . . . Oh hell! That ain't worth a hoot. That's just impossible . . . We tried it in Korea."[12] Senator Morse was also pessimistic about the American ability to make any headway in Vietnam. He had voted against the Tonkin Resolution, one of just two senators who chose to defy the president, and challenged every major assumption underlying Johnson's Vietnam policies. "The policy of what we called helping the Government of South Vietnam control a Communist-inspired rebellion has totally failed," he wrote in February 1965. "I do not foresee a time when any Government in South Vietnam that is dependent upon the United States for its existence will be a stable or popular one." Instead,

George Ball and President Johnson, July 14, 1966. During the Second World War, Ball had been a member of the United States Strategic Bombing Survey (USSB) team that was charged with studying the effects of bombing Germany and Japan. The survey found that "the German capacity to produce armaments of war had increased through the end of 1944 despite progressively expanded allies sorties." In addition, it found that the resolve of both the German and the Japanese population to resist the enemy had not been broken. The conclusion of the survey disturbed Ball and would later affect his thoughts about the bombing of North Vietnam.[13] (LBJ PRESIDENTIAL LIBRARY)

Morse advised, "we should be seeking some kind of settlement that will carry out the 1954 objective of removing foreign domination from the old Indo-China, but this time with an effective guarantee of international enforcement."[14]

Undersecretary of State George W. Ball agreed. As Johnson's "favorite dove," Ball had been an early and consistent opponent of American escalation.[15] Having worked closely with the French during the Indochina war, he had seen firsthand the futility of that conflict. He was also deeply alarmed by the resolution. Sensing that Johnson would win a landslide victory and worried that a decision on Vietnam was fast approaching, Ball wrote his thoughts in October 1964 in a long memorandum titled "How Valid Are Our Assumptions Underlying Our Vietnam Policies."[16]

The main thrust of the memorandum was to show that the Korean War analogy was wrong and even dangerous in thinking about Vietnam. In a section titled "South Vietnam Is Not Korea," Ball argued that Seoul in 1950 had a stable government ruled by a leader who wielded strong political control over the population. This was not the case in South Vietnam in 1964. In South Korea, Americans had fought under a United Nations mandate. No such mandate existed for South Vietnam. Moreover, the Korean War had begun with a massive invasion and was fought as a conventional war. In South Vietnam there was no such clear-cut invasion, only a "slow infiltration that many nations regarded as an 'internal rebellion.'"[17] "In approaching this problem," he wrote, "I want to emphasize one key point at the onset: the problem of South Vietnam is *sui generis*. South Vietnam is not Korea, and in making fundamental decisions it would be a mistake to rely too heavily on this Korean analogy."[18] Instead, Ball argued that the far more valid, and sobering, comparison was the French experience in Indochina between 1945 and 1954. Based on that, he favored a gradual withdrawal of American military forces from South Vietnam.

When Johnson finally gave the memorandum serious consideration in February 1965, it was already clear that Ball never had a chance. Johnson had already made up his mind that an American withdrawal from Vietnam was not a viable option. "It was useless for me to point out the meaning of the French experience," Ball later wrote. "They thought the French experience was without relevance. Unlike the French, we were not pursuing colonialist objectives but nobly waging war to support a beleaguered people. Besides, we were not a second-class nation trying to hang on in Southeast Asia from sheer nostalgic inertia; we were a superpower—with all that implies."[19] Since the purported goal was to help the South Vietnamese defend themselves against communist tyranny, how could moral comparisons between French and American aims in Vietnam even be considered? The strongest arguments for withdrawal, however, actually came from the military. The Joint Chiefs had found themselves in the same position as Ball with regard to the escalation of the war. Johnson's military advisors warned him that "it would take hundreds of thousands of men and several years to achieve military stalemate." If war was to be waged there, then Johnson was urged to mobilize the reserves "and commit the United States to winning the war."[20]

This was essentially the same argument that General Ridgway had given to President Eisenhower in 1954: if the United States was not prepared to pay the cost in blood and treasure that would be incurred by a guerilla war in Vietnam, then such a war *must* be avoided. In effect, the arguments against escalation by both Ball and the JCS wrestled with the Korean War analogy in different ways to make a similar point. Ball said the war in Vietnam was fundamentally *different* from the Korean situation because Saigon in 1964 was not Seoul in 1950. He warned that a war to prop up a failing regime in the face of the Vietcong's increasing success would result in the loss of American prestige. The Joint Chiefs, on the other hand, worried that Vietnam was too much *like* Korea because it would lead to another inconclusive and stalemated war. It might also risk another war with China and lead to World War III.

The president weighed his options carefully before deciding his next move. However, it was the domestic political implications of the Korean War analogy that vexed Johnson the most. "For LBJ," McGeorge Bundy later confided, "the domino theory was really a matter of domestic politics." Vietnam was "an American political problem, not a geopolitical or cosmic matter."[21] Very simply, Johnson did not believe that his administration could survive the loss of South Vietnam. His credibility was at stake. "I am not going to be the President who saw Southeast Asia go the way that China went," he told Henry Cabot Lodge, U.S. ambassador to South Vietnam, shortly after assuming power.[22] As a product of Texas of the 1950s, Johnson was defined by the Korean War era and the fear of appearing "soft" on communism. "Those fears and suspicions of the

Communists had never entirely left him," David Halberstam observed, "and they colored the way he understood the challenge of Vietnam."[23]

At the same time, Johnson was keenly aware that Truman's real fall from grace was brought about by the stalemate in Korea. Eisenhower had capitalized on the Korean tragedy to secure his landslide victory in 1952. "It looks to me like we are getting into another Korea," a distraught Johnson told McGeorge Bundy in the spring of 1964. "I just don't think it's worth fighting for 10,000 miles away from home and I don't think that we can get out. It's just the biggest damn mess I ever saw." Bundy tried to reassure the president. He could fight in Vietnam and still protect his domestic agenda. "Thirty-five thousand soldiers had died in the Korean conflict over a three year period, at a rate roughly comparable to the death toll in Vietnam," he said. "Yet there was no protest." The Korean War had been "a hard choice but incontestably right, both in morals and politics."[24] The American people would see it that way too.

Bundy's assumptions are revealing. The notion that the American people would simply accept the war in Vietnam as a necessary replay of Korea demonstrated the extent to which the legacy of that war still informed the Johnson administration's foreign policy. Bundy declared that "to abandon this small and brave nation to its enemy and to the terror that must follow would be an unforgiving wrong ... [It] would shake the confidence of all these people in the value of the American commitment."[25] What Bundy had failed to address, however, was that the times had changed: the two apparent monolithic constructions of the 1950s were in the process of breaking apart. An overt rebellion by France was taking place in one camp, while another rebellion by China was taking place in another. It was now possible for a member of the Western bloc to be either "American" or "Gaullist" just as it was possible for a member of the Communist Party to be "Russian" or "Chinese."[26] So where did this leave the notion of credibility underlying the domino theory and America's policy in Vietnam?

Years later McGeorge Bundy admitted that he should have challenged the logic of the domino theory when he had the opportunity as national security advisor. In his memoirs, President Johnson claims to have harbored no such doubts. His primary concern had always been how the fate of South Vietnam would adversely affect his domestic agenda.[27]

In February 1965, Johnson ordered a limited bombing campaign of

North Vietnam called Operation Rolling Thunder. Six changes of government in South Vietnam had already occurred in 1964, and three more took place in the spring of 1965. The Vietcong saw their opportunity and had stepped up military pressure, pushing South Vietnam to the verge of collapse. Johnson made the fateful decision of introducing a substantial number of ground troops in March, to protect U.S. air installations. Subsequently, more troops were added to conduct offensive operations in the areas around U.S. air bases. A critical moment of decision had finally been reached. Disastrous South Vietnamese military defeats in the spring led to a series of crisis-driven inspection visits and White House meetings to determine what if anything should be done. By the summer of 1965, the Pentagon requested an increase of 100,000 troops, bringing levels there to 175,000 to 200,000. In six months, the Pentagon projected the need for another 100,000.[28] By the end of 1966 the number was 385,000 and by 1968, at its height, the total U.S. commitment stood at 536,000 military personnel.

Johnson later wrote that his decision to gradually increase the levers of war was due to fear of China's reaction; calling up the reserves and publicly committing the United States to a full-scale war in Vietnam might have precipitated another Korea-like confrontation. Yet it was clear from the beginning that Chinese leaders had sought to avoid a direct Sino-American clash and would only intervene if the United States had invaded North Vietnam. The Chinese had learned from the Korean War experience too, and repeatedly and publicly communicated their intentions so that there would not be any confusion.[29] Moreover, as Ridgway and others later argued, if Johnson had been really worried about such a confrontation, he should have clearly stated the main objectives of the war at its onset. "With our aims loosely described only as 'freedom for the people to choose their way of life' or as 'standing up to communism,'" Ridgway later complained, "we have drifted from a point where we were told, a scant two years ago, that our military task would be largely accomplished and our troops withdrawn by December 1965, to a point where the faint outline of half-million troop commitment becomes a distinct possibility. And even that commitment is not offered as a final limit."[30]

The accumulation of difficulties and the costs of the war also meant that the stakes rose. When his liberal allies began to abandon him,

Johnson felt betrayed. What he had failed to realize was how much the world had changed since the Korean conflict. Had Johnson been truly convinced that the fall of South Vietnam posed an imminent threat to America's national security, as Truman believed about South Korea, he would have embarked on a full-scale commitment to the war from the very beginning. That he failed to do so, deciding instead to wage a major war virtually in secret, speaks volumes not only about his growing doubts regarding the "lessons" of Korea, but also about his impotence in challenging their main assumptions.

Park Chung Hee's Crusade

While a handful of nations sent token forces to Vietnam to join in support of the United States, they did not come close to duplicating the "Uncommon Coalition" of the Korean War. The largest and most meaningful partner was South Korea, which provided both substantial military support and political coverage for the Americans. The height of South Korea's involvement reached its maximum strength in 1968, with over 50,000 military and 15,000 civilian contract workers. The ten-to-one ratio of U.S. to South Korean manpower is misleading because, in fact, 20 percent of the infantry combat forces under U.S. control were South Koreans, a situation rarely appreciated or acknowledged. As during the fighting in Korea, most of the Americans were part of the tail—a tail that also supported the Koreans—while the majority of the Koreans were part of the teeth. Moreover, as U.S. forces began to draw down in 1968, and would be almost all out by early 1973, the South Koreans remained in force until after the Paris Peace Accords were signed in January 1973, effectively serving as the rear guard of the American withdrawal.[31]

These military efforts were led by Gen. Park Chung Hee, who came to power in May 1961, a year after the South Korean people toppled Syngman Rhee in a watershed event known as the April 1960 Revolution. Postwar South Korea in the 1950s was a terribly depressing place, a "hopeless case of poverty, social anomie and political instability."[32] The war had devastated the country. Although Rhee had leveraged South Korea's strategic position in the cold war to wheedle hundreds of millions of dollars in military and economic aid from the United States, he

Park Chung Hee (seated), as a Manchurian Army officer. (SAEMAŬL UNDONG CEN-
TRAL TRAINING INSTITUTE)

had little to show for his efforts, as much of the aid was siphoned off to
line the pockets of corrupt officials. Nearly a decade after the war, the
country, with its tiny domestic market and thoroughly aggrieved population, still lacked sources of domestic capital. The North Korean threat,
which had justified the stationing of large numbers of American troops
in South Korea, was not only a military security concern. In 1961, North
Korea's gross national product (GNP) per capita was $160, twice that of
the South, posing dire psychological and political threats as well.[33] A
review of U.S. policy toward South Korea in 1957 revealed that it was then
"the largest beneficiary of American aid in the third world." The Americans wanted to reduce this dependence but could not do so until South
Korea became able to grow its economy. Postwar South Korea seemed
headed to a future of poverty, dependence, corruption, and despair.[34]

Yet one substantive outcome of the war was the creation of a modern
South Korean military that had swelled from 100,000 in 1950 to well over

600,000 by 1953. The once-fledging force was transformed by the war into an experienced modern formidable fighting organization. It was also adept at solving large-scale logistical problems. This allowed ROK military leaders to boast that their level of managerial skills was "ten years ahead of the private sector." In addition, the military could claim that it was the most democratic institution in South Korean society. Many of its leaders were of humble origins, "and its organization acted as the melting pot for men of diverse social and economic backgrounds."[35] The South Korean military was, in the words of one historian, "the strongest, most cohesive, best-organized institution in Korean life," and by 1961 it had decided to make its power known.[36]

Park Chung Hee became the chosen agent to lead his nation out of its current crisis. After graduating at the top of his class from the military academy of the Japanese puppet state Manchukuo in Manchuria in 1942, he was selected to spend two years at the Japanese Military Academy near Tokyo, where he graduated in 1944. He was then assigned to the Eighth Manchurian Infantry Corps, essentially a Japanese-controlled unit, where he fought anti-Japanese guerilla bands, many manned by Koreans. After Korea's liberation in 1945, Park joined the Korean Constabulary, which subsequently became the ROK Army. His link to the Japanese colonial regime as a soldier in the Japanese military would haunt him after he became president, but it was his membership in the leftist SKWP that almost cost him his life. In the hotbed of postliberation politics, Park followed his older brother, an ardent communist, and became a member of the party. He was later caught up in the purging of leftists and communists from the ROK Army after the Yŏsu-Sunch'ŏn Rebellion in late 1948. Arrested, interrogated, and facing a death sentence, he was saved by then Colonel Paek Sŏn-yŏp, also a graduate of the Manchukuo military academy and in charge of rooting out leftists in the ROK Army, and by KMAG advisor Capt. James H. Hausman. Both sensed something extraordinary about the future president. After serving time in prison, Park returned to work for the ROK Army as a civilian. Given his spotty background, he would probably not have amounted to much had it not been for the outbreak of the Korean War, which gave him the much-needed opportunity to prove his loyalty to South Korea. Just fourteen months after his discharge and days after the North Korean invasion, Park was reinstated into the ROK Army as a major.[37]

Park, however, was not a communist but rather an ardent nationalist and pragmatist. He easily overthrew the corrupt and ineffective government of Rhee's successor, Chang Myŏn, in a bloodless military coup on May 16, 1961. Chang had come to power after the April Revolution, but his administration also floundered. When Park took over, he immediately issued a "revolutionary platform" that called for the eradication of "all social corruption and evil," the creation of a new "national spirit," and a "self-supporting economy." Park sought to change it all, justifying his actions in terms of a "surgical operation." "The Military Revolution is not the destruction of democracy in Korea," he declared in March 1962. "Rather, it is a way of saving it; it is a surgical operation intended to excise a malignant social, political and economic tumor." Koreans, he said, must embark on a "new beginning" by bringing an end to Korea's long history of "slavish mentality" toward strong foreign countries, including the

Thousands of citizens jam City Hall Plaza in Seoul to pledge their support for the military government's anticommunist and austerity programs, May 1961. (AP PHOTOS)

United States, and achieving national independence. In this he shared
with his North Korean nemesis, Kim Il Sung, the same drive for economic and military self-sufficiency that they both linked to overcoming
the people's historical "subservient" mentality toward foreign powers.
Just as Kim had steadfastly worked to increase his independence from
the Soviet Union and China, Park sought to gain independence from the
Americans by "eradicating the corruption of the past and by strengthening the people's ability to be autonomous."[38]

The coup was wildly popular. Most people enjoyed seeing corrupt
officials and businessmen being paraded down the street with dunce caps
and sandwich cards declaring "I am a hoodlum" and "I am a corrupt
swine." Park's cleanup efforts were so effective that even liberal skep-
tics greeted the coup with unabashed admiration. The liberal monthly
journal *Sasanggye* published the kind of laudatory reaction to the military's "clean-up" operation that was typical. It congratulated the coup
leaders "for making the citizens respect the law, reinvigorating sagging
morale, and banishing hoodlums."[39] At the same time, however, Park
needed these businessmen "hoodlums" to help him jump-start the flagging economy, so he offered them a deal: no jail time if they invested
their "fines" in building up new industries to sell products in foreign
markets. Park wanted to build an export-based economy. His efforts paid
off, and in 1963 he legitimately won the presidential election, marking
the end of the junta that had led the nation since the May 1961 coup. This
in turn provided him with the political legitimacy he needed to govern
effectively and with the U.S. backing he would have to rely on to help
fund his national development program. But Park and the nation needed
time to recover. What Park feared most was the withdrawal of American troops from the Korean peninsula before South Korea was ready to
stand on its own against North Korea. His fears were not unwarranted.
In 1961, President Kennedy had seriously considered reducing U.S. forces
in South Korea.

The Vietnam War provided the opportunity for Park to begin to
realize his goal of achieving national independence and security, even
though the price of this autonomy meant aligning South Korea's interests with U.S. security interests in East Asia. Although Park had railed
against his country's dependence on Washington, he was quick to recognize the enormous opportunities afforded by South Korea's commitment

"Hoodlums" are paraded through the streets on May 23, 1961. The sign reads, "We will give up our hooligan lifestyle and lead a clean life." (AP PHOTOS)

of a large combat force to the war in Vietnam. There was the public relations of joining an idealistic and moral anticommunist crusade as a member of the free world. There was also the leverage, from the commitment of Korean blood, he could use to maximize U.S. economic and military aid to fulfill the national priority of securing Korea's autonomy. At the same time, by rallying the nation in support of another war against communism, Park reopened old wounds. His crusade in Vietnam and the ongoing threat from North Korea would become powerful sources of domestic mobilization in support of his economic and national security policies. Park would refight the Korean War in Vietnam to win the nation's economic autonomy from the United States and to secure itself from the threat of another war with the North.

Korea's interest in Vietnam goes back to 1954, when Syngman Rhee offered to send a division to Vietnam in the wake of France's disastrous defeat at Dien Bien Phu in May. Two months later the French were out with the signing of the Geneva Accords. Rhee's motivation was two-fold. The most obvious was to demonstrate Korea's appreciation for the help it had recently received from UN forces in the Korean War. The other motive was more personal: "a burning desire to mobilize an anti-communist front in Asia under his leadership and to court U.S. opinion," as characterized by Ellis O. Biggs, U.S. ambassador in Seoul at the time.[40] Given Rhee's character, it seems rather certain that the latter motive was the dominant one, as he had been under a cloud in American and world opinion, especially over his actions in the final months before the armistice. The Americans at first favorably considered Rhee's offer but ultimately rejected it, owing to the difficulties of supporting the force in Vietnam, but more important was the potential political backlash from the American public, who might question why U.S. troops remained in Korea if South Korea could afford to send forces to Vietnam.[41]

Park also made an early offer of troops, in mid-November 1961, during his visit to Washington, the first by a South Korean head of state. It had barely been five months since the coup, and Park was still a general and the chairman of the junta known as the Supreme Council for National Reconstruction. The CIA's report on his communist ties before the Korean War raised suspicions, but the Kennedy administration gambled that he was the genuine article, and therefore someone who could lead Korea into a democratic and self-reliant nation. Park's visit was a personal triumph and solidified and legitimized his position as Korea's leader. He was greeted upon his return by a wildly cheering, flag-waving crowd of half a million lining the road from the airport.[42] The State Department informed the American embassy in Seoul that "Chairman PAK's [sic] visit successful in achieving results hoped for ... Chairman made very good impression on U.S. officials with whom he came in contact. Appeared dedicated, intelligent, confident, fully in command his govt, and quite aware of magnitude of problems he faces... Informal visits elsewhere in U.S. .... enhanced favorable image of Chairman among Americans generally and together with Washington visit received generally very good press."[43] In response to President Kennedy's question on whether Park had any thoughts about Vietnam, Park responded that he realized the situation was grave and that his country stood ready to assist the United States in sharing the burden to resolve it.[44] Park's motives are uncertain but are suggested by the circumstances of the infancy of his regime, its shaky legitimacy, and the desire to be in America's good graces not only to ensure continued aid but also to reverse its decline, the principle objective of his trip. But there was no explicit American request for troops nor was any given, and by mid-1962 aid levels had gone down, and the United States was considering again a partial drawdown of forces in Korea.[45]

The continuing uncertainties in Korea itself did not help. The junta was still the government, although elections were promised by the end of 1963. Also causing significant problems were the negotiations over the normalization treaty with Japan. Normalization of relations with Japan was an emotional and enormously unpopular issue with the Koreans, who periodically staged mass demonstrations against it. The end of Japanese colonialism was too recent, and the grievances too much to overcome with a simple treaty. But for Park, opening the gates to Japanese grants, loans, and technology was key to fulfilling his economic plans, so he was determined to finalize the treaty. After much uncertainty, a general election was held in November 1963 to choose a president and representatives to the National Assembly. The elections seem to have been fair according to reporting from the American embassy.[46] Park won the presidency, and his party won the majority of seats in the Assembly. Having retired from the army before the elections, Park now had a genuine civilian government, and a political base to achieve his vision for "National Restoration."

After a suspension of talks, owing to the political uncertainties in Korea, negotiations with Japan resumed in early 1964. With the stability of a newly elected civilian government in South Korea, which also represented continuity of the previous junta regime, the Japanese felt secure enough to continue the talks. It also helped that Park was sympathetic to Japan, not only because he had been an army officer in the Japanese colonial regime, but also because he looked to Japan's modernization path since the mid-nineteenth century as a model for Korea. Although Japan saw little to gain from normalizing ties with Korea, indeed it would have to pay compensation for its actions during the colonial period, the United States exerted extraordinary pressure since 1961 on both sides to conclude a treaty. This policy was based purely on the aim of creating a Northeast Asian anticommunist bulwark anchored by Japan and with Korea on the mainland. Ideally, Japan would replace the United States as a proxy of containment in the region, and normalization of Japanese–South Korean relations was sine qua non to getting there.

One final set of issues animated this situation. By the early 1960s Japan had essentially fully recovered from World War II economically. Trade with the United States was a key to sustaining its rapid economic growth. But the economic success of Japan's export machine began to cause friction with its former overseer, and numerous trade and tariff issues began to affect U.S.-Japanese relations. There was also the question of Okinawa, which remained under U.S. occupation and which Japan wanted to get back as soon as possible (it did so in 1972). Improving trade relations with the United States to stay on the path to greater prosperity and reclaiming Okinawa were the two overriding Japanese foreign policy goals at the time.

In 1964–65 the Vietnam War and the Japan-Korea normalization treaty converged. The American escalation and need for troops from Korea, Korea's eagerness to reverse the trend of American aid and open the gates to Japanese funds and technology, and Japan's desire to smooth trade relations with the United States and resolve the Okinawa situation dynamically interacted, creating a situation of great complexity. The best outcomes for Park were a close and beneficial relationship with the United States through support in Vietnam, to ensure South Korea's security, and a treaty with Japan to kick-start economic development.

The opportunity came when Park was asked for a contribution of military aid as part of President Johnson's More Flags campaign in April 1964. Korean support in Vietnam could serve three main purposes, according to historian Jiyul Kim: "to further cement U.S.-ROK relations through alliance and aid; to serve as insurance for that relationship should the normalization talks with Japan break down; and, to increase Korea's and Parks' regional and international importance and influence."[47] Park's offer was a modest one—a mobile army surgical hospital (of 130 personnel) and a ten-person Taekwondo instructor team—but these personnel represented almost a third of the total response (500 from a dozen countries) to the More Flags campaign. Only Australia, with its 167 advisors, exceeded the Koreans in number.[48] By adopting an option for increasing military pressure if North Vietnam remained intransigent in negotiations, a new plan approved by Johnson in December 1964 paved the way for the escalations of 1965.[49] The plan also meant a renewed American effort to solicit additional international assistance. Park, to American elation, agreed to provide a 2,000-person engineer unit for civic projects.[50] This was a substantial addition to the 23,000 Americans in Vietnam at the end of 1964. The renewed U.S. pleas to get "More Flags" from other countries did not do well. South Korea was the only nation to answer the call.[51]

At the end of April 1965, Johnson approved the next dramatic escalation, additional ground forces consisting of nine U.S. battalions (a division), three ROK battalions (a regiment), and an Australian battalion, with the possibility of a further twelve U.S. battalions (division plus regiment) and six ROK battalions (two more regiments to make a ROK division).[52] A Korean contingent thus became an integral and vital part of the overall plan. The deployment of the ROK and Australian forces was not yet confirmed, but 50,000 more Americans were put in the pipeline to join the 23,000 already in Vietnam, to bring the total to almost 75,000. By early June, the military situation had seriously deteriorated, and the Americans anticipated a large-scale Vietcong offensive that threatened to overrun South Vietnam. General William Westmoreland, commander of Military Assistance Command Vietnam (MACV), the top U.S. command in Vietnam, made an urgent request for a further 100,000 soldiers, consisting of thirty-four U.S. battalions (almost four divisions), nine ROK battalions (one division), and one Australian. Westmoreland's plan to use this force to stabilize the situation and then go on the offensive was approved.[53] It was this request that led to intense deliberations and a decision in July 1965 to approve Westmoreland's request for 100,000 troops, then another 100,000 in early 1966, and the possibility of several hundred thousand more beyond, thus decisively committing and escalating the American intervention in Vietnam and opting for a military solution. The number of soldiers in MACV ballooned from 23,000 Americans, 140 Koreans, and 200 Australians in early 1965 to 180,000 Americans, 21,000 Koreans, and 1,500 Australians by the year's end. By the end of 1966 the command would include 385,000 Americans, 45,000 Koreans, and 5,000 Australians, as well as a small force from New Zealand.[54]

In May 1965 Park made a state visit to Washington, his first as presi-

General Creighton Abrams, a U.S. commander in Vietnam, presents the U.S. Presidential Unit Citation to the commander of the Cavalry Regiment of the ROK Capital "Tiger" Division, for actions performed by its Ninth Company, Qui Nhon, Vietnam, September 9, 1968. (U.S. NATIONAL ARCHIVES AND RECORDS ADMINISTRATION)

dent. Dean Rusk recalled later, "There was a personal rapport between President Johnson and President Park."[55] Park provided strong assurances that Korea would be able to send a military division to Vietnam even though no official request had been made, much less approved by the ROK National Assembly. Furthermore, negotiations over the normalization treaty with Japan had progressed sufficiently enough so that a final agreement was imminent. Park could now envision the realization of his grand plan for South Korea.

Nevertheless, doubts about sending South Korean troops to South Vietnam still lingered over the potential cost in lives and the reduced sense of security until the deployed troops could be replaced (and they eventually were, many times over). In a dramatic legislative special session in mid-August 1965, members of the minority party, who opposed both the treaty and the troop bill, resigned and walked out in protest after the majority party, Park's party, forced the treaty legislation to a plenary vote. It passed almost unanimously in their absence. The following day the troop bill also passed unanimously. Interestingly, the troop

Soldiers of the South Korean White Horse Division (Ninth Infantry Division) with Vietnamese prisoners near a village in the Hon Be mountains near Tuy Hoa, November 30, 1966. (AP PHOTOS)

bill was debated before the vote, and pointed questions were raised about the nature of the war and whether it could be won, the same questions that George Ball had raised in opposing escalation. It was an indication that what ultimately mattered was not stopping communism in Vietnam per se, but the leverage that the deployment could provide in obtaining concessions from the United States.[56]

The Korean division-size contingent consisting of two army regiments and a marine brigade deployed just two months later. In 1966, in line with another large expansion of American forces, the More Flags campaign was laid out again. The Koreans responded with another division of 24,000 men. The terms for deploying the second division, emphasizing economic incentives rather than military aid, were qualitatively different from the terms of the first deployment. According to U.S. Ambassador William Porter's testimony to the Senate in 1970, the total direct benefit of the war to South Korea between 1965 and 1970 was approximately $930 million, a significant portion of foreign exchange earnings and of the GNP.[57] By the end of the war, over 5,000 South Koreans had died and 11,000 had been wounded in Vietnam.[58]

When Park came to power in 1961, South Korea was one of the poorest nations in the world in terms of per capita GNP, and it was completely dependent on the United States. By the end of 1966 South Korea was well on its way to becoming a self-sufficient regional economic and political power. James C. Thomson, a key Asia policy advisor on the National Security Council, wrote in June 1966 that "political instability, economic doldrums, and isolation from its neighbors have given way to robust and relatively stable democracy, economic take off, and full participation both in [the] Viet-Nam war and Asian regional arrangements."[59] Two months later in Seoul, Ambassador Porter observed that Korea had "traditionally been a country which looked backward rather than forward, looked inward rather than outward, evaded or deflected relationships with other countries rather than initiated or influenced them . . . [but now] to a new self-confidence has been added a new outlook and a new attitude toward the outside world in which Korea now conceives of herself as playing an important part."[60]

For the first time since the opening of Korea in the late nineteenth century, the nation had garnered the world's respect. The year 1966 was a watershed for South Korea and a personal triumph for Park, owing to the country's role in the Vietnam War and the normalization treaty with Japan. Economically the GNP growth rate increased from 2.2 percent in 1962 to 12.7 percent in 1966, starting a trend for one of the longest sustained periods of high growth of any nation in history.[61] By the end of 1966, the South Korea–Japan trade was the largest in volume in Asia. Complementing the market was U.S. economic aid, which increased from $120 million in 1962 to $144 million in 1966. With regard to security, the ROK armed forces' rapid program of modernization, including new weaponry for ground, air, and naval forces, significantly boosted the nation's capacity to defend against any renewed North Korean hostility. U.S. military aid increased from $200 million in 1961 to $247 million in 1966 and reached $347 million in 1968. Washington also gave a firm promise not to draw down U.S. forces without consultation.[62] Of great symbolic importance was the signing of the Status of Forces Agreement (SOFA) in July 1966, which defined Korean jurisdiction over U.S. troops. Until the agreement was signed, American forces essentially operated under extraterritorial rules. Koreans, therefore, had no legal right to prosecute any crimes committed by American soldiers against a Korean. The State

Department observed that "the question of even-handed treatment was particularly important in early 1965 when we were asking the Koreans to participate to a greater extent in the struggle in Viet-Nam . . . our actions relating to the SOFA were designed to assist the ROK evolve from a client state into a self-reliant and self-confident ally."[63] Perhaps the greatest value to ROK security was the combat experience gained by its armed forces in Vietnam.

The political and diplomatic achievements of 1966 were perhaps even more impressive. In June 1966, Seoul hosted the inaugural meeting of the Asia Pacific Council (ASPAC), with delegations from all noncommunist Asian nations. It was the culmination of Park's dream for it had been his initiative, a venue for South Korea to take a leading role in a new regional organization dedicated to fighting communism and focused on China. ASPAC did not last long—it disbanded in 1975 after the fall of Saigon and the establishment of U.S.-China ties—but it was able to provide one of the strongest statements of Asian-Pacific (Australia and New Zealand were members) support for the U.S. policy in Vietnam. James C. Thomson gleefully reported, "A plethora of regional and sub-regional cooperative initiatives has evolved: *ASPAC, ADB* (Asia Development Bank, to be organized in November) . . . , which hold great promise for future Asian resolution of the region's own problems. Most important, our own view that our presence in Viet-Nam was buying time for the rest of Asia *is now shared by the Asians themselves.*" President Johnson credited Park on the idea for the conference in his memoirs.[64]

At the end of October 1966, after a swing through Southeast Asia, his second for the year, Park participated in the Manila Conference hosted by Johnson "for a review of the war . . . and for a broader purpose—to consider the future of Asia" with countries that had forces in Vietnam. Johnson continued his Asian trip with a state visit to Korea the following week, the first by a serving U.S. president. He reassured the Koreans that the United States was making all possible efforts to harden Korean defenses by modernizing its armed forces and that "the United States has no plan to reduce the present level of United States forces in Korea."[65] It was a triumphal moment for Park. In November the Asia Development Bank was established in Tokyo, with South Korea as one of the charter members.[66] By the end of 1966, though still poor and underdeveloped, South Korea and Park bathed in the glow of these international achievements. Security, prosperity, and influence were now within reach and the possibilities for the future seemed limitless. Vietnam had given South Korea an opportunity to refight the battle against communism, and in the process had laid the foundation for South Korea's spectacular economic growth.

It was under these circumstances that Kim Il Sung, wary that the South would soon catch up to the North, declared renewed provocations to foment a communist revolution in the South. Embarking on a Korean-style "Vietnam strategy" of infiltrating spies and armed guerillas into the South, with the aim of establishing revolutionary bases and inciting instability there, Kim also began to invest a large amount of his nation's resources on a military buildup. It was the beginning of a new phase of the Korean War marked by intense competition and conflict between the Kim Il Sung and Park Chung Hee regimes for the mantle of Korean legitimacy.

PART III

LOCAL WAR

By 1968, the strategic environment that led to America's involvement in Korea and Vietnam had drastically changed. The "surprise" Tet Offensive in January 1968 shocked the American public and turned them against the war. A dispirited President Johnson decided to forgo running for a second term, halt the bombing of North Vietnam, and begin peace talks. At the same time, the threat of monolithic communist power was receding following the Sino-Soviet split, Sino-American rapprochement, and the withdrawal of U.S. forces from Vietnam by early 1973. It was in this new political and strategic environment that the Korean War entered a new phase. This period, from the late 1960s to the late 1980s, saw an intensified "local" struggle between the two Koreas that had little or no impact on the world at large. Faced with a precipitous decline in its economic fortunes, and realizing that South Korea was overtaking North Korea economically, Kim Il Sung launched a series of provocative actions in 1968 and 1969 against South Korea and the United States in a last-ditch effort to foment a South Korean revolution and achieve reunification under his control. The most daring acts were a commando raid to assassinate President Park (which failed) and the capture of the USS Pueblo, within three dramatic days in late January 1968. In October 1968, more than a hundred North Korean commandos landed on the east coast to organize the local peasants and fishermen to spark a communist revolution. In April 1969, the North Koreans shot down an unarmed U.S. reconnaissance plane, killing several-dozen Americans. Between 1967 and 1969, the DMZ was declared a combat zone because of increased North Korean military actions.

The localized confrontations amounted to a competition—economic, military, and psychological—between the two systems and their competing visions of modern Korea. By the late 1960s, peaceful reunification of Korea on P'yŏngyang's terms seemed unlikely. In addition, continued U.S. military presence in South Korea, the strengthening of the South Korean military, and Japan's rapid growth were serious threats to Kim's increasingly shaky regime. With the U.S. and significant South Korean forces committed in Vietnam, Kim saw a chance to try again for reunification by force. Neither the Soviet Union nor China had any interest in Kim's plans. Only once did the situation briefly become of global concern again. This was the ax murder incident in 1976, when North Korean soldiers killed two U.S. officers at the Joint Security Area in the DMZ. The U.S. military response was an overwhelming preparation for large-scale military confrontation.

Kim's provocations had severe repercussions for U.S.-ROK relations. Washington's lukewarm response to the North's attempt on Park's life contrasted with its hyperreaction to the capture of the USS Pueblo. Both responses were based on Washington's desires not to risk renewed fighting in Korea when it was bogged down in Vietnam, and to get the Pueblo crew released. The Nixon doctrine, announced in July 1969, also shocked Park. It essentially stated that nations must rely primarily on their own capacity to secure their defense rather than rely on U.S. power. Park began to think that South Korea must be prepared to defend itself without American support. These feelings were reinforced by Nixon's détente policy with China and the Soviet Union, dramatically demonstrated with a visit to China in February 1972 and to Moscow in May 1972. Soon thereafter, Nixon forced South Vietnam to accept the Paris Peace agreement signed in January 1973, which marked the end of American involvement in Vietnam. For Park, these events signaled America's betrayal of its three principal anticommunist partners in Asia: Taiwan, South Vietnam, and South Korea. In the 1970s Park embarked on a major effort to build up heavy industries tied to an indigenous arms industry. North and South Korea also intensified their diplomatic competition around the world by trying to upstage the other in claiming to be the more legitimate Korean regime.

It was during this "local" phase of the war that America's first post–Vietnam War president was elected to office. Soon after announcing his candidacy in 1975, Jimmy Carter called for a phased and eventually complete withdrawal of U.S. forces from South Korea. Carter's rationale was based not only on a perception of low North Korean threat and the adequacy of South Korean military capacity, but also on his disgust over the Park regime's human rights abuses. Ultimately, President Carter was unable to fulfill his campaign promise. The North Korean threat turned out to be much greater than had previously been known. In addition, the American presence in South Korea had become an indispensable source of regional stability during a period of intensified conflicts among communist nations over national interests and historical issues in Asia. Carter's plan was privately opposed by the Soviet Union and China. Beijing, paranoid about the Soviet threat, was particularly nervous because it saw the removal of American forces as tempting the Soviets to reassert their long-standing interest over the Korean peninsula. The Russians wanted continued American presence to maintain the precarious balance of influence over North Korea and to restrain Kim Il Sung from restarting the war. Ironically, the unfinished Korean War had become necessary to maintaining the peace on the Korean peninsula.

CHAPTER SIXTEEN

Legitimacy Wars

One of the more remarkable feats of Kim Il Sung was that he was able to survive the Korean War at all. The North Korean people rightly wondered what the war had accomplished other than the complete destruction of their country. "So many men of military age perished in the war," wrote the historian Balázs Szalontai, "that women far outnumbered men in North Korea until the 1970s." While soldiers sought refuge from the incessant bombing campaigns in the damp and overcrowded tunnels, they also faced another enemy that proved just as deadly: tuberculosis. It is estimated that as many as a quarter of a million demobilized NKPA soldiers had serious infections. Considering that the total troop strength at the start of the war was roughly 135,000, this is an appalling number. "In the last six months of the war," wrote one North Korean physician, "more people died of tuberculosis than on the front."[1]

The number of civilian deaths from tuberculosis is not known, but without proper equipment—one North Korean hospital treating fifteen hundred tuberculosis patients did not have a single X-ray machine—or adequate medical staff, civilians must have succumbed to the disease by the tens of thousands. One study calculated that the total population of the DPRK in 1949 stood at 9.622 million, but owing to either death or emigration, it decreased by 1.131 million during the war.[2] Hundreds of thousands of acres of farmland had also been decimated, along with nearly three-fourths of residences. Seventy percent of North Korea's trains and 85 percent of its ships had been destroyed during the war, making the country's transportation system almost inoperable.[3]

Despite such destruction, the country had survived, but the North Korean people were aware that it was no thanks to the NKPA or Kim Il Sung. Chinese troops had carried the main burden of the war, while the NKPA had been reduced to a mere supporting role. Chinese influence in North Korean affairs had predictably increased, giving rise to tensions and resentment among North Korean leaders. Ironically, it was the Chinese role in the war that provided new opportunities for Kim to maintain his grip on power. The Soviet Union's domination of North Korean society since 1945 had been severely curtailed by the war and by the Chinese presence on the peninsula. Kim used this situation to his own advantage. Many Soviet Koreans had served as general officers in key positions both during and after the war, and there was a predictable backlash against them, a logical outcome of defeat since Soviet Koreans had never been entirely accepted into North Korean society.

The first sign of Kim's new strategy to strengthen his leadership position was his decision to attack Hŏ Ka-i (Alexei Ivanovich Hegai), the highest ranking Soviet Korean in the North Korean government and a founding member of the North Korean Workers' Party (NKWP). Hŏ was removed from his post as first secretary when China entered the war, and demoted to deputy prime minster, a significant drop in status and power. Taking advantage of the temporary leadership vacuum in the Soviet Union after Stalin's death in March 1953, Kim decided to get rid of Hŏ. On July 2, 1953, Hŏ was found dead, allegedly by his own hand, but the suicide had the appearance of a setup.[4] Shortly after the armistice, Kim also began to target the Yanan faction, Koreans who had served with the Chinese communists during their civil war. Although he was selective in purging leaders of this group, given that Chinese forces continued to remain in North Korea until the late 1950s, Kim nevertheless was bold enough to take on Gen. Mu Chŏng (Kim Mu-chŏng), the best-known member of the Yanan faction, for his alleged role in the unsuccessful defense of P'yŏngyang in October 1950. Mu, however, was able to avoid the fate of a mysterious suicide; he was simply expelled from the party and later sought asylum in China, where he remained for the rest of his life.[5]

Although the removal of Hŏ Ka-i and Mu Chŏng weakened Chinese and Russian influence, Kim waited until 1956 to embark on a wholesale purge of either group, as he was not yet prepared to alienate them and risk cutting off aid or even direct intervention. The South Korean communists who had moved north, however, had no such foreign protector and were thus the first to be completely purged. A week after the armistice was signed, the first show trials began in P'yŏngyang. On August 3,

In the front row, from left to right, Ch'oe Yŏng-gun, Pak Hŏn-yŏng, and Kim Il Sung, P'yŏngyang, 1952. This photo was probably taken by a foreign visitor, which explains the odd composition with Kim barely in the frame. It may also be indicative of the low esteem Kim was held at the time. Also noteworthy is the prominent display of both Stalin and Mao in the background. Fearful of plans to oust him from power, Kim instigated a full-scale attack against the Domestic faction in 1953. This group had originally hailed from the south, and its members had been prominent leaders in the South Korean Workers Party (SKWP) before they were purged or moved north after the ROK's founding in 1948. Foreign Minister Pak Hŏn-yŏng, the most prominent member of the domestic faction, was arrested in 1953. Accused of being an American spy, he was tried and executed in 1955. (COURTESY OF THE HUNGARIAN NATIONAL MUSEUM)

twelve leading members of the SKWP were tried on counts of espionage, sabotage, and conspiracy. Four days later they were found guilty, and in one fell swoop, Kim Il Sung had managed to eliminate the entire southern faction from the North Korean leadership.[6] The North Korean leader spared the leader of the group, his close associate Pak Hŏn-yŏng, however. He was placed in solitary confinement and "tried" two years later. On December 15, 1955, Pak was sentenced to death and executed.

August Purge

In 1955, Kim Il Sung introduced the guiding philosophy of his regime, which remains to this day the foundational political tenet of North Korea. Addressing the Presidium of the Supreme People's Assembly, the highest organ of power according to the North Korean Constitution, on December 28, Kim delivered his first speech about *chuch'e* (literally translated as "master of one's body" or "self-determination").[7] He spoke of the need to study Korean history and culture. Why were Koreans looking at foreign landscapes and studying foreign literature when Korea had its own rich beauty and literary traditions? he asked. He attacked the *Nodong sinmun* newspaper, the NKWP organ, for blindly copying headlines from *Pravda*, and condemned its former editor, Ki Sŏk-bok, a Soviet Korean, for harboring "a subservient attitude toward the Soviet Union." Kim also accused Soviet Koreans of being "dogmatic and fundamentalist in their emulation of the Soviet Union" by their strict adherence to the Moscow line. "To make revolution in Korea we must know Korean history and geography as well as the customs of the Korean people," he declared. "Only then is it possible to educate our people in a way that suits them and to inspire in them an ardent love for their native place and their native motherland."[8] The speech was significant in other ways as well. References to the "glorious Soviet Army that liberated Korea" and "the Soviet Union, savior of all oppressed nations," that had been part of the standard history of North Korea were gone. The "little Stalin" who was "expected to act under the wise protective shadow of the 'big Stalin' in Moscow" was replaced by a man of "unusual naïve spontaneity," loving, innocent, and sincere, in short, a man who embodies truly Korean virtues.[9]

By early 1956, an all-out campaign to weaken Soviet political influence had begun in earnest. Contacts by Soviet Koreans with the Soviet embassy were discouraged. Special permission to meet with "foreigners," a code word for the Russians, had to be obtained. The number of Korean-language Radio Moscow programs was cut in half. The role and presence of the Korean Society for International Cultural Exchange, the primary conduit for spreading Soviet culture, were greatly diminished. "Local branches were closed down, the collection of personal membership fees halted and control of its profitable publishing section was transferred to the Ministry of Culture." Later that spring, the NKWP Central Committee ordered the end of all performances of Russian plays in Korean theaters. The Institute of Foreign Languages, the primary source of Russian-language education, was closed. Russian was no longer taught to college students. Also notable was that the "Month of Soviet-Korean Friendship" was not celebrated in 1956. It had been one of the largest events in North Korea since 1949 and had not even been canceled during the war.[10] Finally, Kim declared that "his partisan activities to have been the vanguard of the Korean communist revolution," sidelining the vital roles that the Soviet Union and the Soviet Koreans had played in the creation of the NKWP.[11] Soviet embassy official S. N. Filatov observed that many Soviet Koreans were growing increasingly worried about the situation in North Korea. According to Filatov, "praise of comrade Kim Il Sung is especially widespread in both oral and print propaganda in Korea and if anyone comments on this matter, they are subject to punishment." Soviet contribution to the liberation of Korea, and its vital role in the founding of the NKWP, were being seriously distorted.[12]

The first overt challenge to Kim's anti-Soviet moves came during the Third Congress of the Workers' Party of Korea, held in P'yŏngyang in late April 1956. Emboldened by Khrushchev's speech in February 1956 denouncing Stalin, critics of the regime began to mobilize themselves against Kim Il Sung's dominance of the NKWP.[13] Pak Ŭi-wan (Ivan Park), a Soviet Korean and the vice premier and minister of light industry, was a leading member of this group."[14] Ch'oe Ch'ang-ik, a prominent leader of the Yanan faction, also began making moves against Kim. He complained that the group's great contributions to the revolutionary

Ch'oe Ch'ang-ik addresses the Third Congress of the Workers' Party of Korea in April 1956. Ch'oe was an early challenger of Kim's personality cult, and he pressed for economic reforms. He was later executed in 1960. (COURTESY OF THE HUNGARIAN NATIONAL MUSEUM)

struggle against Japan and the war effort against the Americans were not being properly recognized by the North Korean leadership.

The biggest source of concern, however, was not simply the marginalization of Soviet Koreans or the Yanan faction, but the distinct "lack of criticism or self-criticism within the North Korean leadership." Opponents of the regime had become wary of Kim's growing personality cult and the uncritical acceptance of his economic directives. "There is no collective leadership in the Korean Worker's Party," Yi Sang-jo, the North Korean ambassador to the Soviet Union, complained. "Everything is decided by Kim Il Sung alone, and the people fawn over him."[15]

The challenge came during the August 1956 NKWP plenum, where Yun Kong-hŭm, another leading member of the Yanan faction, directly criticized Kim. "Yun said that the CC [Central Committee] of the KWP does not put the ideas of Marxism-Leninism into practice with integrity and dedication," Pak Ŭi-wan later recalled. But Kim's supporters vigorously counterattacked. Calling Yun "a dog," they defended Kim and asserted that "the democratic perversion inside the party" was the "legacy of Hŏ Ka-i and did not pertain to the practical work of Kim Il Sung." Yun was immediately condemned as a "counterrevolutionary," and Kim demanded that he be "removed from the ranks of the CC, expelled from the party and put on trial."[16] Soon thereafter, Yun and his band of rebels fled to China. Their "coup" had failed. It was a defining moment for the Great Leader. He had successfully withstood an internal challenge from the party.

Backlash against Kim's foes, real and imagined, ensued. The opposition appealed directly to the Soviet Union and China for help. Ambassador Yi wrote to Khrushchev on September 5 requesting that he send "a senior official of the CC CPSU [Communist Party of the Soviet Union] to Korea to convene a CC Plenum of the [North Korean] Workers Party ... [where the] intra-party situation is to be studied ... and comprehensive and specific steps worked out directed at removing the shortcomings in our party."[17]

Concerned by the developments in North Korea, Khrushchev and Mao decided to act. On September 23, a joint delegation led by Soviet statesman Anastas Mikoyan and the Korean War Chinese commander Peng Dehuai arrived in P'yŏngyang. Peng's contempt for Kim Il Sung was well known. The two had clashed many times during the war, and

Peng, according to a 1966 Soviet report, was "not ashamed to express his low opinion of the military capabilities of Kim Il Sung."[18] Mao was also disdainful of the North Korean leader. According to one Soviet official who accompanied Mikoyan to P'yŏngyang, Mao told Mikoyan that Kim started an "idiotic war and himself had been mediocre."[19] The entire episode was an excruciatingly humiliating experience for Kim Il Sung. He was forced to convene a new party plenum in September, where he had to criticize himself and revoke his decisions from the August plenum and reinstate purged opposition leaders.[20] He was also warned against further purges. When the delegation left a few days later, it appeared that a thoroughly chastised Kim had been forced to mend his ways and embark on a new course.

But Kim was unexpectedly saved by events in Eastern Europe. Stalin's death in 1953 and then Khrushchev's dramatic denunciation of the man and his policies in early 1956 set in motion Eastern European reform movements to gain independence from Soviet domination and liberalization of its political-economic system. Events moved rapidly. Violent public demonstrations in Poland that summer reached a climax in mid-October with the selection of a previously purged moderate communist leader, despite Khrushchev's personal opposition and threat of intervention. Developments in Poland inspired Hungarian students, whose spontaneous demonstrations in support of the new Polish leader sparked a nationwide uprising. Khrushchev faced a mounting crisis in two of the most important members of the Soviet bloc. The new Polish leader was able to assure Khrushchev that greater autonomy and reform did not mean giving up communism or leaving the Soviet orbit, and obtained a modus vivendi. Khrushchev's concession in Poland was also encouraged by his increasing concern over the much larger and more dangerous situation developing in Hungary. By the end of October, reform forces had led an armed insurrection, which violently overthrew the government and announced its intention to withdraw from the Warsaw Pact. A few days later Soviet troops already stationed in Hungary intervened and crushed the uprising, at a cost of twenty thousand Hungarian lives. Several hundred thousand Hungarian refugees fled to the West. Mao, who had bristled at Khrushchev's denunciation of Stalin, had advised a violent suppression of the Hungarian revolt. The limits of Khrushchev's liberalization had been crossed, and the Soviet Union tightened its grip over central Europe.[21]

Fortunately for Kim, the Soviet intervention in Hungary created a backlash in North Korea against the exonerated rebels in the September plenum. The Soviet reaction in Europe raised the possibility of a similar reaction by the Kremlin against North Korea. Would the North Korean rebels who had demanded Kim's removal and called for political liberalization be crushed too? The timing of the Hungarian crisis was fortuitous in other ways as well. China was undergoing its own domestic political turmoil with the launching of its Anti-Rightist campaign. It would be difficult for Mao to support those who railed against the personality cult in North Korea that Mao had embraced for himself in China. Moreover, following the events in Hungary, the Chinese leader began to have second thoughts about the wisdom of backing North Korean dissidents against Kim. Khrushchev's de-Stalinization initiatives had seriously called into question the competence and wisdom of Soviet leadership. Mao was also wary of seeing Kim Il Sung replaced by those who might develop strong ties with the Soviet "revisionists." Hence, by November 1956, Mao had decided to firmly reject these initiatives. There would be no Hungarian Revolution in China nor would China support a similar revolution in North Korea.[22]

Khrushchev was caught by surprise by the events in Hungary and Poland. They were cautionary tales on the dangers of liberalizing too rapidly. He also decided to reject the North Korean dissidents' plea for help. In supporting the status quo, Khrushchev could at least take satisfaction that Kim had eliminated the Yanan faction, an act that presumably increased the Soviet Union's position. Moreover, he could not be sure that in the event of Kim's removal, the new North Korean leader would favor the Soviets over the Chinese. The Soviet leader had little appetite to risk another confrontation with Mao over Korea. For all these reasons, Khrushchev decided not to interfere in North Korea's domestic affairs. "The small spark of the Hungarian uprising was possibly sufficient to burn the buds of the North Korean democracy," observed the Soviet Korean Hŏ Chin, who later fled to the Soviet Union.[23] Henceforth, the purge of real and imagined supporters of the Korean opposition "gained official recognition and unconditional approval."[24]

The scale of the purge between 1958 and 1959 was large. Nearly one hundred thousand "hostile and reactionary elements" were rounded up, imprisoned, and executed. Andrei Lankov noted that this number represented roughly the number of "enemies" exposed between 1945 and 1958. Therefore, "within just nine months of 1958–1959, more people were persecuted on political grounds than during the *entire* first thirteen years of North Korean history."[25] Kim emerged from the August 1956 challenge unscathed and strengthened. Recalling these events in 1965, he saw the moment as a decisive one in North Korean history. It was the moment, he said, when the party had triumphed over "outside forces": "At that time the handful of anti-Party factionalists and die-hard dogmatists lurking within our Party challenged the Party, in conspiracy with one another on the basis of revisions and with the backing of outside forces."[26]

Military Line

By 1961, Kim Il Sung was firmly in control of North Korea. Such a turn of affairs would never have been tolerated under Stalin, but Khrushchev really had no alternatives. When the Hungarian ambassador to North Korea, Jozsef Kovacs, asked Vasily Moskovsky, the newly appointed Soviet ambassador, why the Soviet Union acquiesced to Kim's behavior, he was told that the Soviets were forced to accommodate Kim Il Sung's "idiosyncrasies" because of the Soviet Union's antagonistic relationship with China. "In the policy of the KWP and the DPRK one usually observes a vacillation between the Soviet Union and China," he told Kovacs. "If we do not strive to improve Soviet-Korean relations, these will obviously become weaker, and at the same time, the Chinese connection will get stronger, we will make that possible for them, we will even push them directly toward China."[27] The Sino-Soviet rivalry over North Korea, as elsewhere in the world, was seen as a zero-sum game.

In December 1962, Kim adopted a "military line" that called for "modernizing and strengthening North Korea's military capacity" to reunify the peninsula through an unconventional war unlike the conventional war he tried in 1950.[28] It was the culmination of Kim's thinking about developments in the South since Park Chung Hee's coup in May 1961. Unlike his predecessors, Rhee and Chang, Park was a military man. His ambitious vision for South Korea based on accelerated economic development and expanded military capability was linked to what was undoubtedly a much more competent strategic vision toward the North and the future of the peninsula. Kim thought it inevitable, given Park's background, his vision, and the South's much larger population, that time was running out to reunify the peninsula under his terms. Moreover, ominous signs of economic stagnation in North Korea were beginning to appear in the mid-1960s, owing to faulty economic policies and greatly increased spending on the military. This happened precisely as the South Korean economy began to take off under Park. By the late 1960s it became clear that it would simply be a matter of time before South Korea would catch up with the North, economically and militarily. The longer North Korea waited, the stronger South Korea would become. The North Korean regime, it was reported, was following with "growing anxiety the developments in South Korea where younger, more flexible state leadership has been able to bring the country [back] from the brink of total collapse after the fall of Syngman Rhee."[29] The North Korean Seven-Year Plan (1961–67), introduced with great fanfare in September 1961, was therefore designed to build up the North Korean economy and military to fulfill the goals of the "military line" policy in order to initiate a new war to communize the South. This war was compelled by the ongoing legitimacy wars between Kim in the North and Park in the South. Since each leader claimed to be creating their version of a prosperous and internationally respected nation, the question became which nation, the North or the South, was representative of the "true" Korea. Kim had to make sure to win this legitimacy war before South Korea became too strong to challenge him on that front. "Unification cannot be delayed by one hour," he declared in 1966. "Liberation of the South," he stated, was "a national duty."[30]

During the 1950s, it appeared that North Korea was winning this contest of legitimacy. With the help of the Soviet Union and other socialist states, it had achieved rapid economic strides, recovering from the war and reconstructing the nation. In fact, North Korea had attracted so much attention as a "model" socialist state that many wealthy Korean families living in Japan decided to return to the socialist fatherland and begin a new life there.[31] North Korea's GNP was also higher than the South's and would remain so until the mid-1960s. Nevertheless, there were already signs that this growth rate could not be sustained. Production rates began to slow down or, in some cases, were reversed.[32] Internal deficiencies in the North Korean system and overdependence on foreign aid accounted for much of the decline. The Soviet Union financed the lion's share of nonrepayable assistance, although China also contributed huge sums of aid both during and after the war.[33] This aid had played a decisive role in Kim's reconstruction plans, but it did little to help establish a strong foundation on which to build North Korea's economy, which was becoming overpoliticized. "The issue of political guidance was of single and exclusive importance in resolving any problem," complained one Hungarian official. "The rise of careerists and people of that ilk, and the thrusting of the few technical experts into the background and their designation as politically unreliable on fictitious charges, is a common occurrence."[34] As the pace of economic growth slowed, industrial output declined further. One analysis noted that "in 1966, industrial output had declined 3% over the preceding year, the first time in North Korea."[35]

By this time, it had become clear that Kim's *chuch'e* economy had reached its limits.[36] His dream of creating an autarkic economy turned out to be an unrealizable and self-contradictory enterprise because it led to more dependency, not less. As the historian Erik van Ree pointed out, a country that tries to produce almost everything it needs "spends a tremendous amount of energy in the task of supplying the domestic market." This, in turn, causes problems with productivity and inefficiency. Moreover, the limitation of a small domestic market like North Korea's also makes it very difficult to specialize. Without specialization, it becomes impossible to pursue a vigorous export policy and to take advantage of the international markets. The result is a lack of innovation and a scarcity of funds.[37] Consequently, North Korea had no alternative but to rely on the influx of large amounts of foreign aid as its only strategy for economic growth. But even large influxes of foreign funds could not offset the inevitable slowdown of North Korea's economy, which was caused by the strict adherence to the orthodox Stalinist concept of all-around development and national self-sufficiency.[38] Ironically, Kim's *chuch'e* economy required continuing inputs of foreign funds with no expectation of repayment, the exact opposite of the independent national economy achieved by South Korea.[39] Yet, despite all these problems, the North Korean leadership "thwarted any attempt to reformulate political and economic concepts even within the given socialist model."[40]

At the same time, Kim began to mobilize the entire population for work. In 1958, he launched the *ch'ŏllima* movement, which was based on the massive use of "voluntary labor." The historian Balázs Szalontai noted that "generally speaking, at the end of 1958, people had to do four to five hours of unpaid work every day, in addition to the eight-hour workday." In an ambitious speech Kim Il Sung gave at the Workers' Congress in September, the North Korean leader declared that the Five-Year Plan (1956–61) should be filled in just three and a half years. Agricultural cooperatives pledged to increase harvests, while factories also promised to double their 1958 outputs in just one year. Yet, for all the back-breaking labor, basic living standards hardly improved. Part of the reason for this was the low quality of the yields. In some cases, North Korean factories were mass-producing products that were defective, and yet they continued to produce them anyway to fulfill abstract quotas.[41] While the mobilization campaigns put tremendous strain on the already overworked population, they did not overcome the problems of productivity and inefficiency inherent in a collectivized system.

As the Park regime's political and economic fortunes rose rapidly by the end of 1966, owing to the Vietnam War and the normalization treaty with Japan, the number of incidents along the DMZ underwent a dramatic intensification in 1967, "reaching about 360 by September as opposed to a total of 42 in 1966."[42] Szalontai reported that by July of that year, Kim Il Sung was already preparing for the assassination of Park Chung Hee. Kim's new militant strategy also appeared to be behind his decision to promote military cadres within the NKWP in October 1966, which was then followed by a massive purge of many high-ranking officials as well as several prominent party members in 1967. It is likely that the purge of these leaders was linked to their disagreements with Kim's new militant strategy.[43]

As Kim was escalating his attacks against the South, the battle for legitimacy also took on an international dimension as Park began to directly challenge Kim in the forum of world opinion. Both leaders engaged in diplomatic wars to secure support for their regime in the form of special goodwill missions that crisscrossed the continents and oceans. "The Korean Question" of establishing a unified and democratic Korea through peaceful means had been an agenda item since 1947, but it took on far more significance by the mid-1960s because of the wave of decolonization and new member states in the UN after World War II.[44] From 51 member states at its founding in 1945, the UN had expanded to 122 by 1966.[45] South Korea saw the UN as the most important venue for settling the Korean question and for gaining its legitimacy by becoming a full member.[46] Thus, starting in 1966, South Korea made extraordinary efforts to garner the maximum number of votes for the UN resolution approving South Korean membership by dispatching goodwill missions worldwide, but in particular to young nations in Asia, Africa, the Middle East, and Latin America. North Korea countered with missions of its own starting in 1968, albeit on a smaller scale. Sometimes a keystone cops–like scene took place when a South Korean mission would arrive just as a North Korean mission was departing, or vice versa.[47]

Most importantly, the legitimacy battle waged between the Kim Il Sung and Park Chung Hee was linked to the political question of foreign presence, and especially military forces, in South Korea. Kim had always insisted that the withdrawal of all foreign troops from the Korean peninsula was a prerequisite to achieving peaceful reunification. He had much to gain from this position since the Soviet troops had departed from North Korea in 1948, and the Chinese had by 1958. Furthermore Kim claimed to have purged all those who had worked with the Japanese during the colonial period, while South Korea's Park had himself served in the Japanese army. Kim also claimed that while North Korea had achieved true national autonomy, South Korea was still a "puppet" controlled by and living under the yoke of "foreign occupation." By casting the struggle between North and South Korea in terms of a struggle for national sovereignty, Kim asserted the existence of a "revolutionary movement in South Korea" ready at any moment to topple the Park regime.[48]

Kim seems to have truly believed that the Park regime could be toppled from within. His plan first called for finishing the North Korean revolution by completing its military-industrial base. Simultaneously, the military part of the campaign would begin through the use of unconventional forces (special operations, agitators, and guerillas) to harass the Americans "on every front," including off the peninsula, to strain their commitment to the South by stretching their forces worldwide and thereby break the U.S.-ROK alliance.[49] Once the South Koreans were free of their "puppet master," they would be liberated either by

In this photo, released by the U.S. Navy, crew members of the USS *Pueblo* are seen in captivity. This photo has become an iconic image in North Korean propaganda and is repeatedly used in North Korean posters to show North Korea's "triumph" over a humiliated United States. (AP PHOTOS)

fomenting a revolution or through a conventional invasion.[50] Kim had formulated a fantastically ambitious plan. While completing military and economic goals, he also meant to reunify the peninsula.[51]

The consequences of the new policy were immediate and startling. The share of the military budget "rose from an average of 4.3 percent during 1956–1961 to an astonishing annual average of 31.2 percent in 1967–69."[52] The expansion of the defense sector caused shortages of manpower and raw materials in the nondefense sector of the economy. Production quotas lagged far behind the unrealistic targets of the Seven-Year Plan, and Kim was forced to ask for more Soviet aid. Eager to encourage North Korea's disengagement from China, the Soviets obliged. While Kim "took the Soviet Union for a cow he could usefully milk in order to keep his regime afloat," the Soviet Union was satisfied that it could "keep the North Koreans from the Chinese embrace."[53]

On January 21, 1968, North Korea tested the limits of Soviet friendship when it sent thirty-one commandos across the DMZ on a mission to assassinate Park at his official residence, the Blue House. Two days after the failed assassination attempt, North Korea raised the stakes even higher with the capture of the USS *Pueblo* and its crew off the North Korean coast but still in international waters. Its seizure provoked a condemnation by the Johnson administration and raised the possibility of renewed full-scale fighting on the Korean peninsula.[54]

The Blue House Raid and the Pueblo Incident

"The key question," wrote the *New York Times* on January 28, 1968, was "why did they do it?" Why did North Korea risk war with the United States and invite international condemnation to capture a ship that posed little threat?[55] "What made the *Pueblo* incident particularly disturbing was that it came after more than a year of stepped up North Korean military pressure against South Korea," the *New York Times* continued. There was as yet a lack of understanding or appreciation of Kim's new campaign. There were speculations that Kim was laying the groundwork for greater military action "so that seizure of the *Pueblo* . . . may be a way of testing the readiness of the United States, embroiled as it is in Vietnam, to resist a broadened North Korean offensive," or perhaps the attack was a way "to divert both the United States and South Korea from the Vietnam effort?" Had the Russians and the Chinese put them up to it? The Russians, after all, stood to gain a "great deal from capture and the study of the *Pueblo*'s electronic equipment." There was little doubt in Washington that the attack on the *Pueblo* was part of a coordinated action linked to the broader context of the cold war and Soviet ambitions. The most likely explanation was that it had been prompted by the Soviet Union "to increase pressure on Washington to move to the negotiating table in Vietnam." In his statement to the nation on January 26, President Johnson related the crisis to the "campaign of violence" against South Korean and American troops near the DMZ over the previous fifteen months. Johnson suggested that the attack on the *Pueblo* "may also be an attempt by the Communists to divert South Korean and United States military resources which together are resisting the aggression in Vietnam." Although he did not mention the Soviet Union directly, it was clear that he believed that a conscious effort had been made to open up a second front in Asia. "The attempts to divert American efforts in Vietnam would not succeed," he declared. "We have taken and are taking precautionary military measures [that] do not involve a reduction in any way of our forces in Vietnam."[56]

Contrary to his assessment of Soviet and North Korean intentions, however, the war in Vietnam was not foremost on Kim Il Sung's mind when the *Pueblo* was seized. Rather, it was the failed Blue House raid two days earlier that preoccupied him. Kim had sent commandos to South Korea in January 1968 with an order to assassinate Park Chung Hee. The attempt was a shortcut measure to "liberate" South Korea. Kim had hoped that the assassination would create the necessary political instability in the South to provide an opportunity for pro-North "revolutionary forces" there to usurp power, thus leading to reunification under his rule.[57] Ironically, the operation failed through the commandos' uncharacteristic humanitarian action. A day out from reaching their target, they had been hiding during daylight in the woods when four South Korean woodcutters discovered them. The standing procedure in such a case would have been to kill the witnesses, but after some intense discussion the commandos let the woodcutters go, with a firm warning not to report their discovery to the security forces.

The North Koreans would later come to regret their decision. Immediately after being released, the woodcutters went straight to the police. A massive manhunt was launched. The thirty-one commandos were

Seoul high school students carry a placard depicting the captured USS *Pueblo* that says, "Return the Pueblo now!" The rally was attended by more than a hundred thousand people, with demonstrators burning an effigy of Kim Il Sung. (AP PHOTOS)

nearly on the doorsteps of the Blue House when they were found. In the ensuing firefight and pursuit, all the commandos were killed except one, who was later captured. Sixty-eight ROK soldiers, policemen, and civilians and three American soldiers were killed in the hunt for the would-be assassins. Kim's gamble had backfired, as huge anti–North Korean demonstrations were mounted in Seoul and a wave of anticommunist hysteria swept through the country. On January 30, a hundred thousand students in Seoul braved a nipping cold day to stage a protest against the North Korean regime. The rally included the appearance of "women whose sons had been killed by the Communists and several South Korean veterans of the war in Vietnam who went to the platform and ceremonially nicked their forefingers to write anti-Communist slogans in blood." At the same time, a ten-foot straw effigy of Kim Il Sung was burned.[58] To make matters worse, the surviving North Korean commando, Kim Sinjo, promptly confessed, provided details of the operation, and repented.[59] That same day, thousands of students, parents, and teachers from Poin Technical High School and Kangwŏn Middle School in Kangwŏn province held anticommunist rallies to "denounce the barbarous armed provocations of North Korea" and burned an effigy of Kim Il Sung.[60] The *Kangwŏn ilbo* summed up the defiant mood: "Although the Blue House raid and the *Pueblo* incident were indeed worrisome, we should not shake in fear for this is exactly what North Korea wants." Instead, the paper proclaimed confidence in the people's patriotic spirit: "As we saw with the Blue House raid, our people are thoroughly armed with anti-communism."[61] The Czech embassy in P'yŏngyang reported with a sense of awe how the South Korean government immediately capitalized on the spontaneous anti–North Korea demonstrations, even by leftist laborers, students, and intellectuals, to achieve its main objective: "to turn public attention from criticizing the government, army and police to a more acceptable matter—against the DPRK, which was a complete success."[62]

The failure of the Blue House raid had profound political implications for Kim. The vehement reaction against the raid demonstrated quite clearly that South Koreans had no desire to be "liberated" by the North. Moreover, the myth of a South Korean revolutionary force ready and willing to topple the Park regime and unify the peninsula under Kim's leadership was shattered. It was the second time that Kim had severely miscalculated South Korea's reaction to a North Korean probe.[63] Mortified by the public criticism, Kim responded by blaming the entire affair on South Korean partisans. Less than forty-eight hours later, the *Pueblo* was seized.

The seizure of the *Pueblo* was done without prior knowledge of the Soviet leadership, contrary to White House assumptions. On January 24, North Korean Deputy Foreign Minister Kim Chae-bong simply announced to a group of stunned "fraternal" ambassadors in P'yŏngyang that an American intelligence ship had been captured. Soviet Premier Alexei Kosygin was furious. He later complained that the Soviet Union "learned about [the details of] the *Pueblo* affair only from the press."[64] He was also uncertain about North Korean intentions, but assumed that the seizure was simply a pretext to divert attention from the failed operation in South Korea.[65]

Whether the *Pueblo* had actually trespassed into North Korean waters, as the North Koreans claimed, was viewed as largely irrelevant. American intelligence ships freely operated "near Soviet military bases and the Soviets freely monitored US communications off the American shores." In the April 1968 Soviet Communist Party plenum, General Secretary Leonid Brezhnev, who succeeded Khrushchev after the latter's ouster in 1964, stated that the *Pueblo*'s seizure was "unusually harsh" by international standards.[66] Rather, the bigger issue for the Soviet leader was whether North Korean "adventurism" would lead to war with the United States. Shortly after the *Pueblo*'s seizure, Brezhnev expressed concern that although "comrade Kim Il Sung assured [us] that the [North Korean] friends did not intend to solve the problem of uniting North and South Koreas by military means, and in this connection [did not intend] to unleash a war with the Americans . . . several indications appeared recently that, seemingly, suggested that the leaders of the DPRK have begun to take a more militant road." He was worried that "the North Koreans did not appear to show any inclination toward settling the incident." More alarming still, "DPRK propaganda took on a fairly militant character." The North Korean people are told that "war could begin any day." Brezhnev also noted that the country was on "full mobilization" and that "life, especially in the cities was changed in a military fashion." In addition, "an evacuation of the population, administrative institutions, industries, and factories of Pyongyang" had already begun.[67]

Provoking the United States into a war could have been a primary motive behind the seizure. On January 31, Kim wrote to Kosygin expressing his confidence that the Soviets would come to his aid in the event of a war. "Johnson's clique could at any time engage in a military adventure in Korea," he wrote. "The policy of the American imperialists is a rude challenge to the DPRK, and the Union of Soviet Socialist Republics, who are bound together by allied relations according to the treaty of friendship, co-operation and mutual help between the DPRK and the USSR; [it is] a serious threat to the security of all socialist countries and to peace in the entire world." He concluded that "in case of the creation of a state of war in Korea as a result of a military attack by the American imperialists, the Soviet government and the fraternal Soviet people will fight together with us against the aggressors," and they "should provide us without delay with military and other aid and support, to mobilize all means available."[68]

This brazen attempt to co-opt the Soviet Union into a war with the United States greatly alarmed Brezhnev, who decided that the time had finally come to put Kim Il Sung in his place. "To bind the Soviet Union somehow, using the existence of the treaty between the USSR and the DPRK [as a pretext] to involve us in supporting such plans of the Korean friend about which we knew nothing" was intolerable.[69] On February 26, Brezhnev told North Korean Deputy Premier and Defense Minister Kim Ch'ang-bong, who had come to Moscow instead of Kim Il Sung at Brezhnev's request, that the Soviets would not support a war. "We still base ourselves on the assumption that the Korean comrades maintain a course of peaceful unification of Korea, for we are not aware of [any] changes [to this course]," he told Kim Ch'ang-bong. Moreover, although "we indeed have a treaty, we would like to stress that it has a defensive character and is an instrument of defending the peace loving position of North Korea." He asked North Korea to settle the *Pueblo* incident and the return of the crew "by political means without much delay." Kim Il Sung was forced to acquiesce and soon sent assurances that he was pursuing a political solution, although he confessed it could be protracted. Kim had backed away from war.[70] Still, Kosygin was concerned that the Soviets were getting their information on the *Pueblo* talks only through the open press and were "not aware of the considerations and plans of the DPRK government with regard to further development of events." Kosygin ended with a promising incentive: "We do not have secrets from

you, and we tell you everything frankly." If the North Koreans are cooperative, the Soviets would do their best "to relieve the economic difficulties" caused by a decreased flow of goods from China.[71] Brezhnev was
less conciliatory, warning the North Koreans that "the DRPK could lose
serious political gain obtained at the early stages of this incident."[72]

China's attitude toward the situation is less clear. At the time, China
was embroiled in the Cultural Revolution. Since 1965, Sino–North Korean
relations had been severely strained because of Kim's entirely pragmatic
decision to side with the Soviets in the Sino-Soviet dispute. The fall of
Khrushchev from power in October 1964 had temporarily thawed relations between China and the Soviet Union, but when Khrushchev's successor, Leonid Brezhnev, sent Premier Kosygin to China to smooth over
differences, disputes concerning joint action and aid to North Vietnam
renewed tensions. Beijing, only reluctantly and with constant delays,
allowed railway transit of Soviet aid to North Vietnam through Chinese
territory.[73] Kim repeated Soviet and North Vietnamese complaints that
China was blocking Soviet shipments. It was only natural that North
Korea sided with the wealthier Soviet "revisionists" as opposed to the
poorer Chinese "dogmatists." On January 21, 1967, North Korea issued its
first official statement criticizing Chinese policies. It branded Mao's dictatorship as more disastrous to international communism than Khrushchev's revisionism. The Chinese responded by branding the DPRK as
another revisionist regime. That year, clashes between Chinese Red
Guards and ethnic Koreans in China's Northeast became particularly
grisly and ominous when Korean bodies were displayed "on a freight
train traveling from the Chinese border town of Sinŭiju into the DRPK,
along with graffiti such as 'Look, this will be also your fate, you tiny
revisionists!'" Open retaliation against the Chinese provocations was too
risky. Instead Kim strengthened his personality cult and his brand of
communism in opposition to the Cultural Revolution. He told a Soviet
visitor on May 31, 1968, that North Korea's relationship with China was
"at a complete standstill."[74] Kim knew he could not count on Chinese
support in a war against the Americans.

The problem Kim faced was how to defuse the *Pueblo* crisis without losing face with his own people. He knew that simply releasing the
crew without an official apology from the United States would severely
weaken his position and power by undermining his reputation as a fear-

some revolutionary fighter who had the courage to stand up to foreign powers. It might even lead to his overthrow. Since the mid-1950s, North Korean domestic propaganda had dwelt increasingly on the virtues of national self-determination by touting North Korea's economic success made "without foreign assistance." Kim's talk of self-reliance, which he contrasted to the "lackey" regime in the South, meant that resolving the crisis without an official American apology—in effect, admitting he had backed down to U.S. pressure—would be quite impossible.

The Soviets understood the North Korean leader's dilemma. Over the following months, while Kosygin worked quietly to keep North Korean belligerence from turning into a military confrontation, he also pressured the Americans to yield to North Korean demands for an official apology, which he conveyed to Llewellyn Thompson, U.S. ambassador to Moscow and a longtime Russia hand. Thompson praised Kosygin for acting with "a distinct tone of restraint" in trying to negotiate an end to the crisis, citing his willingness to be a mediator between the two countries.[75] "There were enough conflicts in the world already and there was no need to have a new one," Kosygin told Thompson.[76] Thompson was convinced that the Soviets did not want war.

The result of the delicate triangular finessing and balancing of North Korean, Soviet, and American interests was a long and drawn-out negotiation. North Korea stood its ground not to back away from demanding official admission of "hostile acts and intrusion" into North Korean territory, a "proper apology" and guarantee "against future similar incidents" as a condition for the release of the crew. The Americans balked: "We know, and can prove, that at least some of the documents which they [the North Koreans] have given us are falsified," Dean Rusk told President Johnson. "I firmly believe that we should not admit incursions which we are reasonably certain did not occur."[77] Johnson agreed. He desperately wanted to secure the release of the crew, but without forsaking America's honor and credibility. The impasse was on.

Confessions

The ordeal for the *Pueblo*'s crew, a complement of eighty-three men, contained its share of drama, violence, surprise, and humor. Captain Lloyd

"Pete" Bucher, the commander of the ship, did not know what to expect when they were taken to P'yŏngyang. Some of the men had been injured, and one man, Duane Hodges, was killed in a brief firefight. Bucher, battered and beaten, wondered in his prison cell whether he and his men could withstand the harsh interrogations that would no doubt follow. The ship's intelligence value was staggering. It was full of the most sensitive electronics and classified documents. The men had tried to destroy them, but there was simply too much and too little time. The crew also included specialists who had intimate knowledge of intelligence capabilities and operations. Their personnel files, on the ship and captured, could tell exactly what their specializations were and where they had served.[78]

Bucher was soon taken to the interrogation room. He was relieved when he was not asked about the *Pueblo* ship's equipment, documents, or crew. Instead, the excitable Korean colonel, whom Bucher later nicknamed "Super-C" (for Super Colonel), handed him a confession to sign. "I took advantage of the opportunity to glance through it, catching among the rest of stilted English-Communist composition some specific reference to my admitted association with the CIA in provoking North Korea into a new war. And to promises of great rewards to myself and my family if I succeeded in this infamous mission." Bucher refused to sign and braced himself for a "painful pummeling."[79] Over the next few days, Bucher "puzzled a great deal about the nature of the questions the interrogators had concentrated on so far, wondering why they had asked so little oriented towards obtaining technical information, military intelligence. Instead they seemed completely hung up on a propaganda line for purely political purposes when dealing with me."[80] Other crew members were similarly mystified. Bucher's executive officer, Lieutenant Edward R. Murphy, wondered whether the North Koreans had really "comprehended the importance of their capture. Their questions indicated little interest in the equipment aboard." He observed that they had shown "only undisguised amazement that such a small ship had such a large crew."[81] They seemed to be concerned only with using the *Pueblo* and its crew for propaganda purposes rather than extracting intelligence. "We seemed to be entirely in the custody of propaganda, not intelligence specialists," observed Bucher. "It became obvious to me that the Korean communists had not the slightest intention of going after information of real intelligence value from us."[82]

Initially, Bucher thought the North Koreans were biding their time until Soviet interrogators arrived. They never did. Instead, the North Koreans just repeated their demand for signed confessions and letters of confession and apology to the Korean people, family members, newspaper and magazine editors, political leaders, and the White House. Eventually, Bucher decided to comply. The strain had become too much to bear when the stakes of compliance seemed so low. He was sure that no one in the United States would believe the crew's worthless "confessions." Bucher considered breaking the Code of Conduct, but he did not believe that endangering the life of his men was worth refusing to sign worthless pieces of propaganda. He was not betraying any secrets, after all. He encouraged his men to include in their confessions and letters verbal subterfuges, especially in personal letters to family members, to indicate that they had been written under duress. The subterfuges included mentioning nonexistent relatives, using outlandish or fictitious names, and referencing nonexistent possessions. For example, Bucher concluded his second letter to his wife, Rose, by telling her to send his greeting to his relative "Cythyssa Krocasheidt."[83] When Super-C requested names of influential leaders who "would work on your government for an apology," the men suggested writing to "labor leader Jimmy Hoffa and the Reverend Dr. Hugh Hefner."[84] Visual subterfuge was also used. A group picture inserted in a letter to one family member showed some of the men making the "Hawaiian hand gesture" by extending the middle finger. The prisoners had convinced their captors that the gesture was meant as a good luck sign. The trick worked until one day a family member, puzzled by the picture, released it to the local paper, which was then picked up by the national press. The North Koreans were furious to discover its true meaning.[85]

Meanwhile, the men continued to wonder what the North Koreans hoped to accomplish. Bucher and his men were forced to listen to lectures, lasting hours, about "America's imperialistic sins," the Korean War, the Vietnam War, the CIA, South Korean traitors, the miseries caused by the United States, and so on. It seemed like an attempt at brainwashing, the sort they had heard about from the Korean War, but it was not particularly intense. Sometimes they were asked questions that any ordinary map or encyclopedia could have easily answered. Questions pertaining to the *Pueblo* were even more baffling. The North Koreans wanted to know, for example, about all the supplies that Lieutenant Stephen Harris had ordered for the ship, including the exact amounts and quantities. Harris made them up, and his interrogator "wrote down faithfully every nonsensical figure he gave them."[86] But what they seemed most intensely curious about was American society and social mores, especially sex. James Layton recollected, "If they had questioned the Americans as closely on military matters as they did on American women, the entire U.S. Navy's communications system would have been in jeopardy."[87]

The North Koreans worked hard to keep the prisoners the focus of domestic attention, staging public appearances solely for popular consumption.[88] There was apparently no interest in appealing to the outside world, including Soviet and Chinese audiences. The prisoners appeared in film and television productions that would be seen only by North Koreans. They were taken on public excursions, a concert, a theater production, and even a circus performance, where they were more part of the show for the North Korean public than of the audience. They were featured in "press-conferences" and wrote regularly for the *Nodong sinmun,* the official NKWP newspaper. Bucher and his men did their best to undermine the propaganda. In one joint letter to the Korean people, entitled "Gratitude to the People of Korea for Our Humane Treatment," Bucher inserted this dig at their North Korean captors:

> We, who have rotated on the fickle finger of fate for so long . . . we of the *Pueblo* are sincerely grateful for the humane treatment we have received at the hands of the Democratic People's Republic of Korea and we not only desire to paean the Korean People's Army, but also to paean the Government and the people of the Democratic People's Republic of Korea.[89]

It was only in the last month of their captivity, when the North Koreans caught on to the true meaning of the "Hawaiian hand gesture," that they punished the prisoners mercilessly. By then, however, the game was getting old. After nearly one year in captivity, the prisoners were losing their effectiveness as a propaganda tool. "The North Koreans had exhausted their propaganda efforts," Lieutenant Murphy later explained. "We were no longer an asset to them."[90] The Americans were also becoming increasingly impatient. Something had to be done.

The solution to the crisis came from an unlikely source. James Leon-

Pueblo crew showing the "Hawaiian hand gesture" of good luck. (AP PHOTOS, KCNA)

ard, the country director for Korea in the State Department, had discussed the frustrating situation with his wife, Eleanor. Every American
proposal had been rejected, and North Korea would not back down on
their demand for the "Three A" solution ("admit, apologize, assure").
Eleanor suggested that "if you really make it clear beforehand that your
signature is on a false document, well, then, you remove the deception."[91]
Leonard thought it worth a consideration and took the proposal to Rusk,
who in turn discussed it with President Johnson. They could not see how
it could possibly work, but thought it was worth a try. The proposal was
made on December 15, and two days later it was accepted.[92]

The Americans were stunned. In effect, the Americans had agreed
to sign a Korean-drafted document of apology "for grave acts of espionage" after branding it an outright lie. Moreover, they had repudiated
the document with the full and prior knowledge of the North Koreans, who "had agreed beforehand that the United States would proclaim
their document false and would sign it to free the crew and *only* to free
the crew."[93] Rusk called the resolution bizarre: "It is as though a kidnap-
per kidnaps your child and asks for fifty thousand dollars ransom. You
give him a check for fifty thousand dollars and you tell him at the time
that you've stopped payment on the check, and then he delivers your
child to you."[94] General Charles Bonesteel, commander of U.S. forces

in Korea, noted, "It is difficult to explain its rationality. I don't know whether they've gotten bored with the crew, or possibly thought they had diminishing value as propaganda there."[95] Walt Rostow, who served as Johnson's special assistant for national security affairs, thought the North Koreans were simply "nuts."[96]

But the "nutty" resolution made perfect sense within the context of North Korea's domestic politics. It satisfied Kim Il Sung's one and only condition: a signature on a piece of paper that proved to his isolated domestic audience that he was a great revolutionary fighter who was both feared and respected by the United States. The signed confession was also important in "proving" that, in contrast to the southern "lackey regime," North Korea was strong and brave enough to force the world's greatest military power to bow to its demands. Since the confession mattered only to his own people, who had no access to other sources of information, Kim did not care whether it was discredited by the rest of the world. In the ongoing legitimacy wars with South Korea, this was all that mattered.

On December 23, 1968, as snow fell on the barren hills surrounding P'anmunjom, the remains of Fireman Apprentice Duane Hodges were taken over the Bridge of No Return. Bucher followed, and then the rest of the crew. As the men were repatriated where the armistice had been signed fifteen years earlier, North Korean radio announced the nation's triumph. The American apology represented the "ignominious defeat of the United States imperialist aggressors and constitutes another great victory of the Korean people who have crushed the myth of the mightiness of United States imperialism to smithereens." It was also announced that the ship would not be returned, but "confiscated."[97] Today, the *Pueblo* currently resides on the banks of Taedong River in P'yŏngyang, where it has become a favorite tourist destination.

CHAPTER SEVENTEEN

Old Allies, New Friends

The end of the *Pueblo* crisis was one of the few positive moments in a year, 1968, marked by domestic and global upheavals. First and foremost among American domestic issues was the failing situation in Vietnam, where hundreds of young Americans were dying each week with no indication of progress in the war. American cities were wracked by racial riots. The assassinations of Martin Luther King and Robert Kennedy symbolized a loss of hope for a better future. The rest of the world was hardly doing better. Social and political unrest and anti–Vietnam War riots paralyzed major cities in Europe, Asia, and Latin America. The Czechoslovakian attempt to rise up for democracy and to escape the grip of the Soviet Union was violently crushed by Soviet forces in August 1968. Through it all, the *Pueblo* drama played in the background. "When news first came of the *Pueblo*'s seizure," went a *New York Times* editorial, "fear swept the nation that the incident would lead to a new war on the Asian continent. Fortunately, good sense in Washington prevented that tragedy."[1] The *Chicago Tribune* shared in the nation's relief that the crew had finally come home: "Despite the unprincipled manner in which the release was affected, we are sure everybody in the country will feel a warm glow that the men are finally free."[2] The agreement also received favorable international reactions. Most nations dismissed the apology as meaningless. The *Times of London* described the outcome "as a triumph of patience and diplomacy." The *Berliner Morgenpost* editorialized, "Only a malicious observer could maintain that the American confession had any truth."[3]

The South Korean reaction, however, was different. The failure to forcefully respond to North Korean provocations, and the bizarre conclusion of the *Pueblo* affair, led many South Koreans to begin to question America's commitment to their security. Their fears were first aroused by

Washington's lackluster response to the attempted assassination of President Park. "The incursion into the very heart of the city was what shocked South Koreans the most: it brought the North Korean menace very close." Coming just two days later, the seizure of the *Pueblo* had similarly galvanized the South Korean public, which staged daily demonstrations against the North Koreans."[4] Some of the protests were also directed toward the American government. General Charles Bonesteel reported on January 27 that there was "an expression of strong feeling at all levels of the republic, that US at our governmental level had taken no adequately drastic action following attempted attack on President and Blue House. However, seizure *Pueblo* we had reacted drastically." Park was personally offended and angry. "The depth of feeling over this is very deep," Deputy Secretary of Defense Cyrus Vance told President Johnson after Vance visited Seoul in early February to placate Park. "It was considered a personal affront and a loss of face," because "the raiders got within 300 yards of Blue House," adding "Park wanted to react violently against North Korea." These feelings were compounded by Washington's unprecedented decision to engage in closed negotiations with North Korea without a South Korean presence. On February 7, demonstrators near P'anmunjŏm were turned back by American soldiers who "fired shots in the air," and the next day, a thousand high school students, with posters demanding "Away with Bootlicking Conferences," staged demonstrations in front of the U.S. Information Service Centers at Taegu and Kwangju.[5]

The chairman of the National Assembly's Foreign Affairs Committee, Pak Chŏn-kyu, charged that his nation "was being cut off from discussion of vital interest to its welfare." William Porter, U.S. ambassador to South Korea, reported, "Much ill-feeling had been created by division of the country years ago and current [secret] US talks with NK touching on sovereignty of the country make it impossible to predict how ROK people will react . . . If there is another incident, however, ROK will have to act. They are preparing limited retaliation measures." President Park believed that Johnson did not comprehend or appreciate the magnitude of the threat that South Korea faced. "Indefinite efforts for peaceful solutions will only bring advantages to them rather than to us," he wrote to Johnson on February 5. "I can say through our own experiences that the Communists should be taught a lesson that any aggressive action cannot escape due punitive action."[6]

Tensions between Allies

Park's call for retaliatory action might have been given a more sympathetic ear in Washington a decade earlier. Growing difficulties in Vietnam, however, made it impossible for the Johnson administration to risk another confrontation in Asia. Washington's passive reaction to the Blue House raid had thus opened up a rift. When Johnson decided to reject Park's call for military action following the *Pueblo*'s seizure, American officials in Seoul began to wonder whether U.S.–South Korean relations had reached a crisis point. "I have been deeply disturbed over last several days at growing irrationality in certain areas ROKG [South Korean government] most especially in President Park himself," reported General Bonesteel on February 9. "Inputs in last day have confirmed that Park is almost irrationally obsessed with need to strike now at North Koreans, with sort of 'après moi le deluge' philosophy accentuated by our secret talks with NK at Panmunjom." Bonesteel thought Park might order unilateral air strikes without consulting or informing the United States. "We are taking all feasible preventive measures, which cannot be 100 percent . . . and I feel, or at least hope, ROK Chiefs of Staff would disobey such orders."[7]

The sudden tension also complicated the war in Vietnam. Only a few weeks earlier Park had agreed to send another ten thousand men to Vietnam. He not only withdrew his commitment in the wake of the Blue House raid and the *Pueblo* seizure, but also hinted that he might consider a withdrawal of South Korean troops from Vietnam to shore up defenses at home. To make matters far worse, the Vietcong launched the Tet Offensive in the early morning hours of January 30, 1968, a week after the *Pueblo* was seized, which demonstrated that far from being on the verge of defeat, the communist insurgency was stronger than ever and put in jeopardy any assessment that the Americans were winning or that the war was even winnable. The prospect of losing fifty thousand men in the aftermath of the offensive left Johnson and his staff "aghast."[8] A South Korean retaliatory attack would severely complicate American foreign policy. "We certainly did not want them [the South Koreans] to start another Korean War by launching an attack," recalled Dean Rusk. "After all, we were heavily involved in Vietnam."[9] Ironically, Johnson and

Brezhnev found themselves in almost exactly the same position as Truman and Stalin had just before June 1950: two belligerent Korean regimes
intent on war. The Korean War risked going global all over again.

But Brezhnev had no intention of repeating Stalin's mistake. And Park
ruled over a country very different from the impoverished and backward nation governed by Rhee. "We have tended to be pleased about
economic progress in South Korea over the past few years," Ambassador
Porter wrote to William Bundy on February 27, 1968, "and our satisfaction at this has to some degree obscured the fact that we have concur-
rently been nourishing a tiger, which is becoming difficult to restrain and
confine."[10] This "tiger" could not be appeased by mere soothing words.
Park demanded increased military assistance to improve his defensive
capabilities at home if South Korean troops were to remain in Vietnam.
In early February, Johnson asked Congress to pledge $100 million in spe-
cial military aid to South Korea. "We need to give whatever aid is necessary to South Korea," he told congressional leaders. "They are among
our best allies."[11]

Johnson sent Vance, the president's "soft-spoken troubleshooter," as
a special emissary in mid-February to prevent Park from taking action
against the North while convincing him to keep his troops in Vietnam.
The situation was extremely tense. Vance found Park to be "moody, vol-
atile and . . . drinking heavily." Park was still fuming over the fact that
Washington "did not permit any retaliatory action on the attack on Blue
House." The raid on the Blue House "had an unfortunate psychological
effect on him," Vance continued. "He felt that both he and his country
had lost face and his fears for his own safety and that of his family were
markedly increased."[12] During the four-and-a-half-hour meeting on the
morning of February 12, an angry Park immediately put Vance on the
defensive. "These incidents are clearly preparatory steps for an invasion," Park declared. He believed it was necessary to "threaten the North
with retaliatory action" in order to make the North Koreans "recognize
and apologize for their illegal behavior and obtain their guarantee never
to repeat such actions."

Vance responded that he duly "understood the point" of forcing the
North to apologize. But, he added, "a warning of retaliation can only be
given when one is ready to follow through with it."

"Are you saying there is a difference in severity between an attempt to

President Johnson's personal representative, Cyrus Vance, visits Seoul for talks with Park Chung Hee, February 12, 1968. (U.S. NATIONAL ARCHIVES AND RECORDS ADMINISTRATION)

assassinate a nation's president and his family in Seoul and the bombing of P'yŏngyang?" Park retorted.

"Of course, the killing of the president and his family is an unthinkable act," Vance responded. "But from the world's perspective they will not think of that act as equivalent to the bombing of a city and from that point of view there is a difference."

"They came to assault the presidential residence armed with anti-tank guns and mines!" Park exclaimed. "This cannot be interpreted as anything but an attempt to bring down our country. What would the U.S. do if this happened in the United States?"

"An air attack is a clear attack of aggression," Vance responded calmly. "The UN will recognize it as such. A guerrilla attack is I believe something quite different. I believe these things must be dealt with case by case."

"What is the American government's policy toward the present crisis?" a furious Park shot back. "Don't retaliate, don't give warning, are we to wait to consult each other for every other incident before we decide to do anything!"[13]

Fortunately, cooler heads prevailed when Vance again met with Prime Minister Chŏng Il-kwŏn two days later. Vance told Chŏng that any unilateral South Korean military action would necessitate the immediate withdrawal of American forces because it was "not our interest, or in the interest of the Republic of Korea, to have another all-out war in Korea." But he also warned that "if we fail to reach agreement on the issues before us, there would be serious US domestic reactions in respect to Korea." After some "gasps and sputtering," an agreement between the two sides was finally reached. The South Koreans agreed there would be "no reprisals for the Blue House or *Pueblo*." There would also "be no reprisals in the future without consulting" the Americans. They would "stand by during the closed door sessions with North Korea." In addition, Vance secured "an understanding that they would keep their troops in South Vietnam." The price for restraint and continued support in Vietnam, however, was, as expected, very high. "Park has a large shopping list," Vance reported. It included six Phantom fighter-bomber squadrons and small arms and equipment for one million men in the newly created homeland defense force; four new airfields; expansion of existing airfields; and no reduction in military aid. These measures would require over one hundred million dollars in new funds.[14]

Johnson was prepared to pay the cost. He urged Congress to follow as closely as possible the ROK requests, despite the concerns of some of his military advisors that such a large military procurement might actually embolden Park to take future unilateral actions against the North. The president, however, believed that the overall goal of the wish list was not "to improve combat effectiveness but to maximize the political and psychological impact on South Korea."[15] It was, in effect, an expensive way to give Park and the South Korean people an assurance that the United States was not going to abandon them. On July 8, 1968, Congress approved the wish list with some minor adjustments, for a total aid package of $220 million.[16] The administration also promised to increase business opportunities in South Vietnam for South Korean firms. Park was thus able to reap tremendous benefits from the *Pueblo* crisis despite what he deemed the "ignoble" conclusion of the affair. Kim Il Sung had come away with a worthless piece of propaganda while Park Chung Hee had secured hundreds of millions of dollars in U.S. aid.

Ultimately, Kim's gamble failed. The Blue House raid and the *Pueblo* crisis further strengthened the Park regime, not weakened it. The crisis also made clear that neither the Soviet Union nor the United States was willing to back their respective Korean allies in restarting the Korean War.

Park Chung Hee and Richard Nixon, who was on a private visit, in Seoul, 1966. Nixon's decision to visit Seoul and meet with Park Chung Hee in the run-up to his bid for the presidency in 1968 was indicative of the new status and prestige that South Korea enjoyed as a close ally of the United States. Following years of political reorganization after his narrow defeat to John F. Kennedy in 1960, Nixon won the presidency in 1968 promising to end the Vietnam War. (U.S. NATIONAL ARCHIVES AND RECORDS ADMINISTRATION)

China, embroiled in the Cultural Revolution, also had no appetite for another war on the Korean peninsula, especially if the fighting involved a regime friendly to the Soviet Union. The war that had ushered in the global cold war in June 1950 had thus evolved, by the end of the 1960s, into a series of localized "guerilla" conflicts, mostly along the DMZ.

Opening to China

"It is not often that one can recapture as an adult the quality that in one's youth made time seem to stand still; that gave every event the mystery of novelty; that enabled each experience to be relished because of its singularity."[17] So wrote Henry Kissinger about his first meeting with Chinese Premier Zhou Enlai. On July 9, 1971, Kissinger, President Richard Nixon's national security advisor, secretly arrived in Beijing for a historic meeting that would change the world and pave the way for the normalization of Sino-American relations. Even before his presidency, Nixon had contemplated the possibility of establishing relations with China. In an October 1967 *Foreign Affairs* article titled "Asia after Viet Nam," the arch anticommunist who had established his career during the McCarthy era made a startling proposal to bring China into the folds of the international community. "Taking the long view, we simply cannot afford to leave China forever outside the family of nations, there to nurture its fantasies, cherish its hates and threaten its neighbors," Nixon wrote. "There is no place on this small planet for a billion of its potentially most able people to live in angry isolation."[18]

Shortly after assuming the presidency in 1969, Nixon set out to implement his China policy. The idea was not to improve relations with China at the expense of the Soviet Union, but rather to create a more stable balance of powers by establishing a triangular relationship among the three greatest powers. "We moved toward China," Kissinger later wrote, "to shape a global equilibrium. It was not to collude against the Soviet Union, but to give us a balancing position to use for constructive ends— to give each Communist power a stake in better relations with us."[19] More immediately, Nixon believed a Beijing amicable to Washington could pressure Hanoi to negotiate an end to the Vietnam War.

By 1969, a significant shift in China's security strategy had also begun to occur. The 1968 Soviet invasion of Czechoslovakia, and the outbreak of clashes along the Sino-Soviet border the following year, had led Mao to seriously consider the possibility of a Soviet invasion. It was one reason why Mao approved high-level secret contacts with the United States. He did not encounter internal opposition to his radical new approach toward the United States, but he was nevertheless mindful of the need to prepare the public and the CCP for dramatic changes. In response to a *Time* interview with Nixon in September 1970, which revealed that the president hoped to visit China one day, Mao related through a trusted American intermediary, the journalist Edgar Snow, that he "would be happy to talk to him, either as a tourist or as a president."[20] In April 1971, the pace of change picked up dramatically when Mao invited the American Ping-Pong team to Beijing. The event was a tremendous success. "You have opened up a new chapter in the relations of the American and Chinese people," Zhou Enlai told the players.[21] For the Chinese leadership, the United States was increasingly thought of as a strategic partner to deter the Soviet Union. In this, Mao shared with Nixon a similar approach to triangular diplomacy: "My enemy's enemy is my friend."[22]

Kim Il Sung's reaction to China's sudden shift was at first one of bewilderment. By the time the *Pueblo* affair had run its course, Kim had decided to mend his relations with China. A high-level North Korean delegation was, in fact, in Beijing during Kissinger's secret trip, although the North Koreans were unaware of it at the time.[23] Zhou Enlai flew to P'yŏngyang on July 14, 1971, to personally brief Kim on Nixon's upcoming visit. Kim rationalized the extraordinary development by interpreting Nixon's visit as evidence of America's "accelerating decline" in the face of Chinese power and as representative of a triumph for China and for all small nations fighting against foreign imperialism. "The United States had attempted to isolate China," Kim declared triumphantly at a mass rally, "but China developed into a mighty anti-imperialist revolutionary power in Asia, and the American blockade came to a shameful end." Nixon's visit "proved the bankruptcy of America's anti-Chinese policy." It also represented a "march of the defeated to Beijing."[24]

President Richard Nixon and Premier Zhou Enlai at a state dinner in the Great Hall of the People, Beijing, February 28, 1972. (U.S. NATIONAL ARCHIVES AND RECORDS ADMINISTRATION)

While gloating over America's "defeat," Kim announced his willingness to establish contact with Washington and Seoul.[25] This was an abrupt change in North Korean policy, but after the *Pueblo* incident Kim believed that Nixon's China trip might have gains for North Korea. He now thought the Chinese could assist in securing the withdrawal of American troops from South Korea. A Soviet diplomat in P'yŏngyang observed in early 1972 that North Korean anti-Americanism "solely rests on the U.S. presence in South Korea." If the Americans were to withdraw, "the position of the DPRK vis-à-vis the United States would change as well."[26] Kim could ride on the coattails of "America's humiliation."

In Seoul, Park was deeply dismayed and distressed by the news. The Nixon administration had not notified the Koreans (or the Japanese for that matter) of Nixon's upcoming visit before it was made public. The Sino-American rapprochement was part of a pattern of perceived American betrayals that began with the lackluster response to the 1968 Blue House raid and continued with the establishment of the Nixon Doctrine in 1969, which essentially stated that nations must rely on their own capacity to secure defense rather than on American power. It was also clear by this time that Nixon was ready to do anything to pull U.S. forces out of Vietnam, especially in order to win reelection in 1972. South Vietnam could be betrayed. And establishing ties with China required cutting ties with Taiwan, and so Taiwan would also be betrayed. Park was convinced that the United States was now in the process of abandoning South Korea. Many South Koreans shared these sentiments, as summed up in this editorial in the *Kangwŏn ilbo*:

> For twenty-seven years since World War II, the issue of who has legitimate claim over mainland China, the Nationalists of the Republic of China or the Communists, has been a global issue. Until last year, the Nationalists were recognized as having that legitimacy, but this was shattered by Nixon's visit. Under the power and influence of the U.S., the USSR and Japan, Communist Chinese legitimacy over mainland China has now become a reality in international politics. It is the realization of the "strong eats the weak" principle at work.[27]

The withdrawal in early 1971 of twenty thousand of the sixty-two thousand American troops from South Korea over Park's objections had already intensified the feelings that South Korea would be the next country to be "eaten." Such foreboding was further intensified during

Park's conversation with Ambassador Lam Pham Dang on November 3, 1972. Lam, chief of South Vietnam's Observation Delegation to the Paris Peace Accord talks that began in 1968, had been sent to South Korea by South Vietnamese President Nguyễn Văn Thiệu to convey his country's concerns regarding the terms of the peace accord that was about to be signed by the United States and North Vietnam (it was signed on January 23, 1973, in Paris). Of utmost concern was that the accord did not require the withdrawal of North Vietnamese troops from South Vietnam. "An agreement that doesn't require North Vietnam to withdraw north of the 17th parallel is meaningless," Park told Lam. He also told Lam that Philip Habib, U.S. ambassador to the ROK, had conveyed to him that the Americans were forced to accept this agreement because the peace accord would collapse without it. "I told him [Habib] that if an accord is reached without North Vietnamese troops withdrawing from the south then all of South Vietnam will eventually be taken over by the enemy." Lam shared Park's dismay. Both men wondered whether the U.S. position was constrained by the upcoming presidential elections (on November 7) and whether the U.S. government would change its position after Nixon was reelected. Park was also vexed by Lam's account that the Americans seemed to be prepared to sign the accord only with the North Vietnamese, effectively leaving South Vietnam out in the cold.

"If the U.S. and North Vietnam sign the agreement without South Vietnam's signature, do you see it as being valid?" Park asked.

"I believe the U.S. will stop all military actions based on such an agreement," Lam told Park. "But it will not be able to explain why 40,000 Americans died in Vietnam."

To add to the uncertainty of the situation, Lam confided that before his departure from Saigon, "Dr. Kissinger strongly warned me not to reveal that the U.S. negotiated the terms of the accord without prior consultation with the South Vietnamese during my trip."[28] Apparently, South Koreans were supposed to be kept out in the cold as well. Park was left to make sense of this betrayal and what it might mean for South Korea.

Responding to these events, Park decided that he needed to buy time to strengthen his nation, and in 1971 he quickly moved to approve secret visits between emissaries of Kim Il Sung and himself. Yi Tong-bok, a former member of the ROK National Assembly (1996–2000) who had served in key government positions dealing with North Korea, recalled that the decision to accept the offer for dialogue "had very much to do with a reduced confidence in the United States . . . many officials in the South Korean government as well as the private sector became very worried about the possibility of some kind of political deal between Washington and Beijing about Korea, struck across our shoulders."[29] An inter-Korean dialogue was seen as a temporary measure for Park to build up the country, thus "forestalling the reckless acts of Kim Il Sung."[30] For Kim, believing that the time of U.S. withdrawal from the Korean peninsula was near, talk of peaceful reunification was intended merely as a ploy to oust Park from power. "There are many people in South Korea who want peaceful reunification," confided one North Korean official to the Romanian leader Nicolae Ceaușescu in September 1972. "If we extend our talks, it is likely that at the next presidential elections, Park Chung Hee is eliminated and the position of the president is occupied by the New Democratic Party . . . It is only then that we will be able to create a democratic unified government, through free general elections in both North and South Korea."[31] Kim's plan, in other words, was to lay the foundations for the gradual communization of the South. From the onset, it was clear that neither leader had any illusions that inter-Korean dialogue would lead to peaceful reconciliation.

To no one's surprise, the talks led nowhere and were suspended after only one year. Nixon's historic visit to China took place in February 1972, and three months later he visited Moscow, securing his triangular diplomacy. Kim quickly comprehended that Sino-American rapprochement would not open the path to Korean reunification under his terms as he had hoped. Mao had no interest in jeopardizing his new relationship with the United States by backing the possibility of renewed fighting on the peninsula. Kim had deceived himself with his simplistic assessment of Nixon's visit as simply a "knee-fall before the grand Chinese power." He had, instead, given Park the breathing room he needed to respond to the changing global situation. Even the Bulgarians complained about North Korea's parochial foreign policy perspectives. "The Nixon visit was interpreted as forced upon the American president [and in this way] the Korean leadership attempts to hide from its people the parallel interests of China and the United States," observed one Bulgarian official. "It is pursuing its nationalistic course and fails to notice the anti-Soviet aspect of rapprochement between the Chinese leadership and the United States."[32] Kim, it appeared, did not grasp the full significance of Nixon's "triangular diplomacy" even though he played it so well himself.

Meanwhile, Park tightened his grip on power while pushing forward with his modernization plans. Riding the nationwide wave of fear and apprehension, Park declared martial law. On October 17, 1972, he dissolved the National Assembly and promulgated a new constitution that effectively made him president for life. Inspired by Japan's 1868 revolution, the Meiji *Ishin* (restoration), which ushered in Japan's modernization, Park called his new system *Yusin*, the Korean pronunciation of *Ishin*, thus evoking "restoration" and "revitalizing reforms."[33] While most histories of the period focus on elite Seoul-centered intellectual and student criticism of *Yusin*, in the countryside there appears to have been an overwhelming feeling that *Yusin* was, in fact, an appropriate response to the threats and crises then facing the nation. Although there are no hard numbers to back this claim, a cursory overview of many of the local Korean newspapers published at the time does provide a good feel for what the ordinary Koreans, mostly farmers and fishermen, thought about *Yusin*. Editorials and letters that appear in the *Kangwŏn ilbo* from 1972 to 1974, for example, are almost all overwhelmingly positive. A poem written by a ninth grader in Kangwŏn-do about *Yusin* is indicative of the kind of heart-felt response that frequently appeared in this local paper:

Oh October *Yusin*
You have come to do a great deed
While we flounder against the storm winds.

You will heal the wounds
Made by the devil's nails.

The days go by silently
But our thirty million souls suffer from insecurity and anxiety
Oh, October *Yusin*
You've come to sooth us with a new law.
We will face the future firmly united
At this historical moment

Oh October *Yusin*
You will secure for us
Great benefit, glory and peace.[34]

Park justified his actions on the grounds that South Korea must be united and strong to deter or survive another North Korean attack. The *Yusin* system also sought to achieve political, socioeconomic, and security reforms to maintain South Korea's independence in a changing international environment.[35] Park saw the ultimate aim of *Yusin* as restoration of "the prestige and strength of the Korean nation" that had been lost when Korea lost its sovereignty to Japan in 1910.[36] With an ambitious plan for developing an economy based on heavy industries with the capacity to indigenously produce armaments, Park sought to promote his nation's self-reliance and independence. In 1974, Park authorized a program to develop nuclear weapons technology, but he suspended it in July 1976 under intense U.S. pressure.[37] Ultimately, Park recognized that maintaining a strong alliance with the United States was the most effective deterrent to war, so he would continue to pursue greater self-reliance, but under the protection of the United States.

In the meantime, with hopes for North-South reconciliation now dead—along with Kim's dream of riding the wave of Sino-American rapprochement to achieve his own unification dreams—both Park Chung Hee and Kim Il Sung began concentrating their efforts on developing their nations at home. At the same time, they resorted to fighting the war abroad, through active diplomacy. For Kim, this meant weakening the Park regime through propaganda and diplomatic means and rejecting any action that might confer legitimacy on the ROK, including vigorously opposing South Korea's efforts to gain admission to the United Nations, either independently or under a two-Korea policy. In 1973 alone, Kim Il Sung sent delegations to over eighty countries, and by the mid-1970s ninety member states worldwide recognized the DPRK, almost equaling the number that maintained diplomatic relations with the ROK.[38] In response, Park found it necessary to develop ties with nonaligned member states, since they played a key political force in the UN. But these efforts proved difficult because of Kim's aggressive diplomatic maneuverings and the ideological, anti-imperialist worldview that North Korea naturally shared with other Third World nations.[39] It was another indication of just how "local" the Korean War had become.

CHAPTER EIGHTEEN

War for Peace

The operation was scheduled to begin at 7:00 a.m. As squadrons of fighter jets circled ominously overhead, a sixty-man security platoon of American and South Korean soldiers equipped with side arms and ax handles advanced into the truce village at P'anmunjŏm. The platoon was accompanied by a sixteen-man tree-cutting detail. B-52 strategic bombers from Guam were circling farther south, while three batteries of American 105mm howitzers were stationed north of the Imjin River. A mile from P'anmunjŏm, an ROK infantry reconnaissance company, armed with M16 rifles, mortars, and machine guns, was deployed just outside the Joint Security Area, ready to pounce at the first sign of trouble. Altogether 813 men were involved in the operation. Forty-five minutes later a message was flashed to higher headquarters that the mission was accomplished without incident: a forty-foot-tall Normandy poplar tree had been cut down.[1]

The operation was the climax of a week of tension that began on August 18, 1976, when North Korean soldiers attacked with axes a group of American and South Korean soldiers who were in the Joint Security Area at P'anmunjŏm. The Americans and South Koreans were preparing to prune a tree to clear the line of sight from a guard post. Before they began their work they suddenly found themselves confronted by a large group of angry and armed North Koreans. One South Korean later recalled, "Suddenly they swarmed out of nowhere crowding the Americans, beating them with clubs and kicking them." By the time the attack was over, two American officers, Capt. Arthur Bonifas and Lt. Mark Barrett, were dead of massive head injuries. Four other Americans and five South Koreans were also wounded. The Americans had not fired a shot. "We wanted to avoid escalating any incidents," an American official explained.[2] Within hours, Kissinger was on the phone with

UNC soldiers cut down a poplar tree near the Bridge of No Return, August 21, 1976. (U.S. NATIONAL ARCHIVES AND RECORDS ADMINISTRATION)

the American ambassador in Seoul, Philip Habib: "I want retaliatory action," he told Habib. "We cannot have Americans killed. I hope that is clear."[3] Cooler heads prevailed once the poplar tree was cut down, its removal being a symbol of American resolve and the mass of military power placed on alert a demonstration of its strength. Nevertheless, it was unclear whether the tree cutting would represent the entirety of the American response to the attack. While Kissinger and other American officials believed that the killings were premeditated, they were equally convinced that North Korea did not want to start another war.

Why did the North Koreans commit this heinous attack? The most plausible reason is that it was an act of impulsive passion by North Korean guards who have long been inculcated with hatred for the United States and Americans.[4] However, while the actual killing of the American soldiers may not have been planned, the weight of intelligence, "including the number of Korean reinforcements ready prior to the incident," suggests that it was a calculated political ploy instigated for either domestic or international reasons.[5] On the domestic front, a series of crises had befallen North Korea by 1976. It had been unable to pay back its foreign loans from Japan and European nations, amounting to $1.8 billion, and was on the verge of defaulting. P'yŏngyang had asked for a two-year moratorium, but the debt led to a 63 percent decline in foreign exports during the first five months of 1976.[6] As the economy went into sharp decline, North Korea eventually defaulted. The ax attack may have been an effort to divert domestic attention away from North Korea's failing economy. In addition, there was also the matter of Kim Il Sung's successor. Earlier in the year, Kim had named his son, Kim Jong Il, as his heir apparent. Raising tensions and the threat of renewed war might have been a way for the elder Kim to rally public support for his son during a moment of national crisis. On the international front, the attack could have been staged to draw the world's attention to the Korean situation, as part of a propaganda campaign to condemn the American presence in South Korea and thus eventually force a withdrawal. Within hours of the attack, Kim Jong Il asked the Conference of Nonaligned Nations, meeting in Sri Lanka, to pass a resolution condemning the American presence in South Korea. Kim's "ax diplomacy" could have provoked an American reaction that might have been used to rally support for North Korea at the United Nations. The conference did, in fact, pass the resolution.[7]

As more details of the incident surfaced, however, it became clear that the North Koreans had severely misjudged the situation. No North Koreans had been killed, and the brutal nature of the murders suggested that the North Koreans had been the deliberate instigators of the attack. World opinion swung against North Korea. American reaction had also been swift and strong. The tree-cutting operation unequivocally conveyed the message that Washington was prepared to go to war if necessary. Kim soon issued a statement saying that the killing of the two Americans was "regretful" and that both sides should take steps to ensure that such incidents do not happen again. It was an unprecedented act of contrition for the Great Leader. Washington's initial reaction to Kim's "apology" was harsh. "This expression represented a backhanded acknowledgement that they are in the wrong," Kissinger announced. "However, we do not find this message acceptable because there is no acknowledgement for the brutal, premeditated murder of two Americans."[8] But then Washington abruptly softened its stance. It had concluded that raising further tensions would be counterproductive, and accepted Kim's "conciliatory" message.

South Koreans were appalled by Washington's sudden turnaround. With confidence in American security commitments at its lowest point since the fall of South Vietnam in 1975, they had looked for signs that the Americans would get tough with P'yŏngyang. "In order to guard peace we have to show the North Koreans very strong resolve," Park Chung Hee declared in response to the news that Washington had accepted Kim's "regrets."[9] O Se-yŏng of the opposition New Democratic Party expressed similar concerns, saying he was "worried that the North Koreans may accept it [the American response] as further evidence of their success in their continuous provocations."[10] Washington's decision not to pursue further retaliatory action against North Korea simply reconfirmed in most South Koreans' minds that the American commitment to their security was waning and that they might soon have to face North Korea on their own.

For Americans at home, the brutal killings had, more than any other North Korean provocations since the *Pueblo* seizure, showed them how quickly they could become involved in another Asian land war. In a speech to the Senate on September 15, 1976, Senator George McGovern (D-South Dakota) stated that "the tree cutting incident proved that U.S. forces sent to Korea a generation ago could trip this generation into another war in the wrong place at the wrong time." He then called for the withdrawal of all U.S. forces and the "avoidance of further identification with that disreputable tyrant [Park Chung Hee]."[11]

McGovern's reaction was shared by the first post–Vietnam War president, Jimmy Carter. Carter too was troubled by the "tripwire" danger created by the U.S. forces. He was also deeply troubled by the human rights abuses of the Park regime. For these reasons he was determined to fulfill a campaign pledge to "withdraw our ground forces from South Korea on a phased basis over a time."[12] But keeping this campaign promise proved to be nearly impossible. By the end of his presidency, Carter was forced to confront the reality that an American withdrawal from Korea could have a dangerous impact on the security and stability of the vital Northeast Asian region. The unending Korean War and its unremitting confrontation sparked by continued American presence, paradoxically, now played a vital role in keeping the peace.

Withdrawal

After the trauma of Nixon's resignation in 1974 and South Vietnam's fall in 1975, which was still shocking even if anticipated, the political mood in the United States was deeply skeptical of the government and against further American military ventures in Asia. There was a yearning for moral and righteous governance. Jimmy Carter promised to build "a new world order based on a U.S. commitment to moral values rather than an inordinate fear of communism." The policy, first articulated in May 1977, made human rights a primary issue in how America conducted foreign affairs. Carter based his new approach on his faith in the universality of democracy and American values and principles: "We are confident that democracy's example will be compelling . . . We are confident of our own strength . . . through failure we have now found our way back to our own principles and values, and we have regained our lost confidence."[13] A month later, Carter articulated what this morality-oriented foreign policy might mean for Korea: the withdrawal of U.S. ground forces from South Korea. The mutual defense treaty and commitment of American airpower would remain, but U.S. troops would go home.

On January 26, 1977, six days after his inauguration, Carter ordered a broad review of U.S. policy toward the Korean peninsula, which was set down in Presidential Review Memorandum/NSC 13 (PRM 13).[14] Key national security agencies and officials were tasked to "analyze current developments and future trends bearing on our involvement in Korea," including "possible course of action dealing with . . . the reduction in U.S. conventional force levels on the peninsula."[15] Despite the seemingly open-ended nature of the review, however, officials in the new administration were shocked when Secretary of State Cyrus Vance told the group that the president's mind had already been made up: the group was directed to study not *whether* ground forces should be withdrawn, but *how* it should be carried out.[16] William Gleysteen Jr., Carter's ambassador to South Korea, recalled his dismay: "Some participants threatened to refuse cooperation; others threatened to publicize the issue, perhaps by way of Congress. The angry, fractious session ended in chaos."[17] By asking for recommendations on implementation rather than an assessment of the soundness of the decision, Carter thwarted any opposition to his plan. They thought that for a candidate who had campaigned on the platform of openness and against the overreaching of presidential power, Carter was doing exactly the opposite. In the end, the review group decided to continue by not only framing the study "consistent with the President's instructions," but also allowing the option "to argue for a minimum of withdrawals."[18] Privately, they were concerned that Carter did not understand the risks inherent in a U.S. withdrawal. Doubts would be raised, including by the North Koreans, about whether the U.S. would really fight in the event of another war. This ambiguity could increase the risk of war, as it did in 1949 when the American forces withdrew from the Korean peninsula. Moreover, Carter had announced his plan without any preconditions. There was no incentive for the North Koreans to guarantee that they would not again attempt to use military force against the South by such measures as a nonaggression pact or a reduction in their forces.

Defenders of Carter's plan argued that troop withdrawal was hardly a novel idea. In 1971, Nixon, over the strong objections of the Park regime, had withdrawn the twenty thousand men in the Seventh Infantry Division, of the approximately sixty thousand U.S. troops then on duty in Korea. There was also talk of reducing the remaining U.S. ground combat unit, the Second Infantry Division, to a single brigade. The difference, of course, was that Nixon did not call for the complete withdrawal of U.S. ground forces. This distinction was critical because without troops on the ground, the United States would have an option to intervene in the event of another war or not. Although the Carter administration publicly declared its commitment to South Korea's defense since "the President cannot evade the choice of going to war or not because our Air Force will still be there," privately the president acknowledged that the withdrawal plan would remove the tripwire that would automatically involve the United States in any renewal of fighting. Senator Larry Winn of Kansas stated the concern over the tripwire situation at a House hearing on the ax murder incident: "You don't usually start a war with an ax."[19] The problem was that in Korea you very well could.

These fears were spelled out in another presidential review, Presidential Review Memorandum/NSC 10 (PRM 10), completed on February 18, 1977, which stated that "once the U.S. land forces are out of Korea, the U.S. has transformed its presence in Asia from a land-based posture to an off-shore posture. This . . . provides the U.S. flexibility to determine at the time whether it should or should not get involved in a local war." With the troops gone, "the risk of automatic involvement . . . is minimized. However, should the U.S. decide to intervene, military forces would be readily available." Thus unlike PRM 13, which focused on *how* the withdrawal of U.S. forces should be carried out, PRM 10 provided an acceptable rationale for withdrawing the ground troops. As for deterring North Korea from launching another invasion, "North Korea must take into account powerful U.S. air and naval assets in any decision to attack the South." Nevertheless, its predictions were grim. The North Koreans could not win "a sustained combat" against the South, the report said, but even with U.S. supply comparable to the "initial air and naval support at D-Day," it was possible "that they could at least temporarily attain their most likely major objective, the capture of Seoul."[20]

Within the State Department, Vance's deputies were divided about the withdrawal plan. There was general consensus that given its robust economy, South Korea would be able to make up for a U.S. withdrawal by increasing its military budget, but among the foreign and defense policy community, the reaction was universally negative. Carter's national security advisor, Zbigniew Brzezinski, recalled little support for the idea. The Joint Chiefs of Staff adamantly opposed the withdrawal, fearing that its net effect "could be dangerous for deterrence."[21] Meanwhile, Carter sent Vice President Walter Mondale to Japan in February 1977 to inform the Japanese of his determination to withdraw American ground troops. In yet another slap in the face to the Koreans, the South Koreans received no such courtesy visit.

Many in the Carter administration had serious doubts about the withdrawal plan and also thought that the process of implementing the major policy change was flawed. "No real consultations had been held with any Asian ally; no major strategic or national advantage to the United States had been clearly enunciated or postulated; no extraction of advantage of concessions from those who threatened the stability of Northeast Asia and their vital role to U.S. interest had been obtained." Carter had merely decided that it was "time to go" and seemed to have persuaded himself that it would not result in disaster. Caught between loyalty to the president and a growing perception that the plan carried unnecessary risks to American security, many of the president's advisors simply hoped that the withdrawal process would drag out sufficiently long "so that if concerns did prove real, there would be time for policy adjustments before the U.S. had gone too far."[22]

The public façade of support for Carter's plan broke wide open when Maj. Gen. John Singlaub, chief of staff of U.S. Forces Korea, told the *Washington Post* in May 1977 that "if U.S. ground troops are withdrawn on the schedule suggested, it will lead to war."[23] He was relieved of his duties because his statements were "inconsistent with announced national security policy and have made it difficult for him to carry out" his duties.[24] Singlaub's testimony before a House subcommittee soon thereafter that his views were shared by the military and the diplomatic community created a political firestorm on Capitol Hill. The controversy that had been brewing within the administration for months had been blown wide open. What particularly disturbed conservative leaders like Senators Barry Goldwater and Strom Thurmond was that the administration was pushing a major policy move without congressional or national debate. Goldwater stated on the Senate floor, "The official announcement by the Pentagon said that public statements by General Singlaub . . . were inconsistent with announced national security policy. What I would like to know is where was this official policy defined and announced by the President or by the Pentagon? I can't find such a policy declaration. It has not been presented to the Armed Services Committee of which I am a member . . . and so far as I know it has not been presented in the Committee on Foreign Affairs."[25] Republican critics charged Carter with attempting to hastily and carelessly fulfill an ill-considered campaign promise. Carter had underestimated the obstacles he would face in Washington. He had also misjudged the limits of his powers as the president.

Backlash

Critics of the withdrawal plan loudly voiced their concerns. They pointed to strategic considerations beyond just the risk of a North Korean attack. A precipitous withdrawal of troops from Korea would raise doubts in Japan about America's commitment to Japan's security. Senators Hubert Humphrey (D-Minnesota) and John Glenn (D-Ohio) reported to the Senate Foreign Relations Committee that Japan might expand its military, which could "shatter the fragile balance that now exists in East Asia."[26] The withdrawal might also lead Japan to accommodate Soviet power in the Pacific. China, too, might begin to question American credibility as an Asian-Pacific power willing and able to counterbalance the Soviet Union. Such an uncertainty about America could undermine, as one official put it, the "Chinese interest in normalizing relations with the United States and increase the risk of Sino-Soviet accommodation." South and North Korea would no doubt react to the American withdrawal with an arms buildup and might embark on developing nuclear weapons. The human rights situation in South Korea was likely to worsen. Without American leverage on the Seoul regime, President Park "will undoubtedly use the phase out as further rationalization to intensify repression of his domestic opponents." This was the reason why virtually "the entire South Korean opposition is against American withdrawal."[27] Richard Stilwell, a retired Army general and former commander of the UNC in Korea, summed up the majority opinion in the defense and foreign policy community when he said that "disengagement of American troops entails the gravest of risks, not only on the peninsula but also in Northeast Asia and far beyond," and that the modest investments of men and resources "provide a deterrent that effectively thwarts the North Koreans."[28]

As doubts and opposition to the withdrawal plan became more vocal, Carter responded by sending Secretary of Defense Harold Brown to Seoul to revise the withdrawal schedule. To compensate for the loss of American troops he also promised $1.9 billion in military aid that would be "provided in advance of or parallel to the withdrawals."[29] The military aid package was an essential component of the withdrawal plan. By providing the Park regime with assistance to develop the capacity to defend itself, Carter hoped to assuage fears that South Korea was being abandoned. In December 1977, the State Department published a report that South Korean security would not be harmed by the American withdrawal if it were accompanied by military aid.[30] The aid package, however, required congressional approval, and Korea in the year 1977 was a very unpopular country. Angered and frightened by the abrupt manner in which Carter had announced his withdrawal plan without prior consultation, Park turned to bribing American officials in an effort to buy congressional votes in its favor. The "Korea-gate" scandal, as it came to be known, was a desperate attempt at influence peddling by a regime that was certain it was being abandoned. By the end of 1977, four full-scale congressional investigations of the bribery scandal were under way. Support for South Korea in Congress plummeted so drastically that Carter's proposal to leave weapons behind as insurance when U.S. troops pull out "could not now pass the House." The Korea-gate investigation had paralyzed all legislative actions on Korea. Representative Clement Zablocki, chairman of the House International Relations Committee, announced that "it would be futile to begin hearing this year because of the fall-out from the Korean influence peddling."[31] Robert Rich, the State Department country director for Korea, summed up the feeling on Capitol Hill: "Congress probably could not have passed a bill stating that Korea was a peninsula in North East Asia."[32]

Another obstacle that Carter ran into was self-inflicted. By publicly and relentlessly chastising the Park regime for its human rights abuses, Carter had undercut American popular support for South Korea. It was difficult for him to argue that with the withdrawal of U.S. troops the repressive regime should be provided with a large compensatory military package. Moreover, Carter's emphasis on human rights had emboldened Park's domestic critics. "It's a contest of nerves to see how far we can go," said one opponent of the regime. "With Carter talking human rights, Park doesn't dare arrest all of us. It would mean another whole year of embarrassing sham trials."[33] Questions were raised as to whether the withdrawal should proceed during a period of such political turmoil, as many now believed that North Korea might take advantage of the situation. "We do not face just a frontal, all-out invasion from the North, but a general strategy of revolution in the South," said Kim Kyŏng-wŏn, Park's special assistant for foreign affairs. "The appearance of instability as well as the actual fact would make us run the risk of misleading North Korea to believe that their theories are confirmed. This is a real enough danger."[34] Many in Washington agreed.

While criticism of the withdrawal plan mounted and it became clear that Congress was not going to approve enhanced military aid to South Korea, Senators John Glenn and Hubert Humphrey, two staunch allies of the president, returned from an extensive trip in Asia. The purpose of the trip was to study the withdrawal question as it related to the whole strategic and diplomatic equation in Northeast Asia. Their report, issued on January 8, 1978, created a stir in Congress. It concluded that "the President's decision to withdraw troops from Korea will have a critical impact on the peace and stability of East Asia." With regard to the tripwire effect, "the United States will gain the option not to become involved in another ground war in Asia; but the United States maintaining its commitment, U.S. naval and Air Force personnel would undoubtedly be involved if war broke out."[35] In other words, the best way to ensure that the United States avoided a new Korean War was to prevent such a war from happening in the first place.

But the most devastating, and compelling, finding was the strong opposition to the withdrawal by both China and the Soviet Union.[36] The late 1970s was a period of intense regional change and realignments within the communist world, including China's new relationship with the United States, continuing hostility between China and the Soviet Union, and increasing tensions between China and Vietnam. Instability on the Korean peninsula was the last thing any of the regional powers wanted. Although neither China nor the Soviet Union publicly opposed the withdrawal plan for fear of alienating North Korea, owing to their political rivalry with each other, the report concluded that "both value relations with the United States and Japan above Korean ambitions for reunification." It also found that both countries "seek to disassociate themselves from Kim Il Sung's more rash actions and view the U.S. security commitment to Seoul as a useful ingredient in keeping peace on the peninsula and restraining Japanese rearmament." In particular, the Chinese, paranoid about the Soviet threat, feared that the removal of American forces from the Korean peninsula might tempt the Soviets to reassert their long-standing Russian interests over the peninsula. Humphrey and Glenn observed that "U.S. force reduction, in and of itself, will not lead China to abandon its basic foreign policy strategy of developing a U.S. connection. But it will raise some troublesome implications in Peking [Beijing]. It is widely believed that the Chinese tacitly support a U.S. military presence in South Korea as an element of the strategic counterweight to the threat of Soviet 'encirclement' of China." As for the Soviet Union, "Soviet national interest is best served by a divided, not a unified Korea. Unpredictable Kim could draw the Soviet Union into a conflict with the United States," which is why the Soviet leaders want American troops to remain in the South despite their public utterances to the contrary. The report noted that "Soviet media still refers to 'two Korean states' and the USSR has yet to endorse North Korea's claim to be the 'sole sovereign state' on the Korean peninsula." As for Japan, "it views East Asia strategic politics as tripolar, with the United States, the Soviets and the PRC determining its future . . . the situation in Korea is the vortex of these relationships and thus Japan views its own fate inextricably linked to that of Korea." This is why the Japanese government "was disheartened by Carter's campaign pledges and confidence in the US is at a low point." A withdrawal from Korea would damage Japan's "confidence in the U.S. determination to defend Japan." Under these circumstances, "the rearmament of Japan might develop a situation that would shatter the fragile balance that now exists in Asia." Similar sentiments were voiced by Taiwan, the Philippines, Singapore, Thailand, and Australia. Singapore's President Lee Kuan Yew was particularly critical: "The withdrawal from Korea is part of President Carter's plan for a decreased U.S. presence in Asia."[37]

In South Korea, as expected, the reaction was universally negative. Even staunch domestic opponents of the Park regime were against the withdrawal. The report noted that "every dissident interviewed opposed U.S. troop withdrawal. The Korean National Council of Churches in a recent position paper stated bluntly 'we would like to make clear our belief that the plan to withdraw American troops will deal a death blow to our people's churches in their struggle for freedom, justice and human rights.' They fear that without strong American presence there will be no restraining the government."[38] The regional powers agreed that a sudden American retreat would send the world a political message that the United States was disengaging from an area of potential conflict and abandoning allies.

While these alarming findings were being absorbed by Congress and the administration, behind-the-scene developments would eventually kill the withdrawal plan altogether. A main assumption of the plan was that even after the withdrawal, the military balance of power still favored South Korea. Its larger population, twice that of the North, was seen as a distinct advantage in its long-run economic and military competition with the North.[39] In late 1975, however, John Armstrong, a young army intelligence analyst at Ft. Meade, Maryland, made a startling discovery. Working with imagery of North Korean forces taken by aircraft and satellites, Armstrong determined that North Korean tank forces were nearly double the amount of previous estimates. His initial findings led to a larger effort to completely reassess North Korea's military strength. After two years, the team of three-dozen analysts under Armstrong confirmed a huge increase in North Korean military capability over the previous decade. Ground forces increased by 40 percent, from 485,000 to 680,000, the first time the NKPA had fielded a force larger than the ROK Army. The North Koreans possessed more than a two-to-one advantage in tanks and artillery, and the bulk of this larger force was positioned closer to the DMZ than previously thought and "in such a configuration to suggest offensive intent." The findings electrified the intelligence community, and senior officials recognized the stark implications of the study for Carter's pullout plan. In January 1979, the results of the study became front-page news in the *New York Times* and the *Washington Post*.[40]

Carter questioned the validity of the new assessment (and would continue to do so well after the end of his presidency) and still pressed for withdrawal. The normalization of relations with China on January 1, 1979, raised the possibility of a Sino-American initiative to finalize a settlement between North and South Korea that would permit the withdrawal. During his visit to the United States in late January, Deng Xiaoping, who had succeeded Mao in 1978, two years after the latter's death, agreed to help arrange North-South talks, but when North Korea refused to compromise on the terms of those talks, Deng said that he would not put pressure on North Korea. Carter's scheduled trip to Tokyo in June for the G7 summit provided an opportunity for a visit to Seoul to discuss the situation with Park. Carter's aides proposed such a visit, hoping the outcome would convince Carter that the withdrawal plan was premature. Carter was reluctant to meet Park, whom he despised for his human rights record, much less to discuss the withdrawal plan. Nevertheless, he agreed to make the visit but tied it to an unexpected proposal: a three-way summit with Kim Il Sung and Park in the DMZ. It was an idea born from the Camp David Accords, which had concluded the previous September between Israel and Egypt. Carter would attempt to end the Korean War through diplomacy. A North-South settlement would allow him to keep his campaign promise, since

the long-term presence of American troops after North-South rapprochement would be unnecessary.

It was an idealistic, if not hopelessly naive, proposal that failed to
take into consideration the long and aggrieved history between the two
nations, the regional implications of a withdrawal, and the opposition to
withdrawal by China, Japan, and the Soviet Union. White House aides
thought it might be seen as a "flaky" stunt. Ambassador Gleysteen, who
grew up in China with missionary parents, said he "nearly fell out of my
chair" and "exploded with surprise and anger." A visit meant to symbol-
ize close relations between the United States and South Korea would "be
turned into a circus of events featuring Park's most feared enemy." Asia
experts in the State and Defense Departments were also horrified, realizing that such an event would be seen by the South Koreans as "the first
steps toward a Vietnamese solution for Korea." It would lead to further
suspicion in South Korea that the United States was in the process of
abandoning an old ally. It would also allow Kim to create a wedge between
the Americans and the South Koreans. Park would never agree to such a
summit, and the proposal itself would poison the relations between the
two allies. Gleysteen said that if Carter went ahead with these plans, he
would resign. Through Brzezinski, Carter was convinced to quietly drop
the plan without the South Koreans ever knowing about it.[41]

Like so many of his initiatives, Carter's policies were not part of an
overall strategic design. Each foreign policy initiative, as one observer
put it, "was considered a sacred goal."[42] Focused on the human rights
issue and the tripwire effect, Carter failed to understand the complex
history of Korea's unending war, and America's continued involvement
in it, and how that situation had paradoxically become the basis for
maintaining the peace.

To Seoul

The meeting with Park had initially been proposed as a mechanism to
adjust and refine the withdrawal proposal. Ambassador Gleysteen was
hopeful: "With fingers crossed, I believed we were over the hump in getting President Carter to suspend his troop withdrawal." By this time,
Carter was about the only person in Washington who favored the with-

drawal. Instead of a trilateral summit, Carter accepted a trilateral meeting by lesser diplomats. Gleysteen proposed that "if the president were to tell Park that we would accommodate his concerns by a significant alteration of our troop withdrawal plans, then on that basis of the confidence generated by such a declaration, we could tell him we wished to explore with him the possibility of announcing in Seoul a proposal for a trilateral summit at a later time."[43] Although most of his aides opposed the idea of a trilateral meeting with North Korean diplomats, Park agreed. He saw a possible way to end or reduce the scope of the withdrawal plan, and he was convinced that the North Korean leader would reject the proposal anyway. As it turned out, Park was correct about Kim's reaction, but he miscalculated President Carter's.

On the evening of June 29, 1979, Carter arrived in Seoul after having just finished the G7 summit meetings in Tokyo. Ham Su-yŏng, commander of the presidential guard, recalled later that "the treatment Park received from the [American] visitors was insulting." Because of security concerns, the Secret Service did not notify the Koreans about Carter's exact time of arrival. This meant that Park was forced to wait for nearly an hour at the airport. Moreover, the accompanying press corps was allowed to debark the plane first. As a result, Park, who was short in stature, "was forced to fight his way through a crowd of reporters before finally greeting the U.S. President."[44] After a brief handshake, Carter abruptly departed. In a remarkable defiance of protocol that amounted to a slap in the face against Park, Carter immediately flew to Camp Casey, the headquarters of the U.S. Army's Second Infantry Division near the DMZ, for his first night, rather than stay at the state guesthouse in Seoul. It was an inauspicious start for the visit.

Carter traveled back to Seoul the next morning to meet Park at the Blue House. Gleysteen had advised Park not to bring up the withdrawal issue, at least not right away, in order to set a positive tone for the meeting. Park ignored this advice. Leading off the first session, he delivered "a long, school marmish lecture on the North Korean threat."[45] He asked for U.S. withdrawal plans to be halted: "The most honest desire of every Korean is to avoid the recurrence of war. What is the surest guarantee against the recurrence of war? Continuation of the U.S. presence and end to withdrawals." Park also addressed the president's human rights concerns: "I have great admiration for your human rights," he began, but "every country has unique circumstances. You cannot apply the same yardstick to countries whose security is threatened as to countries whose security is not." He pressed the point on security:

> You went to the front line area, Mr. President, and drove back to Seoul. Our capital is only 25 miles from the DMZ. Right across the DMZ hundreds of thousands of soldiers are poised. We have suffered a tragic war ... Some time ago several members of Congress came to call on me. I told them that if dozens of Soviet divisions were deployed at Baltimore, the U.S. Government could not permit its people to enjoy the same freedoms they do now. If these Soviets dug tunnels and sent commando units into the District of Columbia, then U.S. freedoms would be more limited. We support human rights policy. Respect for human rights is also our concern. I want as much freedom for our people as possible. But the survival of 37 million people is at stake, and some restraint is required.[46]

Carter became furious while Park continued talking for nearly an hour. One of Carter's aides noticed his habit of "working his jaw muscles" to stifle his anger. Passing a note to Vance and Defense Secretary Brown, Carter wrote, "If he goes on like this much longer, I'm going to pull every troop out of the country."[47]

After the meeting, Vance, Brown, Gleysteen, and Brzezinski rode together to the ambassador's residence. Carter vented his anger toward Gleysteen, asking why Park, "in the face of North Korea's huge build-up, was unwilling to increase his country's defense expenditure at least to the American level of 6 percent of the GDP and why Park was so resistant to some real measure of political liberalization." Carter accused his aides of conspiring against him and threatened to continue the withdrawal. Gleysteen tried to defend Park, saying that although his behavior during the session was "ill-advised," he was obviously "upset by Carter's refusal to reassure him about the troop issue." Moreover, the ambassador pointed out that comparing the defense expenditures of the United States with those of South Korea was misleading; South Korea was still a developing nation "and was already carrying a very heavy defense burden." He reminded Carter that in the past "we deliberately refrained from pushing Korea too hard on military expenditures for fear of strengthening the military and their authoritarian tendencies." Vance and Brown joined on Gleysteen's side while Brzezinski remained conspicuously silent. Witnessing the heated exchange through the rear window of the presidential limousine, Nicholas Platt, the National Security Council expert on Asia, turned to a companion and said, "There goes your Korea policy; it's all being decided right there now!"[48]

The mood of the next day's meeting improved considerably after Vance and Gleysteen were able to secure from Park a promise that he would spend more than 6 percent of GDP on defense. Park also said that he "understood" Carter's views on human rights and would make more efforts at liberalization. Carter agreed to reconsider the withdrawal plan and to deal "satisfactorily" with the military question when he got back to Washington. He then made an unusual effort to reach out to Park, asking the South Korean leader about his religious beliefs. Park replied he had none. Carter said, "I would like you to know about Christ," and "proposed to send Chang Hwan (Billy) Kim, an American-based Baptist evangelist who fashioned himself as the Korean Billy Graham, 'to explain our faith'."[49] Despite the initial setback, the summit had been a success. Gleysteen recalled Park's ebullient reaction after Carter's departure: "After Air Force One was airborne, Park, normally rather dour and distant in manner, looked at me, laughed in appreciation, and gave me a big bear hug, an act of spontaneity that astounded his attendants." On July 5, Park sent a message through his Korean CIA chief, Kim Chae-kyu, that he would be releasing 180 political prisoners over the next six months. On July 20, Brzezinski announced that Washington would suspend troop withdrawals from South Korea until 1981, the start of what would have been Carter's second term, in order to reassess the military balance on the peninsula.[50]

That chance did not come. In a sweeping reversal of Carter's policies, his successor, Ronald Reagan, increased the number of American forces in Korea to forty-three thousand, the highest level since 1972. Carter's futile efforts showed that even a resolute president was unable to sever the link between the United States and the Korean peninsula. His two-and-a-half-year withdrawal program ended with a reduction of only three thousand men. Meanwhile, in Seoul, Carter's criticism of Park's human rights record dealt a severe blow to the South Korean president's standing among his own people. The result would lead to another chapter in the unending Korean War.

CHAPTER NINETEEN

End of an Era

LIKE A LONE MAGNOLIA BLOSSOM BENDING TO THE WIND

Under heavy silence
Of a house in mourning
Only the cry of cicadas
Maam, maam, maam
Seem to long for you who is now gone

Under the August sun
The Indian Lilacs turn crimson
As if trying to heal the wounds of the mind

My wife has departed alone
Only I am left
Like a lone Magnolia blossom bending to the wind
Where can I appeal
The sadness of a broken heart
———PARK CHUNG HEE, August 20, 1974,
composed the day after his wife's state funeral[1]

Park Chung Hee awoke every morning to the picture of his wife, Yuk Yŏng-su. On a table under her portrait rested two vases of fresh chrysanthemums and next to them, in a wooden box, was a book about the late First Lady written by the celebrated poet Pak Mok-wŏl. Park missed her dreadfully. In the years after her death, Park had been under a great deal of strain. After a long period of rapid growth, South Korea was experiencing rising political unrest aggravated by an economy that was now stagnant, owing to the 1973 oil crisis and a worldwide recession. Carter's criticism of the regime's human rights record had also emboldened Park's critics. Park's aides were concerned that he was becoming emotionally unstable.

The tragedy took place at the National Theatre on August 15, 1974.

Park was giving a speech to commemorate the twenty-ninth anniversary of the nation's liberation from Japan when shots rang out. Yuk Yŏng-su slumped to the floor. The bullet, fired by a Japanese North Korean assassin, Moon Se-kwang, was meant for Park. Many believed that Park was unable to recover from the shock, and his leadership suffered as a consequence. "Park's power and handling of power changed when she died," observed his biographer Cho Kap-je. "He appeared to become more and more a shell of a man lacking his previous substance. His ability to balance his personality and the use of power had diminished considerably in the last years of his life."[2]

By the time of his death, Park was increasingly isolated. In the 1960s he had been able to travel freely, interacting with people without too much restraint, but since the assassination of his wife, his movements had become severely restricted, depriving him of human contact. Yuk also had had a humanizing influence on him, and without her he felt lost,

Park Chung Hee with his wife, Yuk Yŏng-su, celebrating Park's forty-ninth birthday, on September 30, 1966. Yuk was Park's second wife; the two had married on December 12, 1950, in the midst of the most harrowing phase of the Korean War. Yuk's father was against the match, but Yuk married Park anyway without her father's blessing or approval. (SAEMAŬL UNDONG CENTRAL TRAINING INSTITUTE)

vulnerable, and insecure. In Park's bedroom side drawer, he kept two rifles. "The man who had gained power by the gun," observed Cho, "felt that someday the gun would be turned on him."[3]

That day came sooner than anyone had expected. On the evening of October 26, 1979, while dining in the company of his associates, Kim Chae-kyu, the chief of the Korean Central Intelligence Agency (KCIA), and Ch'a Chi-ch'ŏl, Park's powerful head of Blue House security, Park was shot to death. His demise came not from the hands of a North Korean assassin, but from Kim, an original member of the revolutionary group that took power in May 1961 and one of Park's closest colleagues and advisors. During the investigation and trial, Kim espoused the view that the violent demonstrations and political unrest wracking the nation were an indication of growing public dissatisfaction with Park's rule, and that he believed the time was ripe for a democratic revolution.

However, the real motive for the assassination was something more prosaically personal. Friction between Kim and Park was exacerbated by Kim's growing resentment of Park's body guard, Ch'a Chi-ch'ŏl, who became more powerful and influential after he became the Blue House security chief in 1974 in the wake of Yuk Yŏng-su's death. "That night, it appeared that Kim Chae-kyu was only thinking of killing the president and he had no plan of action for what to do afterwards," wrote Cho Kap-je. "The fact that he had no idea about which command center was most effective for carrying out a coup d'etat shows that the assassination was not premeditated and was a more spontaneous decision."[4] Kim had shot Ch'a first before turning his gun on Park, allegedly saying, "Sir! The reason why the political situation is a mess is because you are served by this worm of a man [Ch'a]!" Subsequent investigations supported the conclusion that Park's murder was a crime of passion and not the result of a conspiracy.[5]

Park's assassination opened a new era of uncertainty in South Korean politics. By the time of his death, vocal critics of the Park regime were demanding greater freedom and democracy. At the same time, the reality of the unending war marked by frequent and violent military confrontations along the DMZ and costly terrorist actions instigated by Kim Il Sung's regime made the possibility of a transition to democracy in the South very unlikely.[6]

Kwangju Uprising

For a time after Park's death, it looked as if Kim Il Sung's cherished dream of fomenting revolution in the South might happen. Taking advantage of the atmosphere of uncertainty following the events of October 26, opposition politicians and student activists began to loudly voice their demands to lift martial law and hold direct presidential elections. The large-scale release of dissidents in July that Park had agreed to during Carter's visit had emboldened Park's critics, and they demanded immediate changes to the *Yusin* constitution. Meanwhile, government and military leaders argued that the *Yusin* charter must remain in effect until the late president's successor could be chosen, to ensure stability and security. Acting President Ch'oe Kyu-ha, a "soft-spoken" former diplomat and Park's prime minister, was formally elected interim president on December 6. But Ch'oe had no independent political backing, and the real power lay with the military.

That power asserted itself on the night of December 12, when Gen. Chŏn Tu-hwan (Chun Doo Hwan), who had taken control of South Korea's intelligence apparatus since Park's assassination, staged a coup. Ambassador Gleysteen and the senior U.S. commander in Korea, Gen. John Wickham, stood by essentially as spectators, having little leverage over the unfolding events. "The era of America's paternal influence over the ROK had passed," Wickham concluded. "Since the United States had significantly reduced its military deployment . . . and had recently threatened to withdraw even those forces, ROK leaders doubted the reliability and continuity of America's commitment." Although President Carter had spent his entire presidency pressuring South Korea to liberalize and reduce the influence of the military, in the end he got exactly the opposite.[7] The events of December 12 put an end to any hope for the emergence of democratic and civilian rule. The South Korean people were outraged.

Chŏn had at first blamed the unrest on a "minority" of student radicals, professors, and intellectuals. However, with daily protests continuing unabated for months on end, he suddenly changed his tune and on May 13 played the North Korea card. Widespread arrests of students and oppositional leaders followed, and martial law was declared on

South Korean soldiers on guard in downtown Kwangju, May 23, 1980. The Kwangju uprising was a pivotal moment in South Korea's struggle for democracy. Swept up by a tide of demonstrations following the death of Park Chung Hee and the military coup that brought Chŏn Tu-hwan to power, the brutality of the new regime's response outraged many Korean citizens. The Kwangju Uprising also tainted South Koreans' view of the United States due to Washington's alleged role in the suppression of the uprising, thus giving rise to fervent anti-Americanism, especially among students. While student dissidents began questioning the U.S. role in Korean affairs, they also began challenging their nation's traditional hostility toward North Korea. (AP PHOTOS)

May 17. The citizens of Kwangju rose up in anger when they received news that Kim Dae-jung, who had almost defeated Park in the 1972 presidential elections, was arrested in the early morning hours of May 18. Kwangju was the capital city of Kim's home region, the South Chŏlla province in southwestern Korea, and Kim was their local hero. This region had been neglected during the economic boom of the 1960s and 1970s because Park had concentrated on developing the southeastern region of Korea, where he was born. Resentment over regional favoritism fueled the anger evoked by the arrest of Kwangju's favorite son. Its citizens responded by seizing weapons from local police, turning the city into a fortress, while demanding the release of Kim and the restoration of democracy. Chŏn responded by ordering the city surrounded by army units. He then unleashed them to retake control. The outcome of the battle between well-armed and organized regular soldiers, many with combat experience in Vietnam, against a hastily assembled citizen militia armed with only a hodge-podge collection of light weapons was predictable.

The city was retaken on May 27. Official government estimates of the number of civilians killed ranged from 170 to 240, but the actual number was likely higher. The brutal put down and killings fueled an intense national opposition to the Chŏn regime, especially from students. Rumors of U.S. complicity also fanned anti-American sentiment.[8] But it was the magnitude of state violence and the complete devastation of democratic forces and processes after the Kwangju uprising that drove many South Korean dissidents and intellectuals to search for the origins of their nation's predicament. While Kim Il Sung continued his efforts to disrupt South Korean society with a new emphasis on terrorism, these students looked to North Korea for answers to their nation's problems.

Students and the Politics of Legitimacy

One way students did this was by openly embracing North Korea's version of the ongoing war between the two Koreas. Accepting Kim Il Sung's view of the conflict as that between Korean revolutionary nationalists in the North and American "imperialists" and their "lackey" South Koreans meant that South Korea was seen as a "puppet" creation of the Americans. Students' embrace of this North Korean line also recycled Kim's *chuch'e* ideology (*chuch'eron*), which stressed North Korea's self-reliance and active resistance to foreign powers.[9] By the mid-1980s, *chuch'eron* had gained widespread influence among student dissidents and intellectuals.

This influence was manifested in two important ways. First, students began to directly challenge and subvert decades of cold war rhetoric that portrayed North Korea as *the* enemy of the South. The officially accepted relationship between friend and foe that had been part of the established South Korean line since the Korean War was turned upside down in *chuch'eron*. Instead, the *real* enemy of the people was the United States, not North Korea. These dissidents saw the U.S. decision to divide, occupy, and establish a military regime in southern Korea as a direct expression of imperialist ambitions in the Korean peninsula. They also questioned the very legitimacy of the South Korean state by playing up Kim Il Sung's resistance to the UN foreign-sponsored elections in 1948, on which the ROK claimed its legal basis. Moreover, whereas state-sponsored histories saw North Korea's menace solely in political and ideological terms, students argued that the United States, the "new" enemy, posed a threat that was much more radical and fundamental. The American capitalist culture represented an invasive force that threatened to undermine the very core of Korean national identity. The decadent individualism of the West, which these dissidents associated with consumerism, sexual promiscuity, and crime, presented external threats that required a nationalist strategy to combat.

Second, the students' rejection of the established South Korean view of North Korea as the main "enemy" forced them to come up with new ways of depicting the North-South relationship. Interestingly, they did this by drawing on a traditional canon of Confucian morality tales about women's steadfast loyalty during periods of loss and forced separation from their husbands. The eighteenth-century *Tale of Ch'unhyang*, Korea's most renowned love story, was especially influential. It concerns the love between the son of an upper-class family named Yi Myong-nyŏng and the daughter of a socially despised *kiseang* (female entertainer) named Ch'unhyang. After their engagement, Yi is called to duty in the capital far away from Ch'unhyang. Shortly thereafter, Ch'unhyang is sent to prison when she refuses the advances of the evil local governor. Finally, her husband returns, rescues her, and punishes the evil governor, and they live happily ever after. Every Korean, North or South, is familiar with this tale. Indeed, it has been the subject of numerous books, dramatic performances, movies, and cartoons in both Koreas.[10]

Students thus used the Ch'unhyang narrative in their portrayal of the division. As an exemplary model of Korean virtues, unwavering, faithful, and determined to undergo whatever tribulations required to resist the forces of evil, the loyal Ch'unhyang came to represent South Korea. Ch'unhyang remains true to her husband (North Korea) by defiantly resisting political authority and not succumbing to the advances of the lascivious evil governor (the United States). Implicit references to the Ch'unhyang story appeared repeatedly in student illustrations and pamphlets. Images of two lovers about to fall into each other's embrace or of a happy couple triumphantly running across the DMZ revealed the connection between marital union and a reunified nation. Indeed, to think of North and South Korea as lovers, struggling to overcome the division of the peninsula, challenged decades of cold war rhetoric.

If marriage represented the unification of the two Koreas and the end of the war, then the division of the peninsula was often compared to

"The Road to Unification," illustration of a man and woman embracing in the shape of the Korean peninsula, used in a Seoul National University student pamphlet, April 1989. (AUTHOR'S COLLECTION)

rape. Rape signaled the breakdown of the marital bond and thus symbolically came to stand for the nation at war with itself. During colonial times, rape was often used to evoke Korea's experience under Japanese colonialism. It was also rooted in the real-life experiences of thousands of Korean women who were forcibly and systematically recruited by the Japanese government to serve as prostitutes (euphemistically referred to as "comfort woman") for Japanese soldiers during World War II. In both colonialism and the division, the image of the violated woman carried with it the values of purity against filth, and of chastity against foreign contamination. A famous poem by the "resistance" poet Kim Nam-ju, "Pulgamjŭng" (1988), shows how prostitution, rape, and violence become interrelated themes in their symbolism for the division:

My elder sister
Is our liberated country's lady of the night.
To borrow one highly venomous tongue,
She is a widely gaped vulva like a
Chestnut burr under the boots of the U.S. Eighth Army.

My little sister is our modernized country's new woman.
To borrow an expression of a common boy,
She is a widely open tourist vulva under the Japanese yen.

How deep did we lapse by rotting.
Not awakening no matter how much [we are shaken].
Not feeling no matter how much [we are pinched].
Ah, my half-piece country,
After 36 years of broken waist, when will you open your eyes from
Your long, long humiliating sleep . . .[11]

The title "Pulgamjŭng," meaning frigidity, refers to a woman's guilt or fear of becoming pregnant or contracting a venereal disease. Rape constituted not only a threat to the marital bond but also a crisis of maternity and female reproduction. For many student dissidents, the danger of Western, and specifically American, cultural contamination was perceived as a threat to the integrity and purity of the Korean nation. To defend the nation's inner "core," Korean women needed to resist the advances of the lascivious foreign male. The reality of American military presence in South Korea exacerbated this perceived crisis. The murder of a Korean prostitute by an American soldier in November 1992 provoked a national outrage igniting large demonstrations in Seoul. Students demonstrated for a full week while even taxi drivers refused to serve American soldiers. The accidental death of two schoolgirls caused by two American soldiers ten years later, on June 13, 2002, caused a similar wave of anti-Americanism that No Mu-hyŏn (Roh Mu-hyun) rode to the presidency in 2003.[12]

The focus on sweeping South Korea clean of America's "putrefying influence" was, of course, a central theme of Kim Il Sung's *chuch'e* ideology. In contrast to North Korea, which was deemed clean and pure and had established itself "without reliance on foreigners," the South was deemed polluted in every way. The description of South Korea in the North Korean novel *Encounter* (*Mannam*) was standard North Korean propaganda: "[South Korea was] the flashiest of American colonies . . . but look under the silk encasing and you see the body of what has degenerated to a foul whore of America." South Korea has been "covered in bruises from where it has been kicked black and blue by the American soldiers' boot."[13] Similar preoccupations with purity and pollution also appeared in South Korea's dissident rhetoric, combining calls for the two Koreas' "national rebirth" with the hope for deliverance from the war and division perpetuated by the United States. This rallying cry for a "liberated" and reunified Korea during a 1989 student demonstration in Seoul was typical of student hyperbole during this period:

> Youth! You who vigorously strike the bell of freedom at dawn, stomp out the dark shadows of the Stars and Stripes with bloody cries, and with longing for the sun-shining Mt. Paektu, work for the independence and reunification of this land. Only then will spring arrive joyously. Let us finish together the incomplete revolution so that we can live in a better world.[14]

The idea that students were struggling toward spring merely recycled North Korean propaganda about the "unfinished" revolution. Korea's spring meant a return to the nation's pristine origins before the peninsula was divided and before the South went from a Japanese colony to an American one. Appropriating Kim Il Sung's propaganda, student

Hours before taking to the streets to do battle with riot policemen, usually at the entrance of the university gate, students put on musical performances, dances, and historical dramas about key events in Korea's modern history. On the occasion of the ninth anniversary of the Kwangju uprising, students at Chŏnnam University in Kwangju recounted those events in a musical performance. Kwangju, May 18, 1989. (AUTHOR'S COLLECTION)

dissidents thus offered a vision of South Korea's *true* liberation from all foreign powers by embracing the *chuch'e* idea as their own.

The naiveté of these fanciful musings aside, by focusing on the virtues of Koreaness versus foreignness, student dissidents had idealized the North Korean regime. North Korean officials were no doubt heartened by the spectacle of South Korean students hurling Molotov cocktails at riot policemen dressed in full battle gear on the streets of Seoul, for it reconfirmed the regime's old propaganda line that the South Korean people were chafing under the yoke of American imperialism and longed to be liberated by their northern brethren. Even as late as the 1980s, Kim Il Sung had still not relinquished the dream of fermenting a nationalist revolution in the South.

In the legitimacy wars between North and South Korea, South Korean student dissidents had thus clearly sided with the North. In their embrace of Kim Il Sung's *chuch'e* thought, which became de rigeur within the mainstream of the student movement during the 1980s, they also condemned the United States and the American-backed "puppet" regime in the South as the main enemy.

Although some of this revolutionary rhetoric later softened and became absorbed into mainstream South Korean society well into the turn of the twenty-first century, it would take P'yŏngyang's economic collapse and the exposure of its nuclear ambitions to rid many South Koreans of their romantic illusions.[15]

PART IV

AFTER THE COLD WAR

The collapse of East European communism and the dissolution of the Soviet Union in 1989–91 spelled disaster for North Korea, which to survive had relied extensively on Soviet aid and concessional pricing for trade. The reality of an impoverished and isolated North Korea was laid bare at a time when South Korea was basking in the afterglow of hosting the 1988 Summer Olympics. The changing geopolitical environment and the stark contrast between the South and the North led South Korea's President No T'ae-u (Roh Tae-woo), elected in 1987, to pursue rapprochement with the communist world, including North Korea. No's Nordpolitik policy aimed to establish close relations with North Korea's allies and thereby induce it to open up to the world. Although Nordpolitik saw considerable diplomatic and economic success, it did not open up the North.

When it was discovered that Iraq had failed to disclose its nuclear program in the aftermath of the first Gulf War in 1991, Hans Blix, the director of the International Atomic Energy Agency (IAEA), the UN agency responsible for enforcing the Nuclear Nonproliferation Treaty (NPT), decided to get tougher in demanding that NPT signatories establish acceptable inspection regimes as soon as possible. North Korea became the first test case, one that the North had not expected. This led to conflicts between North Korean officials and IAEA inspectors and the eventual withdrawal of North Korea from the NPT in March 1993. The possibility of a second Korean War loomed ominously on the horizon.

War was averted when former president Jimmy Carter helped to broker a deal between the United States and North Korea. North Korea agreed that it would abandon its nuclear program if the United States and other allies agreed to provide two light-water reactors (LWRs) for power generation. Signed in October 1994, the Agreed Framework also outlined steps for normalization of relations between the United States and North Korea and assurance that the Americans would never threaten North Korea with nuclear weapons. In 1994, North Korea experienced two catastrophes: the beginnings of a devastating famine and the death of Kim Il Sung. Unable to feed its own people but refusing to initiate necessary reforms, North Korea resorted to provocations and brinkmanship to survive. After discovering that North Korea had secretly begun a uranium enrichment program, the United States declared the Agreed Framework void, and construction of the LWRs stopped. In 2006, North Korea surprised the world by testing a nuclear device. A second nuclear device was tested in 2009. Following the sinking of a South Korean ship in March 2010, allegedly by North Korea, North-South relations have deteriorated to the lowest point in years. North Korea experienced another blow in December 2011 following the unexpected death of Kim Jong Il and the anointment of his younger son, Kim Chŏng-ŭn (Kim Jong-un), as successor. Isolated and impoverished, the P'yŏngyang regime is transitioning under the watchful eye of its only ally and benefactor, China. So what is next for North Korea? How will the Korean War finally end?

CHAPTER TWENTY

North Korea and the World

O n the morning of July 9, 1994, North Koreans woke up to hear that "there will be a critical announcement at noon on TV. Everybody must watch it." When the hour arrived, twenty-one million anxious North Koreans gathered around television sets to see a solemn official, dressed in black, read a prepared statement:

> We, the working class, collective farmers, People's Army soldiers, intellectuals, young students, Central Committee of the Party, Military Commission of the Party, National Defense Commission of the DPRK, Central People's Committee, and Administration Council report with mournful heart to the people that the General Secretary of the Chosun Workers' Party, Premier of the DPRK and Great Leader, Comrade Kim Il Sung, passed away unexpectedly at 2AM on July 8, 1994.

The cause of Kim's sudden demise was a massive heart attack. At the time of his death, North Korea was a failed state. It was, as one observer wrote, "an island of stagnation in a sea of East Asian growth."[1] For most of North Korea's existence, Kim Il Sung had been able to rely on the support of both China and the Soviet Union. Following the turmoil of the Cultural Revolution and Sino-American rapprochement, North Korea depended almost exclusively on the largesse of the Soviet Union, which until 1984 provided more than $1 billion in foreign aid and credits annually, mostly in soft loans that P'yŏngyang did not repay. An Eastern European scholar noted, "A distinctive feature of the creditor-debtor relationship . . . was continuous long-term loans extended by the Soviet Union and frequent deferral of North Korean repayment."[2] North Koreans could not even "produce enough clothing for themselves."[3]

The pattern of defaulting on loans was characteristic of North Korea's trade regime and foreign policy to secure continual and concessional foreign capital. According to the economist Nicholas Eberstadt, this system is distinguished by a "political conception of international economic relations wherein goods and services are understood to flow not so much through voluntary commercial exchange between contractually equal partners, but through a struggle between states and systems." In other words, North Korea viewed the loans not as contractual obligations, but as rewards, "as a sort of tribute from abroad."[4] The North's peculiar triangular relationship with the Soviet Union and China had encouraged this pattern to develop and continue. The "tributary" system, however, ended rather abruptly after the fall of the Berlin Wall in 1989, the dissolution of the Soviet Union in 1991, and the end of the cold war in Europe. Russia and China's abandonment of the "friendship price" system and demand for hard currency for exports resulted in a steep decline in the North Korean economy. The DPRK had fallen into a classic poverty trap. Stagnant economic growth stifled investments to grow the economy. The North's economy was degraded by a lack of innovation and by a dependence on imported raw materials with no resources to pay for them.

Meanwhile, South Korea was booming, its success highlighted by the 1988 Summer Olympics in Seoul, which marked a turning point in the city's status and relationship with the world. South Koreans dramatically showcased to billions around the world that they were no longer the "poverty-stricken Asian war victim" of the past, but a vibrant, rich, and modern society. The contrast with the North could not have been more striking.[5] Furthermore, South Korea had just made a peaceful and successful transition to democracy. On December 16, 1987, after nearly three decades of authoritarian rule, South Koreans chose their first democratically elected president, a former general and Chŏn Tu-hwan's close friend No T'ae-u. This transition was in large part due to students who came together with ordinary citizens during the summer of 1987 to demand a direct presidential election. After weeks of protests, Chun's chosen successor, No T'ae-u, conceded to these demands. But during the election a split in the opposition led to No's victory with just 36 percent of the popular vote. Nevertheless, the election had been fair and democracy secured. The election and the Olympics symbolized South Korea's political and economic coming of age. For the first time in over five decades, the South could claim victory in its legitimacy war with the North. But could this victory end the war?

The time had come to find out. On July 7, 1988, four months after his inauguration and on the eve of the Seoul Olympics, President No announced a new approach to relations with North Korea. In his memoirs, No wrote that he had "agonized over how to resolve the stand-off with the North" and then thought of how the Qin emperor had defeated his enemies at the end of the Warring States period (BCE 475–221) and unified China. "The strategy used by Emperor Qin called for 'establishing close relations with distant states in order to destroy the enemy nearby.'" No therefore "decided to invoke this strategy of making friends with distant enemies." Nordpolitik, as the policy was known, signaled South Korea's new openness to communist nations around the world and led to the South's predominance over the North in a changing international climate. "We would follow the road to P'yŏngyang through Eastern Europe, Moscow and Beijing."[6]

Hungary was the first communist country to respond and establish diplomatic relations. In a dramatic reversal of fortunes, South Korean aid was a key factor. South Korea offered a loan of $625 million to help Hungary's struggling economy. Full diplomatic relations were established on February 1, 1989, over P'yŏngyang's vociferous objections. The Soviet Union soon followed. Until Mikhail Gorbachev came to power in 1985, South Korea was little known and not of any significant concern to the Soviet Union. After the success of the Seoul Olympics, Moscow took steps to establish relations with South Korea. In 1989, trade offices were opened in Moscow and Seoul, and direct sea and air routes established between the two countries.[7] Politically, in a dramatic turnaround, Moscow dropped its opposition to South Korean membership in the United Nations. These developments were, naturally, distressing to the North Korean regime. Hoping to halt Moscow's drift toward Seoul, Kim Il Sung invited Gorbachev to P'yŏngyang. Gorbachev was scheduled to visit China in the spring of 1989, and Kim asked him to stop on his way to Beijing. But despite Kim's desperate pleas, Gorbachev declined.

The rejection was a blow to Kim, who had wanted to obtain Moscow's reassurance of continued support. Gorbachev's trip to China was also disturbing because it signaled the beginning of a closer relation between Moscow and Beijing. North Korea had survived by playing the two communist powers against each other, but this leverage would no longer be available. Gorbachev further inflamed Kim's anxieties by announcing, while in China, his new friendship with Seoul. It was no comfort to Kim that Gorbachev viewed better relations with South Korea as having no effect on Moscow's relations with the North since the main purpose of his Korea policy was "helping the peace process on the Korean peninsula."[8]

In May 1990, Gorbachev met with his senior foreign policy advisor Anatoly Dobrynin, the legendary Soviet ambassador to the United States from 1962 to 1986. He instructed Dobrynin to convey to President No the message that Gorbachev was willing to meet him in San Francisco in June after his summit meeting with President George H. W. Bush in Washington. He also asked Dobrynin to explore the possibility of obtaining a major loan from South Korea. Dobrynin recalled that Gorbachev simply said, "We need some money." The San Francisco meeting was confirmed, and when No and Gorbachev met, the Soviet leader gave his commitment to "peaceful reunification" of the Koreas and the two discussed the normalization of relations between their countries. At the press conference after the meeting, an ebullient No told reporters that "as a result of today's meeting, the cold war ice on the Korean peninsula has now begun to crack." He reaffirmed that "Seoul did not wish to isolate North Korean regime" and that the ultimate goal of Nordpolitik was to induce North Korea to open up to the world.[9]

Events moved quickly after the meeting in San Francisco. On September 30, 1990, Moscow and Seoul established full diplomatic relations. This was originally supposed to have taken place on January 1, 1991, but the Soviets decided to move the date forward due to the extremely rude treatment they received from P'yŏngyang. "The communiqué stated the date of normalized relations as '1 January 1991,'" No recalled, "and Foreign Minister Shevardnadze, with his own pen, crossed it out and wrote '30 September 1990' right at the foreign ministers meeting." It was, the South Korean president wrote triumphantly, "a gift from an angry Shevardnadze."[10]

The Soviet Union also agreed to stop all military aid and cooperation with North Korea in return for South Korea's economic assistance. "The Soviet Union kept its promise and thereafter not a single Soviet fighter jet, tank or missile was shipped to North Korea," No later remarked. "As a result, for $1.4 billion in economic loans, South Korean security gained tens of billions of dollars worth of security."[11] Gorbachev explained his reasons for the abrupt change in North Korean policy in his memoir: "It was clear that we could not, for obsolete ideological reasons (i.e. because of our ties with North Korea), continue opposing the establishment of normal relations with his [No's] country which showed an exceptional dynamism and had become a force to be reckoned with, both in the Asia-Pacific region and in the wider world."[12]

China also moved toward a closer relationship with South Korea. In May 1991, Chinese Premier Li Peng announced that China would not oppose admission of both North and South Korea to the United Nations. This was another huge blow to Kim Il Sung. Since the only possible veto against South Korean membership was the Soviet Union, which had already announced its support for Seoul, Kim had no choice but to follow the winds and announce that North Korea would apply for UN membership too. Kim had long opposed dual membership for North and South Korea, but it was now evident that the world considered the two Koreas as separate sovereign entities. Adding to North Korea's woes was China's announcement in early 1992 that it would normalize relations with Seoul. On August 24, 1992, China and South Korea established diplomatic relations. The previous December the Soviet Union had dissolved.[13]

The dramatic transformation of the geopolitical situation around the divided peninsula at the end of the 1980s and in the early 1990s appeared to spell the doom of the North Korean regime. Its economy in shambles, traditional sources of support all gone, and its founding and inspiring leader dead, few believed that the anachronistic regime could survive much longer. Even South Korean students became disillusioned, knowing full well that Kim's utopia was a chimera and the South had won the war. Yet, despite these setbacks, North Korea did not collapse, nor does it appear likely that it will any time soon. The regime continues to present itself to its people as a defiant power that, in stark contrast to the "Yankee colony in the south," embodies the true spirit of the self-reliant Korean nation. The tenaciousness with which it still clings to the myth of its greatness and fearlessness in the face of great odds defies easy predictions about its future. North Korea's refusal to go the way of other communist states demonstrates the enduring legacy of Kim Il Sung as well as the power of the unending Korean War to shape contemporary events.

Showdown

What is the secret to the extraordinary enduring power of North Korea and the first and only communist dynasty, the Kim family regime? Traditional, historical, and ideological factors—the traditional patriarchal and hierarchical social structure of Korea's Confucian past, Korea's history of isolationism, and the fierce anti-imperialist nationalism that developed during the colonial period—account for part of the answer, but part also lies in Kim Il Sung's strategy for national survival, which provided just enough material sustenance to avert collapse. The strategy was characterized by a unique "aid-maximizing economic strategy" whereby external aid rather than development and economic growth became the indispensable foundation for national viability.[14] Although Kim Il Sung touted self-determination (*chuch'e*) as the fundamental principle of his regime, it was a policy that in reality required dependency. One of the more extraordinary features of Kim's foreign policy was his uncanny ability to navigate between Great Power interests to achieve his own ends. He was the original author of the Korean War, but it was Stalin who made it possible and Mao who largely fought it. After the war, he was able to secure his position by playing China and the Soviet Union against each other, as well as obtain vast amounts of economic aid from both powers. The end of the cold war closed North Korea's sources of support, but Kim again showed his extraordinary ability to leverage competing interests for his gain, this time by playing the nuclear card.

The North Korean nuclear program began in 1985 after three decades of lobbying the Soviet Union for help. During the 1960s and 1970s, the Kremlin had been unwilling to support North Korea's repeated requests for a nuclear power plant because of its suspicion of Kim Il Sung's belligerent intentions. Since P'yŏngyang was hardly a cooperative ally, this refusal was understandable. North Korea's worsening economic condition was another reason for the refusal. The plan was expensive, and North Korea had no means to pay for it. The DPRK made another request in early 1976, even as highly contentious negotiations over North Korea's debt were taking place in Moscow.[15]

Given the frosty relationship between the two communist countries, the dire state of the North's economy, and the long-term pattern of

North Korean belligerence, why did the Soviet leadership finally change its mind and approve of nuclear cooperation with the P'yŏngyang regime in 1985? A major reason was renewed cold war tensions and the increasing international isolation of the Soviet Union during this period. Following the Soviet invasion of Afghanistan in December 1979, the United States decided to increase diplomatic, military, and economic pressures on the Soviet Union during a period when it was already suffering economically. Sino-Soviet relations were also at a standstill. While Moscow's relations with China and the United States worsened, North Korea's strategic importance to the Soviet Union increased. As one observer put it, "Nuclear cooperation between Moscow and P'yŏngyang was one carrot that the Chinese could not match."[16] At the same time, since the Soviets knew they could not maintain effective control over the P'yŏngyang regime, they wanted to be sure that Kim Il Sung's hands were "tied by as many international agreements as possible."[17] The Soviet Union thus agreed to supply four LWRs in 1985, but only if North Korea joined the NPT, which it did in December of that year. The NPT required signatories to sign a safeguard inspection agreement within eighteen months that permitted inspections to identify violations.

However, due to a mix-up in paperwork, the inspection agreements were never signed. By then, the prospects of North Korea receiving the Soviet reactors had dimmed, owing to the waning fortunes of the Soviet economy. Kim Il Sung was stuck with the treaty commitments but without the Soviet reactors. He was thus forced to embark on an indigenous nuclear program at a place called Yŏngbyŏn. It was not until 1991, after the Persian Gulf War (code-named Operation Desert Storm), that pressure to inspect the North Korean nuclear facilities became an international issue. Until then, the IAEA had limited inspections of civilian nuclear sites that NPT signatories had voluntarily reported, but the Gulf War crisis revealed that Iraq, an NPT signatory, had undisclosed secret nuclear sites. Facing "withering criticism" for ineffectiveness and timidity, the IAEA and its new director, Hans Blix, decided to get tough. North Korea became its first target.[18]

When North Korean officials refused to allow the inspection of two installations at Yŏngbyŏn that American intelligence had identified as potential sites for secret nuclear activity, a showdown with the IAEA became inevitable. The IAEA told the North Koreans that if these installations were not open to inspections it would ask the UN Security Council to consider sanctions. The situation, thought Blix, tested the credibility and standing of the IAEA, but more important, allowing North Korea to ignore the required inspections could fundamentally undermine the NPT and the global nonproliferation program. On March 12, 1993, P'yŏngyang made the stunning announcement that North Korea intended to withdraw from the NPT rather than submit to inspections. Three days later, the IAEA Board voted to hand the matter over to the UN Security Council and ordered their inspectors home.

With this defiant act, North Korea had seized the initiative. It was now up to the United States, South Korea, and the international community to persuade P'yŏngyang not to withdraw from the NPT. The United States offered to improve political and economic relations and give security assurances if North Korea remained in the NPT and allowed IAEA inspections. When it became clear that the negotiations were going nowhere, the new Clinton administration decided to ask the United Nations to lay the groundwork for economic sanctions. The move came hours after North Korea threatened war in March 1994 if Washington and Seoul mounted a pressure campaign. In an ominous exchange between North and South Korean officials, captured on video, the North Korean delegate warned his South Korean counterpart that "Seoul is not far away from here. If a war breaks out Seoul will turn into a sea of fire." The statement was so extraordinary that the South Korean government broadcasted it on national television, instantly enflaming anti–North Korean passions. Realizing that the comments had backfired, Kim Il Sung went out of his way to disown the "sea of fire" comment, saying that it had been a "mistake" by the negotiator.[19]

Just three months after his inauguration, in January 1994, President Bill Clinton faced the first international crisis of his administration. As the United States pushed for UN Security Council sanctions against North Korea, the P'yŏngyang regime repeatedly denounced the move, declaring "sanctions are a declaration of war." China and Russia became concerned as the United States and North Korea inexorably moved toward direct confrontation. Prime Minister Li Peng warned that "pressure . . . can only complicate the situation on the Korean peninsula, and it will add to the tension."[20] Russia was also reluctant to support UN sanctions for similar reasons, and it proposed as an alternative a forum with the two Koreas, China, the United States, Japan, Russia, and the IAEA "to work out a balanced approach to denuclearization and international guarantees for North Korea." The Americans were "miffed" mostly because the negotiation track had been tried in vain for over a year and they thought such a conference would lead nowhere.[21]

Unlike the Americans, however, China and Russia had been dealing directly with North Korean recalcitrance for over forty years; both countries had successfully thwarted previous North Korean plans to restart another war on the Korean peninsula. They also understood what Washington apparently did not: that the crisis was neither unique nor isolated but linked to a long series of provocations aiming to bolster Kim Il Sung's hold on power during a period of political uncertainty. The North Korean leadership would view UN sanctions as an international slap in the face that directly challenged the myth of Kim Il Sung as a fearsome and respected leader. It was to uphold and strengthen this myth that had been behind the capture of the *Pueblo* in 1968. Neither China nor Russia wanted to humiliate Kim Il Sung in front of the world. They feared destabilizing the regime, for its collapse would likely result in millions of refugees crossing the Chinese and Russian borders, a calamitous event. If necessary, China and Russia were willing to exercise their veto power in the UN Security Council to stop a sanctions resolution. "It's an international rule now to solve all issues through dialogue," declared Zhang Tingyan, China's ambassador to South Korea. "Why should the North Korean nuclear problem be an exception? China cannot agree to sanctions or any other measures."[22]

Japan too opposed sanctions for a variety of domestic concerns. Sanctions would require stopping the substantial flow of money sent by ethnic Koreans in Japan to their relatives in North Korea. These remittances were estimated to be roughly $600 million annually. Such an action could expose Japan to a severe backlash from pro-North residents, including the possibility of violent acts and terrorism.[23] If the North launched another attack, U.S. bases in Japan would undoubtedly be targeted with missiles. A war or a North Korean collapse also raised the specter of a massive influx of refugees.

South Korea, fearing both war and North Korean collapse, even if the latter resulted in fulfilling the long-cherished dream of reunification, was ambivalent about sanctions as well. Attitudes toward reunification had changed after South Koreans learned the economic and social cost of German reunification. "On the one hand, the absolute majority wants to see reunification," said Kil Jeong Woo, director of policy studies at the Research Institute for National Unification (RINU), a government think tank in Seoul. "That's the emotional side. On the economic side, after witnessing the German experience, we should be more realistic." With estimates for the costs of absorbing North Korea ranging from $200 billion to more than $1 trillion over a decade, many South Koreans had trepidations over what reunification might mean for their newfound prosperity. RINU calculated in 1994 that "raising North Korea's economic level to 60 percent that of the South would take 10 years and cost $40 billion each year, an amount equal to one-eighth of South Korea's annual economic output." Rather than a "big bang" approach to unification, which could result in millions of refugees streaming across the border, the South Korean government began emphasizing "stability, not unity."[24]

In pressing for UN sanctions, the Clinton administration was thus swimming against a strong current of opposition. With Chinese and Russian vetoes of a sanctions resolution certain, North Korea was under no pressure to compromise. Ironically, the same regional concerns that had frustrated Carter's efforts to withdraw U.S. ground troops from South Korea in the 1970s also complicated Clinton's attempts to get tough over the North Korean nuclear program. No one in the region wanted to upset the fragile balance of power on the Korean peninsula and risk another conflict. This was the dilemma that the Clinton administration faced when Kim Il Sung raised the ante and precipitated a showdown that would lead the United States and North Korea to the brink of war.

Defueling Crisis

On April 19, 1994, North Korea notified the IAEA of its intention to withdraw spent fuel rods from a nuclear reactor in Yŏngbyŏn, but without IAEA monitoring. The announcement was a direct rebuff of both the United States and the UN, which had repeatedly warned North Korean authorities not to take this action. Plutonium could be extracted from the rods at a reprocessing plant in Yŏngbyŏn to provide P'yŏngyang with the main ingredient for a nuclear weapon. Secretary of Defense William Perry declared that Washington would seek sanctions if the fuel rods were withdrawn without IAEA scrutiny, calling the situation "a very substantial near-term crisis." The estimate was that there was enough plutonium in the eight thousand rods for four or five nuclear weapons. The removal of the rods without IAEA monitoring posed another serious problem. In essence, the IAEA would not be able to determine the history of previous refueling operations and thus the total number of rods available for reprocessing and the total amount of plutonium North Korea might have accumulated. The agency complained that if the withdrawal was not monitored, "it would result in irreparable loss of the agency's ability to verify that plutonium-laden fuel was not being diverted for use in nuclear weapons." In 1986, for example, the CIA estimated that the Yŏngbyŏn reactor had been shut down for up to 110 days. It was unclear how many of the eight thousand rods might have been replaced at that time, but CIA estimates put the amount of plutonium that might have been obtained to be enough for one or two nuclear bombs. When the actual unloading of the fuel rods began in early May of 1994, the IAEA sent a team led by Dmitri Perricos to witness the operation. According to Perricos, the unloading process was "a big mess," which he believed was deliberate to keep the world guessing on how much plutonium the North possessed, in a high-stakes game of brinkmanship.[25]

The Joint Chiefs were particularly incensed and were asking, in effect, "How long are we going to let them walk all over us?" The Clinton administration once again pressed for UN sanctions, but the difficulty in devising and winning support for sanctions, especially from China and Russia, undercut the message of resolve that the United States sought to convey. In secret, a military option was now put on the table. On June 10, Secretary Perry presented to President Clinton a detailed contingency plan for bombing Yŏngbyŏn. Military considerations included reinforcing military forces in Korea and the region to deter any North Korean military action in response to UN sanctions. These options ranged from two thousand personnel to fill out wartime headquarters staff, to a major force of fifty thousand troops, four hundred aircraft, and fifty ships, an option that would require a reserve call-up and the evacuation of U.S. and foreign noncombatant personnel from South Korea. Clinton was told that renewed war could result in 52,000 U.S. and 490,000 South Korean military causalities in the first ninety days, in addition to a large number of civilian casualties. Furthermore, the inevitable collapse of the

North Korean regime would send millions of refugees flooding across Asia, with destabilizing effects in China, South Korea, and Japan.[26]

On June 16, Clinton and his advisors considered the military options. Perry reminded the group of the danger of starting a cycle of measures and countermeasures that a military contingency to deter North Korean action against sanctions could spark. He evoked Barbara Tuchman's account in *The Guns of August* of such a cycle propelled by "cross-purposes, misunderstandings and inadvertence" in the days leading to World War I. Could this cycle be stopped? The meeting was in its second hour when Clinton was informed that former president Jimmy Carter was on the line from P'yŏngyang. Carter had offered his services to Clinton in a last-ditch effort to resolve the crisis and went to P'yŏngyang ostensibly as a private citizen in response to a standing invitation to visit that Kim Il Sung had extended. Robert Gallucci, assistant secretary of state for political-military affairs, stepped out of the Cabinet Room to take the call. Carter told Gallucci that Kim Il Sung had agreed not to expel the IAEA inspectors and to keep the monitoring equipment in place in return for resuming talks and no sanctions. Kim, in effect, had promised to freeze his nuclear program. He would not place new fuel rods in the reactors, nor would he reprocess the irradiated ones that had already been removed. Carter said that he planned to describe the progress he had made with the North Korean dictator on CNN. Stunned, Gallucci returned to the meeting with the amazing news.[27]

There was skepticism over whether Carter had obtained anything new. Kim did not say he would stop reprocessing or stop producing plutonium. "What we have here is nothing new," one White House official complained. "The problem is that North Korea now has a former president as its spokesperson." The most serious concern was his unexpected public call to "stop the sanctions activity in the United Nations." "In my opinion, the pursuit of sanctions is counterproductive in this particular and unique society," Carter declared. "I don't think the threat of sanctions has any effect at all on North Korea as far as damage to its society or economy is concerned. The declaration of sanctions would be considered by [North Koreans] as an insult to their country . . . and a personal insult to their so-called Great Leader [Kim Il Sung] by branding him a criminal." Kim had played a weak hand brilliantly. Carter's opposition to sanctions and his public pronouncement presented a powerful case to the world. Carter's words humanized the North Korean dictator, making him look rather grandfatherly and quite reasonable; they also fed into the North Korean myth of Kim's respectability during a period of political crisis for the North Korean regime. Carter seemed oblivious to how his efforts might be perceived. By lending respectability that Kim craved, Carter had undercut the strength of the American negotiating position. "President Kim Il Sung understood that I was speaking as a private citizen, not as a representative of the U.S.," Carter later insisted.[28] To most people, Carter was anything but a private U.S. citizen.

Back in Washington after the two-day visit, Carter declared the crisis "over." Although few believed this was the case, since there was still no formal agreement, the visit did provide a breakthrough: the chance to step back from the brink of war and the possibility of a North-South Korean summit. Before he entered North Korea, by ground across the DMZ on June 15, he had met with South Korean President Kim Yŏng-sam, who gave Carter a trump card to play—a proposal for a North-South summit without any preconditions. Carter brought up the proposed summit during a boat ride he and his wife, Rosalynn, took with Kim. On the seven-hour journey down the Taedong River, Kim and Carter "had an interesting conversation," which included discussion on an "unprecedented meeting between him [Kim Il Sung] and South Korean president Kim Young Sam [Kim Yŏng-sam] to be arranged by me at an early date." Thus, quite suddenly, the momentum toward military confrontation was halted. Carter later insisted that North Korea would have gone to war had the United States pursued UN sanctions, conducted an air strike, or sent significant military reinforcement, but in light of North Korea's long history of provocations and backing down when confronted with Armageddon, this seems unlikely. In retrospect, Carter's mission bought time for North Korea, but it also bought time for the Clinton administration to avert a catastrophic showdown on the Korean peninsula. Clinton seized the opportunity made by Carter to negotiate a new deal with P'yŏngyang. Kim Il Sung had survived once again.[29]

Accord

The death of Kim Il Sung in July 1994 did not seriously affect the results of the Carter mission. The U.S.-DPRK nuclear talks began the next day, and the Americans were relieved that the Great Leader's unexpected demise did not change North Korea's desire for a deal nor alter its basic negotiating position. What did change was the prospect for a North-South summit. After weeks of debate on whether an official condolence should be announced, Seoul not only decided not to offer such a condolence but also announced that arrests would be made to anyone who publicly expressed such a sentiment. The stern announcement by the Unification Ministry had followed a North Korean announcement inviting South Korean mourners to come to P'yŏngyang to pay their respects to the Great Leader. The North guaranteed their safety, declaring "they could enter either through Panmunjom [*sic*] or through a third country." The North's invitation to those who found "it hard to repress their bitter grief" was angrily denounced by Seoul. It decided to block a plan hatched by leftist students to send a condolence mission to P'yŏngyang. Seoul suspected that North Korea would use the invitation to exploit the students in order to shore up the regime's legitimacy at home, by showing its citizens how much South Koreans respected the Great Leader. Instead, on the day of Kim's funeral, Seoul released hundreds of Soviet documents, obtained by President Kim Yŏng-sam during a visit to Russia in early June, which conclusively revealed that Kim Il Sung was behind the North Korean attack on June 25, 1950.[30] P'yŏngyang resumed its anti–South Korean rhetoric, which had been suspended because of the anticipated summit. North-South relations rapidly deteriorated and hope for reconciliation evaporated.

Despite the North-South spat, U.S.-DPRK nuclear talks resumed in Geneva on August 5, 1994. By the time of Kim Il Sung's death, it was expected that Kim Jong Il would succeed him in the first dynastic succession in communist history. The short, plump, moon-faced man with a pompadour had a reputation for hard drinking and womanizing. A single portrait of him, a rarity in North Korea, is hung in the entranceway of the Yŏngbyŏn nuclear complex. Beyond the basic elements of the provisional agreement that Carter had negotiated with Kim Il Sung, freezing of the nuclear program and foregoing proliferation-prone nuclear facilities in return for two LWRs, there were a number of other items of concern to both sides. The most contentious issue was what to do with the eight thousand spent fuel rods that North Korea had removed in May. The United States wanted the rods to be moved to a third country so that the plutonium could not be extracted from them in the future.

Another issue was the dismantlement of North Korea's plutonium production facilities, the reactors, and the reprocessing plant. A final issue concerned international inspections of two key nuclear waste sites, which could reveal the amount of plutonium North Korea may already have accumulated. "There'll be no overall settlement until the question of the past has been settled," declared Gallucci, the U.S. official chosen to lead the negotiations with North Korea.[31]

The terms of the accord that was eventually brokered heavily favored North Korea. First, North Korea was not forced to relinquish its eight thousand spent fuel rods to a third country. Instead, the United States and North Korea were to "cooperate in finding a method" to "dispose of the fuel in a safe manner that does not involve reprocessing" in North Korea. There was no provision for dismantling the reactors or the reprocessing plant. Although North Korea agreed to stop work on two other reactors, it was allowed to keep the only working reactor operating until the two promised LWRs were "nearly" complete. Finally, on the most contentious issue, the IAEA's demand for "special inspections" of two nuclear waste sites, North Korea did not have to allow inspections until a significant portion of the LWR project was complete. The agreement did require North Korea to let the IAEA inspect the nuclear sites acknowledged by the North Koreans, "but only after the supply contracts for the LWR project are done." In effect, North Korea would remain in violation of the NPT until the shipment of these "key components" which might take a decade or more.[32]

IAEA officials were furious. North Korea would continue to possess nuclear spent fuel for years. This would leave open the possibility that if it ever renounced the agreement, it could kick out the international inspectors and resume its bomb project. The United States also agreed to supply five hundred thousand tons of heavy fuel oil "to make up for the energy foregone by North Korea before the LWRs came into operation."[33] In effect, the Americans agreed to a new foreign aid program that would help keep North Korean factories running and homes heated for years to come.

North Korea predictably hailed the Agreed Framework, signed on October 21, 1994, as a triumph of North Korean diplomacy. North Korea's domestic propaganda celebrated the agreement as an "abject Yankee surrender" that reinforced the image of cowering Americans who yielded to

North Korea's fearsome power. "America had no choice but to grovel."[34] Seoul was less enthusiastic. As part of the Agreed Framework, the South Korean government was supposed to build the promised LWRs. One aspect of the Agreed Framework was the establishment of a consortium of nations called KEDO (Korean Peninsula Energy Organization), which also included the United States and Japan, that was responsible for implementing the energy-related parts of the Agreed Framework. Although South Korea, as part of this consortium, had been tasked to build the LWRs, it had been given little say in actually formulating the main provisions of the agreement. Many South Koreans felt resentful. In particular, North Korea's rejection of South Korean reactors was especially galling. In the ongoing legitimacy war with the South, the concept of South Korea "aiding" North Korea, much less providing reactors, did not sit well with P'yŏngyang, which continued to belittle the South as puppets of Washington. President Kim Yŏng-sam was equally adamant that Seoul would not foot the bill for reactors from another country. Feeling aggrieved at having been left out of the negotiations, and fearing once again that the United States might sell Seoul short and conclude a separate deal with the North, Kim Yŏng-sam demanded South Korea's inclusion in the process.[35] In the end, Washington persuaded Seoul to accept a compromise. North Korea would accept South Korean reactors if no mention was explicitly made that they were from South Korea.

The Agreed Framework also received a skeptical response in the United States. President Clinton defended it with the argument that North Korea committed to freeze and "gradually" dismantle its nuclear program. More important, the agreement was seen as a necessary step to end North Korea's self-imposed isolation from the international community. Critics, however, insisted that the administration had made a bad deal. A *Washington Post* editorial opined, "How can such an agreement even be defended? . . . It pays North Korea, and handsomely, for returning to the nonnuclear obligations it took on and violated and ideally should not have been paid for at all . . . The accord sets an international precedent that lets the North Koreans keep hiding for years the very facilities whose inspection would show their nuclear cheating to date." The *New York Times* headline simply read, "Clinton Approves a Plan to Give Aid to North Koreans."[36] Faced with a choice between war or compromise, the Clinton administration had opted for compromise.

Three weeks after the agreement was signed, the Republicans took control of both houses of Congress in the fall elections in 1994. Predictably, the Agreed Framework was severely criticized by the new Republican majority. Senator Frank Murkowski of Alaska, the chairman of the Senate Subcommittee on East Asian Affairs, said he would block the United States from purchasing the promised heavy oil. "I don't support the administration's concessions which I find totally unacceptable," he declared. "We have given away the store. I don't know what we've gotten in return other than promises." Other prominent Republicans, including Bob Dole of Kansas and Jesse Helms of North Carolina, also lambasted the agreement. "It is always possible to get an agreement when you give enough away," said Dole.[37] Appropriating funds for the heavy oil was, according to one administration official, like "going through the rings of hell."[38] As a result, the shipments of heavy oil often arrived late. Work on the two LWRs also began falling behind schedule. With the nuclear crisis seemingly behind them, the Americans no longer considered North Korea all that important. Besides, conditions in North Korea were steadily declining. By 1995, reports from travelers and defectors recounted devastating stories of a terrible famine sweeping across the nation. North Korea appeared to be collapsing from within.

CHAPTER TWENTY-ONE

Winners and Losers

S o had South Korea finally won its legitimacy war? Now a prosperous democratic society, how could South Koreans not feel proud of themselves and their accomplishments? The stark contrast between a rich and powerful South Korea and an impoverished and isolated North Korea erased any doubts which nation had emerged triumphant. Yet, at the same time that South Koreans basked in their victory over the North, commemorating the triumph proved tricky. This is because the most pressing issue at that time was to create a usable past that could make the future unification of the two Koreas possible. Recalling the horrors and frustrations of the war, and in particular, North Korea's brutal role in it, was no longer deemed tactful when the primary concern was to finally end the conflict and bring the two separated nations together. A new story of the war had to be constructed, one that would mobilize South Koreans in a tacit forgetfulness of North Korea's "criminal responsibility" for the war while simultaneously commemorating the war as a national tragedy.[1]

Triumph and Forgiveness

The first sign of this new approach occurred in 1994 when the War Memorial, a huge architectural complex located in central Seoul and one of the showpieces of No T'ae-u's presidential legacy, was opened to the public. Whereas earlier narratives of the war had placed the North Korean invasion and brutality at the center of the story, the memorial's various exhibits and displays aimed to promote collective forgiveness by excluding many brutal aspects of the war.[2] This message of forgiveness was clearly apparent in the most iconic structure of the War Memorial:

The Statue of Brothers, War Memorial, Seoul. (PHOTO BY AUTHOR)

The Statue of Brothers. Standing at one corner of the memorial precinct, the first thing that strikes the viewer about the statue is the enormous discrepancy in the size of the two figures. Embracing his smaller brother to his heart, the South Korean soldier's emotion-laden face stares intently at this younger North Korean while the latter looks up at him with admiring, grateful, and, one imagines, tearful eyes.

This theme of brotherly reunion is also reinforced by the cracked base, which is in the shape of an ancient Silla tomb mound. The ancient Silla kingdom unified the Korean peninsula in 668 CE when it conquered the northern kingdom of Koguryŏ. The historical analogy between the ancient past and the divided present is strikingly apparent. "My idea of using a Silla tomb as a pedestal," the statue's sculptor, Chae Yŏng-jip, remarked, "was not intended to evoke the idea of death. On the contrary, it was intended to evoke ideas of hope and rebirth, the cycles of history so to speak. The two brothers are reborn out of the womb of the past to be one again in the future." Rising out of the tomb, a reunified peninsula is reborn as a nation of brothers, although the South Korean elder brother is the more powerful and hence the more legitimate. In my interview with Chae, he remarked that the portrayal of the younger brother as weak and defenseless was deliberate, designed to show "the defeat of communism and the victory of South Korean democracy."[3] President No's reunification message was clear: South Korea's "forgiving embrace" of the North was predicated on the idea that the two Koreas would be united under the South, the authentic and legitimate Korea whose prosperity presented a clear contrast to the poverty-stricken North. Nevertheless, this reconciliation message was evoked on the basis of the South's "forgiveness" of the North, not its explicit triumph over it.

These ideas about reconciliation with the North reached full bloom during President Kim Dae-jung's ascendancy to political power in 1998. Kim was a devout Catholic, and his faith deeply influenced his worldview. In recalling President Park Chung Hee's persecution of him throughout his lifetime, for example, Kim wrote in his memoirs that it was his faith in God that had sustained him. "History only honors those who confess their sins before God, who forgive their enemies and who look after their neighbors."[4] Over and over again in his writings, Kim returned to the virtues of Christian forgiveness. When he became president, Kim declared that he bore no grudge or ill will against the former president or Park's successors, Chŏn Tu-hwan and No T'ae-u, stating, "Only a leader who holds the conviction that forgiveness is the ultimate victory can forgive with confidence."[5] To make good on his promise, one of Kim's first presidential acts was to propose building a memorial hall to honor Park Chung Hee. (It was opened a decade later, in 2012.) And in an unexpected act of clemency, Kim also pardoned Chŏn Tu-hwan and No T'ae-u, who had served just two years of their lifetime sentences in jail.[6]

It was precisely the "higher calling" of Kim's politics that most worried his critics. If love and forgiveness became the catchwords for Kim's attempts to reconcile with his former enemies, these same ideas became the mantra of his "Sunshine Policy" toward North Korea. Naming his new diplomatic efforts after Aesop's fable "The North Wind and the Sun," Kim rejected the idea of putting undue pressure on North Korea as a way to force it to open up to the world.[7] Rather, the essence of his policy was to engage P'yŏngyang out of its isolation by encouraging South Korean companies to do business with the North regardless of their political differences. The impact of this approach would be felt gradually as North Korea became penetrated and influenced by the lib-

Chairman Kim Jong Il meets President Kim Dae-jung, P'yŏngyang, June 12, 2000. Kim received the 2000 Nobel Peace Prize for his efforts to bring about a North-South rapprochement which culminated in the June 13–15, 2000, summit. However, his administration was later criticized when it was discovered that it had secretly paid the Kim Jong Il regime $500 million to attend the summit, causing a major political scandal that eventually led to the downfall of Kim's chief of staff, Pak Chi-wŏn, who was sentenced to prison for his role in the payment scandal. (AP PHOTOS)

eralizing affects of an economy integrated with the global economy. In time, it was hoped, North Korea would have become liberalized enough to make a more open relationship or even unification with South Korea possible.

That moment, it seemed, had finally arrived when Kim Dae-jung flew to P'yŏngyang to attend a historic summit on June 12, 2000. The North Korean leader, he reported, was not crazy after all, but quite sane and even witty. Kim Dae-jung was treated with all the reverence and respect as an "elder brother" should. When Kim returned to Seoul three days later to a hero's welcome, it appeared that the politics of forgiveness had actually worked.

If only it had been that easy. Amid the joyful calls for national reconciliation, a more sinister reality about North Korea was emerging, casting serious doubts on whether Kim Jong Il's regime could really be redeemed after all.

The North Korean Famine

"What is going on over there is simply beyond imagination," Dr. Hu Wanling, a researcher at China's Yanbian University and an ethnic Korean, told Jasper Becker, one of the first Western journalists to write about the North Korean famine. Like many residents living in the border region, Hu believed "hundreds of thousands have died from hunger and the worst is yet to come."[8] In August 1996, U.S. Congressman Tony Hall returned home stunned by what he saw during his four-day visit to North Korea. "Everyone is systematically starving together," he told reporters in Tokyo, it was "a slow starvation on a massive scale." Hall said the evidence included "families eating grass, weeds and bark; orphans whose growth has been stunted by hunger and diarrhea; people going bald for lack of nutrients and hospitals running short of medicine and fuel."[9] Interviews conducted by the humanitarian aid group Médecins Sans Frontières (Doctors Without Borders) in 1998 of scores of North Korean refugees hiding in China painted a dark picture of the most vulnerable victims of the famine: "Children are often too weak to come to class and teachers . . . desert the classroom to look for food . . . Some parents, unable to support their children, abandon them. Children and elderly can be seen lying on the street, too weak to stand."[10] Gangs of abandoned children were often seen at train stations. The trains had all but ceased to operate owing to lack of fuel or electricity, and the stations served as shelters. These children were called *kottjebi*, "flower swallow," because, like the migratory bird, they were in constant search of food and warmth. Hyŏk Kang, who escaped from North Korea in 1998, recalled that "about fifty children from all different backgrounds tried to survive like this, by stealing or begging for food around the station. Some of them lay lifelessly on the ground then dropped dead like flies. People gathered for a few minutes around the body of a child who had just died, as though to witness a spectacle, but then lost interest again almost immediately. In these times of famine, each person only thought of himself."[11]

In an interview with two former *kottjebi* conducted in 1999 by a reporter from the *Wŏlgan Chosŏn*, ten year old Im Ch'ŏl and his eight-year-old sister So-yŏn described their harrowing struggle for survival and their eventual escape to China. After their mother died, both children began living at the market.

"Since we didn't have anything to eat at home we always stayed in the market," said Ch'ŏl. "The market seller would put down a straw mat to sit on and then throw it away at the end of the day. So you'd get a few of those to put over you when you slept.... The kids would fill up the market area because there were so many of them."

"Could you tell me about your friends there and something about them?" asked the reporter.

"Kim Chin-hyŏk was very smart. He was very good at his studies and had a real talent for math. He became a *kottjebi* after his mother disappeared. Although he was very brainy, he still couldn't get enough to eat, so what do you do? Since he didn't get enough to eat, he didn't have the strength to use his brain. He'd beg and then get beaten up and because he slept on the ground and didn't eat, he'd get sick all the time. So he died at the age of ten. He was one year older than me."

"So where did he die? Did he die in the market?"

"Of course he died in the market. Where else would he have died?"

"How did he die?"

"He was begging. Kids died all the time so we got used to it. When I woke up one morning, he couldn't get up. The market sellers don't like it when a *kottjebi* dies. You know the sacks they sit on? They put him in one of those and then put him on a cart used to carry hay on and dumped him near the mountain and came back. Then after that a kid named Chang Ch'ŏl starved to death. He was tall and he had very good penmanship. But good penmanship doesn't help you beg, does it? So he died too, just like Chin-hyŏk. So two of our good friends died...."

"So-yŏn, did you have friends in the market?"

"Yes."

"Tell me about them. What were your friends doing in the market, So-yŏn? Tell me their names."

"I hung around with Hyang-ryo and we picked up scraps. We ate off the ground."

"Where is Hyang-ryo now?"

"She died."

"How did she die?"

"We were walking together and then she peed and died."

Ch'ŏl recalled the day when his sister almost died. Her face began to swell up as did her hands and feet. Her brother managed to steal some noodles from one of the nearby noodle shops and he fed them to her. She eventually recovered.

"That day, two girls lying beside So-yŏn died," he said. "One was six and the other was seven. They had swollen faces and feet just like

So-yŏn, but they didn't have anyone to feed them and so their deaths were unavoidable. When I saw those two being taken away, it was like they were taking away two pigs. The men who took them to the mountains said to us, 'You puppies, if you die, this will happen to you too.' . . ."[12]

There were also grim rumors of cannibalism from escapees claiming to have firsthand knowledge. "People are going insane with hunger," said one former North Korean military officer who fled to China with his family. "They even kill and eat their own infants. This kind of thing is happening in many places," he said. Another North Korean claimed that in his home city of Wŏnsan, a husband and wife had been executed because they had murdered fifty children and stored their salted flesh in a hut.[13] Public executions for these crimes, including stealing government property, became commonplace by 1998, the worst year of the famine crisis. "Last March, they shot 13 people to death who ate humans or cows in Wŏnsan," said a refugee. "The criminals were dangled up high and people were forced to come and look at them. What an unimaginable tragedy! At the present time, Chosŏn [North Korea] is hell on earth."[14] Estimates of the number of deaths caused by famine between 1995 and 1998 range from 600,000 to 1 million, or roughly 3 to 5 percent of the population.[15] Interviews with North Korean refugees suggest that in the northern provinces, 25 percent of the population may have perished from starvation since they were the first to be cut off from the central distribution system. Reports that people were "dropping like flies," including observations of desperate behavior such as foraging for wild plants, tree parts, or anything remotely edible, are simply "too specific and too widespread to be dismissed."[16]

The rest of the world became aware of the food crisis only when North Korea launched the "let's eat two meals a day" campaign in 1991.[17] Over the ensuing years, while sparring with IAEA inspectors, the North Korean regime was fatally slow in responding to the growing food crisis. Much of this had to do with the peculiarities of the North Korean economic system, which was heavily dependent on socialist sources of aid for basic requirements.

Back in 1958, Kim Il Sung abolished private shops, and markets were strictly regulated as "relics of capitalism." Farmers essentially became state employees. They farmed state-owned cooperatives and were forced to sell their produce to the state at fixed prices. Some farmers were allowed to cultivate small private plots of land to grow vegetables and herbs, but in contrast to other communist states the allotted plots were far smaller and resulted in a dearth of privately produced food. It was believed that allowing farmers to cultivate larger private plots would lead to them to ignore their work obligations in the cooperatives.[18] Instead of markets and private shops, food was distributed through the Public Distribution System (PDS), which provided basic necessities at heavily subsidized rates as payment for work. Food rationing levels were determined by a combination of occupation and rank. The PDS reflected the stratification of North Korea's hierarchical system. Senior government and military officials and heavy laborers received the most food. At the bottom were children and the elderly.[19]

Implicit in this system of entitlement was also a political stratification (three-tiered) system, since class background was an important determinant of socio-political hierarchy. Two years after the 1956 coup that had almost toppled Kim Il Sung, the NKWP investigated the population to determine political reliability, which was largely based on family background. This in turn defined the opportunities available for higher education, housing, work assignments, and residency. At the bottom of the three-tiered system was the so-called hostile class. These included families who had been rich peasants or whose family origins hailed from South Korea or Japan. People of this rank were closely watched by neighborhood organizations called the *inminban*, literally "people's group," whose members reported anything suspicious. The second tier, the so-called wavering class, hailed from families of middle-class peasants, traders, or owners of small businesses. The upper tier, the core class, was composed of people whose families had traditionally been workers, soldiers, or party members. Only members of the core class, which constituted roughly 15 percent of the population, were able to live in P'yŏngyang, considered a privilege. By contrast, members of the hostile class were relocated to remote regions of the country beginning in the late 1950s, especially the northeast where most of North Korea's mines and infamous concentration camps were located. This stratified classification system would later have important implications for the famine, as it was precisely these parts of the country that experienced the severest deprivations.[20]

By most accounts, the PDS ceased to function properly by 1993, and the first regions to suffer were the remote northeastern North and South

Hamgyŏng provinces. "The rations stopped in 1993," recounted one refugee. "The government said that every district had to solve its own food
problems."[21] This remote region was particularly dependent on the PDS
because of its mountainous terrain and lack of agricultural land. The
people were forced to go into the hills and mountains to forage for anything to eat. "Our village was feeding itself on weeds like wormwood
and dandelion," remembered Hyŏk Kang. "Weeds, whatever kind, were
boiled up and swallowed in the form of soup. The soup was so bitter that
we could barely keep it down."[22] In 1995, North Korea took the unprecedented step of requesting international food aid, although the magnitude
of the crisis was unknown to the outside world owing to the secretive
and closed nature of the regime. International aid began to flow into the
country in 1996, although these efforts were hampered by North Korean
officials who barred aid workers from monitoring where the aid was going
to ensure it was not being misdirected, for example, to the military. One
of the most frustrating constraints for international aid workers was the
denial of access to the parts of the country that needed the most help.
Refugees all tell the same story: that most of the donated food did not
go to the most vulnerable population and instead was skimmed off by
corrupt officials and sold in the black market or funneled to politically
influential groups. Good Friends, a South Korean organization involved
in the aid program, estimated that as much as "50 percent of Korean aid
went to non-deserving groups, including the military." A survey in 2005
of a thousand North Korean refugees showed that only "63 percent of
the respondents reported even knowing about the *existence* of foreign
humanitarian assistance."[23]

North Korea's restriction on monitoring the distribution of food aid
posed an ethical dilemma for those involved in the effort. Could they
continue to give aid when they could not ensure that it was going to
the needy and not strengthening a repressive regime? One refugee said
that he and others were told in their regular political study classes how
Kim Jong Il "declared that although 30 percent of the population survived the famine, it would be enough to rebuild the country." When Kim
was allegedly told in 1996 that three million had died of famine, he was
suppose to have replied, "Be tough. No uprisings will be allowed. I will
control military power. Have a strong heart. If the people revolt they will
hang us, and if they don't, the South Koreans will."[24]

In 1998 most of the private nongovernmental international aid groups in North Korea withdrew, citing "inadequate access" and "their consequent inability to account for the eventual use of their aid supplies."[25] Their pullout, however, did not adversely affect North Korea's situation. They were but one of three main components of the humanitarian assistance to North Korea, the other two being the UN's World Food Program (WFP) and direct governmental aid. The largest donor was the United States, which gave food aid through the WFP. European countries, Japan, South Korea, and China also donated through the WFP. A U.S. Congressional Research Service report stated that from 1995–2008, "the United States has provided North Korea with over $1.2 billion in assistance, about 60% of which has paid for food and about 40% for energy."[26] In 2008, North Korea signaled that it was again facing food shortages. In May of that year, North Korea and the United States agreed on a protocol allowing for the distribution of up to five hundred thousand tons of food assistance.[27] In the ensuing years, food aid and concessional imports made up more than 90 percent of North Korea's imported grain.[28] North Korea has become an aid-dependent economy, with aid amounting "to approximately two-thirds of recorded merchandise exports, and aid together with revenue from illicit activities such as the exportation of missiles, drug and endangered species trafficking, and counterfeiting, have roughly equaled the total value of exports."[29]

Two countries, however, sent unconditional aid on a bilateral basis. China and South Korea provided "concessional sales," or grants of food, outside of the WFP. This policy met with criticism from some WFP donors and nongovernmental organizations, because it undermined efforts to establish an adequate monitoring system of food distribution. China and South Korea became, in effect, "the suppliers of last resort."[30] Beginning in 1995, South Korea had pursued a restrictive aid policy, but this changed with the inauguration of President Kim Dae-jung in February 1998, and especially after his historic summit with Kim Jong Il at P'yŏngyang in June 2000. Under Kim Dae-jung roughly three-fourths of South Korean food aid was sent with little demand for monitoring its distribution.

In addition to aid, Kim Dae-jung supported inter-Korean business projects aimed at developing economic engagement across the divided peninsula. It is unlikely that South Korean companies ever made any

profits from these projects. Instead, they were more akin to providing state subvention for businesses agreeing to undertake projects that
had little prospect for future gains. For example, Hyundai Corporation
promised North Korea $942 million for the Kŭmgang-san (Diamond
Mountain) tourism venture, but it took government funds to fulfill that
promise. When it was later revealed that Kim Dae-jung's close associates had secretly transferred $500 million to North Korea in return for
securing the June 2000 summit, questions were raised about the legitimacy of Kim's 2000 Nobel Peace Prize, and the South Korean public's
feeling toward North Korea soured. The election of the conservative
Yi Myŏng-bak as president in 2008 was, in part, a negative referendum
on the Sunshine Policy.[31] In the United States, President George W.
Bush's denunciation of North Korea as part of the "axis of evil" in his
State of the Union Address in January 2002 effectively put an end to the
Agreed Framework and the Clinton administration's engagement strategy toward the P'yŏngyang regime.

The Korean public's dissatisfaction with the engagement strategy was
a function of how little the situation changed in North Korea. Major
efforts to engage P'yŏngyang through subsidized trade relations did not
lead to the kind of casual and spontaneous contact between ordinary
North and South Koreans as it had been hoped. South Korea's two large-
scale projects of economic engagement, Diamond Mountain and the
Kaesŏng Industrial Park, were physically isolated from the rest of North
Korea and have had little or no effect on liberalizing North Korea's economic or political stance. Moreover, industrial decline, spurred by lack
of equipment, raw materials, and dilapidated infrastructure, resulted in
large-scale unemployment. The 2009 WFP report on North Korea estimated that 40 percent of its factories stand idle and another 30 percent
are operating well below capacity.[32]

Gulag Nation

The famine and the resulting relaxation of state controls in the 1990s
unleashed drastic changes in North Korea. These changes did not result
from any decision from the top, but rather from the chaotic circumstances at the bottom. As the old economic system began to fall apart,

many North Koreans responded by engaging in surreptitious market activities, selling household items and setting up informal trade networks with Chinese merchants along the border. For the first time, markets began to appear in urban areas. The private markets (*changmadang*, literally "market grounds") grew rapidly as more and more entrepreneurial North Koreans sought alternative means to support themselves and their families. By the mid-1990s, even some luxury foods like fresh fruits and vegetables became available in the markets. Thus, during the death grip of the famine, more food became available, but only to those with hard currency. Corruption was also rife. Foreign-donated rice was sold on the black market by corrupt officials. Travel restrictions, even those to China, could be overcome with a bribe. Out of desperation and hunger, North Koreans reinvented the concept of a free market economy. In the 1990s, North Koreans would say that there were three types of people: "those who starve, those who beg and those who trade."[33]

But the rise of the free market system had dangerous political implications for the regime. Cross-border trade with China and the creation of dense business networks threatened to undermine the government's monopoly on information, especially about South Korea. Once the country was able to recover its equilibrium after the profound chaos created by the famine, mostly with the help of foreign aid and the large infusion of cash from South Korea during the lush "sunshine" years, the regime initiated a direct attack on the emerging market economy beginning in 2005. An indication of the new direction was the decision to reinstate the PDS. The anti-market campaigns were not limited to the food economy, however, but included escalating restrictions on market traders and border-crossing activities. In 2004 and 2007, the North Korean criminal code was changed to expand the definitions of economic crimes, to prohibit a wide range of standard commercial practices. Trading companies also came under greater scrutiny. In April 2008, a team of "200 investigators [was sent] to Sinŭiju in the name of an Antisocialist Conscience Investigation to inspect the books of foreign trade organizations" that impeded market activity. These ad hoc visits, becoming more frequent in the border regions, targeted "illegal internal movement, contraband, and cross-border trade." North Korean refugees living in China also came under greater scrutiny. In cooperation with the Chinese government, North Korean security began to hunt down these refugees to bring them back to North Korea, where they faced incarceration, torture, and even death. One of the major ramifications of the crackdown on private market activity was the expansion of the North Korean prison system and the growing incarceration of citizens for economic crimes.[34]

Prison labor camps, or *kwalliso*, were first established in North Korea after liberation from Japan to imprison enemies of the revolution, land-owners, collaborators, and religious leaders. After the war, these places housed un-repatriated South Korean prisoners of war.[35]

Satellite imagery reveals the massive size of these camps. One camp is large enough to hold fifty thousand inmates.[36] There are six such camps in existence today occupying, according to a May 2011 Amnesty International report, "huge areas of land and located in vast wilderness sites in South Pyŏng'an, South Hamgyŏng and North Hamgyŏng Provinces." A comparison of these latest images with satellite images taken in 2001 also "indicates a significant increase in the scale of the camps."[37] Recent testimonials from North Korean refugees paint a dark picture of life in the camps: widespread deprivation of food, medical treatment, and clothing, along with torture and public executions. Perhaps the most notorious penal colony is *kwalliso* no. 15, or Yodŏk, made infamous by Kang Chŏl-hwan, who was incarcerated there as a child and then escaped to South Korea in 1992 and whose memoir, *The Aquariums of Pyongyang*, has been translated into French and English.[38] A distinctive feature of the North Korean penal system is that inmates and their families are typically incarcerated for long-term or life sentences. Most belong to the hostile and wavering classes, which include a large number of Japanese citizens of ethnic Korean origin who returned to North Korea in the 1950s and 1960s. Although encouraged by the Kim regime to move to North Korea, they were later deemed politically suspect because of their exposure to Japanese liberalism and capitalism. During the 1990s, North Korean students and diplomats, part of the core class, who had been assigned to or studied in Eastern Europe or the Soviet Union, also became suspect.

North Korean authorities continued to find new ways to criminalize market activity, which included the establishment of *kyohwaso*, or reeducation camps for less serious crimes, to supplement the *kwalliso* camps. Still, testimonials and memoirs of former prisoners of *kyohwaso*

Kwalliso no. 15 (Yodŏk). There are currently six operating *kwalliso* in North Korea containing between five thousand and fifty thousand prisoners, totaling between 150,000 to 200,000 people. The encampments themselves are self-contained closed compounds or "villages." A striking feature of the North Korean gulag system is "guilt by association," whereby family members of up to three generations, including children, are incarcerated along with the offending political prisoner. (COURTESY OF THE COMMITTEE FOR HUMAN RIGHTS IN KOREA)

paint a hellish existence of forced labor under brutal conditions, beatings, rampant disease, hunger, torture, and executions. "Everyone moved as a group," recalled Soon Ok Lee, who was released from *kyohwaso* no. 1 (Kaech'ŏn) in 1994 and eventually fled the country to South Korea via

Hong Kong in 1995. "Everyone had to eat, sleep, work or use the toilet at the same time. Until a team was called to use the toilet, team members could not relieve themselves. So new prisoners often wet their pants."[39] The work was brutal, with constant pressure to meet the daily quotas. "At 5:30 a.m. messengers distributed quotas to each prisoner. At 11 pm, the messenger gathered them back and examined each prisoner's activities to see if they had met their quota. Prisoners who could not complete their job had their food reduced to 240 grams (8.4 ounces) for one day of incomplete work, and 210 grams (7.4 ounces) after four days of incomplete work."[40] In camps involving hard labor like mining copper and logging, convicts worked ten to twelve hours a day. One study estimated that "below subsistence level food rations coupled with the harsh conditions and hard labor resulted between 1991 and 1995 in the deaths of one-quarter to one-third of the inmates."[41]

These camps were an important source of hard currency, for the products they made were exported. A former inmate recalled that "every few months, camp authorities trotted out their latest version of the 'Let's Earn Some Dollars for Kim Il Sung Campaign.' These crusades were intended to make us heave with enthusiasm at the idea of harvesting exotic hardwoods, gathering ginseng, or producing whatever else the Party thought might fetch a few dollars on the free and open market."[42] Inmates of *kwalliso* no. 15 (Yodŏk) made brandy (labeled "Yodŏk Alcohol"), textiles, and distilled corn and mined for gold among other things. *Kyohwaso* no. 1 made doilies for Poland, army uniforms for the Soviet Union, sweaters for Japan, and paper flowers for France. Another camp built refrigerators and bicycles.[43] A prisoner from *kyohwaso* no. 77 (Tanch'un) testified about its gold-mining operation: "2,000 out of roughly 7,000–8,000 prisoners died from mining accidents, malnutrition, and malnutrition related diseases" during his two years there in the late 1980s.[44]

A shorter-term detention/punishment system was set up recently to punish the growing number of "petty" criminals. Their crimes include leaving their village, traveling without authorization, not showing up for work, and leaving the country. North Koreans who are caught crossing the border into China or persons forcibly repatriated from China are brought to these detention facilities, where they face the same brutal treatment, hard labor, and subsistence rations as prisoners in the long-term camps. Although most prisoners were incarcerated for less than a year, the death rate was extraordinarily high. One study of former refugees who had been in these detention centers noted that "90 percent reported witnessing forced starvation, 60 percent reported witnessing deaths due to beating or torture, [and] 27 percent reported witnessing executions."[45]

One notable feature about the North Korean penal system is the pervasive experience of deprivation and terror encountered at all levels of contact with authority.[46] As the range of economic activities deemed criminal expands, so does the need to create more detention facilities. Subjecting prisoners to "horrific conditions" from the start may be the state's effort to deter criminal economic activity, but the system might also have led to an unintended effect: the rise of corruption. One survey of North Korean refugees showed that "85 percent of respondents reported that they needed to pay bribes to engage in market activity." If a bribe is not offered or is insufficient to prevent an arrest, officials can always extort money from those who wish to avoid incarceration or those seeking to get out of serving their time. And the more terrifying the incarceration experience, the higher the price to avoid it. In their exhaustive research on North Korea's penal system, Stephan Haggard and Marcus Noland observed that "corruption may act as a safety valve in a fraying socialist system; a means of maintaining support among cadre by providing them access to economic rents." In this predatory society, repression of the people by government, party, and security functionaries appears not to be harnessed by political or even ideological objectives but by private gain, which in turn maintains the regime and its predatory practices.[47]

The Japanese journalist Ishimaru Jiro, who tracks domestic changes in North Korea in his magazine *Rimjin-gang*, which publishes remarkable reports from and interviews by underground North Korean informers, noted that corruption is rampant at all levels of society. Despite the recent government crackdown on private markets (*changmadang*), they continue to flourish mostly because they create a necessary income for corrupt officials. "The government extorts a lot of money from the *changmadang*," related one anonymous office worker to a *Rimjin-gang* reporter.

Suppose I am a shoe salesman at the market. As soon as I put shoes out on my street stall, a space about fifty centimeters [twenty inches] wide, guards will come and calculate my possible day's income according to the goods I have on display. Then they demand a street tax. Maybe that would be 300 to 400 won a day. In the case of a central *jangmadang* [*changmadang*], there are about 10,000 to 15,000 salespeople. Think about it. How much money can they pluck from a *jangmadang* if they take a few won from each merchant![. . .] When the government ordered the ban on the *jangmadang* in October and November of last year [2005], people said, "Everything will restart soon. Just wait for a month and the *jangmadang* will be active again." And it's true. After a month, things were back to business as usual.[48]

Extorting bribes from merchants in the markets or confiscating their goods through crackdowns is common practice among these officials. "If they don't do such things, they can't survive. In other words, they are parasites living off the markets, and in that, they are also excellent examples of the market's power."[49]

These predatory conditions were further exacerbated by North Korea's fiscal policies. In a move that was widely interpreted to consolidate his hold on power, Kim launched a disastrous currency reform in 2009 to crack down on the market economy. On November 30, the regime announced that the "old" 100 North Korean won would be equal to 1 "new" won. The aim of the reform was to punish the rising entrepreneurial class by annihilating private savings earned outside the officially sanctioned state economy. The result was runaway inflation, a widening food crisis, and further deterioration of the North Korean economy.[50]

While most of the world is well aware of the character of the regime and the human rights abuses that go on in North Korea, opening the country up to further scrutiny would expose this corruption and level of abuses on a much wider scale. The more pressure the North Korean regime faces to improve its human rights situation and instituting economic reforms, the harder it becomes to maintain the internal stability and order of the failed system. Since long-term survival of the regime is the leadership's foremost concern, it must continue the policy of national isolation and politics of terror if it is to maintain its hold on power.

How long can such a situation continue? In the short run, engagement with North Korea aimed at reducing the chances of a North Korean collapse through food and other economic aid is a reasonable and rational approach, especially in light of North Korea's continued belligerence and its testing of a nuclear device in 2006 and 2009. It is widely accepted that a renewal of fighting on the peninsula would be disastrous for the region. But what is the long-term prospect of this approach? The longer the North Korean regime continues to exist, the more decrepit its economy will become and the more desperate its people will grow. The contradictory impulses of propping up a failed regime while also seeking to secure stability and peace on the Korean peninsula has not been lost on P'yŏngyang's closest ally, China.

China's Rise, War's End?

Kim Chŏng-ŭn, front right, walks beside the hearse carrying the body of his late father, Kim Jong Il, during a funeral procession in P'yŏngyang on December 28, 2011. Behind Kim Chŏng-ŭn is Chang Sŭng-taek, Kim Jong Il's brother-in-law. (AP/KCNA)

ON THE MORNING OF December 28, 2011, hundreds of thousands of North Koreans lined the snow-covered streets of P'yŏngyang to bid farewell to their Dear Leader, Kim Jong Il.[1] The three-hour funeral event, which was broadcast live on North Korean television, showed wailing crowds of men and women as a tearful Kim Chŏng-ŭn, Kim's youngest son and chosen successor, trudged through the snow alongside the black limousine that carried his father's casket. The snowfall also gave the country's state-run media fresh material with which to eulogize the Dear Leader since his unexpected death was announced on December 19: "The feathery snowfall reminds the Korean people of the snowy days when the leader was born in the secret camp of Mt. Paektu and of the great revolutionary career that he followed through the snowdrifts." The reference to Mt. Paektu, the legendary site where Korea's mythical founder, Tan'gun, had descended from the Heavens and the place where Kim Il Sung had waged his battles against the Japanese, provided a fitting symbol to mark the end of the dictator's life. In his death, the snow imagery also showed the way forward to his rebirth: "The march in the new century of the *Juche* [*Chuch'e*] era," went the joint 2012 New Year's editorial, "is the continuation of the revolutionary march that started up on Mt. Paektu. Steadfast is the will of our service personnel and people to adorn our revolution, pioneered by Kim Il Sung and whose victory after victory they won following Kim Jong Il, with eternal victory following the leadership of Kim Jong Un [Kim Chŏng-ŭn]."[2]

Although the twenty-something Kim Chŏng-ŭn hardly seemed prepared to take over his father's mantle, having just been introduced to the Korean people in 2010, North Korean officials quickly rallied around their new king. But more important to the future of North Korea was that Chinese leaders did too. Just one day after the announcement of Kim Jong Il's death, China moved swiftly to assure its communist ally of its strong support amid the uncertain leadership transition. On December 20, President Hu Jintao visited North Korea's embassy in Beijing to offer his condolences while Foreign Ministry spokesman Liu Weimin offered a crucial endorsement to "Comrade Kim Chŏng-ŭn," calling on him to build a strong Communist country and realize permanent peace on the Korean peninsula."[3] At the same time, a number of PRC Central Committee members, including China's number two, Premier Wen Jiabao, paid their respects to the deceased leader at the embassy. Wen's remarks, in particular, reinforced the strong emphasis that China's leaders have placed on ties with North Korea:

Comrade Kim Jong Il was the North Korean Worker's Party and country's great leader, and a close friend to the Chinese people. Since long ago, he developed the cooperative and friendly relations between China and North Korea, producing great achievements [in that area]. We believe that the Korean Worker's Party under the leadership of Kim Jong Eun [Kim Chŏng-ŭn] the North Korean people will certainly pass through their grief, pushing forward to new successes in socialist construction. The Chinese side wants to take the same road as the Korean side, in order to

further and consolidate and develop the traditional friendship and cooperation between the two countries, striving together.[4]

South Koreans have been concerned about China's rise and growing influence in North Korea for some time. These concerns became
clear in the summit meeting between former South Korean president
No Mu-hyŏn and Premier Wen that was held on September 10, 2006, in
Helsinki. They had come to attend the Asia-European Meeting forum
in order to discuss pressing bilateral issues.[5] Press reports of the meeting reveal that the two leaders spent a good part of their time discussing
ancient history, specifically the history of the Koguryŏ/Gaogouli kingdom. Koguryŏ was one of the three ancient kingdoms of Korea, along
with Paekche and Silla, which existed between the third millennium
and the seventh millennium AD.[6] At the height of its power in the fifth
century, Koguryŏ encompassed a vast area in what is today Northeast
China and North Korea. During his meeting with the Chinese premier,
the South Korean president wanted to discuss recent reports by Chinese
archeologists and historians who claimed that since Koguryŏ's former
territory now resides within the current borders of the PRC, its history
should be considered part of "Chinese history."[7] Official press releases of
the meeting later revealed that President No "had expressed his dissatisfaction with some conclusion of the Chinese archeological teams and
the publication of a provincial research center dealing with events some
two thousand years ago."[8]

President No's concern over China's historical treatment of Koguryŏ
began in 2002, following China's launching of its ambitious Northeast
Asia Project. The ostensible aim of the project was to "strengthen the
association between China proper [all of China] and the northeast
region," which includes three provinces: Heilongjiang, Jilin, and Liaoning. But as the South Korean public soon learned, the Chinese government and scholars associated with the project appeared to be "conducting
a systematic and comprehensive effort to distort the ancient history of
Northeast Asia" by portraying Koguryŏ and the succeeding state of Par-
hae (Korean)/Bohai (Chinese) as Chinese, not Korean, kingdoms. In
April 2004, the South Korean government lodged a formal protest following the appearance on the Chinese Foreign Ministry website that
portrayed Koguryŏ as Chinese and removed references to Koguryŏ as

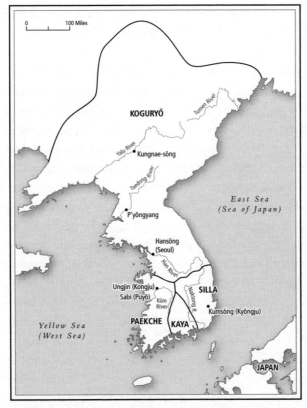

Map of the Three Kingdoms of Korea (AD 300–600) (Kaya was not a kingdom, but a confederation of tribes). In AD 660 Silla conquered Paekche with the help of T'ang China, and eight years later, in 668, Silla and the T'ang subdued Koguryŏ. Turning on its ally, the T'ang then invaded Silla in 674, but Silla was able to finally drive the T'ang from the Korean peninsula in 676, thereby achieving the unification of the peninsula. However, most of Koguryŏ's former territory in Northeast China was not included in Silla's unification.

being part of Korea's Three Kingdom era.[9] Beyond this bickering over history, however, the political ramifications of the dispute have been far-reaching. By claiming Koguryŏ as part of China's ancient past, the South Koreans charge, the Chinese government was surreptitiously undermining the legitimacy and political authority of North Korea whose territory was once part of Koguryŏ.

China's treatment of Koguryŏ has not been all that different from the way it has treated other ancient tribes and states that are now part of the PRC.[10] Knowing that the threat to the integrity of the Chinese nation has

China's Heilongjiang, Jilin, and Liaoning provinces and North Korea.

historically always come from internal challenges to its central authority, China launched an ambitious plan to exert control over its diverse ethnic population by promoting a common Chinese identity under the rubric of being a "multi-ethnic nation."[11] The link made between Koguryŏ and the Northeast provinces like Jilin, whose majority population is ethnic Korean, has clearly been a way to increase the notion of a Chinese identity among ethnic minorities.

But the Northeast Asia Project clearly has another aim: to construct a unitary national history and identity in the Northeast intended to pave the way for the economic intervention and integration of North Korea. Indeed, it is not coincidental that China's concern with Koguryŏ's history began in earnest in 2004 when Premier Wen announced that the Chinese government would embark on an ambitious economic development project for the Northeast provinces. According to Chinese government sources, Chinese investment in North Korea in 2006 topped $135 million and bilateral trade reached $1.69 billion, "an increase of almost seven percent over the $1.58 billion in bilateral trade in 2005."[12] Trade imbalance and North Korea's economic dependence also reached lopsided proportions, with imports from China of crude oil, petroleum, and synthetic textiles amounting to $2 billion while exports, consisting mainly of coal and iron ore, totalling just $750 million.[13] These investments are similar to the contributions to the DPRK's economy during the 1953–60 period, except that China now exerts far greater political leverage over the P'yŏngyang regime because North Korea now has no one to rely on but Beijing.

Despite China's increasing involvement in North Korea, however, Chinese leaders realize that merely propping up the regime without fundamentally transforming its economy will not resolve China's main security dilemma in the region: maintaining stability and peace on the Korean peninsula. Hence, China's ambitious efforts to develop North Korea to prevent the inevitable implosion of its economy while also shielding the North Korean regime from internal collapse. This "grand bargain" is certainly distasteful to the North Korean regime, which is used to getting its own way—thus, Kim Jong Il's decision to conduct a second nuclear test in May 2009. But when the Americans did not respond and the test instead resulted in even more punitive UN sanctions, the friendless regime was forced to make amends with China. "Despite their public rhetoric about the closeness of their ties," confided one observer, "officials in both China and North Korea each tell even American officials how much they dislike each other. North Korean officials have on numerous occasions suggested to American officials that it would be in the interest of our two countries to have a strategic relationship to counter China."[14] North Korean officials privately voiced their wariness of Beijing to South Korean diplomats, and worry about China's "increasing hold on precious minerals and mining rights in the DPRK [and] many oppose mineral concessions as a means to attract Chinese investments." According to one well-placed source, "Disputes with North Korean counterparts develop all the time . . . Investment disputes also occur between competing investors in China." In May 2010, the Saebyŏl Coal Mining Complex in North Hamgyŏng province sealed a contract with a Chinese enterprise. It promised to hand over an "unheard degree of discretion in affairs of personnel management, materials and working methods" to the Chinese. According to one source, the Chinese have been guaranteed "operational independence free from the control of the Saebyŏl party committee, and take 60 percent of net profits." North Korean workers appear to be happy with the arrangements, as they are now guaranteed steady wages and food. But others are far more pessimistic: "The purse strings in the border regions of our country have basically been handed over to China, and our 'socialist pride' is in the hands of China. Any factory where they produce even a small amount of goods has been invested in by the Chinese."[15]

North Korea's increasing dependence on China, however, does not mean that Beijing's leaders are able to exert complete control over their difficult neighbor. North Korea's second nuclear test in May 2009 strained relations between the two countries, but Chinese leaders also know from historical experience that such actions are geared more toward North Korea's domestic audience than the international community. Thus, despite his displeasure with North Korea over the nuclear test, Chinese Premier Wen nevertheless signed an ambitious co-development project with Kim Jong Il the following October.

The project, covering the Chinese cities of Changchun, Jilin, and Tumen, encompasses an area of seventy-three thousand square miles, but it is landlocked by Russia. Kim Jong Il agreed to lease the sea port at Rajin, a gateway to the Pacific, as well as sign on to various economic development projects. In December 2010, for example, China's Shangdi Guanqun Investment Company signed a letter of intent to invest $2 billion in the Rajin-Sŏnbong economic zone, which represents one of the largest potential investments in North Korea.[16] There are already reports that North Korean workers have been dispatched to begin the project, and plans are under way for the building of a new fifty-thousand-kilowatt hydroelectric power plant on the Tumen River.[17] North Korea and China have also recently signed an investment pact on building a highway and laying a railroad between Quanhae in Jilin and Rajin-Sŏnbong.

But more telling to the future relations between North Korea and China has been the swift reopening of the border after Kim Jong Il's passing. When Kim Jong Il's death was announced on December 19, most

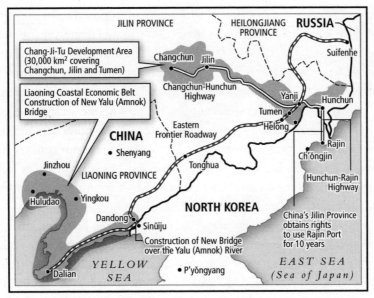

Changchun-Jilin-Tumen River (Chang-Ji-Tu) area.

people assumed that North Korea would close its frontier with China, at least for the short term. However, within forty-eight hours, "many border crossings sprang open again," underlying the reality that the new regime can ill afford to cut off its lifeline to China, even for a few days. Although China's strategy to encourage economic reforms in the North does not appear to be successful, the expansion of trade and investment has nevertheless "unleashed economic forces at least in the border region" as well as created a new group among the country's elite who have a vested interest in expanding trade.[18]

The pressing question that North Korea now confronts in the face of becoming a "fourth province of northeastern China" is how to sell it to the North Korean people. For a regime that has always touted *chuch'e* as the core principle of its nationalist ideology, such dependence would likely trigger a mass legitimization crisis. It would be hard to justify North Korea's *chuch'e* philosophy of self-determination and the regime's repeated denunciation of South Korean "flunkyism" while becoming an economic satellite of China. Hence, the regime's continued efforts to demonstrate its "independence" from China and create international crises to galvanize domestic public support for itself. This has become all the more urgent since Kim Jong Il's death. According to sources familiar

Arirang, North Korea's mass games in 2010, celebrating Sino–North Korean Friendship and the sixtieth commemoration of the "Victorious Fatherland Liberation War." (AP/ KOREAN CENTRAL NEWS AGENCY)

with the North Korean situation, Kim Jong Il was "obsessed with creating political stability to allow orderly succession."[19] Chinese leaders, aware of the delicate situation, had tolerated Kim's antics because they understood he would never actually start a war.

But instigating crises in response to internal domestic turmoil, a familiar North Korean tactic, has done very little to mask the reality of China's growing influence over North Korean affairs. This is where the Korean War story plays a vital role in forging a new relationship between the two countries. In years past, the anniversary of the Chinese intervention in the Korean War, which occurred on October 19, 1950, had been worth just a few lines in the North Korean press, if it was mentioned at all.[20] In recent years, however, China's role in North Korea's Korean War commemorative culture has taken on a strikingly new and prominent role. In August 2010, North Korean officials announced that North Korea's mass games known as *Arirang*, the iconic gymnastic and artistic performance scheduled to be performed as part of the commemorative celebrations, would feature two entirely new scenes: "One of them represents the Korean People's Revolutionary Army and Chinese armed units fighting together against the Japanese imperialists during the anti-Japanese armed struggle. The other portrays the Chinese People's Volunteers joining the Korean army and people in the Korean War against the imperialist allied forces' invasion under the banner of resisting America and aiding Korea, safeguarding the home and defending the motherland." Performers "in Chinese clothes" danced with Chinese props, including "several dozen meter-long dragons, pandas and lions."[21]

If the inclusion of Chinese props and dress was not striking enough for a country that has not overtly acknowledged China's role in the conflict, a grand banquet to commemorate the sixtieth anniversary of the CPV's entrance into the Korean War was held on October 24, 2010. In his address to members of the visiting delegation of the CPV veterans,

On October 26, 2010, Kim Jong Il, center, laid a wreath in front of the grave of Mao Anying, Mao Zedong's eldest son who died during the Korean War. The CPV Martyrs Cemetery, located in Hoech'ang, South P'yŏngan province, has become an important site for ceremonial visits made by Chinese and North Korean officials. Premier Wen Jiabao visited the cemetery during his October 2009 visit to the DPRK. An official visit to the CPV Cemetery in September 2010 was one of the first major events after Kim Chŏng-ŭn was publicly introduced as his father's hereditary successor. In October 2012, DPRK state media reported that a memorial ceremony marking the completion of extensive renovation work of the cemetery was held to mark the sixty-second anniversary of the CPV entry into the Korean War. (AP/KOREAN CENTRAL NEWS AGENCY)

the North Korean vice president of the Presidium of the Supreme People's Assembly, Yang Hyŏng-sŏp, saluted "the CPV's brave men and our people and army [who fought] side by side, to carry forward the courageous spirit and collective heroism" and made "the Fatherland Liberation War a great victory, by gloriously defending Northeast Asia and world peace."[22] This was followed by an unprecedented official visit to the cemetery of Chinese soldiers killed during the Korean War, including Mao Anying, Mao Zedong's son.[23]

Even then, China's role in the war is construed as being one of "reciprocal obligation" since North Korea had once aided the Chinese in their war against Japan. "The tradition of ties of friendship between the peoples of the DPRK and China, sealed in blood in the joint struggle against U.S. and Japanese imperialisms, the two formidable enemies, has steadily developed on the basis of particularly comradely trust and sense of revolutionary obligation of the leaders of the elder generation of the two countries," explained the *Nodong sinmun*, the North Korean party daily, in its October 24, 2010, issue. In short, by equating China's aid against American "imperialists" in the Korean War with the aid of Korean revolutionaries in fighting Japan in China during World War II, North Korean officials drew attention to the *equality* of revolutionary comrades in arms based on the bonds of DPRK-China friendship "sealed in blood," rather than on any indication of super-power "dependence." The "ties of friendship between the people of the two countries" are thus presented in terms of a familial bond of obligation and respect between younger and older generations:

> Kim Il Sung visited China to participate in the function for founding the People's Republic of China in Juche [*chuch'e*] 38 [1949] and had his first meeting with Chairman Mao Zedong and Premier Zhou Enlai. Since then, the leaders of the two countries made great efforts to boost the friendly relations between the DPRK and China . . . In the new century, General Secretary Kim Jong Il paid several visits to China and Chinese party and state leaders including Hu Jintao visited the DPRK, deepening the friendly feelings and comradely fraternity and boosting the DPRK-China friendly and cooperative relations.[24]

What is remarkable about this passage is not only the parallel that is drawn between Kim Il Sung's visits to Mao and Kim Jong Il's visit to Hu Jintao, but also the attempts made to highlight Kim Il Sung's revolutionary struggle in Manchuria. Since Jilin, Heilongjiang, and Liaoning provinces once comprised the Japanese puppet state of Manchukuo, the regime's current "joint" cooperation with China to develop this area is presented as being *foreshadowed* by Kim Il Sung's "hard-fought revolutionary struggle" there. During his visit to Jilin province in August 2010, Kim Jong Il directly linked China's Northeast development project with his father's exploits in Manchuria:

> Jilin and Heilongjiang provinces are a witness to Korea-China friendship and a historical land dear to the Korean people as Comrade President Kim Il Sung waged a hard-fought revolutionary struggle against the Japanese imperialists together with Chinese comrades in this area, leaving indelible footsteps. He in his lifetime had often recollected this historical land and wanted to visit here again. Carrying his desire with us, we have come here today. Entering the northeastern area of China we have felt that this area, which had been trampled down ruthlessly by the Japanese imperialists, is now vibrant with life, enjoying a splendid development in political, economic, cultural and all other fields under the leadership of the Communist Party of China.[25]

Percy Toop, a Canadian tourist, photographed this painting on October 27, 2010, at the Rajin Art Gallery. Many experts believe it is a painting of Kim Chŏng-ŭn. What is remarkable is that the setting and layout are similar to those in depictions of the young Kim Il Sung.[26] (COURTESY OF PERCY TOOP)

This passage is immediately followed by nostalgic reminiscences of Kim Il Sung's revolutionary past, which seek, once again, to demonstrate the "unbreakable" bond of friendship between the two countries.

The explicit linkage made between Kim Il Sung's past exploits in Manchuria and China's future exploits in Heilongjiang and Jilin provinces also provides clues on how P'yŏngyang decided to approach the delicate transition issue. With Kim Il Sung's popularity still intact, it makes sense for the regime to bring the Great Leader back to life in the person of his grandson, Kim Chŏng-ŭn. Such a reincarnation myth would be an effective ploy to ensure a smooth succession, since the Great Leader's untimely death in 1994 has largely absolved him of responsibility for North Korea's disastrous predicament, the famine and the country's economic collapse. This "reincarnation" drama was meticulously planned, with North Korean propaganda skillfully playing up the uncanny resemblance between the Great Leader and his grandson. When official photos of Kim Chŏng-ŭn were first released to the public in October 2010, some North Korea watchers even suggested that Kim Chŏng-un may have undergone plastic surgery to look more like his grandfather. Footage released in the week following the announcement of Kim Jong Il's death showed Kim Chŏng-ŭn visiting a tank division using the same signature mannerisms as his grandfather—walking with his left hand in his pocket and using his right hand to gesture while talking. Kim Chŏng-ŭn also shares the same swept-back hairstyle and protruding belly as the elder Kim; even his gait is reminiscent of the Great Leader's.[27] If Kim Chŏng-ŭn, with Chinese help, can begin a kind of "return to the past," to the days of Kim Il Sung before the famine, he may prove to be a far more effective leader than his own father. Also telling was the decision to introduce the heir apparent at the sixty-fifth anniversary of the NKWP, on October 10, 2010. On the reviewing stand with Kim Chŏng-ŭn and his father was Zhou Yongkang, China's point man in North Korea who is helping to oversee the Northeast Asia Project.[28]

Having embraced Kim Chŏng-ŭn as his father's legitimate successor, China's leaders have signaled that they do not support any drastic change in either Sino-DPRK relations or North Korea's domestic policy, at least in the near future. China will continue to push for economic reforms while exerting pressure on P'yŏngyang's leaders for more access

Kim Jong Il, right, and his son Kim Chŏng-ŭn attend a massive parade to mark the sixty-fifth anniversary of the NKWP in P'yŏngyang, October 10, 2010. (AP PHOTOS)

and faster development of Chinese business interests, particularly in the mineral sector and large projects like at Rajin.

Not surprisingly, South Koreans have become increasingly alarmed by all this talk of Sino–North Korean relations "forged in blood." They remain deeply suspicious of Chinese influence in North Korea and are wary about China's "strategic plot to colonize North Korea economically."[29] Relations between the two countries were made even more tense after North Korea's sinking of the South Korean naval vessel *Ch'ŏn'an* in March 2010.[30] South Korea had initially believed that China, as its largest trading partner, would endorse its position in its quest to seek international justice for the attack. When China wielded its veto power as a UN Security Council member to force a watered-down statement that did not identify North Korean culpability, Seoul responded with anger. Relations between the two countries are currently at their lowest since they established diplomatic ties in 1992.[31] In retaliation for North Korean provocations, the Yi administration cut off all aid to North Korea, including food aid. However, by adopting a hard-line stance toward the Kim Jong Il regime, South Korea essentially surrendered its economic leverage over North Korea to China. Some South Korean lawmakers expressed concern: "I'm worried that North Korea is getting too close and familiar to China in a bid to push third-generation succession," said

Representative An Sang-su, chairman of the ruling Grand National Party. "Would we be able to stop North Korea, if it decides to be under the control of China?"[32]

But the reality is that few South Koreans today are ready to take on the burdens of unification. In the 1990s, more than 80 percent of South Koreans believed that unification was essential; in 2011, that number dropped to 56 percent. Roughly 41 percent of those in their twenties believe unification is imperative, and among teenagers, that figure drops closer to 20 percent.[33] This huge drop in support is in large part due to the failed promises of Kim Dae-jung's Sunshine Policy. In November 2010, the South Korean Unification Ministry released a white paper which declared that the policy was dead. "Despite outward development over the past decade," the white paper said, "inter-Korean relations have been under criticism from the public in terms of quality and process. They have in fact, become increasingly disillusioned with the North and more worried about security as the North continued its nuclear arms program." Furthermore, despite the massive aid from South Korea and inter-Korea exchanges and cooperation over the last decades, no "satisfactory progress has been made in the issue of separated families, South Korean prisoners of war and abduction victims." The paper concluded, "The North has made no positive change in proportion to the aid and cooperation from South Korea."[34]

Few South Koreans harbor illusions about the dire state of the North Korean economy or the tremendous costs of unification. South Koreans also worry about the toll unification will take on the fabric of their society. The Korean Employers Federation predicted that if North Korea collapsed, up to 3.5 million people could flood South Korea. "Even under a conservative estimate, up to 1.6 million North Koreans may move to South Korea, mainly because of the huge difference in wages and employment opportunity," the Federation said. "Such a wholesale movement of people could seriously disrupt the local labor market and cause other social problems."[35] While many older South Koreans give lip service to the ideal of a reunified peninsula, they qualify their support by talking about it taking place over the long term, and preferably after they are dead.[36]

Thus it appears that it will be up to China to drag North Korea into the twenty-first century and finally end the Korean War.[37] North Korean leaders understand this, which is why they have already begun to accommodate China into their national narrative and China's presence into Kim Il Sung's revolutionary past. Hence all the hoopla recently about the Korean War, Kim's Manchurian exploits, and the two countries' bilateral friendship "forged in blood." This does not mean, however, that the new Kim Chŏng-ŭn regime will cease making trouble for China. Since the stability and legitimacy of the regime still rest firmly on the myth of Kim Il Sung, his anti-imperialist exploits, and the principle of *chuch'e*, China knows that it must allow the regime to assert some independence if it is to avoid collapse. Just how much "independence" China will tolerate from its recalcitrant neighbor remains to be seen. Needing both to preserve his rule and to build a "strong and prosperous nation," Kim Chŏng-ŭn is now faced with resolving the perplexing contradictions of instituting vital economic reforms under Chinese guidance while at the same time preserving the *chuch'e* principle so crucial to the legitimacy of the regime during a delicate transition period.

Over one hundred years has passed since China was forced to leave the Korean peninsula after its humiliating defeat in the 1894–95 Sino-Japanese War. That war marked China's decline and Japan's ascendancy in East Asian affairs. In the long aftermath of the war fifty years later, in which China saved North Korea from certain defeat, a revitalized China has returned to the Korean peninsula to reclaim its once-dominant position in Asia. China's rise has many implications for the region, but one of them certainly is the role it will play in ending the war on the Korean peninsula.

The events connected to the ending of the Korean War will be momentous, and the uncertainties surrounding North Korea's potential economic collapse and China's absorption of North Korea's economy are disquieting, as much for the millions of hungry North Koreans as for the prosperous Koreans in the South. How will South Korea react to China's intrusion into North Korea? As for the United States, whose military might and economic power came of age both during and after the Korean War, the specter of a rising China is certainly unnerving, but more worrying, perhaps, than China's role in ending the war in Korea is what this might signal for China's new place on the world stage. Understanding and responding to these changes will require reflection on the lessons and legacies of the unending Korean War and the role this conflict has played, and will continue to play, in shaping the region's past and future.

Addendum

As this book was going to print, it was announced that Pak Kŭn-hye, Park Chung Hee's daughter, was elected president of South Korea on December 19, 2012. As the eldest daughter of Park Chung Hee and Yuk Yŏng-su, Pak Kŭn-hye took on the role of first lady after her mother was tragically killed in a botched assassination attempt on her father's life in 1974. Not only is Pak the first female leader in Korea's millennium-long history (if we do not count the few Silla queens who ruled between the third and seventh century CE), her election also signals another "return of the past" as she must now deal with Kim Chŏng-ŭn, Kim Il Sung's grandson, in the ongoing struggle between North and South Korea. How this legitimacy struggle plays out between the progenies of these two momentous leaders of Korea's history adds a new and ironic twist to the unending war in Korea and China's role in resolving this long-standing family feud.

Appendix

UNC COMBAT FORCES IN KOREA
(Most figures are estimates; conclusive personnel figures are notoriously elusive.)

COUNTRY	CONTRIBUTION AT MAXIMUM STRENGTH	PERSONNEL (NO.)		CASUALTIES (NO.)	
		Peak Ground Strength	Total for 1950-53	Killed/ Missing from All Services	Wounded from All Services
Australia	2 infantry battalions 1 fighter squadron 1 air transport squadron 2 destroyers/frigates 1 aircraft carrier	2,300	17,000	275	1,100
Belgium	1 infantry battalion	950	3,500	97	350
Canada	1 infantry brigade 1 air transport squadron 3 destroyers 1 dry cargo ship	6,200	25,000	309	1,202
Colombia	1 infantry battalion 1 frigate	1,100	6,000	210	610
Ethiopia	1 infantry battalion	1,300	3,500	122	566
France	1 infantry battalion 1 gun boat	1,200	4,000	271	1,008
Greece	1 infantry battalion 1 air transport squadron	1,300	5,000	194	459
Luxembourg	1 infantry platoon	50	90	7	21
Netherlands	1 infantry battalion 1 destroyer	820	5,300	120	645
New Zealand	1 artillery regiment combat team 1 truck transport company 2 frigates	1,400	4,500	39	79
The Philippines	1 infantry battalion combat team	1,500	7,400	128	300

COUNTRY	CONTRIBUTION AT MAXIMUM STRENGTH	PERSONNEL (NO.)		CASUALTIES (NO.)	
		Peak Ground Strength	Total for 1950-53	Killed/ Missing from All Services	Wounded from All Services
South Africa	1 fighter squadron (South Africa did not deploy a ground unit)	210	825	34	16
Thailand	1 infantry battalion 1 frigate 1 air transport flight	1,300	6,500	136	469
Turkey	1 infantry brigade	5,500	15,000	889	2,111
United Kingdom	2 infantry brigades 1 aircraft carrier 2 cruisers 4 destroyers 1 hospital ship 4 frigates 1 HQ ship	14,200	60,000	1,078	2,674
United States	Eighth Army Fifth Air Force Seventh Fleet	330,000	2,000,000	36,574 (7,296 missing as of January 30, 2013)	103,284

UNC MEDICAL UNITS (Non-U.S./ROK)

COUNTRY	UNIT	BEDS (NO.)	PERSONNEL (NO.)
Denmark	Hospital ship *Jutlandia*	360	200
India	60 Parachute Field Ambulance	1,000	345
Italy	Red Cross hospital	150	130
Norway	Mobile army surgical hospital	200	106
Sweden	Red Cross hospital	450	160

OTHER OFFERS

COUNTRY	AID	STATUS
Bolivia	30 officers	Not accepted
Costa Rica	Use of sea and air bases Volunteers	Accepted Not accepted
Cuba	Infantry company	Accepted but not sent
El Salvador	Volunteers	Not accepted
Iran	2 ambulance units	Offer withdrawn
Japan	Use of bases; R&R facilities	Note: Japan regained sovereignty in April 1952 but continued to provide key logistical and infrastructural support for the war
Lebanon	Infantry battalion	Offer withdrawn
Norway	Merchant ship tonnage	Accepted
Pakistan	Infantry regiment	Offer withdrawn
Panama	Free use of bases, roads, and merchant marine space Volunteers	Accepted Not accepted
Taiwan	3 infantry divisions, 20 C47s transport aircraft	Not accepted

HUMANITARIAN AND RECONSTRUCTION AID AS OF 1953

COUNTRY	AID (in 1953 U.S. dollars; the purchasing power of $1 in 1953 was $8 in 2010)
Argentina	$500,000 of corned beef
Australia	$200,000 of barley, $200,000 of medical supplies
Austria	$40,000 of medical equipment
Belgium	$60,000 of sugar
Brazil	$2.7 million cash
Burma	$50,000 of rice
Cambodia	$25,000 of food and timber
Canada	$6.9 million cash
Chile	$250,000 cash
China (Taiwan)	$635,000 of coal, food, DDT, and medical supplies

COUNTRY	AID (in 1953 U.S. dollars; the purchasing power of $1 in 1953 was $8 in 2010)
Cuba	$270,000 of sugar and alcohol
Denmark	$140,000 of medical supplies, $100,000 of sugar
Dominican Republic	$10,000 cash
Ecuador	$100,000 of rice
Egypt	$29,000 cash
El Salvador	$500 cash
Ethiopia	$40,000 cash
France	$75,000 of medical supplies
Germany	$47,000 of medical supplies
Greece	$85,000 of medical supplies, $36,000 of salt, and $31,000 of soap
Guatemala	$153,000 of timber
Honduras	$2,500 cash
Iceland	$45,000 of cod liver oil
India	$168,000 of jute bag
Indonesia	$100,000 cash
Iran	1,000 tons of oil—declined
Israel	$63,000 of medical supplies, $34,000 of food
Japan	$50,000 of clothing and medical supplies
Lebanon	$50,000 cash
Liberia	$25,000 of rubber
Luxembourg	$30,000 cash
Mexico	$350,000 of food and medical supplies
Netherlands	$263,000 cash
New Zealand	$280,000 of food, soap, and vitamins
Nicaragua	Rice and alcohol—Declined
Norway	$70,000 of soap, vitamins, and alcohol
Pakistan	$380,000 of wheat
Paraguay	$10,000 cash
Peru	$59,000 of cotton and wool
Philippines	$2.3 million of rice

COUNTRY	AID (in 1953 U.S. dollars; the purchasing power of $1 in 1953 was $8 in 2010)
Saudi Arabia	$20,000 cash
Sweden	$8,000 of medical supplies
Switzerland	$39,000 of medical supplies
Syria	$11,000 cash
Thailand	$4.4 million of rice
Turkey	Vaccines—declined
United Kingdom	$1.34 million of food, medical supplies, charcoal, and cloth
United States	$253 million of various aid in kind
Uruguay	$2 million cash, $250,000 of blankets
Venezuela	$150,000 of food, medical supplies, clothing, and blankets
Vietnam	$2,000 of rice

Sources: Compiled from *Yearbook of the United Nations*, 1951, 1952, 1953, 1954, 1955, available at http://unyearbook.un.org/ (accessed July 10–20, 2010); Paul M. Edwards, *The Korean War: A Historical Dictionary* (Scarecrow Press, 2003); James I. Matray, ed., *Historical Dictionary of the Korean War* (Greenwood Press, 1991); Gordon L. Rottman, *Korean War Order of Battle: United States, United Nations, and Communist Ground, Naval, and Air Forces, 1950–1953* (Greenwood Publishing, 2002), appendix D: Korean War Casualties; Stanley Sandler, ed., *The Korean War: An Encyclopedia* (Routledge, 1995); Allan R. Millett, "Appendix 2: Selected Statistics, Korean War," *Their War for Korea* (Brassey's, 2002), pp. 266–267; Anthony Farrar-Hockley, *The British Part in the Korean War* (Stationery Office, 1995), vol. 2, p. 491; Walter G. Hermes, *Truce Tent and Fighting Front* (U.S. Government Printing Office, 1966), p. 513; Republic of Korea Ministry of National Defense Institute for Military History Compilation, "6-25 chŏnjaeng t'onggye (Korean War Statistics)," available at www.imhc.mil.kr/imhcroot/data/korea_view.jsp?seq=4&page=1 (accessed October 28, 2012); http://www.dtic.mil/dpmo/summary_statistics/, accessed July 20, 2010, this is the official website of the Department of Defense's Defense Prisoner of War—Missing Person's Office (DPMO); Anne Leland and Mari-Jana Oboroceanu, *American War and Military Operations Casualties* (Congressional Research Service, February 26, 2010); Korea Institute of Military History, *The Korean War: Volume Three* (University of Nebraska Press, 2001), pp. 692–693; and Spencer C. Tucker, ed., *Encyclopedia of the Korean War: A Political, Social, and Military History* (ABL-CLIO, 2000); U.S. Department Of Labor, Bureau of Labor Statistics, Consumer Price Index, July 26, 2010, available at ftp://ftp.bls.gov/pub/special.requests/cpi/cpiai.txt (accessed August 15, 2010); Lawrence H. Officer and Samuel H. Williamson, "Purchasing Power of Money in the United States from 1774 to 2009," *Measuring Worth* (2010), available at http://www.measuringworth.com/ppowerus/ (accessed July 31, 2010).

NOTES

CWIHP: Cold War International History Project, Woodrow Wilson International Center for Scholars, Washington, D.C.

DASJA: Department of the Army Staff Judge Advocate

FEER: *Far Eastern Economic Review*

FRUS: United States Department of State, *Foreign Relations of the United States* (U.S. Government Printing Office, various years)

HUSAFIK: "History of the United States Armed Forces in Korea," unpublished manuscript available in the U.S. Army Center for Military History, Ft. McNair, Washington, D.C., and the Historical Office of Eighth U.S. Army at the Yongsan U.S. Army Base, Seoul, Korea

HMGK: *History of the United States Army Military Government in Korea*, unpublished manuscript available in the U.S. Army Center for Military History,

tory, Ft. McNair, Washington, D.C., and the Historical Office of Eighth U.S. Army at the Yongsan U.S. Army Base, Seoul, Korea

JFK: John F. Kennedy Library, Boston, Massachusetts

LBJ: Lyndon B. Johnson Library, Austin, Texas

MOFAT: Republic of Korea Ministry of Foreign Affairs and Trade (archives), Seoul, South Korea

MHI: U. S. Army Military History Institute, Carlisle, Penn. (archives)

NARA: National Archives and Records Administration, College Park, Md.

NKIDP: North Korea International Documentation Project, Woodrow Wilson International Center for Scholars, Washington, D.C.

NSF: National Security Files, at JFK and LBJ libraries

TRC: Truth and Reconciliation Commission, Republic of Korea ·

INTRODUCTION

1 Ernst Oppert, *A Forbidden Land: Voyages to the Corea* (G. P. Putnam's Son, 1882), p. 3.

2. U.S. policymakers generally have fallen into two main camps in their approach to North Korea. The so-called "optimists" believe that negotiating with North Korea is possible and that the reason the P'yŏngyang regime

has so far been unwilling to abandon its nuclear ambitions is due its legitimate fear for its own national security. By contrast, the so-called "pessimists"
view P'yŏngyang actions far more cynically, identifying a familiar pattern
of behavior with the outside world, which is to "start negotiations, squeeze
aid out of the international community by making incremental concessions
(while trying to cheat), and then walk away from talks and stage a provocation or two—only to return in exchange for more payoffs." For the pessimists, North Korea's main goal is to maintain its hold on power by any means
possible, including using nuclear blackmail. See Andre Lankov, "Changing
North Korea: Information Campaign Can Beat the Regime," *Foreign Affairs*
(November/December 2009), pp. 95–97.

3 Quoted in B. R. Myers, *The Cleanest Race: How North Koreans See Themselves and
Why It Matters* (Melville House, 2010), p. 149. Myers makes a similar point,
that the threat to North Korea is the prosperity and well-being of South
Korea and the legitimization crisis that will ensue if these facts become
known among the North Korean population. However, unlike Myers, I do
not foresee another attempt by the North at "liberating" the South anytime
soon, as I make clear in the epilogue.

ONE: *Liberation and Division*

1 The story is told in Richard Kim, *Lost Names: Scenes from a Korean Boyhood*
(University of California Press, 1988), pp. 164–166. Though written as fiction,
the novel is based on Richard Kim's own childhood experience.

2 *FRUS: Diplomatic Papers, 1945, vol. 6: The British Commonwealth, the Far East* (1969),
p. 1098; Bruce Cumings, *The Origins of the Korean War*, vol. 1: *Liberation and the
Emergence of Separate Regimes, 1945–1947* (Princeton University Press, 1981), pp.
106–109.

3 Cumings, *The Origins of the Korean War*, vol. 1, p. 118.

4 United States Department of Defense, *The Entry of the Soviet Union into the
War against Japan: Military Plans, 1941–45* (U.S. Government Printing Office,
1955), pp. 51–52.

5 Kathryn Weathersby, "Soviet Aims in Korea and the Origins of the Korean
War, 1945–1950: New Evidence from Russian Archives," *CWIHP Working
Paper 8* (November 1993), p. 10.

6 Winston Churchill, *The Second World War: Triumph and Tragedy* (Houghton
Mifflin Harcourt, 1953), pp. 635–639; Tsuyoshi Hasegawa, *Racing the Enemy:
Stalin, Truman, and the Surrender of Japan* (Belknap Press, 2006), p. 141.

7 The Soviets had been aware of the bomb through their wartime espionage
operations in the United States. The Americans were later able to confirm this
through the Venona Project, a highly secret intelligence operation involving
interception of Soviet intelligence messages. At Potsdam, President Truman
was not aware that the Soviets knew about the Manhattan Project. John Earl
Haynes and Harvey Klehr, *Venona: Decoding Soviet Espionage in America* (Yale
University Press, 2000); Richard J. Aldrich, *The Hidden Hand: Britain, America
and Cold War Secret Intelligence* (John Murray, 2001); Stephen Budiansky, *Battle
of Wits: The Complete Story of Code-Breaking in World War II* (Free Press, 2002).

8 Andrei Gromyko, *Memories* (Hutchinson, 1989), p. 109.

9 Hasegawa, *Racing the Enemy*, pp. 178–193; William Stueck, *The Korean War: An International History* (Princeton University Press, 1995), p. 18.

10 *FRUS, 1945*, vol. 6, p. 1039; Cumings, *The Origins of the Korean War*, vol. 1, pp. 120–121.

11 According to historian Kathryn Weathersby, the fate of Korea as a potential "springboard for Japanese invasion onto the Asian continent" and the Soviet Far East was a foremost concern for Stalin. These views were not challenged. The long-held assumption that debate within the Soviet government was limited is correct. She claims that in the hundreds of documents she has studied in the Soviet Central Committee and Foreign Ministry archives, she has never come across a "document indicating a policy debate of any kind." Thus, she concludes, we can assume that the June 1945 report accurately reflected the opinion from the top and that if "its recommendation had not already been approved, the authors would never have written it." Weathersby, "Soviet Aims in Korea and the Origins of the Korean War," p. 11; Cumings, *Origins of the Korean War*, vol. 1, pp. 120–121.

12 Radio Address of Generalissimo Stalin, Soviet Embassy Information Bulletin (Washington, D.C.), September 6, 1945. Quoted in Harold R. Isaacs, *No Peace for Asia* (MIT Press, 1947), p. 256. See also Max R. Beloff, *Soviet Policy in the Far East, 1944–1951* (Oxford University Press, 1953), p. 246.

13 *New York Times*, November 4, 1945.

14 Allan R. Millett, *The War for Korea, 1945–1950: A House Burning* (University Press of Kansas, 2005), pp. 48–50; Henry Chung, *The Russians Came to Korea* (Korean Pacific Press, 1947), p.45.

15 Cumings, *The Origins of the Korean War*, vol. 1, pp. 388–389; Richard E. Lauterbach, *Danger from the East* (Harper & Brothers, 1964), pp. 213–217.

16 Kathryn Weathersby, "Soviet Policy toward Korea: 1944–1946," PhD dissertation, Indiana University, 1990, p. 191.

17 Most scholars who studied the Soviet occupation of North Korea concluded that Soviet policies were well received owing to Soviet authorities' taking popular measures such as prosecuting collaborators, especially those who worked in the detested police, and confiscating Japanese farms and farms belonging to Korean landowners to redistribute them. Recent historians have revised this view of the Soviet occupation. They argue that the Soviet occupation was anything but popular. They also question the alleged discontinuity between the colonial and postcolonial regime in North Korea. These scholars make clear that the Soviet occupation was an *imperialist* occupation and that the Soviets continued many unpopular policies that were identical to Japanese colonial policy such as state purchase of grains. They also argue that many Korean mid-level managers and administrators who had worked for the colonial regime remained and worked for the new government. See Mitsuhiko Kimura, "From Fascism to Communism: Continuity and Development of Collectivist Economic Policy in North Korea," *Economic History Review* 52, no. 1 (February 1999); Kim Ha-yŏng, *Kukchejuŭi sigak eso pon hanbando* [The Korean Peninsula from an International Perspective] (Seoul: Ch'aek pŏlle, 2002); Chung'ang ilbo t'ŭkpyŏl ch'wijaeban, eds., *Pirok chosŏn minjujuŭi inmin konghwaguk* [Secret History of the Democratic People's Republic of Korea] (Seoul: Chung'ang ilbosa, 1992). For recent studies on the

Soviet occupation of North Korea, see Andrei Lankov, *From Stalin to Kim Il Sung: The Formation of North Korea, 1945–1960* (Rutgers University Press, 2002); Andrei Lankov, *Crisis in North Korea: The Failure of De-Stalinization* (University of Hawaii Press, 2005); Erik van Ree, *Socialism in One Zone: Stalin's Policy in Korea, 1945–1947* (Berg, 1989); *CWIHP Bulletin: New Evidence on North Korea,* no. 14/15 (Winter 2003/Spring 2004); Charles K. Armstrong, *The North Korean Revolution, 1945–1950* (Cornell University Press, 2003). The most comprehensive book in English on this period of North Korean history is Robert Scalapino and Chong-sik Lee's monumental two-volume *Communism in Korea* (University of California Press, 1972).

18 Chong-sik Lee and Ki-Wan Oh, "The Russian Faction in North Korea," *Asian Survey* 8, no. 4 (1968), p. 272.

19 Henry R. Huttenbach, "The Soviet Koreans: Product of Russo-Japanese Imperial Rivalry," *Central Asian Survey* 12, no. 1 (1993), pp. 59–69. See also German N. Kim, "The Deportation of 1937 as a Logical Continuation of Tsarist and Soviet Nationality Policy in the Russian Far East," *The Korean and Korean American Studies Bulletin* 12 (2001), pp. 19–43; Dae-sook Suh, ed., *Koreans in the Soviet Union* (University of Hawaii Press, 1987); Walter Kolarz, *The Peoples of the Soviet Far East* (Archon Books, 1969).

20 Lim Ŭn, *The Founding of a Dynasty in North Korea: An Authentic Biography of Kim Il-sŏng* (Tokyo: Jiyusha, 1982), p. 144.

21 Quoted in Van Ree, *Socialism in One Zone,* p. 59.

22 Lankov, *From Stalin to Kim Il Sung,* p. 12. Having good reason to fear reprisal, the Japanese approached local influential Koreans about organizing an interim governing body that could help keep law and order after liberation. Thus was formed the *Chosŏn kŏnguk chunbi wiwŏnhoe,* or Committee for the Preparation of Korean Independence (CPKI). Within weeks of liberation, the CPKI organized tens of thousands of Koreans into local branches aimed to maintain law and order. These self-governing groups, which sprang up throughout the country, eventually evolved into People's Committees. While the Americans disbanded these self-proclaimed governing groups in the South, in North Korea the Soviets chose instead to infiltrate and manipulate them and eventually allying with them to serve the interests of the pro-Soviet North Korean regime. See van Ree, *Socialism in One Zone;* Cumings, *The Origins of the Korean War,* vol. 1, pp. 267–350.

23 Van Ree, *Socialism in One Zone,* p. 54.

24 Nikita Khrushchev, *Khrushchev Remembers* (Little, Brown, 1970), p. 370.

25 Charles K. Armstrong, *The North Korean Revolution: 1945–1950* (Cornell University Press, 2003), p. 53.

26 Hyun-su Jeon with Gyoo Kahng, "The Shtykov Diaries: New Evidence on Soviet Policy in Korea," *CWIHP Bulletin: The Cold War in Asia,* no. 6/7 (Winter 1995), p. 69.

27 Lankov, *From Stalin to Kim Il Sung,* pp. 10–11; Scalapino and Lee, *Communism in Korea,* p. 238.

28 Yu Sŏng-ch'ŏl, "Testimony," installment 6, November 7, 1990, in Sydney A. Seiler, *Kim Il Sung 1941–48: The Creation of a Legend, the Building of a Regime* (University Press of America, 1994), p. 122.

29 Lim, *Founding of a Dynasty in North Korea*, p. 153. See also Lankov, *From Stalin to Kim Il Sung*, pp. 79–80.

30 Yu, "Testimony," p. 105.

31 North Korean propaganda purports that Kim Il Sung led the "Korean People's Revolutionary Army." This force never existed. Wada Haruki, *Kim Il-sŏng gwa manju hangil chŏnjaeng* [Kim Il Sung and the Anti-Japanese Struggle in Manchuria] (Seoul: Changjakkwa pip'yŏngsa, 1992), pp. 136–141. See also Lankov, *From Stalin to Kim Il Sung*, pp. 49–76; Suh Dae Sook, *Kim Il Sung: North Korean Leader* (Columbia University Press, 1988), pp. 37–47; Sydney A. Seiler, *Kim Il Sŏng, 1941–1948: The Creation of a Legend, The Building of a Regime* (University Press of America, 1994), pp. 29–41.

32 Yu, "Testimony," pp. 112–116.

33 Quoted in Scalapino and Lee, *Communism in Korea*, vol. 1, pp. 324–325, from O Yŏng-jin, *So kunjoŏng ha ŭi Pukhan: Hana ŭi chung-ŏn* [North Korea under Soviet Military Government: An Eyewitness Report] (Seoul: Chung'ang Munhwasa, 1952).

34 Yu, "Testimony," pp. 124–125.

35 Van Ree, *Socialism in One Zone*, p. 113; Scalapino and Lee, *Communism in Korea*, vol. 1, p. 331.

36 Scalapino and Lee, *Communism in Korea*, vol. 1, p. 332.

37 Mitsuhiko Kimura, "From Fascism to Communism: Continuity and Development of Collectivist Economic Policy in North Korea," *Economic History Review*, New Series, 52, no. 1 (February 1999), p. 77.

The Land Reform Act of March 5, 1945, was the first major action of the newly formed North Korean Provisional People's Committees. While land reform promoted the distribution of cultivated lands previously owned by the Japanese and a small number of Korean rural gentry to thousands of Korean tenant farmers, Soviet authorities still established price controls that forced these farmers to sell their produce at fixed low prices to state cooperative associations. Immediately after the completion of land reform, the new government also established 25 percent tax-in-kind, "which was to exact approximately 25 percent of the gross produce and constitute the sole burden upon the farmer." Thus, land distribution was just one part of the communist agrarian reform. The other major aspect of land reform was taxation and market policies, which remained essentially unchanged from the Japanese colonial era. See Scalapino and Lee, *Communism in Korea*, part II, pp. 1023–1025. There were other parallels between the colonial and the postcolonial agricultural landholding systems. As the essential element in a capitalist system, private ownership of land derives from the right of the owner to dispose of his property according to his own will. But despite becoming landowners on paper due to land reform, this right was denied to the North Korean farmer. Indeed, the 1945 Land Reform Act strictly *prohibited* the sale or lease of land transferred by deed. "The former tenant was given a legal document guaranteeing ownership of that land, but this had little meaning because of the strict constraints on the disposal of his property." See Kimura, *From Fascism to Communism*, pp. 76–77.

New scholarship on postliberation North Korea is emerging about the extent to which both Stalinist and Japanese imperialist fascism ideology became the main currents of North Korea's economic policy. After August 15, 1945, and despite the Soviet and North Korean leaders' rhetoric about "cleansing" their zone of former Japanese collaborators and influences, many Korean administrators and managers who had worked for the colonial regime at intermediate levels had, in fact, remained to work for the new government and only later defected or were expelled after it was firmly established. The continuity between Japanese and North Korea economic policy was largely due to the apparent sympathy between Soviet and Japanese ideas on economic planning. The conversion of Japanese communists to imperial fascism in the late 1930s had a substantial impact on policy making in the wartime Japanese economy. This conversion was most apparent in Manchuria, where many former Japanese Marxists played an important role in developing the strategic plans for the industries in the Japanese puppet state of Manchukuo. These same Soviet influences, which had helped to shape wartime Japanese economy in Manchuria, also dominated North Korea after 1945. Ibid., p. 82. See also Andrei Lankov, "The Demise of Non-Communist Parties in North Korea (1945–1960), *Journal of Cold War Studies* 3, no. 1 (Winter 2001), pp. 104–109. For a discussion of the relationship between Japanese fascism and North Korean communism, see Brian Myers, *The Cleanest Race: How North Korean See Themselves (and Why It Matters)* (Melville House, 2010), pp. 30–38. Leonid Petrov has also noted that many South Korean intellectuals who had been trained in Japan eventually settled in the north. For example, Paek Nam-ŭn (1894–1979) was a leading North Korean intellectual whose major works were all written in Japanese. It was only after liberation that he translated these works into Korean. After the founding of the Republic of Korea in 1948, Paek Nam-ŭn, and other Japanese-trained intellectuals like him, settled in P'yŏngyang, where they went on to be appointed to high positions within the NKWP and DPRK government. Paek himself held various high administrative posts throughout his career, including educational minister and president of the academy of science. Most of these intellectuals would later come to regret their decision to side with the North Korean regime, as they were later destroyed during the North Korean purges of the late 1950s. See Leonid A. Petrov, "Foreign and Traditional Influences in the Historiography of Paek Nam-un," *Proceedings of the Twelfth New Zealand International Conference on Asian Studies*, Massey University, November 19–26, 1997, pp. 205, available at http://www.north-korea.narod.ru/paek.htm (accessed July 26, 2012).

38   Scalapino and Lee, *Communism in Korea*, vol. 1, p. 336, fn 49. The Sinŭiju uprising on November 23 was the single largest anti-communist demonstration during the "liberation" period. The incident was sparked by the arrest of a school principal who had publicly criticized Soviet soldiers and Korean communists. The arrest became the catalyst for a series of bloody clashes between students and armed Soviet and Korean communists linked to internal Korean security forces, called *poandae*, which was commanded by Kim Il Sung. See Adam Cathcart and Charles Kraus, "Peripheral Influence: The Sinŭiju Student Incident of 1945 and the Impact of Soviet Occupation in North Korea," *Journal of Korean Studies* 13, no. 1 (Fall 2008); Armstrong, *North Korean Revolution*, pp. 62–64. The South Korean historian Kim Ha-yŏng has argued that the uprising was fueled by genuine expressions of popular anger,

which were both deep and widespread. According to her, Soviet occupation forces actually suppressed popular demands for democracy, and their success in doing so was in large part due to the fact that they were able to quickly gain full control over their zone. Moreover, their central aim was to recover the territory and influence that had been lost to the Japanese at the end of the Russo-Japanese War. The basis for Soviet policy toward the Korean peninsula was thus not revolutionary internationalism but the desire for imperialist expansion. Stalin's policy toward Korea, in other words, was simply following the tradition of the tsarist empire. See Kim Ha-yŏng, "The Formation of North Korean State Capitalism," trans. Owen Miller, *International Socialism: A Quarterly Journal of Socialist Theory*, June 1, 2006, available at http://www.isj.org.uk/?id=205 (accessed June 30, 2008). The original Korean version is Kim's *Kukchejuŭi sigak eso pon hanbando* [Korean Peninsula from an International Perspective].

39 *New York Times*, December 6, 1945.

40 Kim Hak-chun, *Pukhan 50 nyŏn-sa* [Fifty Years of North Korean History] (Seoul: Tong'a ch'ulp'ansa, 1995), pp. 96–97; Kim, *Kukchejuŭi sigak eso pon hanbando* [Korean Peninsula from an International Perspective], p. 257; Armstrong, *North Korean Revolution*, pp. 62–63.

41 *New York Times*, July 9, 1947.

42 Van Ree, *Socialism in One Zone*, p. 120.

43 Ibid., pp. 122–123; Scalapino and Lee, *Communism in Korea*, pp. 336–337.

44 John Dower, *Embracing Defeat: Japan in the Wake of World War II* (W. W. Norton, 1999), p. 78. See also D. Clayton James, *The Years of MacArthur*, vol. 3, *Triumph and Disaster, 1945–1964* (Houghton Mifflin, 1985), pp. 287–300.

45 Kenneth Strother, "A Memoir: Experience of a Staff Officer, Headquarters XXIV Corps in the Occupation of Korea, September–November 1945," Miscellaneous Collection S, MHI; James, *The Years of MacArthur*, vol. 3, pp. 287–300.

46 HUSAFIK, vol. 3, chap. 4, pp. 16–17.

47 Strother, "Memoir," pp. 13–14.

48 *FRUS, 1945*, vol. 6, pp. 1045–1050.

49 Ibid., p. 1135.

50 The Korean People's Republic (KPR) was an outgrowth of CPKI peacekeeping activities that had begun immediately after liberation with Japanese support. On September 6, 1945, CPKI members from Seoul and nearby provinces came together to announce the formation of the KPR. It was a direct response to the impending arrival of American occupational forces. CPKI leaders were eager to establish their own provisional government before the arrival of the Americans, "both to show that Koreans could run their own affairs and to forestall either a prolonged American tutelage or the installation in power of other Koreans who might gain American favor." Cumings, *The Origins of the Korean War*, vol. 1, p. 84; Millett, *The War for Korea, 1945–1950*, pp. 46–47.

51 U.S. Army Military Government in Korea (USAMGIK) G-2 Periodic Report no. 1, September 9, 1945, Headquarters XXIV Corps, "Activities of Left-Wing Korean Political Parties," p. 13, H. L. Wolbers Papers, box 1, MHI.

52 *FRUS, 1945*, vol. 6, p. 1064.

53 USAMGIK, "Activities of Left-Wing Korean Political Parties," pp. 15–17.
54 *New York Times*, October 30, 1945.
55 Cumings, *The Origins of the Korean War*, vol. 1, pp. 375–379.
56 Lauterbach, *Dangers from the East*, pp. 218–219.
57 *New York Times*, November 4, 1945.
58 *FRUS, 1945*, vol. 6, pp. 1142–1143.
59 Charles H. Donnelly, "U.S. Military Government in Korea (USAMGIK)," unpublished memoir, pt. 3, 1947–53, p. 960, Charles H. Donnelly Papers, MHI.
60 *New York Times*, December 8, 1945.
61 Donnelly, "U.S. Military Government in Korea," pp. 914, 957–958.

TWO: *Two Koreas*

1 Soon Sung-cho, *Korea in World Politics, 1940–1950, An Evaluation of American Responsibility* (University of California Press, 1967), p. 94.
2 Quoted in Cumings, *The Origins of the Korean War*, vol. 1, p. 200; Ambassador Edwin Pauley to President Truman, June 22, 1946, in *FRUS, 1946*, vol. 8: *The Far East* (1971), pp. 706–709. Truman was impressed with Pauley's letter; see his response, July 16, 1946, in *FRUS, 1946*, vol. 8, pp. 713–714; and in Harry Truman, *Years of Trial and Hope* (Doubleday, 1956), p. 366.
3 Cumings, *The Origins of the Korean War*, vol. 1, pp. 184–187; "Langdon to Secretary of State," November 20, 1945, in *FRUS: Diplomatic Papers, 1945*, vol. 6: *The British Commonwealth, the Far East* (1969), p. 1131.
4 Letter from Mrs. Rhee to Mrs. Frye, May 4, 1947, "Robert T. Oliver File," 79 #13011, Syngman Rhee Presidential Papers (hereafter "Rhee Papers"), Yonsei University, Seoul, Korea. For a complete catalogue of the Rhee papers, see Young Ick Lew and Sangchul Cha, comp., *The Syngman Rhee Presidential Papers: A Catalogue* (Seoul: Yonsei University Press, 2005).
5 "Memorandum of February 5 and May 14, 1945," in *FRUS, 1945*, vol. 6, pp. 1023, 1030.
6 Cumings, *The Origins of the Korean War*, vol. 1, p. 219; Millett, *The War for Korea, 1945–1950*, p. 69.
7 *New York Times*, December 29, 1945.
8 Erik van Ree, *Socialism in One Zone: Stalin's Policy in Korea, 1945–1947* (Berg, 1989), pp. 142–144; Cumings, *The Origins of the Korean War*, vol. 1, pp. 221–223; HUSAFIK, vol. 2, chap. 4, p. 78; Scalapino and Lee, *Communism in Korea*, vol. 1, pp. 276–277.
9 Cumings, *The Origins of the Korean War*, vol. 1, pp. 223–225; Scalapino and Lee, *Communism in Korea*, vol. 1, pp. 276–280.
10 Lim Ŭn, *The Founding of a Dynasty in North Korea: An Authentic Biography of Kim Il-sŏng* (Tokyo: Jiyusha, 1982), pp. 150–151; Scalapino and Lee, *Communism in Korea*, pp. 337–340; Van Ree, *Socialism in One Zone*, p. 143; Andrei Lankov, *From Stalin to Kim Il Sung: The Formation of North Korea, 1945–1960* (Rutgers University Press, 2002), pp. 23–24.
11 Lim, *Founding of a Dynasty in North Korea*, p. 152.
12 Van Ree, *Socialism in One Zone*, pp. 145–146.

13 *New York Times,* January 27, 1946.

14 Quoted in Cumings, *The Origins of the Korean War,* vol. 1, p. 227.

15 *New York Times,* March 11 and 13, 1946.

16 Stalin's instructions to the Soviet delegation stated "that the Commission must consult *only* with those democratic parties and organizations that fully and without any qualifications support the Moscow Decision." See Jongsoo James Lee, *The Partition of Korea after World War II: A Global History* (Palgrave Macmillan, 2006), pp. 96–102.

17 Memorandum, October 26, 1946, Major General Albert E. Brown Papers, Korea, 1946–47, box 3, MHI.

18 HUSAFIK, vol. 3, chap. 2, pp. 212–213. As Kathryn Weathersby demonstrates, briefing papers for the December 1945 conference reveal that Stalin was very concerned about the threat of a resurgent Japan and that his aim for Korea was to eradicate Japanese influence in the peninsula. "If Soviet policy is directed at the destruction of the military capability of the Japanese aggressors, at the eradication of Japanese influence in Korea, at the encouragement of the democratic movement of the Korean people and preparing them for independence, then judging by the activity of the Americans in Korea, American policy has precisely the opposite goal. The Americans have not only retained in Korea the old administrative apparatus, but have also left many Japanese and local collaborators in leadings posts. In the American zone, Japanese enjoy broad political rights and economic possibilities." The Soviets also were well aware that Rhee's political views were staunchly anti-Soviet, and they understood that should a government hostile to the Soviet Union come into power, they would not be able to safeguard their economic and strategic interests there. This concern was highlighted in another briefing report prepared for the December conference which concluded that "the Japanese military and heavy industry in North Korea must be transferred to the Soviet Union as partial payment of reparations, and also as compensation for the huge damage inflicted by Japan on the Soviet Union throughout the time of its existence, including damages from the Japanese intervention in the Far East from 1918–1923." Quoted in Kathryn Weathersby, "Soviet Aims in Korea and the Origins of the Korean War, 1945–1950: New Evidence from Russian Archives," *CWIHP Working Paper 8* (November 1993), pp. 17–20. See also Wada Haruki, "The Korean War, Stalin's Policy and Japan," *Social Science Japan Journal* 1, no. 1 (1998), pp. 5–29.

19 HUSAFIK, vol. 2, pt. 2, p. 29.

20 Hyun-su Jeon with Gyoo Kahng, "The Shtykov Diaries: New Evidence on Soviet Policy in Korea," *CWIHP Bulletin: The Cold War in Asia,* no. 6/7 (Winter 1995), pp. 92–96; Letter from Mrs. Rhee to Mrs. Frye, May 4, 1947, "Robert T. Oliver File," 79 #13011, Rhee Papers.

21 Rhee to Oliver, May 6, 1947, "Robert T. Oliver File," 79 #13011, Rhee Papers.

22 "Statement by Rhee," January 23, 1947, "Robert T. Oliver File," 79 #13004, Rhee Papers.

23 *New York Times,* May 29, 1947.

24 "Draft Report of Special Interdepartmental Committee on Korea, February, 25, 1947, *FRUS, 1947,* vol. 6: *The Far East* (1972), pp. 611–612.

25 Millett, *The War for Korea, 1945–1950*, p. 120.

26 James F. Schnabel and Robert J. Watson, *History of the Joint Chiefs of Staff*, vol. 3, part 1: *The Korean War* (Michael Glazier, 1979), pp. 13–14.

27 "Robert Lovett to V. M. Molotov," October 17, 1947, in *FRUS, 1947*, vol. 6, p. 837.

28 Lankov, *From Stalin to Kim Il Sung*, pp. 45–46; Andre Lankov, "What Happened to Kim Ku?" *Korea Times*, September 4, 2008; "Chronology of Activities of Opposition to the UN Election," Albert E. Brown Papers, Korea, 1946–51, box 3, MHI.

29 An justified the killing by stating that Kim Ku was acting on behalf of the Soviets. An was tried and given a life sentence, but he was pardoned in time to fight in the Korean War, survived it, and became a successful businessman in exile. Many had long suspected that Rhee was ultimately behind An's actions, but it was only in 1992 that An confessed to a major newspaper that Rhee's chief of security had been behind the assassination. In October 1996, at the age of seventy-nine, An was beaten to death by an attacker wielding a club inscribed with the words "Justice Stick." See Lankov, "What Happened to Kim Ku?" An's story took a final strange turn when a U.S. Army Counter Intelligence Corps (CIC) report from July 1, 1949, was discovered in the National Archives (NARA). It clearly states that An was a CIC informant and then an agent. He was also a member of a secret right-wing organization called the "White Clothes Society," whose leader, Yum Dong-jin, supported Rhee and opposed Kim Ku and was considered "our man in Seoul" by the CIC. This raised speculation that the U.S. government might have ultimately been behind the assassination. The CIC report by Maj. George Cilley can be found at http://www.korean-war.com/Archives/2002/06/msg000085.html (accessed August 1, 2010).

30 Allan R. Millett, "Captain James H. Hausman and the Formation of Korean Army, 1945–1950," *Armed Forces and Society*, no. 4 (Summer 1947), p. 510.

31 Ibid., pp. 507–513; James Hausman, John Toland interview transcript, p. 37, Hausman Papers, Yenching Library, Harvard University, Cambridge, Mass.

32 John Merrill, *Korea: The Peninsular Origins of the War* (University of Delaware Press, 1989), p. 67; Bruce Cumings, *The Origins of the Korean War*, vol. 2: *The Roaring of the Cataract, 1947–1950* (Princeton University Press, 1990), p. 254.

33 Merrill, *Korea*, p. 81.

34 HUSAFIK, pt. 3, p. 18.

35 Millett, *The War for Korea, 1945–1950*, p. 161.

36 James Hausman, "Notecards for a Speech on the Early Days of the Korean Constabulary," Hausman Papers. See also Donald Clark, "Before the War—Western Encounters with Korea," unpublished manuscript (author's personal copy), p. 31.

37 James Hausman, "History of the Rebellion, 14th Constabulary," Hausman Papers; Clark, "Before the War," p. 33.

38 Hausman, "History of the Rebellion, 14th Constabulary"; Donald Clark, *Living Dangerously in Korea: The Western Experience, 1900–1950* (Eastbridge, 2001), pp. 335–336.

39 Keyes Beech, *Tokyo and Points East* (Doubleday, 1954), p. 141. Also partly quoted in Cumings, *The Origins of the Korean War*, vol. 2, p. 265.

40 Cumings, *The Origins of the Korean War*, vol. 2, p. 265; Beech, *Tokyo and Points*

East, p. 141; Kim Kye-yu, "Naega kyŏkkun yŏsunsagŏn" [My Experience of the Yŏsu Sunch'ŏn Incident], *Chŏnan munhwa* 4 (1991), pp. 54–57.

41 Hausman, "Notecards for a Speech." The total number killed in Cheju-do is in dispute. Allan R. Millett, for example, doubts it was as high as thirty thousand, based on his own careful analysis. See Millett, *The War for Korea, 1945–1950*, p. 303, no. 74.

42 *New York Times*, May 7, 1949.

THREE: *Momentous Decisions*

1 Kathryn Weathersby, "Should We Fear This? Stalin and the Danger of War with America," *CWIHP Working Paper 39* (July 2002), pp. 3–5.

2 Mao Tse Tung, *Selected Works of Mao Tse-tung* (Foreign Language Press, 1977), vol. 4, pp. 160–163.

3 Sergei N. Goncharov, John W. Lewis, and Xue Litai, *Uncertain Partners: Stalin, Mao and the Korean War* (Stanford University Press, 1993), p. 24.

4 Shi Zhe, " 'With Mao and Stalin: The Reminiscences of Mao's Interpreter,' Part 2; Liu Shaoqi in Moscow," *Chinese Historian* 6, no. 1 (Spring 1993), p. 83. Mao's resentment of Stalin was palpable during his 1956 conversation with the Soviet ambassador: "When armed struggle against the forces of Chiang Kai-shek was at its height, when our forces were on the brink of victory, Stalin insisted that peace be made with Chiang Kai-shek, since he doubted the forces of the Chinese Revolution." "Mao's Conversation with Yudin, 31 March 1956," *CWIHP Bulletin: The Cold War in Asia*, no. 6/7 (Winter 1995), p. 165.

5 Mao, *Selected Works of Mao Tse-tung*, vol. 5, pp. 16–17.

6 Tony Saich, ed., *The Rise to Power of the Chinese Communist Party: Documents and Analysis* (East Gate, 1996), pp. 1368–1369; Chen Jian, *China's Road to the Korean War* (Columbia University Press, 1994), pp. 15–23, 33–57, 64–78.

7 Goncharov et al., *Uncertain Partners*, p. 85.

8 "Conversation between Stalin and Mao, Moscow 16 December 1949," *CWIHP Bulletin: The Cold War in Asia*, no. 6/7 (Winter 1995), p. 5; Goncharov et al., *Uncertain Partners*, pp. 85–88.

9 Sergei Goncharov, "The Stalin-Mao Dialogue," *Far Eastern Affairs*, no. 2 (1992), pp. 109–110. This article features Goncharov's interview with Ivan Kovalev, Stalin's personal envoy to Mao Zedong.

10 Goncharov et al., *Uncertain Partners*, p. 92.

11 *New York Times*, January 2, 1950; Goncharov et al., *Uncertain Partners*, pp. 92–93. See also Vladislav Zubok and Constantine Pleshakov, *Inside the Kremlin's Cold War: From Stalin to Krushchev* (Harvard University Press, 1996), pp. 60–62.

12 "Conversation between Stalin and Mao, Moscow, 22 January 1950," *CWIHP Bulletin: The Cold War in Asia*, no. 6/7 (Winter 1995), p. 8.

13 *New York Times*, January 5, 1950.

14 This interpretation is implied in Goncharov et al., *Uncertain Partners*. Also see John Lewis Gaddis, *We Now Know: Rethinking Cold War History* (Oxford University Press, 1998), pp. 72–73; William Stueck, *Rethinking the Korean War: A New Diplomatic and Strategic History* (Princeton University Press, 2002), p. 73. Lorenz Lüthi has argued, however, that despite the intricate maneuvers

between Mao and Stalin, there was never really a chance of China's rapprochement with the United States simply because Mao did not want it. Lüthi also rejects the notion that Mao was pretending to Stalin that such a rapprochement was possible or that he played the "American card" to get better terms from Stalin. See Lorenz M. Lüthi, *The Sino-Soviet Split: Cold War in the Communist World* (Princeton University Press, 2008). Chen Jian agrees, stating that America's "lost chance" with China is a myth and that the CCP's adoption of its anti-American policy had "deep roots" that went way beyond U.S. support for the Nationalists (p. 48). Sergey Radchenko similarly describes Mao as a "revolutionary realist" who "worked toward one goal alone: China's and his own power" (p. 69). Accordingly, Mao's ultimate goal was to restore the nation's independence and pride and to secure his control over China's state and society. Sergey Radchenko, *Two Suns in the Heaven: The Sino-Soviet Struggle for Supremacy, 1962–1967* (Stanford University Press, 2009); Chen Jian, *Mao's China and the Cold War* (University of Chapel Hill Press, 2001).

15 Gordon Chang, *Friends and Enemies: The United States, China and the Soviet Union, 1948–1972* (Stanford University Press, 1990), pp. 65–66.

16 "Minutes of Conversation between Stalin and Mao, Moscow, 22 January 1950," *CWIHP Bulletin: The Cold War in Asia*, no. 6/7 (Winter 1995), pp. 7–8.

17 Text of the treaty in John W. Garver, *Chinese-Soviet Relations, 1937–1945: The Diplomacy of Chinese Nationalism* (Oxford University Press, 1988), pp. 214–216.

18 Goncharov et al., *Uncertain Partners*, pp. 110–129. Mao also received another gift from Stalin: the Soviet leader provided Mao with a list of Chinese informers within the CCP who reported to Moscow. It was another instance of Stalin's many betrayals that resulted in the purge of hundreds of pro-Soviet communists in the CCP. See Zubok and Pleshankov, *Inside the Kremlin's Cold War*, p. 61.

19 An Sŭng-hwan, "Chupukhan ssoryŏn kunsagomundanŭi pukhangun chiwŏn hwaldong (1946–1953) [Soviet Military Advisory Group Support to the NKPA, 1946–1953]," in *Hanguk chŏnjaengsaŭi saeroun yŏngu* [New Research on Korean War History] (Republic of Korea Ministry of National Defense Institute for Military History Compilation, 2002), vol. 2, p. 371.

20 A list of the number of Soviet advisors assigned to the NKPA reveals the degree of effort to professionalize the NKPA at every level of its command structure in the months before the outbreak of the war:

Division level and higher (total 34)
- Commander (Shtykov)
- Chief advisor to NKPA Supreme Staff
- 10 functional branch advisors
- 18 Supreme Staff operations staff advisors (key group, responsible for war planning and execution)
- 5 division commanders' advisors

Advisors at brigade level and below (total 202)
- 15 brigade advisors
- 68 regimental advisors
- 8 battalion advisors
- 9 military school advisors

- 28 military school faculty advisors
    - 39 advisors to various other units
    - 6 medical advisors
    - 29 military specialists
  From ibid., pp. 370–371.

21 Vladamir Petrov, "Soviet Role in the Korean War Confirmed: Secret Documents Declassified," *Journal of Northeast Asian Studies* 13, no. 3 (1994), pp. 51; Kathryn Weathersby, "The Soviet Role in the Early Phase of the Korean War: New Documentary Evidence," *Journal of American–East Asian Relations* 2, no. 4 (Winter 1993), p. 429.

22 Petrov, "Soviet Role in the Korean War Confirmed," p. 51.

23 Weathersby, "Should We Fear This?" pp. 9–11.

24 Goncharov et al., *Uncertain Partners*, pp. 143–145; Weathersby, "Should We Fear This?" pp. 11–12. Also see Nikita Khrushchev, *Khrushchev Remembers: The Glasnost Tapes*, trans. and edited by Jerrold L. Schecter with Vyacheslav V. Luchkov (Little, Brown, 1990), pp. 86–87; Khrushchev, "Truth about the Korean War: Memoirs," *Far Eastern Affairs*, no. 1 (1991), pp. 63–69.

25 Weathersby, "Should We Fear This?" pp. 12–13; Goncharov et al., *Uncertain Partners*, p. 145.

26 Goncharov et al., *Uncertain Partners*, p. 146. Sources differ as to how reluctant Mao actually was regarding his support of Kim's invasion plans. According to Khrushchev and other Chinese officials close to Mao, it was Mao who convinced Stalin to back Kim because he firmly believed that the United States would not intervene. Thus, far from being manipulated into supporting the war, Mao, according to these accounts, was a strong advocate of Kim's war. See Chen Jian, *China's Road to the Korean War: The Making of the Sino-American Confrontation* (Columbia University Press, 1994), pp. 87–91; Krushchev, *Khrushchev Remembers*, p. 368.

27 The full text of NSC 68 can be found at http://www.fas.org/irp/offdocs/nsc-hst/nsc-68.htm (accessed January 20, 2009).

28 David McCullough, *Truman* (Simon & Schuster, 1992), p. 773; *Public Papers of the Presidents: Harry S. Truman 1950* (U.S. Government Printing Office, 1965), p. 152. For an assessment of the significance of this document, see Ernest R. May, ed., *American Cold War Strategy: Interpretating NCS 68* (St. Martin's Press, 1993).

29 Telegram from Stalin to Shtykov, June 20, 1950, cited in Petrov, "Soviet Role in the Korean War Confirmed," pp. 53–54. Petrov notes that when the NKPA captured Seoul, Stalin forbade General Vasiliev to go there because of its proximity to the front. He "did not want the United States, the United Nations and World opinion to catch him directly participating in the war," although at that time few doubted the degree and nature of Moscow's involvement. An Sŭng-hwan also noted how the Soviet advisory activity was restricted: "Advisors who went to North Korea just before and during the war travelled on their army or navy identification cards rather than with a passport and thus did not register with the Soviet Embassy. Advisors only wore civilian clothing and disguised themselves as *Pravda* correspondents." An, "Chupukhan ssoryŏn kunsagomundanŭi pukhangun chiwŏn hwaldong (1946–1953) [Soviet Military Advisory Group Support to the NKPA, 1946–1953]," p. 369.

30 Weathersby, "Should We Fear This?" p. 14.
31 "Interview of General Razhubayev by Aryuzunov, 29 May 2001," cited in An, "Chupukhan ssoryŏn kunsagomundanŭi pukhangun chiwŏn hwaldong (1946–1953) [Soviet Military Advisory Group Support to the NKPA, 1946–1953]," pp. 439–440.
32 Weathersby, "Should We Fear This?" pp. 14–15. See also Anatoly Torkunov, *The War in Korea, 1950–1953: Its Origins, Bloodshed and Conclusion* (Tokyo: ICF, 2000), p. 68.

FOUR: *War for the South*

 1 Larry Zellers, *In Enemy Hands: A Prisoner in North Korea* (University Press of Kentucky, 1991), p. 1.
 2 "Letter to Lt. Col. Roy E. Appleman from Joseph R. Darrigo," July 2, 1953, Clay Blair Collection, box 78, MHI; Roy E. Appleman, *South to the Naktong, North to the Yalu* (U.S. Government Printing Office, 1961), pp. 23–24.
 3 Appleman, *South to the Naktong*, p. 20.
 4 *FRUS, 1950*, vol. 7: *Korea* (1976), p. 49.
 5 Quoted in Clay Blair, *The Forgotten War: America in Korea, 1950–1953* (Times Books, 1987), p. 55.
 6 *FRUS, 1950*, vol. 7, pp. 121–122.
 7 *U.S. News & World Report*, May 5, 1950, p. 30.
 8 Paik Sun Yup (Paek Sŏn-yŏp), *From Pusan to Panmunjom: Wartime Memoirs of the Republic of Korea's First Four-Star General* (Brassey's, 1992), p. 8.
 9 Ibid., p. 7.
10 Dean Acheson, *Present at the Creation* (W. W. Norton, 1969), pp. 404–405; Harry S. Truman, *Memoirs*, vol. 2: *Years of Trial and Hope* (Doubleday, 1956), p. 332; McCullough, *Truman*, pp. 774–775.
11 *FRUS, 1950*, vol. 7, p. 124; McCullough, *Truman*, p. 777; Truman, *Memoirs*, vol. 2, pp. 332–333.
12 *FRUS, 1950*, vol. 7, p. 129.
13 Marguerite Higgins, *War in Korea: The Report of a Woman Combat Correspondent* (Doubleday, 1951), p. 16.
14 Beech, *Tokyo and Points East*, p. 111; James Hausman, Toland interview transcript, pp. 32–33.
15 Beech, *Tokyo and Points East*, pp. 112–113.
16 Hausman, Toland interview transcript, p. 34.
17 Paik, *From Pusan to Panmunjom*, p. 18.
18 Quoted in D. Clayton James and Anne Sharpe Wells, *Refighting the Last War: Command Crisis in Korea, 1950–53* (Free Press, 1992), p. 138.
19 Blair, *Forgotten War*, p. 76.
20 Douglas MacArthur, *Reminiscences: General of the Army* (Naval Institute Press, 1964), p. 334.
21 *Christian Science Monitor*, June 29, 1950.
22 Anthony Leviero, "U.S. 'Not at War,' President Asserts," *New York Times*, June 30, 1950.
23 John Toland, *In Mortal Combat Korea, 1950–1953* (William Morrow, 1991), pp. 65–68.

24 Eric C. Ludvigsen, "An Arrogant Display: The Failed Bluff of Task Force Smith," *Army* (February 1992), p. 38.

25 A recent study by Thomas E. Hanson suggests that the American soldiers in Japan might have been better prepared than commonly believed. See his *Combat Ready? The Eighth U.S. Army on the Eve of the Korean War* (Texas A&M University Press, 2010).

26 Quoted in *Real Magazine*, October 1952.

27 Michael W. Cannon, "Task Force Smith: A Study in (Un)preparedness and (Ir)responsibility," *Military Review* 68, no. 2 (February 1988), p. 66.

28 Appleman, *South to the Naktong*, p. 75.

29 Letter from Dunn to Appleman, June 17, 1955, Clay Blair Collection, box 72, MHI.

30 *New York Times*, September 3, 1950.

31 Appleman, *South to the Naktong*, p. 110.

32 Comments critical of the ROK Army are found in most standard works in English on the Korean War such as Blair, *Forgotten War*; Appleman, *South to the Naktong*; Cumings, *The Origins of the Korean War*, vol. 2. Allan Millett, however, has sought to correct this bias by focusing on many of the ROK Army's accomplishments, especially at the beginning of the war when the ROK Capital Division and ROK First Division slowed the progress of the NKPA, thereby effectively thwarting Kim's Il Sung's victory drive to Pusan. See Allan R. Millett, *The War for Korea, 1950–1951: They Came from the North* (University Press of Kansas, 2010), pp. 195-201. See also Korean Institute of Military History, *The Korean War*, vol. 1 (University of Nebraska Press, 1999), pp. 374–410.

33 Paik, *From Pusan to Panmunjom*, p. 30.

34 Korea Institute of Military History, *Korean War*, vol. 1, pp. 299–300.

35 "Order from Supreme Commander, NKA, to All Forces, 15 Oct 1950," quoted in James F. Schnabel, *Policy and Direction: The First Year* (U.S. Government Printing Office, 1990), p. 114n.

36 Blair, *Forgotten War*, p. 141.

37 *Korea Times*, October 1, 1999.

38 There are conflicting accounts as to why U.S. soldiers fired on the refugees. Some accounts contend that ill-trained and besieged soldiers had simply panicked, while others believe that they had been ordered. So far, no evidence has been uncovered that U.S. soldiers were given *explicit* orders to shoot the refugees at Nogŭnri; ample evidence supports the contention that there was a policy in place regarding the shooting of refugees. See Sahr Conway-Lanz, "Beyond No-Gun-ri: Refugees and the United States Military in the Korean War," *Diplomatic History* 29, no. 1 (January 2005), p. 59; Charles J. Hanley, Sang-Hun Choe, and Martha Mendoza, *The Bridge at No Gun Ri: A Hidden Nightmare from the Korean War* (Henry Holt, 2001).

39 "One Korean's Account: Too Frighten to Cry," *U.S. News & World Report*, May 22, 2000, p. 52.

40 Department of the Army Inspector General, *No Gun Ri Review*, January 2001, pp. 149–150. An estimate of the number of deaths can be found in ibid., p. 191. The incident gained international attention as a result of a report by Charles J. Hanley, Sang-Hun Choe, and Martha Mendoza, published by the Associ-

ated Press in September 1999, that won the Pulitzer Prize in 2000. The AP team later published a much more extensive revision of their findings in *The Bridge at No Gun Ri.*

41 Donald Knox, *The Korean War,* vol. 1: *Pusan to Chosin, an Oral History* (Harcourt Brace, 1985), pp. 72–73.

42 Millett, *The War for Korea, 1950–1951,* pp. 94–96.

43 Narrative Report of the United States Military Advisory Group to the Republic of Korea, Office of the Chief, USMAG, 1946–1949, Provided by Col. Harold Fischgrund, (Ret.), KMAG, G3 Office, 1949. Copy obtained from Allan R. Millett.

44 Quoted in An Sŭng-hwan, "Chupukhan ssoryŏn kunsa komundangŭi pukhangun chiwŏn hwaldong (1946–1953) [Soviet Military Advisory Group Support to the NKPA, 1946–1953]," p. 443.

45 The soldiers of the ROK Sixth Division held firm and defended the city of Ch'unch'ŏn until noon, June 28. The speed of the North Koreans' advance was seriously retarded and their tight timeline thrown to the winds. As events turned out, the North Korean army failed to execute the most important component of the operation as devised by Soviet planners—the encircle-ment and destruction of the ROK Army. The Soviet planners had envisioned a smaller-scale version of the epic campaigns of encirclement fought on the eastern front during World War II. The destruction of the ROK Army, not territorial advance, was the key to rapid victory. But the North Korean encir-cling forces, delayed by the ROK Sixth Division, were unable to encircle Seoul from the east and south to cut off the retreat route of the bulk of the ROK Army, which was located north of Seoul. See Kim Jwang-so, "The North Korean War Plan and the Opening Phase of the Korean War: A Docu-mentary Study," *International Journal of Korean Studies* (Spring/Summer 2001), pp. 26–27. See also Millett, *The War for Korea, 1950–1951,* pp. 95–96; Korean Insti-tute of Military History, *The Korean War,* vol. 1, pp. 280–282.

46 "26 June 1950, Top Secret Report on Military Situation by Shtykov to Com-rade Zakharov," *CWIHP Bulletin: The Cold War in Asia,* no. 6/7 (Winter 1995), pp. 39–40.

47 Cables from Shtykov to Stalin on June 28, 1950, are cited in An, "Chupukhan ssoryŏn kunsa komundangŭi pukhangun chiwŏn hwaldong (1946–1953) [Soviet Military Advisory Group Support to the NKPA, 1946–1953]," p. 443.

48 "8 July 1950, ciphered telegram, Shtykov to Fyn-Si (Stalin), transmitting let-ter from Kim Il Sung to Stalin," *CWIHP Bulletin: The Cold War in Asia,* no. 6/7 (Winter 1995), pp. 43–44.

49 Cables cited in An, "Chupukhan ssoryŏn kunsa komundangŭi pukhangun chiwŏn hwaldong (1946–1953) [Soviet Military Advisory Group Support to the NKPA, 1946–1953]," p. 449.

50 Ibid., pp. 449–451. An is convinced that Soviet advisors were sent to the front with North Korean troops during the first weeks of the war. He believes that Stalin most likely ordered the withdrawal of most of the advisors before June 25. However, by July 8, realizing that the war was not going well, he agreed to send the requested twenty-five to thirty-five advisors. With regard to the earlier July 4 Shtykov cable requesting assignment of two advisors per two Army Group headquarters, and movement of General Vasiliev and a

group of officers to the front headquarters in Seoul, Stalin replied only that it would be better for Vasiliev to remain in P'yŏngyang. An sees this as a silent consent for the assignment of the Army Group advisors. The South Korean historian Pak Myŏng-nim cites as further evidence the testimony of North Korean POWs. See Pak Myŏng-nim, *Han'guk chongchaengui palbalgwa kiwŏn* [The Korean War: The Outbreak and Its Origins] (Seoul: Nanamch'ulp'an, 1996), vol. 1, pp. 196–197.

51 James, *The Years of MacArthur*, vol. 3, pp. 453–454.

52 Acheson, *Present at the Creation*, p. 422.

53 James, *Years of MacArthur*, vol. 3, pp. 456–458.

54 MacArthur, *Reminiscenses*, p. 349.

55 Former secretary of the army Frank Pace Jr., interview, March 23, 1975, p. 8, MHI.

56 Quoted in James, *Years of MacArthur*, vol. 3, p. 461.

57 Truman, *Memoirs*, vol. 2, p. 356.

58 Almond interview with Capt. Thomas Fergusson, March 28, 1975 (side 1 of tape 4), Edward Almond Papers, box 1, p. 20, MHI.

59 McCaffrey correspondence, September 10, 1978, Roy Appleman Collection, box 20, MHI.

60 O. P. Smith, "Summary of the Situation of 15 November Contained in Letter to Commandant of the Marine Corps," Clay Blair Collection, box 83, MHI.

61 Appleman, *South to the Naktong*, pp. 509–513.

62 Matthew B. Ridgway, *The Korean War* (Doubleday, 1967), p. 42.

63 Clay Blair's interview with Michaelis, April 4, 1984, Clay Blair Collection, box 77, MHI.

64 Oral reminiscences of Major General John H. Chiles, July 27, 1977, interview with D. Clayton James, Clay Blair Collection, box 77, MHI.

65 McCaffrey correspondence, September 10, 1978, Roy Appleman Collection, box 20, MHI.

66 Russell Spurr, *Enter the Dragon: China's Undeclared War against the U.S. in Korea, 1950–51* (Newmarket Press, 1999), p. 105.

67 James, *Years of MacArthur*, vol. 3, p. 482; Schnabel and Robert Watson, *The History of the Joint Chiefs of Staff*, vol. 3, part 1: *The Korean War*, pp. 229–230.

68 Ridgway, *Korean War*, p. 42.

69 Appleman, *South to the Naktong*, p. 587.

70 *New York Times*, October 6, 1950.

71 *Washington Post*, October 4, 1950.

72 *New York Times*, October 6, 1950.

73 *Jefferson City Post*, October 2, 1950.

74 *New York Times*, September 28, 1950.

75 TRC, *Truth and Reconciliation: Activities of the Past Three Years* (Seoul: Ch'ungbuk National University Museum, 2009), pp. 95–96.

76 Appleman, *South to the Naktong*, p. 587.

77 Account of Pvt. Herman G. Nelson in Richard Peters and Xiaobing Li, *Voices from the Korean War: Personal Stories of American, Korean, and Chinese Soldiers* (University Press of Kentucky, 2004), pp. 67–68.

78 Interview with Yi Chun-yŏng, a former guard at Taejŏn prison, November 21, 2007, TRC and Ch'ungbuk National University Museum in *Han'guk*

chŏnjaeng chŏnhu mingan in chipdan hŭisaeng kwallyŏn 2007nyŏn yuhaebalgul pogoso [2007 Report on the Excavations of Human Remains Related to Civilian Massacres before and during the Korean War] (Seoul: Ch'ungbuk National University Museum, 2008) (hereafter *2007 Report on Excavations*), vol. 2, pp. 255–256.

79   *New York Times,* July 14 and 27, 1950.

80   *Time,* August 21, 1950, p. 20.

81   *New York Times,* July 13 and 16, 1950.

82   Higgins, *War in Korea,* p. 89.

83   *New York Times,* July 26, 1950.

84   Muccio to Rusk, July 26, 1950, box 4266, 795.000 Central Decimal Files 1950–1954, RG 59, NARA. The letter, uncovered by the historian Sahr Conway-Lanz, resides in a collection of State Department documents on the Korean War. The document was first cited in Sahr Conway-Lanz, "Beyond No Gun Ri: Refugees and the United States Military in the Korean War," *Diplomatic History* 29, no. 1 (January 2005), p. 59. The letter appears to prove that there was an official policy regarding the shooting of refugees. The revelations are part of a larger probe on the UN handling of the refugee problem during the war. The issue of American killings of Korean civilians is an extremely polemical one and has riled nationalist passions in both the United States and South Korea. An early pioneer in presenting the ferocious nature of the war is Bruce Cumings, whose two-volume study titled *The Origins of the Korea War* is considered a landmark in Korean War historiography. See also Jon Halliday and Bruce Cumings, *Korea: The Unknown War* (Viking Press, 1988); Conrad C. Crane, *American Airpower Strategy in Korea, 1950–1953* (University Press of Kansas, 2000); Sahr Conway-Lanz, *Collateral Damage: Americans, Noncombatant Immunity, and Atrocity after World War Two* (Routledge, 2006). South Korean coverage of civilian killings started even before the September 1999 AP No Gun Ri report and was divided along political lines. In June 1999 the conservative monthly *Wŏlgan chosŏn* published, as part of a series marking the fiftieth anniversary of the beginning of the war, an article detailing the North Korean massacre of South Korean soldiers in hiding and patients at the Seoul National University Hospital in Seoul on June 28, 1950, immediately after the city was captured (pp. 118–130). When the AP report was published, the left-liberal newspapers immediately linked it to a wider issue of U.S. responsibility and culpability and strongly supported the call for apology and compensation. (See, for example, *Tong-a ilbo* articles on September 30 and October 1, 1999. Also see the October 15 interview with Stanley Roth, who was then the assistant secretary of state for East Asia, which portrays a recalcitrant, skeptical, and even defiant American attitude toward U.S. involvement in the killing of civilians during the war; and the *Chung'ang ilbo* story and editorial on October 1, which unequivocally points to U.S. culpability in No Gun Ri and other alleged massacres and pointedly calls for a U.S. apology and compensation for the alleged killings.) On the other hand, the conservative press, while covering the AP story, did so in a matter-of-fact manner that did not immediately point to U.S. culpability and instead highlighted the possible mitigating circumstances—such as untrained troops, fear of North Korean soldiers, and confusion caused by North Koreans disguised as

civilians—to try to conceptualize the incident as something comprehensible while acknowledging it as a tragedy that required an apology and compensation if proved true. (See for example, *Chosŏn ilbo* stories on September 30 and October 11, 1999, and its editorial on October 1, 1999.) The liberal press continued its attacks with further accounts of U.S. complicity in atrocities committed against South Korean civilians, with additional stories on the deliberate destruction of bridges (at Waegwan and Koryŏng) in early August 1950, which blocked refugees from moving south, and another air attack incident at Kwegaegul in January 1951. (See *Chung'ang ilbo*, October 15, 1999, for the Waegwan and Koryŏng story, and *Tong-a ilbo*, December 3, 1999, for the Kwegaegul story.)

85 General Paul Freeman, interview with Colonel James N. Ellis, November 29 and 30, 1973, U.S. Army Military History Research Collection, Senior Officers Debriefing Program, MHI.

86 H. K. Shin, *Remembering Korea 1950: A Boy Soldier's Story* (University of Nevada Press, 2001), p. 44.

87 O. H. P. King, *Tail of the Paper Tiger* (Caxton Printers, 1962), p. 359.

88 *Time*, August 21, 1950, p. 20.

89 In January 2000 a liberal journal in South Korea broke a major story based on newly discovered documents and photographs from the U.S. National Archives that graphically show the execution of eighteen hundred political prisoners by the ROK Military Police and the Korean National Police, an incident that was long believed to be true but unsupported by documentary evidence. The total number believed to have been killed was roughly eight thousand, although this figure is not corroborated by documentary evidence (*Han'gyorae 21*, January 20, 2000, pp. 20–27). Another liberal journal, *Mal*, stoked the flames of anti-Americanism further with a series of articles in its February 2000 issue that provide both documentary and photographic evidence of killings of civilian political prisoners, allegedly communists, by South Korean security forces in Seoul in April 1950 before the war began, at Taejŏn in early July 1950, and at Taegu in August 1950 and April 1951. Both stories strongly implicated the United States, with photos showing American officers calmly observing the executions. The April 1950 incident is made more significant by the fact that it occurred before the war while the country was under peaceful civilian control, and yet the executions were carried out by the ROK Military Police. Also implicated in the killings is Rhee, who is portrayed as being in cahoots with the United States because purging the Left strengthened his dictatorial hold on power. While not the last in this Left-Right debate about wartime culpability, one additional example demonstrates the unending cycle of the accusatory debate, the kind of cycle that the South Korean historian Pak Myŏng-nim calls for an end to. In June 2000, *Wŏlgan chosŏn* published a long article on the North Korean massacre of several thousand civilians and POWs, South Korean and American, at Taejŏn in late September 1950. It happened as the North Korean forces reeled back from the success of the Inch'ŏn landing (pp. 264–287). This was a direct counter to the liberal media coverage of the South Korean killings at Taejŏn in July 1950. The article also made a semantic distinction between *massacre*, which characterizes what the North Koreans committed, and *execution* of prisoners

by the South Korean police. The execution of political prisoners is indi-
rectly justified, because their arrests, as menaces to national security, were
legal under South Korean law at the time (and for a long time afterward).
The debate is far from over. See Sheila Miyoshi Jager, "Re-writing the Past/
Re-claiming the Future: Nationalism and the Politics of Anti-Americanism
in South Korea," *Japan Focus*, July 29, 2005, at http://www.japanfocus.org/
products/details/1772 (accessed January 2010).

90   A compilation of oral histories of massacres can be found in the *2007 Report on
Excavations*.

91   In late 2005, the South Korean government initiated an ambitious project,
the TRC, to bring closure to the many open historical wounds that had been
eating into the soul and fabric of the South Korean people and society. The
TRC was modeled on the many other similar efforts around the world (most
notably in South Africa and Rwanda) that had sprouted since the 1990s as the
end of the cold war opened up space for repressed histories and memories
to come out in the open. The TRC was charged with investigating and finding the truth of contentious issues from the colonial period, the period of
authoritarian rule in the 1960s and 1970s, and the Korean War. Truth could
begin the national healing process. The historical issues concerned were
charged with domestic and international political implications. For the colonial period, the most contentious were collaboration and the assertion that
collaborators were never brought to justice and had instead prospered under
the right-wing rule that controlled South Korea for most of the postliberation period. The focus of the 1960s–1970s period was on the massive human
and civil rights violations that undermined democracy. American support
for that regime, based on cold war logic, is linked to the substantial anti-
Americanism that exists today in South Korea. But it is the alleged killings
and massacres by North Koreans, South Koreans, and Americans before and
during the Korean War that have taken up most of the commission's efforts.
They are also the most sensitive and politically explosive issues attesting to
the enduring impact of the civil conflict that still feeds deep antipathies and
enmities in South Korean society. TRC findings of evidence of massacres in
the South by South Korean security forces made headlines in the summer
of 2008 when excavations of massacre sites, testimonies by perpetrators and
witnesses, and gruesome photographs from American archives were revealed
with the suggestion of American complicity or at least acquiescence. TRC,
Truth and Reconciliation. Also see Charles J. Hanley and Jae-Soon Chang,
"Summer of Terror: At Least 100,000 Said Executed by Korean Ally of US in
1950"; Jae-Soon Chang, "Hidden History: Families Talk of Korean War Executions, Say US Shares Blame"; Charles J. Hanley and Jae-Soon Chang, "U.S.
Okayed Korean War Massacres"; Charles J. Hanley, "Fear, Secrecy Kept 1950
Korea Mass Killings Hidden," all AP reports dated July 4, 2008, all available
at http://japanfocus.org/-Charles_J_-Hanley/2827 (accessed December
2008). The main excavation report is a massive three-volume set, *2007 Report
on Excavations*.

92   *2007 Report on Excavations*, vol. 2, pp. 319–335.

93   Chang, "Hidden History"; Hanley and Chang, "U.S. Okayed Korean War
Massacres"; Hanley, "Fear, Secrecy"; Millett, *War for Korea*, pp. 160–161.

94 *Wŏlgan chosŏn*, June 2000, pp. 264–287. According to Kim Tong-ch'un (Kim Dong-choon), the former commissioner for the Sub-Committee of Investigation of Mass Civilian Sacrifice at the TRC, as many as three hundred thousand suspected communists and leftists may have been executed during the months of June to July 1950 alone. Kim Dong-choon, *Chŏnjaeng'gwa sahoe* [War and Society] (Seoul: Tolpaegae, 2000).

95 *2007 Report on Excavations*, vol. 2, pp. 239–241.

96 Ibid., p. 248.

97 Ibid., p. 236.

98 Ibid., p. 237.

99 Ibid., p. 259.

100 Alan Winnington, *I Saw the Truth in Korea* (People's Press Printing, 1950), pp. 5–6.

FIVE: *Uncommon Coalition*

1 The central pillar of the international coalition, the integration of U.S. and South Korean armed forces, continues to exist today as the foundation for the security of South Korea, a part of the legacy of the unending war.

2 The arrangement of the South Korean military being put under UN/U.S. control lasted until 1994, when peacetime operational command was transferred to South Korea, but wartime operational control still remained with the UN/United States and is not due to be transferred to South Korea until 2015.

3 UN naval and air forces entered the war before ground forces. Two days after the invasion U.S. air and naval forces based in Japan were committed. British naval forces based in Japan followed a day later. Australian air and naval units also based in Japan entered the war on July 1. By the end of July 1950, while the only UN ground forces were American, naval forces from Canada, France, and New Zealand and air forces from Australia and Canada had joined in the effort. By the summer of 1951, additional naval forces from the Netherlands, Thailand, and Colombia as well as a South African fighter squadron and a Greek air transport squadron had joined the coalition. The UN coalition's command structure for controlling air and naval units was straightforward. At the top, the U.S. Far East Command in Japan controlled the coalition as the UNC. The Far East Command's ground, air, and naval components controlled their respective coalition component forces. Air forces were simply organized because coalition contributions were few and small. These units were attached to matching U.S. Air Force units. Coalition naval forces were more substantial, with ships up to the size of aircraft carriers (United Kingdom and Australia) coming from eight nations. They were integrated into the U.S. Naval Forces Far East Command.

4 Walter G. Hermes, *Truce Tent and Fighting Front* (U.S. Government Printing Office, 1966), p. 513.

5 William J. Fox, *Inter-Allied Co-operation During Combat Operations* (Washington, D.C.: Office of the Chief of Military History, Department of the Army, 1952), pp. 10–14.

6 Ibid., pp. 84–85.

7 Ibid., pp. 158–159.

8 Ibid., pp. 155–158.

9 Ibid., pp. 150–155.

10 Appleman, *South to the Naktong*, p. 545.

11 David Curtis Skaggs, "The KATUSA Experiment: The Integration of Korean Nationals into the U.S. Army, 1950-1965," *Military Affairs* 38, no. 2 (April 1974), p. 55; Appleman, *South to the Naktong*, p. 547.

12 Appleman, *South to the Naktong*, p. 503n.

13 James F. Schnabel, *Policy and Direction: The First Year* (U.S. Government Printing Office, 1972), pp. 86, 165–166.

14 Appleman, *South to the Naktong*, p. 492.

15 Schnabel, *Policy and Direction*, p. 167.

16 Skaggs, "KATUSA Experiment," p. 53.

17 Schnabel, *Policy and Direction*, p. 168; Skaggs, "KATUSA Experiment," p. 53; Appleman, *South to the Naktong*, p. 492.

18 Skaggs, "KATUSA Experiment," p. 53; Appleman, *South to the Naktong*, p. 492.

19 Skaggs, "KATUSA Experiment," p. 53.

20 Appleman, *South to the Naktong*, pp. 503–509, 512, 520–523, 527–531, 541; Skaggs, "KATUSA Experiment," pp. 53–54.

21 Appleman, *South to the Naktong*, p. 501.

22 I am indebted to Col. Don Boose (U.S. Army retired) for pointing this out. James A. Field Jr., *History of United States Naval Operations, Korea* (U.S. Government Printing Office, 1962), pp. 232–240. These operations are also covered in more detail in Arnold Lott, *Most Dangerous Sea: A History of Mine Warfare and an Account of U.S. Navy Mine Warfare Operations in World War II and Korea* (U.S. Naval Institute Press, 1959). See also Tessa Morris-Suzuki, "Post-War Warriors: Japanese Combatants in the Korean War," *Asian Pacific Journal* 10, issue 31, no. 1 (July 30, 2012); Reinhardt Drift, "Japan's Involvement in the Korean War," in J. Cotton and I. Neary, eds., *The Korean War in History* (Manchester University Press, 1989), pp. 20–34.

23 Hermes, *Truce Tent*, p. 514.

24 Although there was some talk after the outbreak of the war to directly recruit Japanese soldiers for the war effort, this proposal was immediately squashed by General MacArthur, owing to the sensitive nature of the proposal. Given Stalin's heightened sensitivity about revived Japanese militarism, public evidence of direct involvement by Japan might have led him to risk full-scale Soviet involvement in Korea, something the Americans wanted to avoid at all costs. In addition, South Koreans were adamantly adverse to any Japanese involvement in the war effort because of their recent colonial experience. South Korean backlash and outright defections from the ROK Army were enough concerns to MacArthur that he emphatically stated that "no Japanese were to be employed with the army in Korea." That said, recent evidence suggests that some Japanese nevertheless fought alongside the Americans, although their numbers were quite small. Most had worked for American soldiers in Japan as male cooks, drivers, interpreters, or servants and then later followed their employers to Korea. See Tessa-Morris-Suzuki, "Post-War Warriors," pp. 2–5.

25 Hermes, *Truce Tent*, p. 513

26 And indeed, all U.S. Army units stationed in South Korea to the present day have KATUSAs.

27 Lt. Col. Russell L. Prewittcampbell, "The Korean Service Corps: Eighth Army's Three-Dimensional Asset," *Army Logistician* (March–April 1999), at http://www.almc.army.mil/alog/issues/MARAPR99/MS337.htm (accessed July 15, 2010); Hermes, *Truce Tent*, p. 513; Allan R. Millett, *The War for Korea, 1950–1951: They Came from the North* (University Press of Kansas, 2010), pp. 158–159. Another way to consider the multinational character of the UN army and the significance of the non-U.S. contributions is to quantitatively examine the allocation of the most important fighting elements in the war, the infantry battalions. These units formed the backbone of the front line and provided the overwhelming bulk of men who fought and died. Each nation had its own unique structure, but generally the units were roughly equivalent in terms of battlefield presence. From the beginning of the armistice talks to its conclusion two years later, the UN army nearly doubled in size. These increases were accounted for not only by the growth of the South Korean army but also by a 20 percent increase in U.S. forces and a near doubling of forces from other nations. In the summer of 1951 the Eighth Army had a total of 185 infantry battalions, of which 96 were Korean, 72 American, and 17 from other UN member states. Roughly 10 to 15 percent of all U.S., French, Dutch, and Belgian battalions were also manned by KATUSAs. In other words, conservatively, the KATUSA strength in the U.S. and UN battalions was the equivalent to about eight Korean battalions. The final tally of infantry battalions is then 104 ROK, 65 American, and 16 other nationalities. In percentage terms they are, respectively, 56, 35, and 9 percent. In early 1953, due to a shortage of men, the Commonwealth Division received 1,000 KATUSAs, now dubbed KATCOMs (Korean Augmentation to Commonwealth soldiers), who were integrated down to section (squad) level in the British, Canadian, and Australian infantry battalions. By the summer of 1953, the Eighth Army now had grown to 222 infantry battalions. The ROK number increased to 129, the American contributions stayed the same at 72, and the number from other UN nations increased to 21. The number of KATUSAs remained about the same but was now augmented by the KATCOMs in Commonwealth units. The Korean battalion equivalent in U.S. and other UN units was about 9. After adjustments for this, the final figures (and percentages) are 138 ROK (62 percent), 65 U.S. (29 percent), and 19 from other UN nations (9 percent). If we consider just the U.S. and other UN battalions, the 65 U.S. battalions in 1951 comprised 80 percent of the total (81 battalions), while in 1953 the same number of U.S. battalions (65) comprised 77 percent of the total (84).

A number of general observations can be based on these comparisons and trends from 1950 to 1953. First, the proportion of ROK to UN battalions increased from a little over half to two-thirds. Second, the proportion of U.S. battalions to other UN nations decreased a bit from 80 percent to 77 percent. More important, the share from other UN countries increased from 20 percent to 23 percent. This seems significantly out of proportion to the absolute number of men: 253,000 Americans to 20,000 other UN forces in 1951, to 300,000 Americans to 39,000 other UN forces by 1953. This discrepancy can be explained by the much higher number of Americans who were involved in support functions compared to the number of other UN forces. The "tooth to tail" ratio, in military parlance, was much lower for the American force, a circumstance exaggerated because, except for the Commonwealth units, other nations completely depended on the United States to provide their "tail."

28 Fredrik Logevall, *Embers of War: The Fall of an Empire and the Making of America's Vietnam* (Random House, 2012), pp. 282–283. See also Callum A. McDonald, *Britain and the Korean War* (Blackwell, 1990), pp. 1–4.

29 John M. Vander Lippe, "Forgotten Brigade of the Forgotten War: Turkey's Participation in the Korean War," *Middle Eastern Studies* 36, no. 1 (January 2000), p. 98.

30 Richard Samuels, *Rich Nation, Strong Army: National Security and the Technological Transformation of Japan* (Cornell University Press, 1996), p. 141; John W. Dower, *Embracing Defeat: Japan in the Wake of World War II* (W. W. Norton, 2000), pp. 541–546.

31 Roger Dingman, "The Dagger and the Gift: The Impact of the Korean War on Japan," *Journal of American–East Asian Relations* 1, no. 1 (1993), pp. 29–55; Akagi Kanji, "The Korean War and Japan," *Seoul Journal of Korean Studies* 24, no. 1 (June 2011), pp. 145–184; Akitashi Miyoshita, "Japan," *Encyclopedia of the Korean War*, vol. 1 (ABC-CLIO, 2000), pp. 284–285.

32 Jeffrey Grey, *The Commonwealth Armies and the Korean War* (Manchester University Press, 1988), pp. 182–183; Sri Nandan Prasad, *History of the Custodian Force (India) in Korea* (Historical Section, Ministry of Defence, Government of India, 1976).

SIX: *Crossing the 38th Parallel*

1 Schnabel and Watson, *The History of the Joint Chiefs of Staff*, vol. 3: *The Korean War, Part 1*, p. 244.

2 Ibid., pp. 242–244.

3 Schnabel, *Policy and Direction: The First Year*, p. 182.

4 Schnabel and Watson, *History of the Joint Chiefs of Staff*, vol. 3, p. 243.

5 Korea Institute of Military History, *The Korean War* (University of Nebraska Press, 2000), vol. 1, p. 762.

6 Appleman, *South to the Naktong*, pp. 614–615.

7 Samuel Hawley, *The Imjin War: Japan's Sixteenth-Century Invasion of Korea and Attempt to Conquer China* (University of California Press, 2005), p. 220. For an excellent overview of the Imjin Wars, see also Kenneth M. Swope, *A Dragon's Head and a Serpent's Tail: Ming China and the First Great East Asian War, 1592–1598* (University of Oklahoma Press, 2009); Stephan Turnbull, *The Samurai Invasion of Korea, 1592–1598* (Cassell & Company, 2002).

8 The war would continue over the next few years. While Ming China emerged victorious from the struggle, the heavy financial burden had adversely affected its military capabilities, thus contributing to its fall to the Manchus in 1644. Hideyoshi's misadventure had also cost the Japanese. After the war, Japan would not venture out into the world again until 1894–95, when it fought and won in another war against China.

9 James, *The Years of MacArthur*, vol. 3, pp. 348–349.

10 Omar N. Bradley and Clay Blair, *A General's Life* (Simon & Schuster, 1983), p. 567.

11 Quoted in James, *Years of MacArthur*, vol. 3, p. 503.

12 Ibid., pp. 503–505.

13 Dean Rusk, *As I Saw It* (W. W. Norton, 1990), pp. 168–169.

14 Harry S. Truman, *Memoirs*, vol. 2: *Years of Trial and Hope* (Doubleday 1956), p. 363.

15 Bradley and Blair, *General's Life*, p. 576.

16 McCullough, *Truman*, p. 808.

17 Schnabel and Watson, *History of the Joint Chiefs of Staff*, vol. 3, pp. 275–276; James, *Years of MacArthur*, vol. 3, p. 499. Six months later, General Collins cited this incident as the first instance when MacArthur violated a JCS directive. J. Lawton Collins, *Lightning Joe: An Autobiography* (Louisiana State University Press, 1979), pp. 179–181.

18 Bradley and Blair, *General's Life*, p. 579.

19 Dean Acheson, *Present at the Creation* (W. W. Norton, 1969), p. 468.

20 K. M. Panikkar, *In Two Chinas: Memoirs of a Diplomat* (George Allen & Unwin, 1955), pp. 108–110; *New York Times*, October 2, 1950; *New York Herald Tribune*, October 1, 1950.

21 Truman, *Memoirs*, vol. 2, p. 362.

22 Lim Ŭn, *The Founding of a Dynasty in North Korea: An Authentic Biography of Kim Il-sŏng* (Tokyo: Jiyusha, 1982), pp. 145, 181–184.

23 Alexandre Y. Mansourov, "Stalin, Mao, Kim and China's Decision to Enter the Korean War, September 16-October 15, 1950: New Evidence from the Archives," *CWIHP Bulletin: The Cold War in Asia*, no. 6/7 (Winter 1995), pp. 98, 112.

24 "Ciphered Telegram, Filippov (Stalin) to Mao Zedong and Zhou Enlai, 1 October 1950," *CWIHP Bulletin: The Cold War in Asia*, no. 6/7 (Winter 1995), p. 114.

25 This account of Mao's October 3 communication with Stalin, informing him of China's refusal to enter the war, is based on documents declassified after the fall of the Soviet Union. The message contradicts the purported Mao-to-Stalin message of October 2 that was published in 1987 in an official Chinese document compilation and had since been relied on for numerous scholarly accounts. The official account cites that Mao wrote to Stalin that the Chinese leadership had decided "to send a portion of our troops, under the name of [Chinese People's] Volunteers to Korea, assisting the Korean comrades to fight the troops of the United States and its running dog Syngman Rhee." However, Mao apparently did not send the cable, probably because of the divided opinion among the top CCP leadership. See Shen Zhihua, trans. Neil Silver, *Mao, Stalin, and the Korean War: Trilateral Communist Relations in the 1950s* (Routledge, 2012), pp. 149–158. For the texts of the two versions of Mao's October 2, 1950, telegram, and two interpretations of them, see Mansourov, "Stalin, Mao, Kim and China's Decision," pp. 94–119; Shen Zhihua, "The Discrepancy between the Russian and Chinese Versions of Mao's 2 October 1950 Message to Stalin on Chinese Entry into the Korean War: A Chinese Scholar's Reply," *CWIHP Bulletin*, no. 8/9 (Winter 1996/97), pp. 237–242.

26 "Ciphered telegram from Roshchin in Beijing to Filippov [Stalin], 3 October 1950, conveying 2 October 1950 message from Mao to Stalin," *CWIHP Bulletin: The Cold War in Asia*, no. 6/7 (Winter 1995), pp. 114–115.

27 "Letter, Fyn Si [Stalin] to Kim Il Sung (via Shtykov), 8 [7] October 1950," *CWHIP Bulletin: The Cold War in Asia*, no. 6/7 (Winter 1995), p. 116.

28 Chen Jian, *China's Road to the Korean War: The Making of the Sino-Soviet Alliance* (Columbia University Press, 1995), p. 185.

29 Xiaomin Zhang, *Red Wings over the Yalu: China, the Soviet Union and the Air War over Korea* (Texas A&M University Press, 2002), pp. 74–76.

30 Peng Dehuai, *Memoirs of a Chinese Marshal* (University Press of the Pacific, 2005), p. 473. See also Hao Yufan and Zhai Zhihai, "China's Decision to Enter the Korean War: History Revisited," *China Quarterly*, no. 121 (March 1990), p. 106.

31 Peng, *Memoirs of a Chinese Marshal*, p. 473.

32 Mansourov, *Stalin, Mao, Kim, and China's Decision*, p.101.

33 Chen Jian, "The Sino-Soviet Alliance and China's Entry into the Korean War," *CWIHP Working Paper 1* (June 1992), p. 29; Goncharov et al., *Uncertain Partners*, p. 279.

34 Mansourov, *Stalin, Mao, Kim, and China's Decision*, p. 100; Nikita Khrushchev, *Khrushchev Remembers* (Little, Brown, 1970), pp. 144–152.

35 There are different versions of what took place during the Zhou-Stalin meetings. See Chen, "Sino-Soviet Alliance," pp. 31–32; Mansourov, *Stalin, Mao, Kim, and China's Decision*, p. 103. See also Shen Zhihua, *Mao, Stalin, and the Korean War*, pp. 170–174; Zubok and Pleshankov, *Inside the Kremlin's Cold War*, pp. 67–69.

36 Mansourov maintains that Stalin never betrayed Mao and that the account of Stalin's betrayal is fictional. See Mansourov, *Stalin, Mao, Kim, and China's Decision*, p. 105.

37 Goncharov et al., *Uncertain Partners*, pp. 192–193.

38 Xiaobing Li, Allan R. Millet, and Bin Yu, eds., *Mao's Generals Remember Korea* (University Press of Kansas, 2001), p. 41.

39 Chen, "Sino-Soviet Alliance," p. 32.

40 Chen Jian, *China's Road to the Korean War: The Making of the Sino-American Confrontation* (Columbia University Press, 1994), pp. 222–223.

41 Anthony Farrar-Hockley, "A Reminiscence of the Chinese People's Volunteers in the Korean War," *China Quarterly*, no. 98 (June 1984), p. 295.

42 Clay Blair, *The Forgotten War: America in Korea, 1950–1953* (Times Books, 1987), pp. 387–390; Millett, *The War for Korea, 1950–1951*, pp. 305–306.

43 Blair, *The Forgotten War*, p. 391.

44 Appleman, *South to the Naktong*, p. 677.

45 Schnabel and Watson, *History of the Joint Chiefs of Staff*, vol. 3, p. 281.

46 James, *Years of MacArthur*, vol. 3, pp. 519–520; Truman, *Memoirs*, vol. 2, p. 373. The reason MacArthur seems to have discounted the possibility of a major intervention in Korea, despite ample evidence to the contrary, appears to be linked to his belief that the time had passed for the CPV to have derived any tactical benefits from entering the war at this time. A Far East Command daily intelligence published on October 28 sums up this view: "From a tacti-

cal viewpoint, with victorious U.S. Divisions in full deployment, it would appear that the auspicious time for such [Chinese] intervention has long since passed; it is difficult to believe that such a move, if planned, would have been postponed to a time when remnant North Korean forces have been reduced to a low point of effectiveness." See Schnabel and Watson, *History of the Joint Chiefs of Staff*, vol. 3, p. 281.

47 William T. Y'Blood, ed., *The Three Wars of Lt. Gen. George E. Stratemeyer: His Korean War Diary* (U.S. Government Printing Office, 1999), p. 257.

48 Truman, *Memoirs*, vol. 2, pp. 374–375.

49 Bradley and Blair, *General's Life*, pp. 585–589; Acheson, *Present at the Creation*, p. 464; Schnabel, *Policy and Direction*, pp. 243–246; James, *Years of MacArthur*, vol. 3, pp. 520–522.

50 Schnabel and Watson, *History of the Joint Chiefs of Staff*, vol. 3, pp. 301–302; Bradley and Blair, *General's Life*, pp. 590–591.

51 "Section 7: Chinese Communist Intervention in Korea 6 November 1950," *National Intelligence Council, Selected National Intelligence Estimates on China 1948–1976*, available at http://www.dni.gov/nic/NIC_foia_china.html.

52 Bradley and Blair, *General's Life*, p. 594.

53 An Sŭng-hwan, "Chupukhan ssoryŏn kunsa komundangŭi pukhangun chiwŏn hwaldong (1946–1953) [Soviet Military Advisory Group Support to the NKPA, 1946–1953]," p. 455.

54 Cited in ibid., p. 456.

SEVEN: *An Entirely New War*

1 *Washington Post*, November 23, 1950.

2 *New York Times*, November 23, 1950.

3 Ibid., November 21, 1950.

4 *Chicago Tribune*, November 23, 1950.

5 William T. Y'Blood, ed., *The Three Wars of Lt. Gen. George E. Stratemeyer: His Korean War Diary* (U.S. Government Printing Office, 1999), p. 299.

6 Toland, *In Mortal Combat Korea*, p. 281.

7 Blair, *The Forgotten War*, p. 440; Millett, *The War for Korea, 1950–1951*, pp. 336–337.

8 Beech, *Tokyo and Points East*, p. 196.

9 Oliver P. Smith, "Aide de Memoir . . . Korea, 1950–1: Notes by General O. P. Smith on the Operations during the First Nine Months of the Korean War," 1951, folder 3, pp. 604–610, PD 110, Collection Unit, Marine Corps Historical Center, Washington, D.C.; "Forgotten War," Clay and Joan Blair Collection, Alphabetical Files S-V, box 83, MHI.

10 There are many accounts of the battle of Changjin (Chosin) Reservoir, but the most recent is David Halberstam, *Coldest Winter: America and the Korean War* (Hyperion, 2007). The most detailed military histories of the battle are Roy E. Appleman's *East of Chosin: Entrapment and Breakout in Korea, 1950* (Texas A&M Press, 1987) and Millett, *The War for Korea, 1950–1951*.

11 Almond quoted by Martin Blumenson, "Chosin Reservoir," in Russell A. Gugeler, *Combat Actions in Korea* (U.S. Government Printing Office, 1987), pp. 69–70.

12 Donald Knox, *The Korean War*, vol. 1: *Pusan to Chosin, an Oral History* (Harcourt Brace, 1985), pp. 552–559; Roy E. Appleman, *Disaster in Korea: The Chinese Confront MacArthur* (Texas A&M University Press, 1989), p. 133.

13 *Time*, December 18, 1950, p. 26.

14 Max Hastings, *The Korean War* (Simon & Schuster, 1988), p. 159.

15 *New York Times*, December 11, 1950.

16 *Washington Post*, December 11, 1950.

17 *Time*, December 8, 1950, pp. 26–27.

18 *New York Times*, December 24, 1950; Appleman, *Disaster in Korea*, p. 328.

19 William Whitson, *The Chinese High Command* (Praeger, 1973), p. 96; John J. Tkacik Jr., "From Surprise to Stalemate: What the People's Liberation Army Learned from the Korean War—A Half Century Later," in Laurie Burkitt, Andrew Scobell, and Larry Wortzel, eds., *The Lessons of History: The Chinese People's Liberation Army at 75* (U.S. Army War College Strategic Studies Institute, July 2003), p. 303.

20 Quoted in Chester Cheng, "Through Chinese Eyes: China Crosses the Rubicon," *Journal of Oriental Studies* 31, no. 1 (1993), p. 11.

21 "Telegram, Mao Zedong to Peng Dehuai and Gao Gang, 2 December 1950," in Guang Zhang and Jian Chen, eds., *Chinese Communist Foreign Policy and the Cold War in Asia: New Documentary Evidence, 1944–1950* (Imprint, 1996), p. 211.

22 Quoted in Tkacik, "From Surprise to Stalemate," pp. 302–303.

23 Billy C. Mossman, *Ebb and Flow: November 1950–July 1951* (U.S. Government Printing Office, 1990), pp. 165–176.

24 Bill Gilbert, *Ship of Miracles* (Triumph Books, 2000), pp. 77–157.

25 *Time*, December 11, 1950, pp. 17–18. Fifty-five percent of Americans believed that the United States was in World War III. *Washington Post*, December 6, 1950.

26 *U.S. News & World Report*, December 8, 1950, pp. 16–22; Hugh Baillie, *High Tension* (Harper's & Brothers, 1959), pp. 225–226. See also James, *The Years of MacArthur*, vol. 3, p. 540; *New York Times*, December 1, 1950; Bradley and Blair, *A General's Life*, pp. 601–602.

27 Truman, *Memoirs*, vol. 2, p. 384.

28 James, *Years of MacArthur*, vol. 3, p. 542.

29 Truman, *Memoirs*, vol. 2, pp. 381–382.

30 Bradley and Blair, *General's Life*, p. 603; Matthew B. Ridgway, *The Korean War: How We Met the Challenge; How All-Out Asian War Was Averted; Why MacArthur Was Dismissed; Why Today's War Objectives Must Be Limited* (Doubleday, 1967), pp. 77–78.

31 James Chase, *Acheson: The Secretary of State Who Created the American World* (Harvard University Press, 1998), pp. 306–308; Acheson, *Present at the Creation*, pp. 476–477; George F. Kennan, *George F. Kennan: Memoirs 1950–1963* (Pantheon Books, 1972), pp. 27–35; John Lewis Gaddis, *George F. Kennan: An American Life* (Penguin, 2011), pp. 412–413.

32 Acheson, *Present at the Creation*, p. 476; Kennan, *George F. Kennan*, p. 31.

33 Acheson, *Present at the Creation*, pp. 476–477; Robert L. Beisner, *Dean Acheson: A Life in the Cold War* (Oxford University Press, 2006), p. 418; Kennan, *George F. Kennan*, p. 32.

34 Kennan, *George F. Kennan*, p. 33.

35 J. Lawton Collins, *Lightning Joe: An Autobiography* (Louisiana State University Press, 1979), p. 373; Bradley and Blair, *General's Life*, pp. 606–607.

36 Acheson, *Present at the Creation*, pp. 478–482; M. L. Dockrill, "The Foreign Office, Anglo-American Relations and the Korean War, June 1950–June 1951," *International Affairs* (Royal Institute of International Affairs) 62, no. 3 (Summer 1986), p. 466; Rosemary Foot, "Anglo-American Relations in the Korean Crisis: The British Effort to Avert Expanded War, December 1950–January 1951," *Diplomatic History* 10, no. 1 (Winter 1986), p. 49; *FRUS, 1950*, vol. 7: *Korea* (1976), pp. 1376, 1383, 1431–1432.

37 Acheson, *Present at the Creation*, p. 482.

38 *FRUS, 1950*, vol. 7, pp. 1462–1464, 1473–1475, 1479; Schnabel and Watson, *The History of the Joint Chiefs of Staff*, vol. 3, part 1, p. 379; William Stueck, ed., *The Korean War in World History* (University Press of Kentucky, 2004), p. 140; Beisner, *Dean Acheson*, p. 421.

39 Acheson, *Present at the Creation*, p. 485.

40 *Washington Post*, December 9, 1950.

41 Knox, *Korean War*, vol. 1, p. 659.

42 Appleman, *Disaster in Korea*, p. 318.

43 Knox, *Korean War*, vol. 1, p. 657.

44 Clark, *Living Dangerously in Korea*, p. 395. UN pilots charged with carrying out the strafing and bombing campaigns often justified these sorties by labeling civilians as "disguised troops" or as "supporters" of enemy activity. One pilot recalled, "If we saw civilians in the village, just because they look like civilians, from an airplane you can't tell whether he's a civilian or a soldier, anything in North Korea I consider an enemy. They're definitely not on our side, therefore I have no mercy . . . Anything supporting enemy troops is an enemy of ours; therefore, I consider it worthwhile to strike it." Sometimes, this view was justified. In one case, a pilot had spotted a group of people in a village in white clothing. The presence of women and children in the streets and their friendly waves made him hesitate. But he strafed them and received heavy fire in return from the "peaceful civilians." Raymond Sturgeon was more circumspect about his mission. Dropping napalm and strafing people was a "difficult job," "I can't say I enjoyed it. You're there and that's what you do . . . we were instructed to hit civilians because they did a lot of the work, but I just couldn't do it." John Darrell Sherwood, *Officers in Flight Suits: The Story of American Air Force Fighter Pilots in the Korean War* (New York University Press, 1996), pp. 104–106.

45 Quoted in Clark, *Living Dangerously in Korea*, pp. 393–394.

46 H. K. Shin, *A Boy Soldier's Story: Remembering Korea 1950* (University of Nebraska Press, 2001), p. 143.

47 "Seoul after Victory: Reverse Side to South Korean Rule," *London Times*, October 25, 1950.

48 Peter Kalischer, "2 U.S. Priests Protest as S. Koreans Kill Prsoners," *Washington Post*, December 17, 1950.

49 Muccio to Secretary of State, December 21, 1950, in *FRUS, 1950*, vol. 7, p. 1586.

50 "Atrocities and Trials of Political Prisoners in Korea, British Foreign Office

to Korea and Tokyo, and to Washington and United Kingdom Delegation, New York," December 19, 1950, Telegram no. 125, WO 371/84180, National Archives, Kew, UK.

51 Letter from Private Duncan to Member of Parliament, FO 371/92847, National Archives, Kew, UK.

52 *Washington Post,* December 17, 1950.

53 *New York Times,* December 19, 1950; *Washington Post,* December 18, 1950. Reports of the execution of children were never officially confirmed. Graves opened by UN investigators looking into the allegations did not find children's bodies. Ambassador Muccio also believed the reports to be false, writing on December 20 that "UNCURK had sent a military observer, Colonel White, Canada, to observe exhumation of bodies on December 17, which was conducted under orders of Home Minister and Justice Minister. Exhumation proved allegations re shooting of children wholly false." *FRUS, 1950,* vol. 7, p. 1579.

54 "Mass Executions of Reds in Korea End," *Washington Post,* December 22, 1950. See also "From Foreign Office to Korea," Telegram no. 129, December 21, 1950, WO 371/ 84180, National Archives, Kew, UK.

55 Donald W. Boose Jr., "United Nations Commission for the Unification and Rehabilitation of Korea," in Spencer C. Tucker, ed., *Encyclopedia of the Korean War: A Political, Social and Military History* (ABC-CLIO, 2000), pp. 681–683.

56 Millett, *The War for Korea, 1950–1951,* pp. 374–375. Recent reports provided by South Korea's TRC provide new evidence that children may have indeed been executed. In late 1950 and early 1951, the commission estimates that more than 460 people, including at least 23 children under the age of ten, were executed in Namyangju, about sixteen miles northeast of Seoul. The TRC also reported that children were among the victims in at least six other mass killings during this period. See Charles J. Hanley and Jae-soon Chang, "Children Executed in 1950 South Korean Killings," Associated Press, December 6, 2008. See also Kim Tong-ch'un, *Chŏnjaeng'gwa sahoe* [War and Society]. Kim headed the TRC from December 2005 to its closing in December 2010.

57 *Chicago Daily Tribune,* December 19, 1950.

58 Muccio to Secretary of State, December 20, 1950, in *FRUS, 1950,* vol. 7, p. 1580; *Chicago Tribune,* December 14, 18, and 19, 1950; *New York Times,* December 21, 1950; *Washington Post,* December 17 and 22, 1950.

59 René Cutforth, *Korean Reporter* (Allan Wingate, 1952), p. 52. For other descriptions of the conditions at Sŏdaemun Prison, see Martin Flavin, "Korean Diary," *Harper's Magazine,* March 1951.

60 *Washington Post,* December 21, 1950.

61 Muccio to Secretary of State, December 22, 1950, in *FRUS, 1950,* vol. 7, p. 1587.

62 James Plimsoll, Australian Representative to the UN Commission for the Unification and Rehabilitation of Korea, February 17, 1951, Departmental Dispatch no. 2/51 FO 371/92848, p. 3, National Archives, Kew, UK.

63 Plimsoll, Dispatch no. 2/51, pp. 4–6; *Washington Post,* December 27, 1950; Steven Casey, *Selling the Korean War: Propaganda, Politics and Public Opinion, 1950–53* (Oxford University Press, 2008), pp. 154–168. On December 22, the UNC instructed the Eighth Army Public Information Office (PIO) to check all stories emanating from Korea for security violations. Nevertheless, some

stories did get out. Reprisals against suspected leftists continued through early 1951. The most well-known massacre during this period, the Kŏch'ang Civilian Massacre, took place on the east side of the Chiri Mountains. Although the number of people reported killed during the incident varies widely, it attracted enough attention that Rhee ordered Defense Minister Shin Sŏng-mo and Home Minister Cho Pyŏng-ok to resign. Those who were directly involved in the massacre were later court-martialed and imprisoned. Kim Tong-ch'un, *Chŏnjaeng'gwa sahoe* [War and Society], pp. 301–302.

64 Cited in Richard Fried, *Men against McCarthy* (Columbia University Press, 1976), p. 102; Thomas Reeves, *The Life and Times of Joe McCarthy* (Madison Books, 1997), pp. 347–350.

65 Ronald Steel, *Walter Lippmann and the American Century* (Little, Brown, 1980), p. 474.

66 Dean Acheson, "Memories of Joe McCarthy," *Harper's Magazine*, October 1969, p. 120. Also see Acheson, *Present at the Creation*, p. 366.

67 Acheson, *Present at the Creation*, p. 365.

68 Acheson, "Memories of Joe McCarthy," p. 120; Acheson, *Present at the Creation*, p. 366.

69 Elmer Davis, "The Crusade against Acheson," *Harper's Magazine*, March 1951, p. 24.

70 *Washington Post*, December 20, 1950.

71 Davis, "Crusade against Acheson," p. 29.

72 Acheson, "Memories of Joe McCarthy," p. 124.

73 Almond Diary, December 27, 1950, Edward Mallory Almond Papers, box 10, MHI; Appleman, *Disaster in Korea*, pp. 390–397.

74 Appleman, *Disaster in Korea*, p. 314.

75 Halberstam, *Coldest Winter*, p. 486.

76 James Michener, Draft Article, December 29, 1951, MRP Official Correspondence, series 2, p. 25, MHI. Portions of the draft were later published under the title "A Tough Man for a Tough Job," *Life*, May 12, 1952, pp. 103–118.

77 Interview with Ridgway, March 5, 1988, Matthew B. Ridgway Papers, series 5, Oral Histories, 1964–1987, box 88, MHI; Ridgway, *Korean War*, p. 83.

78 Bradley and Blair, *General's Life*, p. 616.

79 Ridgway interview, "Troop Leadership at the Operational Level: The Eighth Army in Korea," Ft. Leavenworth, Kansas, May 9, 1984, series 5, Oral Histories, box 8, p. 7, MHI.

80 Ridgway, *Korean War*, p. 84.

81 Ibid., pp. 86–87.

82 Clay Blair Collection, box 68, MHI.

83 The Jeter story was well known. Clay Blair interviewed many soldiers who repeated it and it became another Ridgway legend. Blair, *Forgotten War*, p. 574.

84 Ridgway interview, "Troop Leadership at the Operational Level," p. 18.

85 Interview with Maj. Matthew P. Caulfield and Lt. Col. Robert M. Elton, August 29, 1969, Matthew Ridgway Papers, series 5, Oral Histories, box 88, MHI.

86 Interview with General Walter Winton, May 9, 1984, Matthew Ridgway Papers, series 5, Oral Histories, box 8, MHI.

87 Anthony Farrar-Hockley, "A Reminiscence of the Chinese People's Volunteers in the Korean War," *China Quarterly*, no. 98 (June 1984), p. 295.

88 Pingchao Zhu, "The Korean War at the Dinner Table," in Philip West, Steven Levine, and Jackie Hilt, eds., *America's War in Asia: A Cultural Approach to History and Memory* (M. E. Sharpe, 1998), p. 185.

89 Guang Zhang and Jian Chen, eds., *Chinese Communist Foreign Policy and the Cold War in Asia: New Documentary Evidence, 1944–1950* (Imprint, 1996), pp. 214–215; Xiobing Li, Allan R. Millett, and Bin Yu, eds., *Mao's Generals Remember Korea* (University Press of Kansas, 2001), p. 18.

90 Cited in J. Chester Cheng, "The Korean War through Chinese Eyes: China Crosses the Rubicon," *Journal of Oriental Studies* 31, no. 1 (1993), p. 13.

91 Ibid., p. 18.

92 Shen Zhihua, "Sino-North Korean Conflict and Its Resolution during the Korean War," *CWIHP Bulletin*, no. 14/15 (Winter 2003/Spring 2004), p. 10.

93 Ridgway, *Korean War*, p. 93.

94 Li et al., eds., *Mao's Generals Remember Korea*, p. 19.

95 Peng Dehuai, *Memoirs of a Chinese Marshall: The Autobiographical Notes of Peng Dehuai (1898–1974)* (University of Hawaii Press, 2005), p. 478.

96 Zhang Da, "Resist America, Aid Korea!" in Zhang Lijia and Calum MacLeod, eds., *China Remembers* (Oxford University Press, 1999), p. 27.

97 Cited in Roy B. Appleman, *Ridgway Duels for Korea* (Texas A&M University Press, 1990), p. 155.

98 Shen, "Sino-North Korean Conflict," pp. 15–16; Chen Jian, *Mao's China and the Cold War* (University of North Carolina Press, 2001), p. 94.

99 Bradley and Blair, *General's Life*, p. 619; full text of MacArthur's January 10 telegram (quoted in text) in Matthew Ridgway Papers, series 3, Official Papers, Eighth Army, Special Files, December 1950–April 1951, box 68, MHI.

100 Truman, *Memoirs*, vol. 2, p. 492.

101 Acheson, *Present at the Creation*, p. 515.

102 Collins, *Lightning Joe*, pp. 253–254.

103 Bradley and Blair, *General's Life*, p. 623.

104 *Washington Post*, January 15, 1951.

105 Chen, *Mao's China and the Cold War*, p. 94.

106 Acheson, *Present at the Creation*, p. 513.

107 Beisner, *Dean Acheson*, p. 423.

108 *New York Times*, January 13, 1951; Beisner, *Dean Acheson*, pp. 423–424; Bevin Alexander, *Korea: The First War We Lost* (Hippocrene Books, 1986), p. 388.

109 Robert F. Futrell, *The United States Air Force in Korea, 1950–1953* (U.S. Government Printing Office, 1988), p. 273; Blair, *Forgotten War*, p. 652.

110 Ridgway, *Korean War*, p. 105.

111 Evgueni Bajanov, "Assessing the Politics of the Korean War, 1949–1951," *CWIHP Bulletin: The Cold War in Asia*, no. 6/7 (Winter 1995), p. 90.

112 Quoted in Appleman, *Ridgway Duels for Korea*, p. 219.

113 Blair, *Forgotten War*, p. 669; Millett, *The War for Korea, 1950–1951*, pp. 398–399.

114 Ridgway telegram to GHQ, February 3, 1951, Clay Blair Collection, box 68, MHI.

115 Maj. Gen. George Craig Stewart, "My Service with the Second Division during the Korean War," p. 17, Clay Blair Collection, Forgotten War, Alphabetical Files S, box 77, MHI.

116 Blair, *Forgotten War*, p. 690; Paik Sun Yup, *From Pusan to Panmunjom: Wartime Memoirs of the Republic of Korea's First Four-Star General* (Brassey's, 1992), p. 125.

117 Gary Turbark, "Massacre at Hoengsŏng," *Veterans of Foreign Wars Magazine*, February 2001.

118 Blair, *Forgotten War*, pp. 711–712; Millett, *The War for Korea, 1950–1951*, p. 391.

119 Peng, *Memoirs of a Chinese Marshal*, pp. 479–480.

EIGHT: *Quest for Victory*

1 Bradley and Blair, *A General's Life* (Simon & Schuster, 1983), p. 626; Schnabel and Watson, *The History of the Joint Chiefs of Staff*, vol. 3, p. 468; *FRUS, 1951*, vol. 7: *Korea and China, Part 1* (1983), pp. 251–256.

2 *New York Times*, March 24, 1951.

3 *Washington Post*, March 27, 1951; Beisner, *Dean Acheson: A Life in the Cold War*, p. 427.

4 Acheson, *Present at the Creation*, p. 519.

5 Truman, *Memoirs*, vol. 2, pp. 441–442.

6 David McCullough, *Truman* (Simon & Schuster, 1992), p. 837.

7 "Collins Interview with Lt. Col. Charles C. Sperow," 1972, pp. 309–311, Senior Oral History Program Project, MHI.

8 McCullough, *Truman*, p. 837.

9 Acheson, *Present at the Creation*, p. 519.

10 *Washington Post*, April 6, 1951.

11 *FRUS, 1951*, vol. 7: *Part 1*, p. 299.

12 Bradley and Blair, *General's Life*, p. 630.

13 *FRUS, 1951*, vol. 7: *Part 1*, p. 309; Bradley and Blair, *General's Life*, p. 630.

14 Robert H. Ferrell, ed., *Off the Record: The Private Papers of Harry S. Truman* (Harper & Row, 1980), pp. 210–211.

15 Rogers M. Anders, ed., *Forging the Atomic Shield: Excerpts from the Office Diary of Gordon E. Dean* (University of North Carolina Press, 1987), p. 137.

16 Bradley and Blair, *General's Life*, pp. 630–631.

17 Roger Dingman, "Atomic Diplomacy during the Korean War," *International Security* 13, no. 3 (Winter 1988/89), p. 74; Daniel Calingaert, "Nuclear Weapons and the Korean War," *Journal of Strategic Studies* 11, no. 2 (June 1988), pp. 177–202; Steven Casey, *Selling the Korean War: Propaganda, Politics and Public Opinion, 1950–53* (Oxford University Press, 2008), pp. 230–231.

18 Anders, *Forging the Atomic Shield*, p. 140.

19 McCullough, *Truman*, p. 840.

20 James, *The Years of McArthur*, vol. 3, p. 600; Clay Blair, *The Forgotten War: America in Korea, 1950–1953* (Times Books, 1987), pp. 788, 794–797; Robert J. Donovan, *Tumultuous Years: The Presidency of Harry S. Truman, 1949–1953* (W. W. Norton, 1967), pp. 340–362.

21 Matthew Ridgway, *Soldier: The Memoirs of Matthew B. Ridgway, as Told to Harold H. Martin* (Harper, 1956), p. 223.

22 Mathew Ridgway Papers, series 3, "Official Papers," box 72, MHI.

23 James, *The Years of MacArthur*, vol. 3, pp. 602–603.

24 William J. Sebald and Russell Brines, *With MacArthur in Japan: A Personal History of the Occupation Ambassador William Sebald* (W. W. Norton, 1965), p. 235.

25 Frank Tremaine cited in "MacArthur," *American Experience*, PBS, Enhanced Transcript, p. 29, available at http://www.pbs.org/wgbh/amex/macarthur/filmmore/transcript/index.html (accessed October 1, 2010).

26 *Time*, April 30, 1951, p. 23.

27 *Life*, April 23, 1951, pp. 42–46.

28 *Time*, April 23, 1951, p. 28; James, *Years of MacArthur*, vol. 3, p. 610.

29 *Washington Post*, April 12, 1951; McCullough, *Truman*, pp. 846–847; James, *Years of MacArthur*, vol. 3, pp. 607–608; Merle Miller, *Plain Speaking: An Oral Biography of Harry S. Truman* (Berkley, 1974), pp. 311–312; *United Press International*, May 12, 1951.

30 General (Ret) Hong Xuezhi, "The CCPV's Combat and Logistics," in Xiobing Li, Allan R. Millett, and Bin Yu, eds., *Mao's Generals Remember Korea* (University Press of Kansas, 2001), pp. 131–132.

31 Shu Guang Zhang, *Mao's Military Romanticism* (University Press of Kansas, 1995), pp. 145–146.

32 Li et al., eds., *Mao's Generals Remember Korea*, p. 125.

33 Blair, *Forgotten War*, p. 807.

34 Paschal N. and Mary H. Strong, "Sabres and Safety Pins" [Oral History], p. 414, Clay and Joan Blair Collection, "Forgotten War," Alphabetical Files S–V, box 83, MHI; Bittman Barth, "Tropic Lightning and Taro Leaf in Korea" [Oral History], pp. 74–75, MHI.

35 Ridgway, *The Korean War*, pp. 162–164.

36 "Memorandum for Commanding General, Eighth Army," April 25, 1951, Matthew Ridgway Papers, series 3, Official Papers, CINC Far East, 1951–53, box 73, MHI.

37 Ridgway, "Ltr, CINCFE to CG Eighth Army, 25 April 1951, sub. Letter of Instructions," Matthew Ridgway Papers, series 3, Official Papers, CINC Far East, 1951–53, box 73, MHI.

38 Bradley and Blair, *General's Life*, p. 640.

39 "Instructions Given Orally to Colonel Paul F. Smith, in the Presence of Major General Doyle Hickey, Chief of Staff, GHQ, FEC," April 26, 1951, Matthew B. Ridgway Papers, series 3, Official Papers, Commander-in-Chief Far East, 1951–52, box 72, MHI.

40 Interview with General James A. Van Fleet by Colonel Bruce H. Williams, tape 4, March 3, 1973, p. 23, MHI.

41 Quoted in Anthony Farrar-Hockley, *The Edge of the Sword* (Frederick Muller, 1954), p. 49.

42 Ibid., p. 54.

43 E. J. Kahn, "A Reporter in Korea: No One but the Glosters," *The New Yorker*, May 26, 1951, p. 15; Barry Taylor, "Open Road Barred," *Military History* 7, no. 5 (April 1991), pp. 47–52; Brian Catchpole, "The Commonwealth in Korea," *History Today* (November 1988), pp. 33–39.

44 Blair, *Forgotten War*, p. 847.

45 Van Fleet to Ridgway, May 11, 1951, Matthew B. Ridgway Papers, series 2, Correspondence Official, Eighth U.S. Army, January 1951–June 1951, "N-Z," box 13, MHI.

46 *Life*, May 11, 1953, p. 132.

47 Blair, *Forgotten War*, p. 859; Millett, *The War for Korea, 1950–1951*, pp. 443–444.

48 Interview with Lieutenant General Almond (Retired) by Captain Fergusson, March 29, 1975, side 1, tape 5, p. 26, Edward Almond Papers, MHI.

49 *Life*, May 11, 1953, p. 132.

50 Van Fleet interview, p. 53. See also Van Fleet, "How we can win with what we have," *Life*, May 18, 1953, pp. 157–172.

51 Mathew Ridgway Papers, series 3, Official Papers, Commander-in-Chief Far East, 1951–52, box 72, MHI.

52 *Life*, May 11, 1953, p. 127.

NINE: *The Stalemate*

1   *FRUS, 1951*, vol. 7: *Korea and China, Part 1* (1983), p. 547.

2   Quoted in Blair, *The Forgotten War*, p. 925.

3   Stalin to Mao, June 5, 1951, *CWIHP Bulletin: The Cold War in Asia*, no. 6/7 (Winter 1995), p. 59.

4   *FRUS, 1951*, vol. 7: *Part 1*, p. 507.

5   Mao to Stalin, June 13, 1951, *CWHIP Bulletin: The Cold War in Asia*, no. 6/7 (Winter 1995), p. 61.

6   Kathryn Weathersby, "New Russian Documents on the Korean War," *CWIHP Bulletin: The Cold War in Asia*, no. 6/7 (Winter 1995), pp. 34–35.

7   Chen, *Mao's China and the Cold War*, p. 100.

8   Ibid., p. 101.

9   C. Turner Joy, *How Communists Negotiate* (Macmillan, 1955), p. 4.

10 Quoted in Blair, *Forgotten War*, p. 933.

11 Chen, *Mao's China and the Cold War*, p. 100.

12 Walter G. Hermes, *Truce Tent and Fighting Front* (U.S. Government Printing Office, 1988), p. 19.

13 Joy, *How Communists Negotiate*, pp. 4–9.

14 Mao telegram to Stalin, July 3, 1951, *CWIHP Bulletin: The Cold War in Asia*, no. 6/7 (Winter 1995), p. 66.

15 Hermes, *Truce Tent*, pp. 26–35.

16 Mao to Stalin, August 12, 1951, *CWIHP Bulletin: The Cold War in Asia*, no. 6/7 (Winter 1995), p. 68.

17 *FRUS, 1951*, vol. 7: *Part 1*, p. 745.

18 Mao to Stalin, August 27, 1951, *CWIHP Bulletin: The Cold War in Asia*, no. 6/7 (Winter 1995), p. 68; Stueck, *The Korean War: An International History*, pp. 228–229.

19 *FRUS, 1951*, vol. 7: *Part 1*, pp. 848–849, 850–852.

20 Mao to Stalin, August 27, 1951, p. 68.

21 Matthew B. Ridgway Papers, series 3, Official Papers, Commander-in-Chief Far East, 1951–52, box 72, MHI.

22 *FRUS, 1951*, vol. 7: *Part 1*, pp. 774–776.

23 Rosemary Foot, "Anglo-American Relations in the Korean Crisis: The British Effort to Avert Expanded War, December 1950–January 1951," *Diplomatic History* 10, no. 1 (Winter 1986), p. 66.

24 Shiv Dayal, *India's Role in the Korea Question* (Delhi: Chand, 1959), p. 143.

25 Stueck, *Korean War*, pp. 236–237.

26 Quoted in Blair, *Forgotten War*, p. 957; *FRUS, 1951*, vol. 7: *Part 1*, p. 1099.

27 *New York Times*, November 17, 1951.

28 *FRUS, 1951*, vol. 7: *Part 1*, p. 1093.

29 Ibid., p. 618.

30 Ibid., p. 622.

31 Foot, "Anglo-American Relations in the Korean Crisis," p. 88.

32 J. Lawton Collins, *War in Peacetime: The History and Lessons of Korea* (Houghton Mifflin, 1969), p. 340.

33 *FRUS, 1951*, vol. 7: *Part 1*, pp. 857–858.

34 The Geneva Convention of 1949, Convention (III) relative to the Treatment of Prisoners of War, Geneva, August 12, 1949, Article 118, available at http://www.icrc.org/ihl.nsf/FULL/375?OpenDocument (accessed January 2009).

35 U. Alexis Johnson (with Jeff Olivarius McAllister), *Right Hand of Power: The Memoirs of an American Diplomat* (Prentice-Hall, 1984), p. 133; Foot, "Anglo-American Relations in the Korean Crisis," pp. 88–89.

36 Hermes, *Truce Tent*, pp. 135–136. Among the many controversial decisions made at Yalta was the agreement that when World War II ended in Europe, Soviet citizens, regardless of their individuals histories, be sent back to the Soviet Union. Although the agreement reached at Yalta did not specifically state that the Allies must return Soviet citizens against their will, this was what happened in many cases. Rather than return to face the firing squad or the Gulag, many Soviet citizens who were forced to return committed suicide instead. For a heartbreaking account of the forced repatriation of Soviet citizens after the war, see Anne Applebaum's Pulitzer prize–winning book, *Gulag: A History* (Anchor Books, 2003), pp. 435–439.

37 Johnson, *Right Hand of Power*, p. 133.

38 *FRUS, 1952–54*, vol. 15: *Korea, Part 1* (1984), p. 401.

39 Allen Goodman, ed., *Negotiating while Fighting: The Diary of Admiral C. Turner Joy at the Korean Armistice Conference* (Stanford University Press, 1978), p. 137.

40 Hermes, *Truce Tent*, p. 141; Goodman, *Negotiating while Fighting*, p. 154. According to the Hanley Report of November 1951 on North Korean war crimes, compiled by Colonel James M. Hanley, chief of the Eighth Army's war crimes section, 2,513 U.S. POWs and more than 25,000 South Korean POWs were killed. See *Korean Atrocities: Report of the Committee on Government Operations Made through Its Permanent Subcommittee on Investigations by Its Subcommittee on Korean War Atrocities Pursuant to S. Res. 40* (U.S. Government Printing Office, 1954). The report can be accessed at http://www.loc.gov/rr/frd/Military_Law/pdf/KW-atrocities-Report.pdf.

41 Hermes, *Truce Tent*, p. 142.

42 Goodman, *Negotiating while Fighting*, p. 181; Major General (Ret) Chai Chengwen, "The Korean Truce Negotiations," in Xioabing Li, Allan R. Millett, and Bin Yu, eds., *Mao's Generals Remember Korea* (University Press of Kansas, 2001), p. 216.

43 Chai, "Korean Truce Negotiations," p. 217.

44 Goodman, *Negotiating while Fighting*, p. 208.

45 Johnson, *Right Hand of Power*, p. 135.

46 Joy, *How Communists Negotiate*, p. 152.

47 Johnson, *Right Hand of Power*, p. 135.

48 Anthony Eden, March 21, 1952, FO 371/99564, National Archives, Kew, UK.

49 Johnson, *Right Hand of Power*, p. 139.
50 *FRUS, 1952–54*, vol. 15: *Part 1*, pp. 76–77, 58–59.
51 Johnson, *Right Hand of Power*, p. 139.
52 Chai, "Korean Truce Negotiations," pp. 217–224.
53 *Washington Post*, February 26, 1952.

TEN: *"Let Them March Till They Die"*

1 Philip Crosbie, *March Till They Die* (Browne & Nolan, 1955), p. 54.
2 "Maryknoll Missionary Follows in Steps of Missionary Bishop in North Korea," *Catholic News Agency*, May 13, 2008.
3 Philip Crosbie, *Pencilling Prisoner* (Hawthorne Press, 1954), p. 98.
4 Ibid., p. 101.
5 Larry Zellers, *In Enemy Hands: A Prisoner in North Korea* (University Press of Kentucky, 1991), p. 85.
6 Nugent, vol. 4, Department of the Army Staff Judge Advocate (DASJA), p. 692. The bulk of primary sources were obtained from the DASJA through the Freedom of Information Act by Raymond B. Lech, to whom I am indebted for giving me access to them. The material consists of eighty volumes of transcripts of the fourteen U.S. Army court-martial proceedings. Each transcript is formally known by the name of the person being tried. The transcripts are now in the MHI; Nugent, vol. 8, DASJA, p. 2015; vol. 12, DASJA, pp. 139–140; Larry Zellers, *In Enemy Hands: A Prisoner of North Korea* (University of Kentucky Press, 1991), p. 88. Also see Raymond B. Lech, *Broken Soldiers* (University of Illinois Press, 2000).
7 Zellers, *In Enemy Hands*, pp. 90–91.
8 Ibid., p. 100.
9 Clark, *Living Dangerously in Korea*, p. 380.
10 Crosbie, *Pencilling Prisoners*, pp. 141–146.
11 "Testimony of Major Green," Nugent, vol. 8, DASJA, p. 2044.
12 Crosbie, *Pencilling Prisoners*, p. 181.
13 "Testimony of Major Booker," Nugent, vol. 8, DASJA, pp. 2144–2146.
14 Liles, vol. 4B, DASJA, pp. 1817–1818.
15 Fleming, vol. 11, DASJA, pp. 1418, 1477.
16 Ibid., pp. 1497–1500.
17 Ibid., p. 1516.
18 Liles, vol. 2, DASJA, p. 74.
19 "Testimony of Captain Sidney Esensten," Liles, vol. 2B, DASJA, p. 82; "Testimony of Anderson," Liles, vol. 2, DASJA, p. 428. See also Raymond B. Lech, *Broken Soldiers* (University of Illinois Press, 2000), pp. 42–48.
20 Liles, vol. 2, DASJA, p. 86.
21 Liles, vol. 1, DASJA, p. 143.
22 Ibid., pp. 1443–1444.
23 Erwin, vol. 4, DASJA, p. 1146.
24 Liles, vol. 1, DASJA, p. 144.
25 Erwin, vol. 3, DASJA, pp. 815–816.
26 Fleming, vol. 11, DASJA, p. 1544.
27 Olson, vol. 2, DASJA, pp. 29–30.

28   "Testimony of PFC Theodore Hilburn," Olson, vol. 3, DASJA, p. 133.

29   "Testimony of Staff Sergeant Leonard J. Maffioli," Olson, vol. 3, DASJA, p. 175.

30   "Testimony of Master Sergeant Chester Mathis," Olson, vol. 3, DASJA, p. 213.

31   Olson, vol. 3, DASJA, p. 88.

32   "General Court-Martial Order, 10 June 1955," Olson, vol. 2, DASJA, pp. 22–23.

33   "Harrison Testimony," Olson, vol. 3, DASJA, p. 104.

34   Olson, vol. 3, DASJA, p. 278.

35   Fleming, vol. 2, DASJA, p. 305.

36   Liles, vol. 5, DASJA, pp. 279–280.

37   Fleming, vol. 4, DASJA, p. 207; vol. 9, DASJA, p. 1061.

38   Lech, *Broken Soldiers*, p. 124.

39   Liles, vol. 2B, DASJA, p. 724; Lech, *Broken Soldiers*, p. 124.

40   Liles, vol. 3, DASJA, p. 944.

41   Ibid., p. 1053.

42   Farrar-Hockley, *The Edge of the Sword*, p. 192.

43   "Dunn Testimony," Nugent, vol. 5, DASJA, pp. 996–1024.

44   Liles, vol. 1, DASJA, p. 154.

45   "Testimony of Major Harold Kaschko," Liles, vol. 1, DASJA, p. 211.

46   Lech, *Broken Soldiers*, p. 147. "Testimony of Major David McGhee," Fleming, vol. 10, DASJA, p. 1163.

47   Fleming, vol. 10, DASJA, p. 1164.

48   Liles, vol. 1, DASJA, p. 148; "Affidavit of Captain Waldron Berry, 3 Nov 1954," Nugent, vol. 1, DASJA, p. 98.

49   "Affidavit of J. D. Bryant, Captain, United States Air Force, 3 Nov 1954," Nugent, vol. 1, DASJA, p. 98.

50   Fleming, vol. 9, DASJA, pp. 1150–1151.

51   "Testimony of Van Orman," Fleming, vol. 7, DASJA, p. 483.

52   Alley, vol. 4, DASJA, p. 205.

53   "Deposition of Comdr R. M. Bagwell, 10 Sep 1954," Fleming, vol. 4, DASJA, p. 2.

54   "Affidavit of Major Filmore Wilson McAbee, 22 Sep 1954," Nugent, vol. 1, DASJA, p. 354.

55   Cho Ch'ang-ho, *Toraon saja* [Return of a Dead Man] (Seoul: Chiho ch'ulp'ansa, 1995).

56   Pak Chin-hŭng, *Toraon p'aeja* [Return of the Defeated] (Seoul: Yŏksa pip'yŏngsa, 2001), p. 73.

57   Ibid., pp. 78–79, 91–92.

58   Ibid., pp. 94, 98–99.

59   Ibid., pp. 100–101.

60   Ibid., p. 102.

61   Ibid., p. 100.

62   Ibid., p. 104.

63   Ibid., p. 116.

64   Ibid., p. 121.

65   "Hardly Known, Not Yet Forgotten: South Korean POWs Tell Their Story," *Radio Free Asia*, January 25, 2007, at http://www.rfa.org/english/news/politics/korea_pow-20070125.html (accessed March 5, 2010).

66   Cho reiterated this claim in his testimony before the U.S. Congress on April

27, 2006. His testimony stated, "As a POW, I didn't even know that the war ended and the exchange of POWs had been occurred. I've learned that fact long after war ended. All of returned POWs whom I've met were not much different. They didn't know that the exchange of POWs had been occurred either." *North Korea: Human Rights Update and International Abduction Issues: Joint Hearing before the Subcommittee on Asia and the Pacific and the Subcommittee on Africa, Global Human Rights and International Operations of the Committee on International Relations, House of Representatives, 109th Congress, 2nd Session, April 27, 2008* (U.S. Government Printing Office, 2006), p. 43. This congressional hearing provides many more details about Cho's circumstances and stories of other ROK POWs' experience in North Korea.

67 "Hardly Known, Not Yet Forgotten," *Radio Free Asia.*

68 Cho Song-hŭn, *Han'gukchŏn kukkunp'oro silt'aepunsŏk* [An Analysis of the Actual Conditions of South Korean POWs] (Seoul: Kukpangbu kunsa p'yŏnch'an yŏnguso, 2006), p. 103.

69 Ibid., pp. 56–57. See also *2010 White Paper on Human Rights in North Korea* (Korea Institute for National Unification, 2010), pp. 480–485. http://www.kinu.or.kr/upload/neoboard/DATA04/2010%20white%20paper.pdf (accessed October 15, 2012). For an excellent description of the recent plight of former South Korean POWs, see Melanie Kirkpatrick, *Escape from North Korea: The Untold Stories of Asia's Underground Railroad* (Encounter Books, 2012), pp. 117–133.

70 "Soviet Embassy Charge d'Affaire to North Korea S.P. Suzdalev to Foreign Minister Molotov," December 2, 1953, in Yang Chin-sam, "Chŏnjaenggi chungguk chidowa pukhan chidobu saiŭi mosun'gwa kaltung [Contradictions and Discord between the Chinese and North Korean Authorities during the Korean War]," *Hanguk chŏnjaengŭi saeroun yŏngu* [New Research on the Korean War], vol. 2 (2002), p. 619. See also *Yonhap News,* June 16, 2005.

71 Cho, *Han'gukchŏn kukkunp'oro silt'aepunsŏk* [An Analysis of the Actual Conditions of South Korean POWs During the Korean War], pp. 94–95.

72 Pak, *Toraon p'aeja* [Return of the Defeated], p. 199.

73 Ibid., p. 204.

74 Ibid., pp. 218–219.

75 Ibid., pp. 211–212.

76 Ibid., pp. 226–228.

77 Ibid., pp. 232–233.

78 Ibid., p. 206.

ELEVEN: *Propaganda Wars*

1 *FRUS, 1951,* vol. 7: *Korea and China, Part 1* (1983), p. 176.

2 Sahr Conway-Lanz, *Collateral Damage: American, Noncombatant Immunity and Atrocity after World War II* (Routledge, 2006), p. 151. Biographical sketch of Charles Joy at http://www.harvardsquarelibrary.org/unitarians/joy.html (accessed April 6, 2009).

3 Quoted in Balázs Szalontai, "The Four Horsemen of the Apocalypse in North Korea: The Forgotten Side of a Not-So-Forgotten War," in Chris Springer and Balázs Szalontai, *North Korea Caught in Time* (Garnet, 2010), p. xii.

4 Freda Kirchwey, "Liberation by Death," *Nation*, March 10, 1951, p. 216.

5 Harold Ickes, "Sherman's Hell, Korea's Hell," *New Republic*, March 1951, p. 18.

6 Conway-Lanz, *Collateral Damage*, p. 155.

7 John Gittings, "Talks, Bombs and Germs: Another Look at the Korean War," *Journal of Contemporary Asia* 5, no. 2 (1975), p. 214.

8 Soviet journalist Vassili Kornilov, quoted in Springer and Szalontai, *North Korea Caught in Time*, p. 20.

9 *Washington Post*, May 16, 1951.

10 The belief that airpower could have coercive force by itself had existed since the invention of airpower in World War I. But World War II, the first time massive strategic bombing was employed to both destroy and terrorize, demonstrated that it had an opposite effect in both Germany and Japan. The bombing seemed to embolden the bombed even more to fight and resist. In Germany, war production actually increased toward the end of the war even as factories were destroyed. There is significant evidence as well that not even the atomic bombs, the ultimate strategic bombing, convinced the Japanese people to surrender. See, for example, *The U.S. Strategic Bombing Survey* (*USSBS*), a massive detailed assessment of the effects of bombing in Germany and Japan. The report, issued in the fall of 1945, concluded that strategic bombing had a decisive effect, but subsequent analyses concluded otherwise. A good introduction and summary as well as guides for finding the hundreds of *USSBS*s available can be accessed at http://www.ussbs.com/ (accessed May 7, 2009). Tsuyoshi Hasegawa, in *Racing the Enemy Stalin, Truman, and the Surrender of Japan* (Harvard University Press, 2006), argued that rather than the atomic bombs, the Soviet Union's entry into the war was the decisive factor that convinced Japan to capitulate. The debate over the efficacy of airpower still rages today, for example, whether air attacks deterred Serbia in Kosovo in 1999 and the efficacy of the "shock and awe" campaign against Iraq in 2003. Daniel Byman and Matthew Waxman provide good summaries of the advocates of Kosovo airpower in their criticism of it in "Kosovo and the Great Air Power Debate," *International Security* 24, no. 4 (Spring 2000), pp. 5-38.

11 Robert F. Futrell, *The United States Air Force in Korea, 1950-1953* (U.S. Government Printing Office, 1988), pp. 313-340; Robert A. Pape, *Bombing to Win: Air Power and Coercion* (Cornell University Press, 1996), pp. 147-149.

12 Quoted in John J. Tkacik Jr., "From Surprise to Stalemate: What the People's Liberation Army Learned from the Korean War—A Half Century Later," in Laurie Burkitt, Andrew Scobell, and Larry Wortzel, eds., *The Lessons of History: The Chinese People's Liberation Army at 75* (U.S. Army War College Strategic Studies Institute, July 2003), pp. 303-304.

13 Quoted in ibid., pp. 304-305.

14 Quoted in ibid., p. 308.

15 General (Ret.) Yang Dezhi, "Command Experience in Korea," in Xiaobing Li, Allan R. Millet, and Bin Yu, eds., *Mao's Generals Remember Korea* (University Press of Kansas, 2001), pp. 153-155; Tkacik, "From Surprise to Stalemate," p. 311.

16 Yang, "Command Experience in Korea," p. 154.

17 Quoted in Tkacik, "From Surprise to Stalemate," p. 313.

18 By the fall of 1951 eighteen of twenty-two major cities in North Korea had already been at least half obliterated. In early 1952, the Far East Air Force (FEAF) began to target power plants and dams along the Yalu River. The huge Suiho hydroelectrical plant was destroyed in June 1952. The Sokam and Chasan Reservoirs in South P'yŏngan province were destroyed in May 1953, causing huge floods that destroyed hundreds of villages and much livestock and food. See Conrad Crane, *American Airpower Strategy in Korea, 1950–1953* (University Press of Kansas, 2000), pp. 122–124. See also Michael S. Sherry, *The Rise of American Air Power: The Creation of Armageddon* (Yale University Press, 1987).

19 "Crawford Sams Memoir: Medic, 1910–1955," pp. 709–710, Crawford Sams Papers, box 1, MHI.

20 Ibid., p. 715.

21 Ibid., p. 716.

22 Ibid., p. 718; *Renmin Ribao* [People's Daily] published in English in *Foreign Radio Broadcasts*, May 4, 1952.

23 The pioneer work exposing the activities of Unit 731 and subsequent cover-up was done by John W. Powell. See his "Japan's Germ Warfare: The U.S. Cover-up of a War Crime," *Bulletin of Concerned Asian Scholars* 12, no. 2 (1980), pp. 2–17, and "Japan's Biological Weapons, 1930–1945: A Hidden Chapter in History," *Bulletin of Concerned Asian Scholars* 37, no. 8 (October 1981), pp. 43–52. See also Sheldon Harris, *Factories of Death: Japanese Biological Warfare 1932–45 and the American Cover-Up* (Routledge, 1994), p. 54.

24 Milton Leitenberg, "New Evidence on the Korean War Biological Warfare Allegations: Background and Analysis," *CWIHP Bulletin*, no. 11 (Winter 1998), pp. 187–188.

25 Ruth Rogaski, *Hygienic Modernity: Meanings of Health and Disease in Treaty-Port China* (University of California Press, 2004), p. 293.

26 *Renmin Ribao* [People's Daily] published in English in *Foreign Radio Broadcasts*, April 9, 1952.

27 Fang Shih-shan, "Effects of War on the Health of the People," *Chinese Medical Journal* 71, no. 5 (September–October 1953), p. 324.

28 William Dean, *General Dean's Story* (Viking, 1952), p. 276.

29 William E. Banghart, "Court Martial Papers," vol. 1, Department of the Army Staff Judge Advocate (DASJA), pp. 199–200, MHI.

30 Yang, "Command Experience in Korea," p. 166.

31 Rogaski, *Hygienic Modernity*, p. 295.

32 The Three-Anti campaign launched in late 1951 aimed to eradicate (1) corruption, (2) waste, and (3) bureaucracy. The Five-Anti campaign was launched in January 1952 to eliminate (1) bribery, (2) theft of state property, (3) tax evasion, (4) cheating on government contracts, and (5) stealing state economic information. The two campaigns evolved into an all-out war against the bourgeoisie. See also Rogaski, *Hygienic Modernity*, pp. 288–289; Jonathan Spence, *The Search for Modern China* (W. W. Norton, 1990), pp. 536–538.

33 Quoted in Simon Winchester, *The Man Who Loved China* (HarperCollins, 2008), p. 201.

34 Rogaski, *Hygienic Modernity*, pp. 288–289.

35 Lynn T. White, "Changing Concepts of Corruption in Communist China: Early 1950s versus Early 1980s," in Yu-Ming Shaw, ed., *Changes and Continuities in Chinese Communism* (Westview Press, 1988), pp. 327–330.

36 Rogaski, *Hygienic Modernity*, p. 289.

37 A. M. Halpern, "Bacteriological Warfare Accusations in Two Asian Communist Campaigns," in U.S. Air Force, *Project Rand Research Memorandum 25* (April 1952), pp. 54–55.

38 Philip Short, *Mao: A Life* (Henry Holt, 2000), pp. 436–437.

39 *New York Times*, March 13, 1951.

40 "Telegram to V.M. Molotov from Beijing from the Ambassador of the USSR to the PRC, V.V. Kuznetsov, about the Results of a Conversation with Mao Zedong on 11 May 1953 [Not Dated]," *CWIHP Bulletin*, no. 11 (Winter 1998), p. 183.

41 *Department of State Bulletin*, vol. 26, pt. 1, April–June 1952, pp. 427–428.

42 Ibid., pt. 2, April–June 1952, pp. 925–926.

43 Milton Leitenberg, "New Russian Evidence on the Korean War Biological Warfare Allegations: Background and Analysis," *CWIHP Bulletin*, no. 11 (Winter 1998), p. 190. According to Kathryn Weathersby, in anticipation of Acheson's request to the chairman of the ICRC that the ICRC investigate the Chinese and North Korean charges of bacteriological warfare, Soviet Foreign Minister Andrei Gromyko began to immediately prepare for a strategy to refuse such a visit. Citing the Geneva Convention, which specified that "the parties participating in armed conflict would themselves investigate the facts of any alleged violation of the convention," Gromyko advised the North Koreans to refuse any proposal made by the ICRC to conduct on-site investigations. The Soviets at the highest level were also involved in helping the North Koreans avoid inspections proposed by members of the World Health Organization (WHO). When North Korean leaders received the third, and last, telegram from UN Secretary General Trygvie Lie on April 6 requesting that the WHO be allowed to visit North Korea for inspections, the ambassador to North Korea, V. N. Razuvaev, advised that the DPRK respond that "the proposal cannot be accepted because the World Health Organization did not have proper international authority." No doubt, it was because of intense international pressure to prove the truth of allegations, and to fend off further requests for inspections, that the International Scientific Commission, the group organized in 1952 by the Soviet-bloc World Peace Organization, was formed to provide its own on-site investigations. Kathryn Weathersby, "Deceiving the Deceivers: Moscow, Beijing, Pyongyang, and the Allegations of Bacteriological Weapons Use in Korea," *CWIHP Bulletin*, no. 11 (Winter 1998), p. 178.

44 *New York Times*, April 2, 1952.

45 Winchester, *Man Who Loved China*, p. 204.

46 *Report of the International Scientific Commission for the Investigation of the Facts concerning Bacteriological Warfare in Korea and China, with Appendixes* (Commission, 1952), p. 60.

47 Albert E. Cowdrey, "'Germ Warfare' and Public Heath in the Korean Conflict," *Journal of the History of Medicine and Allied Sciences* 39 (April 1984), pp. 169–170.

48 Quoted in Ruth Rogaski, "Nature, Annihilation, and Modernity: China's

Korean War Germ-Warfare Experience Reconsidered," *Journal of Asian Studies* 61, no. 2 (May 2002), p. 403.

49 Ibid., pp. 403–404.

50 Needham to Dr. Alfred Fisk, October 11, 1953, cited in Tom Buchanan, "The Courage of Galileo: Joseph Needham and the 'Germ Warfare' Allegations in the Korean War," *History* 86, no. 284 (October 2001), p. 513.

51 Winchester, *Man Who Loved China*, p. 206.

52 Rogaski, "Nature, Annihilation, and Modernity," p. 402.

53 Cowdrey, " 'Germ Warfare' and Public Health," p. 170.

54 *New York Times*, April 3, 1952.

55 Ibid., May 31, 1952.

56 Weathersby, "Deceiving the Deceivers," p. 177. See also Leitenberg, "New Russian Evidence on the Korean War Biological Warfare Allegations," pp. 185–199.

57 "Explanatory Note from Lt. Gen. V.N. Razuvaev, Ambassador of the USSR to the DPRK and Chief Military Advisor to the KPA, to L.P. Beria," April 19, 1953, *CWIHP Bulletin*, no. 11 (Winter 1998), p. 181; "Explanatory Note from Glukhov, Deputy Chief of the Department of Counterespionage of the USSR Ministry District and Former Advisor to the Ministry of Public Security of the DPRK, to L.P. Beria, Deputy Chairman of the USSR Council of Ministers," April 13, 1953, ibid., p. 180.

58 Weathersby, "Deceiving the Deceivers," p. 179; Chen Jian, *China's Road to the Korean War: The Making of the Sino-American Confrontation* (Columbia University Press, 1994).

59 "Resolution of the Presidium of the USSR Council of Ministers about letters to the Ambassador of the USSR in the PRC, V.V. Kuznetsov, and to the Charge d'Affaire of the USSR in the DPRK, S P. Suzdalev," May 2, 1952, *CWIHP Bulletin*, no. 11 (Winter 1998), p. 183.

60 Weathersby, "Deceiving the Deceivers," p. 177. For the text of the decision by the Council of Ministers to reach a negotiated settlement in Korea, adopted March 19, 1953, see *CWIHP Bulletin: The Cold War in Asia*, no. 6/7 (Winter 1995), pp. 80–82.

61 Matthew B. Ridgway, *The Korean War: How We Met the Challenge; How All-Out Asian War Was Averted; Why MacArthur Was Dismissed; Why Today's War Objectives Must Be Limited* (Doubleday, 1967), p. 204.

62 Stanley Sandler, *The Korean War: An Encyclopedia* (Routledge, 1995), p. 84.

63 Mark Clark, *From the Danube to the Yalu* (Harper & Brothers, 1954), p. 30.

64 Hermes, *Truce Tent*, pp. 233–235.

65 Ridgway, *Korean War*, p. 206.

66 "Sir Esler Dening to British Foreign Office, Feb 25, 1952," FO 371/99638, National Archives, Kew, UK.

67 FO 371/ 99638, April 11, 1952, National Archives, Kew, UK.

68 "Memorandum by P.W. Manhard of the Political Section of the Embassy to the Ambassador of Korea in Korea (Muccio)," March 14, 1952, in *FRUS, 1952–54*, vol. 15: *Korea, Part 1* (1984), pp. 98–99.

69 "Koje POW Camps," May 6, 1952, FO 371/99639, National Archives, Kew, UK.

70 "United Nations Commission Report," March 27, 1952, FO 371/99638, National Archives, Kew, UK.

71 "Summary of Events: Koje-do May 7 through May 10, 1952," FO 371/99639, National Archives, Kew, UK.

72 Wilfred Burchett and Alan Winnington, *Koje Unscreened* (Britain-China Friendship Association, 1953), p. 72. British journalists Burchett and Winnington were well-known communist sympathizers.

73 Zhao Zuorui, "Organizing the Riots on Koje," in Richard Peters and Xiaobing Li, eds., *Voices from the Korean War: Personal Stories of American, Korea and Chinese Soldiers* (University Press of Kentucky, 2004), p. 256. A fictionalized account of this scene also appears in Ha Jin's prize-winning *War Trash* (Pantheon Books, 2004). Ha cites Zhang Zhe-shi's *Meijun Jizhongying Qinli Ji* [Personal Records in the American Prison Camps] (Chinese Archives Press, 1996) as a source for his historical novel.

74 Hermes, *Truce Tent*, p. 250.

75 "Statement of Brig. General Francis T. Dodd," May 12, 1952, FO 371/99638, National Archives, Kew, UK.

76 Hermes, *Truce Tent*, p. 252.

77 Clark, *From the Danube to the Yalu*, p. 46.

78 "Statement of Brig. General Francis T. Dodd," May 12, 1952.

79 Ridgway, *Korean War*, p. 214.

80 Hermes, *Truce Tent*, pp. 253–254.

81 C. H. Johnston, "Conditions in Prisoner of War Camps under the Control of the United Nations Command," May 23, 1952, FO 371/99638, National Archives, Kew, UK.

82 "Record of the Conversation with Mr. Acheson at the United Nations Embassy, Paris," May 28, 1952, FO 371/99638, National Archives, Kew, UK.

83 "Telegram to F.D. Tomlinson from Charles Johnston," June 16, 1952, FO 371/99638, National Archives, Kew, UK.

84 "Confidential 1553/25/52," May 29, 1952, FO 371/99638, National Archives, Kew, UK.

TWELVE: *Armistice, at Last*

1   *New York Times*, January 30, 1952.

2   Ibid., January 12, 1952. Robert and Jerome McGovern's younger brother Charles set up a memorial web site in 2004: http://www.mcgovernbrothers .com/ (accessed December 3, 2011).

3   *New York Times*, February 21, 1952.

4   Emmet J. Hughes, *The Ordeal of Power: A Political Memoir of the Eisenhower Years* (Atheneum, 1963), p. 32.

5   Bradley and Blair, *A General's Life*, p. 656.

6   *New York Times*, November 23, 1952.

7   Memorandum by John Foster Dulles to Dwight Eisenhower, November 26, 1952, in *FRUS, 1952–54*, vol. 15: *Korea, Part 1* (1984), p. 693.

8   Paik Sun Yup (Paek Sŏn-yŏp), *From Pusan to Panmunjom: Wartime Memoirs of the Republic of Korea's First Four-Star General* (Brassey's, 1992), pp. 215–216.

9   Ibid., pp. 216–217.

10 Mark Clark, *From the Danube to the Yalu* (Harper & Brothers, 1954), p. 239.

11 Dwight D. Eisenhower, *Mandate for Change, 1953–1956* (Doubleday, 1963), p. 59.

12 Douglas MacArthur, *Reminiscences: General of the Army* (Naval Institute Press, 1964), pp. 410–411.

13 Eisenhower Oral History Interview, July 28, 1964, pp. 8–9, John Foster Dulles Oral History, Princeton University, Princeton, N.J.

14 *FRUS, 1952–54*, vol. 15: *Part 1*, p. 818.

15 Dingman, "Atomic Diplomacy during the Korean War," p. 81; Edward C. Keefer, "Eisenhower and the Korean War," *Diplomatic History* 10, no. 3 (Summer 1986); H. W. Brand, "The Age of Vulnerability: Eisenhower and the National Insecurity State," *American Historical Review* 94, no. 4 (October 1989); Rosemary Foot, "Nuclear Coercion and the Ending of the Korean Conflict," *International Security* 13, no. 3 (Winter 1988/89).

16 *FRUS, 1952–54*, vol. 15: *Part 1*, pp. 1061–1069.

17 Sarvepalli Gopal, *Jawaharlal Nehru: A Biography*, vol. 2: *1947–1956* (Jonathan Cape, 1979), p. 148; Escott Reid, *Envoy to Nehru* (Oxford University Press, 1981), p. 45.

18 *FRUS, 1952–54*, vol. 15: *Part 1*, p. 1103.

19 Sherman Adams, *First-Hand Report: The Story of the Eisenhower Administration* (Harper & Brothers, 1961), p. 49.

20 David Rees described Eisenhower's "Korea Plan" as the "first vindication of the massive retaliation theory." See also David Rees, *Korea: The Limited War* (St. Martin's Press, 1964).

21 K. M. Panikkar, *In Two Chinas: Memoirs of a Diplomat* (George Allen & Unwin, 1955), p. 108.

22 Vojtech Mastny, *The Cold War and Soviet Insecurity: The Stalin Years* (Oxford University Press, 1998), pp. 172–173.

23 Foot, "Nuclear Coercion and the Ending of the Korean Conflict," pp. 104–107. This does not mean that nuclear threats played no role in bringing the war to an end, but that the claims of its effectiveness, which Eisenhower had used to justify his New Look strategy, had been greatly exaggerated.

24 *New York Times*, July 12, 1953; also William Taubman, *Krushchev: The Man and His Era* (W. W. Norton, 2003), pp. 240–241.

25 Conversation between Stalin and Zhou Enlai, August 20, 1952, *CWIHP Bulletin: The Cold War in Asia*, no. 6/7 (Winter 1995), pp. 12–13; Kathryn Weathersby, "Stalin, Mao, and the End of the Korean War," in Odd Arne Westad, ed., *Brothers in Arms: The Rise and Fall of the Sino-Soviet Alliance* (Woodrow Wilson Center Press/Stanford University Press, 1998), p. 105.

26 Weathersby, "Stalin, Mao, and the End of the Korean War," p. 108. The historian Chen Jian, however, maintains that while Stalin's death might have played a role in changing Chinese attitudes toward the POW issue, it was "more an outgrowth of Beijing's existing policies based on Chinese leaders' assessment of the changing situation than a reflection of altering Soviet directives." After reassessing China's gains and losses in Korea during the spring of 1953, China's leaders had simply decided that nothing more was to be gained from the continuing conflict. By that time, China's social and political transformation under Mao and the promotion of the country's international prestige and influence had already been achieved. Nevertheless, while

domestic concerns certainly played a role in changing Chinese attitudes, this does not explain why these changes came so soon after Stalin's death. See Chen, *Mao's China and the Cold War*, pp. 115–116.

27 Clark, *From the Danube to the Yalu*, p. 241; Hermes, *Truce Tent*, p. 411.

28 "Death of Stalin," July 16, 1953, Office of Current Intelligence, Central Intelligence Agency (HR70-14), p. 3, available at http://www.foia.cia.gov/CPE/CAESAR/caesar-02.pdf (accessed February 3, 2008).

29 Royal Institute of International Affairs (RIIA), ed., *Documents on International Affairs, 1953* (RIIA, 1956), pp. 11–13.

30 Serhy Yekelchyk, "The Civic Duty to Hate: Stalinist Citizenship as Political Practice and Civic Emotion (Kiev, 1943–53)," *Kritika: Explorations in Russian and Eurasian History* 7, no. 3 (Summer 2006), pp. 551–552.

31 Quoted in Walter Isaacson and Evan Thomas, *The Wise Men: Six Friends and the World They Made* (Touchstone, 1986), p. 554.

32 Hermes, *Truce Tent*, p. 412; Charles E. Bohlen, *Witness to History, 1929–1969* (W. W. Norton, 1973), p. 348; Klaus Larres, "Eisenhower and the First Forty Days after Stalin's Death," *Diplomacy and Statecraft* 6, no. 2 (July 1995), p. 436.

33 Weathersby, "Stalin, Mao, and the End of the Korean War," p. 108; "Resolution, USSR Council of Ministers with Draft Letters from Soviet Government to Mao Zedong and Kim Il Sung and Directive to Soviet Delegation at United Nations, 19 March 1953," *CWHIP Bulletin: The Cold War in Asia*, no. 6/7 (Winter 1995), p. 80.

34 Weathersby, "Stalin, Mao, and the End of the Korean War," p. 108.

35 Hermes, *Truce Tent*, p. 412.

36 Clark, *From the Danube to the Yalu*, pp. 241–242.

37 Quoted in Larres, "Eisenhower and the First Forty Days after Stalin's Death," pp. 455–456; J. W. Young, "Churchill, the Russian and the Western Alliance: The Three-Power Conference at Bermuda, December 1953," *English Historical Review* 101, no. 401 (October 1986).

38 Eisenhower, "A Chance for Peace," April 16, 1953, available at http://usa.usembassy.de/etexts/speeches/rhetoric/ikechanc.htm (accessed March 2, 2009).

39 The speech appeared to be part of a larger psychological warfare campaign aimed to weaken and destabilize the new government in Moscow. See Larres, "Eisenhower and the First Forty Days after Stalin's Death"; Kenneth A. Osgood, "Form before Substance: Eisenhower's Commitment to Psychological Warfare and Negotiations with the Enemy," *Diplomatic History* 24, no. 3 (Summer 2000).

40 Adams, *First-Hand Report*, p. 97.

41 Walter Lippmann, "Today and Tomorrow," *New York Times*, April 20, 1953.

42 Bohlen, *Witness to History*, p. 352.

43 Clark, *From the Danube to the Yalu*, p. 256.

44 Hermes, *Truce Tent*, pp. 425–432.

45 Clark to JCS, June 9, 1953, in *FRUS, 1952–54*, vol. 15: *Part 1*, p. 1157.

46 *New York Times*, June 25, 1953.

47 Clark, *From the Danube to the Yalu*, pp. 257–258; U. Alexis Johnson (with Jeff Olivarius McAllister), *Right Hand of Power: The Memoirs of an American Diplomat* (Prentice-Hall, 1984), pp. 166–167.

48 *New York Times,* May 31 and June 9, 1953.

49 Eisenhower, "Letter to President Syngman Rhee of Korea concerning the Acceptance of the Panmunjom Armistice," June 7, 1953, in *Public Papers of the Presidents of the United States: Dwight D. Eisenhower, 1953* (U.S. Government Printing Office, 1960), p. 96.

50 Clark, *From the Danube to the Yalu,* p. 279; Stueck, *The Korean War: An International History,* pp. 335–336.

51 Chŏng Il-kwŏn, Oral History Interview, September 29, 1964, John Foster Dulles Oral History Project, Princeton University Library, Princeton, N.J. The detailed account of how the escape was planned can be found in Ch'oe Tok-sin, *Naega kyokkun p'anmunjŏm* [My Panmunjom Experience] (Seoul: Munhwasa, 1955). Ch'oe wrote that preparation for the release began in early June.

52 *New York Times,* June 21, 1953.

53 *Dong'a ilbo,* June 19, 1953; *New York Times,* June 18, 1953.

54 Dwight D. Eisenhower, *Mandate for Change, 1953–1956* (Doubleday, 1963), pp. 185–186.

55 "Korea: Action in General Assembly," FO 371/105505, National Archives, Kew, UK.

56 *Dong'a ilbo,* June 25, 1953; *New York Times,* June 25, 1953; Yi Han-up, *Yi Sŭng-man 90-nyŏn* [Syngman Rhee: 90 Years] (Seoul: Yonsei University Press, 1995), p. 141.

57 "Dulles Letter to Syngman Rhee June 24, 1953" (emphasis in original text), FO 371/105505, National Archives, Kew, UK.

58 "Public Opinion in Many Countries Demands the Removal of Rhee," FO 371/105505, National Archives, Kew, UK.

59 "Text of a Letter from Marshal Kim Il Sung and General Peng Te-Huai (Peng Dehuai) to General Clark, Handed Over at Panmunjom on July 8, 1953," letter dated July 7, 1953, FO 371/105508, National Archives, Kew, UK.

60 "Telegram: Of the Soviet Chargé to the PRC to the Chairman of the USSR Council of Ministers, 3 July 1953," Document 114, in James Person, ed., "New Evidence on the Korean War," Document Reader, NKIDP, June 2010.

61 *FRUS, 1952–54,* vol. 15: *Part 1,* pp. 1202–1203.

62 Johnson, *Right Hand of Power,* p. 168.

63 *FRUS, 1952–54,* vol. 15: *Part 1,* p. 1307; Edward C. Keefer, "President Dwight D. Eisenhower and the End of the Korean War," *Diplomatic History* 10, no. 3 (July 1986), pp. 267–289.

64 "General Taylor Announced That If the South Korea Decided to Fight Alone, He Would Withdraw US. Troops from the Front," FO 371/105508, National Archives, Kew, UK.

65 *Times of London,* July 3, 1953.

66 Cited in Stephen Jin-Woo Kim, *Master of Manipulation: Syngman Rhee and the Seoul-Washington Alliance, 1953–1960* (Seoul: Yonsei University Press, 2001), pp. 112–114.

67 Paik, *From Pusan to Panmunjom,* p. 241.

68 Clark, *From the Danube to the Yalu,* p. 295.

69 Ibid., p. 296.

70 Paik, *From Pusan to Panmunjom,* p. 245.

71 *New York Times*, July 28, 1953.

72 Stephen E. Ambrose, *Eisenhower*, vol. 2: *The President* (Simon & Schuster, 1984), p. 106.

THIRTEEN: *Lessons of Korea*

1   Nugent, vol. 14, DASJA, p. 3346. See explanation of source in note 6, chap. 10. The scene is also vividly portrayed in Raymond B. Lech, *Broken Soldiers* (University of Illinois Press, 2000), pp. 203–204.

2   Major William E. Mayer, "Why Did Many Captives Cave In?" *U.S. News & World Report*, February 24, 1956, p. 56; Eugene Kinkead, "A Reporter at Large: The Study of Something New in History," *The New Yorker*, October 26, 1957, p. 114.

3   Eugene Kinkead, *In Every War but One* (W. W. Norton, 1959), p. 18. Not everyone agreed with such dire assessments. Lieutenant Colonel Thomas Cameron, one of the army lawyers who participated in Operation Big Switch, asserted that all the talk about American POWs' failings in Korea was utter nonsense. Such harsh judgments about the prisoners' conduct, he claimed, were the result of Chinese propaganda, not American failings. "From what I've seen in my little corner of Big Switch the vast majority of the prisoners were victims of a damnable frame-up . . . The whole thing is mainly lies, clever lies!" (Nugent, DASJA, Appendix "Q," box 9-16). He thought the more serious issue was "the loss of faith and our distrust in the ability of American soldiers to resist Red ideology." Some of America's most prominent social scientists also stepped forward to take issue with popular characterizations of POW conduct during the war and their ominous implications for American society. Drs. Edgar Schein and Albert Biderman, both eminent scientists who were employed by the air force to investigate Korean War POW behavior, adamantly refuted popular condemnation of these soldiers' "moral" failing: "The behavior of the Korean War prisoners did not compare unfavorably with that of their countrymen or with the behavior of other nations who have faced similar trials in the past," they concluded. "It is our opinion that any serious analysis of American society, its strengths and weaknesses, should rest on historically correct data." See Albert Biderman, "The Dangers of Negative Patriotism," *Harvard Business Review* 60 (November 1962), p. 93. See also Biderman's *March to Calumny: The Story of American POWs in the Korean War* (Macmillan, 1963); Edgar H. Schein, "Brainwashing and Totalitarianization in Modern Society," *World Politics* 3, no. 3 (April 1959), pp. 430–441; H. H. Wubben, "American Prisoners of War in Korea: A Second Look at the 'Something New in History' Theme," *American Quarterly* 22, no. 1 (Spring 1970), pp. 3–19; Ron Robin, *The Making of the Cold War Enemy: Culture and Politics in the Military Intellectual Complex* (Princeton University Press, 2001), pp. 162–184.

4   Letter to Secretary of Defense Charles Wilson from Defense Advisory Committee on Prisoners of War, July 12, 1955, NARA, RG 341, box 441.

5   "Presentation to Secretary of Defense from Defense Advisory Committee on Prisoners of War," Part 5, "Conclusion" by General J. E. Hull, Vice Chairman, July 29, 1955, NARA, RG 341, box 441.

6   According to Allan R. Millett, 565 of 3,746 returned American POWs were investigated for possible violation of the Uniformed Code of Military Jus-

tice, with the most serious charges being murder and collaboration with the enemy. The majority (373) of the cases were dismissed on legal or administrative grounds. "Of the remaining 192, the Army convicted six officers and men of crimes and discharged 61 for unsuitability. The Marine Corps reprimanded one and put two on special assignment while the Air Force retired three officers and separated seven for 'misbehavior.'" Memo from Allan R. Millett to the author, June 14, 2011. Regarding the figures for the army, according to Raymond B. Lech in *Broken Soldiers*, the most authoritative and comprehensive study of U.S. Army POWs who were court-martialed, five officers and nine enlisted men were court-martialed, and eleven of them were convicted and punished (pp. 212–213, 264–276).

7 The classic cold war film *The Manchurian Candidate* (1962) also repeats the theme of the dysfunctional American family, represented here by a weak father, an intrusive mother, and an isolated son. In this film the mother is actually a communist agent whose manipulative relationship with her son almost results in the communist takeover of the U.S. government. Like *My Son John*, the *Manchurian Candidate* also sees momism/communism as a threat to the free man and the free nation. Michael Rogin, "Kiss Me Deadly: Communism, Motherhood, and Cold War Movies," *Representations* 6 (Spring 1984), pp. 12–17.

8 Ibid., p. 27.

9 John Foster Dulles, "Address before the Overseas Press Club of America, March 20, 1954," reprinted in *U.S. News & World Report*, April 9, 1954, p. 73.

10 Rosemary Foot, "The Eisenhower Administration's Fear of Empowering the Chinese," *Political Science Quarterly* 3, no. 3 (Autumn 1996), p. 513.

11 Dwight Eisenhower, *Mandate for Change, 1953–1956* (Doubleday, 1963), p. 333.

12 Foot, "Eisenhower Administration's Fear," p. 513.

13 John Lewis Gaddis, *Inquiries into the History of the Cold War* (Oxford University Press, 1987), p. 174.

14 Nancy Bernkopf Tucker, "Cold War Contacts: America and China, 1952–1956," in Harry Harding and Yuan Ming, eds., *Sino-American Relations, 1945–1955: A Joint Assessment of a Critical Decade* (SR Books, 1989), p. 238.

15 *New York Times*, March 30, 1954.

16 Gordon Chang, *Friends and Enemies: The United States, China, and the Soviet Union, 1948–1972* (Stanford University Press, 1990), p. 168.

17 Foot, "Eisenhower Administration's Fear," p. 514.

18 *Life*, May 19, 1952, p. 152.

19 Ibid., p. 154.

20 *New York Times*, March 30, 1954.

21 Ibid., March 22, 1955.

22 *Life*, May 19, 1952, p. 152.

23 Rupert Wilkinson, *The Pursuit of American Character* (Harper & Row, 1988), p. 777; Foot, "Eisenhower Administration's Fear," p. 515.

24 *New York Times*, April 17, 1953.

25 *Life*, May 19, 1952, p. 152.

26 *New York Times*, April 20, 1954.

27 Richard H. Immerman, *John Foster Dulles: Piety, Pragmatism, and Power in U.S. Foreign Policy* (Scholarly Resources, 1999), p. 88.

28 *U.S. News & World Report*, March 5, 1954, p. 55.

29 Ibid., April 16, 1954, p. 21.

30 John Foster Dulles, "Policy for Security and Peace," *Foreign Affairs* 32, no. 3 (April 1954), p. 358.

31 Ibid., pp. 358–359; Richard H. Rovere, *Affairs of State: 1950–1956, The Eisenhower Years* (Farrar, 1956), p. 193.

32 *The Pentagon Papers (Senator Gravel Edition): The Defense Department History of United States Decisionmaking on Vietnam* (Beacon Press, 1971), vol. 1, p. 97.

33 Matthew B. Ridgway, *Soldier: The Memoirs of Matthew B. Ridgway* (Harper & Brothers, 1956), p. 277.

34 Quoted in David H. Petraeus, "Korea, the Never Again Club, and Indochina," *Parameters* (December 1987), p. 64.

35 Yuen Foong Khong, *Analogies at War: Korea, Munich, Dienbienphu, and the Vietnam Decision of 1965* (Princeton University Press, 1992), p. 78.

36 Quoted in Petraeus, "Korea, the Never Again Club," p. 64.

37 *New York Times*, April 3, 1954.

38 Khong, *Analogies at War*, p. 76; FRUS, 1952–1954, vol. 13: *Indochina, Part 1* (1982), pp. 1224–1225.

39 George C. Herring, "Franco-American Conflict in Indochina, 1950–1954," in Lawrence S. Kaplan, Denise Artaud, and Mark Rubin, eds., *Dien Bien Phu and the Crisis of Franco-American Relations, 1954–1955* (Scholarly Resources, 1990), p. 42.

40 Anthony Eden, *The Eden Memoirs: Full Circle* (Casell, 1960), pp. 114–119; George C. Herring and Richard H. Immerman, "Eisenhower, Dulles and Dienbienphu: 'The Day We Didn't Go to War' Revisited," *Journal of American History* 71, no. 2 (September 1984), p. 361. See also Fredrik Logevall, *Embers of War: The Fall of an Empire and the Making of America's Vietnam* (Random House, 2012), pp. 549–554.

41 The armistice that was signed at end of the war on July 27, 1953, required a political conference within three months "to settle through negotiation the questions of the withdrawal of all foreign forces from Korea, the peaceful settlement of the Korean question." This timeline was obviously not met, nor was it clear whether it ever would be met.

42 Evelyn Shuckburgh, *Descent to Suez: Foreign Office Diaries, 1951–1956* (W. W. Norton, 1986), pp. 181–182.

43 U. Alexis Johnson, *The Right Hand of Power*, p. 204.

44 Ibid., p. 204. In his memoirs, Wang Bingnan denied that Dulles refused to shake Zhou Enlai's hand. See Zhai Qing, "China and the Geneva Conference of 1954," *China Quarterly*, no. 129 (March 1992), p. 119.

45 Shuckburgh, *Descent to Suez*, p. 198.

46 Quoted in Zhai, "China and the Geneva Conference of 1954," p. 110.

47 Chen Jian and Shen Zhihua, "The Geneva Conference of 1954: New Evidence from the Archives from the Ministry of Foreign Affairs of the Peoples Republic of China," *CWIHP Bulletin*, no. 16 (Spring 2008), p. 8.

48 Quoted in Zhai, "China and the Geneva Conference of 1954," p. 109. For a similar parallel Zhou made between the conflict in Indochina and China's war in Korea, see Logevall, *Embers of War*, pp. 596–597.

49 Rovere, *Affairs of State*, p. 199.

50 Samuel P. Huntington, *The Soldier and the State: The Theory and Politics of Civil-Military Relations* (Harvard University Press, 1957), p. 345.

51 John Lewis Gaddis, "Was the Truman Doctrine a Real Turning Point?" *Foreign Affairs* 52, no. 2 (January 1974), pp. 392–393.

52 Huntington, *Soldier and the State*, p. 346.

53 *New York Times*, September 26, 1952. Also, A. J. Bacevich, "The Paradox of Professionalism: Eisenhower, Ridgway, and the Challenge to Civilian Control, 1953–1955," *Journal of Military History* 61 (April 1997), p. 308.

54 Quoted in Andrew Bacevich, *The New American Militarism: How Americans Are Seduced by War* (Oxford University Press, 2005), p. 150.

55 Bacevich, "Paradox of Professionalism," pp. 151, 321.

56 Cited in ibid., p. 324.

57 Andrew Bacevich, *Washington Rules: America's Path to Permanent War* (Henry Holt, 2010), p. 61.

58 Ibid., pp. 62–65.

59 George T. McKahin, *Intervention: How America Became Involved in Vietnam* (Alfred Knopf, 1986), pp. 139–140.

60 Michael J. Hogan, *A Cross of Iron: Harry S. Truman and the Origins of the National Security State, 1945–1954* (Cambridge University Press, 1998), p. 472.

61 James L. Clayton, "The Impact of the Cold War on the Economies of California and Utah, 1946–1965," *Pacific Historical Review* 36, no. 4 (November 1967), p. 464.

62 Quoted in Hogan, *Cross of Iron*, p. 472.

63 James L. Clayton, "Defense Spending: Key to California's Growth," *Western Political Quarterly* 15, no. 2 (June 1963), pp. 284–288.

64 *New York Times*, January 5, 1951.

65 By 1955, a fundamental reorientation of NATO and of European security led not only to the granting of full sovereignty to West Germany but also to its rearmament and NATO membership. Germany's rearmament marked a sea change in British and in particular French attitudes. As the instigator of two world wars on the continent and the cause of the death of tens of millions of people, a rearmed Germany, much less making it an integral part of European security, was anathema. But the Soviet threat reinforced by the Korean War had reversed that position. The situation developed even more rapidly with regard to Japan. Japan's sovereignty and rearmament had already taken place a few years earlier, in 1952. In the process, the reversal of priorities in economic policy entailed repudiating many of the original ideals of "demilitarization and democratization" that had seemed so inspiring to a defeated Japanese populace in 1945. That earlier effort proved too radical in the context of the emerging realities of the cold war. By 1947 economic stagnation and social unrest gave rise to fears that the country was ripe for communism. American occupation took a "reverse course," abandoning programs for reform and the creation of a demilitarized and pacifist state. Purged politicians and industrialists from World War II were rehabilitated, the euphemistically named Self Defense Force was created, and a bold effort was made to bring Japan into the Western system of defense as part of the containment ring against communism. The war boom, stimulated by U.S. procurements, put Japan's economy back on track. Arms production and military procure-

ments dominated Japanese industrial production during the war years. Sales worth 7 million yen in 1952 grew to 15 billion by 1954. The impact of U.S. military contracts, however, went far beyond just sales figures. It laid the technological foundation for the post–World War II development of Japanese industry, which became globally dominant by the 1980s. See Samuels, *Rich Nation, Strong Army*, pp. 137–141; also Dower, *Embracing Defeat*, pp. 540–542.

66 *New York Times*, July 23, 1950.

67 President Dwight D. Eisenhower, Farewell Radio and Television Address to the American People, January 17, 1961, available at http://www.eisenhower.archives.gov/all_about_ike/Speeches/Farewell_Address.pdf (accessed December 10, 2011).

FOURTEEN: *Deepening the Revolution*

1 Mao Tse-Tung, *Selected Works of Mao Tse-tung* (Foreign Language Press, 1977), vol. 5, p. 115.

2 William Taubman, *Khrushchev: The Man and His Era* (W. W. Norton, 2003), p. 336.

3 Sergey Radchenko, *Two Suns in the Heavens: The Sino-Soviet Struggle for Supremacy, 1962–1967* (Woodrow Wilson Center Press, 2009), p. 10.

4 Chen Jian and Yang Kuisong, "Chinese Politics and the Collapse of the Sino-Soviet Alliance," in Odd Arne Westad, ed., *Brothers in Arms: The Rise and Fall of the Sino-Soviet Alliance* (Woodrow Wilson Center Press/ Stanford University Press, 1998), pp. 255–257; Taubman, *Khrushchev*, p. 336.

5 Taubman, *Khrushchev*, p. 337.

6 Quoted in Zubok and Pleshakov, *Inside the Kremlin's Cold War*, p. 217.

7 Taubman, *Khrushchev*, p. 337.

8 Sergei Khrushchev, ed., *Memoirs of Nikita Khrushchev*, vol. 3: *The Statesman, 1953–1964* (Pennsylvania State University Press, 2007), p. 417.

9 Chen Jian, *China's Road to the Korean War: The Making of the Sino-American Confrontation* (Columbia University Press, 1994), pp. 220–222; Thomas Christensen, *Useful Adversaries: Grand Strategies, Domestic Mobilization and Sino-American Conflict, 1947–1958* (Princeton University Press, 1996), p. 163.

10 Taubman, *Khrushchev*, p. 337.

11 Khrushchev, *Memoirs*, vol. 3, pp. 421–423. Mao listed his grievances against Stalin during a March 31, 1956, conversation with Soviet ambassador Pavel Yudin. For a transcript of that conversation, see *CWIHP Bulletin*, nos. 6/7 (Winter 1995–1996), pp. 164–167.

12 Li Zhisui, *The Private Life of Chairman Mao* (Random House, 1994), p. 115.

13 Taubman, *Khrushchev*, p. 339; Peter Vamos, "Sino-Hungarian Relations and the 1956 Revolution," *CWIHP Working Paper 54* (November 2006), pp. 23–24.

14 Vamos, "Sino-Hungarian Relations," pp. 24–25.

15 Jerrold L. Schecter with Vyacheslav V. Luchkov, trans. and eds., *Khrushchev Remembers: The Glasnost Tapes* (Little, Brown, 1990), p. 153.

16 Li, *Private Life of Chairman Mao*, pp. 220–222.

17 Khrushchev, *Memoirs*, vol. 3, pp. 436–437.

18 Chen, *Mao's China and the Cold War*, pp. 202–203.

19 Khrushchev, *Memoirs*, vol. 3, p. 455.

20 "Minutes, Conversation between Mao Zedong and Ambassador Yudin, 22 July 1958," *CWIHP Bulletin: The Cold War in Asia*, no. 6/7 (Winter 1995), pp. 155–158.

21 Li, *Private Life of Chairman Mao*, p. 260.

22 Chen and Yang, "Chinese Politics and the Collapse of the Sino-Soviet Alliance," p. 270.

23 Khrushchev, *Memoirs*, vol. 3, pp. 459–461.

24 Li, *Private Life of Chairman Mao*, p. 261.

25 *FRUS, 1958–1960*, vol. 19: *China* (1996), pp. 145–153.

26 Li, *Private Life of Chairman Mao*, pp. 270–271; Taubman, *Khrushchev*, pp. 392–393.

27 Chen and Yang, "Chinese Politics and the Collapse of the Sino-Soviet Alliance," p. 271.

28 Chen, *Mao's China and the Cold War*, p. 180.

29 Wu-Lengxi, "Memoir, Inside Story of the Decision Making during the Shelling of Jinmen," *CWIHP Bulletin*, no. 8/9 (Winter 1996), p. 212.

30 Chen, *Mao's China and the Cold War*, pp. 202–203; Li, *Private Life of Chairman Mao*, p. 262.

31 Khrushchev, *Memoirs*, vol. 3, p. 485.

32 Roderick MacFarquhar, *The Origins of the Cultural Revolution*, vol. 2: *The Great Leap Forward, 1958–1960* (Columbia University Press, 1983), pp. 195–197.

33 Ibid., p. 197.

34 Quoted in Viktor Usov, "Peng Dehuai: Pages from Reminiscences: Confessions of a Chinese General," *Far Eastern Affairs* 5 (1987), pp. 138–139.

35 Quan Yanchi, *Mao Zedong: Man, Not God* (Foreign Language Press, 1992), p. 53.

36 Quoted in Usov, "Peng Dehuai," p. 141.

37 Jurgen Domes, *Peng Te-huai: The Man and the Image* (Stanford University Press, 1985), pp. 123–124; Short, *Mao*, p. 585. According to Usov, Peng died of lung cancer. "In 1974, the illness became acute, the cancerous growth spread to the lungs and caused him great pain, but no one would give him even a pain-killing injection," Usov, "Peng Dehuai," p. 141.

38 By 1978, however, following China's rapprochement with the United States, Peng's reputation began to be rehabilitated. By January 1979, China was swept by a "veritable avalanche of memoirs" in praise of the good general, marking the passing of an era that signaled an apparent "end" of the Korean War and of cold war antagonism between the two superpowers. Yet, while U.S-Sino rapprochement was welcomed by Chinese leaders, Peng's posthumous rehabilitation served to keep alive the memory of China's "victory" in Korea, which did so much to change Chinese perceptions of themselves and the world. Ibid., pp. 127–128.

39 Quoted in Radchenko, *Two Suns in the Heavens*, p. 12. Radchenko's portrayal of Khrushchev as the main culprit of the Sino-Soviet split, due to his insensitivity and his insistence to play the first fiddle, is contrasted to Lüthi's portrayal of the Chinese leader whose Great Power aspirations, personality, and ideology made peaceful coexistence between them impossible. Lorenz M. Lüthi, *The Sino-Soviet Split: The Cold War in the Communist World* (Princeton University Press, 2008).

40 Jonathan Spence, *The Search for Modern China* (W. W. Norton, 1990), p. 583.

41 Estimates of death by famine range from 15 to 32 million. However, the his-

torian Frank Dikötter disputes these numbers, believing that the magnitude of the disaster was much higher, from 43 to 46 million people. See his *Mao's Great Famine: The History of China's Most Devastating Catastrophe, 1958–1962* (Bloomsbury, 2010), p. 325.

42 Chen, *Mao's China and the Cold War*, p. 204

43 *Time*, October 5, 1959, p. 20.

44 Khrushchev, *Memoirs*, vol. 3, p. 169.

45 MacFarquhar, *Origins of the Cultural Revolution*, vol. 2, p. 269; Chen and Yang, "Chinese Politics and the Collapse of the Sino-Soviet Alliance," p. 273.

46 Radchenko, *Two Suns in the Heavens*, p. 14.

47 "M. Suslov, To Members of the CC CPSU Presidium," December 18, 1959, Document 24, in David Wolff, "One Finger's Worth of Historical Events," *CWIHP Working Paper* 30 (August 2000), p. 71.

48 Chen and Yang, "Chinese Politics and the Collapse of the Sino-Soviet Alliance," p. 273.

49 Strobe Talbott, ed. and trans., *Khrushchev Remembers: The Last Testament* (Little, Brown, 1974), p. 473.

50 MacFarquhar, *Origins of the Cultural Revolution*, vol. 2, p. 268.

51 Ibid., pp. 272–273.

52 Quoted in Philip Short, *Mao: A Life* (Henry Holt, 1999), pp. 503–504.

53 Shu Guang Zhang, "Beijing's Aid to Hanoi and the United States–China Confrontations, 1964–1968," in Priscilla Roberts, ed., *Behind the Bamboo Curtain: China, Vietnam and the World beyond* Asia (Stanford University Press, 2006), p. 260; Roderick MacFarquhar, *The Origins of the Cultural Revolution*, vol. 3: *The Coming of the Cataclysm, 1961–1966* (Columbia University Press, 1997), p. 356.

54 David Wolff, "In Memoriam Deng Xioaping and the Cold War," *CWIHP Bulletin*, no. 10 (March 1998), p. 149.

55 Chen Jian, "China's Involvement in the Vietnam War, 1964–69," *China Quarterly*, no. 142 (June 1995), p. 358.

56 Qiang Zhai, *China and the Vietnam Wars, 1950–1975* (University of North Carolina Press, 2000), p. 113.

57 Chen, *Mao's China and the Cold War*, p. 207; Zhai, *China and the Vietnam War, 1950–1975*, pp. 122–129.

58 MacFarquhar, *Origins of the Cultural Revolution*, vol. 3, p. 273.

59 Ibid., p. 283.

60 Ibid., pp. 269–273; Chen, "China's Involvement in the Vietnam War," pp. 361–362.

61 Chen, *Mao's China and the Cold War*, p. 211; Qiang, *China and the Vietnam Wars*, p. 115.

62 MacFarquhar, *Origins of the Cultural Revolution*, vol. 3, p. 334.

63 Chen, *Mao's China and the Cold War*, pp. 210–211.

64 James G. Hershberg and Chen Jian, "Informing the Enemy: Sino-American 'Signaling' and the Vietnam War, 1965," in Roberts, ed., *Behind the Bamboo Curtain*, p. 220.

65 Quoted in ibid., p. 221.

66 Ibid., pp. 224–227

67 The link between the impact of the Korean analogy and Chinese and Ameri-

can decision-making in 1965 is the subject of Hershberg and Chen's pioneering essay, "Informing the Enemy." The analysis set forth in this chapter draws heavily on this work. See also Chen Jian, "Personal-Historical Puzzles about China and the Vietnam War," in Chen Jian, Stein Tonnesson, Nguyen Vu Tungand, and James G. Hershberg, "77 Conversations between Chinese and Foreign Leaders on the Wars in Indochina, 1964–1977," *CWIHP Working Paper 22* (May 1998), p. 26.

FIFTEEN: *Korea and Vietnam*

1 Quoted in Khong, *Analogies at War*, p. 97. Ball was the under secretary of state, the second highest position in the State Department. In 1972, the position was renamed deputy secretary of state.

2 Sin Bum Shik, compiler, *Major Speeches by Korea's Park Chung Hee* (Hollym, 1970), p. 238.

3 W. Averell Harriman, "Sino-Soviet Conflict," *Proceedings of the Academy of the Political Science* 28, no. 1 (April 1965), p. 104.

4 W. W. Rostow, "The Third Round," *Foreign Affairs* 42, no. 1 (October 1963), p. 9.

5 The full text is available at the LBJ Presidential Library web site: http://www.lbjlib.utexas.edu/johnson/archives.hom/speeches.hom/650407.asp (accessed April 15, 2011).

6 William Bundy, "Progress and Problems in East Asia: An American Viewpoint," *Department of State Bulletin*, October 19, 1964, p. 537.

7 *U.S. News & World Report*, April 19, 1965, pp. 79–80.

8 Khong, *Analogies at War*, p. 114. Khong notes that in late 1952, 56 percent of Americans thought the war was a mistake while only 32 percent thought it worthwhile. By September 1956 the proportions began to reverse, with 41 percent thinking it a mistake and 46 percent considering it worthwhile. A poll in liberal Minnesota in March 1965 resulted in 67 percent thinking it had been worthwhile and only 16 percent, a mistake. See also John E. Mueller, *War, Presidents and Public Opinion* (John Wiley and Sons, 1973), pp. 170–171.

9 Quoted in Gordon Goldstein, *Lessons in Disaster: McGeorge Bundy and the Path to War in Vietnam* (Henry Holt, 2008), p. 98.

10 *New York Times*, August 6, 1964.

11 Of the many analogies evoked to justify America's involvement in Vietnam, it was "lessons" of Korea that played the most influential role in the U.S. decision in the summer of 1965. One study found that the Korean analogy and its perceived lessons in the minds of policy makers "can explain why the Johnson administration decided to intervene . . . and took the form that it did." The Korean analogy worked in two ways: one that pushed for action and the other setting the limits of that action. As in Korea, Vietnam was seen as a situation where international communism was threatening the free world. Furthermore, by 1965, in contrast to the opinion in the immediate aftermath of the armistice, the Korean War was seen as a case of success in fighting back and containing communism. The lesson for Vietnam was that not only were the political stakes high, to demonstrate the credibility and will of America and its allies to fight communism, but military intervention was just and necessary and could succeed in preserving peace and freedom.

However, the possibility of Chinese intervention constrained the options for intervention. In terms of strategy, this meant that an invasion of North Vietnam, crossing the 17th parallel, was not an option lest it provoke China's entry with combat forces. Reinforcing the Korean lesson was the lesson of Munich in the 1930s: that aggression must not be appeased. William Bundy, the author of the December 1964 decision for a new Vietnam strategy of escalation, stated publicly in January 1965 that "in essence, our policy derives from (1) the fact of the Communist nations of Asia and their policies [the expansionist policies of China and North Vietnam]; (2) the lessons of the thirties and of Korea; (3) the logical extension of that fact and these lessons to what has happened in Southeast Asia." And that "our action in Korea reflected three elements: a recognition that aggression of any sort must be met early and head-on . . . ; a recognition that . . . our vital interests [in Asia] could be affected by action on the mainland; [and] an understanding that . . . there must be a demonstrated willingness of major external powers both to assist and to intervene if required" (quoted in Khong, *Analogies of War*, pp. 99–100). See George Ball, *The Past Has Another Pattern* (W. W. Norton, 1983); Khong, *Analogies at War*; Ernest R. May, *"Lessons" of the Past: The Use and Misuse of History in American Foreign Policy* (Oxford University Press, 1973); Robert Jervis, *Perceptions and Misperceptions in International Politics* (Princeton University Press, 1976).

12 Quoted in Michael R. Beschloss, *Taking Charge: The Johnson White House Tapes, 1963–1964* (Simon & Schuster, 1997), pp. 367–369.

13 David L. Di Leo, *George Ball, Vietnam and the Rethinking of Containment* (University of North Carolina Press, 1992), p. 22; James A. Bill, *George Ball: Behind the Scenes in U.S. Foreign Policy* (Yale University Press, 1997); pp. 160–161.

14 *U.S. News & World Report*, February 15, 1965, p. 69.

15 James C. Thomson Jr., "How Could Vietnam Happen? An Autopsy," *Atlantic Monthly*, April 1968, p. 48.

16 George W. Ball, "Top Secret: The Prophecy the President Rejected," *Atlantic Monthly*, July 1972, pp. 36–49; Ball, *Past Has Another Pattern*, p. 380.

17 Ball, *Past Has Another Pattern*, p. 381.

18 Ball, "Top Secret," p. 37; Khong, *Analogies at War*, p. 107; Ball, *Past Has Another Pattern*, pp. 380–381.

19 Ball, *Past Has Another Pattern*, p. 376.

20 Larry Berman, *Planning a Tragedy: The Americanization of the War in Vietnam* (W. W. Norton, 1982), pp. 119-120.

21 Quoted in Goldstein, *Lessons in Disaster*, p. 139.

22 Tom Wicker, "The Wrong Rubicon: LBJ and the War," *Atlantic Monthly*, May 1968, p. 139.

23 David Halberstam, *The Best and the Brightest* (Random House, 1969), p. 592.

24 Quoted in Goldstein, *Lessons in Disaster*, pp. 137–138. Dean Rusk also frequently brought up the similarity between Korea and Vietnam in his private and public statements. "In Korea, the international community proved that overt aggression was unprofitable. In Vietnam, we must prove—once again . . . that semi-covert aggression across international boundaries cannot succeed." Even in his approach to the prosecution of the Vietnam War, Rusk drew on the Korean War analogy: "Rusk envisioned the desired end of the

Vietnam war as a negotiation which, as in Korea, would reaffirm the approximate status quo ante." See Thomas J. Schoenbaum, *Waging Peace and War: Dean Rusk in the Truman, Kennedy and Johnson Years* (Simon & Schuster, 1988), pp. 424–425.

25 Quoted in ibid., p. 195.

26 Roberto Ducci, "The World Order in the Sixties," *Foreign Affairs* 42, no. 3 (April 1964), p. 384. In January 1964, France extended diplomatic recognition to the PRC. French President Charles de Gaulle apparently had Vietnam in mind when he opted for recognition since everyone understood that China was a key player in resolving the conflict in Indochina. Recognition of China by France was also an affront to the domino theory and cast doubt on the whole rationale of credibility on which America's Vietnam policy was based. It was, as Averell Harriman bitterly complained to France's ambassador in Washington, "a slap in Lyndon Johnson's face." The move was interpreted as a deliberate insult to the United States in other ways, to demonstrate France's Great Power status and independence vis-à-vis Washington. According to one Western diplomat in Paris, "for de Gaulle, Vietnam is just another lever to cut American influence in Europe to a minimum." See Fredrick Longevall, "The French Recognition of China and Its Implications for the Vietnam War," in Roberts, ed., *Behind the Bamboo Curtain*, pp. 153–159. See also Ball, *Past Has Another Pattern*, p. 378.

27 Goldstein, *Lessons in Disaster*, p. 139; David S. Broder, "Consensus Politics: End of an Experiment," *Atlantic Monthly*, October 1966, p. 62; Doris Kearns Goodwin, *Lyndon Johnson and the American Dream* (Harper & Row, 1976), p. 169; Halberstam, *Best and the Brightest*, p. 501; Robert Dalleck, *Flawed Giant: Lyndon Johnson and His Times* (Oxford University Press, 1998), pp. 252–253.

28 Robert D. Dean, *Imperial Brotherhood: Gender and the Making of Cold War Foreign Policy* (University of Massachusetts Press, 2003), p. 228.

29 James G. Hershberg and Chen Jian, "Informing the Enemy: Sino-American 'Signaling' and the Vietnam War," in Roberts, ed., *Behind the Bamboo Curtain*, p. 231.

30 Matthew Ridgway, "On Viet Nam," in Marcus G Raskin and Bernard B. Fall, eds., *The Viet-Nam Reader* (Random House, 1967), p. 437. The article was originally published in *Look*, April 5, 1966.

31 Jiyul Kim, "U.S. and Korea in Vietnam and the Japan-Korea Treaty: Search for Security, Prosperity and Influence," MA thesis, Harvard University, 1991, pp. 24–30. Much of the discussion on South Korea and Vietnam in this chapter has relied on Jiyul Kim's thesis and the large amount of primary source materials he has made available to me for use in this study. I am indebted to his expertise, his critical review of this chapter, and for allowing me to extensively quote from his work.

32 Taehyun Kim and Chang Jae Baik, "Taming and Tamed by the United States," in Byung-Kook Kim and Ezra F. Vogel, eds., *The Park Chung Hee Era: The Transformation of South Korea* (Harvard University Press, 2011), pp. 60–61.

33 Ibid., p. 60.

34 Ibid., p. 62. Much of the blame for South Korea's stagnant economy also had to do with Rhee's monetary policy. Rhee resisted American efforts to devalue the South Korean currency, insisting that the won be valued at 500 won to the

dollar "despite American claims that the real value of the dollar was as much as twice that." This exchange rate impeded any growth in exports since the prices of Korean goods were too high to attract foreign markets. Meanwhile, import licenses, issued to businessmen by corrupt government officials, strengthened Rhee's hold on power. "Rhee continued to pursue such policies because, although they stunted economic development, they strengthened the power of his regime." See Gregg Brazinsky, *Nation Building in South Korea: Koreans, Americans and the Making of a Democracy* (University of North Carolina Press, 2007), pp. 35–36. For a comprehensive reference source on South Korea's development, see Edward S. Mason et al., eds., *The Economic and Social Modernization of the Republic of Korea* (Harvard University Press, 1980); LeRoy R. Jones and Il Sakong, *Government, Business and Entrepreneurship in Economic Development: The Korean Case* (Harvard University Press, 1980).

35 Yong-Sup Han, "The May Sixteenth Military Coup," in Kim and Vogel, eds., *Park Chung Hee Era*, p. 41.

36 Bruce Cumings, *Korea's Place in the Sun: A Modern History* (W. W. Norton, 1997), p. 302; see also Gregory Henderson, *Korea: The Politics of the Vortex* (Harvard University Press, 1968), pp. 334–360.

37 On Park's life story and the 1961 coup, see Han, "May Sixteenth Coup." For a discussion of Park's involvement in leftist movements and his arrest during the ROK Army purge of 1948, see Cho Kap-je, *Nae mudŏm e ch'imŭl paet'ŏra 2: Chŏnjaeg'gwa sarang* [Spit on My Grave, vol. 2: War and Love] (Seoul: Chosŏn ilbosa, 1998), pp. 215–238. When Park made his coup in 1961, his communist background had temporarily given rise to some worry in Washington. Park was listed in a 1948 CIA report of field-grade officers in the ROK Army who had been "confined for subversive activities." Shortly after the 1961 coup, doubts about Park's political affiliations were raised in a State Department report issued on May 31, 1961: "The declared position of the regime is anti-Communist and available evidence does not support allegations of Pak's continuing ties with the Communists. However, we cannot rule out the possibility that he is a long-term Communist agent, or that he might re-defect." *FRUS, 1961–1963*, vol. 22: *Northeast Asia* (1996), pp. 468–469. Also Bruce Cumings, *The Origins of the Korean War*, vol. 2: *The Roaring of the Cataract, 1947–1950* (Princeton University Press, 1990), p. 266; Kim Kyŏngnae, "Chŏnhyangjanya? aninya? In'gan Pak Chŏng hŭi ui chŏnhyang chubyon [Is he a convert from communism or not? The circumstances of the ideological conversion of Park Chung Hee]," *Sasanggye* (November 1963), pp. 102–110.

38 Cumings, *Korea's Place in the Sun*, p. 348; Kim Hyung-A, *Korea's Development under Park Chung Hee: Rapid Industrialization, 1961–79* (RoutledgeCurzon, 2004), pp. 73–75. The idea of national independence or autonomy (*minjokchŏk chajusŏng*) was the basis on which Park appealed to the public for mass support for his new economic initiatives. This idea referred to Park's pursuit of a "Korean-style" way of life and, especially, independence from the United States. In Park's second book, *Kukka wa hyŏngmyŏng'gwa na* [*The Nation, the Revolution and I*], published in September 1963, he was openly critical of U.S. aid policy and more generally of Korea's traditional reliance on foreign powers (*sadaejuŭi*). The May 16 Revolution, he declared, "was not simply a change of regime. It was a new, mature national debut of spirit" and "the end of

500 years of stagnation of the Chosŏn dynasty (1392–1910), the oppression and bloodshed of 35 years of Japanese rule and the nagging chronic disease bred by the residue of the Liberation." His revolution represented, he declared, "a national debut, inspired by the courage and self-confidence of a people determined never again to be poor, weak or dumb." The revolution, he asserted, was "our last chance for national renaissance." In building the groundwork for this "national renaissance," Park believed it was necessary to create a "spiritual revolution" as the basis for economic construction. These ideas later became the basis for his Secondary Economic Movement, which he launched in 1968. In a speech he gave at a national rally on September 18, 1968, he stated that "we must discard the mental habit of dependency and explore a brighter future image of the fatherland by uniting our strength." See Sheila Miyoshi Jager, *Narratives of Nation Building: A Genealogy of Patriotism* (M. E. Sharpe, 2003), pp. 79–80; Park Chung Hee, *Kukka wa hyŏngmyŏng'gwa na* (Seoul: Tonga ch'ulp'ansa, 1963), p. 22 (this book was later translated under the title *The Nation, the Revolution and I* (Seoul: Hollym, 1970)).

39 Kim, *Korea's Development under Park Chung Hee*, p. 74.

40 Kim, "U.S. and Korea in Vietnam and the Japan-Korea Treaty," pp. 22–23.

41 Ronald H. Spector, *Advice and Support: The Early Years of the U.S. Army in Vietnam, 1941–1960* (Free Press, 1985) p. 198.

42 Kim, "U.S. and Korea in Vietnam and the Japan-Korea Treaty," pp. 41–43.

43 Deptel (Department of State Telegram) 1426, December 4, 1961, National Security Files (NSF), Country, box 128, JFK Library. Quoted in Kim, "U.S. and Korea in Vietnam and the Japan-Korea Treaty," p. 41.

44 Memcon (Memorandum of Conversation), Park-Kennedy, November 14–15, 1961, NSF, Country, box 128, JFK Library, Boston, Mass.; Kim, "U.S. and Korea in Vietnam and the Japan-Korea Treaty," pp. 41–42.

45 Deptel 80 (Seoul), July 27, 1962, NSF, Country, box 129, JFK Library.

46 Seoul Embet 741, November 27, 1963, NSF, Country, box 254, LBJ Library, Austin, Tx.

47 Kim, "U.S. and Korea in Vietnam and the Japan-Korea Treaty," p. 140.

48 Stanley Robert Larsen and James Lawton Collins Jr., *Vietnam Studies: Allied Participation in Vietnam* (U.S. Government Printing Office, 1975), pp. 120–121. Tab C (Third Country Assistance to Vietnam) from "Position Paper on SE Asia," December 2, 1964, NSF, McGB [McGeorge Bundy] Memos to the Pres., box 2, LBJ Library.

49 Khong, *Analogies at War*, pp. 118–120.

50 Deptel 557 (Seoul)/Thomson to McGB, "The Week That Was," December 17, 1964, Thomson Papers, box 11, JFK Library.

51 Kim, "U.S. and Korea in Vietnam and the Japan-Korea Treaty," p. 143; see also *The Pentagon Papers (Senator Gravel Edition): The Defense Department History of United States Decisionmaking on Vietnam* (Beacon Press, 1971), vol. 3, pp. 417–423, 429.

52 *Pentagon Papers*, pp. 451–452; Memo McNamara to LBJ, April 21, 1965, NSF, McGB Memos to the Pres., box 3, LBJ Library.

53 William C. Westmoreland, *A Soldier Reports* (Doubleday, 1976), pp. 136–141; *Pentagon Papers*, pp. 413, 415, 467; William Bundy Oral History, tape 2, p. 29, May 29, 1969, LBJ Library.

54 Kim, "U.S. and Korea in Vietnam and the Japan-Korea Treaty," pp. 11–12, 160, 233–236.

55 Dean Rusk Oral History, interview 3, tape 1, p. 26, January 1970, LBJ Library.

56 *Kukhoe-sa: Chae 4, 5, 6 dae kukhoe* [History of the National Assembly: The 4th, 5th and 6th National Assembly] (ROK National Assembly, 1971), pp. 909–913; Kim, "U.S. and Korea in Vietnam and the Japan-Korea Treaty," pp. 201–202.

57 The terms of agreement for the second ROK division deployed in 1966 were detailed in the "Brown Memorandum" named after Winthrop G. Brown, who was the U.S. ambassador in Seoul at the time. The memo was first made public in the "Symington Hearings" of 1971 when the Senate examined U.S. security policy in Asia. The hearings also provided hard data on the economic benefits for Korea. *U.S. Security Agreement and Commitment Abroad*, vol. 2, pt. 6 (Korea), Hearings before the Committee on Foreign Relations, 91st Congress, 2nd Session (U.S. Government Printing Office, 1971), pp. 1549–1550, 1571, 1708, 1759–1761; see also Sejin Kim, "South Korea's Involvement in Vietnam and Its Economic and Political Impact," *Asian Survey* 10, no. 6 (June 1970), pp. 519–523.

58 Not much is known about North Korea's involvement in the Vietnam War. Balázs Szalontai, however, has uncovered evidence from the Hungarian National Archives of extensive involvement by the P'yŏngyang regime in North Vietnam's war effort. The logic of P'yŏngyang's support of Hanoi apparently stemmed from Kim Il Sung's attempt to undermine U.S. military strength in Asia. For this goal, P'yŏngyang was ready to provide North Vietnam with "substantial quantities of material assistance," which is astonishing given the fact that this was the same period when North Korea was beginning to experience serious setbacks to its own economy. According to Szalontai, "in 1966, P'yŏngyang gave Hanoi a total of 12.3 million rubles of economic and military aid, such as steel, diesel engines, explosives, iron plates, tractors, power generators, and irrigation equipment." The next year, "the value of North Korea aid rose 20 million rubles, including arms, pontoons and military uniforms." These amounts were comparable to what "the more developed East European countries gave to the Democratic Republic of Vietnam, or even exceeded the latter's individual contributions." Kim was apparently willing to provide this aid in order to help Hanoi withstand the massive increases in American combat troops in Vietnam that occurred during 1966. "The more successfully the North Vietnamese fought, the more U.S. troops were tied down in Vietnam, and the less able Washington was to resort to military measures in other countries," including the Korean peninsula. See Balázs Szalontai, "In the Shadow of Vietnam: A New Look at the North Korea's Blue House Raid and the Pueblo," *Journal of Cold War History* 14.4 (Fall 2012), pp. 122–166.

Kim Il Sung also dispatched dozens of North Korean pilots to fight in the Vietnam War. The details of this operation came to light only in 2007 when a Vietnamese newspaper reported that fourteen North Korean air force personnel killed in the Vietnam War had been buried in a special cemetery near Hanoi and had been subsequently disinterred and repatriated to North Korea in 2002. In a letter written to the newspaper, a retired North Vietnamese general who had worked with the North Koreans revealed that a total of

"87 North Korean Air Force personnel had served in North Vietnam between 1967 and early 1969, during which time the North Koreans lost 14 men and had claimed to have shot down 26 American aircraft." In 1966 North Korea agreed to provide pilots and support personnel to man a North Vietnamese Air Force regiment "consisting of two companies (ten aircraft each of MiG-17s) and one company of MiG-21s" that would be under the command of the North Vietnamese Air Force-Air Defense Command to help defend Hanoi against the intensified American bombing campaign called Rolling Thunder. In reality, however, they were volunteer soldiers who maintained their own sovereignty, commanding "their own forces with the assistance of representatives from our [Vietnamese] side." Although the North Vietnamese provided technical support as well as all housing, living supplies, transportation equipment, and medical support, this assistance was hardly comparable to the generous aid package Park was able to secure from Washington for his contribution to the war effort. As far as prestige and benefits accrued from their respective participation in the war, Seoul emerged the clear winner. See Merle Pribbenow, "North Korean Pilots in the Skies over Vietnam," NKIDP, e-Dossier No. 2 (November 2011), pp. 1–3, available at http://www.wilsoncen ter.org/publication/nkidp-e-dossier-no-2-north-korean-pilots-the-skies-over-vietnam (accessed March 7, 2012).

59 Memo, JCT to Rostow, Subj: Elements of Progress in Asia, June 24, 1966, Thomson Papers, box 13, JFK Library.

60 *Administrative History, Department of State*, vol. 7 (East Asia), p. 2g, LBJ Library.

61 Alice H. Amsden, *Asia's Next Giant: South Korea and Late Industrialization* (Oxford University Press, 1989), p. 56.

62 John G. Roberts, "The Spoils of Peace," *FEER*, June 23, 1966, pp. 596–598; Charles Smith and Louise do Rosario, "Empire of the Sun," *FEER*, May 3, 1966, pp. 46–48.

63 *Administrative History, Department of State*, vol. 7 (East Asia), p. F4, LBJ Library; Kim, "U.S. and Korea in Vietnam and the Japan-Korea Treaty," p. 256.

64 *Administrative History, Department of State*, vol. 7 (East Asia), p. 2g, LBJ Library; Memo, JCT to Rostow, Subj: Elements of Progress in Asia, June 24, 1966, Thomson Papers, box 13, JFK Library; Lyndon B. Johnson, *The Vantage Point: Perspectives of the Presidency, 1963–1969* (Holt, Reinhart & Winston, 1971), p. 359. Also quoted in Kim, "U.S. and Korea in Vietnam and the Japan-Korea Treaty," pp. 256–257.

65 Seoul Embtel (Embassy Telegram) 2402, November 2, 1966, NSF, Country, box 255, LBJ Library; Kim, "U.S. and Korea in Vietnam and the Japan-Korea Treaty," pp. 257–258.

66 *Administrative History, Department of State*, vol. 7 (East Asia), p. 2g, LBJ Library; Kim, "U.S. and Korea in Vietnam and the Japan-Korea Treaty," p. 257.

SIXTEEN: *Legitimacy Wars*

1 Balázs Szalontai, "The Four Horsemen of the Apocalypse in North Korea: The Forgotten Side of a Not-So-Forgotten War," in Chris Springer and Balázs Szalontai, *North Korea Caught in Time: Images of War and Reconstruction* (Garnet, 2010), p. xix.

2 Nicholas Eberstadt and Judith Banister, *The Population of North Korea* (University of California, 1999), p. 133; Szalontai, "Four Horsemen of the Apocalypse in North Korea," p. xix.

3 Zhihua Shen and Yafeng Xia, "China and the Post-War Reconstruction of North Korea, 1953–1961," *NKIDP Working Paper* 4 (May 2012), p. 2, available at http://www.wilsoncenter.org/sites/default/files/NKIDP_Working_Pa per_4_China_and_the_Postwar_Reconstruction_of_North_Korea.pdf (accessed May 31, 2012).

4 Andrei Lankov, *From Stalin to Kim Il Sung: The Formation of North Korea, 1945–1960* (Rutgers University Press, 2002), pp. 150–151. In a brief memoir written by Ho K'ai's daughter, Lila, entitled, "Appanŏn amsaldang hayŏtda [My Father Was Assassinated]," she accuses Kim Il Sung of murdering her father in 1953. Although her evidence is circumstantial, she cites the highly suspicious manner in which her father's body was disposed of. She writes that her mother was not allowed to see the body of her husband when she arrived at his residence in Harbin, where he allegedly committed suicide, and was told that her husband had already been buried. See "Biographies of Soviet Korean Leaders," Asian Reading Room, Library of Congress, at http://www .loc.gov/rr/asian/SovietKorean.html (accessed June 1, 2012).

5 Lim Ŭn, *The Founding of a Dynasty in North Korea*, pp. 193–203; Lankov, *From Stalin to Kim Il Sung*, pp. 91–93.

6 Lim, *Founding of a Dynasty*, p. 194; Lankov, *From Stalin to Kim Il Sung*, pp. 94–95.

7 In his memoir written after his defection to South Korea in 1997, Hwang Chang-yŏp, the self-proclaimed architect of *chuch'e* ideology, revealed the circumstances behind the creation of *chuch'e* thought. Born in 1922 and trained as a social scientist and philosopher in Japan (before 1945) and in Moscow (1949–53), Hwang began to devise an ultra-nationalistic ideology that emphasized Korea's unique national characteristics after the war. By revising the orthodox Marxist tenet of class struggle as the driving force of history, Hwang sought instead to show that Korea's history had to be viewed from the perspective of the "people" (*inmin*). Hwang saw the "people's " struggle against foreign powers to achieve independence and self-determination as the main agent of Korean history. In particular, the notion of opposing *sadaejuŭi*, or serving Great Powers, was deemed to be especially important in the Korean people's drive to achieve *chuch'e*. "I decided to use the term 'people,' because I thought that opposing *sadaejuŭi* was not so much linked to the use and adaption of Marxist-Leninist concepts of class struggle, but rather, it had to do with tenaciously upholding the (national) self-determination of the Korean people." The most salient features of *chuch'e* ideology promote hostility against foreign powers while encouraging the sovereignty of Korea's heritage and its people. But as Hwang later explained, *chuch'e* ideology was eventually transformed from its original concept of national self-determination to become "the justification and organizational system for Kim Il Sung's one-man dictatorship." The necessity to inculcate the populace with *chuch'e* had effectively made Kim Il Sung the *sole* keeper and protector of the people's independence and self-determination. For this reason, North Korean propagandists have continually emphasized how Kim Il Sung worked to promote

the idea that the Korean people "not depend on great powers and instead determine their own destiny through self-determination." See Hwang Chang-yŏp, *Hwang Chang-yŏp hoegorok: Nanŭn yŏksaŭi chillirŭl poatta* [Hwang Chang-yŏp Memoir: Witness to History] (Seoul: Hanŭl, 1999), pp. 337–356. In February 1997, Hwang and an aide defected to the South Korean embassy in Beijing and several weeks later arrived in Seoul. After his defection, his wife committed suicide and one daughter died under mysterious circumstances. His other three children, two daughters and one son, as well as his grandchildren are believed to have been sent to labor camps. After his arrival in South Korea, Hwang soon found himself in the cold. Under the new Sunshine Policy of President Kim Dae-jung (1998–2003) that called for engagement with North Korea, few South Koreans, least of all Kim Dae-jung, were receptive to his anti–North Korean message as they feared it would upset the North. As a result, Hwang found himself increasingly isolated. On November 20, 2000, Hwang accused his South Korean hosts of keeping him a virtual prisoner. Nevertheless, Hwang wrote numerous books as well as contributed to the *DailyNK*, an online paper established by North Korean exiles in South Korea. Hwang died in his home on October 19, 2010, of a heart attack. "Hwang Jang-yŏp Hold Press Conference to Explain Why He Defected from North Korea," at http://www.fas.org/news/dprk/1997/bg152.html (accessed January 7, 2012). Also Aidan Foster-Carter, "P'yŏngyang Watch: Hwang Chang-yŏp: An Enemy of Which State?" *Asia Times*, November 30, 2000, at http://www.atimes.com/koreas/bk3odg01.html (accessed January 7, 2012).

8 James F. Person, "We Need Help from the Outside: The North Korean Opposition Movement of 1956," *CWIHP Working Paper 52* (August 2006), pp. 17–18.

9 Tatiana Gabroussenko, "Cho Ki-Ch'ŏn: The Person behind the Myth," *Korean Studies* 29 (2006), p. 67; Brian Myers, *Han Sorya and North Korean Literature: The Failure of Socialist Realism in the DPRK* (Cornell East Asian Series, 1994), pp. 140–141.

10 Andrei Lankov, "Kim Il Sung's Campaign against the Soviet Faction in Late 1955 and the Birth of *Chuch'e*," *Korean Studies* 23 (1999), pp. 60–62. See also Lankov, *Crisis in North Korea* (University of Hawaii Press, 2005), pp. 26–59.

11 Person, "We Need Help from the Outside," p. 18.

12 "Memorandum of Conversation with Vice Premier of the Cabinet of Ministers of the DPRK and Member of the Presidium, KWP CC Park Chang-ok," Filatov S. N., March 12, 1956, Document 1, in ibid., p. 58.

13 Khrushchev said in his secret speech at the Twentieth Party Congress of the Communist Party of the Soviet Union on February 25, 1956, "Stalin acted not through persuasion, explanation, and patient cooperation with people, but by imposing his concepts and demanding absolute submission to his opinion. Whoever opposed this concept or tried to prove his viewpoint, and the correctness of his position was doomed to removal from the leading collective and to subsequent moral and physical annihilation. This was especially true during the period following the 17th party congress, when many prominent party leaders and rank-and-file party workers, honest and dedicated to the cause of communism, fell victim to Stalin's despotism." Taubman, *Khrushchev: The Man and His Era*, pp. 270–277.

14 "Memorandum of Conversation with Vice Premier and Minister of Light Industry Bak Uiwan (Ivan Pak), 5 June 1956," *CWHIP Bulletin*, no. 16 (Fall 2007/Winter 2008), p. 473.

15 "Report by N. T. Fedorenko on a Meeting with DPRK Ambassador to the USSR Li Sangjo, 29 May, 1956," *CWHIP Bulletin*, no. 16 (Fall 2007/Winter 2008), p. 471.

16 "Memorandum of Conversation with Deputy Premier, Pak Ŭi-wan (Ivan Pak), September 6, 1956," translation in Person, "We Need Help from the Outside," pp. 77–78.

17 Letter to Khrushchev from Ambassador Yi Sang-jo via Deputy USSR Minister of Foreign Affairs N. Fedorenko, September 5, 1956, in *CWHIP Bulletin*, no. 16 (Fall 2007/Winter 2008), p. 488.

18 Documents published in Kathryn Weathersby, "From the Russian Archives: New Findings on the Korean War," *CWHIP Bulletin*, no. 3 (Fall 1993), p. 16.

19 Nobuo Shimotomai, "Pyeongyang in 1956," *CWHIP Bulletin*, no. 16 (Fall 2007/Winter 2008), p. 460.

20 James. F. Person, "New Evidence on North Korea in 1956," *CWHIP Bulletin*, no. 16 (Fall 2007/Winter 2008), pp. 448–449. For a description of the plenum as an attempt to replace Kim Il Sung, see Andrei Lankov, "Kim Takes Control: The 'Great Purge' in North Korea, 1956–1960," *Korean Studies* 26, no. 1 (2002), pp. 92–93.

21 John Lewis Gaddis, *The Cold War: A New History* (Penguin Press, 2005), pp. 107–110. Taubman, *Khrushchev: The Man and His Era*, pp. 294–299; Mark Kramer, "New Evidence on Soviet Decision Making and the 1956 Polish and Hungarian Crises," *CWIHP Bulletin*, nos. 8–9 (Winter 1996–1997).

22 James F. Person, "We Need Help from the Outside," pp. 49–50.

23 Hŏ Chin was the pseudonym for Lim Ŭn, author of *The Founding of a Dynasty in North Korea*. Quoted in Andrei Lankov, "Kim Takes Control: The 'Great Purge' in North Korea, 1956–1960," *Korean Studies* 26, no. 1 (2002), p. 102.

24 Ibid., p. 108.

25 Ibid., p. 105.

26 Kim Il Song, *Selected Works* (Foreign Language Publishing House, 1971), vol. 2, pp. 579–580.

27 Quoted in Balázs Szalontai, *Kim Il Sung in the Khrushchev Era: Soviet–DPRK Relations and the Roots of North Korean Despotism, 1953–1964* (Woodrow Wilson Center Press, 2005), p. 190.

28 B. C. Koh, "The *Pueblo* Incident in Perspective," *Asian Survey* 9, no. 4 (April 1969), p. 270; Daniel P. Bolger, "Scenes from an Unfinished War: Low Intensity Conflict in Korea, 1966–1968," *Leavenworth Paper* 19 (Combat Studies Institute, 1991), p. 3.

29 "Ministry of Foreign Affairs, Ministry of National Defense, Ministry of the Interior to the KPCZ CC [Communist Party of Czechoslovakia Central Committee] Presidium and the Czechoslovak Government File no.: 0200.873/68-3, 4 February 1968, Information about the Situation in Korea," Document 15, in Christian F. Ostermann and James F. Person, eds., *Crisis and Confrontation on the Korean Peninsula, 1968–1969: A Critical Oral History* (Woodrow Wilson International Center for Scholars, 2011), p. 186.

30 Bernd Schaefer, "North Korean Adventurism and China's Long Shadow, 1966–1972," *CWIHP Working Paper* 44 (October 2004), p. 19.

31 Most of the Japanese Koreans who immigrated to North Korea in the late 1960s and 1970s later regretted their decision. For a terrifying account of their experiences, see Kang Chol-hwan, *The Aquariums of Pyongyang: Ten Years in the North Korean Gulag* (Basic Books, 2001), and Tessa Morris-Suzuki, *Exodus to North Korea: Shadows from Japan's Cold War* (Rowman & Littlefield, 2007). In her in-depth and moving examination of the mass repatriation of Japanese Koreans (Zainichi) to North Korea, Morris-Suzuki reports that beginning in 1958, Kim Il Sung, together with leaders of Chŏngryŏn (General Association of Korean Residents in Japan), a pro–North Korean organization established in Japan in 1955, began coordinating, with international support, a vigorous propaganda campaign aimed to promote the mass repatriation of Zainichi to North Korea. Remarkably, among the 86,603 ethnic Koreans from Japan who eventually returned to North Korea between 1959 and 1985, the vast majority of them—some 97 percent—had originated from South Korea. While Kim Il Sung's interest in promoting this mass exodus stemmed in part from the labor shortage that North Korea was then experiencing, owing to the withdrawal of Chinese troops from North Korea in 1958, the repatriation of thousands of Zainichi to North Korea also provided the Kim regime with a propaganda victory. What better way to show the world the superiority of the North Korean system than to have thousands of Korean residents, originally from South Korea, "voting with their feet to return to the socialist North." The North Korean leadership certainly framed the repatriation issue in this way. In a meeting with Soviet Deputy Premier Anastas Mikoyan in mid-1959, Foreign Minister Nam Il boastfully proclaimed, "The emergence of the repatriation issue has brought political gains to the DPRK while Syngman Rhee has lost out. He is not only unable to accept [returnees] to South Korea, but on the contrary, is prepared to export unemployed people from South Korea to Latin America" (Morris-Suzuki, *Exodus to North Korea*, pp. 181–184). Sadly, while unknown numbers of those who left Japan for the DPRK would later end up in North Korean concentration camps, the mass exodus was hailed as evidence of the superiority of the North Korean system.

32 Joseph Sang-hoon Chung, " 'Seven Year Plan' (1961–1970): Economic Performance and Reforms," *Asian Survey* 12, no. 6 (June 1972), p. 529. One striking finding of more recent assessments of North Korea's economy is that the economic slowdown occurred much sooner, starting as early as the early 1960s. Comparison of growth rates between the two Koreas shows that only in the late 1950s was the growth rate in North Korea higher than that in the South. By the mid-1960s, South Korea's GNP per capita had already begun to surpass that of the North. These assessments run counter to the traditional view of high economic growth until the mid-1970s. See Byung-yeon Kim, Suk Jin Kim, and Keun Lee, "Assessing the Economic Performance of North Korea, 1954–1989: Estimates and Growth Accounting Analysis," *Journal of Comparative Economics* 35 (2007), pp. 564–582; Nicholas Eberstadt, *Policy and Economic Performance in Divided Korea during the Cold War Era: 1945–91* (AEI Press, 2010), pp. 78–80.

33 As one Soviet official stated, "The intensity of the two countries' rapproche-

ment was in direct proportion to the volume of all kinds of aid to the DPRK from the Soviet Union." Sergey S. Radchenko, "The Soviet Union and the North Korean Seizure of the USS *Pueblo*: Evidence from Russian Archives," *CWHIP Working Paper 47* (2005), p. 10. According to Russian sources, the Soviet Union rendered extensive aid to North Korea by November 1945. An aid package of 74 million rubles was provided in 1946; in 1947 that figure doubled to 140 million. After the war, in 1953 Moscow announced that it would grant 225 million rubles in free financial aid. The assistance dispensed by the Soviet Union and by other socialist states to North Korea accounted for 77.6 percent of all imports entering North Korea during 1954–56, which were financed through this free aid. For a detailed account of Soviet development aid to North Korea from 1945 to 1960, see George Ginsburg, "Soviet Development Grants and Aid to North Korea, 1945–1980," *Asia Pacific Community* (Fall 1982), pp. 43–63. According to Erik van Ree, the Soviets provided grants and credits roughly to the tune of $690 million for the period between 1953 and 1959. Long-term credits from Moscow between 1961 and 1976 were provided on at least eight occasions in the amount of approximately $300 million. Although assistance declined year by year, van Ree believes that Moscow may have provided P'yŏngyang assistance for the whole period of 1953–76, with credits and grants in the order of $1.3 billion. Soviet sources also suggest that "P'yŏngyang never repaid anything" (p. 68). The total of $1.3 billion average out to roughly $55 million in grants and aid per year that Soviet invested into North Korea's industry. North Korea's "economic miracle" was a chimera financed by foreign inputs from the Soviets and other communist bloc countries. See Erik van Ree, "The Limits of *Juche*: North Korea and Soviet Aid, 1953–1976," *Journal of Communist Studies* 5, no. 1 (1989); George Ginsburg, "The Legal Framework of Soviet Investment Credits to North Korea," *Osteuropa-Recht* 29, no. 4 (1983), pp. 256–277. Chinese documents uncovered from the PRC Ministry of Foreign Affairs archives also show the extensive amount of food aid China provided to North Korea after the war. From January 1954 to September 1955, for example, China transferred 300,000 tons of grain to North Korea. The Chinese also provided extensive monetary aid. In November 1953 Kim Il Sung arrived in Beijing to hammer out an economic pact with Chinese leaders that heavily favored North Korea: Beijing offered 800 million yuan in grants to be used for food, textiles, cotton, coal, reconstruction supplies, and other equipment. Kim also learned, "much to his delight," that the Chinese had "cancelled all of North Korea debts from the Korean War." China also became the largest supplier of consumer goods to North Korea, "flooding the market with clothing, toiletries and utensils." Apart from this aid and the delivery of important reconstruction equipment and supplies, perhaps the most important assistance P'yŏngyang received was from Chinese troops who were stationed in North Korea from 1953 to 1958. These soldiers made up for significant labor shortages and rebuilt infrastructure, and "their importance in reconstruction should not be underemphasized." See Adam Cathcart, "The Bonds of Brotherhood: New Evidence of Sino-North Korean Exchanges, 1950–1954," *Journal of Cold War Studies* 13, no. 3 (Summer 2011), pp. 27–51. China's aid also included the cancellation of North Korea's war debt, which amounted to 729 million Chinese yuan. According to Zhihua Shen and Yafeng Xia, "China's aid to North Korea in 1954 was equal to 3.4 percent of China's 1954 budget." See Shen and Xia, "China and the Post-War Reconstruction of North Korea, 1953–1961," p. 7.

34 "Report, Embassy of Hungary in North Korea to the Hungarian Foreign Ministry, August 1962," *CWIHP Bulletin*, no. 14/15 (Winter 2003/Spring 2004), p. 127.

35 Chung, " 'Seven-Year Plan'," p. 528. See also Scalapino and Lee, *Communism in Korea*, Part 2, pp. 1257–1262.

36 Ibid.

37 Van Ree, "Limits of *Juche*," pp. 55–56. Since domestic producers were protected from the foreign competition, there was no real incentive for increasing efficiency or productivity. In order to cope with these problems, North Korea was forced to resort to mass mobilization drives for longer working hours. This was essentially the strategy behind the *ch'ŏllima* movement that was launched in 1958, which was intended to promote rapid economic development. However, the mobilization of domestic labor alone cannot sustain a high level of growth in an economy limited by the constraints of a small domestic market that is bound to be monopolized by one or two producers. This is because there is very little incentive to improve productivity and efficiency through innovation in a seller's market. The result is decreased productivity and declining economic growth.

38 Erik van Ree, "Limits of *Juche*," p. 56. Van Ree also notes the irony that the *chuch'e* concept was original to North Korea. In fact, the idea behind all-around development and national self-sufficiency was in keeping with the standard, orthodox Stalinist concept of comprehensive economic development that was propagated after 1945. But this idea soon ran into trouble owing to the creation of unnecessary duplication of industries in the Soviet bloc countries. Although Khrushchev attempted to reverse this trend after 1953 by introducing the principle that small states should not strive for all-around development but instead begin a program of international specialization, North Korea never really got on board with that new program. As van Ree notes, "During the 1960s and 1970s, the construction of an autarkic, all-round economy remained the official goal." Ibid., p. 61; Sang-chul Suh, "North Korean Industrial Policy Today," in Robert A. Scalapino and Jun-yop Kim, eds., *North Korea Today: Strategic and Domestic Issues* (Center for Korean Studies, 1983), pp. 197–213.

39 By the 1970s, the Kim regime attempted to make some fundamental changes in its development strategy when it began to borrow heavily from Japan and Western Europe to finance the importation of new technology and foreign plants. However, it soon found itself unable to meet payments on external debts and defaulted. As a result of its debt problem, North Korea has been unable to obtain Western sources of credit since 1976. See Suh, "North Korean Industrial Policy Today," p. 213; Aidan Foster-Carter, "Korea and Dependency Theory," *Monthly Review* (October 1985), pp. 27–34.

40 Karoly Fendler, "Economic Assistance and Loans from Socialist Countries to North Korea in the Postwar Years, 1953–1963," *Asien: The German Journal on Contemporary Asia* 42 (January 1992), p. 4; V. Andreyev and V. Osipov, "Rela-

tions of the USSR and the European Socialist Countries with the DPRK in the 1970s," *Far Eastern Affairs* 1 (1982), pp. 52–56.

41 Szalontai, *Kim Il Sung and the Khrushchev Era*, pp. 121–123. The *ch'ŏllima* movement was modeled after Mao's Great Leap Forward. Like China, Kim also launched a patriotic hygiene campaign to eliminate the four "pests" (mice, sparrows, flies, and mosquitoes). The DPRK also introduced small-scale steelmaking projects, and in rural areas it "carried out the policy of merging cooperatives and operating mess halls," following China's practice of making "every citizen a soldier." See Shen and Xia, "China and the Post-War Reconstruction of North Korea, 1953–1961." Also, Scalapino and Lee, *Communism in Korea*, Part 2, pp. 1115–1120.

42 Balázs Szlontai, "In the Shadow of Vietnam: A New Look at North Korea's Militant Strategy, 1962–1970," *Journal of Cold War History* (forthcoming).

43 Ibid. Also Suh Dae-suk, *Kim Il Sung, the North Korean Leader* (Columbia University Press, 1988), pp. 231–234.

44 MOFAT: C21/F6/134, October 1967. The format for referencing MOFAT archival material, available only on microfilm, is microfilm roll number/file number/frame number, date.

45 Each year the UN General Assembly reaffirmed, through an overwhelming majority, its support for "The Korean Question" resolution. "Growth in United Nations Membership, 1945–Present," available at http://www.un.org/en/members/growth.shtml (accessed March 15, 2011).

46 See resolutions passed in 1965 and 1966: UN General Assembly, 20th Session (September–December 1965), Resolution 2132 (XX) "The Korean Question," December 21, 1965; UN General Assembly, 21st Session (September–December 1966), Resolution 2224 (XXI) "The Korean Question," December 19, 1966, available at http://www.un.org/documents/resga.htm (accessed March 15, 2011).

47 MOFAT: the following selected archival references to ROK/DPRK goodwill missions in 1967, 1968, 1970, and 1972 provide a good overview of the scale and variety of these missions especially those from South Korea.

   1967 ROK Goodwill missions: C21/F6/1-146 (Middle East), October 17–November 7, 1967; C21/F7/1-372 and C21/F8/1-135 (East Africa), August 24–October 5, 1967; C21/F9/1-382 (West Africa), August 23–September 29, 1967; C22/F1/1-132 (Southeast Asia), August 13–September 9, 1967; C22/F2/1-39 (Central America), October 16–26, 1967.

   1968 ROK Goodwill missions: C27/F4/1-111 (North Africa), January 22–February 1, 1968; C27/F5/1-236 (South/Southeast Asia), August 19–September 11, 1968; C27/F6/1-417 (Middle East), August 1–31, 1968; C27/F7/1-184 (Central America), August 1–24, 1968; C27/F8/1-258 (East Africa), August 1–September 8, 1968; C27/F9/1-284 (West Africa), August 1–September 1, 1968.

   1968 DPRK Goodwill missions: D6/F18/1-15 (Africa), November 7–December 19, 1968; D6/F19/1-216 (Southeast/Southwest Asia), June 15–August 1, 1968.

   1970 ROK Goodwill missions: C41/F5/1-66 (Middle East, Cyprus), July 9–August 6, 1970; C41/F6/1-155 (Latin America), July 23–August 15, 1970; C41/F7/1-23 (East Africa), July 25–August 19, 1970; C41/F8/1-62 (West Africa), July 23–August 17, 1970.

1970 DPRK Goodwill missions: D8/F31/1-142 (Africa), January 22–February 24, June 27–August 5, 1970.

1972 ROK Goodwill missions: C56/F9/1-221 and C56/F10/1-219 (Asia), July 8–23, 1972; C56/F10/1-189 (Middle East), December 5–21, 1972; C57/F11/1-66 (West Africa), December 5–18, 1972; C57/F5/1-209 (North Europe, Ethiopia), August 4–18, 1972.

1972 DPRK Goodwill missions: C56/F10/1-219 (ROK discussion of North Korean missions to East Europe, Middle East, Africa, Asia), July 8–23, 1972.

48 North Korean propaganda spread the message that South Koreans wished for nothing more than to rid themselves of their foreign "oppressors" and to be reunited with their northern brethren under the benevolent rule of Kim Il Sung. North Korea therefore needed "to be on constant alert and eventually seize the right opportunity to act." See Schaefer, "North Korean 'Adventurism'," p. 19. An East German report also confirms North Korean thinking: "More and more often they [North Koreans] repeat their readiness to act on the order of the party and the leader, to destroy the enemy and liberate South Korea. Ideological propaganda addressed to the population for armed liberation of South Korea has increased. At the same time, reports in the DPRK press about revolutionary movements and events in South Korea have proliferated. They are portraying a picture of a revolutionary upsurge already in motion." Quoted in ibid., p. 42.

49 The North Korean pilots and air defense forces sent to North Vietnam were part of this effort. According to a recently declassified CIA report, North Korea had offered an infantry division, but it was apparently rejected by Hanoi. CIA Intelligence Report, *Kim Il-Sung's New Military Adventurism* (TOP SECRET), November 26, 1968 (declassified with redactions on May 2007), p. 6, available at http://www.foia.cia.gov/CPE/ESAU/esau-39.pdf (accessed March 15, 2011).

50 Ibid., pp. 1–11; Bolger, *Scenes from an Unfinished War*, pp. 33–36.

51 B. C. Koh, "North Korea and the Sino-Soviet Schism," *Western Political Quarterly* 22, no. 4 (December 1969), pp. 957–958.

52 Chung, " 'Seven-Year Plan'," p. 538.

53 Radchenko, "The Soviet Union and the North Korean Seizure of the USS *Pueblo*," p. 10. The Soviet Union's abundant military aid for North Korea was an open secret. The *New York Times* reported in January 1968, for example, that "over the course of the last twelve months Moscow provided North Korea with 21 MIG-21 and 350 MIG-17 aircrafts, 80 MIG-15 fighters plus 80 IL-28 bombers." It also reported that "the North Korean army of 350,000 to 400,000 men is equipped almost exclusively with Soviet equipment, including medium tanks." *New York Times*, January 31, 1968. In 1968, Kim introduced a new slogan: "Vietnam is breaking one leg of the American bandit, we are breaking the other one." Quoted in Schaefer, "North Korean 'Adventurism'," p. 12.

54 *New York Times*, January 28, 1968.

55 Mitchell B. Lerner, *The Pueblo Incident: A Spy Ship and the Failure of American Foreign Policy* (University Press of Kansas, 2002), p. 99; also *New York Times*, January 28, 1968.

56 *New York Times,* January 27, 1968.

57 Radchenko, "The Soviet Union and the North Korean Seizure of the USS *Pueblo,*" p. 12.

58 *New York Times,* February 1, 1968; *Chosŏn ilbo,* February 1, 1968.

59 A year later, Kim was pardoned and released. In 1970 he became a South Korean citizen. He is today a well-known Protestant minister and an outspoken critic of the North Korean regime. John M. Glikona, "The Face of South Korea's Boogeyman," *Los Angeles Times,* July 18, 2010.

60 *Kangwŏn ilbo,* January 30, 1968, p. 3.

61 Ibid., January 25, 1968, p. 2. The *Kangwŏn ilbo* was the only province-wide newspaper published in Kangwŏndo province until 1992, when the *Kangwŏn domin ilbo* was established. Kangwŏndo is the only province that was split in half by the 38th parallel and the DMZ. Its border with North Korea, rugged terrain, and coastline, which is contiguous with North Korea, made it vulnerable to frequent North Korean provocations, including infiltration, murder, kidnapping of farmers and fishermen, capture of fishing boats, and even an attempt to incite a revolutionary uprising. Kangwŏndo was and still is predominantly populated by farmers and fishermen. Their tight-knit communities, tied to the soil and the sea and the constant threat of North Korean provocations, fostered a deeply anticommunist and anti–North Korean attitude and values. Kangwŏndo remains today one of the most conservative areas of South Korea. What sets the *Kangwŏn ilbo* apart from the more established national newspapers published in Seoul is that because it is far away from Seoul, the seat of power, and its major concern was economic development and the success of farming and fishing, it received relatively little scrutiny from the central government. As a result its contents were more open and often critical of Seoul's policies during the authoritarian period of the 1960s–70s.

62 "9 February 1968, [from] The Embassy of Czechoslovak Socialist Republic SM-021712/68, Pyongyang, [to] Ministry of Foreign Affairs, [subject] Pueblo and American-South Korean Relations," Document 17, in Ostermann and Person, eds., *Crisis and Confrontation on the Korean Peninsula,* pp. 207–208.

63 The first time Kim had severely miscalculated was when he had assured Stalin that "200,000 South Korean partisans" would rise up to greet the NKPA after it launched its invasion of the South. During the spring of 1968, Park approved the creation of the Homeland Reserve Force (*hyangt'o yebigun*), a people's militia. Although primarily designed to deal with the increasing North Korean guerilla threat in the countryside, it was, in essence, the first nationwide mass mobilization of the Park era. The Homeland Reserve Force quickly grew to include 2.5 million citizens and "created a hierarchically organized armed men in every village, town, city, and county" (Jiyul Kim, "War, Diplomacy, Mobilization and Nationbuilding in South Korea, 1968," unpublished paper [Harvard University, 2004], p. 4). The militia proved to be invaluable in detecting North Korean guerilla infiltration activity. In addition, Park established "reconstruction villages" just south of the DMZ. These villages, inhabited by armed ex-soldiers and their families on the model of Israeli border kibbutzim, "created a band of fiercely loyal people squarely in the path of any likely northern infiltrators" (Bolger, *Scenes from an Unfinished*

War, p. 83). ROK soldiers were also directed to work with local villages, building roads and doing civil engineer projects. The aim of the new ROK civic-action effort was to promote closer ties between the military and the civilian population. One of the most important ROK civic-action efforts entailed the creation and dispatch of "Medical/Enlightenment Teams" into the harsh T'aebaek and Chiri Mountains, where many North Korean infiltrations had taken place. These teams conducted medical screenings, inoculations, and minor surgery while promoting anticommunism. The success of the Homeland Reserve Force can be measured by the complete failure of Kim Il Sung's last major infiltration effort, which occurred in October 1968, just ten months after the Blue House raid. One hundred and twenty members of the elite 124th Army unit landed at eight separate locations on the east coast of South Korea, between the towns of Samchŏk and Ulchin. Their aim was to create guerilla bases in the South, but the scheme collapsed thanks to local villagers who quickly alerted the police to the North Korean presence. A force of seventy thousand, including thirty-five thousand Homeland Reserve Force members, was mobilized to track down the intruders. Within two weeks, they had all been captured or killed. As General Bonesteel observed about the incident, "It was a losing game to begin with for the North because of a miscomprehension of the situation in the South." Bolger, *Scenes from an Unfinished War*, pp. 86–87; Kim, "War, Diplomacy, Mobilization, and Nation-Building in South Korea, 1968," pp. 26–27.

64 Radchenko, "The Soviet Union and the North Korean Seizure of the USS *Pueblo*," p. 14.

65 Schaefer, "North Korean 'Adventurism'," p. 22.

66 Radchenko, "The Soviet Union and the North Korean Seizure of the USS *Pueblo*," p. 14.

67 Ibid., Document 23, "Excerpt from a Speech by Leonid Brezhnev," April 9, 1968, pp. 62–64. Similar observations were made by the Romanian ambassador to the DPRK, N. Popa, about the general state of tension, troop movements, neighborhood anti–air defense drills, night alarms, and evacuation of major cities in North Korea. "The archives of central institutions, a significant part of the State Library and of the Academy, more than half of the machinery used in the Typographic Complex and probably many other factories have been moved out of Pyongyang." Telegram from Pyongyang to Bucharest, TOP SECRET, no. 76.051, February 27, 1968, in Mitchell Lerner and Jong-Dae Shin, *NKIDP e-Dossier* No. 5: "New Romanian Evidence on the Blue House Raid and the USS Pueblo Incident," Document 23, available at http://www.wilsoncenter.org/publication/nkidp-e-dossier-no-5-new-romanian-evidence-the-blue-house-raid-and-the-uss-pueblo (accessed April 24, 2012).

68 Radchenko, "Soviet Union and the North Korean Seizure of the USS *Pueblo*," Document 23, p. 65.

69 Radchenko, "Soviet Union and the North Korean Seizure of the USS *Pueblo*," p. 15. Documents from the Romanian archives reinforce this view. S. Golosov, second secretary of the Soviet embassy in P'yŏngyang, reported that "Soviet diplomats were extremely worried with respect to the unrestrained actions undertaken by the DPRK against the ROK (the January 21 attack in Seoul)

and against the USA, manifested in the capturing of the military vessel AGER-2 [the USS *Pueblo*]. The Soviet diplomat pointed out that if the DPRK continued to undertake such initiatives to speed up the reunification of the country, it would be possible for the Soviets to be presented with a fait accompli in the sense of the resumption of an all-out war." S. Golosov also complained to Romanian officials that "when we try to moderate this warmongering state of mind on many occasions, our position is not taken into account." Telegram from P'yŏngyang to Bucharest, TOP SECRET, no. 76. 017, January 25, 1968, in Lerner and Shin, NKIDP e-Dossier No. 5: "New Romanian Evidence," Document 5.

70 Radchenko, "Soviet Union and the North Korean Seizure of the USS *Pueblo*," Document 23, pp. 66–67.

71 Ibid., Document 24, "Record of Conversation between Chairman of the Council of Ministers of the USSR Aleksei Kosygin and North Korean Ambassador in the USSR Chon Tu-hwan," May 6, 1968, p. 70.

72 "Excerpt from Leonid Brezhnev's Speech at the April (1968) CC (Central Committee) CPSU (Communist Party of the Soviet Union) Plenum, April 9, 1968," Document 13, in Mitchell B. Lerner, " 'Mostly Propaganda in Nature:' Kim Il Sung, the Juche Ideology, and the Second Korean War," *NKIDP Working Paper 3* (December 2010), p. 97.

73 Qiang Zhai, *China and the Vietnam Wars, 1950–1975* (University of North Carolina Press, 2000), p. 150; Radchenko, "Soviet Union and the North Korean Seizure of the USS *Pueblo*," p. 160.

74 Schaefer, "North Korean 'Adventurism'," pp. 5–15.

75 Lerner, *Pueblo Incident*, p. 140.

76 Radchenko, "Soviet Union and the North Korean Seizure of the USS *Pueblo*," pp. 18–19.

77 "Memorandum from Secretary of State Rusk to President Johnson, Washington, March 14, 1968," in *FRUS, 1964–1968*, vol. 29: *Korea, Part 1* (2000), p. 665.

78 *New York Times*, January 24, 1968; Lerner, *Pueblo Incident*, p. 118.

79 Lloyd M. Bucher, *Bucher: My Story* (Doubleday, 1970), p. 231.

80 Ibid., p. 249.

81 Edward R. Murphy, *Second in Command: The Uncensored Account of the Capture of the Spy Ship Pueblo* (Holt, Rinehart & Winston, 1971), p. 162.

82 Bucher, *Bucher*, p. 311.

83 Ibid., p. 324.

84 Stephen Harris, *My Anchor Held* (Fleming H. Revell, 1970), p. 108.

85 *Time*, October 18, 1968, p. 38.

86 Ed Brandt, *The Last Voyage of the USS Pueblo: The Exclusive Story, Told by 15 Members of the Crew* (W. W. Norton, 1969), pp. 84–85.

87 Ibid., p. 176.

88 Lerner, *Pueblo Incident*, p. 119.

89 Bucher, *Bucher*, p. 344.

90 Mitchell B. Lerner, "A Dangerous Miscalculation: New Evidence from Communist-Bloc Archives about North Korea and the Crisis of 1968," *Journal of Cold War Studies 6*, no. 1 (Winter 2004), p. 20.

91 Trevor Armbrister, *A Matter of Accountability: The True Story of the* Pueblo *Affair* (Coward-McCann, 1970), p. 334.

92 Ibid., p. 335.

93 *New York Times*, December 23, 1968.

94 Lerner, "Dangerous Miscalculation," p. 19.

95 *New York Times*, December 26, 1968.

96 Lerner, "Dangerous Miscalculation," p. 19.

97 *New York Times*, December 23, 1968.

SEVENTEEN: *Old Allies, New Friends*

1   *New York Times*, December 23, 1968.

2   *Chicago Tribune*, December 24, 1968.

3   Lerner, *Pueblo Incident*, p. 221.

4   *New York Times*, February 18, 1968.

5   Lerner, *Pueblo Incident*, p. 131.

6   Cables and letters between Seoul and Washington, in *FRUS, 1964–1968*, vol. 29: *Korea, Part 1* (2000), pp. 315–330.

7   "Telegram from the Commander in Chief, United States Forces, Korea (Bonesteel) to the Commander in Chief, Pacific (Sharp), Seoul, February 9, 1968," in *FRUS, 1964–1968*, vol. 29: *Part 1*, p. 356.

8   Kim, "U.S. and Korea in Vietnam and the Japan-Korea Treaty," pp. 243–249; Lerner, *Pueblo Incident*, p. 133.

9   Lerner, *Pueblo Incident*, p. 133.

10 "Letter from the Ambassador to Korea (Porter) to the Assistant Secretary of State for East Asian and Pacific Affairs (Bundy), Seoul, February 27, 1968," in *FRUS, 1964–1968*, vol. 29: *Part 1*, p. 392.

11 Lerner, *Pueblo Incident*, p. 134.

12 "Memorandum from Cyrus R. Vance to President Johnson, Washington, February 20, 1968," in *FRUS, 1964–1968*, vol. 29: *Part 1*, pp. 384–385. Key U.S. cables and reports pertaining to the Vance visit are in *FRUS, 1964–1968*, vol. 29: *Part 1*, pp. 347–395. Records of the visit from the South Korean archives are in MOFAT, C28/10 (C21-1/7-7/7) and C28/F11 (C22-1/1).

13 MOFAT, "First Park-Vance, Park Meeting," C28/F10 (C21-1/7-7/7)/42-58, February 12, 1968.

14 The details of what South Korea wanted as printed in *FRUS* ("Notes of the President's Meeting with Cyrus R. Vance," February 15, 1968, in *FRUS, 1964–1968*, vol. 29: *Part 1*, pp. 378–379) appear to be incorrect with regard to one item. The *FRUS* transcript of Vance's meeting with Johnson immediately after his return states, "One million dollars to augment his anti-guerilla forces." In actuality, the issue concerned providing small arms and equipment for one million men of the homeland security forces. The more accurate details come from the letter Vance signed at the conclusion of his visit (MOFAT, "Letter from Cyrus Vance to Foreign Minister Ch'oe Kyu-ha," C28/F10 (C21-1/7-7/7)/243-244, February 15, 1968).

15 Lerner, *Pueblo Incident*, p. 136.

16 Ibid., pp. 134–166.

17 Henry Kissinger, *White House Years* (Little, Brown, 1979), p. 742.

18 Richard Nixon, "Asia after Viet Nam," *Foreign Affairs* 46, no. 1 (October 1967), p. 121.

19 Walter Isaacson, *Kissinger: A Biography* (Simon & Schuster, 1992), p. 336.

20 National Security Archive, *New Documentary Reveals Secret U.S., Chinese Diplomacy behind Nixon's Trip*, National Security Archive Electronic Debriefing Book 145, William Burr, ed., December 21, 2004, Document 4: "Front page of People's Daily, 25 December 1970, showing from left, Edgar Snow, interpreter Ji Chaozhu, Mao Zedong, and Lin Biao, at a reviewing stand facing Tiananmen Square on 1 October 1970," available at http://www.gwu.edu/~nsarchiv/NSAEBB/NSAEBB145/index.htm (accessed March 16, 2011).

21 Isaacson, *Kissinger*, pp. 338–339.

22 Philip Short, *Mao: A Life* (John Murray, 2004), p. 583.

23 Bernd Schaefer, "North Korean 'Adventurism' and China's Long Shadow, 1966–1972," *CWIHP Working Paper 44* (October 2004), p. 32.

24 Ibid., pp. 34–35.

25 Don Oberdorfer, *The Two Koreas* (Addison-Wesley, 1997), p. 12.

26 Schaefer, "North Korean 'Adventurism'," p. 38.

27 *Kangwŏn ilbo*, September 30, 1972, p. 2.

28 MOFAT, *Lam, Pham Dang, Visit of South Vietnamese Special Envoy*, C58/F5/77-87, November 2–4, 1972.

29 Christian F. Ostermann and James F. Person, eds., *The Rise and Fall of Détente on the Korean Peninsula, 1970–1974*, History and Public Policy Program, Critical Oral History Conference Series (CWIHP, 2011), pp. 14–15.

30 Seongji Woo, "The Park Chung-hee Administration amid Inter-Korean Reconciliation in the Détente Period: Changes in the Threat Perception, Regime Characteristics and the Distribution of Power," *Korea Journal* (Summer 2009), p. 54. The South Koreans had good reason to worry. In his conversation with Zhou Enlai on July 9, 1971, Kissinger gave hope that North Koreans would have something to gain from a Sino-U.S. rapprochement: "If the relationships between our countries develop as they might, after the Indochina war ends and the ROK troops return to Korea, I would think it quite conceivable that before the end of the next term of President Nixon, most, if not all, American troops will be withdrawn from Korea." "Memcon (Memorandum of Conversation), Zhou Enlai-Kissinger 9 July, 1971," in *FRUS, 1969–1976*, vol. 17: *China 1969–1972* (2006), p. 390. See also Bernd Schaefer, "Overconfidence Shattered: North Korean Unification Policy, 1971–1975," *CWIHP Working Paper 2* (December 2010), p. 6.

31 James Person, "New Evidence on Inter-Korean Relations, 1971–1972," Document 28 (September 22, 1972), *NKIPD Document Reader 3*, CWIHP, October 15, 2009.

32 Schaefer, "Overconfidence Shattered," p. 31. Also Schaefer, "North Korean 'Adventurism'," p. 37.

33 See Yong-Jick Kim, "The Security, Political, and Human Rights Conundrum, 1974-1979," in Kim and Vogel, eds., *Park Chung Hee Era*, 2011), pp. 457–482; see also Ch'oe Ho-il, "Kukga anbo wigiwa yusinch'eche [National Security Crisis and the Yusin System]," in Cho Yi che and Carter Eckert, eds., *Han'guk kundaehwa, kichŏkŭi kwachŏng* [Modernization of the Republic of Korea: A Miraculous Achievement] (Seoul: Wŏlganchosŏnhoe, 2005), pp. 149–179. Ch'oe makes the interesting point that South Korea's economic suc-

cess was a direct result of the threat posed by North Korea and that rapid industrialization under Park's *Yusin* system can aptly be described as "crisis development." This situation was not unlike what Japan's leaders experienced at the end of the nineteenth century when Commodore Mathew Perry and his armed "black ships" sailed into Edo (Tokyo) Bay in 1853. Japan's new Meiji leaders quickly recognized the Western threat to their nation and, in response, launched the Meiji Revolution in 1868. Not surprisingly given his background as a former lieutenant in the Japanese Kwantung Army, Park saw himself as a "Korean" Meiji reformer and considered his *Yusin* system to be the Korean equivalent of Japan's Meiji Revolution.

34 Yi P'il–nam, "The October *Yusin*," *Kangwŏn ilbo*, February 27, 1973.

35 Oberdorfer, *Two Koreas*, p. 37.

36 Kim Hyung-a, *Korea's Development under Park Chung Hee: Rapid Industrialization, 1961–79* (Routledge, 2004), p. 139.

37 Recent evidence indicates that the nuclear program continued under cover and in reduced scale in response to President Carter's threat to withdraw all U.S. forces from Korea. See Sung Gul Hong, "The Search for Deterrence: Park's Nuclear Option," in Kim and Vogel, eds., *Park Chung Hee Era*, pp. 483–510; Peter Hayes and Chung-in Moon, "Park Chung Hee, the CIA, and the Bomb," Nautilus Institute, September 23, 2011, available at http://www .nautilus.org/publications/essays/napsnet/reports/Hayes_Moon_Park ChungHee_Bomb (accessed October 10, 2011).

38 Schaefer, "Overconfidence Shattered," p. 28.

39 Pak Ch'i-young, *Korea and the United Nations* (Springer, 2000), pp. 49–50. The Nonaligned Movement (NAM) originated at the Asia-Africa Conference held in Bandung, Indonesia, in 1955. The conference, convened at the invitation of the prime ministers of Burma, Ceylon, India, Indonesia, and Pakistan, brought together leaders of twenty-nine states, mostly former colonies, from the two continents of Africa and Asia to discuss "similar problems of resisting the pressures of the major powers, maintaining their independence and opposing colonialism and neo-colonialism, specially western domination." In 1961, it was formally established as an intergovernmental organization of states that represented nearly two-thirds of the United Nations' members. See http://www.nam.gov.za/background/history.htm, the official NAM web site (accessed April 15, 2011).

EIGHTEEN: *War for Peace*

1 John Singlaub, *Hazardous Duty: An American Soldier in the Twentieth Century* (Summit Books, 1991), pp. 376–379; *New York Times*, August 25, 1976; *Time*, August 30, 1976, pp. 42–43; *Newsweek*, August 30, 1976, pp. 50–52.

2 *New York Times*, August 19, 1976.

3 "Response to Ax Killing, Memorandum of Telephone Conversation, August 18, 1976," *The United States and the Two Koreas from Nixon to Clinton (1969–2000)*, item K000213, Digital National Security Archives (accessed February 2, 2010).

4 I am indebted to retired U.S. Army Col. Don Boose for this point. Colonel Boose served at the Joint Security Area as a member of the UN Command Military Armistice Commission and was present in the Joint Security Area

when the ax incident took place, and participated in its investigation and negotiations with the North Koreans. He stated, "Having studied the incident intensely, I am convinced that the murder of the two U.S. officers was not planned, but was the result of a fight instigated by the NKPA guard force officer on the scene that got out of hand. The most compelling evidence is that the North Koreans were totally unprepared to take advantage of the incident for propaganda purposes and were unprepared to deal with any military escalation that might have resulted." Comment for the author, July 13, 2011.

5 "Minutes of Washington Special Actions Group Meetings, Washington, August 19, 1976, 8:12-9:15 a.m.," Document 285, Chapter 6, in *FRUS, 1969–1976*, vol. E-12: *Documents on East and Southeast Asia, 1973–1976*. Available only online at History.state.gov/historicaldocuments/frus1969-76ve12/d285 (accessed November 16, 2011).

6 *New York Times*, August 11, 1976.

7 Ibid., August 29, 1976. During the first half of 1976, P'yŏngyang took several steps to heighten international tensions. In February, two North Korean diplomats publicly announced that the DPRK possessed nuclear weapons. On April 7, two North Korean tanks entered the DMZ and remained there for four hours, "an act unprecedented since the 1953 armistice." The killing of the two American soldiers in August was thus the culmination of a series of provocative actions timed to coincide with the NAM conference in Sri Lanka. Such provocations were, as the historian Balázs Szalontai has observed, "often planned well in advance and were carefully coordinated with diplomatic maneuvers, indicating that KWP leaders were more rational actors than it is sometimes assumed." See Balázs Szalontai and Sergey Radchenko, "North Korea's Efforts to Acquire Nuclear Technology and Nuclear Weapons: Evidence from Russian and Hungarian Archives," *CWIHP Working Paper 53* (August 2006), pp. 13–15.

8 *New York Times*, August 22, 1976.

9 Ibid., August 25, 1976.

10 Ibid., August 23, 1976.

11 Robert Rich, "U.S. Ground Forces Withdrawal from Korea: A Case Study in National Security Decision Making," *Executive Seminar in National and International Affairs*, U.S. Department of State, Foreign Service Institute, June 1982, p. 6.

12 *New York Times*, June 24, 1976; Don Oberdorfer, "Carter's Decision on Korea Traced Back to January 1975," *Washington Post*, June 12, 1977.

13 *U.S. News & World Report*, June 6, 1977, p. 17; *New York Times*, May 23, 1977. Also, James V. Young, *Eye on Korea: An Insider Account of Korean American Relations* (Texas A&M Press, 2003), pp. 41–42.

14 Presidential Review Memorandum (PRM) 13 available at http://www.fas.org/irp/offdocs/prm/prm13.pdf (accessed April 1, 2011).

15 "Top Secret, Presidential Directive, May 5, 1977," *The United States and the Two Koreas from Nixon to Clinton (1969–2000)*, item K000228, Digital National Security Archives; Oberdorfer, *Two Koreas*, p. 87.

16 Oberdorfer, *Two Koreas*, p. 87; Cyrus Vance, *Hard Choices: Critical Years in America's Foreign Policy* (Simon & Shuster, 1983), p. 128.

17 William Gleysteen Jr., *Massive Entanglement, Marginal Influence: Carter and Korea in Crisis* (Brookings Institute Press, 1999), p. 22.

18 Ibid., p. 23.

19 *Deaths of American Military Personnel in the Korean Demilitarized Zone: Hearing before the Subcommittees on International Political and Military Affairs and International Organizations of the Committee on International Relations, House of Representatives, 94th Congress, 2d Session, September 1, 1976* (U.S. Government Printing Office, 1976), p. 22.

20 PRM 10 *Comprehensive Net Assessment Force Posture Review*, February 18, 1977. PRM 10 was one of the largest strategic reviews of the cold war. Neither the PRM 10 task force reports nor the overview reports have been declassified. Portions of the report and its findings have been published as an annex to the final PRM 10 report. See PRM 10 (February 18, 1977), available at http://www.fas.org/irp/offdocs/prm/prm10.pdf (accessed April 1, 2011); Joe Wood and Philip Zelikow, "Persuading a President: Jimmy Carter and American Troops in Korea," *Kennedy School of Government Case Program*, Harvard University, C1-96-1319.0, p. 7; Rowland Evans and Robert Novak, "PRM 10 and the Korean Pull-out," *Washington Post*, September 7, 1977; PRM/NSC-13 (January 26, 1977), p. 23, available at http://www.fas.org/irp/offdocs/prm/prm13 .pdf (accessed April 1, 2011). For an excellent overview of PRM 10, see Brian J. Auten, *Carter's Conversion: The Hardening of America's Defense Policy* (University of Missouri Press, 2009), pp. 154–165.

21 Wood and Zelikow, "Persuading a President," p. 9.

22 Rich, "U.S. Ground Forces Withdrawal from Korea," p. 14. See also Vance, *Hard Choices*, pp. 127–130.

23 *New York Times*, May 26, 1977; Oberdorfer, *Two Koreas*, p. 89.

24 *Time*, May 30, 1977, p. 14.

25 *New York Times*, May 29, 1977.

26 *U.S. Troop Withdrawal from the Republic of Korea, a Report to the Committee on Foreign Relations, United States Senate*, by Senators Hubert H. Humphrey and John Glenn, January 9, 1978 (hereafter the *Humphrey and Glenn Report*), 95th Congress, 2d Session (U.S. Government Printing Office, 1978), p. 13.

27 *New York Times*, July 2, 1977.

28 Ibid., May 30, 1977.

29 Oberdorfer, *Two Koreas*, p. 91.

30 Wood and Zelikow, "Persuading a President," p. 15.

31 *Washington Post*, October 28, 1977. See also Chae-Jin Lee, *A Troubled Peace: U.S. Policy and the Two Koreas* (Johns Hopkins University Press, 2006), pp. 98–103, and Kim Han-cho, *Robisŭt'ŭ Kim Han-cho ch'oe ch'o kopaek koria geit'e* [*Very First Confessions of Lobbyist Kim Han-cho*] (Illim wŏn, 1995). Although ten members of Congress and several Korean businessmen, including Pak Tong-sŏn and Kim Han-cho, were implicated in the scandal, in the end only U.S. Congressman Richard T. Hanna (D-CA) and Kim Han-cho were convicted by the U.S. Department of Justice for their roles in the affair. (Pak was granted immunity in exchange for his testimony). Kim Han-cho served a six-month prison sentence in the United States and later wrote a memoir about his experiences. In it, he blamed Kim Hyŏng-uk, one of Park Chung Hee's close associates and KCIA director from 1963–1969, of

offering false testimony against him. Kim Hyŏng-uk also implicated Park Chung Hee in the lobbying scandal. Nevertheless, no definitive evidence has ever been uncovered directly linking the South Korean president to illegal lobbying activities, and is it still unclear how much Park Chung Hee knew about the affair. On October 7, 1979, Kim Hyŏng-uk disappeared in Paris. It was widely rumored that he was killed by ROK agents. See Chong Hŭi-sang, "Kim Hyŏng ukŭn naega chukyŏtta" ["I Killed Kim Hyŏng-uk"], *Sisa chŏnŏl*, December 18, 2005, http://www.sisapress.com/news/articleView .html?idxno=23992 (accessed December 17, 2012).

During his testimony, Kim Hyŏng-uk heavily criticized Park. Kim was also going to publish his memoirs, which would have been extremely damaging to Park, so the latter tried to silence him with a bribe. Kim took Park's money but still gave a friend in New York the only copy of the manuscript. Excerpts of the manuscript were originally published in Japan. The entire manuscript was eventually smuggled into South Korea and published in 1985. See Kim Hyŏng-uk, *Kim Hyŏng-uk heorok* [*Memoir of Kim Hyŏng-uk*], 3 vols. (Tosŏ ch'ulp'an ach'im, 1985). For the complete transcripts of the congressional hearings, including Kim Hyŏng-uk's testimony, see Committee on International Relations, *Investigation of Korean-American Relations: Hearing before the Subcommittee on International Organizations*, 95th Cong., 1st sess., in seven parts from June 22, 1977, to August 15, 1978 (Government Printing Office, 1978), http://catalog.hathitrust.org/Record/002939983 (accessed December 17, 2012).

32 Quoted in Oberdorfer, *Two Koreas*, p. 92.

33 *New York Times*, April 10, 1977.

34 Ibid., March 11, 1977.

35 *Humphrey and Glenn Report*, p. v; Rich, "U.S. Ground Forces Withdrawal from Korea," p. 22.

36 China's strong opposition to the withdrawal plan was made clear in a report from the Hungarian embassy in P'yŏngyang in July 1975: "We know from Soviet and Chinese sources that—primarily in China—Kim Il Sung considered the possibility of a military solution. According to the Chinese ambassador, the DPRK wants to create the kind of military situation in South Korea that came into being in South Vietnam before the victory. Taking advantage of the riots against the dictatorial regime of Park Chung Hee, and invited by certain South Korean [political] forces, the DPRK would have given military assistance if it had not been dissuaded from doing so in time. This dissuasion obviously began as early as [Kim Il Sung's visit] in Beijing [April 18–26, 1975], for it is well-known that—primarily in Asia—*China holds back and opposes any kind of armed struggle that might shake the position of the USA in Asia* [author's emphasis]. A new Korean War would not be merely a war between North and South [Korea]. With this end in view, during the Korean party and government delegation's stay in Beijing, the Chinese side strongly emphasized the importance of the peaceful unification of Korea." Document No. 26, "Report, Embassy of Hungary in North Korea to the Hungarian Foreign Ministry, 30 July 1975," in Szalontai and Radchenko, "North Korea's Efforts to Acquire Nuclear Technology and Nuclear Weapons," pp. 52–53.

37 *Humphrey and Glenn Report*, pp. 9–16.

38 Ibid., pp. 9, 62.

39 Rich, "U.S. Ground Forces Withdrawal from Korea," p. 3.

40 Oberdorfer, *Two Koreas*, p. 103. In a similar intelligence assessment of the military balance on the Korean peninsula, the CIA warned that "the static military balance between North and South Korea alone now favors the North by a substantial margin" and that "the US military presence in South Korea represents an in-place affirmation of the US commitment to help to defend the South and remains a key factor in the balance of deterrence on the Korean peninsula." "Military Balance on the Korean Peninsula (Secret)," CIA NFAC (National Foreign Assessment Center), May 10, 1978, in *The United States and the Two Koreas from Nixon to Clinton (1969–2000)*, item K00259, Digital National Security Archives.

41 Oberdorfer, *Two Koreas*, pp. 101–105; Rich, "U.S. Ground Forces Withdrawal from Korea," p. 22; Gleysteen, *Massive Entanglement*, p. 43.

42 Michael A. Ledeen, "Trumping Asian Allies," *Harper's Magazine*, March 1979, p. 28.

43 Gleysteen, *Massive Entanglement*, pp. 38–43; Oberdorfer, *Two Koreas*, p. 105.

44 Cho Kap-je, *Nae mudŏm e ch'imŭl paet'ŏra: Ch'oin ŭi norae* [Spit on My Grave: Hymn of a Great Man] (Seoul: Choson ilbosa, 1998), vol. 1, p. 108.

45 Gleysteen, *Massive Entanglement*, p. 46.

46 "Conversation between President Carter and South Korean President Park Chung Hee, July 5, 1979," in *The United States and the Two Koreas from Nixon to Clinton (1969–2000)*, item K00317, Digital National Security Archives (accessed March 2, 2010).

47 The scene is vividly painted by Oberforder, *Two Koreas*, p. 106.

48 Gleysteen, *Massive Entanglement*, pp. 47–48.

49 Oberdorfer, *Two Koreas*, p. 108.

50 Gleysteen, *Massive Entanglement*, p. 50.

NINETEEN: *End of an Era*

1 Chŏng Chae-gyŏng *Wiin Pak Chŏng-hŭi* [The Great Man Park Chung Hee] (Seoul: Chipmundang, 1992), pp. 295–296.

2 Cho, *Nae mudŏm e ch'imŭl paet'ŏra: Ch'oin ŭi norae* [Spit on My Grave: Hymn of a Great Man], pp. 62–63.

3 Ibid., p. 20.

4 Ibid., p. 169.

5 Ibid., p. 119. According to the South Korean Joint Investigation Team of the Martial Law Command that investigated the incident, Kim Chae-kyu did not give instructions to mobilize military units nor were other KCIA men alerted to his plan. The official report concluded that Kim's anger at the president's reprimands over his handling of the political turmoil in Pusan and Masan, together with his deep hatred of Ch'a Chi-ch'ŏl, whom he saw as having an unhealthy and negative influence on Park, drove Kim to kill both men. On the other hand, Kim allegedly also told his attorneys that the assassination was premeditated because he was intent on preventing bloodshed in Seoul, where large demonstrations were expected in the wake of the political turmoil in Pusan and Masan. For an excerpt of the report in English, see *New*

York Times, November 7, 1979. A detailed account of the assassination and its aftermath is recounted in Cho's *Nae mudŏm e ch'imŭl paet'ŏra* [Spit on My Grave].

6 Between 1966 and 1972 North Korean forces caused the deaths of 329 South Korean military, 91 civilians, and 75 American military personnel. North Korean terrorism continued into the 1980s with devastating results. On October 9, 1983, North Korea attempted to assassinate President Chŏn Tu-hwa), Park's successor, and his cabinet members in Rangoon, Burma (Myan-mar). The president survived the attack, but four members of his cabinet, including two senior presidential advisors and the ambassador to Burma, were killed in the blast. In September 1986, a North Korean bomb at Seoul's Kimp'o International Airport killed five and wounded thirty. A year later, on November 29, 1987, two North Korean agents planted a bomb on Korean Air flight 858 bound for Seoul from Abu Dhabi. It exploded in mid-flight, kill-ing all 115 on board. North Korea was condemned as a terrorist state by the international community. See Narushige Michishita, "Calculated Adventur-ism: North Korea's Military-Diplomatic Campaigns," *Korea Journal of Defense Analysis* 16, no. 2 (Fall 2004), pp. 188–197; Joseph S. Bermudez Jr., *Terrorism: The North Korean Connection* (Crane Russak, 1990), p. 43.

7 John A. Wickham, *Korea on the Brink: From the "12/12/ Incident" to the Kwangju Uprising, 1979–1980* (National Defense University, 1999), pp. 61–65; Oberdorfer, *Two Koreas*, pp. 117–119.

8 Oberdorfer, *Two Koreas*, 125; Wickham, *Korea on the Brink*, 128. Nearly a decade later, after an extensive investigation due to enormous political pressure from South Korean and American human rights activists and politicians, the U.S. government concluded that Ambassador Gleysteen and General Wick-ham had no prior knowledge of nor aided and abetted the December 12 coup, the declaration of martial law, or the Kwangju crackdown, and that they had tried their utmost to prevent political and human rights abuses through the unauthorized and misuse of military forces. See *U.S. Government Statement on the Events in Kwangju, Republic of Korea, in May 1980* issued by the Ameri-can embassy in Seoul on June 19, 1989, available at http://seoul.usembassy .gov/p_kwangju.html (accessed July 30, 2011).

9 For a detailed examination of student *chuch'e* ideology (*chuch'eron*), see Sheila Miyoshi Jager, *Narratives of Nation Building in Korea: A Genealogy of Patriotism* (M. E. Sharpe, 2003), especially chaps. 4 and 6. I am grateful to M. E. Sharpe for allowing me to use portions of these and other chapters in this book. Copyright, 2003, M. E. Sharpe. All rights reserved. Reprinted by permission of M. E. Sharpe, http://www.mesharpe.com/.

10 The link between national unification and romantic reunion is laid out in detail in Sheila Miyoshi Jager, "Woman, Resistance and the Divided Nation: The Romantic Rhetoric of Korean Reunification," *Journal of Asian Studies* 55, no. 1 (1996).

11 Kim Nam-ju, Nongbuŭi pam [The Farmer's Night] (Seoul: Kidok Saeng-hwal Tongjihoe, 1988). Translation in Jager, *Narratives of Nation Building*, pp. 69–70.

12 Sheila Miyoshi Jager and Jiyul Kim, "The Korean War after the Cold War: Commemorating the Armistice Agreement in South Korea," in Sheila Miyo-

shi Jager and Rana Mitter, eds., *Ruptured Histories: War, Memory and the Post-Cold War in Asia* (Harvard University Press, 2007), pp. 262–265.

13 Quoted in B. R. Myers, *The Cleanest Race*, pp. 155–156.

14 Jager, *Narratives of Nation Building*, p. 103.

15 On how these perceptions of North Korea were absorbed in mainstream South Korean society, see Jager and Kim, "Korean War after the Cold War." In *Swiri* [Shiri] (1999), for example, Korea's first Hollywood-style big-budget blockbuster, the reunification drama is examined from the perspective of a doomed love story between a South Korean security agent and a secret North Korean agent. *Joint Security Area* (2000) and *Taegguki* [T'aegukki] (2004), both also blockbuster hits, explored the Korean War in terms of the relationship between brothers. Like *Swiri*, both films were sympathetic in their portrayal of North Korea.

TWENTY: *North Korea and the World*

1 Nicholas Eberstadt, *The End of North Korea* (American Enterprise Institute Press, 1999), p. 118.

2 Karoly Fendler, "Economic Assistance from Socialist Countries to North Korea in the Postwar Years: 1953–1963," in Han S. Park, ed., *North Korea: Ideology, Politics, Economy* (University of Georgia Press, 1996), p. 166.

3 *Christian Science Monitor*, July 10, 2003.

4 Eberstadt, *End of North Korea*, p. 100.

5 After P'yŏngyang's unsuccessful attempts to persuade the Soviet Union and other Soviet-bloc countries to boycott the Seoul Olympics, Kim suggested that North Korea co-host the games and asked for a fifty-fifty split of all events. Seoul and the International Olympic Committee (IOC) rejected the proposal but, under pressure from North Korea's allies, suggested instead that North Korea be allowed to host some events, including table tennis and fencing. North Korea responded that the offer was insufficient. As negotiations stalled, the IOC and Seoul eventually decided to go ahead with their planning without P'yŏngyang's participation. Angered by this turn of events, North Korea decided to disrupt the games and on October 7, 1987, sent two highly trained espionage agents to destroy Korean Air flight 858. The plane blew up on its way from Abu Dhabi to Seoul, killing all 115 persons on board. In wake of the bombing of flight 858, North Korea was placed on a list of countries practicing terrorism, further deepening its international isolation. See Oberdorfer, *Two Koreas*, pp. 180–186; see also Kim Hyun-hui, *The Tears of My Soul* (William Morrow, 1993).

6 No T'ae-u, *No T'ae-u hoegorok* [Memoirs of No T'ae-u], vol. 2: *Chŏnhwangiŭi taejŏllyak* [Grand Strategy of a Turning Point] (Seoul: Chosŏn nyusŭ p'resu, 2011), p. 140.

7 Carolyn Ekedahl and Melvin Goodman, *The Wars of Eduard Shevardnadze* (University of Pennsylvania Press, 1997), p. 216.

8 Oberdorfer, *Two Koreas*, p. 207.

9 Quoted in ibid., pp. 209–212.

10 No T'ae-u, *No T'ae-u hoegorok* [Memoirs of No T'ae-u], vol. 2, p. 209.

11 Ibid., p. 217.

12 Mikhail Gorbachev, *Memoirs* (Doubleday, 1995), p. 544.

13 Oberdorfer, *Two Koreas*, p. 246.

14 Eberstadt, *End of North Korea*, p. 100.

15 Document No. 30, "Report, Embassy of Hungary in North Korea to the Hungarian Foreign Ministry, 15 April 1976," in Balázs Szalontai and Sergey Radchenko, "North Korea's Efforts to Acquire Nuclear Technology and Nuclear Weapons: Evidence from Russian and Hungarian Archives," *CWIHP Working Paper 53* (August 2006), p. 56.

16 Szalontai and Radchenko, "North Korea's Efforts to Acquire Nuclear Technology and Nuclear Weapons," p. 29.

17 Ibid., p. 21.

18 Oberdorfer, *Two Koreas*, pp. 254–255, 267–269; International Institute for Strategic Studies (IISS), *North Korea's Weapons Program: A Net Assessment* (Palgrave Macmillan, 2004), pp. 34–35.

19 " 'Sea of Fire' Threat Shakes Seoul," *Financial Times*, March 22, 1994; *Washington Post*, May 1, 1994.

20 *New York Times*, March 23, 1994.

21 *Washington Post*, May 1, 1994.

22 *New York Times*, March 19, 1994; Peter D. Zimmerman, "Nuclear Brinkmanship Redefined," *Los Angeles Times*, June 5, 1994.

23 *Washington Post*, April 6, 1994; Oberdorfer, *Two Koreas*, p. 319.

24 *New York Times*, July 24, 1994.

25 *Washington Post*, May 19 and 20, 1994; Oberdorfer, *Two Koreas*, p. 309.

26 *Washington Post*, May 19, 1994; Joel Wit, Daniel Poneman, and Robert Gallucci, *Going Critical: The First North Korean Nuclear Crisis* (Brookings Institution, 2004), p. 205; Oberdorfer, *Two Koreas*, p. 315.

27 Wit et al., *Going Critical*, pp. 227–228; Oberdorfer, *Two Koreas*, pp. 306, 332.

28 Wit et al., *Going Critical*, p. 228; *Washington Post*, June 18, 19, and 20, 1994; Myers, *The Cleanest Race*, p. 142; *New York Times*, June 19, 1994.

29 Jimmy Carter, *Sharing Good Times* (Simon & Schuster, 2004), pp. 129–130; Oberdorfer, *Two Koreas*, p. 336.

30 *New York Times*, July 15, 1994; Oberdorfer, *Two Koreas*, pp. 344–345.

31 Myers, *Cleanest Race*, p. 51; *New York Times*, August 31, 1994.

32 *Washington Post*, November 23, 1994; Oberdorfer, *Two Koreas*, pp. 352–354.

33 Oberdorfer, *Two Koreas*, p. 357.

34 Myers, *Cleanest Race*, p. 144.

35 *Chosŏn ilbo*, September 4, 1994; *Washington Post*, September 5, 1994.

36 "The Content of the Korea Accord," *Washington Post*, October 21, 1994; "Clinton Approves a Plan to Give Aid to North Koreans," *New York Times*, October 19, 1994.

37 *New York Times*, November 26, 1994.

38 "Kim's Nuclear Gamble," *Frontline*, PBS, 2003, directed by Marcela Gaviria and written by Martin Smith.

TWENTY-ONE: *Winners and Losers*

1 Sheila Miyoshi and Jiyul Kim, "The Korean War after the Cold War," in Jager and Mitter, eds., *Ruptured Histories*, p. 242. I am grateful to Harvard University Press for giving me permission to reprint portions of this chapter in this book. Copyright, 2007, Harvard University Press. All rights reserved. Reprinted by permission of the present publisher, Harvard University Press, http://www.hup.harvard.edu/.

2 A detailed treatment of the War Memorial can be found in my "Monumental Histories: Maniless, the Military and the War Memorial," *Public Culture* 14, no. 2 (Spring 2002), pp. 387–409; *Narratives of Nation Building in Korea: A Genealogy of Patriotism* (M. E. Sharpe, 2003); and Jager and Kim, "Korean War after the Cold War." I am grateful to Duke University Press for giving me permission to reprint portions of my article "Monumental Histories" in this book. Copyright, 2002, Duke University Press, http://www.dukeupress .edu/.

3 Jager, *Narratives of Nation Building*, pp. 136–138. The interview with Chae Yŏng-jip was conducted by the author on March 25, 1997. See also Jager and Mitter, eds., *Ruptured Histories*, pp. 248–249.

4 Kim Dae-jung, *Tashi saeroŭn sichakŭl wihayŏ* [Again, in the Interest of a New Beginning] (Seoul: Kim Yongsa, 1998), p. 173; Jager, *Narratives of Nation Building*, p. 144.

5 Kim, *Tashi saeroŭn sichakŭl wihayŏ* [Again, in the Interest of a New Beginning], p. 116; Jager, *Narratives of Nation Building*, p. 144.

6 Former President Chŏn Tu-hwan had been sentenced to life in prison and No T'ae-u to seventeen years in 1995 during Kim Yŏng-sam's administration, for their role in the 1979 military coup that brought Chŏn to power. They were also tried and found guilty for their role in the brutal suppression of the Kwangju uprising in May 1980 as well as for the collection of million-dollar bribes.

7 In Aesop's tale, the North Wind and the Sun boast that each is more powerful than the other. To settle the question, they both agreed that the one who could first strip clothes off a wayfaring man would be declared the victor. The North Wind tried first. Blowing with all his might, the blast succeeded only in making the traveler wrap his cloak closer around him. It was then the Sun's turn. Shining his rays on the earth, the traveler soon began to take off one garment after another, until at last, overcome with heat, he undressed altogether. Persuasion is stronger than force.

8 Jasper Becker, "Letters Highlight Horror of Famine: Victims Caught in Desperate Struggle for Help as Worse Feared to Be Yet to Come," *South China Morning Post*, May 12, 1997.

9 "Scores of Children Dead in North Korea Famine," *CNN World*, April 8, 1987, available at http://articles.cnn.com/1997-04-08/world/9704_08_korea .food_1_food-crisis-food-and-medicine-pyongyang?_s=PM:WORLD (accessed May 30, 2011).

10 Médecins Sans Frontières (Doctors Without Borders), "North Korea: Tes-

timonies of Famine," August 1, 1998, available at http://www.doctorswithout borders.org/publications/article.cfm?id=1468 (accessed May 30, 2011).

11 Hyŏk Kang, *This Is Paradise: My North Korean Childhood* (Abacus, 2007), p. 125. For other testimonials about life in the North Korean gulags see Blaine Harden, *Escape From Camp 14: One Man's Remarkable Odyssey from North Korea to Freedom in the West* (Viking, 2012). See also Barbara Demick's masterful *Nothing to Envy: Ordinary Lives in North Korea* (Spiegel & Grau; 2009) and Melanie Kirkpatrick, *Escape from North Korea: The Untold Story of Asia's Underground Railroad* (Encounter Books, 2012).

12 So Kae-mal, "Im Ch'ŏl-Im-So-yŏn onuiŭi yuksŏng chŭngŏn (nogŭm t'aep'u nokch'wi kirok)" [Oral testimony of brother and sister, Im Ch'ŏl and Im So-yŏn (transcript of a taped interview)] *Wŏlgan Chosŏn,* September 1999, pp. 304–319. After living in the market for several months, Chŏl decided to make the hazardous journey to China with his sister. After crossing the Tumen River in April 1999, they were eventually taken in by a Chinese family. The secret interview took place somewhere in China.

13 Jasper Becker, "North Koreans Turning to Cannibalism, Say Refugees," *South China Morning Post,* October 1, 1997.

14 Andrew S. Natsios, *The Great North Korean Famine: Famine, Politics, and Foreign Policy* (United States Institute of Peace, 2001), p. 220.

15 Given the secrecy of the North Korean regime, it is not surprising that estimates of the number of deaths by famine vary enormously. North Korean officials put the estimated number of deaths between 1995 and 1998 at 220,000, but interviews with party defectors have said that that number is greatly deflated, suggesting that internal estimates range from 1 to 1.2 million. The South Korean nongovernmental organization Good Friends Center for Peace, Human Rights, and Refugees puts the number of famine-related deaths as high as 3.5 million, or 16 percent of the population (Good Friends Center for Peace, Human Rights, and Refugees, "Human Rights in North Korea and the Food Crisis," March 2004). A team from Johns Hopkins School of Public Health working from 771 refugee interviews sought to determine the mortality rates in North Hamgyŏng province, which was widely seen as the most affected province. The study concluded that nearly 12 percent of the province's population had died of starvation. Extrapolating from these numbers for the whole country (which the Johns Hopkins team did not do) would yield an estimate of more than 2.6 million deaths, which is certainly too high given that not all provinces were affected as traumatically as North Hamgyŏng province. See Stephan Haggard and Marcus Noland, *Hunger and Human Rights: The Politics of Famine in North Korea* (U.S. Committee for Human Rights in North Korea, 2005), p. 18, available at http://www.hrnk.org/download/Hunger_and_Human_Rights.pdf (accessed May 30, 2011); Bradley Martin, *Under the Loving Care of the Fatherly Leader* (Thomas Dunne Books, 2004), pp. 557–573; see also Amnesty International, "Starved of Rights: Human Rights and the Food Crisis in the Democratic Republic of Korea (North Korea)," January 17, 2004, p. 9, available at http://www.amnesty.org/en/library/info/ASA24/003/2004 (accessed May 30, 2011). In 1994, the North Korean government reportedly stopped sending food ship-

ments to these remote northeastern provinces, which were highly dependent on the PDS. The failure of already poor domestic production of food was also compounded by severe floods in 1995 and 1996. As a result, mortality rates from the famine vary considerably according to region. Médecins Sans Frontières, "North Korea: Testimonies of Famine"; Haggard and Noland, *Hunger and Human Rights*, p. 17; Natsios, *Great North Korean Famine.*

16 Scott Snyder, "North Korea's Decline and China's Strategic Dilemmas," United States Institute of Peace Special Report (October 1997), p. 2, available at http://www.usip.org/files/resources/SR27.pdf (accessed May 31, 2011).

17 Amnesty International, "Starved of Rights," p. 9.

18 Andre Lankov, *North of the DMZ: Essays on the Daily Life in North Korea* (McFarland, 2007), p. 315.

19 Haggard and Noland, *Famine in North Korea*, pp. 53–54.

20 Ibid., pp. 54–55. This sociopolitical classification system, or "*sŏngbun*," impacts every facet of people's daily lives, from housing and food to education and healthcare. *Sŏngbun* literally means "ingredient" or "material substance," and North Koreans use the term to refer to one's sociopolitical background based on one's family history. Whereas other societies practice "discrimination based on religion, ethnicity and other factors, the primary source of discrimination in North Korean society is defined by the regime to be one's presumed value as a friend or foe to the Kim regime" (p. 6). It is also the root cause of discrimination and humanitarian abuses in North Korea. In his exhaustive study of the *sŏngbun* system, Robert Collins demonstrates how the institution of *sŏngbun* has created "a form of slave labor for a third of North Korea's population of twenty-three million citizens and loyalty-bound servants out of the remainder" (p. 1). See Robert Collins, *Marked for Life: Sŏngbun, North Korea's Social Classification System* (The Committee for Human Rights in North Korea, 2012), http://www.hrnk.org/uploads/pdfs/HRNK_Songbun_Web.pdf (accessed November 1, 2012); Chon Hyun-joon, Lee Keum-soon, Lim Soon-hee, Lee Kyu-chang, and Hong Woo-taek, *White Paper on Human Rights in North Korea* (Korea Institute for National Unification, 2011), pp. 220–227.

21 Médecins Sans Frontières, "North Korea: Testimonies of Famine," p. 7.

22 Kang, *This Is Paradise*, p. 89.

23 Haggard and Noland, *Hunger and Human Rights*, p. 28.

24 Jasper Becker, *Rogue Regime: Kim Jong Il and the Looming Threat of North Korea* (Oxford University Press, 2005), pp. 205–206.

25 Amnesty International, "Starved of Rights," p. 18.

26 Mark E. Manyin and Mary Beth Nikitin, "U.S. Assistance to North Korea," Congressional Research Service Report for Congress, July 31, 2008, available at http://www.fas.org/sgp/crs/row/RS21834.pdf (accessed May 31, 2011).

27 World Food Program, "Emergency Operation Democratic People's Republic of Korea (1 September 2008–30 November 2009)," Executive Summary, pp. 5–6, available at http://one.wfp.org/operations/current_operations/proj ect_docs/107570.pdf (accessed May 31, 2011).

28 Haggard and Noland, *Hunger and Human Rights*, p. 16.

29 Marcus Noland, "Between Collapse and Revival: A Reinterpretation of the

North Korean Economy," paper presented at a conference on Economic Development in North Korea and Global Partnership, Cheju, South Korea, March 15–16, 2001, p. 1, available at http://www.iie.com/publications/papers/paper.cfm?ResearchID=401 (accessed May 31, 2011).

30 Haggard and Marcus, *Hunger and Human Rights*, p. 17.

31 Nicholas Eberstadt, *The North Korean Economy: Between Crisis and Catastrophe* (Transaction, 2007), p. 170; "South Korea Mourns Kim Dae Jung's Death," *Bloomberg Businessweek*, August 18, 2009, at http://www.businessweek.com/blogs/eyeonasia/archives/2009/08/south_korea_mourns_kim_dae_jungs_death.html (accessed May 31, 2011); Haggard and Noland, "Sanctioning North Korea: The Political Economy of Denuclearization and Proliferation," *Peterson Institute for International Economics Working Paper Series* (July 2009), pp. 17–18, available at http://www.iie.com/publications/interstitial.cfm?ResearchID=1268 (accessed May 31, 2011).

32 Stephan Haggard and Marcus Noland, "North Korea's External Economic Relations," *Peterson Institute for International Economics Working Paper Series* (August 2007), p. 19; Haggard and Noland, "Sanctioning North Korea," p. 3; World Food Program, "Emergency Operation," p. 2.

33 Lankov, *North of the DMZ*, p. 320.

34 Stephan Haggard and Marcus Noland, "The Winter of Their Discontent: Pyongyang Attacks the Market," Peterson Institute for International Economics (January 2010), pp. 3–9, available at http://www.piie.com/publications/pb/pb10-01.pdf (accessed May 31, 2011). For the most up-to-date examination of the North Korean surveillance and prison system, see Ken E. Gause, *Coercion, Control, Surveillance, and Punishment: An Examination of the North Korean Police State* (The Committee for Human Rights in North Korea, 2012), http://www.hrnk.org/uploads/pdfs/HRNK_Ken-Gause_Web.pdf (accessed November 1, 2012).

35 The adoption of the three-tiered political structure of loyal, wavering, and hostile classes in the 1950s led to whole groups of citizens being imprisoned for political crimes based solely on family ties. "Group punishment in the form of incarceration of extended family and confiscation of property is a distinctive feature of the management of political crimes" in North Korea, a tradition that goes back to feudal times when "three generations" were punished along with the condemned. David Hawk, *The Hidden Gulag: Exposing North Korea's Prison Camps* (U.S. Committee for Human Rights in North Korea, 2003), p. 27, available at http://www.hrnk.org/download/The_Hidden_Gulag.pdf (accessed May 31, 2011); Helen-Louise Hunter, *Kim Il Sung's North Korea* (Praeger, 1999), pp. 3–13.

36 Stephan Haggard and Marcus Noland, "Economic Crime and Punishment in North Korea," *Peterson Institute for International Economics Working Paper Series* (March 2010), p. 4, available at http://www.piie.com/publications/wp/wp10-2.pdf (accessed May 31, 2011).

37 Amnesty International, "Images Reveal Scale of North Korean Political Prison Camps," May 3, 2011, available at http://www.amnesty.org/en/news-and-updates/images-reveal-scale-north-korean-political-prison-camps-2011-05-03 (accessed June 1, 2011).

38 Chŏl-hwan Kang, *Aquariums of Pyongyang: Ten Years in the North Korean Gulag*

(Basic Books, 2001). Since his 2003 publication, *The Hidden Gulag*, David Hawk wrote a second edition that chronicles in greater detail the conditions of Camp 15 as well as other political penal labor camps, owing to a substantial increase in the amount of available testimony from former prisoners. In 2002 and 2003 there were roughly three thousand former North Koreans who resettled in South Korea. That number has increased to over twenty thousand in 2009–10. These testimonies, together with many more and clearer-resolution satellite photographs, corroborate and reconfirm the findings and analysis of the first edition. See David Hawk, *The Hidden Gulag*, 2d ed. A Report by the Committee for Human Rights in North Korea (Committee for Human Rights in North Korea, April 2012), available at http://hrnk.org/wp-content/uploads/HRNK_HiddenGulag2_Final_Web_v4.pdf (accessed April 13, 2012).

39 Hawk, *Hidden Gulag* (2003), p. 44; Soon Ok Lee, *Eyes of a Tailless Animal: Prison Memoirs of a North Korean Woman* (Living Sacrifice Book, 1999), p. 60.

40 Lee, *Eyes of a Tailless Animal*, p. 60.

41 Hawk, *Hidden Gulag* (2003), p. 53.

42 Kang, *Aquariums of Pyongyang*, p. 92.

43 Becker, *Rogue Regime*, p. 87.

44 Hawk, *Hidden Gulag* (2003), p. 48.

45 Ibid., pp. 56–58; Haggard and Noland, "Economic Crime and Punishment in North Korea," p. 12. Numerous witnesses have also offered detailed accounts of pregnant women forced to undergo abortion and infanticide upon their repatriation to North Korea. According to David Hawk, North Korean officials have made no secret of racially motivated abortions and infanticide forced upon Korean women in order to prevent them from giving birth to "half-Chinese" babies. There also appears to be little difference between forced abortions and infanticide as many of the fetuses are born viable. According to one account from a sixty-six-year-old grandmother who was held in a detention center in Sinŭiju after being forcibly repatriated in 1997, all the babies she was assigned to help deliver were killed shortly after birth. "The first baby was born to a twenty-eight-year-old woman named Lim who had been married to a Chinese man," she recalled. "The baby boy was born healthy and unusually large, owing to the mother's ability to eat well during pregnancy in China." She then "assisted in holding the baby's head during delivery and cut the umbilical cord." However, when she held the baby "and wrapped him in a blanket, a guard grabbed the newborn by one leg and threw him in a large plastic-lined box." When the box was full of babies, it was taken outside and buried. See David Hawk, *The Hidden Gulag*, 2nd ed., (2012), pp. 122–125.

46 Hawk, *Hidden Gulag*, 2d ed. (2012), p. 121.

47 Haggard and Noland, "Economic Crime and Punishment in North Korea," pp. 12–16; Shin Joo Hyun, "Bribery and Extortion Are Common in North Korean Commerce," *DailyNK*, December 31, 2010, at http://www.dailynk.com/english/read.php?cataId=nk01500&num=7196 (accessed May 31, 2011). When bribery becomes the unofficial exchange between state officials and the population, a certain equilibrium in the system is maintained. In this case, the dictator who is unable to pay government officials a living wage "condones corruption as the price he must pay to maintain his loyalty." At

the same time, however, government officials such as police officers and security agents are granted more discretionary power when they deal with cracking down on informal market activities. Since market traders understand that police and other government officials have the power to punish, they are incentivized to bribe their way out of arrest or harsh punishment. "Equilibrium is established between government officials and market participants as bribe-takers and bribe-givers, respectively, and even strong collusion may develop." However, such a system is fragile, since members of the police and other officials may want to increase the amount of bribes they receive, thus increasing the discontent among the population. Byung-Yeon Kim, "Markets, Bribery, and Regime Stability in North Korea," *East Asia Institute Security Initiative Working Paper* 4 (April 2010), p. 21.

48 Ishimaru Jiro, *Rimjin-gang: Reports by North Korean Journalists within North Korea* (Asiapress, 2010), pp. 97–98.

49 Ibid., p. 170.

50 Although the reform effectively wiped out all private savings from black-market operators, it also caused hyperinflation. Merchants with goods for sale wanted to convert their merchandise into hard currency like Chinese yuan or U.S. dollars or into durable items such as rice. Those who wanted to buy goods were unable to do so since the retail prices for all goods skyrocketed. The situation caused open dissension among the North Korean populace, the first time that such open and public criticism of the regime had ever occurred. The regime later publicly acknowledged that the currency reform was a massive failure and pinned the blame on Pak Nam-gi, director of the Planning and Finance Department of the KWP. Pak was arrested in January 2010 and executed by firing squad two months later. See Ishimaru, *Rimjin-gang*, p. 175; "N. Korean Technocrat Executed for Bungled Currency Reform: Sources," Yonhap News Agency, March 18, 2010; Scott Snyder, "North Korea Currency Reform: What Happened and What Will Happen to Its Economy?" paper presented at the 2010 Global Forum on North Korea Economy, Korea Economic Daily and Hyundai Research Institute, Seoul, Korea, March 31, 2010, available at http://asiafoundation.org/resources/pdfs/SnyderDPRK-Currency.pdf (accessed March 25, 2012).

EPILOGUE: *China's Rise, War's End?*

1 An earlier version of this chapter was previously published in the online *Asia-Pacific Journal* 9, no. 2 (January 24, 2011), available at http://japanfocus.org/-Sheila_Miyoshi-Jager/3477. I am grateful to Mark Selden, the journal's coordinator, for granting me permission to reuse portions of the article in this book.

2 "DPRK Leading Newspapers Publish Joint New Year Editorial," Korea Central News Agency (KCNA), January 1, 2012, at http://www.kcna.co.jp/item/2012/201201/news01/20120101-15ee.html (accessed January 2, 2012).

3 Stephanie Ho, "China Recognizes Kim Jong Un as North Korea's Next Leader," Voice of America, December 19, 2011, at http://www.voanews.com/english/news/asia/China-Recognizes-Kim-Jong-Un-as-North-Koreas-Next-Leader-135914943.html (accessed December 22, 2011).

4   Adam Cathcart, "Beijing-P'yŏngyang: Developments in and around North Korea from the Chinese Media," *Sino-UK*, December 22, 2011, at http://sinonk.wordpress.com/2011/12/22/beijing-pyongyang-developments-in-and-around-north-korea-from-the-chinese-media/ (accessed January 7, 2012).

5   Andrei Lankov, "The Legacy of Long-Gone States: China, Korea and the Koguryo Wars," *Asia-Pacific Journal*, September 28, 2006, p. 1, available at http://www.japanfocus.org/-Andrei-Lankov/2233 (accessed May 1, 2011).

6   Traditional dating of Koguryŏ is 37 BC–AD 668, but recent archeological evidence suggests that state formation on the Korean peninsula occurred around AD 300, much later than 37 BC. This means that the Three Kingdoms of Koguryŏ, Paekche, and Silla were established after the Chinese Han Lelang period (108 BC–AD 313), when Han Dynasty commanderies occupied the northwestern part of the Korean peninsula and introduced to Korea the most important "traits of civilization," including intensive wet rice agriculture, iron technology, and writing. These traits of civilization spread to other parts of the peninsula to create the basis for the emergence of new Korean states that comprised Koguryŏ, Paekche, and Silla. Sarah Milledge Nelson, *The Archeology of Korea* (Cambridge University Press, 1993); Gina Barnes, *State Formation in Korea: Historical and Archaeological Perspectives* (Curzon, 2001); Hyung Il Pai, "Lelang and the Interaction Sphere: An Alternative Approach to Korean State Formation," *Archaeological Review from Cambridge* 8, no. 1 (1989), pp. 64–75.

7   Yonson Ahn, "Competing Nationalisms: The Mobilization of History and Archeology in the Korea-China Wars over Koguryo/Gaogouli," *Asia-Pacific Journal*, February 9, 2006, p. 2, available at http://www.japanfocus.org/-Yonson-Ahn/1837 (accessed May 1, 2011).

8   Lankov, "The Legacy of Long-Gone States," p. 2.

9   Ahn, "Competing Nationalisms," p. 5.

10 Lankov, "The Legacy of Long-Gone States," p. 5.

11 Sheila Miyoshi Jager, "The Politics of Identity: History, Nationalism and the Prospect for Peace in Post-Cold War Asia," U.S. Army Strategic Studies Institute (April 2007), pp. 21–22, available at http://www.strategicstudiesinstitute.army.mil/pdffiles/pub770.pdf (accessed May 1, 2011).

12 Bonnie Glaser, Scott Snyder, and John S. Park, "Keeping an Eye on an Unruly Neighbor: Chinese Views of Economic Reform and Stability in North Korea," *United States Institute of Peace Working Paper* (January 3, 2008), p. 10, available at http://www.usip.org/files/resources/Jan2008.pdf (accessed May 1, 2011).

13 Scott Snyder, "Pyŏngyang Tests Beijing's Patience," *Comparative Connections* (July 2009), p. 5, available at http://csis.org/files/publication/0902qchina_korea.pdf (accessed May 1, 2011).

14 Choe Sang-hun, "South Korea Risks Driving North into China's Embrace," *International Herald Tribune*, April 29, 2010, p. 2.

15 Min Cho Hee, "Chinese Take Complete Control of Mines," *DailyNK*, May 11, 2010, at http://www.dailynk.com/english/read.php?cataId=nk01500&num=6352 (accessed May 1, 2011).

16 "Company's $2 Billion Pledge Would Mark One of the Largest Deals with

Neighbor; Pact Was Signed after Yeongpyeong Shelling," *Wall Street Journal*, January 19, 2011.

17 "China's Industrial Expansion near North Korea Stirs Fears," *Korea Times*, August 7, 2010; "Kim Jong Il's China Visit Was about Economy," *Korea Times*, September 6, 2010. The ambitious plan that emerged in 1991 aims to convert an area from the Chinese town of Yanji to the Sea of Japan and from Ch'ŏnjin in North Korea to Vladivostok in Russia into a $30 billion trade and transport complex. The goal is to create a free economic zone in Northeast Asia over the next twenty years involving China, the two Koreas, Russia, and Japan. While the development project poses great potential economic benefits, implementing it has been very complicated because of political issues and the fact that the area in question will require border countries to relinquish some of their land if the overall project is to succeed. Mark J. Valencia, "Tumen River Project," *East Asian Executive Reports* 14, no. 2 (1993), available at http://www1.american.edu/TED/tumen.htm (accessed May 1, 2011); Joseph Manguno, "A New Regional Trade Bloc in Northeast Asia?" *China Business Review* 20 (March/April 1993).

18 Jeremy Page, "Trade Binds North Korea to China," *Wall Street Journal*, December 24, 2011. For China's failed efforts to put North Korea on the path to economic reform, see Stephan Haggard, Jennifer Lee, and Marcus Noland, "Integration in the Absence of Institutions: China-North Korea Cross-Border Exchanges," *Peterson Institute for International Economics Working Paper Series* (August 2011), available at http://www.iie.com/publications/wp/wp11-13.pdf (accessed December 26, 2001). Also see Carla Freeman and Drew Thompson, "The Real Bridge to Nowhere: China's Foiled North Korea Strategy," *United States Institute of Peace Working Paper* (April 22, 2009), available at http://www .usip.org/files/resources/1%282%29.PDF (accessed December 26, 2011).

19 The April 27, 2009, cable from the American embassy in Seoul, in "U.S Embassy Cables: Reading the Runes on North Korea," *Guardian*, November 29, 2010, at http://www.guardian.co.uk/world/us-embassy-cables-docu ments/204174 (accessed May 1, 2011).

20 Tessa Morris-Suzuki pointed out that the North Korean Victorious Fatherland War Museum portrays the war as a battle between the United States and North Korea, with almost no reference to the involvement of any other countries in the war: "The emphasis throughout is on US imperialism and aggression, and the war, in short, is narrating as a resounding victory of the DPRK over the United States" (p. 11). Tessa Morris-Suzuki, "Remembering the Unfinished Conflict: Museums and the Contested Memory of the Korean War," *Asia-Pacific Journal* (July 27, 2009), available at http://www.japanfocus .org/-Tessa-Morris_Suzuki/3193 (accessed May 1, 2011). However, as B. R. Myers has pointed out, this does not mean that China's contribution to the war has been completely ignored. Chinese visitors, for example, are taken to specific exhibits that do acknowledge their country's enormous sacrifice in the war, but these exhibits are off-limits to North Koreans, who "are taken on another route where they see and hear no mention of it." Myers, *The Cleanest Race*, p. 130.

21 "Arirang Has a New Scene Reflecting DPRK-China Friendship," *Korean Central News Agency of the DPRK* (hereafter *KCNA*), October 22, 2010, at http://

www.kcna.co.jp/item/2010/201010/news22/20101022-12ee.html (accessed May 2, 2011).

22 "DPRK Arranges Banquet to Mark Entry of CPV into Korean Front," *KCNA*, October 24, 2010, available at http://www.globalsecurity.org/wmd/library/news/dprk/2010/dprk-101024-kcna04.htm (accessed May 2, 2011).

23 "Floral Tribute Paid to Mao Anying and Fallen Fighters of the CPV," *KCNA*, October 24, 2010. One interesting (and amusing) side note regarding Korean War memory: During the White House state banquet hosted on January 19, 2010, in honor of President Hu Jintao, the Chinese pianist Lang Lang played "My Mother Land," which was a very popular song during the Korean War. The song encouraged the Chinese to fight the American invaders. See http://news.backchina.com/viewnews-124030-gb2312.html (accessed May 3, 2011).

24 *Nodong sinmun*, October 24, 2010.

25 Speech of Kim Jong Il at Banquet," *KCNA*, August 30, 2010, at http://www.kcna.co.jp/item/2010/201008/news30/20100830-23ee.html (accessed May 4, 2011).

26 According to the Korea scholar Rüdiger Frank, the building in the picture appears to be the Catholic church on the bank of the Songhua River in Jilin City. He suggests that the painting is linked to the increasingly frequent allusions to Kim Il Sung's youth in Northeast China in what is clearly a campaign to emphasize traditional Sino–North Korean closeness. "So the painting might actually be part of the new policy of emphasizing the two countries joint revolutionary past" (p. 3). On the other hand, he is not entirely convinced that this is, in fact, a painting of Kim Chŏng-ŭn. Rather, it appears to be a portrait of a young Kim Il Sung in Northeast China. Frank Rüdiger, "Harbinger or Hoax: The First Painting of Kim Jung Un?" *Foreign Policy*, December 9, 2010, at http://www.foreignpolicy.com/articles/2010/12/09/harbinger_or_hoax_the_first_painting_of_kim_jung_un (accessed May 2, 2011). Other North Korea experts, however, are convinced that the portrait was indeed the first glimpse of the new leader Kim Chŏng-ŭn. See Mark McKinnon, "North Korea's Kim Jong-un: Portrait of a Leader in the Making," *Globe and Mail*, December 4, 2010.

27 *Korea Times*, January 6, 2012.

28 *Dong-a ilbo*, October 11 and 13, 2010; *Telegraph*, October 5, 2010; Aidan Foster-Carter, "North Korea: Embracing the Dragon," *Asia Times*, October 28, 2010.

29 *New York Times*, April 29, 2010. For an excellent overview and analysis of South Korea's reaction to China's economic influence in North Korea and the political challenges of future Sino-South Korean relations, see Scott Snyder, *China's Rise and The Two Koreas: Politics, Economics, Security* (Lynne Rienner Publishers, 2009).

30 South Korean President Yi's current position toward North Korea is that it must apologize for the *Ch'ŏn'an*'s sinking and the Yŏnp'yŏng shelling before serious negotiations can resume. Since North Korea has refused to acknowledge its responsibility for the sinking of the South Korean corvette and has justified the shelling of the island as a retaliatory move, Yi will presumably have to wait a long time.

31 *Korea Times*, September 9, 2010.

32 Ibid., November 2, 2010.

33 Chico Harlan, "South Korea's Young People Are Wary of Unification," *Wash-ington Post*, October 17, 2011. Every year the Institute of Peace and Reunifica-tion Studies at Seoul National University conducts extensive polling data on unification issues. In the 2010 survey, South Koreans of all ages were asked about their views on the personal benefits from unification. The responses were startling, with 75.2 percent of South Koreans replying that unification would have no or very little impact for them personally, while just 3.6 percent responded that it would benefit them "very much" and 21.2 percent "some-what." These results compare with the findings in 2008, in which 72.3 percent replied "very little" or "none at all." In 2009, the percentage was higher, at 76.1, most likely due to North Korea's decision to test a nuclear device on May 25 of that year. See *2010 T'ongil ŭisik chosa* [2010 Investigation on Per-ceptions on Unification], Institute of Peace and Unification Studies, Seoul National University, 2010, available at http://tongil.snu.ac.kr/xe/index.php?document_srl=6147 (accessed March 18, 2012).

34 *Choson ilbo*, November 18, 2010.

35 *Korea Times*, January 27, 2012.

36 Andre Lankov, "South Korea Harbors Unification Heresy," *Asia Times*, Sep-tember 9, 2011.

37 Foster-Carter, "How North Korea Was Lost to China," *Asia Times*, Septem-ber 10, 2010.

INDEX

Page numbers in *italics* refer to illustrations and maps.